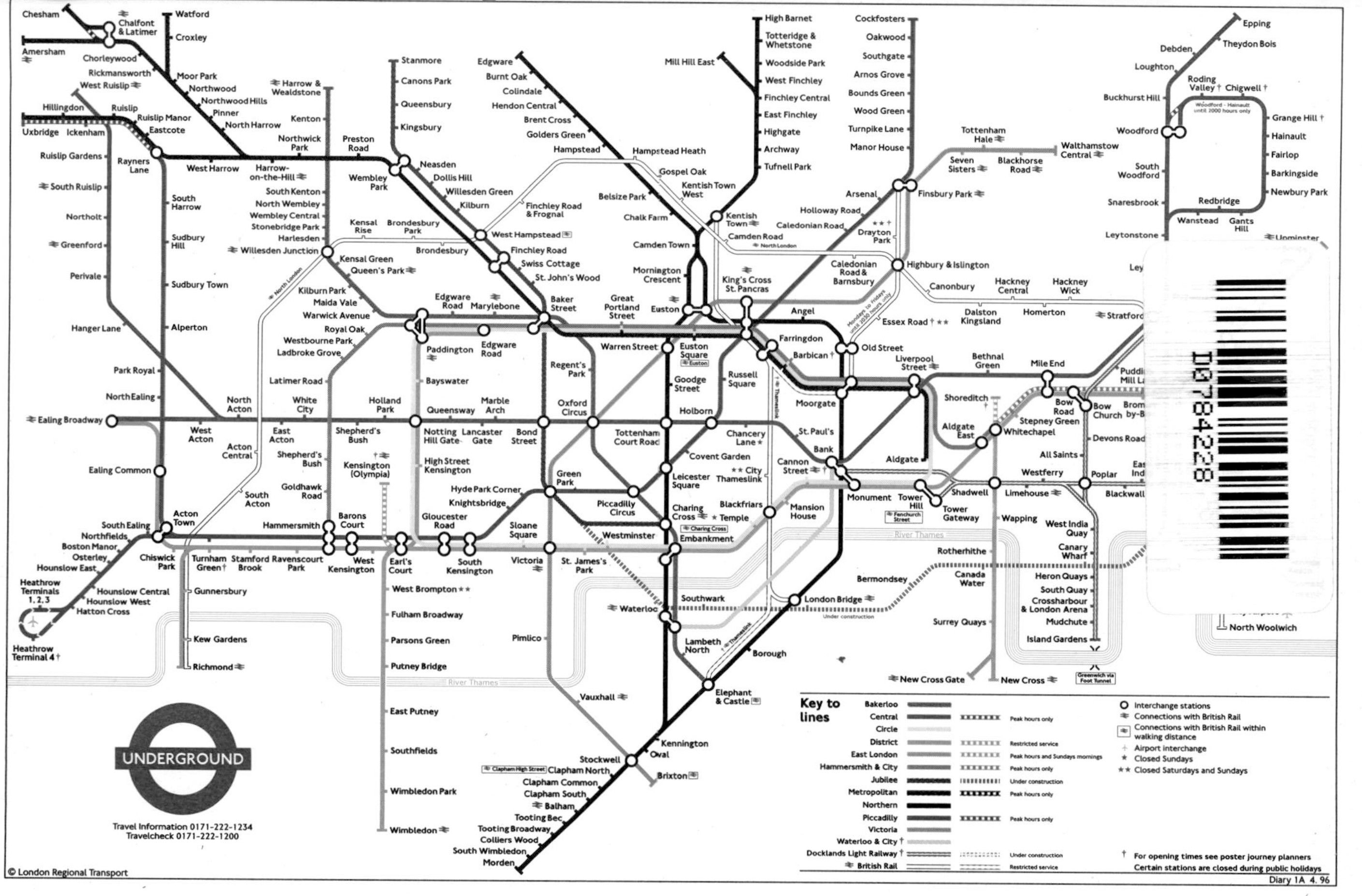

LRT Registered User No. 97/2726

London: Overview

King's Cross
Station
Pentonville Rd.
City Rd.
St. Pancras
Station
King's
Cross
Rd.
Gray's Inn Rd.
Judd St.
Rosebery Ave.
St. John's
St.
Goswell Rd.
Lever St.
Bath St.
East Road
Hoxton St.
Kingsland Rd.
Old
St.
Gt. Eastern St.
Shoreditch
High
St.
Commercial
St.
Coram's
Fields
Guilford St.
Woburn
Pl.
Farringdon Rd.
Aldersgate
City Rd.
Southampton
Row
Theobalds Rd.
Clerkenwell Rd.
Barbican
Centre
ritish
seum
Charterhouse St.
Smithfield
Market
London Wall
Moorgate
Liverpool St.
Station
Holborn
Chancery La.
Fetter La.
Holborn
Viaduct
New
Oxford St.
High
Kingsway
Drury La.
Newgate
St.
Old Bailey
St. Paul's
Bank of
England
Bishopsgate
Houndsditch
Cheapside
Cornhill
Gracechurch
St.
Leadenhall St.
Fenchurch St.
Ave.
Charing Cross Rd.
Aldwych
Law
Courts
Fleet St.
Queen
Victoria
St.
Cannon St.
Eastcheap
Strand
Victoria
Embankment
Blackfriars Br.
Blackfriars
Station
Southwark Br.
Cannon St.
Station
London Br.
Upper
Thames St.
Tower Hill
The Tower
National
Gallery
Charing
Cross Stn.
Waterloo Br.
National
Theatre
River Thames
Tower Br.
algar
uare
Stamford St.
Southwark St.
Tooley St.
Royal Festival
Hall
Whitehall
Blackfriars Rd.
Union St.
St. Thomas St.
London Bridge
Station
Borough High St.
York Rd.
The Cut
Waterloo
Rd.
Waterloo
Station
Long La.
Bridge
Rd.
Tower
Westminster Br.
Houses of
Parliament
ster
bey
Westminster Br. Rd.
Borough Rd.
Great Dover St.
Harper Rd.
Tabard St.
Abbey
St.
Millbank
Lambeth Palace Rd.
London Rd.
Lambeth Rd.
New Kent Rd.
Willow Walk
rseferry Rd.
Lambeth Br.
Imperial
War
Museum
Kennington Rd.
Rodney
Pl.
Albert Embankment
Black Prince Rd.
Crampton
St.
Flint St.
East St.
Old Kent Rd.
Tate
Gallery
Walworth Rd
Rd.
Vauxhall Br.
Kennington Park Rd.
Manor Pl.
Portland St.
Thurlow St.
Kennington La.
N
Braganza
St.
Albany Rd.
Vauxhall
Station
Kennington
Oval
0
1/2 mile
0
1/2 kilometer

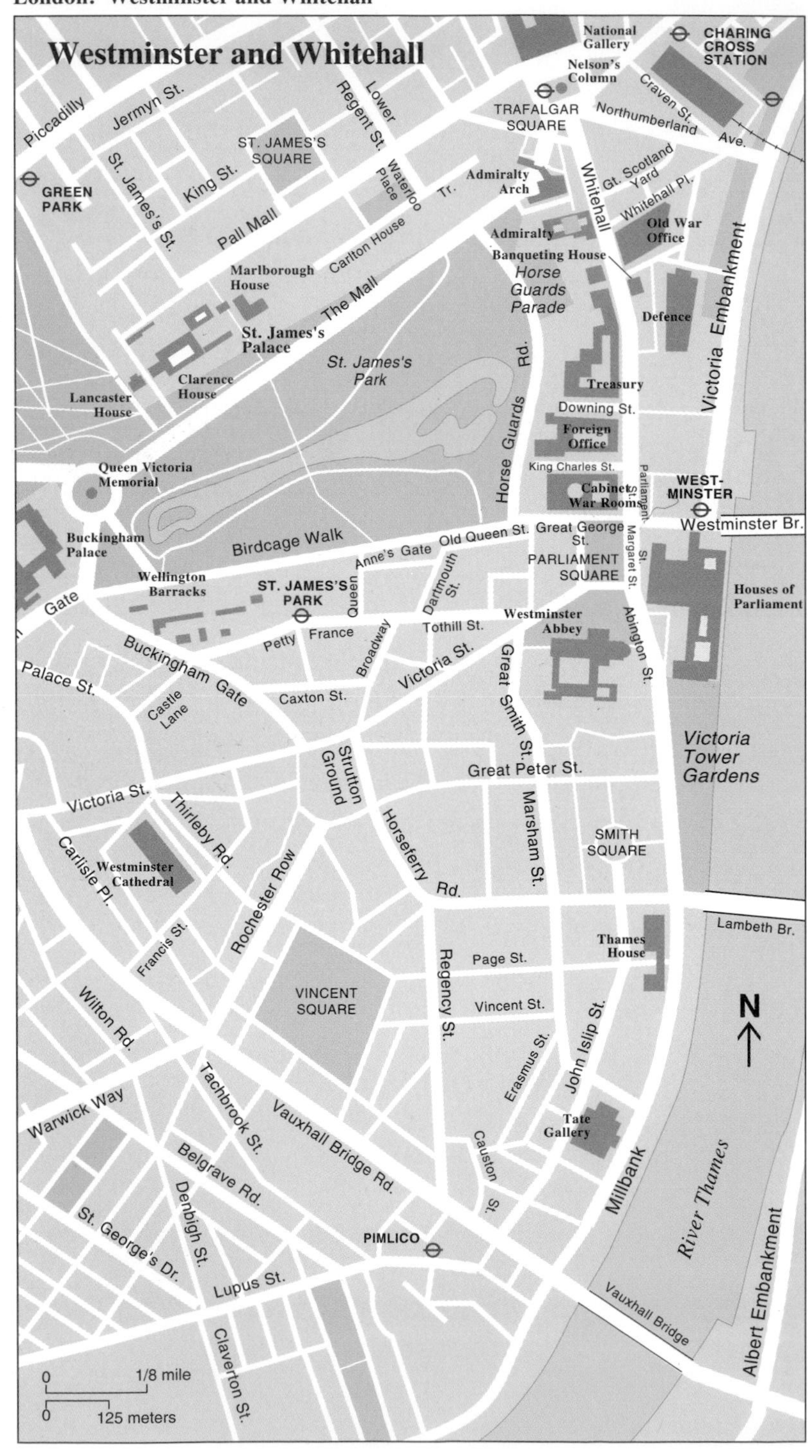
Westminster and Whitehall
National Gallery
CHARING CROSS STATION
Nelson's Column
TRAFALGAR SQUARE
Craven St.
Northumberland Ave.
Piccadilly
Jermyn St.
Lower Regent St.
ST. JAMES'S SQUARE
GREEN PARK
St. James's St.
King St.
Waterloo Place
Admiralty Arch
Whitehall
Gt. Scotland Yard
Whitehall Pl.
Pall Mall
Carlton House Tr.
Admiralty
Old War Office
Banqueting House
Horse Guards Parade
Marlborough House
The Mall
Defence
Victoria Embankment
St. James's Palace
St. James's Park
Horse Guards Rd.
Clarence House
Lancaster House
Treasury
Downing St.
Foreign Office
Queen Victoria Memorial
King Charles St.
Parliament St.
Cabinet War Rooms
WEST-MINSTER
Westminster Br.
Buckingham Palace
Birdcage Walk
Old Queen St.
Great George St.
Anne's Gate
Dartmouth St.
PARLIAMENT SQUARE
St. Margaret St.
Houses of Parliament
Wellington Barracks
Gate
ST. JAMES'S PARK
Queen
Westminster Abbey
Tothill St.
Petty France
Broadway
Abingdon St.
Buckingham Gate
Victoria St.
Great Smith St.
Palace St.
Castle Lane
Caxton St.
Victoria Tower Gardens
Strutton Ground
Great Peter St.
Victoria St.
Thirleby Rd.
Horseferry Rd.
Marsham St.
SMITH SQUARE
Carlisle Pl.
Westminster Cathedral
Rochester Row
Lambeth Br.
Francis St.
Thames House
Page St.
Regency St.
VINCENT SQUARE
Vincent St.
Wilton Rd.
N
John Islip St.
Erasmus St.
Warwick Way
Tachbrook St.
Vauxhall Bridge Rd.
Tate Gallery
Causton St.
Belgrave Rd.
Millbank
River Thames
Denbigh St.
St. George's Dr.
PIMLICO
Albert Embankment
Lupus St.
Vauxhall Bridge
Claverton St.
0 1/8 mile
0 125 meters

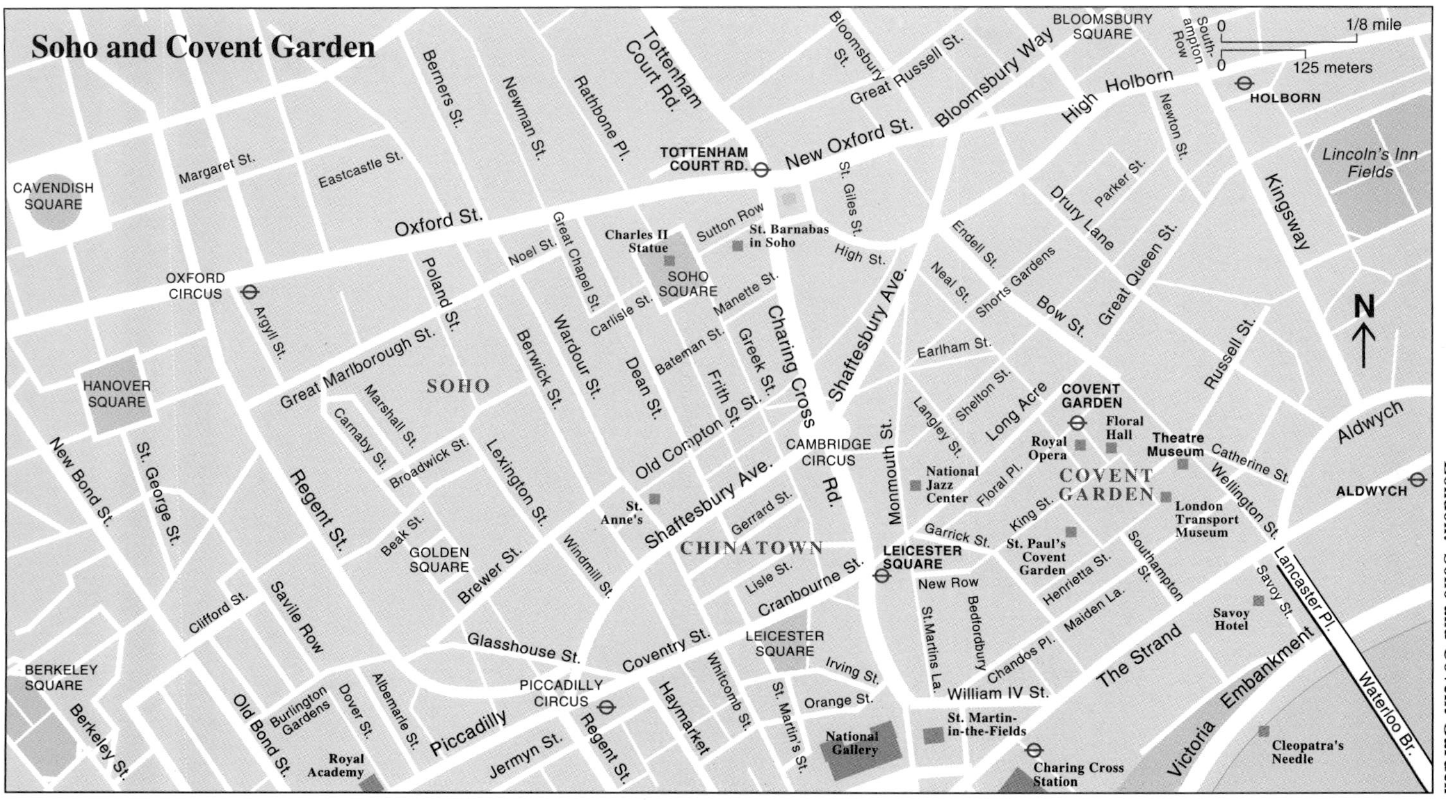
Soho and Covent Garden
CAVENDISH SQUARE
Margaret St.
Eastcastle St.
Berners St.
Newman St.
Rathbone Pl.
Tottenham Court Rd.
TOTTENHAM COURT RD.
New Oxford St.
Bloomsbury St.
Great Russell St.
Bloomsbury Way
BLOOMSBURY SQUARE
South-ampton Row
0
1/8 mile
0
125 meters
HOLBORN
High Holborn
Newton St.
Lincoln's Inn Fields
Kingsway
Oxford St.
OXFORD CIRCUS
Argyll St.
Noel St.
Great Chapel St.
Charles II Statue
SOHO SQUARE
Sutton Row
St. Barnabas in Soho
St. Giles St.
High St.
Endell St.
Drury Lane
Parker St.
Great Queen St.
Neal St.
Shorts Gardens
Bow St.
N
Poland St.
Carlisle St.
Manette St.
Bateman St.
Greek St.
Charing Cross Rd.
Shaftesbury Ave.
Earlham St.
Russell St.
HANOVER SQUARE
Great Marlborough St.
SOHO
Marshall St.
Carnaby St.
Berwick St.
Wardour St.
Dean St.
Frith St.
Old Compton St.
Langley St.
Shelton St.
Long Acre
COVENT GARDEN
Floral Hall
Royal Opera
Theatre Museum
Catherine St.
Aldwych
ALDWYCH
New Bond St.
St. George St.
Regent St.
Broadwick St.
Lexington St.
CAMBRIDGE CIRCUS
Monmouth St.
National Jazz Center
Floral Pl.
COVENT GARDEN
Wellington St.
London Transport Museum
St. Anne's
Shaftesbury Ave.
Gerrard St.
King St.
Beak St.
GOLDEN SQUARE
Brewer St.
Windmill St.
CHINATOWN
Garrick St.
LEICESTER SQUARE
St. Paul's Covent Garden
Southampton St.
Lancaster Pl.
Savoy St.
Clifford St.
Savile Row
Lisle St.
Cranbourne St.
New Row
Henrietta St.
Maiden La.
Savoy Hotel
Glasshouse St.
Coventry St.
LEICESTER SQUARE
St.Martins La.
Bedfordbury
Chandos Pl.
The Strand
BERKELEY SQUARE
Irving St.
William IV St.
Victoria Embankment
Waterloo Br.
PICCADILLY CIRCUS
Berkeley St.
Old Bond St.
Burlington Gardens
Dover St.
Albemarle St.
Piccadilly
Jermyn St.
Regent St.
Haymarket
Whitcomb St.
St. Martin's St.
Orange St.
National Gallery
St. Martin-in-the-Fields
Charing Cross Station
Cleopatra's Needle
Royal Academy

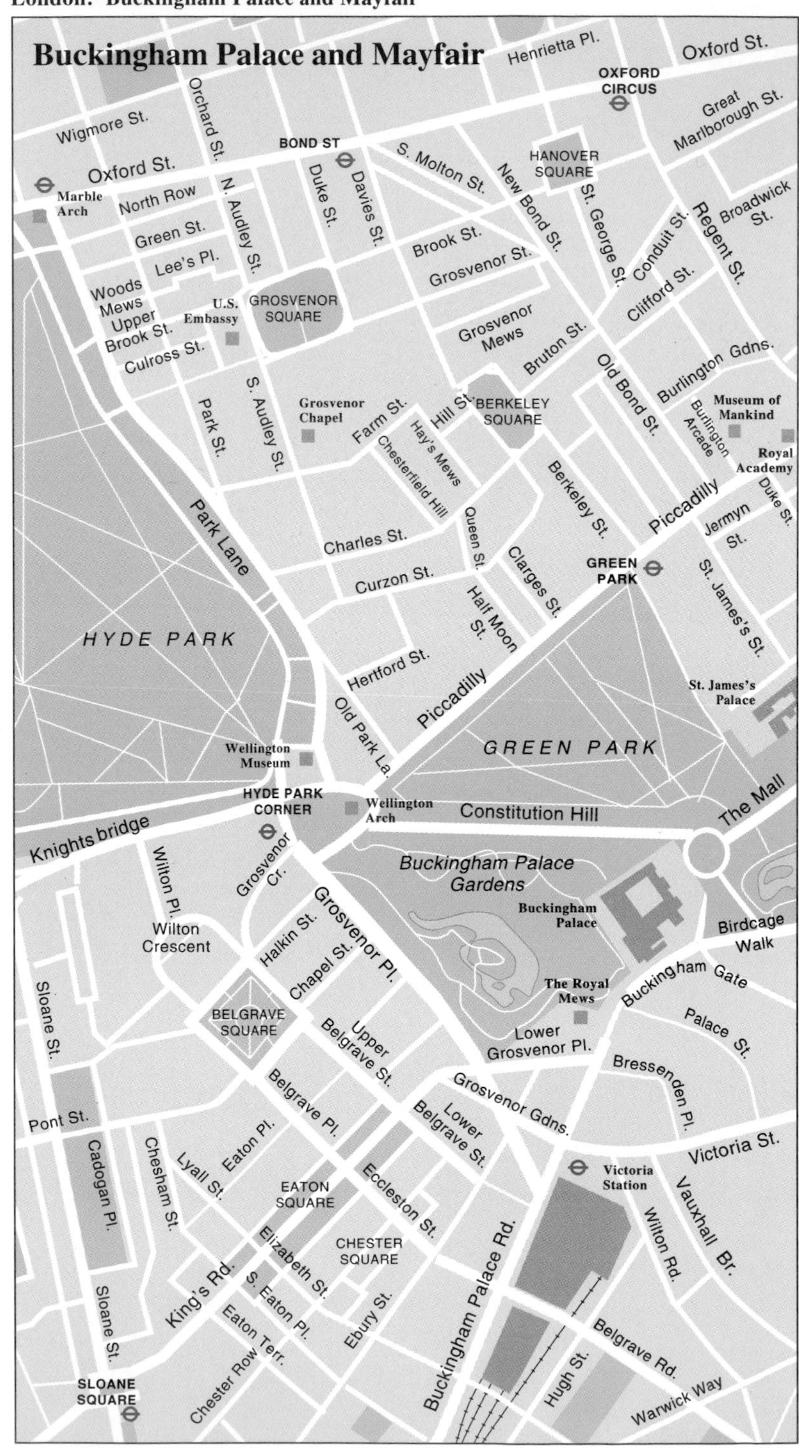
Buckingham Palace and Mayfair
Henrietta Pl.
Oxford St.
OXFORD CIRCUS
Great Marlborough St.
Wigmore St.
Orchard St.
BOND ST
S. Molton St.
HANOVER SQUARE
Oxford St.
Marble Arch
North Row
N. Audley St.
Duke St.
Davies St.
New Bond St.
St. George St.
Regent St.
Broadwick St.
Green St.
Lee's Pl.
Brook St.
Grosvenor St.
Conduit St.
Clifford St.
Woods Mews
Upper Brook St.
U.S. Embassy
GROSVENOR SQUARE
Grosvenor Mews
Bruton St.
Culross St.
Old Bond St.
Burlington Gdns.
S. Audley St.
Park St.
Grosvenor Chapel
Farm St.
Hill St.
BERKELEY SQUARE
Burlington Arcade
Museum of Mankind
Royal Academy
Hay's Mews
Chesterfield Hill
Berkeley St.
Piccadilly
Jermyn St.
Duke St.
Park Lane
Charles St.
Queen St.
Curzon St.
Clarges St.
GREEN PARK
St. James's St.
Half Moon St.
HYDE PARK
Hertford St.
Piccadilly
St. James's Palace
Old Park La.
GREEN PARK
Wellington Museum
HYDE PARK CORNER
Wellington Arch
Constitution Hill
The Mall
Knights bridge
Wilton Pl.
Grosvenor Cr.
Buckingham Palace Gardens
Buckingham Palace
Wilton Crescent
Halkin St.
Grosvenor Pl.
Birdcage Walk
Chapel St.
The Royal Mews
Buckingham Gate
Sloane St.
BELGRAVE SQUARE
Upper Belgrave St.
Lower Grosvenor Pl.
Palace St.
Bressenden Pl.
Belgrave Pl.
Grosvenor Gdns.
Lower Belgrave St.
Pont St.
Eaton Pl.
Chesham St.
Cadogan Pl.
Lyall St.
Victoria St.
Victoria Station
EATON SQUARE
Eccleston St.
Vauxhall Br.
Wilton Rd.
Elizabeth St.
CHESTER SQUARE
Buckingham Palace Rd.
King's Rd.
S. Eaton Pl.
Ebury St.
Sloane St.
Eaton Terr.
Belgrave Rd.
Hugh St.
Chester Row
Warwick Way
SLOANE SQUARE

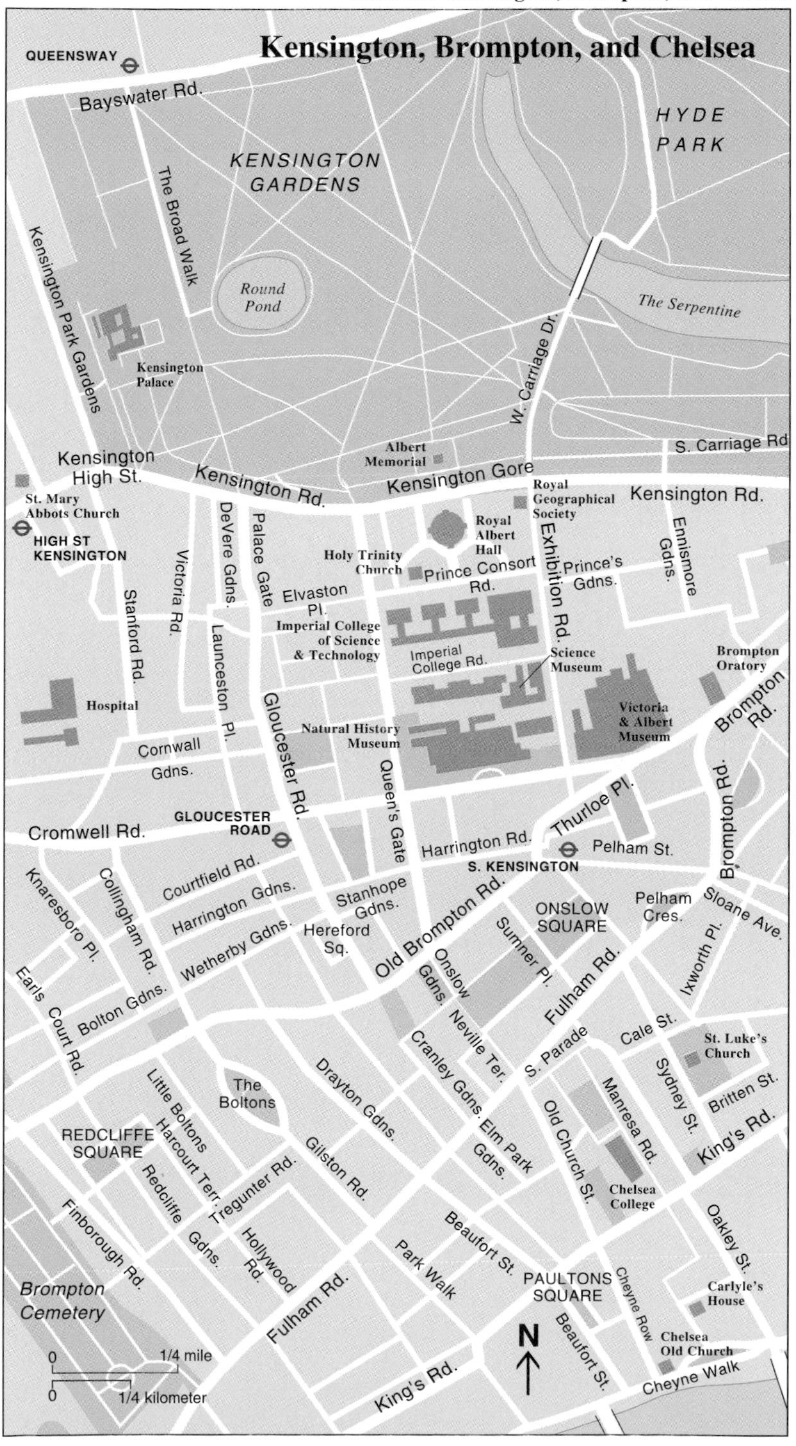
Kensington, Brompton, and Chelsea
QUEENSWAY
Bayswater Rd.
HYDE PARK
KENSINGTON GARDENS
The Broad Walk
Kensington Park Gardens
Round Pond
The Serpentine
Kensington Palace
W. Carriage Dr.
Albert Memorial
S. Carriage Rd
Kensington High St.
Kensington Rd.
Kensington Gore
Royal Geographical Society
Kensington Rd.
St. Mary Abbots Church
HIGH ST KENSINGTON
DeVere Gdns.
Palace Gate
Royal Albert Hall
Exhibition Rd.
Ennismore Gdns.
Victoria Rd.
Holy Trinity Church
Prince Consort Rd.
Prince's Gdns.
Stanford Rd.
Elvaston Pl.
Imperial College of Science & Technology
Launceston Pl.
Imperial College Rd.
Science Museum
Brompton Oratory
Hospital
Gloucester Rd.
Victoria & Albert Museum
Brompton Rd.
Natural History Museum
Cornwall Gdns.
Queen's Gate
Thurloe Pl.
Brompton Rd.
Cromwell Rd.
GLOUCESTER ROAD
Harrington Rd.
Pelham St.
S. KENSINGTON
Knaresboro Pl.
Collingham Rd.
Courtfield Rd.
Harrington Gdns.
Stanhope Gdns.
Old Brompton Rd.
ONSLOW SQUARE
Pelham Cres.
Sloane Ave.
Hereford Sq.
Wetherby Gdns.
Sumner Pl.
Ixworth Pl.
Earls Court Rd.
Bolton Gdns.
Onslow Gdns.
Fulham Rd.
Neville Ter.
Cale St.
S. Parade
St. Luke's Church
Cranley Gdns.
Sydney St.
The Boltons
Drayton Gdns.
Little Boltons
Manresa Rd.
Britten St.
Old Church St.
REDCLIFFE SQUARE
Harcourt Terr.
Elm Park Gdns.
King's Rd.
Gilston Rd.
Redcliffe Gdns.
Tregunter Rd.
Chelsea College
Finborough Rd.
Oakley St.
Beaufort St.
Hollywood Rd.
Park Walk
Brompton Cemetery
Fulham Rd.
PAULTONS SQUARE
Cheyne Row
Carlyle's House
N
Beaufort St.
Chelsea Old Church
0
1/4 mile
0
1/4 kilometer
King's Rd.
Cheyne Walk

London: City of London

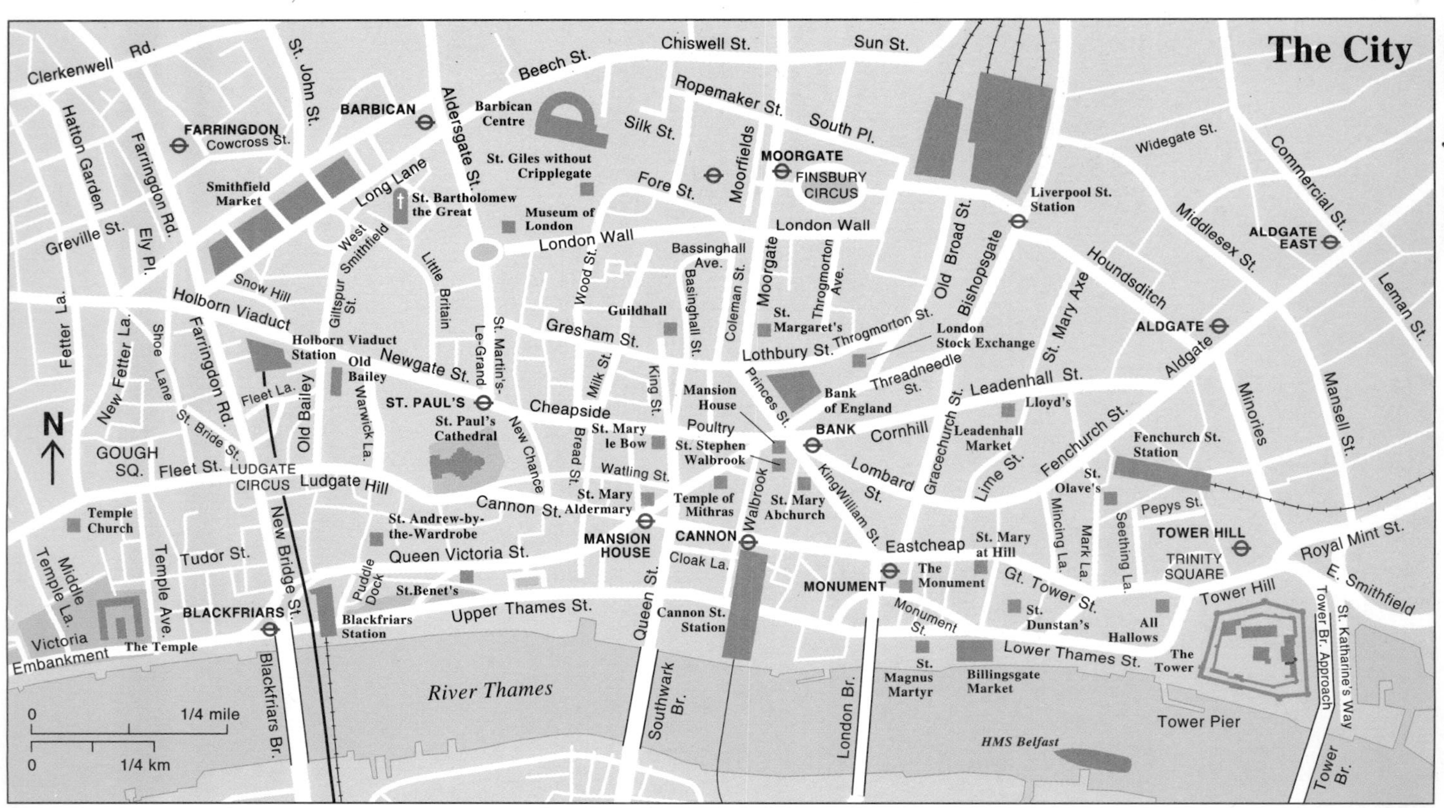

LET'S GO
London

Let's Go writers travel on your budget.

"Guides that penetrate the veneer of the holiday brochures and mine the grit of real life."

—The Economist

"The writers seem to have experienced every rooster-packed bus and lunar-surfaced mattress about which they write."

—The New York Times

"All the dirt, dirt cheap."

—People

Great for independent travelers.

"The guides are aimed not only at young budget travelers but at the independent traveler, a sort of streetwise cookbook for traveling alone."

—The New York Times

"Flush with candor and irreverence, chock full of budget travel advice."

—The Des Moines Register

"An indispensable resource. *Let's Go*'s practical information can be used by every traveler."

—The Chattanooga Free Press

Let's Go is completely revised each year.

"Only *Let's Go* has the zeal to annually update every title on its list."

—The Boston Globe

"Unbeatable: good sight-seeing advice; up-to-date info on restaurants, hotels, and inns; a commitment to money-saving travel; and a wry style that brightens nearly every page."

—The Washington Post

All the important information you need.

"*Let's Go* authors provide a comedic element while still providing concise information and thorough coverage of the country. Anything you need to know about budget traveling is detailed in this book."

—The Chicago Sun-Times

"Value-packed, unbeatable, accurate, and comprehensive."

—Los Angeles Times

Let's Go Publications

Let's Go: Alaska & the Pacific Northwest 1999
Let's Go: Australia 1999
Let's Go: Austria & Switzerland 1999
Let's Go: Britain & Ireland 1999
Let's Go: California 1999
Let's Go: Central America 1999
Let's Go: Eastern Europe 1999
Let's Go: Ecuador & the Galápagos Islands 1999
Let's Go: Europe 1999
Let's Go: France 1999
Let's Go: Germany 1999
Let's Go: Greece 1999 **New title!**
Let's Go: India & Nepal 1999
Let's Go: Ireland 1999
Let's Go: Israel & Egypt 1999
Let's Go: Italy 1999
Let's Go: London 1999
Let's Go: Mexico 1999
Let's Go: New York City 1999
Let's Go: New Zealand 1999
Let's Go: Paris 1999
Let's Go: Rome 1999
Let's Go: South Africa 1999 **New title!**
Let's Go: Southeast Asia 1999
Let's Go: Spain & Portugal 1999
Let's Go: Turkey 1999 **New title!**
Let's Go: USA 1999
Let's Go: Washington, D.C. 1999

Let's Go Map Guides

Amsterdam
Berlin
Boston
Chicago
Florence
London
Los Angeles
Madrid
New Orleans
New York City
Paris
Rome
San Francisco
Washington, D.C.

Coming Soon: *Prague, Seattle*

Let's Go Publications

Let's Go London 1999

Shanya J. Dingle
Editor

Researcher-Writers:
Rachel Greenblatt
Ben Jackson
Tobie Whitman

St. Martin's Press New York

HELPING LET'S GO

If you want to share your discoveries, suggestions, or corrections, please drop us a line. We read every piece of correspondence, whether a postcard, a 10-page email, or a coconut. Please note that mail received after May 1999 may be too late for the 2000 book, but will be kept for future editions. **Address mail to:**

Let's Go: London
67 Mount Auburn Street
Cambridge, MA 02138
USA

Visit Let's Go at **http://www.letsgo.com**, or send email to:

feedback@letsgo.com
Subject: Let's Go: London

In addition to the invaluable travel advice our readers share with us, many are kind enough to offer their services as researchers or editors. Unfortunately, our charter enables us to employ only currently enrolled Harvard-Radcliffe students.

Distributed outside the USA and Canada by Macmillan.

ISBN: 0-312-19489-7

First edition
10 9 8 7 6 5 4 3 2 1

Let's Go: London is written by Let's Go Publications, 67 Mount Auburn Street, Cambridge, MA 02138, USA.

Printed in the USA on recycled paper with biodegradable soy ink.

ADVERTISING DISCLAIMER

All advertisements appearing in Let's Go publications are sold by an independent agency not affiliated with the production of the guides. Advertisers are never given preferential treatment, and the guides are researched, written, and published independent of advertising. Advertisements do not imply endorsement of products or services by Let's Go. If you are interested in purchasing advertising space in a Let's Go publication, contact: Let's Go Advertising Sales, 67 Mount Auburn St., Cambridge, MA 02138, USA.

How to Use This Book

London is one of the most popular tourist destinations in the world—as it well should be, with an innumerable number of museums, a vast array of cultural offerings, and the most entertaining royal family in the world. The city is a vast metropolis, filled with obvious and hidden wonders. But fear not—*Let's Go* is here to help you navigate the London maze.

London: An Introduction provides a brief history of London, along with an overview of politics, music, art, architecture, film, and more. Each section is arranged chronologically, so it's easy to follow the progression of say, music, from Henry Purcell to the Spice Girls. **Essentials** provides the details and references to make planning your trip to London and getting around the city once you're there trouble-free. In the Essentials chapter, **Planning Your Trip** offers information on money, packing, and specific concerns for disabled travelers, minority travelers, women, seniors, and families with children. **Getting There** lists a variety of budget travel services, including courier and consolidator companies. **Once There** lists emergency services and a detailed introduction to the different methods of transportation around the city.

Accommodations provides detailed information on hostels, halls of residence, and bed and breakfasts in a variety of neighborhoods—there's something to suit every budget and taste. **Food and Drink** describes the cuisine available in London and lists a variety of restaurants throughout the city. After restaurants, you will find a list of popular chain eateries, along with supermarkets and groceries. Groceries are followed by a description of London pub culture and detailed information on pubs in every corner of the city. The Food and Drink chapter concludes with a list of tea houses and wine bars.

Sights begins with an overview of London's major sights, followed by a list of suggested itineraries for whatever length your visit. Sights are divided into main geographic areas: Central, West, North, East, South, and Greater London. There you can find full descriptions of the neighborhoods located in each area (for instance, Central London: Westminster). After the neighborhoods is a short list of enjoyable parks, gardens, and views of the city. **Museums** gives detailed information on everything from the British Museum and the National Gallery to the Bethnal Green Museum of Childhood.

Entertainment describes the theater, film, music, and nightclub offerings around the city, followed by information on spectator and participatory sports and some off-the-beaten-path activities. **Shopping** details where to pick up everything from crazy club clothes to Doc Martens to a volume of Shakespeare. The **Bisexual, Gay, and Lesbian** chapter provides listings of gay-friendly bars, pubs, restaurants, cafes, dance clubs, and shops. **Families with Children** lists activities around the city to enthrall the kiddies and offer an endless number of Kodak moments.

Daytrips lists respites from the city of London and provides details on transportation, accommodations, and sights. Finally, the **Appendix** lists holidays and festivals, climate and phone code information, and more.

A NOTE TO OUR READERS

The information for this book was gathered by *Let's Go*'s researchers from May through August. Each listing is derived from the assigned researcher's opinion based upon his or her visit at a particular time. The opinions are expressed in a candid and forthright manner. Other travelers might disagree. Those traveling at a different time may have different experiences since prices, dates, hours, and conditions are always subject to change. You are urged to check beforehand to avoid inconvenience and surprises. Travel always involves a certain degree of risk, especially in low-cost areas. When traveling, especially on a budget, always take particular care to ensure your safety.

Table of Contents

Maps

Color Maps

Let's Go Picks

Best Restaurants:
Line up for noodle soups at Wagamama (p.97) and take in the best of French cuisine: crêpes! at Le Crêperie de Hampstead (p.117).

Best Pubs:
Enjoy the music and madness of Covent Garden at the Lamb and Flag (p.125), or revel in history at The Shakespeare (p.127), in the City of London.

Best Churches:
Westminster Abbey (p.140) offers not only beauty, but a chance to visit the graves of some of the most influential people in history. St. Paul's Cathedral (p.165) provides a stunning view of the city, and doesn't look half-bad itself.

Best Museums:
The National Gallery (p.222) offers an endless display of incredible paintings, while the British Museum (p.220) provides historical insight from ancient cultures to modern Britain.

Best Sights:
Hampton Court Palace (p.212) is a sumptous residence, fit for a king. The Houses of Parliament (p.145) are not only beautiful, but offer the opportunity to see British government at work.

Best Store:
No doubt, Harrods (p.255) wins this hands down, with everything from clothing to food to grand pianos. Even if you haven't thought of it yet, it's here.

Best Entertainment:
At Shakespeare's Globe Theatre (p.201), pretend that you are one of the Renaissance masses. Take in a concert at the Royal Albert Hall (p.174), or visit Speaker's Corner, which offers the endless delights of raving derelicts (p. 218).

London: An Introduction

At first, London fulfils the expectations of visitors stuffing their mental baggage with bobbies and Beefeaters, "Masterpiece Theatre" and Sherlock Holmes. The Thamescape is still bounded by the over-familiar Big Ben in the west and the archetypal Tower Bridge in the east; St. Paul's and the Tower of London pop up in between. And the whole world and all its double-decker red buses *do* seem to spin around the mad whirl of Piccadilly Circus.

But even the most timid of tourists will notice that those tube lines spider out a long way from the Circle Line—central London is just a speck on the Greater London map. Beyond Tower Bridge looms the glossy, pyramid-tipped Canary Wharf skyscraper, centerpiece of one of the world's largest and most controversial redevelopments. The Victorian doorway inscribed with an Anglican piety may belong to a Sikh or a Muslim in a city internalizing its imperial past. A glance between the bus fenders at peers and punks swirling around Piccadilly, or at a newsagent overflowing with music and style mags, reveals that "culture" means more than the Royal Opera.

History

ROMAN TIMES

Personal enterprise and ownership have defined London since its founding as the **Roman Empire's** farthest outpost. Although Roman officials laid out merely the skeleton of a town in 43 AD—a bridge, roads, a mint—the city soon became a thriving purchase and shipping hub for wool, wheat, and metals. Within just a few years, Tacitus described the new **Londinium** as "a great trading center, full of merchants." With the Romans for protection, the locals were able to concentrate on commerce. But in 61 AD, the Romans failed to prevent **Queen Boudicca's** Iceni warriors from attacking, looting, and burning the town. The Queen was incensed that the Romans had seized the kingdom left her by her husband and whipped her in public. To protect it from future raids, the Romans built a large stone fort on the edge of the town. In 200 AD, they added a wall and a wooden stockade, but in 410, with Rome in decline, they left altogether.

CHRISTIANITY AND THE NORMANS

Christianity officially arrived in 597 when eager missionary **Augustine** successfully converted King Æthelbert of Kent. Even though subsequent kings were not as receptive to the new religion, **Christianity** was all the rage soon enough. By the end of the 7th century, the religion had a solid foothold in England: its path was immortalized by the Venerable Bede in 731 with his *Ecclesiastical History of the English People*. In the late 9th century, **King Alfred the Great** of Wessex sought to unify the different regions of England against the threat of invasion by Vikings. Alfred repelled the onslaught, succeeded in unifying Southern England politically and economically, and established centers of learning throughout his kingdom. The Danes managed to seize the city from Alfred's successor, Ethelred the Unready. In response, Ethelred enlisted the help of his better-prepared friend Olaf (later a saint), who led a fleet up the Thames to the bridge in 1014. Olaf tied ropes to the bridge supports and rowed away, pulling down the rickety bridge. The Danes fell into the Thames—and the nursery rhyme "London Bridge is Falling Down" was born.

The English and the Danes maintained an uneasy truce until 1066, when **William the Conqueror** of Normandy invaded England in order to seize the throne from Harold, Earl of Wessex; William slaughtered Harold and, for good measure, his two brothers. To protect his unruly subjects, and protect himself from them, he built the White Tower (in the **Tower of London**) immediately after his Christmas Day coronation as King of England.

THE MIDDLE AGES

Henry I first chartered the city of London in 1130, thus allowing it to self-govern. After Henry II revoked London's new autonomy, **Richard I** (better known as the Lion-Heart) aimed to increase the city's revenue in order to finance a crusade to Jerusalem. He appointed the first mayor of London, Henry Fitzailwin, who reigned for 24 years until powerful nobles forced King John to sign the **Magna Carta** in 1215. The document's emphasis on preserving the rights of the Church and royal respect for laws laid the foundation for democracy in Britain. The first Parliament convened 50 years later in 1265, during the reign of Henry III.

History took a sad turn in 1290, when Edward I expelled the entire **Jewish population** of England. In London, Lombard Italians replaced the substantial Jewish community which had flourished through money-lending and finance. The **Black Plague** ravaged the city during the 14th century, eventually decimating over one-third of its residents. As Richard II ascended the throne, another exorbitant poll tax was levied on the people, who countered with the **Peasants' Revolt** of 1381. Wat Tyler, leader of the rebels, was murdered by Lord Mayor William Walworth, who was knighted for his service to the crown.

While King Richard II was on an Irish holiday in 1399, Henry Bolingbroke invaded Britain and snatched the throne. This bold move put the Lancaster (or Plantagenet) house in Buckingham Palace, and gave Shakespeare something decent to write about. In 1415, **Henry V** defeated the French in the Battle of Agincourt, a victory for the British underdogs that soon became legendary. His son Henry VI blew it and was executed in the **Tower of London,** allowing Richard III to get his murderous paws on the crown. The merchant guilds, which arose after the Norman Conquest, took charge of elections and other municipal functions, set quality standards, and watched over sick and elderly workers.

REFORMATION AND RENAISSANCE

The second King of the Tudor Family, **Henry VIII** was such a devout Catholic that Pope Clement VII named him "Defender of the Faith." However, his political ambition soon overrode religious obligations. Convinced that his first wife **Catharine of Aragon** would not give birth to a son, he asked the Pope to grant him a separation. When the Pope refused, he called Parliament and requested that England break from the papacy. In 1534, he formed the **Church of England** and married **Anne Boleyn.** In establishing the new Church, Henry VIII called for the dissolution of the monasteries, causing vast unemployment in London and placing the burden of the sick and the aged upon the city government. Despite his creation of the new Church, Henry was without a male heir eight marriages later. Ironically, Anne's daughter, **Elizabeth I,** would turn out to be the most powerful Tudor monarch.

Queen Elizabeth I became a symbol for the **English Renaissance:** she spoke French, Italian and Spanish fluently, played the lute, wrote poetry, and was a domineering diplomat. During her rule, the British fleet **defeated the Spanish Armada,** establishing Britannia's dominion over the seas. Joint stock ventures such as the Virginia Company sent the British flag fluttering across the seas. With Sir Thomas Gresham as an advisor, Elizabeth established the **Royal Exchange.** In 1581 John Lyly declared that London "may be called the storehouse and mart of all Europe," as the city became the center of the financial world and European commerce. Coffeehouses cropped up, brewing business deals alongside literary and political discussions. Playwrights and poets amused commoners in the outdoor theaters of Southwark, including Shakespeare's **Globe Theatre.** However, the new Anglican Church was unstable and lacked the people's full support.

THE PROTECTORATE AND THE RESTORATION

In the 17th century, political and religious turmoil climaxed in a clash between **Oliver Cromwell's** Puritan forces and **King Charles I's** Anglican army during the English Civil War. Royalists attempted to attack the capital, but the city stood firmly on the side of Parliament: on January 30, 1649 Charles was tried for the crime of treason and became the first and only English king to be publicly executed. Cromwell was named Lord Protector of the Commonwealth in 1653, but died of malaria five years later. Cromwell's short reign had a profound effect on the country; he sent troops to Northern Ireland starting a conflict that still exists today. He also allowed Jews to return to England, ending three centuries of expulsion. In London his Puritanism resulted in the end of all music and theatre in the capital: in fact, Cromwell's Parliament outdid themselves when they announced the abolishment of Christmas Day in 1652. His son Richard was unable to sustain the government and was soon replaced by Charles' son, **King Charles II.** Charles II returned to an enthusiastic London, where he restored the lost merriment of the city. Political turmoil was followed by natural disasters as the Plague in 1665 and the **Great Fire** which ravaged the city in 1666 caused economic collapse. Under the guiding hand of Sir Christopher Wren and the new King, Londoners energetically rebuilt (see **Architecture,** p. 10).

The **Restoration** did not, however, signal the end of troubles with the Stuarts: although Charles II was pliant enough to suit Parliament, there was heated debate about whether to exclude Charles II's fervently Catholic brother James II from the succession. Debate during the **Exclusion crisis** spawned the establishment of two political parties, the **Whigs** (who were firmly Protestant) and the **Tories** (who likened their opponents to the lately discredited Puritans). The bloodless **Glorious Revolution** erupted in 1688 to prevent James II from achieving a Catholic monarchical dynasty; Dutch Protestant William of Orange and his wife Mary were crowned when they assented to the Bill of (Parliamentary) Rights. The ascension of William and Mary marked the end of a century of violent upheaval. Supporters of James II (Jacobites) remained only a distant threat, and became less so in 1746 when James II's grandson "Bonnie Prince Charlie" failed in his bold attempt to invade and recapture the throne. But the Bill of Rights did far more than end debate about who would hold the Crown; it also quietly revolutionized the relationship between Crown and Parliament, bringing a triumphant Parliamentary leadership to the fore. Over the 18th century, the office of Prime Minister, held at the beginning of the century by master negotiator Robert Walpole, gradually eclipsed the monarch as the head of government. In London, King William increased the city's role as financial center, establishing a Bank of England based on the Amsterdam model, much to the thrill of London merchants.

The 18th century witnessed one of the greatest social changes in British history: massive portions of the rural populace migrated to towns, including a substantial portion which relocated to London, pushed off the land by the **Enclosure Acts** and lured by rapidly growing opportunities in industrial employment. Over the next hundred years, industrialization irreversibly altered the texture of British as well as global society as Britain expanded into Empire. The gulf between workers and owners that began as early as the 11th century was replaced by a wider gap between factory owners and their laborers.

THE VICTORIAN ERA

As Britannia's rule expanded under **Victoria,** London enthusiastically took up its position as the center of the Empire. **The Great Exhibition,** a fair celebrating and displaying British and imperial products along with Queen Victoria's Golden and Diamond Jubilees and Prince Albert's South Kensington Museums, would long stand as symbols of the pinnacle of Britain's technological and imperial prowess.

By the 1830s, the combined forces of class division and frightening workplace conditions spurred the beginnings of domestic industrial regulation. A century of reform was inaugurated by a moderate franchise reform in 1832. At the same time, some morally stringent Victorian Liberals such as **William Gladstone** picked up where free-traders like **Robert Peel** left off, extending the economic notion of a free market to encompass a more open attitude toward different religions. The **Chartist movement** of the mid-19th century dramatically pressed for universal manhood suffrage regardless of class, but modest reforms and a boom in the 1840s effectively curbed more radical reform until later in the century.

While the empire burgeoned, the city became increasingly crowded. Rampant growth in the 18th and 19th centuries worsened structural problems (horse-drawn traffic jams and street pollution) that the government was unable to address. Increasing **pollution** of the Thames river led to the "Big Stink" of 1858. Private enterprise stepped into the gap; the first underground **tube** line was financed by private backers. But the London County Council, created in 1889, provided a more substantial public transit solution. It developed public motor-buses to reduce congestion and would eventually pass clean air legislation. The grimy, foggy streets that Holmes and Watson had once rattled down would never be the same again.

By the end of the century, trade union organization strengthened, assuming its modern form during the 1889 strike of the East London dockers and eventually finding a political voice in the **Labour Party.** Despite the gains of organized labor, the quality of urban life declined alarmingly. In the capital, three out of four children did not live beyond the age of five, and an outbreak of cholera struck many of the city's poor. Perched comfortably on divans, the Victorian elite took up aid to the poor as its pet project. This paved the way for a slew of welfare programs established by the Liberal government in 1910. The peers drew the line at Prime Minister **Lloyd George's** "people's budget" and provoked a constitutional crisis. Meanwhile, pressures to alter the position of different marginalized groups proved largely ineffectual. The **Suffragettes** moved their headquarters to London, but failed to win women the vote through radical strategies such as hunger strikes.

WORLD WAR I AND DEPRESSION

The Great War, Britain's first continental military action in a century, scarred the British spirit with the loss of a generation and dashed Victorian dreams of a peaceful, progressive society. London endured 25 air raids, and hope for a new beginning within England was generally lost; though women gained **suffrage** at this time, a sense of aimlessness overtook the nation's politics. A succession of amusing mediocrities came to power: Bonar Law, Ramsay MacDonald, and Stanley Baldwin. The 1930s brought **depression** and mass unemployment (inertially presided over by Baldwin's National government), as well as the appeasement of Hitler, led by **Neville "peace in our time" Chamberlain.** After WWI, the "Homes for Heroes" program, which failed to deliver fully its promise of adequate housing, nevertheless expanded the map of London fourfold.

WORLD WAR II AND SWINGIN' LONDON

"We would rather see London laid in ruins and ashes than that it should be tamely and abjectly enslaved," **Winston Churchill** declared in 1940. During the **Battle of Britain,** the city endured bombing every night except one for three straight months. Many Londoners took refuge in the underground tube stations. When Hitler finally transferred the Luftwaffe to the Russian front, London emerged from the Blitz, battered but unbowed.

After the war, the second Empire reached its peak and immediately lost its power: The British took control of the old Gamin and Ottoman Empires, only to forfeit them to the forces of democracy and nationalism which the Allies themselves had unleashed. The post-war era's growing affluence and diversity propelled Britain to the center stage of international popular culture, with **Swingin' London** as its center, and gave rise and fall to countless subcultures clustered around pop music and fashion. Queen Elizabeth II, who continues to reign today, was coronated in 1953. Harold Wilson's Labour government introduced a number of crucial **social liberalizations,** including reform of divorce and homosexuality laws and the abolition of capital pun-

London Underground

While today, most give little thought to the Underground public transit system, aside from bemoaning its rush hour delays, those who survived World War II probably know the Tube system far more intimately than anyone could ever ask for. During the war, over 150,000 people found shelter on the platforms of London's tube stations. The government originally forbade the camping out of London residents in spaces designed for people to momentarily stand upon. During the German air raids, however, it soon became apparent that many of the city's inhabitants intended to avoid falling bombs by getting as far away from them as possible—namely, by burrowing underground. Once the government realized that the platform squatters were there to stay, fear that an epidemic would result from the squalid conditions prompted the emergence of British hospitality. Bathrooms were provided, refreshments and tea were served, lights were dimmed in the evenings, and bunks were provided for added comfort. A spirit of community began to evolve among the Underground inhabitants beneath London's surface. Over 50 lending libraries were created to provide entertainment. Recorded music was played. Mini-schools and day-care centers were arranged. Ever obsessed by the news, some of the tube stations began their own newspapers. For instance, the Swiss Cottage tube station published the *Swiss Cottager,* perhaps one of the few examples of an underground press.

ishment. Wilson also sought to drive the nation forward with the "white heat" of technological advance, but toward the end of the 60s became mired in the government's decreasingly reciprocal relationship with organized labor, which now represented middle-class clerical workers as much as railwaymen and miners. The London County Council became the Greater London Council in 1965, and the Council's authority over the city was gradually diminished.

Britain gradually relinquished the majority of its colonial holdings in Africa, the Middle East, and South Asia, and retreated tail-between-legs from the Suez Canal crisis. Visionary Conservative **Harold Macmillan** heard "the winds of change" blowing and paved the way for the denouement of the Empire. He hoped to win Britain its place in the **European Community (EC),** a task completed in 1974 by Edward Heath.

Increasing economic problems that stemmed from Britain's colonial retreat led to increased belief in the 70s of the theorization of "decline." Would Britain be able to prosper without the income from her former empire? Conservative and Labour governments alike floundered in their attempts to curtail unemployment while maintaining a certain base level of social welfare benefits. The discovery of oil in the North Sea lifted hopes prematurely, but plummeting prices hobbled its market value. Government after government wrangled with labor unions, culminating in a series of public-service strikes in early 1979, the **"Winter of Discontent,"** which stymied the Labour government.

THE THATCHER YEARS AND BEYOND

It was against this backdrop that Britain grasped at what looked like a chance for change: the admonishing "Victorian values" and nationalism of **Prime Minister Margaret "The Iron Lady" Thatcher.** Her first term seemed doomed by the painful economic recession, but by 1983 the victory in the **Falklands** (smelling of the former glory of British imperialism) and embarrassing disarray in the Labour Party clinched her second term. Thatcher turned from the war in the islands to "the enemy within," referring to the bitter miners' strike of 1983-84, while denationalizing industries and dismantling the welfare state with disarming quips like "There is no such thing as society." Unlike her Tory and Labour predecessors, Thatcher neither believed nor succumbed to the long-standing view that the government should focus its economic policies on reducing unemployment. The first Prime Minister to break with the post-war consensus, she advocated privatization and preferred to control inflation by cutting taxes and welfare programs.

By 1987, the Tories had won over a contented sector of the affluent working class with such popular policies as the sale of public housing to its occupants, even as others shuddered at the mention of "that bloody woman's" name. Thatcher's policies brought dramatic prosperity to many, but sharpened the divide between those who benefitted from the changes and those who didn't.

Thatcher prided herself on "politics of conviction," but her stubbornness was her undoing, as she clung to the unpopular **poll tax** and resisted European integration. In London, conflicts with Lord Mayor Ken Livingstone led her to completely abolish the Greater London Council. A 1990 leadership challenge led to her resignation and the election of **John Major** as Prime Minister representing the **Conservative Party.** The soft-spoken Major quietly jettisoned the poll tax and stepped more carefully around Europe. His **"Citizen's Charter"** tried to continue the reform of public services, though less radically, by gently speaking of Health Service "customers" and promising refunds to delayed rail passengers. But Major's cabinet became more occupied with predicting the end to a deep recession resulting partly from the credit-fueled 80s boom. In 1993, the British pound toppled out of the EC's monetary regulation system, embarrassing Major's government and casting doubt on Britain's place in the Community. Finally, in August of the same year, after severe division between Major and anti-treaty rebels within the Conservative Party, Britain became the last member of the EC to ratify the **Maastricht Treaty** on a closer **European Union (EU).**

Even with these Conservative debacles, Labour failed again to shed the image gained during 70s recessions, and the Tories under John Major won another five years in April 1992. Labour's defeat spurred the election of a new leader, Scotsman **John Smith,** and the pursuit of reform, but the beloved Smith's untimely death in May 1994 dashed Labour hopes once more. From 1992-97, Major struggled with constant unpopularity; the aftermath of the 1991-92 recession, the 1993 tax increases, and continuing strife within the Conservative Party over relations with Europe all accounted for drops in support. By 1995, Major's ratings were so low that he resigned as leader of the Party in order to force a leadership election. Major won the election, restoring some semblance of authority, but as the Conservatives began to lose parliamentary seats and continued to languish in the polls, the Labour Party, under the leadership of charismatic **Tony Blair,** refashioned itself into the alternative for discontented voters and began to rise in popularity after years in decline.

Politics

London has always been at the fore of British politics, as home to the **Houses of Parliament** and all of the Royal Palaces. Since Henry I first chartered the city in 1130, it has struggled to maintain its own autonomy within England, a struggle which culminated this year in the descision of London residents to elect their own mayor. Its role within British politics has always been a powerful one – every monarch has acknowledged the necessity of appeasing the capital in order to maintain leadership. While London was often recognized as a **seat of rebellion,** overall political and social change has occurred (relatively) calmly in Britain—give or take a 17th-century regicide. Politics has long been a civilized affair joined in by public-minded artists, writers, and scholars. William Pitt, Benjamin Disraeli, and Winston Churchill chastised opponents and praised friends with eloquence and grace.

Another salient feature of British politics is its **partisanship.** In the tumultuous 17th century, before organized parties even existed, the religious floundering of the Stewart monarchs divided MPs (members of Parliament) into **Tories,** who wished to preserve a steady line of succession regardless of religion, and **Whigs,** who wanted an Anglican king regardless of the line of succession. As time passed, Tories became more generally conservative and loyal to the monarch, while the Whigs became a group of reformers and progressives. In the 19th century, the **Conservative** and **Liberal** Parties formed along these ideological lines. Today, the word Tory is still used to indicate a Conservative Party member. The dismal industrial conditions of the late 19th and early 20th centuries prompted not only moderate governmental regulation, but also cries for reform. Trades unions became increasingly organized, a phenomenon crystallized in the strike of the East London dockers in 1889, and continuing in today's London. In 1906, the almost 2,000,000 trade union members found political voice in the newly formed **Labour** party, which finally bumped the **Liberal Party** off as the official second party after WWI.

Parliament is divided into two houses, the **House of Lords** and the **House of Commons.** The MPs convene in the House of Commons and are elected to their positions; the Lords are either born into families with Lordships or receive honorable appointments (for example, Lord Andrew Lloyd Webber). The House of Lords has no power over taxation which severely reduces their legislative importance. However, their Parliament tea rooms are rumored to be more plush than those of the Commons.

There is no such thing as a minor **sex scandal** in London politics. The steamy **Profumo affair,** on which the film *Scandal* was based, involved some high-profile House of Lords types and a mistress allegedly shared by the Minister of Defense and a KGB agent. The British sex scandal fixation took an interesting turn before the 1992 election, when the revelation of an affair by Liberal Democrat leader Paddy Ashdown shot his opinion poll ratings up by 15%. In 1993, the peculiarities of British political scandal met the (equally peculiar) intricacies of British libel law; when the *New Statesman* suggested that **John Major** was having an affair with a Downing Street caterer, Major sued for libel, placing the magazine in a precarious financial position.

There are no set dates for Britain's general **parliamentary election.** The responsibility for setting a date falls on the Prime Minister, who must "request" that the queen dissolve the Parliament and hold an election at least every five years. The Prime Minister must give only three weeks notice, a rule which keeps elections short and inexpensive. The leader of the majority party is then formally invited by the Queen to form a government. Each of the parties has a specific means of nominating a candidate, involving party MPs and sometimes others. Candidates for Prime Minister are nominated by their specific parties and elected in a general election. The main opposition party is constantly poised to move into office. The Opposition leader (an officially paid position currently held by William Hague of the Conservative Party) forms a **"shadow cabinet"** that mirrors the Cabinet in government, and prepares to set up a ministry should they win a majority.

Though such a system is ostensibly a two-party one, **"third parties"** persist. The Liberal Democrats (LDs) were formed from the old Liberal Party and the Social Democratic Party, a moderate Labour splinter group. The LDs, led by Paddy Ashdown, champion a bill of rights and open government, as well as libertarian economics. Other important parties include the Social Democratic and Labour Party (SDLP), the Greens, Sinn Fein, the Scottish Nationalist Party, Plaid Cymru (the Welsh nationalist party), and the Ulster Unionists.

It is **Parliament** that has served as the voice of authority ever since political power moved from the House of Lords to the House of Commons during the 19th century. It expanded male suffrage grudgingly, but made social welfare a priority. Publicity surrounding Jack the Ripper in U.S. papers brought poverty into the limelight, spurring on the first social reformers. During the same period, British women, led by suffragette Emmeline Pankhurst, sought their own political rights; women gained full voting rights in 1928.

After WWII, the Labour Party introduced a **national health system,** fondly known as the NHS, nationalized industries, and initiated a period of vaguely social-democratic "consensus." Some 30 years later, politics took on a new direction, when **Margaret Thatcher** brought the country's movement towards socialism to an abrupt halt. She claimed to have revitalized the nation's economy, increased competitiveness, and created a new style of affluence for the money-managers. Her opponents counter that she left growing social tensions, staggering dole lines (Britain's form of welfare), and a tattered educational system in her wake. One of her most controversial (and last) actions as Prime Minister was to abolish local tax rates based on property value in favor of rates based on number of inhabitants over the age of 18 per dwelling—a poll tax. Euphemistically referred to by the government as "Community Charge," this tax was an undeniably regressive form of legislation which has since been repealed.

Thatcher's replacement, **John Major,** was confirmed in a close general election in 1992. Elected as a right-winger, and as somebody who was neither Thatcher nor her nemesis Michael Hesseltine, Major became a self-described centrist. This confusion about his stance was fundamental and ultimately detrimental to his political profile: critics complained that he tried to please everyone and failed, of course, to entirely please even one of the many and multiplying factions. One thing few disagreed on was the fact that Major replaced Thatcher's voluble resistance to the **European Community (EC)** with cautious negotiation, a stance that divided his party and gravely threatened their majority.

In May 1997 party infighting and lack of direction proved too much for Major's fledgling campaign. After nearly 18 years, the conservative party was ousted from power in the worst loss since 1832, when **Tony Blair,** leader of the **Labour Party,** was elected Prime Minister. Despite his party affiliation, Blair is in some ways continuing the centrist tendencies of his predecessor. To woo conservative Middle England voters, he has gone on a quest to form a "New Labour" party free from the socialist vestiges of traditional labour politics. Blair has publicly stated his admiration for some of Thatcher's ideals and has subsequently reformed Labour's stance on trade unions and nationalization. His somewhat toothless approach to politics has earned him the nickname "Tony Blur" from enemies, but has also brought tens of thousands of new members into the party. As Blair pushes forth an image of "Cool Britannia," his popularity only continues to grow. These traits have spawned numerous comparisons to U.S. president Clinton; indeed, the current political climate in the U.K. is remarkably similar to that in the U.S. in 1992, when anti-incumbent fervor propelled Clinton to the White House.

This Year's News

On March 25, 1998 the British government revealed its plans for the creation of a new position of **London mayor.** John Prescott, Deputy Prime Minister, declared that "for the first time, a local authority in Britain will have a directly elected Mayor and a new form of assembly acting as a check and balance to the Mayor." According to the "White Paper," which details the organization of the new city government, the mayor, along with a **Greater London Assembly,** wil be directly elected by 5 million London residents by the year 2000. The new mayor will have control of a £3 billion budget, and will control the city police and fire services, transportation, and tourism. Though current city councillors fear that concentrating such authority in a single individual could spell trouble (including a loss of their own power), Londoners voted to support the plan in the May 7 **London Referendum,** the first such vote since 1975. High-profile contenders from both parties have begun to make their appeals for the position – but a recent poll suggested that **Richard Branson,** head of the Virgin empire, is the most favoured candidate among London residents.

While in 1996, the EU's ban of British beef strained the island's already tenuous relationship with the Continent, Tony Blair's six-month **EU presidency** (from Jan. to June, 1998) abandoned the confrontational approach of the Conservative party and aimed to unite British and European interests. Nevertheless, Labour endured criticism for poor foreign policy and economic integration. In May 1998, 11 European nations met the criteria for the establishment of the **euro**, a single European currency, and plan to adopt a single monetary policy on January 1, 1999, Britain has declined to join. A single currency means no loss when purchasing items across borders. A croissant, sauerkraut, and bubble n'squeak dinner could become a lot cheaper, if not exactly appetizing. Parliament is concerned that there will be a decrease in economic independence and national sovereignty. For example, if inflation in England unexpectedly skyrockets, Europeans might only be eating croissants and sauerkraut.

Red Ken and the Race to Run London

Unlike most major cities in the world, London does not have a Mayor. This anamolous situation is about to be rectified, however, thanks to the crusading zeal of Britain's Labour government. As part of his program of constitutional reforms, Tony Blair has decided to introduce a directly elected, American-style mayor to the nation's capital by the year 2000. There's just one small problem: Mr. Blair can't stand the front-runner for the Labour Party's nomination, Ken Livingstone. Christened "Red Ken" by the tabloid newspapers, Mr. Livingstone is just the kind of traditional socialist that Blair has tried to eradicate from the Labour party. Livinstone is, however, harder to marginalize than your average left-wing critic of the Blair regime. Not only is he extremely popular, but he also possesses that most prized of assets—a proven track record in London local government. During his time in office, as head of the (no longer existent) Greater London Council (GLC), Livingstone undertook an ambitious program of reforms, most notably a visionary public transport policy that included the now ubiquitous Travelcard.

National sovereignty has become a key issue on the domestic front as well. In a September 1997 referendum, Scotland voted for a **Scottish devolution,** providing the Scots with their own Parliament and allowing them to eventually become an independent nation. In Elections for the newly devolved Congress would occur in May 1999. Perhaps not as strong are recent moves towards a **Welsh devolution.** This would follow Scotland's example, but Wales would retain 40 MPs in Parliament. The current Welsh MPs are split on whether devolution is a good idea, so prospective dates have yet to be set.

Royal London

It's not easy being Queen. Lots of money, to be sure, but no end of unabashedly publicized disaster. The sad spectacle of royal life took a tragic turn in August 1997 as a car carrying **Princess Diana** crashed in a tunnel in Paris. The princess, the driver (later declared drunk at the time of the accident by officials), and her companion, Dodi Fayed, were killed. In an ironic twist, it appears that the accident occurred as the princess was fleeing press paparazzi—the same tabloid reporters and photographers whose screaming headlines and shocking photos have tormented the Royal family for years.

Many hope that Diana's tragic death will be the final chapter in a saga of royal slump begun in 1992, pronounced an *annus horribilis,* or "horrible year" by the Queen. The last few years have witnessed behavior which falls short of elegant: divorce proceedings between Charles and Diana; the alleged discovery and broadcast of Charles's indiscretions with his lover Camilla Parker-Bowles by M15 while spying on Charles and Diana; the separation of Fergie and Andrew; a massive fire in the summer castle; Fergie's photographed romp with a Texas tycoon. Indeed, it is not entirely surprising that London bookmaking organization William Hill laid odds at one-in-six chance that the Windsors would soon be jobless.

Though Diana played a crucial role in shaping modern perceptions of the **British Monarchy,** it's uncertain how her passing will affect the monarchy's longevity—it is only certain that it will. The public outpouring of grief, crystallized in photos of Buckingham Palace drowned in flowers, has been likened to the public reaction to the death of John F. Kennedy or Winston Churchill. However, the fate of the royals after the flowers wilt will depend on whether the Monarchy embraces Diana's fervent populism or retreats to the private realm with traditional composure and aloofness.

Still, despite much complaint, the British seem to be unable to give the royals that greatest of insults, namely to ignore them. News that Charles and Diana were discussing divorce pushed news of an IRA cease-fire off of the front pages (this in the middle of a renewed series of IRA bombings). And despite the recent furor there are still many traditionalists who feel that the royals are a way of affirming a connection to a glorious history. Besides, there may be a more base motive than national pride for subsidizing the royal presence—queens and princes add to a mystique that draws millions of tourists to London each year. At some level, the tourist experience in London would be quite different were there no monarchy. *Maclean's* magazine makes an observation for Canadians which holds equally true for all foreigners: as non-taxpayers we get all the fun of watching the royals without spending a cent.

The current queen, **Elizabeth II,** is not to be confused with her mother, the **Queen Mum,** who was once queen, but is no longer. Elizabeth's children are **Charles, Prince of Wales** (next in line for the throne, has two children, William and Henry), **Andrew, Duke of York** (resting after a tumultuous marriage to the notorious Sarah Ferguson), **Anne,** and **Edward** (who's about to get hitched).

Recent events aside, the Queen is still the Queen, and unless your first name is Duke, getting to see her is not easy. Her public engagements (several hundred each year) are published daily in the Court Circular in *The Times, The Daily Telegraph,* and *The Independent.* You can see the Queen at one of the numerous annual pageants she attends, such as the **Trooping the Colour** ceremony in the middle of June. This is a celebration of the Queen's "official birthday"—never mind that she was born on April 21. In October, at the **State Opening of Parliament,** another occasion not without a fancy robe or two, the Queen gives a speech prepared by the government that outlines proposed legislation for the new session. The Queen rides to and from Parliament via the Mall and Whitehall in the state coach. A large division of the Royal Family usually turns out for the **Remembrance Day Service** (Sun. nearest Nov. 11), held at the Cenotaph in Whitehall to honor the war dead. A more cheerful occasion is the distribution of Maundy Money, on **Maundy Thursday** (the day before Good Friday). In a demonstration of royal humility, the Queen distributes a special silver coin to randomly selected pensioners, the number of which equals her age (73 in 1999). Originally, this ancient ritual (which dates back to around the 12th century) involved the monarch washing the feet of the poor, but the Plague put an end to that.

The Many Faces of London

It's difficult not to notice the many ethnic groups and communities from around the globe that inhabit the city—today's Londoners are just as likely to worship at a Hindu mandir as at a Gothic Wren church, and newstands feature dailies in Chinese alongside the *Times* and the *Daily Telegraph.* The diversity began with the vast British empire, which once stretched across the globe, and was intensified in London as the government encouraged the immigration of Commonwealth citizens to compensate for the labor shortage caused by World War II. But London's cosmopolitan identity has always been shaped by newcomers—the Normans exerted a strong influence on the city during the reign of William the Conqueror, and Lombard Italians took the place of Jews who were expelled from Britain by Edward I in 1290. The expansion of the British empire paved the way for the immigration of West Indians, Hong Kong Chinese, and South Asians, who arrived via the South Asian sub-continent and sub-Saharan Africa. During World War II, Jews fled to the city to escape fascist persecution and immediately after the war, Eastern Europeans anticipating a dismal future beneath the Iron Curtain migrated to London in large numbers. The wide variety of cultures and backgrounds is evident in vibrant ethnic areas such as Brixton, home to a large Caribbean community, the East End, a thriving Southeast Asian neighborhood, and Golders Green, center of the Jewish community.

■ Architecture

The Angles and the Saxons began the confusing story of English building with a style that combined the severe Roman and simple Celtic approaches. They built small monasteries and churches with several towers and wooden or stone roofs. Their mark on London building history exists for the most part under the ground; the Roman London amphitheater was recently excavated during tube construction. The Normans brought the first distinctive national style in the 11th century: churches with endlessly long naves and rectangular east wings. These Romanesque elements survive in the 12th-century church of St. Bartholomew the Great.

In the Middle Ages, Gothic architecture became the design of choice for clerical buildings. Ribbed vaulting, pointed arches, and flying buttresses became immensely popular. The predecessor to today's St. Paul's Cathedral was one of Europe's largest Gothic churches. In the early 17th century, Court Architect **Inigo Jones** introduced Italian stylings: English manor houses began to be laid out symmetrically and surrounded by manicured gardens. Inspired by Italian Andrea Palladio, Jones spread the Palladian style throughout England. He coated James I's Banqueting House in Whitehall with gleaming Portland stone, constructed the airy Covent Garden Piazza, and built the first classical church in England for Charles I's Spanish fiancée.

The **Great Fire of 1666** provided the next opportunity for large-scale construction. In its aftermath, as most of London lay an ashy wasteland, ambitious young architect **Christopher Wren** presented his blueprints for a new city to Charles II. Wren envisioned broad avenues and spacious plazas: London would no longer be a medieval hodgepodge of streets and buildings. But the pragmatic king was well aware that the plan, which took no account of existing property lines, would incense local landowners. So he vetoed Wren's design and the city was rebuilt in the same piecemeal way that it had risen. Wren built 51 new churches, flooding the skyline with a sea of spires leading up to St. Paul's, his masterwork. St. Paul's was Wren's final church—he used the earlier ones as experiments to work out anticipated design problems.

The lyrical styles begun by Jones and Wren continued to shape London's architecture for much of the next century. Other designers, like **James Gibbs, Colin Campbell,** and **William Kent,** refined their styles and integrated them with the new baroque trend sweeping the Continent. The tower and steeple plan of St. Martin's-in-the-Fields proved a popular model for Gibbs' colonial churches, particularly in the United States. Kent, a painter, designed the walls and pseudo-Pompeiian ceiling of Kensington Palace, and the interior of the Palladian Chiswick House. Campbell built early mansions such as Burlington House, now home of the Royal Academy.

By the late 1700s, builders yearned for something more exotic. Tired of London's stout brick face, **John Nash** covered the town with fanciful terraces and stucco facades. He wanted to create a massive garden city for the nobility. His plan was never realized in full, but the romantic pediments, triumphal arches, and sweeping pavilions of Regent's Park provide a glimpse of his rich vision. The discovery of Pompeii and Lord Elgin's pilfering of the Parthenon inspired the next trend—mock Greek and Roman ruins. Architects **Robert Adam, William Chambers,** and **John Soane** went on columnic rampages, grafting Doric, Tuscan, Ionic, and Corinthian pillars onto a variety of unlikely structures.

This enthusiasm for Neoclassicism faded under the reign of Victoria. Victoria's dark propriety and the Romantics' flair combined to usher in a spirited Gothic revival: pubs, villas, and banks were oddly festooned with Italian Gothic pillars. The design contest for the new House of Commons in 1894 required that the style be Gothic or Elizabethan. An immense Gothic cathedral soon rose at St. Pancras Station. While many architects insisted on bringing back Gothic, others ushered in Italian Renaissance, French, and Dutch forms; still others latched onto Tudor, and some lonely pioneers discovered new building possibilities in iron and glass. **Sir Joseph Paxton** created the splendid Crystal Palace for the World's Fair of 1851. The inspirational (1600 ft. long) building burned down at the time of Edward's abdication.

In 1944, the city gained the right to purchase all areas razed by the bombing; on this land they built hundreds of blocks of towering Council housing. In 1947 the Town and Country Planning Act provided for the creation of a "green belt" on the outskirts of the city. While the **London Building Act of 1939** limited heights of buildings to 100 ft. "unless the Council otherwise consent," the office blocks of central London suggest that the Council has consented to the reforms.

After WWII, the face of building in London, perhaps exhausted by the demolition of the war, took a harsher turn. The 1951 Festival of Britain, a centennial celebration of the Great Exhibition and postwar "Tonic to the Nation," created such buildings as the **Royal Festival Hall.** The hopes of postwar utopian planning, and their varying degrees of fulfillment, are embodied in the vast and interplanetary **Barbican Centre.** Then came the early 60s and a building boom in which the post-Blitz face of the City was established. Hulking monoliths now neighbor Victorian door pillars and spiraling chimneys. The medley of building continues: Modern, Neoclassical, and/or postmodern. Lloyd's of London's 1986 tower is remarkable for being decked on the *outside* with elevators and ducts. Contemporary London continues to be the city planner's nightmare—beginning in 1981, the London Docklands Development Corporation was given free reign to develop eight miles of wasteland, causing a frenetic race to create offices and luxury apartments on the Thames. At the center of this showcase of modern architecture is the dazzling **Canary Wharf,** the tallest building in Britain.

Art

Religious art went out of vogue with the Reformation in the 16th century, distinguishing Britain from its still-Roman Catholic counterparts. An early republican revolution (Cromwell's in 1649) led to a more diverse group of British patrons—gentry and wealthy members of the bourgeoisie began commissioning artworks.

Despite these distinguishing marks, many of England's early stars were imported. In the 16th century, the German **Hans Holbein** worked in London as the official painter to the king. A century later, **Sir Anthony Van Dyck** played the same role, painting dramatic royal portraits of Charles I. Partly in reaction to these foreign artists who had helped shape the conventions of British painting, 18th-century painter and Londoner **William Hogarth** prided himself on his distinctly English sense of style. *A Harlot's Progress* and *A Rake's Progress,* two series of morally instructive engravings, established his reputation and broadened the audience for British art.

From the mid-18th to mid-19th century, portraiture continued to thrive under the influence of painters **Thomas Gainsborough** and **Joshua Reynolds.** The **Royal Academy** which Reynolds founded currently holds summer Academy exhibits in Piccadilly. The mid-19th century also saw the emergence of British landscape painting. London was home to **J.M.W. Turner,** who painted mythic, light-filled landscapes in both watercolor and oil paint. He is famed for the visual records of his travels, including a set of engravings entitled *Picturesque Views of England and Wales.* The Tate has a magnificent collection of Turner's work (see **Tate Gallery,** p. 224). In the same period, **John Constable** lovingly painted the smaller details of English landscape.

This period was followed by an eclectic visual feast ranging from **William Blake's** fantastical paintings and illustrations, to the retro-Renaissance paintings of the Pre-Raphaelites **John Everett Millais, Dante Gabriel Rossetti,** and **Edward Burne-Jones,** to the Pop Art and later 'Op' Art of the 60s. Disturbing meat-filled portraits by **Francis Bacon** and the oddly unrealistic "realism" of **Lucien Freud** transformed Britain's tradition of portraiture in the last half of this century.

London is filled with art forms other than painting and engraving, including sculpture, photography, and constantly reinvented mixtures of media. Britain's sculptural tradition can be traced in London's architectural details, stone and brass tomb carvings, and abundant public monuments. Beginning in the 1930s, **Henry Moore's** rounded and abstracted human forms and **Barbara Hepworth's** carved elemental materials catapulted modern British sculpture into international fame. During the same period, **Bill Brandt's** photographs (collected in *The English at Home* and *Night in London*) described London in visual essays. British photography since then has ranged from the intensely personal work of radical feminist **Jo Spence** to **Nick Waplington's** photos of working-class interiors and the families that live in them.

Literary London

EARLY DRAMA AND TRAVELING TALES

Geoffrey Chaucer, the son of a well-to-do London wine merchant, initiated the tradition that British tales commence in London. The pilgrims in *Canterbury Tales* set off from the Tabard Inn in Southwark on the South Bank. Since then London has cast a long shadow over the British literary imagination.

Rowdy dramatist **Ben Jonson** held sway in the English court scene of the early 17th century. He planned balls for Queen Elizabeth and her friends, creating original music, choreography, and special effects. Meanwhile, **William Shakespeare** (and his colleagues **Marlowe** and **Webster**) catered to aristocracy and groundlings alike in the circular Rose and Globe theaters across the Thames, the heart of the red-light district.

SATIRE AND THE NOVEL

Many writers found London a degenerate, morally disturbing place, though they could not resist incorporating it into their art. **John Donne,** who became Dean of St. Paul's in 1621, wrote poetry while meting out advice to his parishioners. He set his first and fourth satires in London, drawing attention to urban evils. As a market for books developed in the 1700s, literary society began to resemble today's marketplace of trends: it welcomed **Alexander Pope** as a prodigy at the age of 17, but his disillusionment came quickly. In London, "nothing is sacred…but villainy," he wrote in the epilogue to his *Satires.* Pope drank away his gloom with professional genius and renowned conversationalist **Samuel Johnson** in the Cheshire Cheese pub, while **James Boswell** scurried around collecting crumbs for his grand biography, the *Life of Johnson.* **Daniel Defoe, Henry Fielding,** and **Samuel Richardson** also explored themes of urban injustice, using journalism, satire, and sermons as their tools.

Poets of the Age of Reason fantasized about a city different from the crime-filled one that they unhap'ly inhabited, but few moved away. London remained a haven for publishing and literary cliques wrestling with ideas of social justice. In the early 18th century, **Joseph Addison** and **Richard Steele** attacked urban ills in a new way: the *Tatler* and *Spectator* delivered moral and political essays to subscribers, while **Johnathan Swift** suggested in his *Modest Proposal* that to curb urban poverty, hunger, and over-crowding, the poor should eat children.

PLEASE SIR, MAY I HAVE SOME MORE?

As a gray haze settled over the city's houses and the beggars on the streets swelled into what **Marx** referred to as the capitalists' "reserve army," the wretchedness attracted the empathy and creative interest of a number of writers, most famously **Charles Dickens.** Dickens—whose name has elicited titters from generations of schoolboys—described his characters' wendings through the 19th century's filthy back allies, poorhouses, and orphanages. These fictional characters served to warn readers that too much time in industrial London does wretched things to one's nerves. The Romantic poets had the same idea. They abandoned the classical idealization of the urban and left the city. **John Keats** and **William Wordsworth** lived in Hampstead and Westminster, both distant suburbs at the time. **Percy B. Shelley** wrote, "Hell is a city much like London," and **William Blake** doubted the existence of a new Jerusalem "amongst these dark Satanic mills."

By the close of the 19th century, when reforms began to mitigate the effects of industrialization, some writers turned to purely aesthetic issues. In the 1890s, **W.B. Yeats** joined the London Rhymers' Club. **Lewis Caroll** went into the looking glass with Alice. The relentlessly quotable **Oscar Wilde** proclaimed that art could only be useless. Fellow dramatist and Fabian socialist **George Bernard Shaw** allowed his politics to find expression in his vision of art, with plays more didactic than decadent.

THE MODERNISTS

In 1921, Missouri-born T.S. Eliot turned London into an angst-ridden modern *Waste Land*, an "Unreal City." The poem follows a crowd over London Bridge into the City, wondering how many of them the war has "undone." Both Eliot and Yeats did their time in the high modernist Bloomsbury group. This erudite crowd included **Virginia Woolf, Vanessa and Clive Bell,** the multitalented **John Maynard Keynes, Lytton Strachey,** and **E.M. Forster** (recently re-popularized by Merchant-Ivory). Meanwhile, a concerned **George Orwell** was meeting street people and telling yarns of urban poverty in his ultimate tale of budget travel, *Down and Out in Paris and London.* Orwell put forth his disturbing and compelling critique of the direction of modern life in *1984* while living in Notting Hill; much of this book is a reflection of Orwell's somewhat sordid surroundings and consequent misgivings about city life.

POSTMODERNISM AND BEYOND

Aside from Orwell's haunting account and **Anthony Burgess's** description of the "ultra-violence" of future life in *A Clockwork Orange,* much of London's modern literature is witty and bright. **P.G. Wodehouse** wrote a clever and light novel for each of the 70-some years of his long life. **Kingsley Amis** and his now famous son **Martin** write well-loved satirical novels. **Sue Townsend's** *Diaries of Adrian Mole* sets brilliant adolescence in Thatcherite England, while **Stephen Fry's** *The Liar* exploits that bastion of Britain education, the elitist boarding school. London has become a publishing center for writers in English from the former colonies and other lands, such as **Salman Rushdie, V.S. Naipaul, Kazuo Ishiguro,** and **Timothy Mo. Helen Fielding** recently made a splash with her witty and revealing account of the life of a single woman in England in *Bridget Jones's Diary.* While questions about London's future European and world status in the emerging order may be open for discussion, a survey of recent titles—Amis's *London Fields,* **V.S. Pritchett's** *London Perceived,* **Doris Lessing's** *London Observed*—tells us that it retains a distinguished place in the world's intellectual and literary life. Writers keep coming to this irresistible town—as a publishing center and an inexhaustible topic, they can't seem to avoid it.

The Press

In a culture not yet completely addicted to the telly, the influence of papers is enormous. The **Sun,** a daily Rupert Murdoch-owned tabloid better known for its **page-three pinup** than for its reporting, was widely credited with delivering victory to Margaret Thatcher in her re-election campaign (no, she did not pose). Ambitious English journalists aspire to finish their apprenticeships in the provinces and join "the Fleet Street hacks" (who now inhabit the old Wapping docks). With the exception of the Manchester-born **Guardian,** national papers originate from London.

The **Financial Times,** printed on pink paper, does more elegantly for the City what the *Wall Street Journal* does for Manhattan. The **Times,** has remained a model of thoughtful discretion and mild infallibility for centuries. The **Daily Telegraph** (dubbed "Torygraph") is fairly conservative and old-fashioned. The **Independent** lives up to its name. Of the screaming tabloids, the **Daily Mail,** the **Daily Express,** and the **Evening Standard** (the only evening paper) make serious attempts at popular journalism, while **News of the World,** the **Star,** the **Daily Mirror,** and **Today** are as shrill and lewd as *The Sun.* The best international news shows up in *The Guardian, The Times, The Financial Times,* and *The Independent.*

On Sundays, *The Sunday Times, The Sunday Telegraph, Independent on Sunday,* and the highly polished *Observer* publish multi-section papers with glossy magazines, detailed arts, sports, and news coverage, together with a few more "soft bits" than their daily counterparts. Sunday papers, although they share close association with their sister dailies, are actually distinctly styled, separate newspapers.

The immensely popular satirical publications, **Viz** and **Private Eye,** parody modern prejudices and hypocrisies with unashamedly outrageous comic-strips and biting political comedy—look to Private Eye for serious political satire, and seek out Viz for a laugh. World affairs are covered with a surreptitious wit by the **Economist.** The **New Statesman** on the left and the **Spectator** on the right cover politics and the arts with verve and sense. England also boasts some of the best music rags in the world: **Melody Maker** and **New Musical Express** trace the latest trends with often hilarious wit (check these for concert news), **Q** covers a broader spectrum in excellent detail, while **Grammophone** focuses on classical music. The indispensable London journal **Time Out** is the most comprehensive calendar/guide to the city and features fascinating pieces on British life and culture.

Radio and Telly

The **BBC** established its reputation for fairness and wit with its radio services: BBC1 has ceded responsibilities of news coverage to its cousin BBC4, but continues to feature rock and roll institution John Peel. BBC2 has easy listening and light talk shows; BBC3 broadcasts classical music (undoubtedly the finest station of its kind anywhere). AM is called Medium Wave (MW) in England. Each town and region in England is equipped with a variety of local commercial broadcasting services.

TV-owners in England have to pay a tax; this supports the advertisement-free activities of BBC TV. Close association with the government has not hampered innovation and risque programming. While days may be filled with interminable cricket matches, the evening's fare could include a *Friends* marathon, or the *X-Files.*

Home of *Monty Python's Flying Circus,* BBC TV broadcasts on two national channels. BBC1 carries news at 1, 6, and 9pm as well as various Britcoms. Cultural and political commentary is telecast on BBC2, along with the excellent Newsnight, a news and current affairs program. ITV, Britain's established commercial network, carries much comedy along with its own McNews. Channel 4, the newest channel, has highly respected arts programming and a fine news broadcast at 7pm on weeknights—Salman Rushdie once worked for it. At press time there were rumblings of the BBC picking up *The Simpsons,* currently available only on Sky TV, Britain's satellite network. Cable television has been recently added to select English dials. Parliament was introduced to television in 1989: try to catch a session of Question Time, the regular, refreshingly hostile, parliamentary interrogation of the Prime Minister

Music

CLASSIC. TOTALLY CLASSIC.

England was long called "a land without music," a tag which is not entirely deserved. Morley, Weelkes, and Wilbye revamped madrigals; John Dowland wrote lachrymose works for lute. **Henry Purcell** was England's best-known composer for centuries; his opera *Dido and Aeneas* is still performed. London welcomed Handel, Mozart (who wrote his first symphony in Chelsea), and Haydn (whose last cluster of symphonies was named "London"). **Gilbert and Sullivan's** operettas are loved for their puns, social satire, farce, and pomp. Though the pair allegedly hated each other, they collaborated on such gems as *The Mikado, H.M.S. Pinafore,* and *The Pirates of Penzance.* Serious music began a "second renaissance" under **Edward** *(Enigma Variations)* **Elgar,** whose bombast is outweighed by moments of quiet eloquence. Delius redid impressionism, while **Gustav** *(The Planets)* **Holst** adapted neoclassical methods and folk materials to his Romantic moods.

William Walton and **Ralph Vaughan Williams** brought musical modernism to England in the 20th century. **Benjamin Britten's** *Peter Grimes* turned a broader audience on to opera, and his *Young Person's Guide to the Orchestra* continues to introduce classical music to young and old alike. **Michael Tippett** wrote operas, four symphonies, and the oratorio *A Child of Our Time,* for which he asked T.S. Eliot to write the words; Eliot told Tippett he could do better himself.

THE BRITISH INVASION

After WWII, imported American rock and jazz led to the first wave of "British Invasion" bands. **The Beatles** spun out the songs your mother should know and seemed at the front of every musical and cultural trend; the **Rolling Stones** became their nastier, harder-edged answer, while the **Kinks** voiced horror at the American vulgarity that seemed, to them, to have crushed Little England. **The Who** began as Kinks-like popsters, then expanded into "rock operas" like *Tommy* (consequently produced as a Broadway hit) and *Quadrophenia,* which chronicled the famous fights in Brighton between "rockers" (who liked leather jackets and America) and "mods" (who liked scooters, speed, androgyny, and the Who).

SWINGIN' LONDON

Psychedelic drugs and high hopes produced a flurry of great tunes by bands like the short-lived **Creation** from '66 to '68. White British adapters of African-American blues—most famously the **Yardbirds**—spawned guitar heroes such as **Eric Clapton** (Cream) and **Jimmy Page** (Led Zeppelin), who dominated mass markets in the early 70s. The same period's **"art-rock"** (Yes, Pink Floyd, Roxy Music) was at times exciting, at times dreadful. Working-class "skinheads" adopted the sounds and rhythms of Jamaican reggae and ska adding to it their own aggression; later skins would split into socialist, anti-racist and right-wing, neo-fascist factions, both propelled by stripped-down rock called "oi." While **David Bowie** flitted through personae, "pub rock" groups tried to return rock to the people—and in London, a King's Road entrepreneur organized the **Sex Pistols** to publicize his boutique, "Sex."

PUNK

With "Sex"'s clothes and Johnny Rotten's snarl, the Pistols changed music and culture forever. **The Clash** made their punk explicitly anti-Thatcherite and political; the all-female **Slits** mixed theirs with reggae. "Do it yourself" was the order of the day: untouched, and often untouchable, by the big corporations, the second wave of punks started their own clubs, record labels, distributors, and studios, creating the International Pop Underground that persists to this day.

Industrial unemployment gave Northerners the time to form bands and a harsh landscape to inspire them. The fans who sent it up the charts were surprised to learn that the **Buzzcocks'** Pete Shelley wrote "Ever Fallen in Love?" about a man. **Joy Division** and **Factory Records** made Manchester echo with gloomily poetic rock and graphic design. Birmingham's **Au Pairs** asked feminist questions over a hooky backbeat, and that grim city's leftist ska bands, like the **Selecter** and the **Specials**, took their "two-tone" style to the people. **Elvis Costello, Squeeze,** and the **Jam** found that punk and ska had cleared the ground for smart pop, which stayed persistently and bitingly English even as it took over world charts.

NEW PUNK AND RAVE

Melancholy stylishness like **Felt** and **Eyeless in Gaza** passed sadly unnoticed through the 80s, but the **Smiths** of Manchester took up the slack and shook teens everywhere. Oxford's **Tallulah Gosh** idealized childhood in million-mile-an-hour pop; regrouped as **Heavenly,** they and Bristol-based **Sarah Records,** inspired self-proclaimed "boys" and "girls" to cast aside volume and swagger for last-chance tries at innocence. **The Police** exploded onto the international music scene with the reggae/punk hit "Don't Stand So Close to Me."

Even current dance trends spring from punk: the **Human League** and **Cabaret Voltaire** (whose native Sheffield had no clubs to play in) learned to play synths to make assaultive noise before they used them to shake up clubgoers. **Yaz, Depeche Mode,** and **New Order** soon joined them. A decade later, unemployed kids and easy access to the drug **ecstasy** created rave culture's all-night, all-day, sweaty, anaesthetic gatherings and the faceless electronic music that accompanied them.

BLUR, SPICE, AND EVERYTHING NICE

National trends are made and unmade by London-based music weeklies. An unknown band can make "single of the week," graduate to the papers' covers, sell 600,000 CDs, and then vanish. "Indie" bands like **Pulp, Blur,** and **The Verve** continue to wrestle with the same credibility problems as their American "alternative" counterparts. **Oasis,** vanguard of the more straight-ahead, shiny "Britpop" sound, have captured the sound and hype (minus the creativity) of the Beatles to win the hearts of tabloids and 14-year-olds alike. The studio-manufactured **Spice Girls** have won/conquered the world over with their bubblegum pop; Baby Spice is Prince Henry's favorite. Much to the despair of 8-year-old girls throughout the UK, **Geri Halliwell** (better known as Ginger Spice) has chosen to leave the group and embark on a solo career, but the group in its entirety can be seen again and again by purchasing the girls' film debut, *Spice World.*

Electronic music enjoys a large following in the London music scene with popular bands like **Prodigy** and the **Chemical Brothers.** Hip-hop's burgeoning popularity in Europe is reflected by British trip-hop bands like **Massive Attack, Portishead** and **Tricky.** Despite this, London's sole momentous contribution to rap remains the fact that it served as the birthplace and childhood home of Ricky Walters, aka **Slick Rick (the Ruler).** Swingin' London was recently resurrected by lounge star/satirist extraordinaire **Mike Flowers Pops.**

Film

British Film has suffered an uneven history, marked by cycles of confidence and expansion followed by decline and stagnation. Unlike French or Australian cinema which is often partially subsidized by the government, the conservative upsurge in the late 70s and 80s lead to a decrease in production and a drain of talent to Hollywood. Nevertheless, British film, whether assisted by outside investors and talent, has had a formidable impact on world cinema.

The New Wave movement in the 1960s focused on the contemporary working class experience, producing such cinematic adaptations as **John Osborne's** play *Look Back in Anger* (1959) directed by **Tony Richardson.** Allied Film Makers, a company formed by Bryan Forbes and actor **Richard Attenborough,** produced such films as *Whistle Down the Wind* (1961) (now an Andrew Lloyd Webber musical) and *The L-Shaped Room* (1964). **John Schlesinger** directed such films as *Billy Liar* (1963), deflecting working class angst into fantastical comedy.

With the success of Richardson's *Tom Jones* (1963) which starred **Albert Finney,** the New Wave movement ended, eclipsed by the phenomenon of "Swingin' London" and an upsurge in international interest in British culture. As Twiggy walked the world's fashion runways, American director **Richard Lester** made rock stars into film stars with the Beatles' *A Hard Day's Night* (1963), **Michael Caine** shagged his way to the top in **Lewis Gilbert's** *Alfie* (1966), and **Sean Connery** drank the first of many martinis, shaken not stirred, as **James Bond** in *Dr. No* (1962). Hollywood began investing in British talent, allowing director **David Lean** to direct the international epics *Lawrence of Arabia* (1962) and *Doctor Zhivago* (1965). Established foreign auteurs, intrigued by fashionable Britain, began passing through London. Italian director **Michelangelo Antonioni** satirized the fickle nature of trendy London with *Blowup* (1966), ex-patriate **Stanley Kubrick** went beyond the infinite without leaving England in *2001* (1969), and **Francois Truffaut** heated up Britain in his much-maligned adaptation of *Fahrenheit 451* (1966). As the hopes and promises of the decade began to look a little tarnished, elements of British cinema took on a darker edge. **Lindsay Anderson's** *If...* (1968) and Kubrick's *A Clockwork Orange* (1971) both exposed the restlessness of British youth and their discontent with society.

In 1969, 90 percent of the investment in British cinema came from America. Following a number of British commercial failures, Hollywood effectively pulled out, leaving the British industry bereft of a major part of its production finance. During this slow period, ex-Beatle **George Harrison** formed HandMade pictures to produce *Monty Python's Life of Brian* and **Terry Gilliam's** surprise success *Time Bandits* (1981) and surprise flop *Brazil* (1986). Then, on Oscar night in 1982, **Hugh Hudson's** *Chariots of Fire* received best picture. The next year Attenborough's *Ghandi* (1982) swept the Oscars and British film was again thrust to the forefront of international cinema. More recently, **Neil Jordan's** *The Crying Game,* **Sally Potter's** *Orlando,* and **Mike Newell's** phenomenally successful *Four Weddings and a Funeral* been well-received without sacrificing their "Englishness." Last year's fashionable *Trainspotting* directed by **Danny Boyle** was all the rage, while **Mike Leigh's** small film *Secrets and Lies* made a sizable impression on an international audience. These new trends cannot disguise Britain's groovin' past; "Swingin' London" returned this past spring in the **Mike Myers** spy thriller *Austin Powers: International Man of Mystery*. Actress Judi Dench immortalized Queen Victoria in **John Madden's** critically acclaimed *Mrs. Brown.* The period epics of **Anthony Minghella's** *The English Patient* and **Ian Softley's** *Wings of the Dove* were featured in theaters alongside smaller films such as **Peter Hewitt's** *Sliding Doors* and Leigh's *Career Girls*.

Essentials

The title above says it all. At best, the information below will get you to and from London cheaply and with minimum fuss; at worst, it will keep you out of prison and the hospital. Either way, it's fairly important. The chapter is divided into three self-explanatory sections: **Planning Your Trip, Getting There,** and **Once There.**

PLANNING YOUR TRIP

When To Go

Traveling during the off-season will save you money, as airfares drop and domestic travel becomes less congested. You'll have more room to yourselves in the city, and your pockets will benefit from lower rates and prices. Hotel owners generally consider November to March the off-season, although business may be slow enough in October, April, and May for you to bargain for a discount. For sights, October to April is the off-season and opening hours are sometimes shortened. For climate information, see **Appendix,** p. 306.

At-Home Resources

GOVERNMENT INFORMATION OFFICES

British Tourist Authority (BTA): In **Australia,** Level 16, Gateway Bldg., 1 Macquarie Pl., Sydney NSW 2000 (tel. (02) 9377 4400). In **Canada,** 111 Avenue Rd., Ste. 450, Toronto, Ont. M5R 3J8 (tel. (888) VISIT UK (847-4885) or (416) 925-6326). In **New Zealand,** Dilworth Bldg., Ste. 305, Corner Customs & Queen St., Auckland 1 (tel. (09) 303 14 46). In **South Africa,** Lancaster Gate, Hyde Ln. Manor, Hyde Park, Sandton 2196 (tel. (011) 325 03 43; fax 325 03 44). In the **U.S.,** 551 5th Ave., Ste. 701, New York, NY 10176-0799 (tel. (800) GO2 BRIT (462-2748) or (212) 986-2200).

British Consulates and Embassies: In **Australia,** British High Commission, Commonwealth Ave., Yarralumla, Canberra, ACT 2600 (tel. (02) 6270 6666). In **Canada,** British Consulate-General, British Trade & Investment Office, 777 Bay St., Ste. 2800, Toronto, Ont. M5G 2G2 (tel. (416) 593-1290). In **Ireland,** British Embassy, 29 Merrion Rd., Ballsbridge, Dublin 4 (tel. (01) 205 3700; fax 205 3885). In **New Zealand,** British Consulate-General, 17th fl., Fay Richwhite Bldg., 151 Queen St., Auckland 1 (tel. (09) 303 2973). In **South Africa,** British High Commission, Liberty Life Pl., Glyn St., Hatfield 0083, Pretoria. In the **U.S.,** British Consulate, 19 Obervatory Circle, NW, Washington, D.C. 20008. British Embassy, 3100 Massachusetts Ave., NW, Washington D.C. 20008 (tel. (202) 462-1340).

TRAVEL ORGANIZATIONS

American Automobile Association (AAA) Travel Related Services, 1000 AAA Dr. (mail stop 100), Heathrow, FL 32746-5063 (tel. (407) 444-7000; fax 444-7380). Provides road maps and travel guides free to members. The International Driving Permit (IDP), for most countries worldwide is available for purchase from local AAA officers. To become a member, call (800) 222-4357.

Council on International Educational Exchange (CIEE), 205 East 42nd St., New York, NY 10017-5706 (tel. (888) COUNCIL (268-6245); fax (212) 822-2699; http://www.ciee.org). A private, non-profit organization, Council administers work, volunteer, academic, internship, and professional programs around the world. They also offer identity cards, (including the ISIC and the GO25) and a range of publications, among them the useful (and free!) magazine *Student Travels.* Call or write for further information.

Federation of International Youth Travel Organizations (FIYTO), Bredgade 25H, DK-1260 Copenhagen K, Denmark (tel. (45) 33 33 96 00; fax 33 93 96 76; email mailbox@fiyto.org; http://www.fiyto.org), is an international organization promoting educational, cultural, and social travel for young people. Member organizations include educational travel companies, national tourist boards, accommodation centers and other suppliers of travel services to youth and students. FIYTO sponsors the GO25 Card (http://www.go25.org).

International Student Travel Confederation (ISTC), Herengracht 479, 1017 BS Amsterdam, The Netherlands (tel. (31) 20 421 2800; fax 20 421 2810; http://www.istc.org; email istcinfo@istc.org). The ISTC is a nonprofit confederation of student travel organizations whose focus is to develop, promote, and facilitate travel among young people and students. Member organizations include International Student Surface Travel Association (ISSTA), Student Air Travel Association (SATA), IASIS Travel Insurance, the International Association for Educational and Work Exchange Programs (IAEWEP), and the International Student Identity Card Association (ISIC).

USEFUL PUBLICATIONS

Time Out, a widely available weekly magazine (£1.80) detailing everything there is to do in and around London—consider it your new best friend. Check local newstands and bookstores, or view their website (http://www.timeout.co.uk).

Blue Guides, published in Britain by A&C Black Limited, 35 Bedford Row, London WC1R 4JH, in the U.S. by W.W. Norton & Co. Inc., 500 5th Ave., New York, NY 10110, and in Canada by Penguin Books Canada Ltd., 10 Alcorn Ave., #300, Toronto, Ontario N4V 3B2. Blue Guides provide invaluable and unmatched historical and cultural information as well as sightseeing routes, maps, tourist information, and listings of pricey hotels.

Bon Voyage!, 2069 W. Bullard Ave., Fresno, CA 93711-1200 (tel. (800) 995-9716, from abroad (209) 447-8441; fax 266-6460; email 70754.3511@compuserve.com). Annual mail order catalogue offers a range of products. Books, travel accessories, luggage, electrical converters, maps, and videos. All merchandise may be returned for exchange or refund within 30 days of purchase, and prices are guaranteed (lower advertised prices will be matched and merchandise shipped free).

The College Connection, Inc., 1295 Prospect St. Suite B, La Jolla, CA 92037 (tel. (619) 551-9770; fax 551-9987; email eurailnow@aol.com; http://www.eurailpass.com). Publishes *The Passport,* a booklet listing hints about every aspect of traveling and studying abroad. This booklet is free to *Let's Go* readers; send your request by email or fax only. The College Rail Connection, a division of the College Connection, sells railpasses with student discounts.

Forsyth Travel Library, Inc., 1750 East 131st St., P.O. Box 480800, Kansas City, MO 64148 (tel. (800) 367-7984; fax (816) 942-6969; email forsyth@avi.net; http://www.forsyth.com). A mail-order service that stocks a wide range of maps and guides for rail and ferry travel in Europe. Also sells rail tickets and passes, and offers reservation services. Sells the *Thomas Cook European Timetable* for trains, a complete guide to European train departures and arrivals (US$28, or $39 with full map of European train routes; $4.50 postage for Priority shipping). Call or write for a free catalogue or visit their web site.

Transitions Abroad, P.O. Box 1300, 18 Hulst Rd., Amherst, MA 01004-1300 (tel. (800) 293-0373; fax 256-0373; email trabroad@aol.com; http://transabroad.com). Invaluable magazine lists publications and resources for overseas study, work, and volunteering (US$25 for 6 issues, single copy $6.25). Also publishes *The Alternative Travel Directory,* a comprehensive guide to living abroad (US$20; postage $4).

Wide World Books and Maps, 1911 N. 45th St., Seattle, WA 98103 (tel. (206) 634-3453; fax 634-0558; email travel@speakeasy.org; http://www.ww-books.com).1 A good selection of travel guides, travel accessories, and hard-to-find maps, including Puget Sound's largest selection of travel books.

INTERNET RESOURCES

There is a vast amount of information available through the **Internet.** Commercial providers such as **America Online** (tel. (800) 827-6364) and **CompuServe** (tel. (800) 433-0389) offer many travel-related services to their subscribers. Among the most accessible Internet resources are the **Usenet Newsgroups.** Try **rec.travel.europe, rec.travel.air, soc.culture.british, alt.politics.britain, uk.politics, clari.world.europe.british-isles.uk.**

The easiest way to find information on the Internet is via the **WorldWide Web.** You can accomplish a search by pointing your browser to a service such as http://www.yahoo.com. Another good way to explore is to find a good site and go from there, through links from one web page to another. **British Tourist Authority** (http://www.visitbritain.com) is a good place to start. Lots of specialized pages (cyclists, movie buffs, shoppers) and links abound. Check out **Let's Go's web site** (http://www.letsgo.com) and find our newsletter, information about our books, an always-current list of links, and more. **Rent-A-Wreck's Travel Links** (http://www.rent-a-wreck.com/raw/travlist.htm) is a very complete list of excellent links. **Big World Magazine** (http://www.paonline.com/bigworld), a budget travel 'zine, has a web page with a great collection of links to travel pages. **TravelHUB** (http://www.travel-hub.com) is a great site for cheap travel deals. For communication info, see **Keeping in Touch,** p. 71.

Documents and Formalities

When traveling, always carry two or more forms of ID on your person, including at least one photo ID. A passport combined with a driver's license or birth certificate usually serves as adequate proof of your identity and citizenship. Many establishments, especially banks, require several IDs before cashing traveler's checks. It is useful to carry extra passport-size photos for the various IDs you will eventually acquire.

ENTRANCE REQUIREMENTS

You must have a valid **passport** to enter Britain and to re-enter your country. Citizens of Australia, Canada, New Zealand, and the U.S. may enter the U.K. without a visa. The standard **period of admission** is six months in Britain. To stay longer, you must show evidence that you can support yourself for an extended period of time, and a medical examination is often required. Admission as a visitor from a non-EU nation does not include the right to work, which is authorized only by the possession of a work permit (see **Alternatives to Tourism,** p. 42). Entering Britain to study does not require a special visa, but immigration will want to see proof of acceptance by a British school, proof that the course of study will take up most of your time in the country, and proof that you can support yourself. Possession of a round-trip airline ticket (proof that you'll eventually leave) is also advisable.

PASSPORTS

Before you leave, photocopy the page of your passport that contains your photograph, passport number, and other identification information. Carry one photocopy in a safe place apart from your passport, and leave another copy at home. These measures will help prove your citizenship and facilitate the issuing of a new passport if you lose the original document. If you do lose your passport, immediately notify the local police and the nearest embassy or consulate of your home government.

Australian citizens must apply for a passport in person at a post office, a passport office, or an Australian diplomatic mission overseas. An appointment may be necessary. **Passport offices** are located in Adelaide, Brisbane, Canberra City, Darwin, Hobart, Melbourne, Newcastle, Perth, and Sydney. A parent may file an application for a child who is under 18 and unmarried. Adult passports cost AUS$120 (for a 32-page passport) or AUS$180 (64-page), and a child's is AUS$60 (32-page) or AUS$90 (64-page). For more info, in Australia call toll-free 13 12 32, or visit http://www.austemb.org.

Canadian citizens can pick up application forms in English and French at all passport offices, Canadian missions, many travel agencies, and Northern Stores in northern communities. Citizens may apply in person at any 1 of 28 regional **Passport Offices** across Canada. Travel agents can direct applicants to the nearest location. Canadian citizens residing abroad should contact the nearest Canadian embassy or consulate. Children under 16 may be included on a parent's passport. Passports cost CDN$60, plus a CDN$25 consular fee, are valid for 5 years, and are not renewable. Processing takes approximately 5 business days for applications in-person; allow 3 weeks for mail delivery. For additional information, contact the Canadian Passport Office, Department of Foreign Affairs and International Trade, Ottawa, ON, K1A 0G3 (tel. (613) 994-3500; http://www.dfait-maeci.gc.ca/passport). Travelers may also call (800) 567-6868 (24hr.); in Toronto (416) 973-3251; in Vancouver (604) 775-6250; in Montréal (514) 283-2152. Refer to the booklet *Bon Voyage, But...*, free at any passport office or by calling InfoCentre at (800) 267-8376 (within Canada) or (613) 944-4000 for further help and a list of Canadian embassies and consulates abroad. You may also find entry and background information for various countries by contacting the **Consular Affairs Bureau** in Ottawa (tel. (800) 267-6788 (24hr.) or (613) 944-6788). There is no charge for re-entering Canada with an expired passport.

New Zealand citizens can pick up application forms for passports in New Zealand from travel agents and Department of Internal Affairs Link Centres in the main cities and towns. Overseas, forms and passport services are provided by **New Zealand embassies,** high commissions, and consulates. Applications may also be forwarded to the Passport Office, P.O. Box 10526, Wellington, New Zealand. Standard processing time in New Zealand is 10 working days for correct applications. The fees are adult NZ$80, under 16 NZ$40. An urgent passport service is also available for an extra NZ$80. Different fees apply at overseas post: 9 posts, including London, Sydney, and Los Angeles, offer both standard and **urgent services**—a passport will be issued within 3 working days. Children's names can no longer be endorsed on a parent's passport—they must apply for their own, which are valid for up to 5 years. An adult's passport is valid for up to 10 years. More information is available on the internet at http://www.govt.nz/agency_info/forms.shtml or http://www.undp.org/missions/newzealand.

South African citizens can apply for a passport at any **Home Affairs Office** or **South African Mission.** Tourist passports, valid for 10 years, cost SAR80. Children under 16 must be issued their own passports, valid for 5 years, which cost SAR60. If a passport is needed in a hurry, an **emergency passport** may be issued for SAR50. An application for a permanent passport must accompany the emergency passport application. Time for the completion of an application is normally 3 months or more from the time of submission. Current passports less than 10 years old (counting from date of issuance) may be **renewed** until December 31, 1999; every citizen whose passport's validity does not extend far beyond this date is urged to renew it as soon as possible to avoid the expected glut of applications as 2000 approaches. Renewal is free, and turnaround time is usually 2 weeks. For further information, contact the nearest Department of Home Affairs Office.

United States citizens may apply for a passport at any federal or state **courthouse** or **post office** authorized to accept passport applications, or at a **U.S. Passport Agency,** located in Boston, Chicago, Honolulu, Houston, Los Angeles, Miami, New Orleans, New York, Philadelphia, San Francisco, Seattle, Stamford, or Washington, D.C. Refer to the "U.S. Government, State Department" section of the telephone directory or the local post office for addresses. Parents must apply in person for children under age 13. You must apply in person if this is your 1st passport, if you're under age 18, or if your current passport is more than 12 years old or was issued before your 18th birthday. Passports are valid for 10 years (5 years if under 18) and cost US$65 (under 18 US$40). Passports may be **renewed** by mail or in person for US$55. Processing takes 3-4 weeks. **Rush service** is available for a surcharge of US$30 with proof of departure within 10 working days (e.g., an airplane ticket or itinerary), or for travelers leaving in 2-3 weeks who require visas. Given proof of citizenship, a U.S. embassy or consulate abroad can usually issue a new passport. Report a passport lost or stolen in the U.S. in writing to Passport Services, 1425 K St., N.W., U.S. Department of State, Washington D.C. 20524 or to the nearest passport agency. For more info, contact the U.S. Passport Information's **24-hour recorded message** at tel. (202) 647-0518. U.S. citizens may receive consular information sheets, travel warnings, and public announcements at any passport agency, U.S. embassy, or consulate, or by sending a self-addressed stamped envelope to: Overseas Citizens Services, Room 4811, Department of State, Washington, D.C. 20520-4818 (tel. (202) 647-5225; fax 647-3000). Additional information (including publications) about documents, formalities and travel abroad is available through the Bureau of Consular Affairs homepage at http://travel.state.gov, or through the State Department site at http://www.state.gov.

CUSTOMS: GOING HOME

Upon returning home, you must declare all articles acquired abroad and pay a **duty** on the value of articles that exceed the allowance established by your country's customs service. Goods and gifts purchased at **duty-free** shops abroad are not exempt from duty or sales tax at your point of return; you must declare these items as well. "Duty-free" merely means that you need not pay a tax in the country of purchase. Contact your government agency to find out alcohol and cigarette import limits.

Australian citizens may import AUS$400 (under 18 AUS$200) of goods duty-free, in addition to 1.125L alcohol and 250 cigarettes or 250g tobacco. You must be over 18 to import alcohol or tobacco. There is no limit to the amount of Australian and/or foreign cash that may be brought into or taken out of the country, but amounts of AUS$10,000 or more, or the equivalent in foreign currency, must be reported. All foodstuffs and animal products must be declared on arrival. For information, contact the Regional Director, Australian Customs Service, GPO Box 8, Sydney NSW 2001 (tel. (02) 9213 2000; fax 9213 4000; http://www.customs.gov.au).

Canadian citizens who remain abroad for at least 1 week may bring back up to CDN$500 worth of goods duty-free any time. Citizens or residents who travel for a period between 48hr. and 6 days can bring back up to CDN$200. Both of these exemptions may include tobacco and alcohol. You are permitted to ship goods except tobacco and alcohol home under the CDN$500 exemption as long as you declare them when you arrive. Goods under the CDN$200 exemption, as well as all alcohol and tobacco, must be in your hand or checked luggage. You must be of legal age (which varies by province) to import tobacco and alcohol; the value of these products is included in the CDN$200 or CDN$500. For more information, write to Canadian Customs, 2265 St. Laurent Blvd., Ottawa, Ontario K1G 4K3 (tel. (613) 993-0534), phone the 24hr. Automated Customs Information Service at (800) 461-9999, or visit Revenue Canada at http://www.revcan.ca.

New Zealand citizens may import up to NZ$700 worth of goods duty-free if they are intended for personal use or are unsolicited gifts. Only travelers over 17 may import tobacco or alcohol. For more information, contact New Zealand Customs, 50 Anzac Ave., Box 29, Auckland (tel. (09) 377 3520; fax 309 2978).

South African citizens pay a 20% duty on goods more than SAR10,000 above the duty-free limit. Such goods are also exempted from payment of VAT. Items acquired abroad and sent to the Republic as unaccompanied baggage do not qualify for any allowances. You may not export or import South African bank notes in excess of SAR25,000. For information, consult the free pamphlet *South African Customs Information,* available in airports or from the Commissioner for Customs and Excise, Private Bag X47, Pretoria 0001 (tel. (12) 314 99 11; fax 328 64 78).

United Kingdom citizens or visitors arriving in the U.K. from outside the EU must declare goods in excess of prescribed allowances including UK£145 worth of all goods including gifts and souvenirs. You must be over 17 to import liquor or tobacco. For duty-free purchases within the EU, allowance is UK£75. Goods obtained duty and tax paid for personal use (regulated according to set guide levels) within the EU do not require any further customs duty. More information is available from Her Majesty's Customs and Excise, Custom House, Nettleton Road, Heathrow Airport, Hounslow, Middlesex TW6 2LA (tel. (0181) 910 3602, 910 3566; fax 910-3765) and on the web at http://www.open.gov.uk.

United States citizens may import US$400 worth of accompanying goods duty-free and must pay a 10% tax on the next US$1000. You must declare all purchases, so have sales slips ready. The US$400 personal exemption covers goods purchased for personal or household use (this includes gifts) and cannot include more than 100 cigars, 200 cigarettes (1 carton), or 1L of wine or liquor. You must be over 21 to bring liquor into the U.S. If you mail home personal goods of U.S. origin, you can avoid duty charges by marking the package "American goods returned." For more information, consult the brochure *Know Before You Go,* available from the U.S. Customs Service, Box 7407, Washington D.C. 20044 (tel. (202) 927-6724; http://www.customs.ustreas.gov).

YOUTH, STUDENT, AND TEACHER IDENTIFICATION

The **International Student Identity Card (ISIC)** is the most widely accepted form of student identification. Flashing this card can procure discounts for sights, theaters, museums, accommodations, meals, as well as train, ferry, bus, and airplane transportation, and other services. Present the card wherever you go and ask about discounts even when none are advertised. It also provides insurance benefits, including US$100 per day of in-hospital sickness for a maximum of 60 days, and US$3000 accident-related medical reimbursement for each accident (see **Insurance,** p. 34). In addition, cardholders have access to a toll-free **24-hour ISIC helpline** whose multilingual staff can provide assistance in medical, legal, and financial emergencies overseas (in the U.S. and Canada tel. (800) 626-2427; in the UK tel. (0181) 666 9025; elsewhere call collect (44) 181 666 9025).

Many student travel agencies around the world issue ISICs, including STA Travel in Australia and New Zealand; Travel CUTS and the ISIC website (http://www.isic-canada.org) in Canada; USIT in Ireland and Northern Ireland; SASTS in South Africa; Campus Travel and STA Travel in the U.K.; Council Travel, Let's Go Travel, STA Travel, and the Council website (http://www.ciee.org/idcards/index.htm) in the U.S.; and any of the other organizations under the auspices of the International Student Travel Confederation (ISTC). When you apply for the card, request a copy of the *International Student Identity Card Handbook,* which lists some of the available discounts by country. You can also write to Council for a copy. The card is valid from September to December of the following year and costs US$20, CDN$15, or AUS$15. Applicants must be at least 12 years old and degree-seeking students of a secondary or post-secondary school. Because of the proliferation of phony ISICs, many airlines and some other services require other proof of student identity, such as a signed letter from the registrar attesting to your student status and stamped with the school seal or your school ID card. The **International Teacher Identity Card (ITIC)** offers the same insurance coverage and similar but limited discounts. The fee is US$20, UK£5, or AUS$13. For more information on these cards, consult the organization's website at http://www.istc.org; email isicinfo@istc.org.

Federation of International Youth Travel Organizations (FIYTO) issues a discount card to travelers who are under 26 but not students. Known as the **GO25 Card,** this one-year card offers many of the same benefits as the ISIC, and most organizations that sell the ISIC also sell the GO25 Card. A brochure that lists discounts is free when you purchase the card. To apply, you will need a passport, valid driver's license, or copy of a birth certificate; and a passport-sized photo with your name printed on the back. The fee is US$20. Information is available on the web at http://www.ciee.org, or by contacting Travel CUTS in Canada, STA Travel in the U.K., Council Travel in the U.S., or FIYTO headquaters in Denmark (see **Useful Organizations,** p. 46).

DRIVING PERMITS AND CAR INSURANCE

If you plan to attempt to drive in London, you must have an **International Driving Permit (IDP).** Your IDP, valid for one year, must be issued in your home country before you depart and must be accompanied by a valid driver's license from your own country. Contact the national automobile association in your home country for details and application information.

HOSTELS

For info specific to London, see **Accommodations,** p. 74. If you have Internet access, check out the **Internet Guide to Hostelling** (http://hostels.com). Reservations for over 300 **Hostelling International (HI)** hostels (see listing below) may be made via the **International Booking Network (IBN),** a computerized system which allows you to make hostel reservations months in advance for a nominal fee (in the U.S., tel. (202) 783-6161). Consider becoming a member of Hostelling International to receive various services and discounts. Although you can join HI in London, it is much easier to do so at home. Here are some of the national associations:

Australian Youth Hostels Association (AYHA), Level 3, 10 Mallett St., Camperdown NSW 2050 (tel. (02) 9565 1699; fax 9565 1325; email YHA@yha.org.au; http://www.yha.org.au). Memberships AUS$44, renewal AUS$27; under 18 AUS$13.

Hostelling International-Canada (HI-C), 400-205 Catherine St., Ottawa, Ontario K2P 1C3, Canada (tel. (613) 237-7884; fax 237-7868; email info@hostellingintl.ca; http://www.hostellingintl.ca). IBN booking centers in Edmonton, Montreal, Ottawa, and Vancouver. Membership packages: 1-year, under 18 CDN$12; 1-year, over 18 CDN$25; 2-year, over 18 CDN$35; lifetime CDN$175.

ESSENTIALS

An Óige (Irish Youth Hostel Association), 61 Mountjoy St., Dublin 7 (tel. (353) 1 830 4555; fax 1 830 5808; email anoige@iol.ie; http://www.irelandyha.org). 1-year membership is IR£7.50, under 18 IR£4, family IR£7.50 for each adult with children, under 16 free.

Youth Hostels Association of England and Wales (YHA), Trevelyan House, 8 St. Stephen's Hill, St. Albans, Hertfordshire AL1 2DY, England (tel. (01727) 85 52 15; fax 84 41 26; email yhacustomerservices@compuserve.com; http://www.yha.org.uk). Enrollment fees are adults UK£10, under 18 UK£5, UK£20 for each parent with children under 18 enrolled free, UK£10 for one parent with children under 18 enrolled free, UK£140 for lifetime membership.

Youth Hostels Association of New Zealand (YHANZ), P.O. Box 436, 173 Cashel St., Christchurch 1 (tel. (643) 379 9970; fax 365 4476; email info@yha.org.nz; http://www.yha.org.nz). Annual membership fee NZ$24.

Hostelling International Northern Ireland (HINI), 22-32 Donegall Rd., Belfast BT12 5JN, Northern Ireland (tel. (01232) 32 47 33 or 31 543 5; fax 43 96 99; email info@hini.org.uk; http://www.hini.org.uk). Prices range from UK£8-12. 1-year UK£7, under 18 UK£3, family UK£14 for up to 6 children, lifetime UK£50.

Scottish Youth Hostels Association (SYHA), 7 Glebe Crescent, Stirling FK8 2JA (tel. (01786) 89 14 00; fax 89 13 33; email syha@syha.org.uk; http://www.syha.org.uk). Membership UK£6, under 18 UK£2.50.

Hostelling International South Africa, P.O. Box 4402, Cape Town 8000 (tel. (021) 24 25 11; fax 24 41 19; email info@hisa.org.za; http://www.hisa.org.za). Membership SAR50, group SAR120, family SAR100, lifetime SAR250.

Hostelling International-American Youth Hostels (HI-AYH), 733 15th St. NW, Ste. 840, Washington, D.C. 20005, tel. (202) 783-6161, ext. 136; fax 783-6171; email hiayhserv@hiayh.org; http://www.hiayh.org). Maintains 35 offices in the U.S. Memberships can be purchased at many travel agencies (see p. 46) or the national office in Washington, D.C. 1-year membership US$25, under 18 US$10, over 54 US$15, family cards US$35.

Money

CURRENCY AND EXCHANGE

US$1 = 0.61 British pounds	£1 = US$1.63
CDN$1 = £0.41	£1 = CDN$2.42
IR£1 = £0.85	£1 = IR£1.18
AUS$1 = £0.38	£1 = AUS$2.66
NZ$1 = £ 0.31	£1 = NZ$3.18
SAR1 = £0.10	£1 = SAR10.42

A Note on Prices and Currency:
The information in this book was researched in the summer of 1998. Since then, inflation may have raised the rates considerably. The exchange rates listed were compiled on July 8, 1998. Since rates fluctuate considerably, confirm them before you go by checking a national newspaper or the web (http://www.bloomberg.com).

Nothing is certain in London but expense.
—William Sherstone, *Curiosities of Literature*

Even if you stay in hostels and prepare your own food, expect to spend US$45-50 per person per day. Transportation will increase these figures. No matter how low your budget, if you plan to be in London for more than a couple of days, you will need to keep handy a larger amount of cash than usual. Carrying it around with you, even in a money belt, is a risky but necessary precaution.

Those lucky enough to have money may still have trouble holding on to it as they make their way through the web of commissions and conversion rates. Remember that pounds will be less costly in Britain than at home. Observe commission rates closely when abroad. Banks will ordinarily offer better rates than those of travel agencies, restaurants, hotels, and the dubious bureaux de change. Don't be lured by bureaux that scream "No Charge—No Commission." If it makes you wonder how they make their money, just look at the rates. Since you lose money with every transaction, convert in large sums, but don't convert more than you need, because it may be difficult to change it back to your home currency or to a new one. If you are using traveler's checks or bills, be sure to carry some in small denominations (US$50 or less), especially for times when you are forced to exchange money at disadvantageous rates.

The British pound sterling (£) is divided into 100 pence (p). Coins are issued in denominations of 1p, 2p, 5p, 10p, 20p, 50p, and £1; notes are issued in denominations of £5, £10, £20, and £50. If you hear the term "quid," don't stress—it's merely slang for £1 (as in a quid). Furthermore, if you are given Scottish money as change, don't worry—Scotland's pound notes are legal tender throughout the U.K.

Most banks are closed on Saturday, Sunday, and all public holidays. Britain enjoys "bank holidays" several times a year (see **Appendix,** p. 305, for dates). Usual bank hours in Britain are Monday to Friday from 9:30am to 3:30pm, although many banks, especially in central London, remain open until 5pm and on Saturday mornings. Personal checks from home will probably not be acceptable no matter how many forms of identification you have.

TRAVELER'S CHECKS

Traveler's checks are one of the safest and least troublesome means of carrying funds as they can be refunded if stolen. Several agencies and many banks sell them, usually for face value plus a small percentage commission. (Members of the American Automobile Association, and some banks and credit unions, can get American Express checks commission-free; see **Travel Organizations,** p. 19.) **American Express** and **Visa** are the most widely recognized, though other major checks are sold, exchanged, cashed, and refunded with almost equal ease. If you're ordering your checks, do so well in advance, especially if large sums are being requested.

Each agency provides refunds **if your checks are lost or stolen,** and many provide additional services. (Note that you may need a police report verifying the loss or theft.) Inquire about toll-free refund hotlines, emergency message relay services, and stolen credit card assistance when you purchase your checks.

You should expect a fair amount of red tape and delay in the event of theft or loss of traveler's checks. To expedite the refund process, keep your check receipts separate from your checks and store them in a safe place or with a traveling companion, and record check numbers when you cash them. Leave a list of check numbers with someone at home and ask for a list of refund centers when you buy your checks. Keep a separate supply of cash or traveler's checks for emergencies. Never countersign your checks until you're prepared to cash them, and always bring your passport with you when you plan to use the checks.

American Express: in Australia call (800) 25 19 02; in New Zealand (0800) 44 10 68; in the U.K. (0800) 52 13 13; in the U.S. and Canada (800) 221-7282). Elsewhere, call U.S. collect (801) 964-6665. AmEx traveler's checks are readily available in British pounds and 9 other currencies. They are the most widely recognized worldwide and the easiest to replace if lost or stolen. Checks can be purchased for a small fee (1-4%) at American Express Travel Service Offices, banks, and American Automobile Association offices (AAA members can buy the checks commission-free). Cardmembers can also buy checks at American Express Dispensers at Travel Service Offices at airports, or order them by phone (tel. (800) ORDER-TC (673-3782)). AmEx offices cash their checks commission-free (except where prohibited by national governments), although they often offer slightly worse rates than banks. You can also buy *Cheques for Two,* which can be signed by either of two people traveling together. Request the booklet "Traveler's Companion," which lists travel office addresses and stolen check hotlines for each European country. Visit their on-line travel offices at http://www.aexp.com.

Citicorp: in the U.S. and Canada call (800) 645-6556; in Europe, the Middle East, or Africa (44) 171 508 7007; from elsewhere call U.S. collect (813) 623-1709. Sells both Citicorp and Citicorp Visa traveler's checks in British pounds, along with several other currencies. Commission is 1-2% on check purchases. Citicorp's World Courier Service guarantees hand-delivery of traveler's checks when a refund location is not convenient. Call daily 24hr.

Thomas Cook MasterCard: For 24hr. cashing or refund assistance: from the U.K. call (0800) 622 101 free or (1733) 318 950 collect; from the U.S., Canada, or Caribbean (800) 223-7373; elswhere call collect (44) 1733 318 950. Offers checks in British pounds, and other currencies. Commission 2% for purchases. Thomas Cook offices will cash checks commission-free; banks will make a commission charge. Thomas Cook MasterCard Traveler's Checks are also available from **Capital Foreign Exchange** (see **Currency and Exchange,** p. 27).

Visa: in the U.K. call (0800) 895 078; in the U.S. (800) 227-6811; elsewhere call collect (44) 1733 318 949. The above numbers can tell you the location of their nearest office. Any Visa traveler's checks can be reported lost at the Visa number.

CREDIT CARDS

As in most major cities, a credit card can be your best friend in London. Businesses, excepting the most budget, welcome plastic. Using major credit cards (**MasterCard** and **Visa** are the most widely accepted) you can instantly extract cash advances from associated banks and teller machines throughout the city. Provided you pay your bill quickly, this is a great bargain because credit card companies get the wholesale exchange rate, which is generally 5% better than the retail rate used by banks and even better than that used by other currency exchange establishments. **American Express** cards also work in some ATMs, as well as at AmEx offices and major airports. All such machines require a **Personal Identification Number (PIN),** which credit cards in the United States do not usually carry. You must ask your credit card company to assign you a PIN before you leave; without it, you will be unable to withdraw cash with your credit card outside the U.S. Keep in mind that MasterCard and Visa might be called "Access" and "Barclaycard," respectively, in Britain.

Credit cards are also invaluable in an emergency—an unexpected hospital bill or ticket home or the loss of traveler's checks—may leave you temporarily without other resources. Furthermore, credit cards offer an array of other services, from insurance to emergency assistance, that depend completely on the issuer.

American Express (in the U.S., tel. (800) 843-2273) has a US$55 annual fee but offers a number of services. AmEx cardholders can cash personal checks at AmEx offices outside the U.S., and Global Assist, a **24-hour hotline** with medical and legal assistance in emergencies, is also available (tel. (800) 554-2639 in U.S. and Canada; from abroad call U.S. collect (202) 554-2639). Cardholders can use the American Express Travel Service; benefits include assistance in changing airline, hotel, and car rental reservations, baggage loss and flight insurance, sending mailgrams and international cables, and holding your mail at one of the more than 1700 AmEx offices around the world.

Visa (Telephone Assistance Center tel. (800) 336-8472 in the U.S.) and **MasterCard** are issued in cooperation with individual banks and some other organizations; ask the issuer about services which go along with the cards.

CASH CARDS

Cash cards—popularly called ATM (Automated Teller Machine) cards—are widespread in London. Depending on the system that your bank at home uses, you can probably access your own personal bank account whenever you need money. (Be careful, however, and keep all receipts—even if an ATM won't give you your cash, it may register a withdrawal on your next statement.) Happily, ATMs get the same wholesale exchange rate as credit cards. Despite these perks, do some research before relying too heavily on automation. There is often a limit on the amount of money you can withdraw per day (usually about US$500, depending on the type of card and account), and computer networks sometimes fail. Also, if your PIN is longer than four digits, ask your bank whether the first four digits will work, or whether you need a new number. Many ATMs are outdoors; be cautious and aware of your surroundings.

The two major international money networks are **Cirrus** (U.S. tel. (800) 4-CIRRUS (424-7787)) and **PLUS** (U.S. tel. (800) 843-7587; http://www.visa.com). Cirrus has cash machines in 80 countries and territories. It charges US$3-5 to withdraw non-domestically depending on your bank. PLUS covers 115 countries. Carrying one card for each network will provide maximum coverage.

GETTING MONEY FROM HOME

One of the easiest ways to get money from home is to bring an **American Express** card. AmEx allows its cardholders to draw cash from their checking accounts at any of its major offices and many of its representatives' offices, up to US$1000 every 21 days (no service charge, no interest). AmEx also offers Express Cash, with over 100,000 ATMs located in airports, hotels, banks, office complexes, and shopping areas around the world. Express Cash withdrawals are automatically debited from the Cardmember's checking account or line of credit. Green card holders may withdraw up to US$1000 in a seven-day period. There is a 2% transaction fee for each cash withdrawal, with a US$2.50 minimum and $20 maximum. To enroll in Express Cash, Cardmembers may call (800) CASH NOW (227-4669). Outside the U.S., call collect (336) 668-5041. Unless using the AmEx service, avoid cashing checks in foreign currencies; they usually take weeks and a US$30 fee to clear.

Money can also be wired abroad through international money transfer services operated by **Western Union** (tel. (800) 325-6000). In the U.S., call Western Union any time at (800) CALL-CASH (225-5227) to cable money with your Visa, Discover, or MasterCard within the domestic U.S. and the U.K. The rates for sending cash are generally US$10-11 cheaper than with a credit card, and the money is usually available in the country you're sending it to within an hour, although this may vary.

Some people choose to send cash abroad via **Federal Express** to avoid fees and taxes. FedEx is reasonably reliable; however, this method may be illegal, it involves an element of risk, and it requires that you remain at a legitimate address for a day or two to wait for the money's arrival. In general, it may be safer to swallow the cost of wire transmission and preserve your peace of mind.

In emergencies, U.S. citizens can have money sent via the State Department's **Overseas Citizens Service,** American Citizens Services, Consular Affairs, Room 4811, U.S. Department of State, Washington, D.C. 20520 (tel. (202) 647-5225; nights, Sundays, and holidays (202) 647-4000; fax (on demand only) (202) 647-3000; email ca@his.com; http://travel.state.gov). For a fee of US$15, the State Department will forward money within hours to the consular office, which will disburse it according to instructions. The office serves only Americans in the most dire of straits abroad; non-American travelers should contact their embassies for information on wiring cash. Check with the State Department or the nearest U.S. embassy or consulate for the quickest way to have the money sent.

VALUE-ADDED TAX

Britain charges value-added tax (VAT), a national sales tax of 17.5%, on many services (such as hairdressers, hotels, restaurants, and car rental agencies) and on all goods (except books, medicine, food, and children's clothes). The prices stated in *Let's Go* include VAT unless otherwise specified. Visitors to the U.K. can get a VAT refund through the **Retail Export Scheme.** Ask the shopkeeper for the appropriate form, which immigration officials will sign and stamp when you leave the country. Keep purchases in carry-on luggage so a customs officer can inspect the goods and validate refund forms. Both Heathrow and Gatwick airports offer on-site cash refunds; look for the Tax-Free Refund desk and leave at least an exra hour at the airport as lines can be long. To obtain the refund by check or credit card, send the form back in the envelope provided and the shop-keeper will then send your refund; note, however, that a service charge will be deducted from your refund. Many shops have a purchase minimum of £50-100, that you will have to meet before they fill out a VAT form for you;

stores may try to fob you off because of the inconvenience, but insist and the prices you pay for goods may become much more reasonable. You must leave the country within three months of your purchase in order to claim a VAT refund.

OPENING A BANK ACCOUNT

For a long stay in London, an English **sterling bank account** may be a convenient way to manage funds. If you're planning on working for a year in the city, you should have no problems. The head branches of the five big U.K. banks are: **Barclays Bank,** 54 Lombard St., EC3 (tel. 699 5000); **Lloyd's Bank,** 71 Lombard St., EC3 (tel. 626 1500); **Midland Bank,** 27-32 Poultry, EC2 (tel. 260 8000); and **National Westminster Bank,** 41 Lothbury, EC2 (tel. 606 6060). (Tube: Bank, for all addresses.) **Abbey National,** head office at 201 Grafton Gate East, Central Milton Keynes (tel. (01908) 343 000), will refer you to your nearest branch or a special branch set up to deal with short-term customers. Decisions concerning opening accounts and extended credit privileges are ultimately at the discretion of the branch manager. In all cases you should contact your home bank a few months before coming to London. Obtain a letter of introduction from your bank and find out if it can make arrangements in advance for an account to be opened at a bank in the U.K. so that it is available for use on arrival. Once in London, it may be harder to have your home bank help you open an account. When opening an account, you must show your passport and your bank's letter of introduction, a letter from an employer confirming the tenure of employment in Britain and a regular salary, or a letter from your school (in Britain) confirming your status as a full-time student.

While proof of employment almost guarantees an account, students are screened rigorously. Students of American colleges studying abroad should contact their home school's bursar's office, which may have a special arrangement with a bank in London. When opening an account for a student, the bank generally requires a large deposit to be placed in the account, which could ideally support the student for the full period of study. Alternatively, they may accept proof that regular payments would be made into the account (e.g., from parents).

Once you have made your way through all the red tape, the bank will generally issue you a checkbook, a check guarantee card (vouching for checks of up to £50 or £100), and a cash machine card. They may be rather reticent about handing out credit cards to temporary visitors—which should not matter as long as you can arrange to have your own credit card bills paid back home. Note that Barclaycard acts as both a Visa card and a check guarantee card for Barclay's checks. If the obstacles prove too great, try a **building society,** the British version of a savings and loan, which is less likely to require proof of employment.

ESSENTIALS

Safety and Security

Travelers can feel safer in London than in many large American cities. After all, even the bobbies (police officers) are unarmed. It's hard to wander unwittingly into unnerving neighborhoods—these areas, in parts of Hackney, Tottenham, and South London, lie well away from central London.

To avoid being robbed, keep all valuables on your person, preferably stowed away in a money belt or neck pouch, which hide your money from prying eyes. Never ever put your wallet in your back pocket. Women should sling purses over the shoulder and under the opposite arm. Carry all your treasured items (including your passport, railpass, traveler's checks, and airline ticket) either in a money belt or neck pouch stashed securely inside your clothing. When sitting in public, keep your bags directly underfoot or hooked under the leg of your chair if possible. Never count your money in public, and keep a sharp eye out for fast-fingered pick-pockets, dastardly con artists, and conniving packs of hustlers masquerading as angel-faced children. Be alert in public telephone booths. If you must say your calling-card number, do so very quietly. Making photocopies of important documents (passport, ID, driver's license,

health insurance policy, traveler's checks, credit cards) will allow you to replace them in case they are lost or stolen. Carry one copy separate from the documents and leave another copy at home.

Unattended packages will be taken by thieves or the police (for fear of IRA bombs), so hold your parcels tight. Report any suspicious, unattended packages.

At night, the areas around King's Cross/St. Pancras and Angel tube stations are a bit seedy, and parks, heaths, and riverbanks in all areas should be avoided. Late trains on the tube out of central London are usually crowded and noisy. Waiting at less central stations, on the other hand, can be unsettling. On night buses, sit on the lower deck next to the driver, who has a radio. When walking after dark, stride purposefully on busy, well-lit roads. Keep to the right, facing oncoming traffic. Avoid shortcuts down alleys or across wasteground. Women may want to carry a rape alarm or whistle. For more safety tips, order Maggie and Gemma Moss's *Handbook for Women Travellers* (see **Women Travelers,** p. 34).

Especially when **traveling alone,** be sure that someone at home knows your itinerary. Never say that you're traveling alone. Steer clear of empty train compartments. Ask the manager of your hotel, hostel, or B&B for advice on specific areas and consider staying in places with a curfew or night attendant. Some cheap accommodations may entail more risk than savings; when traveling alone, you may want to forego dives and city outskirts.

For the love of god, look right! British drivers travel on the opposite side of the road, meaning that they'll be speeding towards pedestrians from a different direction than most visitors will expect. It's a testament to the competence of London drivers that more tourists aren't killed by stepping unwittingly into traffic. Don't go out like a sucker—signs at your feet tell you which way to look. Obey them.

Drugs and traveling can be a bad combination. If you carry **prescription drugs** while you travel, it is vital to have copies of the prescriptions themselves readily accessible. As for **illegal drugs,** the safest bet is to avoid them. It may seem "square," but little can ruin a vacation faster than a narcotics charge.

In an emergency, call 999 (the emergency number in England), a free call. The operator will ask whether you require police, ambulance, or fire service.

Self-defense classes, may prove helpful, but expensive. **Model Mugging,** a national organization with offices in several major U.S. cities, teaches a very effective, comprehensive course on self-defense (course prices vary from US$400-500). Women's and men's courses are offered. **Impact, Prepare, Model Mugging, and Fight Back** can refer you to local self-defense courses in the United States (tel. (800) 345-KICK (345-5425)). Course prices vary from $50-400. **Community colleges** frequently offer self-defense courses at much lower prices. For an official **Department of State Travel Advisory** on England, call the 24-hour hotline at (202) 647-5225. To order publications, including a pamphlet entitled *A Safe Trip Abroad,* write them at Superintendent of Documents, U.S. Government Printing Office, Washington, D.C. 20402.

Health

Common sense is the simplest prescription for good health while you travel: eat well, drink and sleep enough, and don't overexert yourself. Wearing sturdy shoes and clean socks and using talcum powder can help comfort your feet through days of pounding the London pavement. To minimize the effects of jet lag, "reset" your body's clock by adopting British time immediately upon arrival. Most travelers feel acclimated to a new time zone after two or three days.

AIDS AND HIV

All travelers must be concerned about sexually transmitted diseases (STDs), especially HIV infection; HIV is the virus that leads to AIDS (Acquired Immune Deficiency Syndrome). To protect yourself from HIV infection and other STDs while traveling, follow all the precautions that you should follow at home. Never have unprotected sex with people that you are not certain are HIV negative (on the basis of test results from six months after the person's last risky contact). An upsurge in heroin use across Britain has also led to needle-sharing and its attendant risks. For more information on AIDS, call the UK's 24-hour hotline (tel. (0800) 567 123), sponsored by the **National Aids Trust,** New City Cloisters, 188-196 Old St., London EC1 9FR. In the U.S., call the **U.S. Center for Disease Control's** 24-hour hotline at (800) 342-2437. Council's brochure, *Travel Safe: AIDS and International Travel,* is available at all Council Travel offices (see **Budget Travel Agencies,** p. 46).

Sexually transmitted diseases (STDs) such as gonorrhea, chlamydia, genital warts, syphilis, and herpes are a lot easier to catch than HIV, and can be just as deadly. When having sex, condoms may protect you from certain STDs, but oral or even tactile contact can lead to transmission.

BIRTH CONTROL AND ABORTION

If you are straight and sexually active, you will need to think about contraception. Women on the Pill should bring enough to allow for possible loss or extended stays and should bring a prescription, since forms of the Pill vary a good deal. If you use a diaphragm, be sure that you have enough contraceptive jelly on hand. Though condoms are available, you may want to bring your favorite national brand before you go; availability and quality vary.

Abortion is legal in Britain. Your consulate can give you a list of ob/gyn doctors who perform abortions. For general information on contraception, condoms, and abortion worldwide, contact the **International Planned Parenthood Federation,** European Regional Office, Regent's College Inner Circle, Regent's Park, London NW1 4NS (tel. 487 7900; fax 487 7950; email info@ippf.org; http://www.ippf.org).

Insurance

Beware of buying unnecessary travel coverage—your regular insurance policies may well extend to travel-related medical problems and property loss. **Medical insurance** (especially university policies) often covers costs incurred abroad; check with your provider. Canadians should check with the provincial Ministry of Health concerning extent of coverage. Australia has a Reciprocal Health Care Agreement (RHCAs) with the U.K.; Australian citizens are entitled to many of the services that they would receive at home. The Commonwealth Department of Health and Family Services can provide more information. Your **homeowners' insurance** (or your family's coverage) often covers theft during travel. Homeowners are generally covered against loss of travel documents (passport, plane ticket, railpass, etc.) up to US$500 in value.

ISIC and **ITIC** provide basic insurance benefits; cardholders have access to a toll-free, 24-hour helpline whose multilingual staff can provide assistance in medical, legal, and financial emergencies overseas (in the U.S. and Canada call (800) 626-2427; elsewhere call the U.S. collect (713) 267-2525). Most **American Express** cardholders receive automatic car rental (collision and theft, but not liability) insurance and ground travel accident coverage of US$100,000 on flight purchases made with the card (customer service tel. (800) 528-4800).

Remember that insurance companies usually require a copy of the police report for thefts, or evidence of having paid medical expenses (doctor's statements, receipts) before they will honor a claim. Time limits on filing for reimbursement may apply. Always carry policy numbers and proof of insurance. Check with each insurance carrier for specific restrictions and policies.

Specific Concerns

WOMEN TRAVELERS

Women exploring any area on their own inevitably face additional safety concerns. In all situations, it is best to trust your instincts: if you'd feel better somewhere else, don't hesitate to move on. You may want to consider staying in hostels that offer single rooms that lock from the inside or religious organizations that offer rooms for women only. Stick to centrally located accommodations and avoid late-night treks or rides on the Underground. Remember that hitching is *never* safe for lone women, or even for two women traveling together.

To escape unwanted attention, foreign women in London should follow the example of local women; in many cases, the less you look like a tourist, the better off you'll be. Look as if you know where you're going and ask women or couples for directions if you're lost or if you feel uncomfortable. Your best answer to verbal harassment may be no answer at all. Seek out a police officer or a female passerby before a crisis erupts and don't be afraid to scream for help. *Always* carry change for the phone and extra money for a bus or taxi. Carry a whistle on your keychain and don't hesitate to use it in an emergency. **London Women's Aid** (tel. 392 2092) offers 24-hour support for victims of violence, and the **Rape and Sexual Abuse Support Center** (tel. (0181) 239 1122) hotline is answered from Monday to Friday noon-2:30pm and 7-9:30pm, weekends and bank holidays 2:30-5pm. The **London Rape Crisis Center** (tel. 837 1600) is open sporadically and provides a similar service. These warnings and suggestions shouldn't discourage women from traveling alone—avoid unnecessary risks, but keep your spirit of adventure.

The **Audre Lorde Clinic,** at the Ambrose King Centre, Royal London Hospital, E1 (tel. 377 7312; tube: Whitechapel), and the **Bernhard Clinic,** Dept. of Gen. Medicine, Charing Cross Hospital, Fulham Palace Rd., W6 (tel. (0181) 846 1576; tube: Baron's Court or Hammersmith), are female-staffed facilities offering smear tests, screenings for STDs and vaginal infections, breast exams, HIV tests, advice, and counseling for lesbians. (Audre Lorde open F 10am-5pm, Bernhard open W 2-4:30pm, and 5:30-7pm; call for appointments M-F.) **Lady Cabs** (tel. 241 4780; fax 272 1992) is a London-based women's taxi service (drivers are female, riders are both sexes; open M-Th 7:30am-12:30am, F 7:30am-1am, Sa 9am-2am, Su 10am-midnight). For more general information on women and travel, consult these publications:

Handbook For Women Travellers, by Maggie and Gemma Moss (UK£9). Encyclopedic and well-written. Available from Piatkus Books, 5 Windmill St., London W1P 1HF (tel. (0171) 631 0710).

A Journey of One's Own: Uncommon Advice for the Independent Woman Traveler, by Thalia Zepatos, (US$17). Interesting and full of good advice, with a bibliography of books and resources. **Adventures in Good Company: The Complete Guide to Women's Tours and Outdoor Trips,** on group travel by the same author, costs US$17. These books are available in bookstores across North America or can be ordered directly from the publisher. (US$2 shipping for the 1st book, $0.50 for each additional order). Available from The Eighth Mountain Press, 624 Southeast 29th Ave., Portland, OR 97214 (tel. (503) 233-3936; fax 233-0774; email soapston@teleport.com).

Women's Travel in Your Pocket, Ferrari Guides, P.O. Box 37887, Phoenix, AZ 85069 (tel. (602) 863-2408; email ferrari@q-net.com; http://www.q-net.com), an annual guide for women (especially lesbians) traveling worldwide. Hotels, night life, dining, shopping, organizations, group tours, cruises, outdoor adventure and lesbian events (US$14, plus shipping).

More Women Travel: Adventures, Advice & Experience, by Miranda Davies and Natania Jansz (Penguin, US$16.95). Essays by women travelers in several foreign countries plus a decent bibliography and resource index. From Rough Guides, 345 Hudson St. 14th fl., New York, NY 10014 (tel. (212) 366 2348; fax 414 3395; email rough@panix.com; http://www.roughguides.com/women).

A Foxy Old Woman's Guide to Travelling Alone, by Jay Ben-Lesser (Crossing Press, US$11). Info, informal advice, and a resource list on solo budget travel.

OLDER TRAVELERS

A wide array of discounts (called **concessions**) are available with proof of senior citizen status. These are often denoted "OAP" (old-age pensioners).

Elderhostel, 75 Federal St., 3rd fl., Boston, MA 02110-1941 (tel. (617) 426-7788; email Cadyg@elderhostel.org; http://www.elderhostel.org). For those 55 or over

(spouse of any age). Programs at colleges, universities, and other learning centers in over 70 countries on varied subjects lasting 1-4 weeks.

The Globe Piquot Press, P.O. Box 833, Old Saybrook, CT 06475-0833 (tel. (800) 243-0495; fax (800) 820-2329; email info@globe-piquot.com; http://www.globe-piquot.com). Publishes *Europe the European Way: A Traveler's Guide to Living Affordably in the World's Great Cities* (US$14), which offers general hints for the budget-conscious senior considering a long stay or retiring abroad.

Pilot Books, 127 Sterling Ave., P.O. Box 2102, Greenport, NY 11944 (tel. (516) 477-1094 or 1 (800) 79PILOT (797-4568); fax (516) 477-0978; email feedback@pilot-books.com; http://www.pilotbooks.com). Publishes a large number of helpful guides, including *Doctor's Guide to Protecting Your Health Before, During, and After International Travel* (US$10, postage US$2) and *Have Grandchildren, Will Travel* (US $10, postage US$2). Call or write for a complete list of titles.

No Problem! Worldwise Tips for Mature Adventurers, by Janice Kenyon. Advice and info on insurance, finances, security, health, and packing. Useful appendices. US$16 from Orca Book Publishers, P.O. Box 468, Custer, WA 98240-0468.

A Senior's Guide to Healthy Travel, by Donald L. Sullivan (US$15; can be found at http://www.amazon.com).

Unbelievably Good Deals and Great Adventures That You Absolutely Can't Get Unless You're Over 50, by Joan Rattner Heilman. After you finish reading the title page, check inside for some great tips on senior discounts. US$10 from Contemporary Books or on-line at http://www.amazon.com.

ESSENTIALS

BISEXUAL, GAY, AND LESBIAN TRAVELERS

The following organizations and publications provide general travel information. For London-specific information, see **Bisexual, Gay, and Lesbian London,** p. 264.

Damron Travel Guides, P.O. Box 422458, San Francisco, CA 94142-2458 (tel. (415) 255-0404 or (800) 462-6654; fax (415) 703-9049 or 703-8308; email damronco@damron.com; http://www.damron.com). Publishers of the *Damron Address Book* (US$15), which lists bars, restaurants, guest houses, and services in the U.S., Canada, Mexico, and Europe which cater to gay men. The *Damron Road Atlas* (US$16) contains color maps of 70 major North American and European cities and gay and lesbian resorts and listings of bars and accommodations. *The Women's Traveller* (US$13) lists over 7500 bars, restaurants, accommodations, bookstores, and services catering to lesbians. *Damron's Accommodations* lists gay and lesbian hotels around the world (US$19). Mail order is available for an extra US$5 shipping.

Ferrari Guides, P.O. Box 37887, Phoenix, AZ 85069 (tel. (602) 863-2408; fax 439-3952; email ferrari@q-net.com; http://www.q-net.com). Gay and lesbian travel guides: *Ferrari Guides' Gay Travel A to Z* (US$16), *Ferrari Guides' Men's Travel in Your Pocket* (US$16), *Ferrari Guides' Women's Travel in Your Pocket* (US$14), *Ferrari Guides' Inn Places* (US$16). Available in bookstores or by mail order (postage and handling US$5 for the 1st item, US$1 for each additional item mailed within the U.S. In Canada, 1st item $10. Overseas, call or write for shipping cost.)

Giovanni's Room, 345 S. 12th St., Philadelphia, PA 19107 (tel. (215) 923-2960; fax 923-0813; email giophilp@netaxs.com). An international feminist, lesbian, and gay bookstore with mail-order service; they also accept email orders.

International Gay and Lesbian Travel Association, 4331 N. Federal Hwy., Ste. 304, Fort Lauderdale, FL 33308 (tel. (954) 776-2626 or (800) 448-8550; fax (954) 776-3303; email IGLTA@aol.com; http://www.iglta.org). An organization of over 1350 companies serving gay and lesbian travelers worldwide. Call for lists of travel agents, accommodations, and events.

Spartacus International Gay Guides (US$32.95), published by Bruno Gmunder, Verlag GMBH, Leuschnerdamm 31, 10999 Berlin, Germany (tel. (49) 030 615 00 30; fax (49) 030 615 90 07; email bgvtravel@aol.com). Lists bars, restaurants, hotels, and bookstores around the world catering to gays. Also lists hotlines for gays in various countries and homosexuality laws for each country. Available in bookstores and in the U.S. by mail from Lambda Rising, 1625 Connecticut Ave. NW, Washington D.C., 20009-1013 (tel. (202) 462-6969).

The Gay Vacation Guide: The Best Trips and How to Plan Them, by Mark Chesnut. Carol Publishing, 120 Enterprise Ave., Secaucus, NJ 07094 (tel. (800) 447-2665; fax (201) 866-8159). Provides a complete listing of tour operators and travel companies along with advice on how to use gay-friendly businesses and how to avoid problems while traveling (US$14.95, shipping US$4 for the 1st order, $1 for each additional title).

MINORITY TRAVELERS

Since the empire-building days of the 19th century, Great Britain has prided itself on a racially diverse population; in the 1991 census, 3 million Britons (roughly 5.5% of the total population) did not categorize themselves as white. Ian McAuley's *Passport's Guide to Ethnic London* (US$15) details immigrant contributions to English culture. While minority travelers are unlikely to experience any blatant racism, subtle slights are not uncommon, especially towards those of Indian, Arab, and African descent. There are few resources specifically oriented toward minority travelers in Britain; in cases of harassment or assault, contact the police or the Commission for Racial Equality, Elliot House, 10-12 Allington St., London SW1E 5EH (tel. (0171) 828 7022; http://www.open.gov.uk/cre/crehome.htm).

Go Girl! The Black Woman's Book of Travel and Adventure, Elaine Lee, editor. The Eighth Mountain Press, 624 SE 29th Ave., Portland, OR 97214. (tel. (503) 233-3936; fax 233-0774; US$18). Includes travelers' tales, advice on how to travel inexpensively and safely, and a discussion of issues of specific concern to black women. With essays from Maya Angelou, Alice Walker and Gwendolyn Brooks, it's a good read for any traveler.

The Jewish Traveler, Alan M. Tigay, editor. Published by *Hadassah Magazine* (US$30). Covers Jewish history of cities worldwide. Also includes accommodations, kosher restaurants, synagogues, and sights of interest. Available for purchase on the web at http://www.amazon.com.

The Jewish Travel Guide, published by Ballantine Mitchell Publishers. Available for purchase through Sepher-Hermon Press, 1265 46th St., Brooklyn, NY 11219 (tel. (718) 972 9010; US$15, shipping US$2.50).

DISABLED TRAVELERS

Many transportation companies in Britain are very conscientious about providing facilities and services to meet the needs of travelers with disabilities. It is strongly recommended that you notify a bus or coach company of your plans ahead of time so that they will have staff ready to assist you; British Rail requires advance notice especially for those using wheelchairs. **British Rail** also offers a discounted railcard for disabled British citizens, with up to 50% discount on BR tickets. Not all stations are accessible, though; write for the pamphlet *British Rail and Disabled Travelers.* Several **car rental agencies,** such as Wheelchair Travel in Surrey (tel. (01483) 233 640; fax (01483) 237 772; email info@wheelchair-travel.co.uk) can provide hand-controlled cars, but at a hefty price. These companies can also deliver cars to London itself. Britain imposes a six-month quarantine on animals entering the country—this includes seeing-eye dogs (called "blind-dogs" in England). The owner must also obtain a veterinary certificate (consult the nearest British Consulate for details). You can write to the British Tourist Authority for free handbooks and access guides.

A phenomenally useful guide to London for people with any sort of mobility impairment is Couch's *Access in London,* an in-depth guide to accommodations, transport, and accessibility. (Order from Access Project, 39 Bradley Gardens, West Ealing, London W13 8HE. £7.95 donation.) Another excellent resource is *Tripscope* (tel. (0181) 994 9294; fax (0181) 994 3618; email tripscope@cableinet.co.uk.), a not-for-profit agency that provides excellent, free advice and helpful phone numbers for travel throughout the UK. *London For All* is a booklet on transport, tours, and hotels published by the London Tourist Board and available at Tourist Information Centres.

There are networks of **Mobility Buses** in outer London, which are fully wheelchair accessible and available to anyone getting on and off. One route, Bus #139, which covers central London, has **low-floor Buses,** which are accessible to those in wheelchairs and are also available to parents pushing prams. The **Stationlink** coaches are fully accessible low-floor buses which run at hourly intervals along a route between the main line terminals. Another good method of transport is the **Docklands Light Railway,** which is fully wheelchair accessible, including all stations. In the last year the Underground has yielded and allowed wheelchair users to ride the Tube, though would-be riders are warned that few, if any, of the ancient stations are easily navigated. The newer stations being built for the Jubilee and East London extensions will be fully wheelchair accessible. For further information on **travel by Underground and bus,** pick up the free booklet *Access Around London* from Tourist Information Centres and London Transport Information Centres, or by post from the Unit for Disabled Passengers (London Transport, 172 Buckingham Palace Rd., London SW1W 9TN; tel. 918 3312; fax 918 3876). London Transport's 24-hour travel information hotline is also useful (tel. 222 1234). Perhaps your best bet for traveling around central London is by black cab, most of which can accommodate wheelchairs (see **Taxicabs,** p. 69)

A resource that may make your trip to London easier is the RADAR Toilet Key, which is a key that literally opens the door to thousands of disabled loos throughout the U.K. For more information, contact RADAR, 12 City Forum, 250 City Rd., London EC1V 8AF (tel. 250 3222). Send £2.50 along with a letter stating your disability.

For equipment repair and hire, try **Homecare Equipment Hire,** 93 Northcote Rd., Clapham SW11 6PL (tel. 924 4058). Their list of products is geared toward outpatients, so it extends beyond wheelchairs, and they offer a free delivery service.

The **"Arts Access"** section at the beginning of the London telephone books details special services available at theaters, cinemas, and concert halls around London. Call **Artsline,** 5 Crowndale Rd., NW1 (tel. 388 2227), for entertainment accessibility information (M-F 9:30am-5:30pm). **Shape** (tel. 700 8138) offers very cheap tickets to accessible arts events through a membership scheme, as well as providing transport and escorts to these events. The following organizations may also be helpful:

Facts on File, 11 Penn Plaza, 15th Fl., New York, NY 10001 (tel. (212) 967-8800). Publishes of *Resource Directory for the Disabled,* a reference guide for travelers with disabilities (US$45 plus shipping). Available at bookstores or by mail order.

Graphic Language Press, P.O. Box 270, Cardiff by the Sea, CA 92007 (tel. (760) 944-9594; email niteowl@cts.com; Contact person: A. Mackin). Publishes *Wheelchair Through Europe,* a guide covering accessible hotels, transportation, sightseeing, and resources for disabled travelers in many European cities. Available for $12.95 (includes shipping); check payable to Graphic Language Press.

Mobility International USA (MIUSA), P.O. Box 10767, Eugene, OR 97440 (tel. (541) 343-1284 voice and TDD; fax 343-6812; email info@miusa.org; http://www.miusa.org). Sells the 3rd Edition of *A World of Options: A Guide to International Educational Exchange, Community Service, and Travel for Persons with Disabilities* (individuals US$35; organizations US$45).

Moss Rehab Hospital Travel Information Service, (tel. (215) 456-9600, TDD (215) 456-9602). A telephone information resource center on international travel accessibility and other travel-related concerns for those with disabilities.

Twin Peaks Press, P.O. Box 129, Vancouver, WA 98666-0129 (tel. (360) 694-2462; fax (360) 696-3210; email 73743.2634@compuserve.com; http://netm.com/mall/infoprod/twinpeak/helen.htm). Publishers of *Travel for the Disabled,* which provides travel tips, lists of accessible tourist attractions, and advice on other resources for disabled travelers (US$20). Also publishes *Directory of Travel Agencies for the Disabled* (US$20), *Wheelchair Vagabond* (US$15), and *Directory of Accessible Van Rentals* (US$10). Postage US$4 for first book, US$2 for each additional book.

Flying Wheels Travel Service, 143 W. Bridge St., Owatonne, MN 55060 (tel. (800) 535-6790; fax 451-1685). Arranges trips in the U.S. and abroad for groups and individuals in wheelchairs or with other sorts of limited mobility.

The Diabetic Traveler, P.O. Box 8223 RW, Stamford, CT (tel. (203) 327-5832). A short quarterly offering advice to diabetics on flying, eating abroad, and visiting extreme climates. Subscription ($18.95) includes list of organizations worldwide.

TRAVELERS WITH CHILDREN

Children under two generally fly for 10% of the adult airfare on international flights. International fares are usually discounted 25% for children from two to eleven. Most sights, as well as many restaurants and accommodations in London, have reduced fees for children, sometimes listed under the name "concessions." Always have children carry a passport or other ID in case of emergency if they get lost. You might want to refer to the following publications:

A Directory of Mothers' Rooms, by Susan Townend, N.C.H. Action for Children, 85 Highbury Park, London, NS, IVA (tel. (0171) 226-2033; fax 226-2537; £2). Compilation of public places with "mothers'" rooms that facilitate breastfeeding.

Backpacking with Babies and Small Children (US$9.95). Published by Wilderness Press, 2440 Bancroft Way, Berkeley, CA 94704 (tel. (800) 443-7227 or (510) 843-8080; fax 548-1355; email wpress@ix.netcom.com; http://wildernesspress.com). The 3rd edition was scheduled for release in August 1998.

Take Your Kids to Europe, by Cynthia Harriman (US$16.95, shipping US$3.95). Family budget-travel guide. Published by Globe-Pequot Press, 6 Business Park Rd., Old Saybrook, CT 06475 (tel. (800) 285-4078; fax (860) 395-1418).

Travel with Children by Maureen Wheeler (US$12, postage US$2.50). Published by Lonely Planet Publications, 150 Linden St., Oakland, CA 94607 (tel. (800) 275-8555 or (510) 893-8555; fax 893-8563; email info@lonelyplanet.com; http://www.lonelyplanet.com). Also at P.O. Box 617, Hawthorn, Victoria 3122, Australia.

How to take Great Trips with Your Kids, by Sanford and Jane Portnoy (US $9.95, shipping and handling US$3). Advice on how to plan trips geared toward the age of your children, packing, and finding child-friendly accomodations. Harvard Common Press, 535 Albany St., Boston, MA 02118 (tel. (888) 657-3755; fax 695-9794).

Have Kid, Will Travel: 101 Survival Strategies for Vacationing With Babies and Young Children, by Claire and Lucille Tristram. Published by Andrews & McMeel for US$9; available at http://www.amazon.com.

DIETARY CONCERNS

Vegetarians should have no problem finding exciting cuisine. Most restaurants have vegetarian selections on their menus, and some cater specifically to vegetarians. *Let's Go* often notes restaurants with good vegetarian selections. Travelers to London should only note that many explicitly vegetarian restaurants tend to close early.

The International Vegetarian Travel Guide (UK£2) was last published in 1991. Order back copies from the Vegetarian Society of the UK (VSUK), Parkdale, Dunham Rd., Altringham, Cheshire WA14 4QG (tel. (0161) 928 0793; fax (0161) 926 9182; email veg@minxnet.co.uk; http://www.vegsoc.org). VSUK also publishes other titles, including *The European Vegetarian Guide to Hotels and Restaurants.* Call or send a self-addressed, stamped envelope for a listing.

Travelers who keep kosher should contact synagogues in larger cities for information on kosher restaurants; your own synagogue or college Hillel should have access to lists of Jewish institutions across the nation. If you are strict in your observance, consider preparing your own food on the road. **The Jewish Travel Guide** lists kosher restaurants (see **Minority Travelers,** p. 38).

Packing

Pack lightly; the rest is commentary. Remember that you can buy anything you'll need in London. One tried-and-true method of packing is to set out everything you think you'll need, then pack half of it—and twice the money, if you can.

For a long stay in London, you might prefer a suitcase to a conspicuous backpack. If you'll be on the move frequently, go with the pack. Bring along a small daypack for carrying lunch, a camera, and valuables. Keep your money, passport, and other valuables with you in a purse, neck pouch, or money belt. Label every article of baggage both inside and out with your name and address. For added security, bring a combination lock for your main bag and for London hostel lockers.

Nothing will serve you more loyally in London than comfortable walking shoes and a folding umbrella. Bring a light sweater (even in summer), an alarm clock, and a raincoat. Despite its rainy reputation, London can get gruelingly sunny in summer—pack sunglasses. A single-sheet sleeping sack is free in all London HI hostels.

Any electrical gadget will need an adapter and a converter. The voltage in England is 240 volts AC (North American appliances are 110 volts AC). Converters and adapters are available worldwide in department and hardware stores (US$10-15).

If you take expensive **cameras** or equipment abroad, it's best to register everything with customs at the airport before departure. If you're coming from the U.S., buy a supply of film before you leave; like almost everything, it's more expensive in Britain. Unless you're shooting with 1000 ASA or more, airport security x-rays should not harm your pictures. Pack film in your carry-on, since the x-rays employed on checked baggage are much stronger. Though fiercely contested, many allege that x-rays damage floppy disks—if you're bringing a laptop or notebook computer, you may want to have both computer and floppy disks hand-inspected, lest stray x-rays wipe out your as-yet-unpublished *magnum opus.* Officials may ask you to turn it on, so be sure the batteries are fully loaded. A warning: lost baggage is common and not always retrieved. Keep all valuables in your carry-on.

Alternatives to Tourism

If the often madcap, train-changing, site-switching pace of tourism loses its appeal, consider a longer stay in London. Study, work or volunteering will help you get a better sense of aspects of the city that are often unavailable to the short-term visitor.

STUDY

It's not difficult to spend a summer, term, or year studying in London under the auspices of a well-established program. Enrolling as a full-time student, however, is somewhat trickier; admission requirements can be hard to meet unless you attended a British secondary school; only a limited number of foreign students are accepted each year. **Council** sponsors over 40 study abroad programs throughout the world. Contact them or one of the following organizations to start your hunt:

American Field Service (AFS), 310 SW 4th Ave., Ste. 630, Portland, OR 97204-2608 (tel. (800) 237-4636; fax (503) 241-1653; email afsinfo@afs.org; http//www.afs.org/usa). AFS offers summer, semester, and year-long homestay international exchange programs for high school students and graduating high school seniors. Financial aid available.

American Institute for Foreign Study, College Division, 102 Greenwich Ave., Greenwich, CT 06830 (tel. (800) 727-2437 ext. 6084; http://www.aifs.com). Organizes programs for high school and college study in universities. Summer, fall, spring, and year-long programs available. Scholarships available.

Association of Commonwealth Universities, John Foster House, 36 Gordon Sq., London WC1H OPF, England (tel. (0171) 387 8572; fax (0170) 387 2655; email info@acu.ac.uk; http://www.acu.ac.uk). Administers scholarship programs such as the British Marshall scholarships and publishes information about Commonwealth universities.

Beaver College Center for Education Abroad: 450 S. Easton Rd., Glenside, PA 19038-3295 (tel. (800) 755-5607 or 888-BEAVER; fax (215) 572-2174; email cea@beaver.edu; http://www.beaver.edu/cea). Operates summer-, semester- and year-long programs; applicants must have completed three full semesters at an accredited university. Call for brochure.

Central College Abroad, Office of International Education, 812 University, Pella, IA 50219 (tel. (800) 831-3629; fax (515) 628-5375; email studyabroad@central.edu; http://studyabroad.com/central/). Offers semester- and year-long study abroad programs. US$25 application fee. Scholarships available. Applicants must be at least 18 years old, have completed their 1st year of college, and have a minimum 2.5 GPA.

Council sponsors over 40 study abroad programs throughout the world. Contact them for more information (see **Travel Organizations,** p. 19).

Institute of International Education (IIE), 809 United Nations Plaza, New York, NY 10017-3580 (tel. (212) 984-5413; fax 984-5358). For book orders: IIE Books, Institute of International Educations, P.O. Box 371, Annapolis Junction, MD 20701 (tel. (800) 445-0443; fax (301) 953-2838; email iie-boks@iie.org). Publishes *Academic Year Abroad* (US$43, US$4 postage) and *Vacation Study Abroad* (US$37, US$4 postage). Write for a complete list of publications.

International Association for the Exchange of Students for Technical Experience (IAESTE), 10400 Little Patuxent Pkwy. #250, Columbia, MD 21044-3510 (tel. (410) 997-3068; fax (410) 997-5186; email iaste@aipt.org; http://www.aipt.orgl). Operates 8- to 12-week program for college students who have completed two years of study in a technical field. Non-refundable US$50 application fee; apply by Dec. 16 for summer placement.

Peterson's, P.O. Box 2123, Princeton, NJ 08543-2123 (tel. (800) 338-3282; fax (609) 243-9150; http://www.petersons.com). Their comprehensive Study Abroad annual guide lists programs in countries all over the world and provides essential information on the study abroad experience in general. Purchase a copy at your local bookstore (US$27) or call their toll-free number in the U.S. 20% off the list price when you order through their website.

Universities and Colleges Admissions Services, Fulton House, Jewssop, Cheltenham GL50 3SH (tel. (01242) 22 77 88). Provides information and handles applications for admission to all full-time undergraduate courses at universities and their affiliated colleges in the United Kingdom. Write to them for an application and the extremely informative *U.C.A.S. Handbook*.

UKCOSA/United Kingdom Council for International Education, 9-17 St. Albans Pl., London N1 0NX (tel. (0171) 226 3762; fax 226 3373; http://www.britcoun.org/website/ukcosa/index.htm). Advises prospective and current students on immigration, finance, and more.

WORK

One foolproof way to immerse yourself in a foreign culture is to become part of its economy. It's easy to find a **temporary job,** especially with London's booming economy, but it will rarely be glamorous and may not even pay for your plane fare, let alone your accommodation. Furthermore, officially, you can hold a job in the U.K. only with a **work permit** which may be difficult to obtain, unless you're a citizen of a Common Market or British Commonwealth nation. Citizens of Commonwealth nations between the ages of 17 and 27 may work in Britain during a visit if the employment they take is "incidental to their holiday" by obtaining a working holiday visa. Commonwealth citizens with a parent born in the U.K. may apply for a certificate of entitlement to the right of abode, which allows them to live and work in Britain without other formalities.

Non-Common Market and Commonwealth job-seekers must have their prospective employers apply for a work permit or apply themselves with supporting papers from the prospective employers. The real catch-22 is that normally one must physically enter the country in order to have immigration officials validate your work permit papers and note your status in your passport. This means if you can't set up a job from afar and have the permit sent to you, you must enter the country to look for a job, find an employer, have them start the permit process, then *leave* the country until the permit is sent to you (up to 6 weeks), and finally return and start work.

If you are a U.S. citizen and a full-time, degree-seeking student at a U.S. university, the simplest way to get a job abroad is through work-permit programs run by **British Universities North America Club (BUNAC)** and its member organizations. For a US$225 application fee, BUNAC can procure six-month work permits and offers information and assistance in finding work and housing, along with other perks. BUNAC also admisters programs for residents of Australia, New Zealand, and South Africa. For more information contact BUNAC at 16 Bowling Green Ln., London EC1 0BD (tel. (0171) 251-3472 or (800) GO-BUNAC (462-8622); email BUNAC@easynet.co.uk; http://www.bunac.org.uk). The helpful resource *Summer Jobs: Britain 1999* (US$17), published by **Peterson's Guides** (see **Study,** p. 43), lists roughly 30,000 jobs in England, Scotland, Wales, and Northern Ireland.

Childcare International, Ltd., Trafalgar House, Grenville Place, London NW7 3SA (tel. (0181) 959 3611 or 906 3116; fax 906 3461; email office@child-int.demon.co.uk; http://www.ipi.co.uk/childint), offers *au pair* positions in the UK and provides information on qualifications required. UK£60 application fee. The organization prefers a long placement but does arrange summer work. Member of the International *Au Pair* Association.

International Schools Services, Educational Staffing Program, P.O. Box 5910, Princeton, NJ 08543 (tel. (609) 452-0990; fax 452-2690; email edustaffing@iss.edu; http://www.iss.edu). Recruits teachers and administrators for schools. Applicants must have a bachelor's degree and 2 years of relevant experience. Nonrefundable US$100 application fee. Publishes *The ISS Directory of Overseas Schools* (US$35).

Office of Overseas Schools, A/OS Room 245, SA-29, Dept. of State, Washington, D.C. 20522-2902 (tel. (703) 875-7800; http://www.state.gov/www/aboutstate/schools/), keeps a list of schools abroad and agencies that arrange placement for Americans to teach abroad.

Surrey Books, 230 E. Ohio St., Chicago, IL 60611 (tel. (800) 326-4430; fax (312) 751-7330; email SurreyBk@aol.com, http://www.surreybooks.com), publishes *How to Get a Job in Europe: The Insider's Guide* (1995 edition US$18).

Transitions Abroad, P.O. Box 1300, 18 Hulst Rd., P.O. Box 1300, Amherst, MA 01004-1300 (tel. (800) 293-0373; fax 256-0373; email trabroad@aol.com; http://www.transabroad.com). Magazine lists resources for overseas study, work, and volunteering (US$20-42 per 6 issues, depending on location). Also publishes *The Alternative Travel Directory,* a comprehensive guide to living, learning, and working overseas (US$20 plus $4 postage).

Vacation Work Publications, 9 Park End St., Oxford OX1 1HJ, U.K. (tel. (01865) 24 19 78; fax 79 08 85). Publishes a wide variety of guides and directories with job listings and info for the working traveler, including *Teaching English Abroad* (UK£10, postage UK£2.50, £1.50 within U.K.) and *The Au Pair and Nanny's Guide to Working Abroad* (UK£9, £2.50 and £1.50 postage). Opportunities for summer or full-time work in numerous countries. Write for a catalogue.

Uniworld Business Publications, Inc., 257 Central Park West, 10A, New York, NY 10024-4110 (tel. (212) 496-2448; fax 769-0413; email uniworld@aol.com; http://www.uniworldbp.com). Check your local library for *The Directory of American Firms Operating in England* (1998; US$89) and *The Directory of American Firms Operating in Foreign Countries* (1998; US$250).

VOLUNTEERING

Volunteer jobs are readily available almost everywhere. You may receive room and board in exchange for your labor; the work can be fascinating (or stultifying). You can sometimes avoid the high application fees charged by the organizations that arrange placement by contacting your prospects directly; check with the organizations. Try the listings in Vacation Work Publications's *International Directory of Voluntary Work* (UK£9; postage UK£2.50, £1.50 within U.K.)

Council has a Voluntary Services Dept., 205 E. 42nd St., New York, NY 10017 (tel. (888) COUNCIL (268-6245); fax (212) 822-2699; email info@ciee.org; http://www.ciee.org), which offers 2- to 4-week environmental or community services projects in over 30 countries. Participants must be at least 18 years old. Minimum US$295 placement fee; additional fees may also apply for various countries.

Service Civil International Voluntary Service (SCI-VS), 5474 Walnut Level Rd., Crozet, VA 22932 (tel. (804) 823-1826; fax 823-5027; email sciivsusa@igc.apc.org; http://wworks.com/Ìsciivs). Arranges placement in workcamps in Europe (ages 18 and over). Local organizations sponsor groups for physical or social work.

Volunteers for Peace, 43 Tiffany Rd., Belmont, VT 05730 (tel. (802) 259-2759; fax 259-2922; email vfp@vfp.org; http://www.vfp.org). A nonprofit organization that arranges speedy placement in 2-3 week workcamps comprising 10-15 people. VFP offers over 1000 programs in 70 nations. Complete and up-to-date listings are in the annual International Workcamp Directory (US$15). Registration fee US$200. Some work camps are open to 16- and 17-year-olds for US$225. Free newsletter.

GETTING THERE

Budget Travel Agencies

The following budget travel organizations typically offer discounted flights for students and youths, railpasses, ISICs and other identification cards, hostel memberships, travel gear, travel guides, and general expertise in budget travel. Students and people under 26 ("youth") with proper ID qualify for enticing reduced airfares.

Campus Travel, 52 Grosvenor Gardens, London SW1W 0AG (http://www.campus-travel.co.uk). 46 branches in the U.K. Student and youth fares on plane, train, boat, and bus travel. Skytrekker, flexible airline tickets. Discount and ID cards for students and youths, travel insurance for students and those under 35, and maps and guides. Puts out travel suggestion booklets. Telephone booking service: in Europe call (0171) 730 3402; North America (0171) 730 2101; worldwide (0171) 730 8111; Manchester (0161) 273 1721; Scotland (0131) 668 3303.

Council Travel (http://www.ciee.org/travel/index.htm), the travel division of Council, is a full-service travel agency specializing in youth and budget travel. They offer discount airfares on scheduled airlines, railpasses, hosteling cards, low-cost accommodations, guidebooks, budget tours, travel gear, and international student (ISIC), youth (GO25), and teacher (ITIC) identity cards. In **London,** at 28A Poland St. W1V 3DB (tel. (0171) 287 3337; tube: Oxford Circus), **Paris** (146 55 55 65), and **Munich** (089 39 50 22). U.S. offices include: Emory Village, 1561 N. Decatur Rd., **Atlanta,** GA 30307 (tel. (404) 377-9997); 2000 Guadalupe, **Austin,** TX 78705 (tel. (512) 472-4931); 273 Newbury St., **Boston,** MA 02116 (tel. (617) 266-1926); 1138 13th St., **Boulder,** CO 80302 (tel. (303) 447-8101); 1153 N. Dearborn, **Chicago,** IL 60610 (tel. (312) 951-0585); 10904 Lindbrook Dr., **Los Angeles,** CA 90024 (tel. (310) 208-3551); 1501 University Ave. SE #300, **Minneapolis,** MN 55414 (tel. (612) 379-2323); 205 E. 42nd St., **New York,** NY 10017 (tel. (212) 822-2700); 953 Garnet Ave., **San Diego,** CA 92109 (tel. (619) 270-6401); 530 Bush St., **San Francisco,** CA 94108 (tel. (415) 421-3473); 1314 NE 43rd St. #210, **Seattle,** WA 98105 (tel. (206) 632-2448); 3300 M St. NW, **Washington, D.C.** 20007 (tel. (202) 337-6464). **For U.S. cities not listed,** call 800-2-COUNCIL (226-8624).

Council Charter, 205 E. 42nd St., New York, NY 10017 (tel. (212) 661-0311; fax 972-0194). Offers a combination of inexpensive charter and scheduled airfares from a variety of U.S. gateways to most major European destinations. One-way fares and open jaws (fly into one city and out of another) are available.

CTS Travel, 220 Kensington High St., W8 (tel. (0171) 937 33 66 for travel in Europe, 937 33 88 for travel world-wide; fax 937 90 27). Tube: High St. Kensington. Also at 44 Goodge St., W1 (tel. 637 5601). Tube: Goodge St. Specializes in student/youth travel and discount flights.

Educational Travel Centre (ETC), 438 North Frances St., Madison, WI 53703 (tel. (800) 747-5551; fax (608) 256-2042; email edtrav@execpc.com; http://www.edtrav.com). Flight information, HI-AYH cards, Eurail, and regional rail passes. Write for their free pamphlet *Taking Off.* Student and budget airfares.

Eurolines, 52 Grosvenor Gardens, Victoria, London SW1W 0AU (tel. (0171) 723 8235 in London, or (01580) 240 4511 main office). Specializes in coach travel throughout Western and Eastern Europe.

Let's Go Travel, Harvard Student Agencies, 17 Holyoke St., Cambridge, MA 02138 (tel. (617) 495-9649; fax 495-7956; email travel@hsa.net; http://hsa.net/travel). Railpasses, HI-AYH memberships, ISICs, ITICs, FIYTO cards, guidebooks, maps, bargain flights, and a complete line of budget travel gear. All items available by mail; call or write for a catalogue.

Rail Europe Inc., 226 Westchester Ave., White Plains, NY 10604 (tel. (800) 438-7245; fax 432-1329; http://www.raileurope.com). Sells all Eurail products and passes, national railpasses including Brit Rail and German Rail passes, and point-to-point tickets. Up-to-date information on all rail travel in Europe, including Eurostar, the English Channel train.

STA Travel, 6560 Scottsdale Rd. #F100, Scottsdale, AZ 85253 (tel. (800) 777-0112 nationwide; fax (602) 922-0793; http://sta-travel.com). A student and youth travel organization with over 150 offices worldwide offering discount airfares for young travelers, railpasses, accommodations, tours, insurance, and ISICs. In the U.K., 6 Wrights Ln., **London** W8 6TA (tel. (0171) 938 4711 for North American travel), and 117 Euston Rd., London NW1 (tel. (0171) 361 6161). In Australia, 222 Faraday St., **Melbourne** VIC 3050 (tel. (03) 349 6911). In New Zealand, 10 High St., **Auckland** (tel. (09) 309 9723). 16 offices in the U.S. include: 297 Newbury St., **Boston,** MA 02115 (tel. (617) 266-6014); 429 S. Dearborn St., **Chicago,** IL 60605 (tel. (312) 786-9050; 7202 Melrose Ave., **Los Angeles,** CA 90046 (tel. (213) 934-8722); 10 Downing St., Ste. G, **New York,** NY 10003 (tel. (212) 627-3111); 4341 University Way NE, **Seattle,** WA 98105 (tel. (206) 633-5000); 2401 Pennsylvania Ave., **Washington, D.C.** 20037 (tel. (202) 887-0912); 51 Grant Ave., **San Francisco,** CA 94108 (tel. (415) 391-8407), **Miami**, FL 33133 (tel. (305) 284-1044).

Travel CUTS (Canadian Universities Travel Services Limited), 187 College St., Toronto, Ont. M5T 1P7 (tel. (416) 979-2406; fax 979-8167; email mail@travelcuts). Canada's national student travel bureau and equivalent of Council, with 40 offices across Canada. Also in the U.K., 295-A Regent St., **London** W1R 7YA (tel. (0171) 637 3161). Discounted domestic and international airfares open to all; special student fares to all destinations with valid ISIC. Issues ISIC, FIYTO, GO25, and HI hos-

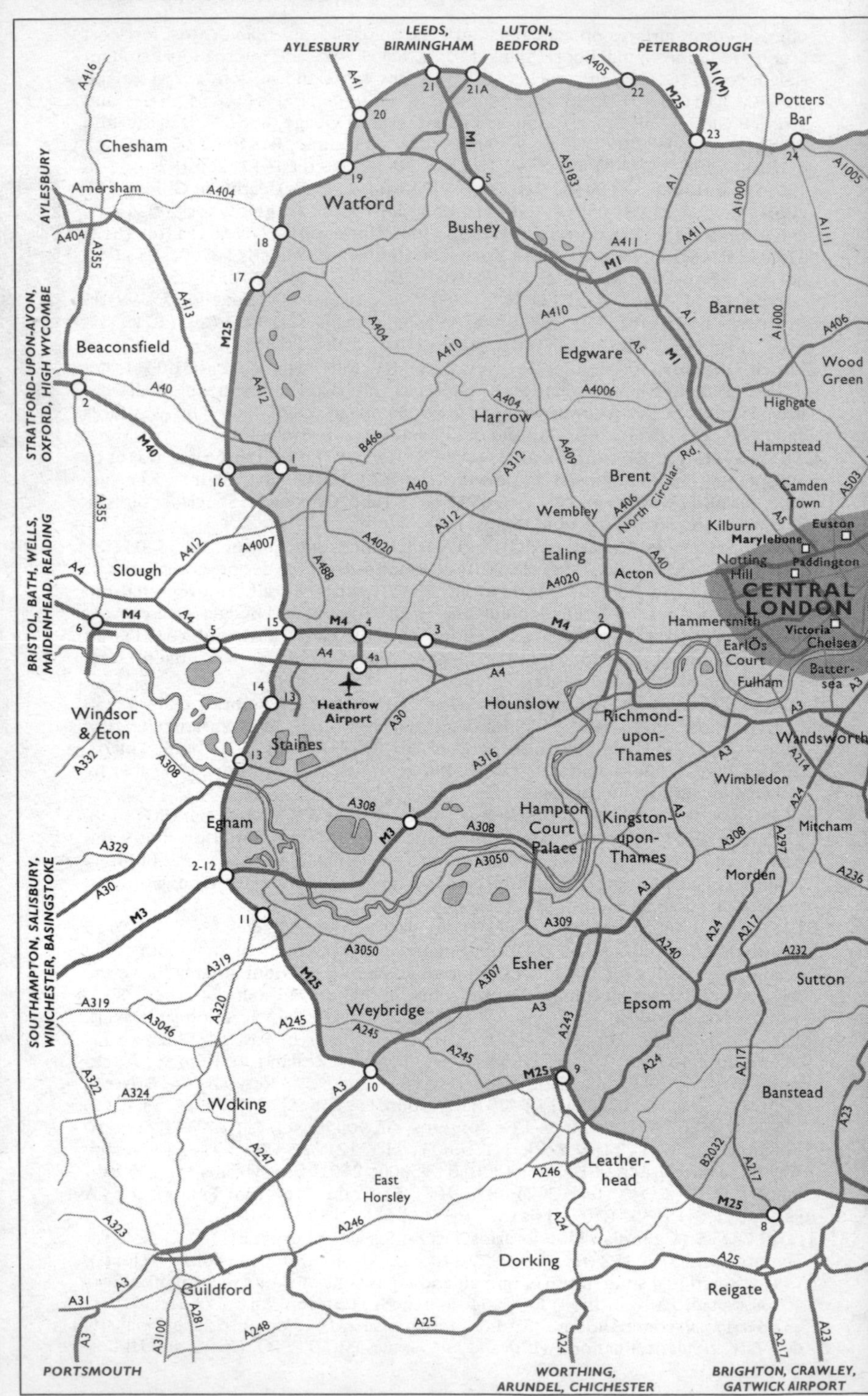
AYLESBURY
LEEDS, BIRMINGHAM
LUTON, BEDFORD
PETERBOROUGH
Potters Bar
Chesham
Amersham
Watford
Bushey
Barnet
Beaconsfield
Edgware
Wood Green
Highgate
Harrow
Hampstead
Brent
Camden Town
Wembley
Kilburn
Euston
Marylebone
Slough
Ealing
Notting Hill
Paddington
Acton
CENTRAL LONDON
Hammersmith
Victoria
Earl's Court
Chelsea
Battersea
Fulham
Windsor & Eton
Heathrow Airport
Hounslow
Richmond-upon-Thames
Wandsworth
Staines
Wimbledon
Egham
Hampton Court Palace
Kingston-upon-Thames
Mitcham
Morden
Esher
Sutton
Weybridge
Epsom
Banstead
Woking
Leatherhead
East Horsley
Dorking
Guildford
Reigate
AYLESBURY
STRATFORD-UPON-AVON, OXFORD, HIGH WYCOMBE
BRISTOL, BATH, WELLS, MAIDENHEAD, READING
SOUTHAMPTON, SALISBURY, WINCHESTER, BASINGSTOKE
PORTSMOUTH
WORTHING, ARUNDEL, CHICHESTER
BRIGHTON, CRAWLEY, GATWICK AIRPORT
M25
M1
M40
M4
M3
A1(M)
North Circular Rd.

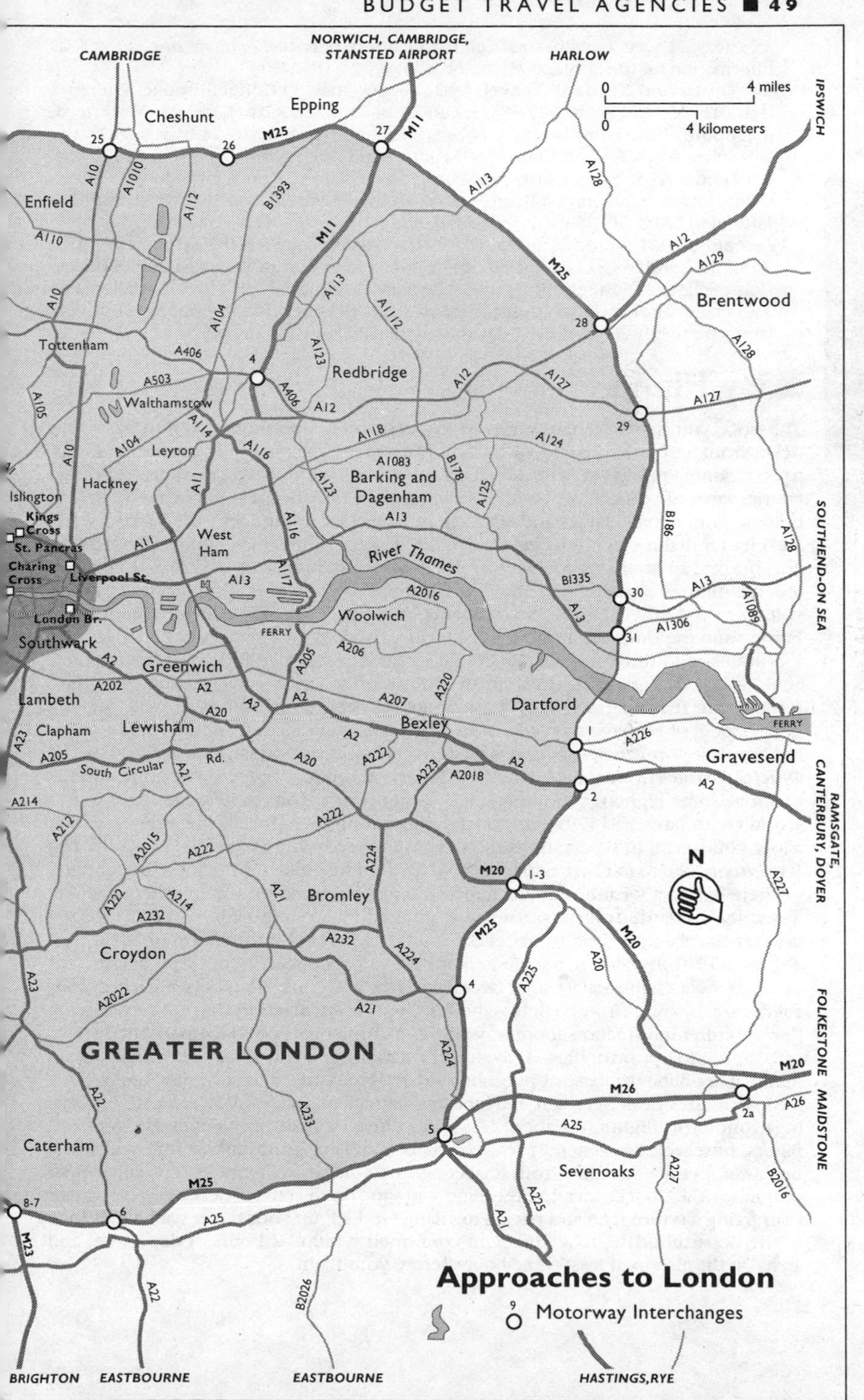

Approaches to London

Motorway Interchanges

tel cards, as well as railpasses. Offers free *Student Traveller* magazine, as well as information on the Student Work Abroad Program (SWAP).

Usit Youth and Student Travel, 19-21 Aston Quay, O'Connell Bridge, Dublin 2 (tel. (01) 677-8117; fax 679-8833). Offices in Cork, Galway, Limerick, Waterford, Maynooth, Coleraine, Derry, Athlone, Jordanstown, Belfast, and Greece. In the U.S.: New York Student Center, 895 Amsterdam Ave., New York, NY, 10025 (tel. (212) 663-5435; email usitny@aol.com). Specializes in youth and student travel. Offers low-cost tickets and flexible travel arrangements all over the world. Supplies ISIC and FIYTO-GO 25 cards in Ireland only.

Wasteels, 7041 Grand National Drive #207, Orlando, FL 32819 (tel. (407) 351-2537; in **London** (0171) 834 70 66). A huge chain in Europe, with 200,000 locations. Sells the Wasteels BIJ tickets, which are discounted (30-45% off regular fare) 2nd-class, international, point-to-point train tickets with unlimited stopovers (must be under 26 on the 1st day of travel); sold *only* in Europe.

By Plane

The price you pay for airfare varies widely depending on whom you purchase your ticket from and how flexible your travel plans are. Understanding the airline industry's byzantine pricing system is the best way of finding a cheap fare. Very generally, courier fares (if you can deal with restrictions) are the cheapest, followed by tickets bought from consolidators and stand-by seating. Last minute specials, airfare wars, and charter flights can often beat these fares, however. Always get quotes from different sources; an hour or two of research can save you hundreds of dollars. Call every toll-free number and don't be afraid to ask about discounts, as it's unlikely they'll be volunteered. Knowledgeable **travel agents,** particularly those specializing in travel to Europe and the U.K., can provide excellent guidance.

Students and others under 26 should never need to pay full price for a ticket. Seniors can also get great deals; many airlines offer senior traveler clubs or airline passes with few restrictions and discounts for their companions as well. Sunday newspapers often have travel sections that list bargain fares from the local airport; London is a popular destination. Outsmart airline reps with the phone-book-sized *Official Airline Guide* (check your local library; at US$359 per year, the tome costs as much as some flights), a monthly guide listing nearly every scheduled flight in the world (with fares US$479), and toll-free phone numbers for all the airlines which allow you to call in reservations directly. More accessible is Michael McColl's *The Worldwide Guide to Cheap Airfare* (US$15), a useful guide for finding cheap airfare.

There is also a wealth of travel information to be found on the Internet. The **Air Traveler's Handbook** (http://www.cs.cmu.edu/afs/cs.cmu.edu/user/mkant/Public/Travel/airfare.html) is an excellent source of general information on air travel. **TravelHUB** (http://www.travelhub.com) provides a directory of travel agents that includes a searchable database of fares from over 500 consolidators (see **Ticket Consolidators,** below). Groups such as the **Air Courier Association** (http://www.aircourier.org) offer information about traveling as a courier and provide up-to-date listings of last-minute opportunities. **Travelocity** (http://www.travelocity.com) operates a searchable online database of published airfares that you can reserve on-line.

Most airfares peak between mid-June and early September. Midweek (M-Th morning) round-trip flights run about US$40-50 cheaper than on weekends; weekend flights, however, are generally less crowded. Traveling from hub to hub will win a more competitive fare than from smaller cities. Return-date flexibility is usually not an option for the budget traveler; traveling with an "open return" ticket can be pricier than fixing a return date and paying to change it. Pick up your ticket well in advance of the departure date, have the flight confirmed within 72 hours of departure, and arrive at the airport at least three hours before your flight.

COMMERCIAL AIRLINES

The airlines' published airfares should be just the beginning of your search. Even if you pay an airline's lowest published fare, you may waste hundreds of dollars. For the adventurous or the bargain-hungry, there are other, perhaps more inconvenient or time-consuming options. But before shopping around it is a good idea to find out the average commercial price in order to measure just how great a "bargain" you are being offered.

The commercial airlines' lowest regular offer is the **Advance Purchase Excursion Fare (APEX);** specials advertised in newspapers may be cheaper, but have more restrictions and fewer available seats. APEX fares provide you with confirmed reservations and allow "open-jaw" tickets (landing in and returning from different cities). Generally, reservations must be made seven to 21 days in advance, with seven- to 14-day minimum and up to 90-day maximum stay limits, and hefty cancellation and change penalties (fees rise in summer). Book APEX fares early during peak season; by May you will have a hard time getting the departure date you want.

Days of the Week

While round-trip tickets may be cheaper during the week than on weekends, they also mean crowded flights, which in turn means competition for frequent-flier upgrades. Scheduling weekend flights is more expensive, but less crowded, and proves the best bet for using frequent-flier upgrades. Most business travelers travel on Thursdays, which makes stiff competition for upgrade hunters. Saturdays and Sundays present the best opportunities for frequent fliers.

TICKET CONSOLIDATORS

Most airlines in the world are heavily regulated, which means that their published fares may be significantly more expensive than the market price available from a **ticket consolidator.** Ticket consolidators resell unsold tickets on commercial and charter airlines at unpublished fares; a 30-40% price reduction is not uncommon. Consolidator tickets provide the greatest discounts over published fares when you are traveling on short notice (you bypass advance purchase requirements, since you aren't tangled in airline bureaucracy) or in the peak season, when published fares are way up. There are rarely age constraints or stay limitations, but unlike tickets bought through an airline, you won't be able to use your tickets on another flight if you miss yours and you will have to go back to the consolidator rather than the airline to get a refund. Keep in mind that these tickets are often for coach seats on connecting (not direct) flights, and that frequent-flyer miles may not be credited. Decide what you can and can't live with before shopping.

Not all consolidators deal with the general public; many only sell tickets through travel agents. **Bucket shops** are retail agencies that specialize in getting cheap tickets. Although ticket prices are marked up slightly, bucket shops generally have access to a larger market than would be available to the public and can also get tickets from wholesale consolidators. Generally, a dealer **specializing** in travel to the country of your destination will provide more options and cheaper tickets. The **Association of Special Fares Agents (ASFA)** maintains a database of specialized dealers for particular regions (http://www.ntsltd.com/asfa). Look for bucket shops' tiny ads in the travel section of weekend papers; in the U.S., the Sunday *New York Times* is a good source; in Australia, try the *Sydney Times.* In London, a call to the Air Travel Advisory Bureau (tel. (0171) 636 5000) can provide names of reliable consolidators and discount flight specialists. Kelly Monaghan's *Consolidators: Air Travel's Bargain Basement* is an invaluable source for more information and lists of consolidators by location and destination (US$8 plus $3.50 shipping) from the Intrepid Traveler, P.O. Box 438, New York, NY 10034 (email info@intrepidtraveler.com).

Be a smart shopper; check out the competition. Among the many reputable and trustworthy companies are, unfortunately, some shady characters. Contact the local Better Business Bureau to find out how long the company has been in business and its track record. Although not necessary, it is preferable to deal with consolidators close to home so that you can visit in person if necessary. Ask to receive your tickets as quickly as possible so you have time to fix any problems. Get the company's policy in writing: insist on a **receipt** that gives full details about the tickets, refunds, and restrictions, and record who you talked to and when. It may be worth paying with a credit card (despite the 2-5% fee) so you can stop payment if you never receive your tickets. Beware the "bait and switch" gag: shyster firms will advertise a super-low fare and then tell a caller that it has been sold. Although this is a viable excuse, if they can't offer you a price near the advertised fare on *any* date, it is a scam to lure in customers—report them to the Better Business Bureau. Also ask about accommodations and car rental discounts; some consolidators have fingers in many pies.

Always try to contact specialists in your region, but the following agents provide general services. For destinations in **Europe,** try **Rebel,** Valencia, CA (tel. (800) 227-3235; fax (805) 294-0981; email travel@rebeltours.com; http://www.rebeltours.com) or Orlando, FL (tel. (800) 732-3588). For destinations **worldwide,** try **Airfare Busters;** offices in Washington, D.C. (tel. (202) 776-0478), Boca Raton, FL (tel. (561) 994-9590), and Houston, TX (tel. (800) 232-8783); **Pennsylvania Travel,** Paoli, PA (tel. (800) 331-0947); **Cheap Tickets;** offices in Los Angeles, CA, San Francisco, CA, Honolulu, HI, Seattle, WA, and New York, NY (tel. (800) 377-1000); **Interworld** (tel. (305) 443-4929; fax 443-0351); or **Travac** (tel. (800) 872-8800; fax (212) 714-9063; email mail@travac.com; http://www.travac.com). **NOW Voyager,** 74 Varick St. #307, New York, NY 10013 (tel. (212) 431-1616; fax (212) 334-5243); email info@nowvoyagertravel.com; http://www.nowvoyagertravel.com) acts as a consolidator and books discounted international flights, mostly from New York, as well as courier flights (see **Courier Companies and Freighters,** p. 55), for an annual fee of US$50. For a processing fee, depending on the number of travelers and the itinerary, **Travel Avenue,** Chicago, IL (tel. (800) 333-3335; fax (312) 876-1254; http://www.travelavenue.com), will search for the lowest international airfare available, including consolidated prices, and will even give you a 5% rebate on fares over US$350.

STAND-BY FLIGHTS

Airhitch, 2641 Broadway, 3rd Fl., New York, NY 10025 (tel. (800) 326-2009 or (212) 864-2000; fax 864-5489) and Los Angeles, CA (tel. (310) 726-5000), will add a certain thrill to the prospects of when you will leave and where exactly you will end up. Complete flexibility in the dates and cities of arrival and departure is necessary. Flights to Europe cost US$159 each way when departing from the Northeast, $239 from the West Coast or Northwest, $209 from the Midwest, and $189 from the Southeast. Travel within the USA and Europe is also possible, with rates ranging from $79-$139. The snag is that you buy not a ticket, but the promise that you will get to a destination near where you're intending to go within a window of time (usually 5 days) from a location in a region you've specified. You call in before your date-range to hear all of your flight options for the next seven days and your probability of boarding. You then decide which flights you want to try to make and present a voucher at the airport which grants you the right to board a flight on a space-available basis. This procedure must be followed again for the return trip. Be aware that you may only receive a monetary refund if all available flights which departed within your date-range from the specified region are full; future travel credit, however, is always available. There are several offices in Europe, so you can wait to register for your return; the main one is in Paris (tel. (1) 47 00 16 30).

AirTech.Com, 588 Broadway #204, New York, NY 10012 (tel. (212) 219-7000; fax 219-0066; email fly@airtech.com; www.airtech.com) offers a very similar service. Their travel window is one to four days. Rates to and from Europe (continually updated; call and verify) are: Northeast US$169; West Coast US$229; Midwest/Southeast US$199. Upon registration and payment, AirTech.Com sends you a FlightPass with a contact date falling soon before your travel window, when you are to call them for flight instructions. Note that the service is one-way—you must go through the same procedure to return—and that no refunds are granted unless the company fails to get you a seat before your travel window expires. AirTech.Com also arranges courier flights and regular confirmed-reserved flights at discount rates.

Be sure to read all the fine print in your agreements with either company—a call to The Better Business Bureau of New York City may be worthwhile. Be warned that it is difficult to receive refunds, and that clients' vouchers will not be honored when an airline fails to receive payment in time.

CHARTER FLIGHTS

Charters are flights a tour operator contracts with an airline (usually one specializing in charters) to fly extra loads of passengers to peak-season destinations. Charters are often cheaper than flights on scheduled airlines, especially during peak seasons, although fare wars, consolidator tickets, and small airlines can often beat charter prices. Some charters operate nonstop, and restrictions on minimum advance-purchase and minimum stay are more lenient. However, charter flights fly less frequently than major airlines, make refunds particularly difficult, and are almost always fully booked. Schedules and itineraries may also change or be cancelled at the last moment (as late as 48hr. before the trip, and without a full refund), and check-in, boarding, and baggage claim are often much slower. As always, pay with a credit card if you can; consider traveler's insurance against trip interruption.

Many consolidators such as **Interworld, Rebel, Travac,** and **Travel Avenue** (see **Ticket Consolidators,** p. 51), also offer charter options. Don't be afraid to call every number and hunt for the best deal. Eleventh-hour **discount clubs** and **fare brokers** offer members savings on travel, including charter flights and tour packages. Research your options carefully. **Travelers Advantage,** Stamford, CT (tel. (800) 548-1116; http://www.travelersadvantage.com; US$49 annual fee) specializes in European travel and tour packages. Study these organizations' contracts closely; you don't want to end up with an unwanted overnight layover.

ESSENTIALS

COURIER COMPANIES AND FREIGHTERS

Those who travel light should consider flying internationally as a **courier,** where ridiculously low fares often come at the price of heavy restrictions. The company hiring you will use your checked luggage space for freight; you're usually only allowed to bring carry-ons, though some firms allow you to check luggage, depending on your trip. You are responsible for the safe delivery of the baggage claim slips (given to you by a courier company representative) to the representative waiting for you when you arrive—don't screw up or you will be blacklisted as a courier. You will probably never see the cargo you are transporting—the company handles it all—and airport officials know that couriers are not responsible for the baggage checked for them. Restrictions to watch for: you must be over 21 (18 in some cases), have a valid passport, and procure your own visa (if necessary); most flights are round-trip only with short fixed-length stays (usually one week); only single tickets are issued (but a companion may be able to get a next-day flight); and most flights out of the U.S. are from New York. Round-trip fares to London range from $160 to 280. Keep in mind that last-minute deals for all courier flights can get you significantly cheaper or even free flights. Becoming a member of the **Air Courier Association** (tel. (800) 282-1202; http://www.aircourier.org) is a good way to start; they give you a listing of all reputable courier brokers and the flights they are offering, along with a hefty courier manual and a bi-monthly newsletter of updated opportunities ($30 one-time fee plus $28 annual dues). For an annual fee of $45, the **International Association of Air Travel Couriers,** 8 South J St., P.O. Box 1349, Lake Worth, FL 33460 (tel. (561) 582-8320; email iaatc@courier.org; http://www.courier.org), informs travelers (via computer, fax, and mailings) of courier opportunities worldwide. **NOW Voyager,** 74 Varick St. #307, New York, NY 10013 (tel. (212) 431-1616; fax 334-5243; email info@nowvoyagertravel.com; http://www.nowvoyagertravel.com), acts as an agent for many courier flights worldwide (primarily from New York) and offers special last-minute deals to London for as little as US$200 round-trip plus a US$50 registration fee. (They also act as a consolidator; see **Ticket Consolidators,** p. 51.) Another agent to try is **Halbart Express,** 147-05 176th St., Jamaica, NY 11434 (tel. (718) 656-5000; fax 917-0708; offices in Chicago, Los Angeles, and London).

You can also go directly through courier companies in New York, or check your bookstore, library, or on-line at http://www.amazon.com for handbooks such as *Air Courier Bargains* (US$15 plus $3.50 shipping from the Intrepid Traveler, tel. (212) 569-1081; email info@intrepidtraveler.com; http://intrepidtraveler.com). The *Courier Air Travel Handbook* (US$10 plus $3.50 shipping) explains how to travel as an air courier and contains names, phone numbers, and contact points of courier companies. It can be ordered directly from Bookmasters, Inc., P.O. Box 2039, Mansfield, OH 44905 (tel. (800) 507-2665).

By Train

In May 1994, the **Channel Tunnel** (Chunnel) was completed, physically connecting England and France, to the horror of some and the delight of many. This union is symbolized by the attendants on the new *Eurostar* trains. They speak fluent English and French, and sport uniforms by the French designer Balmain. *Eurostar* operates rather like an airline, with similar discounts, reservations, and restrictions. Major railpasses are not tickets to ride, but do entitle you to discounts, as does being a youth. In the U.K., call (01233) 617 575 or (0345) 881 881 for more information. Also call (800) EUROSTAR (387-6782) to purchase your ticket.

By Ferry

To travel between Britain and the Continent, consider crossing the English Channel by **ferry.** You must book the crossing a day in advance. Arrive an hour in advance, and remember your passport. Ask ahead where to board the ferry. Arrange connections in order to spare yourself the misery of sitting by an empty wharf for 10 hours because you forgot to book a bus ticket from Pembroke Dock to London. Ask about reduced fares—flashing a hostelling card or ISIC with TravelSave stamps might win a 25-50% discount on your fare. Some travelers ask car drivers to let them travel as one of the four free passengers allotted to a car. This can reduce costs considerably, but consider the risks before getting into a stranger's car. Try **Stena Sealink Line,** Head Office, Charter House, Park St., Ashford, Kent TN24 8EX (tel. (01233) 64 70 47).

ONCE THERE

Emergencies and Help

Emergency medical care, psychological counseling, crash housing, and sympathetic support can often be found in London free of charge.

Britons receive largely free health care from the National Health Service (NHS). Foreign visitors do not, of course, get such favorable terms, but are nevertheless eligible for some free treatment, including: outpatient treatment in the Accident and Emergency (A&E) ward of an NHS hospital; treatment of communicable diseases (such as V.D., typhoid, or anthrax); and "compulsory" mental treatment. Unfortunately, many of the hospitals are shrinking their operations and no longer offer 24-hour care, so make sure you check where you are going before rushing out for help.

AIDS: National AIDS Helpline (24hr. tel. (0800) 567 123). Toll-free for information on testing, health care, or to simply answer questions and listen (for more on AIDS/HIV and travelling, see **AIDS and HIV,** p. 33).

Alcoholics Anonymous: London Helpline (tel. 352 3001) answered daily 10am-10pm; answering machine from 10pm-10am.

Automobile Breakdown: Members can call the 24hr. AA breakdown service (tel. (0800) 887 766) or RAC Breakdown Service (tel. (0800) 828 282).

British Diabetic Association: 10 Queen Anne St., W1M OBD (tel. 323 1531). Offers information on diabetic treatment and services and free travel guides specifically for diabetic concerns covering much of the world. Careline (tel. 636 6112) open M-F 9am-5pm to answer questions and concerns.

Citizen's Advice Bureaux: Holborn Library, 32-38 Theobald's Rd., WC1 (tel. 404 1497). Tube: Holborn. Several branches dot London and offer suggestions on anything from housing to silencing your neighbor's doberman. Telephone advice M-W and F 2-4pm.

Dental Care: Eastman Dental Hospital, 256 Gray's Inn Rd., WC1 (tel. 915 1000; fax 915 1012). Tube: Chancery Ln. or King's Cross. Phone for emergency treatment availability and times.

Discrimination: Liberty: the National Council for Civil Liberties, 21 Tabard St., SE1 4LA. Tube: Borough. Advice on dealing with discrimination excluding education and housing issues, by letter only.

Domestic Violence/Rape: Women's Aid, 52-54 Featherstone St., EC1 (tel. 392 2092). 24hr. helpline provides aid, advice, and emergency shelter for victims of domestic and sexual abuse. **The London Rape Crisis Centre's Rape Crisis Hotline,** P.O. Box 69, WC1 (tel. 837 1600) allows you, emergency or not, to talk to a woman, receive legal or medical information, or obtain referrals. They'll send someone to accompany you to the police, doctor, clinic, and court upon request. Hours vary—call for more information.

Emergency (Medical, Police, and Fire): Dial 999; no coins required.

Family Planning Association: 2-12 Pentonville Rd., N1 (Helpline tel. 837 4044; staffed M-F 9am-7pm). Tube: Angel. Informational services: contraception, pregnancy test, and abortion referral.

Gay and Lesbian Information: see **Bisexual, Gay, and Lesbian London,** p. 264.

Hospitals: In an emergency, you can be treated at no charge in the Accidents and Emergencies (A&E) ward of a hospital. You have to pay for routine medical care unless you work legally in Britain, in which case NHS tax will be deducted from your wages and you will not be charged. Socialized medicine has lowered fees here, so don't ignore any health problem merely because you are low on cash. The following have 24hr. walk-in A&E (also known as casualty) departments: **Royal London Hospital,** Whitechapel Rd., E1 (tel. 377 7000; tube: Whitechapel); **Royal Free Hospital,** Pond St., NW3 (tel. 794 0500; tube: Belsize Park or BR: Hampstead Heath); **Charing Cross Hospital,** Fulham Palace Rd. (entrance St. Dunstan's Rd.), W6 (tel. (0181) 846 1234; tube: Baron's Ct. or Hammersmith); **St. Thomas' Hospital,** Lambeth Palace Rd., SE1 (tel. 928 9292; tube: Westminster); **University College Hospital,** Gower St. (entrance on Grafton Way), WC1 (tel. 387 9300). Tube: Euston or Warren St. For others, look under "Hospitals" in the gray Businesses and Services phone book.

Information for Travelers with Disabilities: see Disabled Travelers, p. 38.

Legal Advice: Release, 388 Old St., EC1 (tel. 729 9904; 24hr. emergency number 603 8654). Tube: Liverpool St. or Old St. Specializes in criminal law and advising those arrested on drug charges. Open by appointment only M-F 10am-6pm. **Legal Aid Board,** 29-37 Red Lion St., WC1 (tel. 813 5300). Tube: Holborn. Provides representation (upon a solicitor's referral) for minimal fees. Open M-F 9am-5pm.

Narcotics Anonymous: Call 730 0009. Hotline answered daily 10am-10pm.

Victim Support National: Cranmer House, 39 Brixton Rd., SW9 (tel. 735 9166). Tube: Oval. Trained volunteers based in 378 local schemes in England, Wales, and Northern Ireland offer emotional support, information, and practical help to victims of crime. Details available from the national office. Open M-F 9am-5:30pm, answering machine at other times.

Pharmacies: Every police station keeps a list of emergency doctors and chemists in its area. Listings under "Chemists" in the Yellow Pages. **Bliss Chemists** at Marble Arch (5 Marble Arch, W1; tel. 723 6116) is open daily, including public holidays, 9am-midnight.

Police: Stations in every district of London, including: Headquarters, New Scotland Yard, Broadway, SW1 (tel. 230 1212; tube: St. James's Park); West End Central, 10 Vine St., W1 (tel. 437 1212; tube: Piccadilly Circus); Islington (tel. 704 1212). For emergencies, dial 999.

Police Complaints: If the problem is the police, contact the **Police Complaint Authority,** 10 Great George St., SW1 (tel. 273 6450). Be sure to note the offending officer's number (worn on the shoulder).

Shelter: *Sleeping in the open is highly dangerous.* Several organizations provide emergency shelter in London. The **Salvation Army** has a battery of emergency hostels: the **Booth House,** Whitechapel Rd., E1 (tel. 247 3401; tube: Whitechapel) and **Parkway,** 12 Inverness Terr., W2 (tel. 229 9223; tube: Bayswater), are men-only. **Hopetown,** 60 Old Montague St., E1 (tel. 247 1004) is women-only; all will do their best to accommodate you or refer you to a place that will. The **Shelter Nightline** (tel. (0800) 446 441), a volunteer-run helpline, offers free advice on emergency accommodations. Open M-F 6pm-9am, Sa-Su 24hr.

Samaritans: 46 Marshall St., W1 (tel. 734 2800). Tube: Oxford Circus. Highly respected 24hr. crisis hotline provides listening (rather than advice) for suicidal depression and other problems.

Sexual Health: Jefferiss Wing Centre for Sexual Health, St. Mary's Hospital, Praed St., W2 (tel. 725 6619). Tube: Paddington. Free and confidential sexual health services. Drop-in for free condoms and dental dams, STDs testing, and AIDS and HIV tests and counseling. Open M 8:45am-7pm, Tu and F 8:45am-6pm, W 10:45am-6pm, Th 8am-1pm, Sa 10am-noon.

Women's Health: see **Women Travelers,** p. 34.

Tourist Offices

London Tourist Board Information Centre, Victoria Station Forecourt, SW1 (tel. (0839) 123 432; recorded message only, 39-49p per min., available within U.K. only). Tube: Victoria. Offers information on London and England, a well-stocked bookshop, theater and tour bookings, and an accommodations service (a hefty £5 booking fee, plus 15% refundable deposit; tel. 932 2020; fax 932 2021; MC, Visa only). Expect long waits at peak hours (around noon). Their cheapest rooms cost

ESSENTIALS

£22, most run £25-30. Victoria Station center open Apr.-Nov. daily 8am-7pm; Dec.-Mar. M-Sa 8am-7pm, Su 8am-5pm. Additional tourist offices located at **Heathrow Airport** (open daily Apr.-Nov. 9am-6pm; Dec.-Mar. 9am-5pm), **Liverpool St. Underground Station** (open M 8:15am-7pm, Tu-Sa 8:15am-6pm, Su 8:30am-4:45pm), and **Selfridges** department stores during store hours (see **Department Stores,** p. 255).

British Travel Centre, 12 Regent St., SW. Tube: Piccadilly Circus. Down Regent St. from the Lower Regent St. tube exit. Run by the British Tourist Authority (tel. (0181) 846 9000) and ideal for travelers bound for destinations outside of London. Combines the services of the BTA, British Rail, and a Traveler's Exchange with an accommodations service. £5 surcharge for booking and a required deposit (either 1 night's stay or 15% of the total stay depending on the place; does not book for hostels). Also sells maps, theater tickets, books, and pamphlets translated into many languages. Pleasantly relaxed compared to LTB, but equally long queues. Open M-F 9am-6:30pm, Sa-Su 10am-4pm.

City of London Information Centre, St. Paul's Churchyard, EC4 (tel. 606 3030). Tube: St. Paul's. Specializes in information about the City of London but answers questions on all of London. Helpful, knowledgeable staff. Open daily 9:30am-5pm.

London Transport Information Offices, (24hr. tel. 222 1234). At Euston (open M-Sa 7:15am-6pm, Su 8:30am-5pm); Victoria (open M-Sa 7:45am-9pm, Su 8:45am-9pm); King's Cross (open M-Sa 8am-6pm, Su 8:30am-5pm); Liverpool St. (open M-Sa 8am-6pm, Su 8:45am-5:30pm); Oxford Circus (open M-Sa 8:45am-6pm); Piccadilly (open daily 8:45am-6pm); St. James's Park (open M-F 8am-5:30pm); Heathrow Central station (open M-Sa 6:30am-7pm, Su 7:15am-7pm); Heathrow Terminal 1 (open daily 7:15am-10pm); Heathrow Terminal 2 (open M-Sa 7:15am-5pm, Su 8:15am-5pm); Heathrow Terminal 4 (open M-Sa 6am-3pm, Su 7:15am-3pm); Hammersmith (open M-F 7:15am-6pm, Sa 8:15am-6pm); and West Croydon Bus Station (open M-F 7:30am-6pm, Sa 8:15am-5pm). Helpful agents offer advice on travel by underground or bus. Free maps. Booths sell helpful brochures, guidebooks, and the museum Whitecard (see **Museums,** p. 226).

Greenwich Tourist Information Centre, 48 Greenwich Church St., SE10 (tel. (0181) 858 6376). Offers information on sights in Greenwich and surrounding areas. Open daily 10am-5pm.

Southwark Tourist Information Centre, Hay's Galleria, Tooley St., SE1 (tel. 403 8299). Helpful advice in navigating the newly dynamic areas south of the muddy Thames. Open daily 10am-5pm.

Embassies and High Commissions

If anything goes seriously wrong, inquire first at your country's consulate. Consulary offices are housed within each country's London embassy or high commission. The distinction between an embassy and a consulate is nevertheless significant: an embassy houses the ambassador's office and staff; you won't gain access unless you know someone inside. All facilities for dealing with nationals are in the consulate. If your passport is lost or stolen, go to the consulate as soon as possible to get a replacement. The consulate keeps lists of local lawyers and doctors, will notify family members of accidents, and has information on how to proceed with legal problems, but its functions end there. Don't ask the consulate to pay for your hotel or medical bills, investigate crimes, obtain work permits, post bail, or interfere with standard legal proceedings. If you are arrested during your stay, there is little, if anything, that your own government can do to help you, so behave yourself. All embassies and High Commissions close on English holidays (see **Bank Holidays** listing, p. 305).

United States Embassy, 24 Grosvenor Sq., W1 (tel. 499 9000). Tube: Bond St. Phones answered 24hr.

Australian High Commission, Australia House, The Strand, WC2 (tel. 379 4334). Tube: Aldwych or Temple. Recorded visa info tel. (0891) 600 333, 50p per min. Open M-F 9:30am-3:30pm.

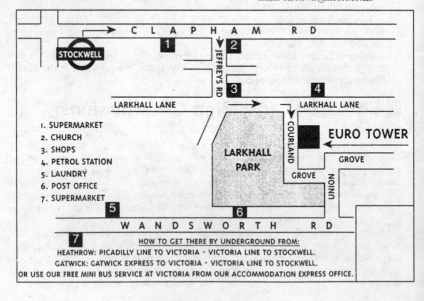

Canadian High Commission, MacDonald House, 1 Grosvenor Sq., W1 (tel. 258 6600). Tube: Bond St. or Oxford Circus. Visas M-F 8-11am.
Irish Embassy: 17 Grosvenor Pl., SW1 (tel. 235 2171). Tube: Hyde Park Corner. Open M-F 9:30am-1pm and 2:30-5pm.
New Zealand High Commission, New Zealand House, 80 Haymarket, SW1 (tel. 930 8422). Tube: Charing Cross. Open M-F 10am-noon and 2-4pm.
South African High Commission, South Africa House, Trafalgar Sq., WC2 (tel. 451 7299). Tube: Charing Cross. Open M-F 10am-noon and 2-4pm.

Getting In and Out of London

FROM THE AIRPORT

With planes landing every 47 seconds, **Heathrow Airport** (tel. (0181) 759 4321) in Hounslow, Middlesex, is the world's busiest international airport. The bureaux de change in each terminal are open daily. The most recognizable bureaux are the red **Thomas Cook** booths which are found in every terminal. The easiest way to reach central London from Heathrow is by **Underground** (Piccadilly line; about 45min. to central London), with one stop for terminals 1, 2, and 3, and another for terminal 4. To reach **Victoria Station,** transfer at Gloucester Rd. or South Kensington to a District Line or Circle Line train heading east. At Victoria, you'll find a blue **Tourist Information Centre** with an accommodations service, currency exchange, and help with transportation connections (see **Getting Around,** p. 65). Introduced in the summer of 1998, the **Heathrow Express** travels between Heathrow and Paddington Station every 15 minutes (15min., 5:10am-11:40pm, one-way £10); the express train departs from Heathrow terminal #1, 2, 3, and 4.

London Regional Transport's **Airbus** (tel. 222 1234) makes the 1-hr trip from Heathrow to central points in the city. The Airbus A1 runs to Victoria, stopping at Hyde Park Corner, Harrods, and the Earl's Ct. tube station (daily 5am-9pm). Airbus A2 runs to Russell Sq. and King's Cross stations, with stops at Euston, Baker St., Marble Arch, Paddington, Bayswater, Queensway, Notting Hill Gate, Holland Park, and Shepherd's Bush (to King's Cross daily 6:40am-10:40pm, to Russel Sq. daily 5:20am-10:50pm). (Prices for both buses £6 one-way, round-trip £10; children £4, £6.) **Airbus Direct** is a faster bus service (same prices as Airbus) stopping only in the center of the City & Hyde Park Corner.

Gatwick Airport in West Sussex (tel. (01293) 535 353) is London's second-busiest airport. Heathrow is not close to the city and Gatwick is even farther. A number of 24-hour restaurants and bureaux de change are located in both the North and South Terminals. From Gatwick, take the **BR Gatwick Express** (tel. (0345) 484 950) train to Victoria Station (daily 5am-midnight every 15min., midnight-5am approx. every 30min.; one-month open return £19, day return £8.30-11). **National Express coaches** run between Gatwick and Victoria (1hr., 5:05am-8:20pm every hr., £8.50, return £11).

Taxis that congregate outside the terminals charge a fee based upon distance, which is designed for short hops in the city. Fares from central London to Heathrow run at least £30; from central London to Gatwick, expect to pay £50-60. Travelers who have too much luggage to negotiate public transport should consider using **Airport Transfers,** a private chauffeur service (tel. 403 2228). For a flat rate, London Airways will take up to four people from either airport to any central London destination (£20-30 per car from Heathrow, £47 per car from Gatwick).

Major international flights are now arriving in **Stansted Airport,** northeast of London in Stansted, Essex (tel. (01279) 680 500). Stansted is served by British Rail's **Stansted Express** to Liverpool St. Station (40min., 3 per hr., M-Sa 5am-11pm, Su 7am-11pm, £10.40, under 15 £5.20).

FROM THE TRAIN STATIONS

British Rail (BR) trains leave London from several stations on the perimeter of Central London. All BR stations are served by Tube as well. To begin your journey, you must first find out which of the stations your train will be leaving from, which can be a surprisingly difficult task at times. The new, centralized **British Rail information number,** which functions 24 hours, is (0345) 484 950. **To Europe,** try (0990) 84 88 48, or for **Eurostar** (thru the Chunnel), call (0345) 88 18 81.

To get a **Young Person's Railcard** (£18), you must be under 26 or a full-time student in the U.K. A **Senior Railcard** for persons over 65 also costs £18. Both will save you one-third on off-peak travel for one year. A **Network Card** gives the same discount for travel in the Network Southeast area. The **Network Rover** allows unlimited travel on Network Southeast for the daytripper (3 weekend days £47; 7 days £69; children half-price). Ask at any mainline station.

FROM THE BUS STATIONS

Victoria Coach Station (tube: Victoria), located on Buckingham Palace Rd., is the hub of Britain's coach network. **National Express coaches** (tel. (0990) 80 80 80) service an expansive network which links cities big and small. Coaches are considerably less expensive than trains but also take longer. National Express offers a **Discount Coach Card** (£8) to students, youths age 16 to 25, and seniors (over 50). Other coach companies compete with National Express; their routes often overlap and prices are almost identical.

Much of the commuting area around London, including Hampton Court and Windsor, is served by **Green Line** coaches, which leave frequently from Eccleston Bridge behind Victoria Station. (For information, call (0181) 668 7261 M-F 8am-8:30pm, Sa-Su 9am-5pm; or try the information kiosk on Eccleston Bridge.) Purchase tickets from the driver. Prices for day returns are higher before 9am Monday through Friday. Discounts include the one-day **Rover** ticket (£7, children and seniors £4; valid on almost every Green Line coach and London Country bus M-F after 9am, Sa-Su all day).

HITCHHIKING AND RIDE SHARING

> *Let's Go* strongly urges you to seriously consider the risks before you choose to hitch. We do not recommend hitching as a safe means of transportation, and none of the information presented here is intended to do so.

Women, even in a group, should never hitchhike. Men should consider all of the risks involved before hitching. Anyone who values safety will take a train or bus out of London. Ask at youth hostels for possibilities. Hitching can be quite difficult within central London and reasonably easy from places like Cambridge and Oxford to the city.

Freewheelers is a **"lift agency"** which can match you up to a driver going your way at no charge. The price for the trip itself is agreed between the passenger and driver based on fuel costs. The agency requires that members abide by a safety procedure to confirm each other's identity and keeps records of all members and matches made. Single-sex matching can be arranged. But Freewheelers does not take responsibility for members' safety—you are still getting in a car with a stranger. For more details, email freewheelers@freewheelers.co.uk, or look at their website at http://www.freewheelers.co.uk/freewheelers.

Orientation

Greater London is a colossal aggregate of distinct villages and anonymous suburbs, of ancient settlements and modern developments. As London grew, it swallowed adjacent cities and nearby villages and chewed up the counties of Kent, Surrey, Essex, Hertfordshire, and Middlesex. "The City" now refers to the ancient, and much smaller, "City of London," which covers but one of the 620 square miles of Greater London. London is divided into boroughs and postal code areas. The borough name and postal code appear at the bottom of most street signs. Areas and neighborhoods are more vaguely delineated, but correspond roughly to the numbered postal areas; the district names are used frequently in non-postal discourse.

Most of the sightseer's London falls within the five central boroughs: the **City of London,** the **City of Westminster, Kensington and Chelsea, Camden,** and **Islington.** This region north of the river Thames is bounded roughly by the Underground's Circle line. The center of most visits to London is usually the **West End,** an area primarily within the borough of the City of Westminster. The West End incorporates the elegant Georgian facades of Mayfair, the crowded shopping streets around Oxford St., the vibrant labyrinth of gay and fashion-conscious Soho, and the chic market in Covent Garden. All distances in London are measured from **Charing Cross,** the official center of London, on the south side of Trafalgar Square.

East of the West End, toward the City of London, lies **Holborn,** the center of legal activity, and **Fleet Street,** until recently, the center of British journalism. Though the **City of London** is no longer the hub of central London, it continues to function as the metropolis's financial heart. Here, St. Paul's Cathedral is skirted by newer, taller buildings. The Tower of London, at the eastern boundary of the City, stands between central London and the vast **Docklands** building site stretching down the Thames—once port to the Empire, now the face of a new commercial Britain.

Northeast of the West End, **Bloomsbury** harbors the British Museum, the core of University of London, and scores of bookshops and art galleries. North and northwest of the West End, tidy terraces cling to the streets bordering Regent's Park in the districts of **Marylebone, Camden Town,** and **St. John's Wood. Islington** to the northeast harbors an artsy intellectual image and a growing gay community. One stage farther north, **Hampstead** and **Highgate** are separated from each other by the enormous Hampstead Heath. Two of London's most expensive residential areas, they command exceptional views of the city. Lying west of the West End, the faded squares of Paddington and Bayswater give way to Notting Hill, home each August bank holiday to the largest street carnival in Europe.

South and southwest of the West End, still in the City of Westminster, is the actual district known as **Westminster.** This is England's royal, legislative, and ecclesiastical center, home of Buckingham Palace, the Houses of Parliament, and Westminster Abbey. Belgravia, packed with embassies, nestles between Westminster and the semi-gracious borough of **Kensington** and **Chelsea.** The shops of Knightsbridge and Kensington High St., the excellent museums of South Kensington, the "posers" stalking King's Road in Chelsea, and the Australians and the large gay male population in Earl's Court ensure that this borough has no single image.

London's suburbs extend for miles in all directions. To the southwest, **Kew** luxuriates in its exquisite botanical gardens. In adjacent **Richmond,** the expansive deer park brings wildlife to the capital. Toward the southeast, **Greenwich** takes pride in its rich navigational and astronomical history on the privileged path of the Prime Meridian. **Brixton,** just south of the river, is home to a large African and Caribbean community. Farther south lies the residential suburb of **Wimbledon,** site of the famed tennis tournament. Far out on the northeast fringe of London, ancient **Epping Forest** preserves a degree of wildness and straddles the eastern and western hemispheres.

At times you'll need the ingenuity of Sherlock Holmes to find one of London's more obscure addresses. Some homeowners favor names rather than numbers, and the owner of a house on a corner is free to choose either street name as an address. Numbering starts at the end of the street nearest the center of London, but note that house numbers on opposite sides of large streets increase at different rates; house no. 211 may face no. 342. Numbers occasionally go up one side of the street and down the other. Some streets abruptly change names, disappear, and then materialize again after a hundred yards, while others twist through and around greens. You might find yourself in a tangle of Eaton Mews, Eaton Square, Eaton Gate, Eaton Place, and Eaton Terrace. There are 31 variations on Victoria Road and 40 streets named Wellington. To navigate this mess, get a comprehensive street map or guide with a complete index, such as **London A to Z** ("A to Zed," as streetwise Londoners call it), **ABC Street Atlas,** or Nicholson's

London Streetfinder (from £2) at any newstand or bookstore. Even if you only intend to stay in London for a week or so, the outlay is well worth it.

Postal code prefixes, which often appear on street signs and in street addresses, may help guide you. The letters stand for compass directions, with reference to the central district (itself divided into WC and EC, for West Central and East Central). All districts bordering this central district are numbered "1." There are no S or NE codes.

Getting Around

London's public transit system, operated by **London Regional Transport (LRT),** is impressively comprehensive. The **Underground** (known as "the tube") is supplemented by **buses,** the **Docklands Light Railway (DLR),** and by **British Rail (BR).** Because government subsidies for public transport are very low, London's public transport system is expensive to ride when compared to other world capitals.' Nevertheless, London Transport is the busiest system in western Europe, and public transport is always cheaper than a taxi.

In general, fares on all modes of public transportation in Britain are either "single" (one-way) or "return" (round-trip). When riding the tube or buses, a return ticket costs exactly twice as much as a single. BR offers significant savings for "day returns" (both legs traveled same day) and slightly less spectacular savings on "period returns" (requiring you to return within a specific number of days).

Information on both buses and the tube is available on the **24-hour help line** (tel. 222 1234). The line is busy in the early mornings, but you should get an operator within two to three minutes during all other times. Pick up free maps and guides at **London Transport's Information Centres.** Look for a lowercase "i" beside the distinctive "roundel" logo at information windows and on signs (see **Government Information Offices,** p. 19). For recorded information on how the buses and Underground trains are currently running, phone 222 1200 (24hr.). London Transport's **lost property office** (tel. 486 2496) lies just down the road from Holmes and Watson at 200 Baker St., W1 (tube: Baker St.; open M-F 9:30am-2pm). Allow three working days for articles lost on buses or the tube to reach the office.

London is divided into six concentric transport zones. Central London, including most of the major sights, is covered by zone 1; Heathrow Airport is zone 6. Fares depend on the distance of the journey and the number of zones crossed. The **Travelcard,** because of its price and the flexibility of both its duration and the zones it covers, is a must for budget travelers. It can be bought for one day's, one week's, or one month's worth of travel. One-day Travelcards have certain restrictions: they cannot be used before 9:30am Monday through Friday, and are not valid on night buses (adult **one-day Travelcard,** zones 1 and 2, £3.50). The one-week and one-month Travelcards can be used at any time and are valid for Night Bus travel. You will need a passport-sized photo in order to purchase a one-week or one-month Travelcard. Photo booths can be found in major tube stations, including Victoria, Leicester Sq., Earl's Ct., and Oxford Circus (about £3 for 4 pictures). Most tourists will find the zones 1 and 2 cards the most useful and economical. All Travelcards can be used on the Underground, regular buses, British Rail within London, and the Docklands Light Railway. Travelcards can be purchased at Underground ticket offices, London Transport Information Centres, and PASS agents throughout the city; credit cards are accepted. (**Adult 1-week Travelcard,** zones 1&2, £16.60; **adult 1-month Travelcard,** zones 1&2, £65.80.) **Weekend travelcards** (adult, zones 1&2, £5.20) consist of two valid one-day travelcards for Saturday and Sunday (or any two consecutive days on a holiday weekend) that cannot be used on Night buses. A valid Travelcard will save you money on tube and BR trains regardless of zone—ask for an extension ticket before boarding.

Travel agents in your home country can sell you Travelcards or vouchers for Travelcards before you leave. Prices in your country's currency are calculated in April and, based upon April's exchange rate, cost the same as buying with pounds. Of course, as the exchange rates fluctuate, buying in home currency may be a bit of a bargain or a loss, though these alterations are apt to be small. Travelcards purchased abroad can be for two to six days (whereas only 1- and 7-day travelcards are available in London), which may mean savings if you're here for a short trip.

UNDERGROUND

The color-coded **Underground** railway system, or the **tube,** is the easiest way to get around London, with 273 stations (give or take) on 11 lines (Bakerloo, Central, Circle, District, East London, Hammersmith and City, Jubilee, Metropolitan, Northern, Piccadilly, and Victoria). Call the **24-hour tube info line** for help (tel. 222 1234). Small but invaluable "Journey Planner" maps are available at all stations and inside the front and back cover of *Let's Go: London.* The stylization reduces above-ground geographic accuracy, but greatly increases lucidity.

Fares depend on the number of zones passed through—a journey within central zone 1 will cost much less than a trip to a distant suburb. On Sundays and Bank Holidays (see **Appendix,** p. 305), trains run less frequently. All transfers are free. Bicycles are allowed on the above-ground sections of the Circle, District, Metropolitan, and Piccadilly lines for a child's fare except during morning and evening rush hours. A single adult ticket will cost between £1.60 and £3.30, with most central London trips costing £1.60 to £1.80. Return tickets cost exactly double the price of a single ticket. If you plan to make more than two trips in a day, a Travelcard will save you money (see above). You may also consider buying a **Carnet** (£10), which is a booklet entitling you to 10 one-way trips within Zone 1, if you'll be using the tube sporadically.

You can buy your ticket either from the ticket window or from a machine. The ticket allows you to go through the automatic gates; keep it until you reach your final destination, where the exit gates will collect it. Inspectors are becoming rather strict about enforcing the tube's new on-the-spot £10 fine for travel without a valid ticket. Acting the befuddled foreigner may not get you off the hook.

Most tube lines' **last trains** leave Central London between midnight and 12:30am; service resumes around 6am. The gap in service is bridged by Night buses. The tube, unremittingly packed during rush hour (M-F roughly 7-10am and 4:30-7:30pm) and high season (July-Aug.), earns its share of flak due to delays, dirt, and diverted trains; the Northern line has been nicknamed "the misery line" because of its rush-hour bedlam, though the Central line rivals it in sheer congestion. Bear in mind that some distant suburban stations close on Sundays and other off-peak periods. Smoking is not allowed anywhere in or on the tube.

Some of London's deepest tube stations were used as air-raid shelters during the Blitz. At the worst of the bombing, as many as 175,000 people took shelter in them in one night; some were unable or unwilling to leave for days on end. While some stations may still bring bomb shelters to mind, others are quite jazzy with their intricate, colorful mosaics, often cryptically related to their name. London Transport continues its tradition of stylish poster art by commissioning paintings from contemporary artists for its "By Tube" posters, and has expanded to posting poems by writers from Middle English scrawlers to contemporary versifiers.

Many stations feature labyrinthine tunnels and steep staircases so, if you're carrying a lot of luggage, you may fare better on a longer route that requires fewer transfers. Fitness zealots may wish to tackle the 331-step climb at Hampstead station, London's deepest. Remember to stand to the right and walk on the left on escalators, or risk a rude tumbling from commuters in full stride.

BUSES

> *The way to see London is from the top of a bus—the top of a bus, gentlemen.*
>
> —William Gladstone

If you're in a hurry, don't take a bus. Take the tube; it's faster, easier, and generally more consistent. However, being shuttled about underground tunnels can hardly match the majesty of rolling along the street on top of a double-decker. Riding the buses is a great way to orient yourself to the city's layout and to soak up its atmosphere and sights. A number of buses in central London provide excellent sight-seeing opportunities at discount rates. **Bus 11,** beginning at Liverpool Street station, takes in St. Paul's, Fleet St., the Strand, Trafalgar Sq., Westminster, Sloane Sq., and all of King's Rd. **Bus 14** originates in Riverside-Putney and coasts down Fulham Rd., past the South Kensington museums, Knightsbridge, Hyde Park Corner, Piccadilly Circus and Leicester Sq., and terminates on Tottenham Court Rd. in Soho.

Unfortunately, double-decker **Routemaster** buses, with their conductors and open rear platforms, are being replaced to save money. On modern double-deckers and single-deck "hoppa" buses, you pay your fare to the driver as you board, and you must have exact change. On Routemasters, take a seat and wait for the conductor, who can tell you the fare and let you know when to get off. Smoking is not permitted on London's buses. **Bus stops** are marked with route information; at busy intersections or complicated one-way systems, maps tell where to board each bus. A warning: each stop is marked with route numbers and only those buses stop there. On stops marked "request," buses stop only if you flag them down (to get on) or pull the bell cord (to get off). While waiting, you must form a queue (line up); bus conductors may refuse some passengers at the stop with withering looks of scorn during crowded periods. Service is notoriously sporadic during the daytime; it is perfectly common to wait 20 minutes only to be greeted by a procession of three identical buses in a row. Regular buses run from about 6am to midnight.

Night buses (the "N" routes) now run frequently throughout London from 11:30pm until the first day buses get going. When the tube goes to sleep (last trains run between midnight and 12:30am), Night buses provide an inexpensive and convenient alternative to taxis. All Night bus routes pass through Trafalgar Sq. and many stop at Victoria as well. (See **Inside Back Cover** for a list of Night Bus destinations.)

London Transport's information offices put out a free brochure about Night buses, which includes times of the last British Rail and Underground trains. Call London Transport's 24-hour information line (tel. 222 1234) for fares and schedules; see Tourist Offices for office location and hours (p. 19).

The bus network is divided into four zones. In and around central London, one-way **fares** range from 50p to about £1.20, depending on the number of zones through which you pass. Be sure to carry change to pay your fare; drivers will not accept bills. Travelcards purchased for the Underground are valid on buses; armed with a Travelcard, you may hop on or off as often as you like. Weekly and monthly **bus passes** are generally less practical and barely cheaper than Travelcards.

If you're planning on utilizing the bus network, London Transport issues a free bus map for London called the *All-London Bus Guide,* which is available at most tube stations and LRT information offices. The *Central Bus Guide* is a more manageable pamphlet, describing only bus routes in zone 1. If you require more detailed info about bus routes, there are 35 different *Local Bus Guides* which will help you navigate specific neighborhoods. To find out whether buses are running on schedule or whether routes have changed call 222 1200. To acquire free local guides, call 371 0247.

Wheelchair accessible **Mobility Bus** routes, numbered in the 800s and 900s, service most of outer London. **Stationlink,** a wheelchair accessible bus, travels hourly between the major train stations. For information on either service, call 918 3312. For more information, see **Disabled Travelers,** p. 38.

BRITISH RAIL

Most of London is fully served by buses and the tube. Some districts, however, notably southeast London, are most easily reached by train. The BR is speedy and runs frequently to suburbs and daytrip areas around London, functioning as a commuter rail that is often cheaper than the tube. Its old-fashioned compartments are roomy and comfortable. The North London Link, stretching across north London from North Woolwich to Richmond, often deposits travelers closer to sights (such as Keats's house) than the tube. Trains (every 20min.) scoot from Hampstead Heath to Kew in 25 minutes. However, BR is used by most visitors for its service from Gatwick Airport to Victoria (see **Getting In and Out of London,** p. 61).

TAXICABS

In order to earn a license, London taxicab drivers must pass a rigorous exam called "The Knowledge" to demonstrate that they know the city's streets by heart; the route taken by a cabbie is virtually certain to be the shortest and quickest. Although the London cab appears clumsy and vaguely old-fashioned, these specialized vehicles comfortably seat five and are able to dart in and out of traffic jams unperturbed. Most of the distinctively shaped cabs are black, although a few come in other colors, including *Financial Times* pink and *Evening Standard* newsprint pattern.

You are most likely to find cabs at large hotels or at major intersections, but cabs abound throughout Central London and are easy to hail except in rain. A taxi is available if its yellow light is aglow. You can catch a cab yourself or call a radio dispatcher for one (tel. 272 0272, 253 5000, or look in the Yellow Pages under "Taxi"); beware that you may be charged extra for ordering a cab by phone. Drivers are required to charge according to the meter for trips within London. A 10% tip is expected, with a surplus charge for extra baggage or passengers. Taxis in London are notoriously expensive. If you believe that you have been overcharged, get the driver's number.

Apart from the licensed cabs, there are many **"minicab"** companies, listed in the Yellow Pages. Ladycabs (tel. 241 4780) has only female cabbies. (Open M-Th 7:30am-12:30am, F 7:30am-1am, Sa 9am-2am, Su 10am-midnight.) Be sure to ask the price when you order a minicab. Reclaim **lost property** (tel. 833 0996) you have left in a taxi at 15 Penton St., N1 (tube: Angel; open M-F 9am-4pm).

The cheapest way to get to and from the airports (besides public transportation of course) is to call a cab company that will dispatch an ordinary car (not the snazzy and distinctive London cabs) for a set fee (see **Getting In and Out of London,** p. 61).

DOCKLANDS LIGHT RAILWAY

The **Docklands Light Railway (DLR),** London's newest transport system, connects the flashy developments of the old docks with the City of London. Call the 24-hour **London Transport Hotline** (tel. 918 4000) for information. The semi-automatic trains run on elevated tracks, providing an unusual perspective on both the dilapidation and the frenetic construction in the area. DLR cars are a little smaller and lighter than their plain vanilla Tube counterparts. The tube's zone system applies to the DLR; DLR lines appear on all tube maps. Fares are the same as for the tube; Travelcards apply. There are three lines: the **red line** running north-south (connecting with the tube at Bow Church and Stratford); the **green line** running west-east to merge with the red line (connecting with the tube at Bank, Shadwell, and Tower Hill/Gateway); and the new **Beckton** line, which starts at Poplar Station (on the red line) and extends 5 mi. to the east. The expansion of the transportation services required by the Docklands is expected to cost over £4 billion. (The rail cars run M-F 5:30am-12:30am, Sa 6:30am-12:30am, Su 7:30am-11:30pm.) The area is also served by a network of buses that run during the same hours and have similar prices to the DLR rail cars. The N50 Night bus from Trafalgar serves the Docklands area late at night.

BICYCLES

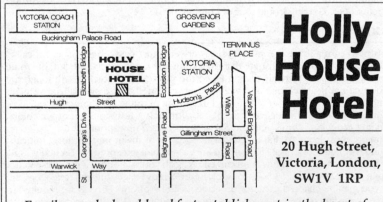

London's roads are in excellent condition, but on weekdays both the volume and temper of its traffic may seem homicidal. However, bicycling has its advantages and there are few better ways to spend a Sunday than pedaling through the parks of the city. Great deals on second-hand bikes can be found at the **General Auction** (see below). Also check outdoor markets, classified ads, and the University of London's bulletin board at 1 Malet St., WC1 (tube: Russell Sq.). Bikes are allowed on BR trains and on the above-ground sections of the Circle, District, Metropolitan, Hammersmith, and City lines (M-F before 7:30am, 9:30am-4:30pm, and after 7pm, Sa-Su all day). Many London cyclists wear breathing masks while riding to lessen the effects of the miasmal fumes polluting the London streets. The *Green Screen* (£6) is a cheaper and less-effective mask, while the *Respro* (£20-25) is the mask of choice for cyclists in the know; both are available at virtually all bike shops.

General Auction, 63 Garrat Ln., Wandsworth, SW18 (tel. (0181) 874 2955). Tube: Tooting Broadway, then Bus #44 or 220. Police auction 50-100 used bikes every Monday at 11am. Prices range from £5 to £400, working bikes begin at £40. Examine bikes M 9-11am, Sa 10am-3pm. Examine the £1 ones with particular care.

Mountain Bike and Ski, 18 Gillingham St., SW1 (tel. 834 8933). Tube: Victoria. From station, go down Wilton Rd., turn right on Gillingham St. Mountain bikes £7 per day, £13 per weekend, £1 per day for insurance. £150 deposit or £50 if you buy insurance. Open M-Th and Sa 9:30am-5:30pm, F 9:30am-6:30pm. AmEx, MC, Visa.

On Your Bike, 5254 Tooley St., SE1 (tel. 357 6958). Tube: London Bridge. 3-speeds £8 per day. Mountain bikes £15 per day, £25 per weekend. Tandems £60 per week. Will take credit card imprint, passport, driver's license, or check for value of bike as deposit. Open M-F 9am-6pm, Sa 9:30am-5:30pm, Su 11am-4pm. MC, Visa.

Scootabout Ltd., 1-3 Leek St., WC1 (tel. 833 4607). Tube: King's Cross. Serious touring motorcycles (500cc) from £45 per day, £225 per week, including helmet, insurance, and unlimited miles. Credit card or £500 deposit. Open M-F 9am-5pm.

CARS

London is not the place to go pouncing about in your Mini—parking is next to impossible, traffic is deplorable, gas is painfully expensive, and the gear shift (not to mention your car) is on the left. When all's said and done, you can bike, bus, tube, or walk. **Renting a car** will not save you time, money, or hassle compared to public transport in London. Big rental firms like Avis and Hertz may be convenient, but they are quite expensive. Small cheap companies can be dodgy. Drivers must usually be over 21 and under 70. Make sure you understand the insurance agreement before you rent; some agreements require you to pay for damages that you may not have caused. If you are paying by credit card, check to see what kind of insurance your company provides free of charge. You have been warned.

BOATS

The **River Thames** no longer commands as much traffic as in the Middle Ages, but if you venture out in a boat you can still sense the pulse of a major lifeline. **Catamaran Cruisers** (tel. 839 3572) offers cruises with commentary. Tours run from Charing Cross to Greenwich pier (every 30min., 10:30am-5:15pm; £6, return £8, day pass £8.50, children £3, £4, £4.25).

The following destinations are served by **Westminster Pier** (tube: Westminster): **Greenwich** (tel. 930 4097), **Hampton Court, Kew,** and **Richmond** (tel. (0181) 940 3891), and the **Thames Barrier** (tel. 930 3373). For more information on these worthy destinations, see **Greater London,** p. 204.

Call the London Tourist Board's **help line** for more information on boat tours and transportation at (0839) 12 34 32.

Keeping in Touch

MAIL

Airmail from London to anywhere in the world is speedy and dependable. A letter will reach the East Coast of the U.S. or urban Canada in about a week and may arrive in as few as three days. **Surface mail,** while much cheaper than airmail, takes up to three months to arrive. It is adequate for getting rid of books or clothing you no longer need in your travels (see **Customs,** p. 17). In summer 1998, an airmail letter to destinations outside Europe cost 63p, a postcard 37p. The cheapest way to write overseas is by aerograms, which are sold in packs of six for £2, making them cheaper than postcards. Single aerograms are 36p. Postage within the U.K. is 26p.

If you have no fixed address while in London, you can receive mail through the British post offices' **Poste Restante** (General Delivery) service. If you were sending a letter to Måns Larsson in Nottingham, you'd mark the envelope "HOLD," and address it like this: "Måns LARSSON, Poste Restante, Nottingham, England NG1 2BN." Include the county and the postal code if you know them. Try to have your Poste Restante sent to the largest post office in a region. When in London, send mail to Poste Restante, Trafalgar Square Post Office, 24-28 William IV St., WC2N 4DL (tel. 930 9580; tube: Charing Cross; open M-Th and Sa 8am-8pm, F 8:30am-8pm)—all general delivery to unspecified post offices ends up here.

Postcards and aerograms sent from the U.S. cost US$0.50. Airmailed letters under 5oz. can be sent to the UK for US$0.60. Many U.S. city post offices offer Express Mail service, which sends packages up to 66 lbs. to Britain in 40 to 72 hours (under 5 oz. US$16.50, and it's straight up from there). Private mail services provide the fastest, most reliable overseas delivery. **DHL, Federal Express,** and **Airborne Express** can get mail from North America to London in two days.

American Express receives and holds mail for up to 30 days, after which they return it to the sender. If you want to have it held longer, write "Hold for x days" on the envelope. The envelope should be addressed with your name in capital letters; "Client Letter Service" should be written below your name. The London office at 445 Oxford St. (open M-F 9:30am-5:30pm) provides this service free of charge for AmEx cardholders and Traveler's Checks users, and can refer you to other London offices that do the same.

TELEPHONES

For a list of country codes, see **Appendix,** p. 306. Within London, if you are dialing from one 0171 or 0181 number to another, you don't need to dial the prefix. If you are dialing from 0171 to 0181 or vice versa (or from another phone code in Britain), you do. If dialing from outside Britain, you need only dial 171 or 181. **In *Let's Go: London,* numbers have 0171 codes unless otherwise noted.**

The new, polite British payphone (known locally as the "callbox") lights up with the words "Insert Money" when you lift the receiver. Payphones do not accept coins smaller than 10p and they don't give change, so use 10p and 20p coins. When the initial time period is exhausted, a series of beeps warns you to insert more money and the digital display ticks off your credit in penny increments.

More convenient than carrying tons of pocket-destroying English change is the **British Telecom (BT) Phonecard,** available in denominations of £2, £4, £10, and £20. The entire country is in the process of changing from an older version of the card (inserted larger edge first) to a newer version (inserted skinnier end first). It's rare to find a phone that accepts both; keep an eye out for which cards the phones in your area take and buy accordingly. Both old and new cards are available everywhere: main post offices, almost any news agent, or the W.H. Smith and John Menzies stationery chains stock them. BT calls are charged in 10p units. It costs £1.30 per minute to use a BT Phone card to call the U.S. If you use the private line of an acquaintance who is a BT residential customer, prices will be far more affordable.

For **international calls,** dial the international code (00), the country code, the city code (if necessary), and then the local number. BT publishes a simple pamphlet about how to make international calls from any phone (available at tourist offices and most hotels, printed in several languages). Consider calling through U.S. long-distance companies, which offer significantly cheaper rates. To access a U.S. AT&T operator from Britain, dial their **USA Direct** number (0800) 89 00 11. You can then call collect or with an AT&T calling card. You can also use calling cards from **MCI** (tel. (0800) 89 02 22) or **Sprint** (tel. (0800) 89 08 77). The first minute (to the US) costs about US$4.20-4.40, additional minutes cost US$1.20-1.30. Calling collect costs much more. For Canadian Calling Card holders, **Canada Direct** is (0800) 89 00 16.

Reduced rates are available for most international calls from Britain (M-F 8pm-8am, Sa-Su all day; to Australia and New Zealand, daily midnight-7am and 2:30-7:30pm). Within Britain, three rate periods exist: the lowest (M-F 6pm-8am, all day Sa-Su); middle (M-F 8-9am and 1-6pm); and most expensive (M-F 9am-1pm).

Important numbers in Britain include **999** for police, fire, or ambulance emergencies, **100** for the telephone operator, **192** for London and Britain directory inquiries, **155** for the international operator, and **153** for international directory assistance. Directory assistance is free from public phones only. Translation assistance for international calls is available at (0181) 889 6363. Area codes for individual British cities are listed in telephone directories. Telephone area codes range from three to six digits, and local telephone numbers range from three to seven. The code **(0800)** indicates a toll-free number. If you call an advertised number beginning with **0898, 0836,** or **0077,** be aware that you will be charged at an extortionary rate.

OTHER COMMUNICATION

Domestic and international **telegrams** offer an option slower than phone but faster than post. Fill out a form at any post or telephone office; cables arrive in one or two days. Telegrams can be quite expensive. **Western Union,** (tel. (800) 325 6000), for example, adds a surcharge to the per-word rate depending on the country. You may wish to consider **faxes** for more immediate, personal, and cheaper communication. Major cities have bureaux where you can pay to send and receive faxes.

Between May 2 and October, **EurAide,** P.O. Box 2375, Naperville, IL 60567 (tel. (630) 420-2343; fax (630) 420-2369; http://www.cube.net/kmu/euraide.html), offers Overseas Access, a service useful to travelers without a set itinerary. The cost is US$15 per week or US$40 per month plus a US$15 registration fee. To reach you, people call, fax, or email to leave a message; you receive it by calling Munich, which is cheaper than calling overseas. You can leave messages for callers to get by phone.

Daily **newspapers,** including the London *Times,* the *Wall Street Journal* (International Edition), and the *New York Times* are available at train stations and kiosks. The *International Herald Tribune* is available just about everywhere.. *The Economist* and international versions of *Time* and *Newsweek* are also easy to find.

If you're spending a year abroad and want to keep in touch with friends or colleagues in a college or research institution, **email** is an attractive option. Free email access is possible. One option is to befriend college students as you go and ask if you can use their email accounts. If you're not the finagling type, Traveltales.com (http://www.traveltales.com) provides free, web-based email for travelers and maintains a list of cybercafes and travel links and chat rooms. Other free, web-based email providers include Hotmail (http://www.hotmail.com), RocketMail (http://www.rocketmail.com), and USANET (http://www.usa.net). Search through http://www.cyberiacafe.net/cyberia/guide/ccafe.htm to find a list of cybercafes around the world from which you can drink a cup of joe and email him, too.

If you're already hooked up to the *infobahn* at home, you should be able to find access numbers for London; check with your internet provider before leaving. If you're not connected, one comparatively cheap, easy-to-use provider is America Online, (tel. (800) 827-6364). The interactive computer service now offers "GLOBALnet," making it possible for American net-junkies to access the internet, sexy chat rooms, and of course email through their home accounts while traveling in 70 countries. The only hurdles for budget travelers are the US$6-12 per hour surcharge and the fact that GLOBALnet only works on computers with AOL software already installed; in other words, to use the service you must travel with your own portable computer or install the software on computers as you go and log on as a guest.

Travelers who have a laptop with them can use a modem to call an internet service provider. Long-distance phone cards intended for such calls can defray high phone charges. Check with your long-distance provider to see if they offer this option; otherwise, try a C.COM Internet PhoneCard (tel. (888) 464-2266), which offers Internet connection calls for US$0.15 per minute, with a minimum initial purchase of US$5.

Accommodations

To sleep in London, however, is an art which a foreigner must acquire by time and habit.

—Robert Southey, 1807

No matter where you plan to stay, it is essential to plan ahead, especially in July and August when London's hotels are bursting with visitors. It is often worth the price of a phone call or fax to secure a confirmed booking. The proprietor should specify the deposit amount (usually one night's stay). The hotel will advise the best way to make the deposit. More and more hotels and most HI hostels accept credit card reservations over the phone, so if you don't have time to make written reservations, it's well worth calling ahead. The **Tourist Information Centre Accommodations Service** at Victoria Station can help you find a room (see **Tourist Offices,** p. 57).

In the listings below, the accommodations near the top of the listing for each region generally offer more pleasant lodgings at a better price than those at the bottom of the listing. Listings which feature a **thumbs-up** (👍) are exceptional values, worthy of special mention.

TYPES OF ACCOMMODATIONS

London offers a wide range of accommodations to suit travelers with different social needs, attachments to privacy, and capacities for roughing it. There are three major categories of accommodation in the following listings: Hostels, B&Bs, and Halls of Residence.

Hostels are low-priced, dorm-style accommodations generally geared toward young travelers. If you are traveling alone or in a small group, a hostel will be your cheapest bunking option. You will be sleeping on a bed in a room with at least three fellow travelers (who may be strangers and who may snore) and, in rare cases, as many as 10 or 15 fellow travelers. Some hostels offer private rooms for two at a slightly higher cost per person. You will be sharing a bathroom with your new roommates and sometimes with travelers from several rooms. Hostels are places where globetrotters can swap information and meet new traveling companions. This social dimension is a selling point as important as hostels' low prices.

There are two flavors of hostel: **Hostelling International (HI) hostels** and **private hostels.** HI hostels generally cost more than private ones, but are usually cleaner and often have spectacular locations. The HI hostels require membership (see HI Hostels listings below for more information) and some have curfews. The staff in HI hostels are usually extremely knowledgeable about the area and many can arrange activities for guests. Bathrooms and other common spaces unfailingly sparkle. On the other hand, many travelers prefer the less expensive private hostels, which tend to attract a more bohemian crowd.

Bed and Breakfasts are smallish hotels run by a family or a proprietor who will provide—surprise!—a bed in which to sleep and breakfast to eat. The term "B&B" encompasses budget hotels of varying quality and personality. Some are nothing more than budget hotels that serve breakfast—don't expect snug, quaint lodgings. Rooms in these lesser-quality B&Bs are small, dreary, and provide few amenities (although you can usually count on a sink and tea/coffee-making facilities). However, some B&Bs are quite cozy, sporting warm comforters, charming decorative details, friendly management, and the occasional pet. Due to the variable character of B&Bs, investigate all of your options before choosing a hotel. A **basic room** means that you share the use of a shower and toilet in the hall. A room **with bath** contains both a private shower and toilet (or "W.C."), and costs several pounds more. Be aware, however, that in-room showers are often awkward prefab units jammed into a corner. **Family room** in B&B lingo generally means a quad or quint with at least one double bed and some single beds. A group of two or more may find that sharing a room in a moderately-priced B&B costs less than staying in some hostels.

Most B&Bs (and some hostels) serve the full **English breakfast**—eggs, bacon, toasted toast, fried toast, baked beans, a peculiarly prepared tomato (baked or stewed), and tea or coffee. **Continental breakfast,** on the other hand, means only some form of bread and hot beverage.

B&Bs generally take reservations (by phone, fax, or letter) with one night's deposit unless we state otherwise. Most accept credit cards. However, if you pay with plastic a **surcharge** may be added to your bill. If you are making reservations in person, be sure to look at a room before agreeing to take it—test the bed, faucets, and toilet. If you arrive on a hotel's doorstep in the afternoon or evening looking for a night's lodging, **haggling** over the price can often save you a few quid—after all if you don't take the room, it'll likely go empty. Some proprietors grant **rate reductions** for stays over a week or during the off season. Off season is from October through March (although September, April, and May are slow enough that you may be able to wrangle a few pounds' discount). In winter, be sure to check whether the room will be heated. If you don't like climbing stairs, keep in mind that "first floor" means second floor to Americans—few B&Bs in the budget range have lifts (elevators).

London's colleges and universities rent out rooms in their **Halls of Residence** over the summer. If you have a student ID, you can often find stupendous bargains—in some cases, you can get a private single for the same price that you would pay for a bed in a hostel dorm. Rates are a bit higher for those without student ID, but are still an affordable option for those traveling alone. Rooms tend to be fairly spartan—standard student digs—but clean. Many Halls of Residence are filled with large groups of adults or teens in London as part of a course or conference. Generally the halls offer rooms to individuals for two or three months over the summer, so calling or writing ahead is advisable. Some halls reserve a few rooms for travelers throughout the year.

ACCOMMODATION DISTRICTS

When contemplating where to stay, tourists should take into consideration what sorts of fun they'll be having in London. Some districts are better for those interested in being close to the sights, others more geared toward those who seek the nightlife, baby. What follows is a thumbnail sketch of the areas in which tourists are most likely to bunk down. Keep in mind that London is not very well served by public transportation after midnight, so if you're staying in the outskirts you'll have to swallow a huge wait for a night bus or an expensive cab ride.

Bloomsbury. Quiet residential streets lined with B&Bs, a few Halls of Residence, and a few hostels. Close to the massive British Museum. This moderately expensive area is within walking distance of Drummond St. (home of outstanding Indian restaurants) to the north and Covent Garden (an exciting nightlife and shopping district) to the south. The West End theaters are within reach, either a longish walk or short bus ride away.

Near Victoria Station. Contains a wide variety of B&Bs and a few hostels as well. **Belgrave Rd.** is covered with cheap B&Bs of varying quality, while pricier **Ebury St.** offers more luxurious accommodations. The area around Victoria is near Buckingham Palace and some of the city's bigger museums, and is also fairly close to major sights such as Westminster Abbey, Parliament, and Whitehall. Theater and nightlife districts are not very far.

Paddington and Bayswater. These neighborhoods don't contain any of London's major sights, but they're a reasonable distance from nearly all of them. The Bayswater/Queensway area sustains a raucous, touristy pub scene, as well as some excellent cheap restaurants. Whiteley's, London's first large, indoor shopping mall, is within walking distance. Lovely Hyde Park and Kensington Gardens are just to the south. Nightlife districts, such as Soho and Covent Garden are a slight haul.

Earl's Court. Emerging from the tube station onto Earl's Court Rd., travelers carrying bags will be harassed by hustlers hawking the area's budget accommodations (though authorities are cracking down on such activities). The beautiful Victorian area feeds on the budget tourist trade, spewing forth travel agencies, souvenir shops, and currency exchanges. Some streets seem to be solely populated by B&Bs and hostels. The area has a vibrant gay and lesbian population and is also a tremendously popular destination for Aussie travelers cooling their heels in London. This is the destination of choice for backpackers looking for dirt-cheap hostels.

Kensington and Chelsea. Elegance comes at a price, and unfortunately, the level of elegance in Kensington and Chelsea puts it almost out of the budget traveler's reach. Still, there are a few B&Bs and hostels that offer outstanding value and allow a visitor to stay in this graceful area for an affordable price. Hyde Park and Kensington Gardens are just to the north, as are the fantastic museums (V&A, Natural History, and Science) that line the Park's southern border. Some of the city's best, and priciest, shopping is in nearby Knightsbridge (a short bus ride away). West End theaters and nightlife are a moderately long bus or tube ride away.

North London and Belsize Park. This huge area contains a few pleasant B&Bs, a few hostels, and a number of residence halls. The prices tend to offer outstanding value, although the long, expensive commute tends to diminish the savings. Some areas of North London can be fairly dreary, though Belsize Park and Hampstead are enclaves of wealth and comfort.

HI/YHA HOSTELS

Each of the Hostelling International/YHA hostels in London requires a **Hostelling International** or **Youth Hostel Association membership card.** Overseas visitors can buy one at YHA London Headquarters or at the hostels themselves for £10.20, under 18 £5. An **International Guest Pass** (£1.70) permits residents of places other than England and Wales to stay at hostel rates without joining the hostel association. After you purchase six Guest Passes, you attain full membership. A membership card for residents of England and Wales costs £10.20. (See also Essentials, p. 19.)

The cheerful staff members, often international travelers themselves, keep London HI/YHA hostels clean and refreshingly well-managed. They can also often provide a range of helpful information on the environs of the hostel. Plan ahead, since London hostels are exceptionally crowded. During the summer, beds fill up months in advance. In recent years, hostels have not always been able to accommodate every written request for reservations, much less on-the-spot inquiries. But hostels frequently hold some beds free until a few days before—it's always worth checking. To secure a place, show up as early as possible and expect to stand in line. With a Visa or MasterCard, you can book in advance by phone. Or you can write to the warden of the individual hostel. There is a new **central reservations number** for all London hostels (tel. 248 6547; open M-Sa 9am-5pm).

For hostel information, visit or call the jumbo-market **YHA London Information Office and Adventure Shop,** 14 Southampton St., WC2 (tel. 836 8541 or 374 0547 for office; tube: Covent Garden; shop open M-Th 10am-6pm, F 10am-7pm, Sa 9:30am-6pm, Su 11am-4pm); 174 Kensington High St. (tel. 938 2948; tube: High St. Kensington; M-W 10am-6pm, Th-F 10am-7pm, Sa 9am-6:30pm, Su 11am-5pm); 52 Grosvenor Gdns. (tel. 823 4739; tube: Victoria; office open M-W and F 8:30am-6pm, Th 8:30am-8pm, Sa-Su 10am-5pm. Shortened winter hours). Cardholders receive a 10% discount on anything in the Adventure Shop.

All hostels are equipped with large **lockers** that require a padlock. Bring your own or purchase one from the hostel for £3. London hostels do not charge for a sheet or sleeping bag. Most have laundry facilities and some kitchen equipment. Theater tickets and discounted attraction tickets are available.

Oxford Street, 14-18 Noel St., W1 (tel. 734 1618; fax 734 1657). Tube: Oxford Circus. Walk east on Oxford St. and turn right on Poland St.; the hostel stands next to a blue and green nature mural entitled "Ode to the West Wind." As close as you can possibly get to the Soho action. An elevator takes you 3 flights up. Facilities include spacious TV lounge with plenty of comfortable couches, clean and fully equipped **kitchen** with microwave, **laundry** facilities and **currency exchange.** 75 beds in small, clean rooms of 2-4 with pink walls. Rooms have large **storage lockers,** but you must bring your own padlock. Packed breakfast £2.10. Superb location makes up for the expense: 3-4 bed £18.70, under 18 £15.25; double £40.60. Book at least 3-4 weeks in advance—very few walk-ins accepted. Full payment required to secure a reservation. No children under 6. Reception open 7am-11pm. 24hr. security; no curfew. MC, Visa.

Hampstead Heath, 4 Wellgarth Rd., NW11 (tel. (0181) 458 9054 or 458 7096; fax 209 0546). Tube: Golders Green, then bus #210 or 268 toward Hampstead, or on foot by turning left from the station onto North End Rd., then left again onto Wellgarth Rd. (10min.). A beautiful, sprawling hostel in a former nursing school that looks like a convent. **Kitchen** and **laundry** facilities. Lovely backyard and outdoor walkway covered with clinging grape vines. Video games and outdoor foosball. Internet and fax access. 200 beds in surprisingly sumptuous 2- to 6-bed dorms £15.60, under 18 £13.35. Family rooms: doubles £38.50; triples £55; quads £71; quints £87; 6-bed £103.50 (breakfast included with all rooms). 24hr. security and reception. No curfew. Book in advance. MC, Visa.

City of London, 36 Carter Ln., EC4 (tel. 236 4965; fax 236 7681). Tube: St. Paul's. (See map of Bloomsbury, Holburn, and Fleet Streets.) From the City Information Centre on the opposite side of St. Paul's Cathedral, go left down Godliman St., then take the 1st right onto Carter Ln. (a helpful sign outside the Centre points you in the right direction). Sleep in quiet comfort a stone's throw from St. Paul's. Scrupulously clean, with a full range of services, including secure luggage storage, currency exchange, **laundry** facilities, and theater box office. Rooms contain between 1 and 15 beds; the average room has 5 beds. Larger rooms feature the less-than-ideal triple-decker bunk beds ubiquitous in London hostels. Single-sex rooms only. Dorms £19, under 18 £17; 5- to 8-bed dorms £21.30, £17.90. Singles £25, under 18 £21.50; doubles £49, £41; triples £67.50, £90; quads £57, £76. 24hr. security. Reception open 7am-11pm. Best to call at least a week in advance, especially for the dorms. Make bookings for other UK hostels at reception. A canteen offers inexpensive set lunches and dinners. Major credit cards.

Earl's Court, Earl's Ct., 38 Bolton Gdns., SW5 (tel. 373 7083; fax 835 2034). Tube: Earl's Ct. Exit from the tube station onto Earl's Ct. Rd. and turn right; Bolton Gdns. is the 5th street on your left. A converted townhouse in a leafy residential neighborhood. 155 beds in rooms of 4-16. Lounge has TV and a soft drink machine. Currency exchange. Meals available in the large, colorful cafeteria 5-8pm. **Kitchen** and **laundry** access. Very clean. All rooms single-sex. £18.70, under 18 £16.45. Nonmembers £1.70 extra. Student discount £1. Continental or full English breakfast. Reception open 7am-11pm. 24hr. security. No curfew. MC, Visa.

Holland House, Holland Walk, W8 (tel. 937 0748; fax 376 0667). Tube: High St. Ken. A handsome 1607 Jacobean mansion nestled in Holland Park offers lovely green views and a multi-lingual staff. The reception is large and functional, and the rooms are clean and relatively spacious, using standard hostel beds with built-in **storage lockers**—bring a padlock. **Laundry** and **kitchen** facilities. Free daytime luggage storage. HI membership required. Dorms £18.70, under 18 £16.45. Cooked breakfast included. 24hr. access. The restaurant offers a set dinner for £4.45 from 5-8pm each evening. MC, Visa.

King's Cross/St. Pancras, 79-81 Euston Rd., N1 (tel. 388 9998; fax 388 6766). Tube: King's Cross/St.Pancras or Euston. This spanking-new 8-story hostel boasts a convenient location between 2 major tube stations. Beneath the unremarkable facade are new, comfortable beds and sparkling bathrooms. Some rooms even come with the unheard-of amenity of air-conditioning—ask in advance. "Premium" rooms include bathroom, TV, and coffee/tea facilities. **Laundry** and **kitchen** facilities. Game room lounge. Restaurant serves affordable meals from 6-9pm (£5). Numerous family rooms are excellent for parents with children (who must be present for you to stay there). 4-5 bed dorm £21.30, under 18 £17.90; 2-bed rooms £22.50, £19.40, with bath £24.30, under 18 £20.90; 4-bed family rooms £80; 5-bed £97.50. Luggage storage. No curfew. Book in advance. Max. stay 1 week. MC, Visa.

Rotherhithe, Island Yard, Salter Rd., SE1 (tel. 232 2114; fax 237 2919). Tube: Rotherhithe. (See map of The East End.) A 15-min. walk down Brunel Rd., then onto Salter. Welcome to *2001, A Space Odyssey:* Chrome, glass, and stucco make this modern, somewhat impersonal, 320-bed hostel a trip into futuristic living. The only big problem: being in the Docklands means you're in the boondocks. Transportation into the city takes around 30min. Facilities include a restaurant, a lounge, and a bar. No curfew. 6- to 10-bed dorms £21.30, under 18 £17.90; 4-bed dorms £21.75, £18; 2-bed dorms £24.50, £20.50. Breakfast included. Wheelchair accessible. MC, Visa.

Epping Forest, Wellington Hall, High Beach, Loughton, Essex 1G10 (tel./fax (0181) 508 5161). Tube: Loughton (zone 6, 45min. from central London), then a brisk 35-min. walk. Follow Station Rd. as it crosses Epping High Rd. and becomes Forest Rd. Continue along Forest Rd. as it becomes Earl's Path, straight through the roundabout, keep right until the King's Oak pub, turn left and then right at the "Wellington Hall" sign; the hostel will be on your left. A cab from the tube station costs £3 per carload. Set in the heart of 6000 remote acres of ancient woodland. Simple washing facilities and no laundry, but large **kitchen.** Dorms £8, students £7, under 18 £5.40; 4-bed family rooms (2 adults, 2 children) £30.50; 6-bed family rooms £42. **Camping** (tents not supplied) £4 per person. Reception open 7:30-10am. 5-11pm lockout. Curfew 11pm. Don't make the long journey for nothing—call ahead. Open Mar.-Nov. MC, Visa.

PRIVATE HOSTELS

Bloomsbury

Ashlee House, 261-65 Gray's Inn Rd., WC1 (tel. 833 9400; fax 833 6777; email ashleehouse@tsnxt.co.uk). Tube: King's Cross. From King's Cross, turn right onto Pentonville Rd. and then right again onto Gray's Inn Rd.; the hostel is a few blocks up the road on the right. Newly opened, Ashlee House offers clean, bright rooms within easy walking distance of King's Cross. 140 beds. Offers a range of facilities, including **laundry, kitchens,** and secure luggage room. The rooms are small but functional: all have washbasins and central heating. Dorms £13; 4- and 6-bed rooms £17; twins £22. Generous breakfast (served M-F 7:30-9.30am, Sa-Su 8-10am). Spacious reception area open 24hr. No curfew or lockout. Check-out 10am.

Central University of Iowa Hostel, 7 Bedford Pl., WC1 (tel./fax 580 1121). Tube: Holborn or Russell Sq. From Holborn Rd., head right on Southampton Rd. Walk 2 blocks, take the 2nd street on the left (Bloomsbury Pl.), then take the 1st right. From Russell Sq., head left and turn left onto Southampton Row, then turn right onto Russell Sq.; Bedford Pl. is the 1st left. On a quiet street near the British Museum. Spartan rooms with bunk beds. Wood bunks in some rooms are superior to the metal variety. **Laundry** facilities, towels and linen, TV lounge. Singles £21; twins £19; 4-5 bed room £17. £10 key deposit. Continental breakfast. Reception 9am-1pm and 3-8:30pm. No curfew. Open May 20-Aug. 20. AmEx, MC, Visa.

Astor's Museum Inn, 27 Montague St., WC1 (tel. 580 5360; fax 636 7948). Tube: Holborn, Tottenham Ct. Rd., or Russell Sq. Off Bloomsbury Sq. Across the street from the British Museum. Decorated with colorful murals. **Kitchen** facilities and cable TV. Coed dorms almost inevitable. Dorms £14; 6-bed dorms £14; 4-bed dorms £15; 3-bed dorms £16; doubles £17. Discounts available Oct.-Mar. Continental breakfast. Linens provided. 24hr. reception. If they're full, they'll direct you to 1 of 3 other Astor's hostels. No curfew. Book 1 month ahead. MC, Visa.

Tonbridge School Clubs, Ltd. (tel. 837 4406), Judd and Cromer St., WC1. Tube: King's Cross/St. Pancras. Follow Euston Rd. to the site of the new British Library and turn left onto Judd St.; the hostel is 3 blocks down. Students with non-British passports only. A clean, no frills place to sleep and shower. Men sleep in basement gym, women in karate-club hall. Blankets and foam pads provided. Pool tables, TV, video games. Floor space £5. Daytime storage space. Lockout 9am-9pm; lights-out 11:30pm; midnight curfew. Use caution when walking in the area at night.

Paddington, Bayswater, and Notting Hill Gate

Hyde Park Hostel, 2-6 Inverness Terr., W2 (tel. 229 5101; fax 229 3170). Tube: Bayswater or Queensway. New as of July 1998, this conveniently located hostel is being converted from a methodist chaplaincy. Clean rooms feature high ceilings and new red bunks. Pool room/lounge. Color TV lounge, and plans for addition of a bar. **Kitchen, laundry** facilities. 10-bed dorms £12.50; 6- to 8-bed dorms £14; 4-bed dorms £15. Weekly rate £70. £5 key deposit. Continental breakfast served at school desks downstairs. 24hr. reception. MC, Visa (min. charge £40).

Quest Hotel, 45 Queensborough Terrace, W2 (tel. 229 7782). Tube: Queensway. From the tube, turn right onto Bayswater; walk along Bayswater for 2 blocks and then turn left onto Queensborough Terrace. The hostel, a terraced house, is on your left. 60-70 beds. Communal, clean, and sociable, the multinational staff throws one theme party a month. The bathrooms are cleaned daily, the kitchen twice daily. Pool room and **kitchen** available. Satellite TV in lounge. 4- to 8-bed dorms (coed and 1 women-only) £15; 2-bed dorm £18. Ask about weekly rates during winter. Continental breakfast (served 8-9:45am) and sheets included (changed daily). Check-out 10am. No curfew or lockout. Key deposit £3. MC, Visa.

Dean Court Hotel, 57 Inverness Terr., W2. See p. 88 for more details.

ACCOMMODATIONS

Kensington, Chelsea, and Earl's Court

Albert Hotel, 191 Queens Gate, SW7 (tel. 584 3019; fax 823 8520). Tube: Gloucester Rd., or Bus #2 or 70 from South Kensington. A substantial walk from the tube; take a right on Cromwell and a left on Queen's Gate. The hotel is approximately ¼ mi. up Queen's Gate on your right, deliciously close to Hyde Park. The bus, which stops near the Royal Albert Hall on Kensington Gore, is much quicker. This wood-paneled hostel with sweeping staircases seems more like a quality hotel. Rooms range from large dorms to intimate doubles, most with bath. **Laundry.** Dorm (single-sex or coed) £12; 4- to 6-bed dorm £15; singles or doubles £40. Weekly: dorm only, £72. Continental breakfast and sheets provided. 24hr. reception. No lockout or curfew. Luggage storage £1 per day. Reserve with 1 night's deposit. MC, Visa.

Curzon House Hotel, 58 Courtfield Gdns., SW5 (tel. 581 2116; fax 835 1319). Tube: Gloucester Rd. Turn right onto Gloucester Rd., right again on Courtfield Rd., and right on Courtfield Gdns. TV lounge features groovy, plush, velour-checked couches. No bunk beds. Bathrooms are basic, but functional. **Kitchen.** 4-bed dorm (single-sex) £17. Singles £30; doubles £44; triples £39. Weekly and seasonal discounts as low as £70 per week in winter. Breakfast included. MC, Visa.

Court Hotel, 194-196 Earl's Ct. Rd., SW5 (tel. 373 0027; fax 912 9500). Tube: Earl's Ct. Sister hostel at 17 Kempsford Gardens (tel. 373 2174). All single, double, and twin rooms have TV and tea/coffee set. Full **kitchen** facilities and spacious TV lounge. Safe available for valuables. 3- to 4-bed dorm (single-sex) £15; singles £26; doubles £35. Weekly: dorm £91; singles £165; doubles £210. Linen provided. Off-season and long-term discounts. Key deposit £10. Reception open 8am-9pm. No curfew. Reservations not accepted; call for availability. AmEx, MC, Visa.

O'Callaghan's Hotel, 205 Earl's Ct. Rd., SW5 (tel. 370 3000; fax 370 2623). Tube: Earl's Ct. A bare bones place to hit the hay; guests like the relaxed atmosphere as well as the prices. 32 beds in neat blue-painted rooms. Friendly management will pick you up from Victoria and drive you to two other branches if first hostel is full. Connection with Stafflink (tel. 373 5400), a local temp agency, offers employment preference to hostel residents. Rooms have big windows and bunk beds. Dorm £10; doubles £24. Weekly: dorm £60; doubles £140. Winter discounts. 24hr. reception. Same management operates the aptly-named **O'Callaghan's II,** 64 Holland Rd., W14 (tel. 603 0743). Tube: Olympia. From the station, cross the bridge, 1st left, then 1st right onto Holland Rd. Large kitchen, ironing facilities, and BBQs several times a month. Same prices as O'Callaghan's. Same management also runs **Table Mountain,** 109 Warwick Rd., SW5 (tel. 370 4474). Tube: Earl's Ct. Offers the same services as above. Rooms are adequate and may include a fridge and TV. Same prices as O'Callaghan's.

Chelsea Hotel, 33-41 Earl's Ct. Sq., SW5 (tel. 244 6892 or 244 7395; fax 244 6891). Tube: Earl's Ct. Turn right onto Earl's Ct. Rd., then right again at Earl's Ct. Sq. A tattered union jack flag hangs in the window of this no-frills establishment. 300 dorm beds. Stark rooms generally feature bunk beds. May be a line for the bathrooms. **Laundry.** Fax available. Dorms £10; doubles £15, with shower £16; triples £13; quads £12. Weekly: 7 nights for the price of 6. Continental breakfast. Linens provided. 24hr. reception. No lockout or curfew. Luggage storage £1 per day; store valuables in downstairs safe for 50p. £1 winter discount. Reserve ahead in writing.

Ayer's Rock Hotel, 16 Longridge Rd. (tel. 373 2944). Tube: Earl's Ct. Large reception and lounge area. Free tea and coffee. Basic accommodations which cater to a backpacker crowd. 4- to 6-bed dorm from £10; doubles from £25. Weekly: dorms from £50; doubles from £130. No credit cards.

Near Victoria Station

Victoria Hotel, 71 Belgrave Rd. SW1 (tel. 834 3077; fax 932 0693). Tube: Victoria or Pimlico. Closer to Pimlico. From the station, take the Bessborough St. (south side) exit and go left along Lupus St., then take a right at St. George's Sq. Belgrave Rd. starts on the other side. A clean, friendly, bohemian hostel with cool pool room and broad video selection for TV. 70 beds. Shower stalls are oddly constructed, but clean. **Kitchen.** 6-8 bed dorm rooms £12.50-15. Continental breakfast. Luggage storage. 24hr. reception. MC, Visa.

O'Callaghans, 92 Ebury St. (tel. 730 6776). From Victoria Station make a left onto Buckingham Palace Rd., then a right onto Eccleston St., then a left onto Ebury St. Updated, spare doubles and dorm rooms have been whitewashed and puffy maroon backboards attached to the beds. Shared bathrooms. **Kitchen** facilities. 4-bed dorms £15; doubles £30-35; triples £15. Higher rates for single-night stays. Winter discounts. Luggage storage. 24hr. reception.

Near North London

International Student House, 229 Great Portland St., W1 (tel. 631 8300, -8310; fax 631 8315). Tube: Great Portland St. (See map of Regents Park and Marylebone.) At the foot of Regent's Park, across the street from the tube station's rotunda. 60s exterior hides a thriving international metropolis with its own films, concerts, discos, study groups, athletic contests, expeditions, and parties. Over 500 beds. The Una Mundo bar in the lobby has a huge TV and serves £1.80 pints from 5-11pm weekdays, F-Sa 5pm-2am. Lockable cupboards in dorms, **laundry** facilities, money changing services (£3 flat fee). No curfew. Dorms (without breakfast) £10; singles £28; doubles £20; triples £16.50. With ISIC card: singles £21; doubles £16; triples £13. Rooms with W.C. and telephones £4 extra. Continental breakfast. Reserve at least 1 month ahead, earlier during academic year. MC, Visa.

Barbican YMCA, 2 Fann St., EC2 (tel. 628 0697; fax 638 2420). Tube: Barbican. Turn left out of the station then right onto Fann St. 240 rooms and 26 nationalities represented says it all: institutional feeling offset by international flair. Spacious fitness center with free weights. Singles £23; doubles £40. Weekly rates: singles £140; doubles £244; breakfast and dinner included. Check-out 9:30am. No curfew. Call 24hr. ahead. MC, Visa.

HALLS OF RESIDENCE

Bloomsbury

High Holborn Residence, 178 High Holborn, WC1 (tel. 379 5589; fax 379 5640). Tube: Holborn. 10min. walk down High Holborn. This 3-year-old London School of Economics hall offers comfort and affordability. Singles are spacious and well-furnished. Each room has a phone with free incoming calls and voice mail. Lounge and bar. **Laundry** and **kitchen** facilities. Singles £27; twins £45, with bath £52. Discounts for longer stays. Continental breakfast. Reception daily 7am-11pm. Excellent disabled access. Open July to mid-Sept. Book in advance. MC, Visa.

Carr Saunders Hall, 18-24 Fitzroy St., W1 (tel. 323 9712; fax 580 4718). Tube: Warren St. Turn right off Tottenham Ct. Rd. onto Grafton Way, then left onto Fitzroy St. 134 single study bedrooms, 12 doubles. Singles £25; doubles £44. Under 12 ½-price. English breakfast. Reception Su-Th 8:30am-midnight, F-Sa 8:30am-2am. MC, Visa.

Connaught Hall, 36-45 Tavistock Sq., WC1 (tel. 387 6181; fax 383 4109). Tube: Russell Sq. Head left from the station and turn right onto Woburn Pl.; the 1st left is Tavistock Sq. Quiet atmosphere. 200 small, single study bedrooms on long, narrow, typical college dorm hallways. Rooms feature sinks, wardrobes, desks, and tea-making facilities. **Laundry,** reading rooms, private garden, and an elegant green marble lobby. Singles £21.50. English breakfast. Reception daily 8am-midnight. Reservations recommended. Open July-Aug. and Easter.

Passfield Hall, 1-7 Endsleigh Pl., WC1 (tel. 387 3584 or 387 7743; fax 387 0419). Tube: Euston. Head left on Euston Rd., then take the 1st right onto Gordon St. Endsleigh Pl. is the 2nd left. 100 singles, 34 doubles, 10 triples; rooms vary in size, but all have desks and phones that can only receive incoming calls. **Laundry** and **Kitchen.** Singles £21; doubles £42; triples £54. Under 12 ½-price. English breakfast. Call by Mar.-Apr. for July. Open July-Sept. and Easter 8am-midnight. MC, Visa.

John Adams Hall, 15-23 Endsleigh St., WC1 (tel. 387 4086; fax 383 0164). Tube: Euston. Head right on Euston Rd., take 1st right onto Gordon St. and 1st left onto Endsleigh Gdns.; Endsleigh St. is the 2nd right. Elegant Georgian building with small wrought-iron balconies. 124 singles, 22 doubles. Singles are small and simple, with desks, wardrobes, and sinks. **Laundry** facilities, TV lounge, Ping-Pong table, 5 pianos, and quiet reading room. Singles £22; doubles £38. 6 or more nights: doubles £35. English breakfast. Reception daily 8am-1pm and 2-10pm. Open July-Aug. and Easter, but a few rooms kept free for travelers all year. MC, Visa.

Hughes Parry Hall, 29 Cartwright Gdns., WC1 (tel. 387 1477). Tube: Russell Sq. Head right from the station, turn left onto Marchmont St., and Cartwright Gdns. will appear just past Tavistock Pl. Another mammoth, modern London University hall with 13 floors of 300 smallish, sparse singles, outfitted with desks and fairly large wardrobes. Squash and tennis, **laundry** facilities, libraries, TV lounge, bar (pint £1.40). Singles with breakfast £18.50, with breakfast and dinner £22. 24hr. porter. Reception M-F 8:30am-5:30pm. Reservations with deposit. Open July-Aug. and Easter. MC, Visa.

Commonwealth Hall, 1-11 Cartwright Gdns., WC1 (tel. 387 0311). Tube: Russell Sq. (See directions to Hughes Hall, above.) Not too different from Hughes Parry Hall. 420 small singles with institutional decor. Ask for a room overlooking Cartwright Gardens. Squash and tennis, **kitchen** and **laundry** facilities, Ping-Pong, (satellite) TV lounges, library, music rooms, and a pleasant bar (pint £1.40). Single with breakfast £20, with breakfast and dinner £24. £2 student discount. 24hr. porter, no curfew. Reservation required. Open July-Aug. No credit cards.

Kensington, Chelsea, and Earl's Court

The **King's Campus Vacation Bureau** (write to 127 Stamford Street, SE1 9NQ; tel. 928 3777), controls bookings for a number of residence halls where students at **King's College** of the University of London live during the academic year. Rooms are available from early June to mid-September. All have 24-hour security and offer breakfast, linen, soap, towel, and **laundry** facilities. All offer a 10% discount for stays over seven days. Remember: these are dorm rooms and generally are not as elegant or tasteful as many private B&Bs. It's a good idea to bring thongs with you for the bathroom. The college has opened a brand new set of self-catering flats. For information about the **Stamford Street Apartments,** or the **Great Dover Street Apartments,** call the King's Campus Vacation Bureau at the number listed above (see also p. 82).

Wellington Hall, 71 Vincent Sq., Westminster, SW1 (tel. 834 4740; fax 233 7709). Tube: Victoria. Walk 1 long block along Vauxhall Bridge Rd.; turn left on Rochester Row. Convenient to Westminster, Big Ben, Buckingham Palace, and the Tate Gal-

ACCOMMODATIONS

lery, this hall is the most central and expensive of the King's College halls. Spacious rooms come with desks. English breakfast. 2 lounges, library, conference room, and bar. Reserve through **King's Campus Vacation Bureau** (see Kensington, Chelsea, and Earl's Ct., p. 79) Singles £25; doubles £38.50. Discounts for longer stays. Book in advance. Rooms generally available June-Sept. and Easter.

Other halls of residence not affiliated with King's College which let rooms include:

Queen Alexandra's House, Kensington Gore, SW7 (tel. 589 3635; fax 589 3177). Tube: South Kensington, or Bus #9, 10, or 52 to Royal Albert Hall; the hostel is just behind the Royal Albert Hall to the left. Women only. Magnificent Victorian building with ornate bars and staircases running through the lobby. **Kitchen, laundry,** sitting room, and 20 piano-laden music rooms. Cozy singles £25. Continental breakfast. Weekly rates for stays over two weeks (£125 per week) upon availability. No credit cards. Write weeks in advance for a booking form. Fax is best.

More House, 53 Cromwell Rd., SW7 (tel. 589 6754 or 584 2040). Tube: Gloucester Rd. Exit left onto Gloucester Rd. then turn right on Cromwell Rd. Unmarked Victorian building across from Natural History Museum. It doubles as the West London Catholic Chaplaincy Center. Full English breakfast. **Laundry** and **kitchen** facilities available. Dorm £15; single £25; double £40. Weekly rates for stays over a month. Open July-Aug. Reserve ahead with a £10 non-refundable deposit deductible from final bill. No credit cards.

North London

Hampstead Campus, 23 Kidderpore Ave., NW3 (tel. 435 3564; fax 431 4402). Tube: Finchley Rd. or West Hampstead, then Bus #13, 28, 82, or 113 to the Platt's Ln. stop on Finchley Rd. Turn onto Platt's Ln. then take an immediate right on Kidderpore Ave. Beautiful residential surroundings with singles at dorm room prices. Game rooms, music room, **kitchen,** and TV lounge. All rooms have basins, desks, and wardrobes. Singles £15.50; twins £26.50. 10% off 7 nights or more. 24hr. security. Reserve through King's Campus Vacation Bureau (see **Kensington, Chelsea, and Earl's Court,** p. 80). MC, Visa.

Walter Sickert Hall, 29 Graham St., N1 (tel. 477 8822; fax 477 8825). Tube: Angel. Exit the station heading left. Turn left onto City Rd.; Graham St. will be on the left just before the canal. Fresh blue carpeting and white-painted halls. All rooms come with bath, hot pot, phone, desks, and bookshelves. About 220 units. TV rooms, **laundry** facilities. Office-building feel prevents sense of hostel community but ensures cleanliness. Most rooms have TVs. Singles £30; doubles £50. Prices subject to change, so call ahead. Continental breakfast delivered to the room every morning. 24hr. security. Open July-Sept.—call ahead for winter months. MC, Visa.

University of North London, The Arcade, 385-401 Holloway Rd., N7 (tel. 607 5415; fax 609 0052; email summerlets@unl.ac.uk). Tube: Holloway Rd. Head left from the tube station. Dorms located above the Hogshead Pub right before Parkhurst Rd. Over 365 single rooms in 4- to 6-person flats. Each flat has its own **kitchen** and bathroom. Single beds £11, with linen £16; £70 per week with linens. Open July 6 to mid-Sept. Book months in advance (in writing or via email) because low prices make these rooms very popular for long guest stays. AmEx, MC, Visa.

South of the Thames

Stamford Street Apartments, 127 Stamford St., SE1 (tel. 873 2960; fax 873 2962). Tube: Waterloo. (See map of Lambeth, South Bank, and Southwark.) From Waterloo station, take the exit marked "Waterloo Bridge." Take the pedestrian subway marked "Subway to York Road," and follow it around the circle to reach Stamford St. 560 spacious singles come replete with wood furniture, refrigerators, blue carpeting, and an attached bathroom. **Kitchen** and color TV lounge. **Laundry** facilities. Use of on-site gym £5 per week. Singles with bath £32.50. 10% discount for stays over 7 days. 24hr. reception. Disabled access. Open July-Sept. MC, Visa.

Great Dover Street Apartments, 165 Great Dover St., SE1 (tel. 407 0068 or 407 0069; fax 378 7973). Tube: Borough. (See map of Lambeth, South Bank, and Southwark.) Rooms offer new furniture, dark blue rugs, refrigerators, and tiny, yet clean bathrooms. **Kitchen** and color TV lounge. **Laundry** facilities. Over 750 rooms. Singles with bath £29.50, concessions £25; doubles £46. 10% discount for stays over 1 week. 24hr. reception. Wheelchair accessible. Open July-Sept. MC, Visa.

BED AND BREAKFAST HOTELS

BED AND BREAKFAST AGENCIES

Bed & Breakfast (GB), P.O. Box 66, Henley-on-Thames, Oxon, England RG9 1XS (tel. (01491) 578 803; fax (01491) 410 806). Comprehensive UK B&B booking service (see **Budget Travel Agencies,** p. 46).

Primrose Hill Agency, 14 Edis St., NW1 8LG, (tel. 722 6869; fax 916 2240). Gail O' Farrell books charming accommodations in 10 homes in the beautiful Hampstead and Primrose hill areas. From £20-37 per person per night.

London Home-to-Home, 19 Mt. Park Crescent, Ealing, London W5 2RN (tel./fax (0181) 566 7976). Anita Harrison and Rosemary Richardson will book you a room in a London home. Singles £30; doubles £46 for areas like Hammersmith and Chiswick, higher for more central locales. Family rooms. 2-night min. stay.

Bloomsbury

GOWER STREET

Budget hotels line one side of **Gower Street.** From the tube station head left on Tottenham Ct. Rd., turn right onto Torrington Rd., and take the third right onto Gower St. With the British Museum just down the street and loads of fabulous eateries around the tube station, Gower St. B&Bs offer a great combination of comfort and convenience in Bloomsbury. Keep in mind that Gower St. is a main thoroughfare, so light sleepers may wish to request a room away from the road. **Tube: Goodge St.**

Arosfa Hotel, 83 Gower St., WC1 (tel./fax 636 2115). The name is Welsh for "place to rest," and the charming couple who have turned this B&B around over the last 2 years ensure that it lives up to its name. All furnishings and fixtures are close to new, the rooms are spacious, and the facilities are immaculate. Singles £31; doubles £44, with bath £58; triples £59, £70. MC, Visa.

Ridgemount Hotel, 65-67 Gower St., WC1 (tel. 636 1141 or 580 7060; fax. 636 2558). Ongoing renovations have improved the quality of the hospitality. Radiantly clean. Snug singles with TVs. **Laundry** facilities, garden in back, free tea and coffee in the TV lounge. Singles £30, with bath £40; doubles £44, £55; triples £57, £72; quads £64-68, £78; quints £75. English breakfast. Call in advance. No credit cards.

The Langland Hotel, 29-31 Gower St., WC1 (tel. 636 5801; fax 580 2227). Clean, spacious rooms, although sparsely furnished. Some with TV, some with shower. Cable TV lounge with comfy blue sofas. Singles £35; doubles £45, with bath £75; triples £65; quads £85. Winter discounts. English breakfast. MC, Visa.

RUSSELL SQUARE

The grass grows a little greener and the traffic jams a little less on the other side of the British Museum—but the rates run a little higher. **Tube: Holborn or Russell Sq.**

Ruskin Hotel, 23-24 Montague St., WC1 (tel. 636 7388; fax 323 1662). From the Holborn tube station, take Southampton Row, then the 2nd left onto Great Russell St.; Montague St. is the 2nd right. Prime position across the street from one side of the British Museum. Meticulously clean and well-kept rooms sport vaguely institutional, motel-type furnishings, hot pots, and hair dryers. TV lounge with elegant glass lamps. Pretty back garden. Singles £42; doubles £60, with bath £75; triples £75, £85. English breakfast. AmEx, MC, Visa.

Celtic Hotel, 62 Guilford St., WC1 (tel. 837 9258 or 837 6737). Go left when exiting the station. Take a left onto Herbrand St., and another left onto Guilford. Family-run establishment provides basic, sparsely furnished rooms and clean facilities. They don't give room keys, but will open the door for guests 24hr. Streetside rooms can be a bit noisy. TV lounge. Singles £36.50; doubles £48.50; triples £68; quads £78; quints £100. English breakfast.

Cosmo/Bedford House Hotel, 27 Bloomsbury Sq., WC1 (tel. 636 4661; fax 636 0577). From Holborn tube station, take Southampton Row, then the 2nd left onto Bloomsbury Pl.; the hotel is on your right. Clean, comfortable rooms with color TVs. Rooms in the back overlook a tree-filled garden; some in the front look out onto the square. TV lounge with beverage machines and sofas. Singles £34, with bath £45; doubles £55, £65; triples £75, £80. Continental breakfast. AmEx, DC.

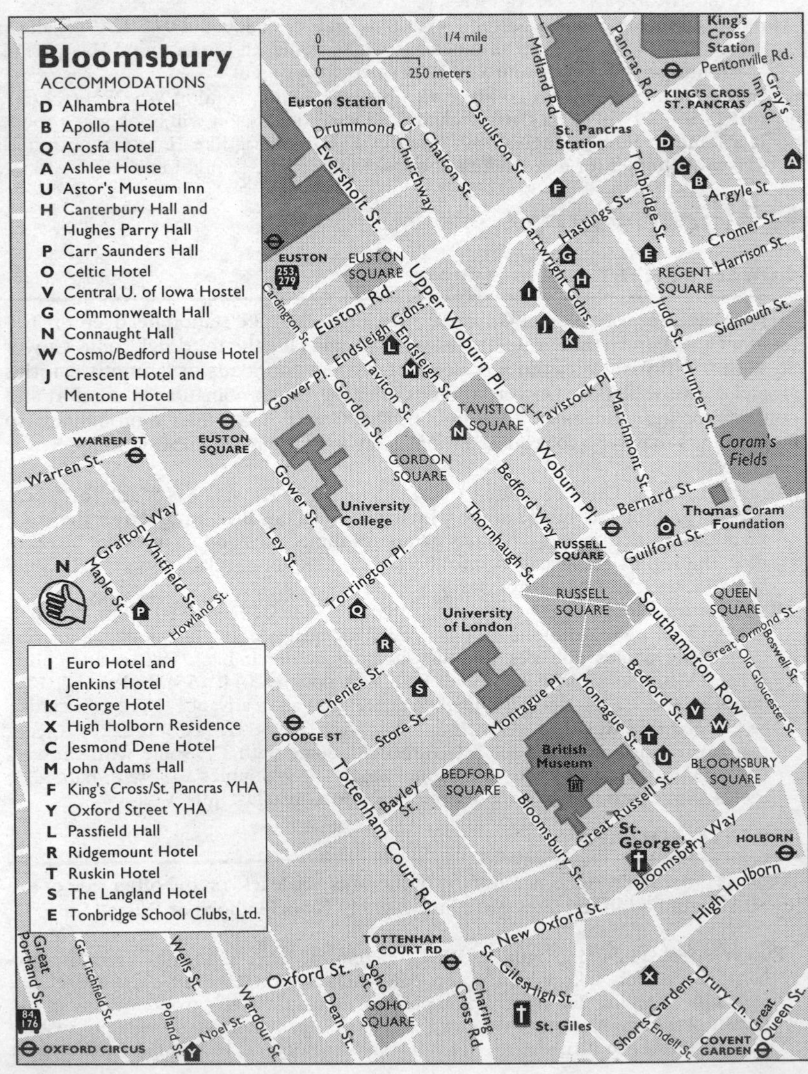

CARTWRIGHT GARDENS

Accommodations encircle the crescent-shaped **Cartwright Gardens.** From the tube station, follow Marchmont St. for two blocks until Cartwright Gdns. appears on the left. Only local B&B guests and University hall residents have access to the gated lawns and tennis courts—another bonus to already excellent digs. **Tube: Russell Sq.**

Euro Hotel, 51-53 Cartwright Gdns., WC1 (tel. 387 4321; fax 383 5044). Large rooms with cable TV, radio, hot pot, phone, and sink. Immaculate bathroom facilities are spacious for a London B&B. Free use of **email** at reception. Singles £46, with bath £68; doubles £63, £82.50; triples £76, £96; quads £84, £104. Under 13 £9.50. 10% discount for stays over 1 week. Flexible winter discounts. Full English breakfast in the dining room/lounge/reception room. AmEx, MC, Visa.

Mentone Hotel, 54-55 Cartwright Gdns., WC1 (tel. 387 3927; fax 388 4671). Pleasantly decorated and newly renovated, with a bright, cheery atmosphere. All rooms with color TV and tea/coffee makers. Singles £42, with bath £60; doubles £60, £75; triples with bath £85; quads with bath £90. Reduced rates Dec.-Apr. English breakfast. AmEx, MC, Visa.

George Hotel 60 Cartwright Gdns., WC1 (tel. 387 8777; fax 387 8666; email ghotel@aol.com). Homey dining hall, high ceilings, track lighting, and pastel hallways. All rooms have cable TV and kettles. Hair dryers, irons available upon request. Singles £43.50; doubles £59.50, with shower £64.50, with bath £75; triples £73, £79, £87; quads £80. Children stay free on weekends; £9.50 otherwise. 10% discount for stays of 1 week or longer. English breakfast. MC, Visa.

Jenkins Hotel, 45 Cartwright Gdns., WC1 (tel. 387 2067; fax 383 3139). Family-run B&B featured in the Agatha Christie TV series *Poirot.* Tidy rooms with pastel wallpaper, floral prints, phones, teapots, TV, hairdryers, and fridges. No smoking. Singles £45, with bath £59; doubles £59, £69; triples with bath £80. Winter discount available. English breakfast. Book ahead. MC, Visa.

Crescent Hotel, 49-50 Cartwright Gdns., WC1 (tel. 387 1515; fax 383 2054). Family run for 30 years. Tea/coffee makers in each room, hair dryers and alarm clocks on request. Color TVs in each room. Also TV lounge/sitting room. Singles £40, with shower £45, with bath £60; doubles with bath £75; triples with bath £85; quads with bath £96. Discounts for stays over 1 week. English breakfast. MC, Visa.

ARGYLE SQUARE

The area due south of the **King's Cross/St. Pancras** rail complex is being revitalized as the station makes steps towards becoming a Chunnel terminus in 2007. Budget hotels lining **Argyle Street,** directly south of the tube station, feature rock-bottom prices. Any sights are quite a walk away, but the tube station is well-connected, serving five lines. Be cautious of King's Cross to the northeast (a notorious red-light district), and exercise caution at night. **Tube: King's Cross/St. Pancras.**

Alhambra Hotel, 17-19 Argyle St., WC1 (tel. 837 9575; fax 916 2476). The singles in the main building are sparkling clean and modest; refurbished annex is pricier and posher. TVs in all rooms. Cozy dining room, French-speaking owner, and new furniture. Singles £30, with shower £40; doubles £40, with shower £45, with bath £55; triples £55, £60, £70; quads with bath £90. English breakfast. AmEx, MC, Visa.

Jesmond Dene Hotel, 27 Argyle St., WC1 (tel. 837 4654; fax 833 1633; http://www.scoot.co.uk/jesmond-dene). Newly-renovated hotel offers spotless, tasteful rooms with TVs, modern furniture, and black-and-white prints of Marilyn Monroe. Singles £28; doubles £38, with shower £55; triples £55, £66; quads £75, £85; quints £85. English breakfast. MC, Visa.

Hotel Apollo, 43 Argyle St., WC1 (tel. 837 5489; fax 916 1862). Small hotel indicative of most offers on Argyle. The bright white with blue trim face of this hotel stands out from the others on the street. All rooms with sinks and TVs. Singles £28, with shower £40; doubles £38, £50. Winter discounts. English breakfast. MC, Visa.

Near Victoria Station

Many of the major thoroughfares in this area seem to be populated solely by budget hotels. Naturally, competition is fierce—try to take advantage of this. Show reluctance to take a room, and you may see prices plummet. If your first choice is full, shop around. Don't be surprised if the proprietor asks you to pay up front for your first night—many are burned by overeager reservation-makers who fail to show up.

BELGRAVE ROAD

In an area chock full of budget hotels, this is the main drag. B&Bs on Belgrave Rd. tend to be a bit less luxurious than those in the other areas around Victoria station, though they are priced accordingly. From the Victoria tube station (Victoria St. exit), head left past the bus bays and around the corner onto Buckingham Palace Rd. Turn left onto Eccleston Bridge, which becomes Belgrave Rd. Beware that addresses higher than 45 are a bit of a walk down Belgrave Rd., which continues on the other side of Warwick Sq. A ride on Bus #24 from Victoria Station or a tube hop over to Pimlico Station is advisable.

Melbourne House, 79 Belgrave Rd., SW1 (tel. 828 3516; fax 828 7120). Past Warwick Sq. Closer to Pimlico than Victoria; from Pimlico station take the Bessborough St. (south side) exit and go left along Lupus St. Turn right at St. George's Sq.; Belgrave Rd. starts on the other side of the square. Extraordinary cleanliness and recent refurbishments have improved an already top choice. The modern, private custom-designed showers have smashing water pressure and glass doors. Sparkling rooms have TV, phone, and hot pot. Singles £30, with bath £50; doubles or twins with bath £70; triples with bath £95; family quad with bath £110. Winter discount. English breakfast (served 7:30-8:45am). Book ahead. No credit cards.

Luna and Simone Hotel, 47-49 Belgrave Rd., SW1 (tel. 834 5897; fax 828 2478), past Warwick St. Tube: Victoria or Pimlico. Immaculate and well-maintained. The rooms, decorated in shades of blue, all come with TV, phones, hair dryers, and firm mattresses. Singles £25; doubles £50, with bath £60; triples with shower £75. 10% discount for long-term stays. Winter discount. English breakfast. Luggage storage.

Alexander Hotel, 13 Belgrave Rd., SW1 (tel. 834 9738; fax 630 9630). White and gold paisley wallpaper and sumptuous carpeting. Rooms are slightly crunched, but

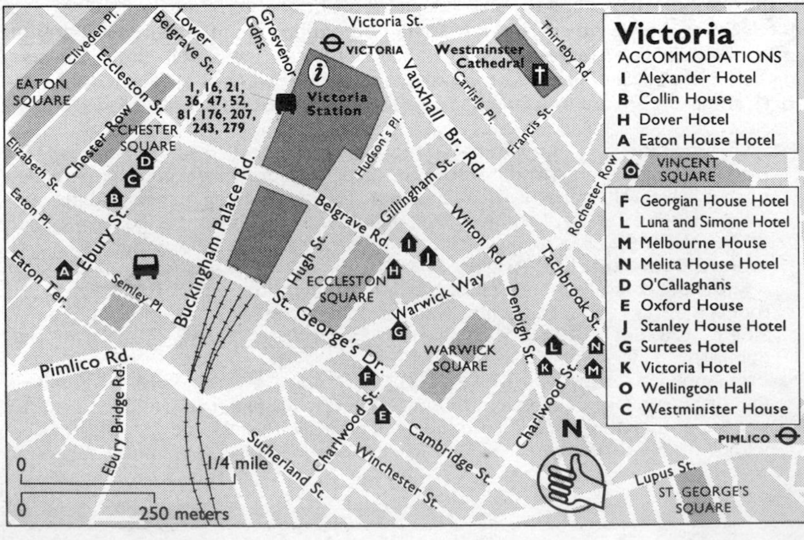

Special Features

Just dial the AT&T Access Number for the country *you are in* and follow the instructions listed below.

- To call U.S. 800 numbers: Enter the 800 number you are calling. (Note: Based upon the 800 number dialed, calls may be toll-free or AT&T Direct℠ Service charges may apply for the duration of the call; some numbers may be restricted.)
- To set up conference calls: Dial AT&T TeleConference Services at 800 232-1234. (Note: One conferee must be in the U.S.)
- To access language interpreters: Dial AT&T Language Line® Services at 408 648-5871.
- To record and deliver messages: Dial #123 if you get a busy signal or no answer, or dial AT&T True Messages® Service at 800 562-6275.

Here's a time-saving tip for placing additional calls: When you finish your conversation, or if there is a busy signal or no answer, <u>don't hang up</u> – press # and wait for the voice prompt or an AT&T Operator.

To Call the U.S. and Other Countries Using Your AT&T Calling Card* or credit card,∞ Follow These Steps:

1. Make sure you have an outside line. (From a hotel room, follow the hotel's instructions to get an outside line, as if you were placing a local call.)
2. If you want to call a country other than the U.S., make sure the country *you are in* is highlighted in blue on the chart like this: ▭
3. Enter the AT&T Access Number listed in the chart for the country *you are in*.
4. When prompted, enter the telephone number you are calling as follows:
   - For calls to the U.S., dial the Area Code (no need to dial 1 before the Area Code) + 7-digit number.
   - For calls to other countries,† enter 01+ the Country Code, City Code, and Local Number.
5. After the tone, enter your AT&T Calling Card* or credit card number (not the international number). If you need help or wish to call the U.S. collect, hold for an AT&T Operator.

* You may also use your AT&T Corporate Card, AT&T Universal Card, or most U.S. local phone company cards.

† The cost of calls to countries other than the U.S. consists of basic connection rates plus an additional charge based on the country you are calling.

∞ Credit card billing subject to availability.

Calling From Specially Marked Telephones

Throughout the world, there are specially marked phones that connect you to AT&T Direct℠ Service. Simply look for the AT&T logo. In the following countries, access to AT&T Direct Service is *only* available from these phones: Ethiopia, Mongolia, Nigeria, Seychelles Islands.

Public phones in Europe displaying the red 3C symbol also give you quick and easy access to AT&T Direct Service. Just lift the handset and dial ✻60 (in France dial M60) and you'll be connected to AT&T.

Pay phones in the United Kingdom displaying the New World symbol provide easy access to AT&T. Simply lift the handset and press the pre-programmed button marked AT&T.

Customer Care

If you have any questions, call 800 331-1140, Ext. 707.

When outside the U.S., dial the AT&T Access Number for the country *you are in* and ask the AT&T Operator for Customer Care.

108-25 Printed in the U.S.A. on recycled paper.

For your calling convenience tear off and take with you!

AT&T

AT&T Direct℠ Service

Wallet Guide

Inside you'll find simple instructions on how to use AT&T Direct Service to place calling card or collect calls from outside the U.S.

All you need are the AT&T Access Numbers when you travel outside the U.S., because you can access us quickly and easily from virtually anywhere in the world. And if you need any further help, there's always an AT&T English-speaking Operator available to assist you.

www.att.com/traveler

attractive and relatively clean. All with TV, radio, and private bath. TV lounge. Singles £40; doubles £60; triples £75. Winter discount. English breakfast (served 7:30-9am). Check-out 11am. MC, Visa.

Stanley House Hotel, 19-21 Belgrave Rd., SW1 (tel. 834 5042 or 834 8439). Nearer to Victoria station than many on Belgrave Rd. Clean rooms and efficient management make this a fine choice. Ceilings lower and rooms smaller as you go up. English breakfast. TV lounge. Singles £36, with shower £46; doubles £45, £55; triples with shower £75. 10% discount with *Let's Go*. AmEx, MC, Visa.

Dover Hotel, 44 Belgrave Rd., SW1 (tel. 821 9085; fax 834 6425). You'll pay a little more than elsewhere on Belgrave, but there's a full lineup of extras: satellite TV, clock/radio, phone, hair dryer, tea/coffee maker, and bath. Private showers with sliding glass doors. The rooms and facilities are sparkling clean. Singles from £55; doubles from £69; triples from £75; quads from £100; quints from £110. Continental breakfast (served 7:30-9:30am). Check-out 11am. AmEx, DC, MC, Visa.

ST. GEORGE'S DRIVE

Parallel to Belgrave Rd., **St. George's Drive** tends to be quieter than its neighbor. From Buckingham Palace Rd., continue one block farther past Eccleston Bridge. Turn left at Elizabeth Bridge, which turns into St. George's Drive. From Belgrave Rd., take a right at Eccleston Sq., then left onto St. George's Dr. B&Bs also line **Warwick Way,** which crosses both Belgrave Rd. and St. George's Dr. near Victoria. **Tube: Victoria or Pimlico.**

Georgian House Hotel, 35 St. George's Dr., SW1 (tel. 834 1438; fax 976 6085). Terrific discounts on "student rooms" on the 3rd and 4th floors (you don't even need to be a student, just be willing to walk up the long flights of stairs). Spacious rooms decorated with personality—some with ceiling moldings, striped curtains, blond wood furnishings, or armchairs. Showers vary as well, ranging from metal stalls in the corner to newly refurbished bathing units. All rooms come with TV, phone, and hot pot. Rooms in the annex (about a block away) are older but cheaper and quieter. Reception 8am-11pm. Singles £29, students £19, with bath £36-39; doubles with bath £49-55, students £32; triples with bath £63-68, students £45; quads £69-75, students £54. Huge English breakfast includes fruit and cereal. MC, Visa.

Surtees Hotel, 94 Warwick Way, SW1 (tel. 834 7163 or 834 7394; fax 460 8747). Cheerful, well-kept flowers brighten the front of this family run hotel. Sparkling clean rooms pleasantly decorated in muted colors, with comfy beds. All rooms come with radio and color TV. Singles with bath £45; doubles £50, with bath £60; triples with bath £60; quads with bath £80. £5 discount for stays over 5 days. Winter discount. AmEx, MC, Visa.

For a hotel off the noisy main thoroughfares, but still within walking distance of Victoria Station, try one of these:

Oxford House, 92-94 Cambridge St., SW1 (tel. 834 6467; fax 834 0225), close to the church. From St. George's Dr. (see directions above to St. George's), turn right onto Clarendon St., then take the 1st left onto Cambridge St. Set in a quiet residential area, it's more homey than most B&Bs in the vicinity. Bask next to the cat in the cushy, plant-filled TV lounge or go outside to pet the family's 2 rabbits. Commodious, clean rooms with flowered wallpaper. Singles £36; doubles £46-48; triples £56-59; quads £76-80. Fabulously well-prepared English breakfast. Reserve 3-4 weeks ahead. Reservations only and 5% surcharge with credit card. MC, Visa.

Melita House Hotel, 33-35 Charlwood St., SW1 (tel. 828 0471 or 834 1387; fax 932 0988). 2nd left off Belgrave Rd. from Pimlico station, or Bus #24 from Victoria, which stops around the corner on Belgrave Rd. Multilingual. Pleasant rooms with small private bathrooms. TV, hairdryer, and telephone in each room. Downstairs rooms have been refurbished and cost slightly more. Singles £36, upstairs with bath £45, downstairs with bath £50; doubles upstairs with bath £65, downstairs with bath £75; triples £80, £90; quads £95, £105; quints with bath £110. English breakfast. Discount for stays over 1 week. AmEx, MC, Visa, with 5% surcharge.

EBURY STREET

Historic **Ebury Street** lies west of Victoria Station in the heart of Belgravia, between Victoria and Sloane Sq. tube stations. Those who can afford to stay here will enjoy a peaceful respite from the bustle of the station while remaining close to many of London's major sights. From Victoria, head left on Buckingham Palace Rd. and turn right onto Eccleston St., then take the second left onto Ebury St. **Tube: Victoria.**

Eaton House Hotel, 125 Ebury St., SW1 (tel./fax 730 8781). Kind hosts (former tour guides) serve up Belgravian comfort at very reasonable prices. Multilingual. Large, clean rooms have dark wood chairs, TV, and tea/coffee maker. Singles £35, with bath £55; doubles £55, £70; triples £70, £85. Discount for stays over 3 days. 10% winter discount. English breakfast; no smoking in breakfast room. AmEx, MC, Visa.

Collin House, 104 Ebury St. SW1 (tel. 730 8031) Fragrant, well-kept B&B, with pine headboards, plenty of shelf room, and some renovated bathrooms. Singles with shower £42; doubles £55, with bath £65; triples with bath £80. English breakfast. No credit cards.

Westminster House, 96 Ebury St., SW1 (tel./fax 730 4302). Large bathrooms are rough around the edges, though refurbishment is planned. Modestly sized rooms have TV, tea/coffee makers, and plush carpets. Singles £48; doubles £60, with bath £70; triples or quads with bath £80. Discounts for stays over 1 week and in winter. English breakfast in homey breakfast room with pictures of the owner's family. AmEx, MC, Visa.

Paddington and Bayswater

B&Bs of variable quality cluster around Norfolk Sq. and Sussex Gdns. (Tube: Paddington, unless otherwise noted.)

Hyde Park Rooms Hotel, 137 Sussex Gdns., W2 (tel. 723 0225 or 723 0965). Family run hotel with exceptionally large, airy rooms. All come with TVs and washbasins, some with balconies. The baths are spic and span. An outstanding value. There are only 14 rooms—book in advance. Singles £26, with bath £38; doubles £38, £48; triples £57, £72. Occasional discount for small children. English breakfast. AmEx, MC, Visa with 5% surcharge.

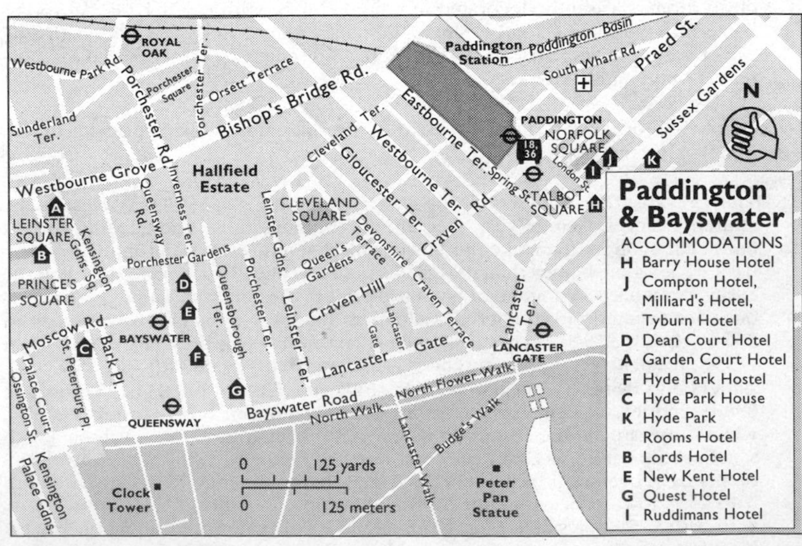

Dean Court Hotel, 57 Inverness Terr., W2 (tel. 229 2961; fax 727 1190). Tube: Bayswater or Queensway. From Queensway, make a right onto Bayswater Rd., walk left along Bayswater, and Inverness is your 1st left. This hotel offers clean, functional rooms with firm mattresses, English breakfast (served 7:30-8:30am, weekends 8:30-9:30am), full-pressure showers, and a friendly atmosphere. **The New Kent** next door offers the same rooms, prices, and management. Over half the beds are in the hostel-like dorm rooms (no bunk beds). No private facilities. Dorms £14 per night, £79 per week; doubles £38; twins £49; triples £54. AmEx, MC, Visa.

Garden Court Hotel, 30-31 Kensington Gdns. Sq., W2 (tel. 229 2553; fax 727 2749). Tube: Bayswater. From the Tube, make a left onto Queensway, a left onto Porchester Gdns., and then a right onto Kensington Gdns. Sq. A larger hotel in a pleasant, leafy area, every room is equipped with a TV, phone, washbasin, and hair dryer. A common area with coffee, tea and TV keeps guests comfortable, when they're not out in the ivy-covered courtyard. Expect the installation of a lift by 2000. Singles £34, with bath £48; doubles £48, £74; triples £68, £82; family rooms £78, £88. English breakfast. £25 deposit required. Check-out 11am. MC, Visa.

ACCOMMODATIONS

Compton House Hotel, Millard's Hotel, and **Tyburn Hotel,** 148-152 Sussex Gdns., W2 (tel. 723 2939, 262 5755, or 723 1352; fax 723 6225). Turn right when you exit Paddington Station, then make a right onto London St. followed by a left onto Sussex Gdns. A clean, slightly worn establishment. Soft beds feature wooden headboards, and the bathrooms are basic but sparkling. Carpeted stairwells lead to spacious rooms, all with tea/coffee set, washbasin, closet, and color TV (including satellite channels). Singles £27-30, with bath £40; doubles £35, £50-58; triples (all with bath) £75. English breakfast. DC, MC, Visa.

Hyde Park House, 48 St. Petersburgh Pl., W2 (tel. 229 1687). Tube: Queensway or Bayswater. From Queensway, take a right onto Bayswater, then turn right again onto St. Petersburgh Pl. From Bayswater, take an immediate left when exiting the station (onto Moscow Rd.), and then turn left again onto St. Petersburgh Pl. Just north of the new West End Synagogue and just east of the hulking St. Matthew's Church, this inconspicuous, consistent B&B blends right into its residential surroundings. Family-run, giving the place a friendly atmosphere. Sunny rooms with TVs, washbasins, and an occasional fridge. Singles £26; doubles £38; family rooms from £60. Reservation with deposit. Continental breakfast. No credit cards.

Barry House Hotel, 12 Sussex Pl., W2 (tel. 723 7340; fax 723 9775; email bhhotel@liaison.demon.co.uk; http://www.hotel.uk.com/barryhouse). One of the UK's first on-line B&Bs. Bright, smallish rooms with TVs, phones, tea sets, and desks or vanity tables. English breakfast (served 7:30-9am). Theater, taxi and sightseeing tour reservations available at reception. Safe available. Clearly a place on its way up—sadly, so are its rates. Singles £35, with bath £48; doubles with bath £74; triples with bath £85-90; quads £110-120. Ask about Jan.-Feb. discounts. AmEx, DC, MC, Visa with 3% surcharge.

Lords Hotel, 20-22 Leinster Sq., W2 (tel. 229 8877; fax 229 8377). Tube: Bayswater. From the Tube, make a left onto Queensway, a quick left onto Moscow Rd., and right onto Ilchester Gdns. Keep walking down Ilchester, and it eventually becomes Prince's Sq. and then Leinster Sq. Lords is a large hotel boasting a range of small but comfortable rooms. Virtually all have a TV and bathroom, and a few even offer balconies. Phone, coffee/soft drinks machine in the lobby. Singles £30, with bath £40; twins £44, £60; triples £55, £72; quads £66, £82. Discounts available Nov.-Mar. and for groups over 15. Continental breakfast served (7:30-9:30am). Secure booking with credit card or deposit. Check-out 11am. AmEx, DC, MC, Visa.

Ruddimans Hotel, 160-62 Sussex Gdns., W2 (tel. 723 1026; fax 262 2983; http://www.characom.com/ruddhotel.co.uk). Dark, cozy rooms. Washbasin, phone, and satellite TV in each room. Tiny, clean bathrooms. Singles £28, with bath £38; doubles £45, £55; triples £57, £68; quads (2 twin beds and a double bed) £78. English breakfast. 24hr. reception. Checkout 11am. AmEx, DC, MC, Visa.

Earl's Court

The Piccadilly tube line travels directly between Heathrow and **Earl's Court.** Underground exits are on Earl's Ct. Rd. and Warwick St., which run parallel to each other: Turn right from the Warwick St. exit to reach Philbeach Gdns.; turn right from the Earl's Ct. exit to Earl's Ct. Sq. or to Barkston Gdns., where the hotels are more pleasant but more expensive. The police have recently installed closed-circuit video cameras around the neighborhood, but be careful at night. Also, beware of overeager guides willing to lead you from the station to a hostel. Some B&Bs in this area conceal grimy rooms behind fancy lobbies and well-dressed staff. Always ask to see a room.

York House Hotel, 27-28 Philbeach Gdns., SW5 (tel. 373 7519; fax 370 4641). French, Spanish, and Arabic are spoken in this dependable hotel. Special features include a mod, 60s-style TV lounge and a lovely garden. Hallway facilities are

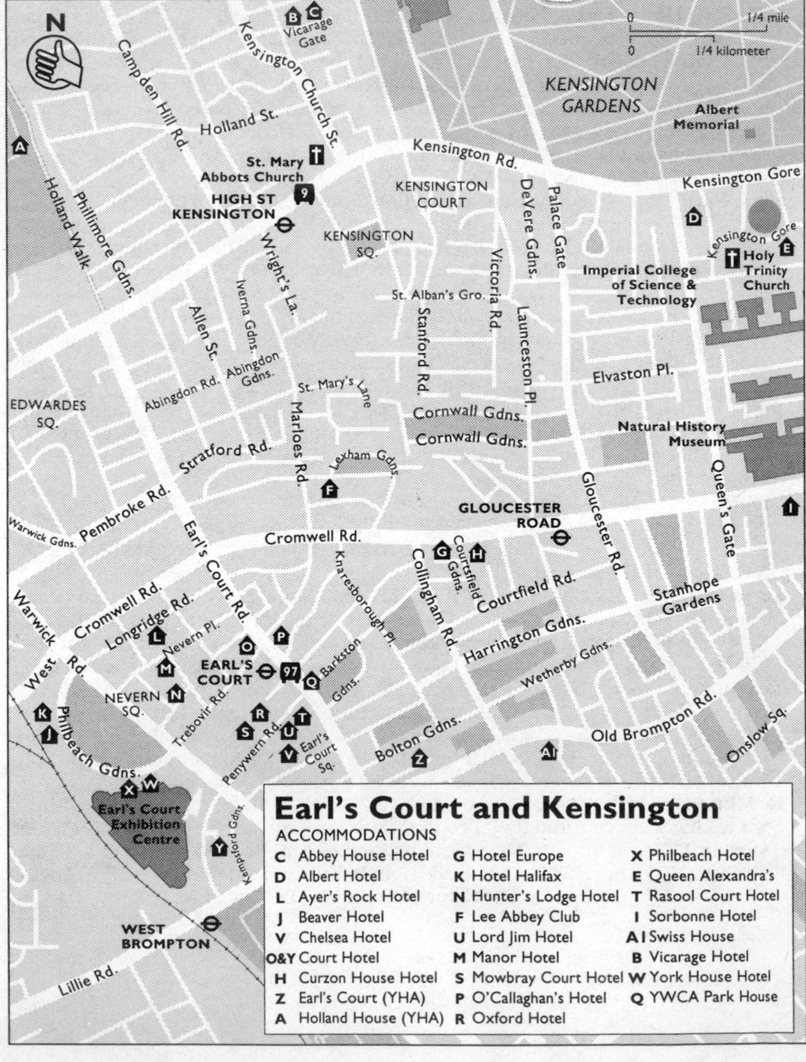

extraordinarily clean, as are the rooms. Friendly staff, surroundings, and low prices. Singles £30; doubles £47, with bath £66; triples £58, with bath £79; quads £67. English breakfast. AmEx, DC, MC, Visa.

Mowbray Court Hotel, 28-32 Penywern Rd., SW5 (tel. 373 8285 or 370 3690; fax 370 5693; email mowbraycrthot@hotmail.com). Distinctive striped reception area leads to a lounge decorated in 70s swinger style, complete with full bar and cigarette machine. Manager-brother team Tony and Peter greet everyone who walks through the door. Staff this helpful is a rarity in London; wake-up calls, tour arrangements, taxicabs, theater bookings, and dry cleaning are all available. Rooms are equipped with firm mattresses, towels, shampoo, hair dryers, TV, radio, trouser press, telephone, the *Bible,* and *The Teachings of Buddha.* Suites with **kitchens** are on the way. In-room safes cost £2 per day. A lift serves all floors. Singles £40, with bath £48; doubles £50, £60; triples £63, £72; family rooms for 4 people £76, £85; for 5 £90, £100; for 6 £106, £110. Negotiable discounts. Superb continental breakfast. Reserve ahead if possible; no deposit required. AmEx, DC, MC, Visa.

Oxford Hotel, 24 Penywern Rd., SW5 (tel. 370 1161; fax 373 8256; email Oxfordhotel@btinternet.com). Musty orange bedspreads are mitigated by soaring ceilings and flamboyant moldings. The stylish dining room has been recently refurbished to include a bar. All rooms have TV. Extra guests may be put in the annex 3 doors down. Singles with shower £32, with bath £45; doubles £50, £60; triples £60, £69; quads £72, £79; quints with bath £90. Winter and weekly rates may be 10-15% lower. Reserve ahead. No credit cards.

Beaver Hotel, 57-59 Philbeach Gdns., SW5 (tel. 373 4553; fax 373 4555). Rooms with facilities are too expensive to mention, but if you don't mind hall showers and you desire a touch of luxury, look here. Plush lounge with polished wood floors and remote-control TV—a 2nd lounge upstairs is non-smoking. All rooms have desks, phones, and coordinated linens. Located on an absolutely beautiful street. Singles £30, with bath £45; doubles £45, £70; triples with bath £85. Breakfast served in lovely room. Reserve several weeks ahead. AmEx, DC, MC, Visa.

Philbeach Hotel, 30-31 Philbeach Gdns., SW5 (tel. 373 1244; fax 244 0149). The largest gay B&B in England, popular with both men and women. Elegant lounge sports Asian porcelain and varnished wood moldings. Gorgeous garden and an award-winning, upscale restaurant (see "Wilde About Oscar," p. 260) complement the sumptuous, uniquely decorated rooms. Singles £45, with shower £55; doubles £58, with bath £75. Continental breakfast. 1 week advance booking recommended. AmEx, DC, MC, Visa.

Half Moon Hotel, 10 Earl's Ct. Sq., SW5 (tel. 373 9956; fax 373 8456). Graceful mirrors on every landing and inexpensive rooms. Amenities include hair dryer, telephone, and Sky TV in every room. Singles £25, with shower £40; doubles £35, £60; triples £55, £75; quads with shower £90. Continental breakfast. MC, Visa with 4% surcharge.

Lord Jim Hotel, 23-25 Penywern Rd., SW5 (tel. 370 6071; fax 373 8919; email taher_taheb@compuserve.com). If you don't mind small bedrooms, this hotel offers prices about £5-10 lower than competitors. Large-windowed lounge with TV. Super-clean rooms include phone, TV, and hair dryer. Singles £25-32, with shower £48; doubles £35-45, £52, with bath £59; triples £39-55, with bath £68. Group rates from £12 per person. Continental breakfast. 1 night deposit required to secure reservation. AmEx, MC, Visa.

Rasool Court Hotel, 19-21 Penywern Rd., SW5 (tel. 373 8900; fax 244 6835). Top-floor rooms have unique sloping ceilings. Curious lounge has red curtains, red couches, and red chairs. Rooms include TV, phone, desk, closet, and colorful wall-hangings. Singles £29, with shower £32, with bath £35; doubles £40, £44, £46; triple with shower £54, with bath £59; family room with bath £68. Continental breakfast. Reserve 3-4 weeks in advance; 1 night's deposit required. AmEx, MC, Visa.

Manor Hotel, 23 Nevern Place, SW5 (tel. 370 6018; fax 244 6610). A hunter's palace. Plush red staircase runs beneath a knight's armor and a deer's head. Newly-refurbished rooms with soft beds; nothing too fancy, but you'll get your money's worth. Singles £30, with shower £45; doubles £50, £60; triples £55, £70. MC, Visa.

Hotel Halifax, 65 Philbeach Gdns., SW5 (tel. 373 4153). You can't miss the bright yellow-and-white gate of this small gay hotel. Mostly men. Color TVs, radios, and washbasins in large, well-appointed rooms with firm mattresses. Most rooms have a bathroom. Leafy garden. Singles £30-45; doubles £45-58. Continental breakfast. Full payment upon arrival. Secure reservations with 2 weeks notice. AmEx, MC, Visa.

Hunter's Lodge Hotel, 38 Trebovir Rd. SW5 (tel. 373 7331; fax 460 3524) A pleasant, clean, small B&B. The lobby is nice and the rooms quite livable. Singles £30, with bath £35; doubles £40, £59; triples £48, £75; shared rooms £12. Weekly: shared rooms £60. Breakfast served from 8-9am. Check-out 10:30am. 1 night non-refundable deposit required for reservations. AmEx, MC, Visa.

Kensington and Chelsea

These hotels will prove convenient for those who wish to visit the stunning array of museums that line the southwest side of Hyde Park. Prices are higher, but the appointments at these hotels are so outstanding that several rank among the best values in London. These hotels deliver a modicum of luxury at surprisingly affordable prices. Vicarage Gate lies off Kensington Church St.

Abbey House Hotel, 11 Vicarage Gate, W8 (tel. 727 2594), off Kensington Church St. Tube: High St. Kensington. The elegant black and white marble entrance into this historical house makes you feel like royalty when you enter. After you check in, the owners or 1 of their 2 assistants, will spend 20min. giving you an introduction to London. After a series of renovations, the hotel has achieved a level of comfort that can't be rivaled at these prices. 24hr. tea, coffee, and ice room. Palatial pastel rooms with color TVs, washbasins, towels and soap, and billowing curtains. Hall bathrooms decorated with Laura Ashley furnishings. English breakfast. Singles £40; doubles £65; triples £78; quads £90; quints £100. Weekly rates in winter only. Book ahead. No credit cards.

Vicarage Hotel, 10 Vicarage Gate, W8 (tel. 229 4030; fax 792 5989). Tube: High St. Kensington. The immaculate stone entrance combines Greek marble columns with Victorian, Sherlock Holmesian lights. The stately breakfast room is only surpassed by the comfortable, immaculate bedrooms and spotless bathrooms. TV room for guests to watch or deposit daytime luggage. Singles £40; doubles £63; triples £80; quads £88. English breakfast 7:30-9am. No credit cards.

Swiss House, 171 Old Brompton Rd., SW5 (tel. 373 2769; fax 373 4983; email recep@swiss-hh.demon.co.uk). A beautiful B&B with airy, spacious rooms, most with fireplaces. Omnipresent cleaning staff keeps things spic and span. 14-channel cable TV, telephone, towels, shampoo, and soap included. Singles £42, with bath £59; doubles with bath £75, with third person £87. Extra bed £12. Continental breakfast included, as well as coffee and snacks, which are available all day. English breakfast £5. 10% discount if staying over 1 week.

Still farther south you can stay in trendy **Chelsea,** but you'll have trouble finding many moderately priced hotels south of King's Rd. Be aware that Chelsea is not well served by the Tube, though buses pass through frequently.

Oakley Hotel, 73 Oakley St., SW3 (tel. 352 5599 or 352 6610; fax 727 1190). Tube: Sloane Sq. or Victoria, then Bus 11, 19, or 22; or South Kensington. (See map of Hyde Park, Belgravia, and Chelsea.) Turn left onto Oakley St. from King's Rd. at the Chelsea Fire Station. Lovely bedrooms with large windows and matching bedspreads. TV and VCR lounge doubles as a dining room. Amiable staff invites guests to use the **kitchen** at any hour of the day or night. Singles £32; twins £48, with bath £58; triples £63, £72; quads £72; quints £80. 4-bed dorms (women only) £14, £75 per week. English breakfast. Reserve ahead several weeks. AmEx, MC, Visa.

The area around **Cromwell** and **Gloucester Rd.** is less staid than the adjacent South Kensington and Chelsea neighborhoods and remains relatively convenient to the Kensington museums and attractions (tube: Gloucester Rd.). Be aware that Cromwell Rd., though centrally located, is a very busy, noisy, and dirty street.

Hotel Europe, 131-137 Cromwell Rd., SW7 (tel. 370 2336; fax 244 6985). Professional hotel cleanliness, unfortunately often at the mercy of swarming tour groups. Can be a bit noisy along this main drag. Bar, lounge and continental breakfast. Singles £40, with shower or bath £45; twins or doubles £50, £55; triples £50, £60; families £60, £70. AmEx, MC, Visa.

Belsize Park

This affluent suburb in North London is full of tree-lined residential streets. It is quite removed from both the historic district and the bumpin' nightlife scene but the values are unbeatable if you're willing to be a little off the beaten path.

Dillons Hotel, 21 Belsize Pk., NW3 (tel. 794 3360; fax 431 7900). Tube: Belsize Pk. or Swiss Cottage. Or head right on Haverstock Hill and take the 2nd left onto Belsize Ave., which becomes Belsize Pk. 15 large, well-furnished, and bright rooms. Cheery yellow breakfast room and deluxe TV lounge. Singles £26, with shower £34; doubles £38, with bath £46; triples £44, with shower £52; quads with shower £58. Every 7th night free. Continental breakfast. For stays over a week, they accommodate with a fridge and microwave for the room. Book in advance. One-night deposit required for reservation. MC, Visa.

Buckland Hotel, 6 Buckland Crescent (tel. 722 5574; fax 722 5594). Tube: Swiss Cottage. Exit station and head straight, then right onto Buckland Crescent. 16 clean, modern rooms sport colorful comforters and bathrooms. Satellite TV in all rooms. Convenient to Finchley Rd. shops. Price is very negotiable. Singles £22-29, with bath £45; doubles with bath £65. Groups of 4 or more £18-19 per person. Continental breakfast. Deposit required. AmEx, MC, Visa.

CAMPING

Camping in London is the cheapest way to travel, and the showers and toilets are similar to the ones in most hostels. In summer months, the few campsites near London fill up. You'll have to make reservations one to two weeks in advance.

Tent City—Acton, Old Oak Common Lane, East Acton, W3 (tel./fax (0181) 743 5708). Tube: East Acton. Turn left out of station and left on Wulfstan Rd., Tent City is a 10min. walk. You can pitch your own tent, or sleep in one of the dormitory-size big top tents (no bearded ladies though). Showers, snack bar, baggage storage, **laundry,** and cooking facilities. Deservedly popular—basic but cheap. £6 per person, children £3, under 5 free. Discounts for extended stays. Open June 1-Sept. 7.

Tent City—Hackney, Millfields Rd., Hackney Marshes, E5 (tel. (0181) 985 7656). Bus 38 from or Piccadilly Circus to Clapton Pond, and walk down Millfields Rd.; or Bus #22a from Liverpool St. to Mandeville St., and cross bridge to Hackney Marshes. 4mi. from London. Pitch your own or rest under their big top tents. Free hot showers, baggage storage, shop, snack bar, laundry, and cooking facilities. No caravans. A inconvenient by public transport. £5 per person, children £2.50, under 5 free. Open 24hr. Open June-Aug.

Crystal Palace Caravan Club Site, Crystal Palace Parade, SE19 (tel. (0181) 778 7155). Tube: Brixton, then Bus #3. BR to Crystal Palace. 8mi. from London. Wonderfully close to the healthful activities at the Crystal Palace National Sports Centre. Showers and laundry facilities. Unlike Tent City, you must bring your own tent. 21-day max. stay. Wheelchair accessible. £4 per person, children £1.20. All visitors (even pedestrians) must pay additional parking fees: caravan £5 (£4 for members—ask about membership at the site); tent with car £3; tent with motorcycle £2.50; tent with backpacker £1. Lower fees Oct.-Apr. Open year-round. Prices may have changed by 1999.

LONG-TERM STAYS

Finding a flat in London is easy; finding an affordable one is an entirely different game. Consider renting a **bed-sit,** anything from a studio apartment to a small room in a private house, with access to a kitchen and bathroom. Bed-sits run at the very least £40 per week, and most landlords won't lease for less than a month. You will generally be required to pay a month's rent in advance, and put up a month's rent for a deposit.

Begin your search at the wonderful **University of London Accommodations Office**, University of London Senate House, Room B, Malet St., WC1 (tel. 862 8880; fax 862 8084; email ulao@accom.lon.ac.uk; tube: Russell Sq). Student ID required. They put out lists of private accommodations available for summer stays beginning in June, and have similar lists of University-affiliated housing for the summer, Christmas, and Easter holidays. Bear in mind: summer lets don't usually begin until late June, and Easter constitutes a six-week period from mid-March to April. Sometimes "summer listings" actually want tenants for the long haul, so search carefully. The helpful staff gives free advice on the intricacies of London flatting, from tenant/landlord responsibilities to inventories and deposits. Before you sign anything, come here (open M and W-F 9:30am-5:30pm, Tu 10:30am-5:30pm).

Do-it-yourselfers willing to put in some time and footwork should rush to the newsagent the morning that London's **ad papers** are published, and immediately begin calling. **Loot** (tel. 328 1771; www.loot.com) is published daily, while the weekly **Relocator** (tel. (0181) 994 9444) comes out on Thursdays. All allow private clients to **place ads for free.** Check their extensive listings and consider placing an ad of your own. Bulletin boards in small grocery shops frequently list available rooms and flats, as do the classified sections of the major newspapers. Beware of ads placed by accommodations agencies; they often try to sell you something more expensive when you call.

Slackers will find it easier to enlist the aid of an **accommodations agency,** but at a cost—they generally charge one or two weeks' rent as a fee, and it's in their interest to find high-priced accommodations. **Jenny Jones Accommodations Agency,** 40 S. Molton St., W1 (tel. 493 4801; tube: Bond St.), charges the fee to the landlord instead of the tenant and has bed-sits starting from £60-65 for something suburban. You may have to check several times for a central location (£80-100). Check which transport zone the flat is in; this will determine the bus or tube fare you'll be charged during your stay (open M-F 10am-5:30pm). **Universal Aunts,** P.O. Box 304, SW4 0NN (tel. 738 8937; fax 622 1914), has central locations for about £75-150 plus a service charge.

Barbican YMCA, 2 Fann St., EC2 (tel. 628 0697; fax 638 2420). Tube: Barbican. (For details, see p. 80.) Spacious fitness center with free weights, Nautilus machines, treadmills, and bikes provides a compelling perk for long-term guests. Singles £23; doubles £40. Short-term (under 12 weeks) weekly rates: singles £140; doubles £244; two meals per day included. Long-term (12 weeks or more) weekly rates: singles £114.46 1st week, £103.88 weeks 2-4, £94 thereafter; twins £197.12 1st week, £175.96 weeks 2-4, £160 thereafter. Breakfast and dinner included. Check-out 9:30am. No curfew. Call 24hr. ahead for short-term, 2 months in advance for long-term. MC, Visa.

International Student House, 229 Great Portland St., W1 (tel. 631 8300, -8310; fax 631 8315). Tube: Great Portland St. (For details, see p. 80.) This privately run non-profit organization, in addition to offering short-term stays, also offers very reasonable rates to students who will be staying over 3 months. Must have letter from a university to be eligible. A lack of kitchen facilities is the only drawback. Weekly: dorm £38.50; single £80.50; double £71.75; triple £55.65. The first month's rate will be between £3-10 higher, depending upon room type. MC, Visa.

Holland House, Holland Walk, W8 (tel. 937 0748; fax 376 0667). Tube: High St. Kensington. (For details, see p. 77.) The average stay is around 3 months, with a couple of rooms available for short stays. Price includes breakfast and a 3-course dinner. Weekly: dorm £68.50; single £104; double £82.50. MC, Visa. Holland House is the main office for the **London Hostels Association (LHA)** which operates 10 long-term stay hostels throughout the city. LHA central office (tel. 828 3263 or 834 1545; fax 834 7146; out of office inquiries tel. 727 5665).

Lee Abbey International Students' Club, 57-67 Lexham Gdns., W8 (tel. 373 7242; fax 244 8702). Tube: Earl's Ct. Left onto the Earl's Ct. Rd., cross Cromwell Rd., then right on Lexham Gdns.—the club's on your right. An international crowd; you must be at least 18 to stay here. Student status required during the school year. The recently renovated rooms are quite pleasant. Some rooms with bath. Singles £18-21.50; doubles £15.50, with bath £17; triples £13, £14. Weekly: singles £113-159; doubles £98-117; triples £81-99.50. English breakfast, evening meal, and Sa-Su lunch included. Linens provided. Inquire about reservations 1 month in advance.

YWCA Park House, 227 Earl's Court Rd., SW5 (tel. 373 2851). Tube: Earl's Court. This high-security block provides long-term stays for single women ages 16-25yrs. 6-month min. stay, 3-year max. stay. Requires an interview and selection process which takes 3-7 days. 117 beds. Guests rent single bedrooms in 2- to 3-bedroom flats with living room, kitchen, and bathroom. Visitors allowed from 10am-11pm. Feels like a women's college dorm. Telephones, laundry, and TV. £71.64 per week. No credit cards.

Food and Drink

Once upon a time, British cuisine was something of a joke among international know-it-alls. "Going to England?" one's globe-trotting friends might say, "Stick to McDonald's, heh-heh-heh." Well, smart guys, now the joke's on you. While British cooking persists in all its boiled glory, food from around the world has breathed new life into London's kitchens. Lebanese, Greek, Indian, Chinese, Thai, Italian, Cypriot, African, Malaysian, and West Indian flavors have considerably spiced up London.

Of these different cuisines, London is perhaps most famous for its **Indian restaurants,** most of which are quiet and dimly lit. Dishes here are spicier (and often smaller) than their American counterparts. In general, Indian restaurants are cheaper around Westbourne Grove and Euston Square, and cheaper still on Brick Lane in the East End. Though spellings vary among restaurants, **bhel poori** in the title means strictly vegetarian; **Balti** means your order will be served in the same dish used to cook it; and **Tandoori** is a method of cooking ingredients in a traditional Indian clay oven. Keep in mind that you will be asked to pay extra for orders of rice and *naan,* the traditional bread that complements Indian meals. **Bangladeshi** cuisine is essentially synonymous with Indian, due to a great deal of social and political history which is not, in the context of Food and Drink, germane. Still it's worth seeking out other unique South Asian cuisines, such as Nepalese, South Indian, and Sri Lankan.

London's wealth of international restaurants shouldn't deter you from sampling Britain's own infamous cuisine. **Pubs** have always offered cheap, filling English classics like meat pastries ("Cornish pasties" and "pies"), potatoes, and shepherd's pie (a meat mixture topped with mashed potatoes and baked). Recently, the Renaissance in cuisine has infiltrated even the most pubby pubs. Quality has improved markedly, and some wood-paneled ale joints even offer gourmet options like vegetable pancakes with ricotta and spinach ragout. Other cheap, quick dining options include **fish-and-chip shops** and **kebab shops,** which may be found on nearly every corner. They vary little in price but can be oceans apart in quality. Look for queues out the door and hop in line. **Sandwich shops** are handy for a quick bite and differ little from their kind in any country. Many serve filling, inexpensive breakfast foods all day. Be warned—visitors may not share the British worship of **mayonnaise,** which is rivaled only by a love of **pure, rich butter.** You may have to ask several times to get a sandwich without gobs of buttery goodness or mayonnaisey love.

In **restaurants,** watch the fine print: a perfectly inexpensive entree may be only one item on a bill supplemented with side dishes, shamefully priced drinks, VAT, minimum per-person charges, and an occasional 50p–£2 cover charge. You don't have to tip in those restaurants that include a service charge (10-12½%) on the bill. The menu or the bill should clearly state whether service has been included in the total. And if the service has disappointed you, you can complain to the manager and then legally subtract part or all of the service charge. When the service charge is not included in the bill, you should tip about 10%.

For a cheaper alternative to restaurant dining, try a meal in a **caff**—the traditional British equivalent of a U.S. diner. Caffs serve an odd mix of inexpensive English and Italian specialties (£4.50-6 for a full meal). Interiors may be dingy, and tables may be shared, but the food is often very good.

If you want regular **coffee,** ask for a **filter coffee. White coffee** is coffee with a good deal of milk in it, what Americans call café au lait. As for **tea,** Brits assume it is taken with milk, so if you drink plain tea (or black coffee), specify this clearly. Because most people add milk, coffee in England tends to be brewed strong and dark. Iced coffee is virtually unheard of in London, even in summertime (if you see it on a menu, it almost always refers to a shake-like coffee and ice cream drink). Restaurants have to provide non-smoking sections, though you might find the rule honored mostly in the breach. In most eateries, smoking is permitted at any table (with the exception of vegetarian and whole food restaurants, where it is usually banned entirely).

Open-air markets pop up all over central London, vending fresh produce and raw fish at lower prices than stores. **Groceries** and **supermarkets** provide by far the cheapest option for a filling snack, including ubiquitous but consistent boxed sandwiches. Remember that it is always cheaper to eat **take-away**, rather than having a sit-down meal. Almost all restaurants have take-away service; by eating your meal elsewhere, you can sometimes save up to 40% on service and VAT charges.

The restaurants are arranged both by type and by location. **Restaurants: By Type** provides a list of restaurants cross-referenced by food and location. Every restaurant listed in this section is followed by an abbreviated neighborhood label; turn to **Restaurants: By Location** for the full write-up. In the listings by location, the restaurants towards the top of the list tend to offer a better combination of taste, ambience, and value than the ones towards the bottom of the list. Thumbs-up restaurants are **Let's Go Picks,** and represent the restaurants that we wouldn't miss on a trip to London. The following is a code to the abbreviated neighborhood labels:

B	Brixton	*H*	Hampstead
B&E	Bloomsbury and Euston	*HSK*	High St. Kensington
B&Q	Bayswater and Queensway	*I*	Islington
C	Chelsea	*K&HP*	Knightsbridge and Hyde Park Corner
CG	Covent Garden	*NH&LG*	Notting Hill and Ladbroke Grove
CH	Chinatown	*NC*	Notable Chain
City	The City	*S&PC*	Soho and Piccadilly Circus
CT	Camden Town	*SK*	South Kensington
D	Docklands	*ST*	South of the Thames
EC	Earl's Court	*V*	Victoria
EE	East End	*W&E*	Windsor and Eton
GG	Golders Green	H	*Let's Go* Pick

RESTAURANTS: BY TYPE

AFRICAN

Asmara Restaurant, *B*
The Bel Air, *NH&LG*
Calabash Restaurant, *CG*
Le Petit Prince, *CT*

AMERICAN

Chorister's, *City*
Kim's Cafe, *B*
Hard Rock Cafe, *K&HP*
Sticky Fingers, *HSK*
Tinseltown, *City*

ASIAN/PACIFIC REGIONAL

Hotei, *S&PC*
Makan, *NH&LG*
Nam Bistro, *I*
The New Culture Revolution, *I*
Penang, *B&Q*
Rasa Sayang, *S&PC*
Satay Bar, *B*
Sushi & Sozai, *City*
Vietnamese Restaurant, *S&PC*
Wagamama, *B&E, S&PC*

BREAKFAST

Benjy's, *EC*
Prost Restaurant, *NH&LG*
Tinseltown, *City*
Vingt Quatre, *SK*
The Well, *V*

CAFES AND SANDWICH SHOPS

Al's Café, *City*
Aroma, *CG*
Barbican Grill, *City*
Beverly Hills Bakery, *K&HP*
Bluebird Cafe, *C*
Café Deco, *EC*
Café Emm, *S&PC*
Café Floris, *SK*
Café Pushkar, *B*
Chelsea Bun Diner, *C*
Chelsea Diner, *C*
Choristers, *City*
Coffee Cup, *H*
The Coffee Gallery, *B&E*
The Courtyard Coffee Shop, *W&E*
Crank's, *CG and B&E*
Delice de France, *EC*

Farmer's Kitchen, *D*
Field's Sandwiches, *City*
Frank's Café, *CG*
Freshly Maid Café, *ST*
Gallery Café, *NH&LG*
The Gallery Café Bar, *City*
Glad's Café, *W&E*
Goodfella's Delicatessen, *B&E*
Kim's Café, *B*
Knightsbridge Express, *K&HP*
Kool Eddy's Music Cafe, *S&PC*
Leigh St. Café, *B&E*
Marks & Spencer, *NC*
Marie's Café, *ST*
Marino's, *B&E*
Mima's Café, *K&HP*
Monmouth Coffee Company, *CG*
Neal's Yard Bakery Co-op, *CG*
Neal's Yard Salad Bar, *CG*
Neal's Yard World Food Café, *CG*
October Gallery Café, *B&E*
Patisserie Valerie, *S&PC*
Phoenix, *B*
Polly's Cafe/Tea Room, *H*
Presto, *S&PC*
Pret a Manger, *NC*
Saints Cafe/Lab, *City*
St. Georges of Mayfair Sandwich, *D*
The Star Café, *S&PC*
Stop Gap, *B*
SWTen, *C*
Troubador Coffee House, *EC*
Webshack, *S&PC*
The Well, *V*
Wren Café at St. James, *S&PC*

CARIBBEAN

The Bel Air, *NH&LG*
Jacaranda, *B*

CHINESE

Camden Friends Restaurant, *CT*
Chuen Cheng Ku, *CH*
The Dragon Inn, *CH*
Golden Dragon, *CH*
Harbour City, *CH*
Hong Kong Chinese Restaurant, *EC*
Kowloon Restaurant, *CH*
Lido Chinese Restaurant, *CH*
Lok Ho Fook, *CH*
Royal China, *B&Q*
Wong Kei, *CH*

CLASSIC ENGLISH

See also Pubs, p. 122.
Chelsea Kitchen, *C*
Cockney's, *NH&LG*
Neal's Yard Dairy, *CG*
Norman's, *B&Q*
The Pier Tavern, *D*
The Stockpot, *S&PC*
The Two Brewers, *W&E*
The Waterman's Arms, *W&E*

FISH AND CHIPS

Alpha One Fish Bar, *S&PC*
The Fryer's Delight, *B&E*
Geale's, *NH&LG*
The Hi-Tide Fish&Chips Restaurant, *EC*
The Rock&Sole Plaice, *CG*
Upper St. Fish Shop, *I*

FRENCH

Ambrosiana Crêperie, *SK*
Café Deco, *EC*
Cafe Dome, *NC*
Le Crêperie de Hampstead, *H*
Delice de France, *EC*
Entre Nous, *C*
Jules Rotisserie, *SK, C*
Kramps Crêperie, *EC*
Le Mercury, *I*
Paris-London Cafe, *H*
Le Petit Prince, *CT*
Pierre Victoire, *NC*

GREEK AND MIDDLE EASTERN

Apadna, *HSK*
Cosma's Taverna, *B&E*
Gaby's Continental Bar, *S&PC*
Jimmy's Greek Taverna, *S&PC*
Manzara, *NH&LG*
Nontas, *CT*
Phoenicia, *HSK*
Sofra, *CG*

INDIAN/SOUTH ASIAN

Aladin Balti House, *EE*
Ambala Sweet Centre, *B&E*
Bengal Cuisine, *EE*
Bharat, *CT*
Chutney's, *B&E*
Diwana Bhel Poori House, *B&E*
Eastern Eye, *EE*
Govinda's, *S&PC*
Great Nepalese Restaurant, *B&E*
Gupta Sweet Center, *B&E*
Indian Veg Bhelpoori House, *I*
Khan's, *B&Q*
Lahore Kebab House, *EE*
Mandeer, *S&PC*
Muhib, *EE*
Nazrul, *EE*
Nusa Dua, *S&PC*
Rasa Sayang, *S&PC*
Shampan, *EE*
Sheraz, *EE*
West End Tandoori, *S&PC*

ITALIAN

Arco Bar, *K&HP*
Asmara Restaurant, *B*
Bonavita, *CT*
Bistro Benito, *EC*
Cafe Pasta, *NC*
Calzone, *H, I, NH&LG*
Ciaccio, *V*
Cosmoba, *B&E*
Il Falconiere, *SK*
Frank's Café, *CG*
Lorelei, *S&PC*
Mamma Conchetta, *CT*
Marine Ices, *CT*
Mille Pini Restaurant, *B&E*
O, Sole Mio, *V*
Parson's Restaurant, *SK*
The Pasta Place, *H*
Piazza Bar, *S&PC*
Pollo, *S&PC*
Trattoria Aquilino, *I*
Trattoria Mondello, *B&E*

KOSHER/DELI

Al's Deli, *H*
Bloom's, *GG*
Brick Lane Beigel Bake, *EE*
Carmelli, *GG*
Daniel's Bagel Bakery, *GG*
Dizengoff, *GG*
The Nosherie, *City*

OPEN LATE

Alpha One Fish Bar, *S&PC*
Lido Chinese Restaurant, *CH*
Lord's Food and Wine, *K&HP*
Nyam's, *B*
Piazza Bar, *S&PC*
Tinseltown, *City*
Vingt Quatre, *SK*

PIZZA

Broadway Pizza, *CT*
Gourmet Pizza Company, *ST*
Parkway Pizzeria, *CT*
Piazza Bar, *S&PC*
Pizza Express, *NC*
Pucci Pizza Vino, *C*

RUSSIAN

Borshtch 'n' Tears, *K&HP*
Wodka, *HSK*

S.AMERICAN/ PORTUGEUSE/ TAPAS/

Bar Gansa, *CT*
Café Olé, *I*
Lisboa Patisserie, *NH&LG*
Montesol, *H*
Nando's, *EC*
O'Porto Patisserie, *NH&LG*
La Piragua, *I*

SWEETS

Ambala Sweet Centre, *B&E*
Beverly Hills Bakery, *K&HP*
Canadian Muffin Co., *K&HP*
Gupta Sweet Centre, *B&E*
Lisboa Patisserie, *NH&LG*
Marine Ices, *CT*
Michael's The Eton Bakery, *W&E*
O'Porto Patisserie, *NH&LG*
Patisserie Valerie, *S&PC*
Perry's Bakery, *EC*
Rumbold's Bakery, *H*
Thompson's Bakery, *B*

THAI

Jewel of Siam, *B&Q*
Penang, *B&Q*
Tuk Tuk, *I*

VEGETARIAN

Alara Wholefoods, *B&E*
Café Pushkar, *B*
The Cherry Orchard Café, *EE*
Chutney's, *B&E*
Crank's, *CG, B&E*
Diwana Bhel Poori House, *B&E*
Food for Thought, *CG*
Futures!, *City*
Gaby's Continental Bar, *S&PC*
Gallery Café, *NH&LG*
Govinda's, *S&PC*
The Grain Shop, *NH&LG*
Indian Veg Bhelpoori House, *I*
Jacaranda, *B*
Mandeer, *S&PC*
Mildred's, *S&PC*
Neal's Yard Bakery Co-op, *CG*
Neal's Yard Salad Bar, *CG*
The Place Below, *City*
Woolley's Wholefood and Take Away, *B&E*
The Wren at St. James's, *S&PC*

OTHER EATS

Belgo Centraal, CG
The Fire Station, *ST*
Henry J. Bean's Bar and Grill, *C*
Jazz Bistro, *City*
My Old Dutch Pancake House, *C*
Mezzo, *S&PC*
Roxy Café Cantina, *I*
Ruby in the Dust, *CT, I*

RESTAURANTS: BY NEIGHBORHOOD

Soho and Piccadilly Circus

Scads of unimpressive pizza and fast food joints cluster around Piccadilly Circus. A trip a few blocks down Shaftesbury Ave. and left onto Wardour or Dean St. rewards the hungry with the smart cafes and cheaper sandwich shops of Soho. **Old Compton St.,** one of Soho's main drags, lies off Wardour St. one block north of and parallel to Shaftesbury Ave. For fresh fruit, check out old **Berwick Market** on Berwick St.

Mandeer, 8 Bloomsbury Way (tel. 242 6202). Tube: Tottenham Ct. Rd. A few streets off New Oxford St., Mandeer offers some of the best Indian food around and the chance to learn about owner Ramesh Patel's Ayurvedic Science of Life. The owners brought the tasty, healthy vegetarian cuisine of their home province in Northern India to London—soon after opening, their restaurant became the center of a Bohemian expatriate community. Food is fresh, organic, and vegetarian. In accordance with Hindu philosophy, kitchen doors remain open so you can observe the calm chefs in their immaculate culinary workshop. The best deals in the house are the lunch buffet options, which begin at a mere £3.50. The restaurant is also affordable and well worth it. Open M-Sa for lunch (self-service) noon-3pm, dinner 5-10pm.

The Stockpot, 18 Old Compton St., W1 (tel. 287 1066), by Cambridge Circus. Tube: Leicester Sq. or Piccadilly Circus. Beloved by locals, who pack the sidewalk tables, it's the cheapest place in Soho to soak up some style. Menus are handwritten daily but always represent a simply marvelous value. Entrees £2.20-3.95. Fresh strawberries and cream in season £1.65. Open M-Tu 11:30am-11:30pm, W-Sa 11:30am-11:45pm, Su noon-11pm. Also at 40 Panton St. (Tube: Leicester Sq.). No credit cards.

West End Kitchen, 5 Panton St., SW1 (tel. 839 4241). Tube: Picadilly Circus. Perhaps the best deals going in London. Choose from a variety of ethnic and English dishes while relaxing in the cozy wooden booths. A 3-course set lunch £3.50, spaghetti bolognese £1.85, and moussaka £3. This is the place to come for "good food at great value." Open daily 7am-11:45pm.

The Wren Café at St. James's, 35 Jermyn St., SW1 (tel. 437 9419). Tube: Piccadilly Circus or Green Park. Whole food and vegetarian delights served in the shadow of a Christopher Wren church. Tranquil and gorgeous backdrop for lunch or tea in the shady courtyard. Overflows with customers after free afternoon concerts in the church. Casserole of the day with brown rice £4, fresh quiche £2. Open M-Sa 8:30am-6pm, Su 9am-5pm.

Café Emm, 17 Frith St., W1 (tel. 437 0723). Tube: Leicester Sq. Large portions are served in an unpretentious and soothing atmosphere where the largest fuss is made over 2 outdoor tables. A cheap and palatable way to sample Soho cafe-culture. All dishes on the rotating special menu, from vegetarian casseroles to sausages and mash, are £5. Last orders 30min. before close. Open M-Th noon-3pm and 5:30-11pm, F noon-3pm and 5:30pm-1am, Sa 5pm-1am, Su 5:30-11pm.

Govinda's Vegetarian Restaurant, 9 Soho St., W1 (tel. 437 3662). Tube: Tottenham Ct. Rd. Next to their Radha Krishna Temple, the International Society for Krishna Consciousness serves deliciously wholesome, vegetarian Indian food for very little money. No eggs, meat, or seafood are used, though some dishes contain milk or cream. The cafeteria-style, all-you-can-eat buffet fills stomachs for a mere £5. Open M-Sa 7am-8pm.

Mildred's, 58 Greek St., W1 (tel. 494 2392). Tube: Tottenham Ct. Rd. or Leicester Sq. Small, simple, and cozy, this restaurant has a menu that changes daily, but you can always order the stir fry vegetables with rice (£4.50) and the falafel with *tahini* (£4.70). The art on the wall, like the menu, is in a constant state of flux, but the clientele remains the same—young, artsy Soho diners gorging themselves with well-presented, healthy food. Take-away discount 40p. Open M-Sa noon-11pm, Su 12:30-6:30pm. No credit cards.

Alpha One Fish Bar, 43 Old Compton St., W1 (tel. 437 7344). Tube: Leicester Sq. or Piccadilly Circus. Good, greasy fun in a slightly uptown chippie, replete with marble tables beneath precariously hanging shellfish in a fish net. A humungous slab of cod with chips is £4.10 (take-away). The fish is delivered fresh every day from Scotland. Open M-Th 11:30am-1am, F-Sa 11:30am-2am, Su 11:30am-midnight.

Saigon, 45 Frith St. (tel. 437 1672). Tube: Picadilly Circus or Tottenham Ct. Rd. Classy decor and mouth-watering aromas are the norm at this renowned Vietnamese restaurant. Large chicken with lemon grass or coconut curry (£5.35) are both fresh and savory. Seasonal vegetable stir-fry £4.35. Open daily noon-11:30pm.

Presto, 4-6 Old Compton St., W1 (tel. 437 4006). Tube: Leicester Sq. A 35-year-old hyper-trendy cafe where Derek Jarman ate at least once every day, Presto fills with locals each night at suppertime. Busy waitstaff serves up pastas (£3.20-3.50). Jarman dug on spaghetti carbonara (£3.35) and eggs (£3.20-3.65). Thick chocolate mud pie £1.85. Open M-Sa 11am-11pm. MC, Visa.

The Star Café and Bar, 22 Great Chapel St., W1 (tel. 437 8788). Tube: Oxford Circus. A British approximation of the red-checkered, tableclothed American diner. Pasta of the day £2.95 (take-away). Daily specials include swordfish steaks (£3.95), a welcome alternative to the standard mayonnaise fare. Open M-F 7am-5pm.

Café Roma, 37 Berwick St., W1 (tel. 437 1076). Tube: Oxford Circus. This tiny neighborhood shop offers delicious Italian *ciabatta* sandwiches for around £2. Savor the *panino vegetariano,* enticingly smothered with thick slabs of avocado, tomato, and mozzarella. Full breakfast and hot entrees £3. Open daily 7am-7pm.

Jimmy's Greek Taverna, 23 Frith St., W1 (tel. 437 9521). Tube: Piccadilly Circus or Tottenham Ct. Rd. Subterranean Jimmy's is fun, hot, and sweaty, and portions are heaping. Tasty vegetarian *moussaka* £5, chicken kebab £5.50. All main dishes include rice, chips, and salad. Make reservations for parties over 4. Open M-W noon-11pm, Th-Sa noon-11:30pm.

Mezzo, 100 Wardour St., W1 (tel. 314 4000). Tube: Leicester Sq. Ultra-swank, 2-story mega-restaurant on the former site of the renowned Marquee Club. Doormen, cigarette girls—the whole nine. Priced accordingly, but come from 5:30-7pm and get a £7, 2-course meal in the upstairs "mezzonine." Also offers a 2-course meal with an Odeon movie ticket for £12.50. Mezzonine open for lunch M-F noon-3pm, Sa noon-4pm; dinner M-Th 5:30pm-1am, F-Sa 5:30pm-3am. Restaurant open for lunch M-F noon-3pm, Su 12:30-3pm; dinner M-Th 6pm-midnight, F-Sa 6pm-1am, Su 6-10pm. Bar open until 3am Friday and Saturday.

Patisserie Valerie, 44 Old Compton St., W1 (tel. 437 3466). Tube: Leicester Sq. Opened in 1926, this place introduced the continental patisserie to the English. An immediate success, it became the meeting place for starving artists and bohemians. It still bustles today with a mixed crowd of young and old who come to enjoy the fresh tarts, cakes, breads, and truffles. Tasty sandwiches also available (£1.30-2.70). Open M-F 8am-8pm, Sa 8am-7pm, Su 10am-6pm.

Nusa Dua, 11-12 Dean St., W1 (tel. 437 3559). Tube: Leicester Sq. or Tottenham Ct. Rd. Comfy, high wicker chairs ready diners for their adventure into the rewarding realm of Indonesian cuisine. Set lunches begin at £6; noodle and take-away specials (noon-8pm) go for £4. Open M-Th noon-2:30pm and 6-11:30pm, F noon-2:30pm and 6pm-midnight, Sa 6pm-midnight, Su 6-11pm.

West End Tandoori, 5 Old Compton St., W1 (tel. 734 1057). Tube: Leicester Sq. Unusual lighting and languid Indian music create a serene atmosphere. Chicken curry £5, vegetarian dishes £3.50-3.75. Open daily noon-2:30pm and 6-11:30pm. AmEx, DC, MC, Visa.

Gaby's Continental Bar, 30 Charing Cross Rd., WC2 (tel. 836 4233). Tube: Leicester Sq. Right next to the tube station. This deli-restaurant serves great Middle Eastern and vegetarian food. Hefty falafel sandwich £2.40 (take-away). Large selection of delectable salads. 60 seats in air-conditioning. Take-away discount 18-20%. Open M-Sa 9am-midnight, Su 11am-10pm.

Kool Eddy's Music Cafe, 146 Charing Cross Rd., WC2. Tube: Tottenham Ct. Rd. or Leicester Sq. Dirt-cheap prices and 24hr. service make this a welcome haven for club kids, especially come 4 or 5 in the morning. This upper-story hideout also features a dance floor and DJ, but most come to enjoy the pasta special (includes salad, bread, and a glass of wine; £2.50). Open daily 24hr.

Webshack, 15 Dean St., W1 (tel. 439 8000). Tube: Leicester Sq. or Tottenham Ct. Rd. Cool, blue Internet cafe with bumpin' music offers sandwiches for £1.85-3.30, as well as 90p espresso. The big draw, however, is the score of PC terminals, offering a range of net services, including WorldWideWeb, telnet, AOL, IRC, Netscape, fax, download to disk, and guest email send (£3 for 30min., £5 for hr., 10% student discount). Open M-Sa 10:30am-11pm. AmEx, MC, Visa.

Lorelei, 14 Bateman Rd., W1 (tel. 734 0954). Tube: Leicester Sq. This unassuming pizzeria offers a superb value to the famished traveler, especially with the aptly named "Poorman" pie (tomato and basil; £3.60). Other pizzas £3.50-5. Open M-Sa. noon-11:30pm.

The Global Café, 15 Golden Sq. (tel. 287 2242). Tube: Picadilly Circus. A funky cybercafe with delicious coffee, salads, and sandwiches. French staff makes a scrumptious *tarte aux pommes*. £2.75 for 30min. on-line; a 10min. email check is £1. Open M-F 8am-midnight, Sa 10am-midnight, Su 11am-midnight.

Offshore Café, 8 Sackville St. (tel. 734 1590). Tube: Picadilly Circus. Panini sandwiches and veggie specials abound at this hip black and white cybercafe. Vegetable curry £3.40, sandwiches £1.85. Computers are £3 for 30 min., £5 for 1hr. Minimum charge £1.50. If hunger strikes, use the handy phones installed at each computer to order food from upstairs. Open M-Sa 8am-7pm.

Chinatown

Dozens of traditional, inexpensive restaurants are crammed into London's **Chinatown** (tube: Leicester Sq.), which occupies the few blocks between Shaftesbury Ave. and Leicester Sq. **Gerrard Street,** the pedestrian-only backbone of Chinatown, is one block south of Shaftesbury Ave. Because of the pre-1997 Hong Kong connection, Cantonese cooking and language dominate. Most restaurants serve *dim sum* every afternoon, and many keep their doors open incredibly late. The **Golden Gate Cake Shop,** 13 Macclesfield St., W1, off Gerrard St. (open daily 10am-10pm), and the bakery at the **Kowloon Restaurant** (see below) sell pork buns and other delectable Chinese pastries. If your sole interest is cramming your gullet, a number of restaurants also offer all-you-can-eat buffets at lunchtime, most for around £5. These include **Luxuriance,** 40 Gerrard St. (tel. 437 4125), **Yee Tung,** 20 Gerrard St. (tel. 287 2539), the always reliable **Mr. Wu,** 28 Wardour St. (tel. 287 3885), and others. An automatic 10% service charge is standard for all meals except buffets, so you needn't worry about tipping.

Golden Dragon, 28-29 Gerrard St., (tel. 734 2763). One of the best Chinese restaurants in Chinatown; regular meals are expensive, but the *dim sum* is affordable, delicious, and unique (served M-Sa noon-5pm, Su 11am-5pm). Such delicacies as fish balls and turnip in pot (£2.20) and shark's fin dumpling in soup (£2.20) are worth the splurge. Open M-F noon-11:30pm, Sa noon-midnight, Su 11am-11pm. AmEx, DC, MC, Visa.

Lok Ho Fook, 4-5 Gerrard St., W1 (tel. 437 2001). Busy place with good prices and a welcoming atmosphere. Extensive offerings with lots of seafood, noodles, and vegetarian dishes. Vegetarian hot and sour soup £1.55. *Dim sum* (before 6pm £1.35-2.55) is made fresh when you order and not strolled around on carts. Helpful staff will aid the novice in selection. Not to be confused with a nearby (and more expensive) place called Lee Ho Fook. Open daily noon-11:45pm. AmEx, DC, MC, Visa.

Kowloon Restaurant, 21-22 Gerrard St., W1 (tel. 437 0148). Meal-sized portions of vermicelli, wheat, or *ho-fun* rice noodles (£2.50-6) are served steaming and cheap in this Chinatown institution. Rice dishes also under £4. Tea service available 11:30am-6pm. Satisfy your sweet tooth in the bakery. Open daily noon-11:45pm.

Harbour City, 46 Gerrard St., W1 (tel. 439 7859 or 287 1526). A wonderful place for *dim sum* (served daily noon-5pm; £1.60-5 per dish). Food is light and expertly prepared. The *cheung fun* (rice noodles surrounding various fillings in sweet soy sauce; £2.40) are delectable. Open M-Th noon-11:30pm, F-Sa noon-midnight, Su 11am-11pm. AmEx, DC, MC, Visa.

Vietnamese Restaurant, 34 Wardour St., W1 (tel. 494 2592). This well-known Vietnamese eatery serves *pho* (£3.80), spring rolls (£2.60), and fried frogs' legs (£3.10) in record time to a hungry local crowd. Set meals are also available for as little as £5.90 per person. The huge windows make this a pleasant place to sit and watch the world go by. Open daily 11am-11:30pm. AmEx, DC, MC, Visa.

The Dragon Inn, 12 Gerrard St., W1 (tel. 494 0870 or 494 0869). Plain, diner-like setting, and traditional Cantonese home cooking. Delicious *dim sum* dishes served daily 11am-5pm, including a set *dim sum* for £5.50 per person. "The best duckling in town," £6. You might like to try their special glutinous rice: it's soaked for 24 hours, wrapped in a lotus leaf and slow steamed—the results are delicious. Open daily 11am-11:45pm. AmEx, MC, Visa.

Wong Kei, 41-43 Wardour St., W1 (tel. 437 3071). Three stories of busy waiters and one of the best values in Chinatown. A waterfall trickles on the first floor and dumbwaiters zoom food up to the other floors. Solo diners should expect to share tables. Rice entrees £3-3.50. Set dinner £6 per person (min. 2 people). Open M-Sa noon-11:30pm, Su noon-10:30pm. Cash only.

Lido Chinese Restaurant, 41 Gerrard St., W1 (tel. 437 4431). Unobtrusive dark wood paneling and wall-set aquariums make this a serene setting in which to recover from a night of Soho revelry. Chicken, beef, and vegetable dishes (£4.50-7) and *dim sum* (£1.60-1.70) are served into the wee hours. Open daily 11:30am-4:30am. AmEx, DC, MC, Visa.

The Immortals, 58-60 Shaftesbury Ave., W1 (tel. 437 3119). Newish, pleasant Cantonese restaurant, notable largely because it disproves the ancient axiom that set menus in Chinese restaurants should be ignored at all costs. Lunchtime set menu served noon-4pm, £6. Choose from a range of chicken, beef, or vegetable dishes. More expensive set menus available, as well as a range of entrees. Open M-Sa noon-11:30pm, Su 11:30am-10:30pm.

Covent Garden

Covent Garden offers an enticing array of eateries to playgoers and tourists in the heart of London's theater district. Don't let the expensive looks deceive you—good food at reasonable prices can be found. Tucked away from the tourist labyrinth, the **Neal's Yard** area, off Neal St., overflows with sumptuous vegetarian joints among herbal healers and colorful window boxes. Beware that these restaurants, and many others in the area, close relatively early. **Tube: Covent Garden.**

Neal's Yard Salad Bar, 2 Neal's Yard, WC2 (tel. 836 3233). Take-away or sit outside at this simple vegetarian's nirvana. Get a plateful of the hearty and wholesome hot vegetable dishes for £4.50-5 (take-away discount 50p). Tempting mix 'n' match salads from £2. Open daily 11am-9pm.

Neal's Yard Bakery Co-op, 6 Neal's Yard, WC2 (tel. 836 5199). Only organic flour and filtered water are used in the delicious breads here. A small, open-air counter offers a plethora of baked goods, sandwiches, and salads—all vegetarian with many vegan options. Large loaf £1.90. Bean burger £2.20, take-away £1.80. 50% discount on day-old breads. No smoking. Open M-Sa 10:30am-4:30pm

Belgo Centraal, 50 Earlham St., WC2 (tel. 813 2233). Second branch called **Belgo Noord** in Camden Town on 72 Chalk Farm Rd., NW1 (tel. 267 0718; tube: Chalk Farm Rd.). Waiters in monk's cowls, bizarre 21st-century beerhall interior, and great specials make this one of Covent Garden's most popular restaurants. Mondays noon-3pm, all dishes, from lobster halves to 6oz. steak, is £5.55. During "lunchtime" (daily noon-5pm), £5 buys you wild boar sausage, Belgian mash, and a BEER (the inimitable *Hoegaarten*). Weekday specials 5-6:30pm. Open M-Sa noon-11:30pm, Su noon-10:30pm. Wheelchair access. AmEx, DC, MC, Visa.

Café Sofra, 26 Wellington St., WC2 (tel. 836 4726). This Turkish cafe serves fresh meat and vegetarian dishes. The mouth-watering quiche (£2.50) and wide array of mediterranean dishes will satiate the palate. Take-away discount 50p-£2. Finish your meal with some of the best *baclava* (60p) in the city. Open M-Sa 7am-11pm (take-away 7am-10pm), Su 8am-10pm.

Food for Thought, 31 Neal St., WC2 (tel. 836 0239). Verdant foliage decorates this tiny, aromatic restaurant, which offers large servings of excellent vegetarian and vegan food at moderate prices. Soups, salads, and stir-fries. Tasty daily specials like chick pea ratatouille from £3.40. You can sit at slightly cramped wooden tables or take-away a 40-50p discount. Open M-Sa 9:30am-9pm, Su noon-4:30pm.

Neal's Yard World Food Café, 14-15 Neal's Yard, WC2 (tel. 379 0298). In this airy upstairs cafe, you know you're eating fresh vegetarian food because you can see it being prepared—the kitchen is the center of the restaurant. Features a la carte and world meals, such as Indian, West African, Mexican, and Turkish (£7.45). Open M-Sa noon-5pm.

The Rock and Sole Plaice, 47 Endell St., WC2 (tel. 836 3785). Fortunately, the fish (£4) and chunky chips (£1-1.20) are better than the puns. Sit under the trees at picnic tables or downstairs where the underwater scene shows you just what you're eating. If ye lack sealegs, have the spicy sausage and chips (take-away £1.70). Open M-Sa 11:30am-11:30pm, Su 12:30-9:30pm.

Neal's Yard Dairy, 17 Shorts Gdns., WC2 (tel. 379 7646). In close contact with dairies in Britain and Ireland, this world-class cheese shop makes regular buying trips to the farms, then keeps the huge cheeses fresh with a colossal humidifier. Don't miss the fresh milk and homemade yogurt (£1.75 for about a quart). Wholesale location at 28 Park St. (tube: London Bridge) now also does retail (open M-F 10am-6pm). Main shop open M-Sa 9am-7pm, Su 10am-5pm.

Monmouth Coffee Company, 27 Monmouth St., WC2 (tel. 379 4337 or 836 5272; fax 379 3801). Can't decide on a roast? Sit in the back sampling room, and taste the many brews (25p per taste). Or slide into one of the 4 small booths with a full cup (£1.10, take-away 80p). Some of the best coffee in Britain. No smoking. Cafe/sampling room open M-Sa 9am-6pm, Su 11am-4:30pm (no pastries on Su). Shop open M-Sa 9am-6:30pm, Su 11am-5pm.

Calabash Restaurant, 38 King St., WC2 (tel. 836 1976), in the cool basement of the Africa Centre. The savory pan-African menu features *doro wat* (chicken in hot pepper sauce served with eggs and rice or *injera* bread, £6.95). Open M-F. 12:30-3pm and 6-11:30pm, Sa 6-11:30pm. AmEx, MC, Visa

Frank's Café, 52 Neal St., WC2 (tel. 836 6345). An old Italian cafe with a mural of Amalti covering the wall. Serves delicious homemade pastas at bargain prices (£2.80-3.80). Pizza, sandwiches, and breakfast foods available all day. Try the apple pie with custard (£1.60) for an artery-hardening treat. Take-away discount. Open M-Sa 7:30am-7:30pm.

Bloomsbury and Euston

Superb Greek, Italian, and vegetarian restaurants line Goodge St., conveniently close to the British Museum. Northwest of Bloomsbury, around Euston Sq., a vast number of the city's best and most traditional Indian restaurants ply their trade. Try to avoid the restaurants on Woburn Pl., Southampton Row, and Great Russell St., which cater to swarms of tourists.

NEAR GOODGE STREET

This food-filled neighborhood runs the gamut of culinary temptations: upscale French cuisine, informal Mediterranean fare, and modest sandwich shops and cafes. **Goodge Street** (to the right of the tube station) and **Tottenham Street** (to the left of the station) are the major avenues, but those who meander down side streets will make delicious discoveries. **Tube: Goodge St.,** unless otherwise noted.

The Coffee Gallery, 23 Museum St. (tel. 436 0455). Tube: Tottenham Ct. Rd. or Holborn. Sandwich prices (mozzarella, tomato, and basil £2.90) are comparable to the other cafes flanking the British Museum, but the crowd here is less touristy and the atmosphere miles ahead. Within the bright blue walls lies a gallery of ceramics and paintings, in which delicious, fresh, Italian garden food is served. Menu changes daily. Open M-F 8am-5:30pm, Sa 10am-5:30pm.

Crank's Restaurant/Take-Away, 9-11 Tottenham St., W1 (tel. 631 3912). Another branch of London's original health food restaurant, founded in 1961, now an 8-store chain. Enjoy the art exhibits on the wall, which are also for sale. Large vegetarian and vegan dishes made with fresh ingredients, including free-range eggs and organic flour. Entrees ranging from vegetarian lasagna to polenta with roast vegetable and 2 side salads (£4.95). Healthy yogurt drinks. No smoking. Open M-Sa 8am-7:30pm, Su 11-5pm. AmEx, MC, Visa.

Trattoria Mondello, 36 Goodge St., W1 (tel. 637 9037). An array of zesty, but pricey Sicilian dishes served in a rustic, seaside-style dining room with open-beam ceilings and discreet seating alcoves. Pasta as a side or main dish, the side serving is generous; try the *fettucine al salmone* (£5). Cappuccino £1. Open M-F noon-3pm and 5:30pm-11:30pm, Sa noon-midnight. AmEx, MC, Visa.

Marino's, 31 Rathbone Pl., W1 (tel. 636 8965). From Goodge St., turn left onto Charlotte St., which turns into Rathbone Pl. Restaurant and sandwich bar bustling with a young, hip crowd. Large seating area, yet maintains a cafe feel. Grab a paper and order a cappuccino. Pizzas, omelettes, and grilled meats £3.30-5.95. Salads and sandwiches from £1.60. Take-away available. Open M-F 7am-7pm, Sa 9am-3pm.

AROUND RUSSELL SQUARE

Immediately around Russell Sq. and the British Museum, eateries tend to be predictably dull and overpriced. A few blocks to the east, on **Theobald's Rd.** (from Holborn, turn right onto Southampton Row and make first right) and **Lamb's Conduit** (from Russell Sq., walk two blocks and take a right off of Guilford St., or take left off of Theobald's Rd.) non-touristy cafes and bakeries line the walkways.

Wagamama, 4A Streatham St., WC1 (tel. 323 9223). Tube: Tottenham Ct. Rd. Go down New Oxford St. and left onto Bloomsbury St. Streatham St. is the 1st right. "Positive Eating+Positive Living." Fast food with a high-tech twist: waitstaff take your orders on hand-held electronic radios that transmit directly to the kitchen. Strangers slurping happily from their massive bowls of ramen sit elbow-to-elbow at long tables, like extras from *Tampopo.* Not the place for a long, quiet meal: average turnover time is 20min. Pan-fried noodles, rice dishes, and vegetarian soup bases also available. Noodles in various combinations and permutations (£4.50-5.70). Try the raw juice (£2). No smoking. Open M-Sa noon-11pm, Su 12:30-10pm. MC, Visa. Another, less crowded branch has opened in Soho at 10a Lexington St., W1 (tel. 292 0990; fax 734 1815). Tube: Piccadilly Circus. From Piccadilly, head down Shaftesbury Ave., turn left on Great Windmill St. which turns into Lexington. Go late to avoid theater crowds, but still expect to wait on line. Open M-Sa noon-11pm, Su 12:30-10pm. MC, Visa.

Woolley's Salad Shop and Sandwich Bar, 33 Theobald's Rd., WC1 (tel. 405 3028). Tube: Holborn. Healthy and delicious picnic fare for take-away, mostly vegetarian. Mix and match their 10 fresh salads in a variety of sizes (70p-£6.30 for a huge party pot). The adjoining sandwich shop offers everything from chicken *saag* to smoked salmon lovingly swaddled in fresh rolls (90p-£2.30). Dried fruit, nuts, herbal tea, and muesli also for sale. Open M-F 7am-3:30pm.

The Fryer's Delight, 19 Theobald's Rd., WC1 (tel. 405 4114). Tube: Holborn. One of the best chippies around. Popular with British Library scholars and assorted locals. Retro buffs will gladly pay some extra pence to submerge themselves in authentic orange, red, and blue formica. Large portions of fish and chips £3.10 take-away. Walk out with a Cornish pastie or a chicken pie for £1.10. Open M-Sa noon-10pm, until 11pm for take-away.

Goodfella's Delicatessen, 50 Lamb's Conduit, WC1 (tel. 720 4457). Tube: Russell Sq. Clean, bright sandwich shop offers a frozen yogurt machine and wide variety of fresh, made to order sandwiches (from £1.50), bins of olives, shelves of fresh bread, and assorted ripe ingredients. Salad buffet plates £3 or £3.50 (take-away £2 or £2.50). Open M-F 8am-7pm, Sa 10am-6pm.

Mille Pini Restaurant, 33 Boswell St., WC1 (tel. 242 2434). Tube: Holborn. Take Southampton Row and turn right onto Theobald's Row. Boswell St. is the second left, with a brick entrance. Wine racks on the walls and chandelier lights provide the decor; sepia-tone floor tiles add a rustic feel. Offers terrific brick-oven pizza, pasta (£4.50-5.50), and homemade pastries. Divine *tiramisu* £2.40. Open M-F noon-3pm and 6pm-midnight, Sa 6pm-midnight.

Cosmoba, 9 Cosmo Pl., WC1 (tel. 837 0904). Tube: Russell Sq. On a pedestrian thoroughfare off Old Gloucester St., this simple restaurant has welcomed the hungry of Bloomsbury with low prices and Italian hospitality for nearly 40 years. Choose from spaghetti, tagliatelle, or penne with a variety of sauces (£3.45-5.30). Succulent specials like *pollo cosmoba* (chicken in mushroom and wine sauce, £7.20). Perfect cappuccinos £1. Open M-Sa 11:30am-3pm and 5:30-11pm. MC, Visa.

Leigh St. Café, 16 Leigh St., WC1 (tel. 387 3393). Tube: Russell Sq. A bright student- and local-filled cafe serving creative sandwiches and pastries. Elegant decor and marble tables inside, enclosed garden in back. Sandwiches from 70p, daily pasta selections £3.25. Take-away available. Open M-Sa 7am-6pm, Su 9am-5pm.

Alara Wholefoods, 58/60 Marchmont, WC1 (tel. 837 1172). Tube: Russell Sq. A good staple store offering dried fruit, nuts, grains, and a little wholefood propaganda. Lots of healthy foods for the cupboard, and the take-away kitchen in the back is practically giving away jacket potatoes (from 90p) and generous slices of quiche (£1.60). Open M-F 9am-7pm, Sa 10am-6pm.

October Gallery Café, 24 Old Gloucester St., WC1 (tel. 242 7367). Tube: Holborn. Take Southampton Row and turn right at Theobald's Rd. Old Gloucester St. is the 1st left. A high-ceilinged, chic cafe with wood floors and wicker seats. Adjacent to the October Gallery (see p. 190). Exciting menu changes daily and reflects the multi-cultural artwork on display. Recent offerings included Roman Style chicken, cooked from an ancient Roman recipe recovered by the British Museum (£3.50). Open M-F 12:30-2:30pm. Closed in Aug.

NEAR EUSTON

Restaurants specializing in Western and Southern Indian cuisine cluster along **Drummond Street.** Many are *bhel poori,* or vegetarian. From the Warren St. tube station, head up Hampstead Rd. until it meets Drummond St. From the Euston Sq. station, take N. Gower St. until Drummond St. crosses it. **Tube: Warren St.** or **Euston Sq.**

Diwana Bhel Poori House, 121 Drummond St., NW1 (tel. 387 5556). Tube: Warren St. Tasty Indian vegetarian food in a clean and airy restaurant. Strict vegetarians (including liberal kosher eaters) find this place a dining haven. Spicy sauces and chutneys make for creative use of vegetables. The specialty is *thali* (an assortment of vegetables, rices, sauces, breads, and desserts; £3.80-4.10). Lunch buffet includes 4 vegetable dishes, rice, savories, and dessert (served noon-2:30pm; £4). Open daily noon-11:30pm. AmEx, MC, Visa.

Chutney's, 124 Drummond St., NW1 (tel. 338 0604). Tube: Warren St. A cheerful cafe serving vegetarian dishes from western and southern India. Paintings in deep royal hues and spiral brass lamps decorate the walls. Delicious chutneys. Organic wines for vegetarians and vegans (£7 per bottle). Delicious mango milkshakes £2. All-you-can-eat lunch buffet (served M-Sa noon-2:45pm; £5). Su buffet (served noon-10:30pm; £5). *Dosas* (filled pancakes; £3.50-4.30). Take-away available 6-11:30pm. Open M-Sa noon-2:45pm and 6-11:30pm, Su noon-10:30pm. MC, Visa.

Great Nepalese Restaurant, 48 Eversholt St., NW1 (tel. 338 6737). Tube: Euston Sq. From the station, head left up Eversholt St. Walls covered with accolades from food critics and restaurant guides. Try Nepalese specialties like *bhutuwa* chicken, prepared with ginger, garlic, spice, and green herbs (£4.60). Delicious vegetarian dishes like *aloo bodi tama* (potato, bamboo shoots, beans; £2.85). Food is spicy, but the staff is sweet in this family-owned restaurant. Don't pass up the Nepalese Rum (£1.65) poured from the bottle shaped like the *kukri* knife—the national weapon of Nepal. 10% take-away discount. Open M-Sa noon-2:45pm and 6-11:45pm, Su noon-2:30pm and 6-11:15pm. AmEx, DC, MC, Visa.

Gupta Sweet Centre, 100 Drummond St., NW1 (tel. 380 1590). Tube: Warren St. Excellent Indian sweets and savories to take away. A refreshingly neighborly sort of shop that hasn't gone industrial in any way; you'll forget you're in London. Delicious *chum-chum* (sweet cottage cheese; 30p). *Samosa* 30p. Open M-Th 11am-7pm, F-Sa 10am-7pm, Su noon-7pm.

Ambala Sweet Centre, 112 Drummond St., NW1 (tel. 387 7886). The original shop of the 32-branch chain has been selling to sweet tooths since 1965. Check out the ever-popular *halwa habshi* (sticky nuts, milk, sugar; £3.30 per lb.). The *sohan salwa* (£2.70 per lb.) is like English toffee, but better—and a thick circle of it will leave you only 60-70p poorer. Open daily 9am-9pm.

Victoria, Kensington, and Chelsea

VICTORIA

Culinary prospects in the areas immediately surrounding the Victoria station megaplex may seem a bit grim. The avenues radiating north and east from the station (Buckingham Palace Rd., Victoria Rd., and Vauxhall Bridge Rd.) are populated with mediocre sandwich shops and chain restaurants catering to desperate and famished (i.e. non-discriminating) tourists. Follow the suits and count on local office workers to find the cheapest lunch spots, or pick up some fresh fruit at the stands on Tachbrook St. and head elsewhere.

Ciaccio, 5 Warwick Way, SW1 (tel. 828 1342). An intimate Italian eatery whose prices and spices make it a giant for budget eaters. Handsome portions make for an unbeatable value. Pick a container of pasta and one of about 10 sauces (pesto, veggie, tomato and meat), and they'll heat it up in the microwave for £1.69-2.85 (take-away even less). Open M-F 10am-7pm, Sa 9:30am-6pm.

The Well, 2 Eccleston Place, SW1 (tel. 730 7303). A large open eatery dispensing sandwiches (£1.55-1.80) and good cheer (free). Breakfast especially cheap. All profits and tips go to good works and charity. Open M-F 9am-6pm, Sa 9:30am-5pm.

O Sole Mio, 39 Churton St. (tel. 976 6887). From Victoria, take a left off Belgrave Rd. Cozy, clean basement eatery serves healthy portions of pasta at reasonable prices (£5.30-6); pizza's a good deal too (£5.90-6.20). Convenient to Belgrave Rd. hotels. Open M-F noon-2:30pm and 6-11:30pm, Sa 6-11:30pm.

The Little Bay, 47 Lupus St., SW1 (tel. 837 9075 or 233 9828). Tube: Pimlico. From thc station, turn right on Bessborough St., which leads towards Lupus St. 15min. walk. Unpretentious exterior hides an intimate, bohemian interior. 3-course meal £6 (served noon-7:15pm). Chicken with black peppercorn sauce £4, homemade tiramisu £1.65. Open M-Sa noon-3pm and 6pm-midnight, Su noon-11pm.

KNIGHTSBRIDGE AND HYDE PARK CORNER

Epicurean stomachs-on-a-budget teased by the sumptuous outlay of the Harrods food court may growl with disappointment at the dearth of affordable eateries near Knightsbridge (tube: Knightsbridge). **Knightsbridge Green,** which connects Brompton Rd. and Knightsbridge Rd. just past their divergence, offers several sandwich shops, in addition to fresh fruit and vegetable stands where you can procure provisions for a picnic.

Mima's Café, 9 Knightsbridge Green, SW1 (tel. 589 6820). Understandably packed during lunch hours. Practically every sandwich under the sun, each £2.70 or less, including delicious chicken and sweet corn and numerous creations involving mozzarella. Huge salads £4.40-6. Take-away discount. Open M-Sa 6am-5:30pm.

Knightsbridge Express, 17 Knightsbridge Green, SW1 (tel. 589 3039). Crowds of businessfolk and weary shoppers pack this upbeat eatery during lunch hours. The upstairs seating area is more placid. Most sandwiches £1.50-2.40. Pasta platters £3.80. The hearty omelette sandwich (£2.80) is good in the morning or afternoon. Take-away discount. Open M-Sa 6am-5pm.

Arco Bars, 46 Hans Crescent, SW1 (tel. 584 6454). Cheap, hearty Italian food. Several pleasant outdoor tables. Large portions of pasta or eggs are all £4 take-away. Generously filled sandwiches on excellent bread £1.30-2.20 take-away. Open M-F 7am-6pm, Sa 8am-6pm.

Borshtch 'n' Tears, 46 Beauchamp Pl., SW3 (tel. 589 5003 and 584 9911). Dining here provides an evening's entertainment for every comrade. Although the restaurant is not budget, the enjoyment is priceless, as the management of this Russian restaurant collectively scoffs at Knightsbridgean reserve and Russian stereotypes. Starters £3-6. Most entrees £7-9. Try a shot from one of the 16 different vodkas in Baron Benno von Borshtch's bewildering collection (around £2.50). Live music nightly. Last orders 1am. Cover £1. Service charge 10%. Open daily 6pm-2am.

Beverly Hills Bakery, 3 Egerton Terrace, SW3 (tel. 584 4401). All things Californian, from the sunny, colored walls to the natural ingredients in the goodies. Everything baked on the premises. Pecan pie, carrot cake, and cheesecake slices £2.20, take-away £1.80. Muffins £1.10; buy 6 and get the 7th free. Espresso 80p take-away. Open M-Sa 7:30am-6:30pm, Su 8am-6pm.

Lord's Food and Wine, 209 Brompton Rd., SW7 (tel. 589 8851). A 24hr. supermarket offering cheap, tasty take-away. Serves a wicked good whole roast chicken for only £4, fresh Thai dishes for £2.59, and potatoes with cheese for £1.39. Something for everyone, all the time.

Hard Rock Cafe, 150 Old Park Ln., W1 (tel. 629 0382). Tube: Hyde Park Corner. This little-known neighborhood restaurant serves burgers and fries (£7.25) to a small local crowd in an intimate and quiet atmosphere. The perfect eatery for those wishing to avoid lines, loud music, and rock 'n' roll memorabilia. The madness first began here in 1971. Open Su-Th 11:30am-12:30am, F-Sa 11:30am-1am.

SOUTH KENSINGTON

This is the unofficial French quarter of London; it is also one of the ritziest areas in the city. As one might expect, South Ken (as it's called by those in the know) is not brimming with bargains. For budget dining, Old Brompton Rd. and Fulham Rd. are the main thoroughfares in this graceful area—Fulham Rd. is especially lively in the evenings. South Kensington tube station lies closest, but some of the restaurants below require a substantial hike from there; others can easily be reached from the Earl's Ct. tube station. Old Brompton Rd. is served by Buses #74 and C1; Fulham Road by Buses #14, 45a, and 211.

Café Floris, 5 Harrington Rd., SW7 (tel. 589 3276). A bustling cafe offering large, fresh sandwiches (£1.50-2) and filling breakfasts. Colossal breakfast special for £3.50 is a better value than anything for miles. Open daily 7am-7pm.

Jules Rotisserie, 6-8 Bute St., SW7 (tel. 584 0600; fax 584 0614). This lively, pleasant restaurant with indoor and outdoor seating serves roasted free-range poultry. Quarter chicken with potatoes and green salad £6.25. Free delivery (tel. 221 3331). Open M-Sa noon-11:30pm, Su noon-10:30pm.

Luigi's, 359-361 Fulham Rd., SW10 (tel. 351 7825). Chaotic and tasty, enjoy this Italian deli-style restaurant's authentic salads, pastas, and desserts at one of its large outdoor tables. The wafting scent of the flower stand next door transports you to the south of Italy. Amazingly large pizzas for around £5. Open daily 8am-11pm.

Parson's Restaurant, 311 Fulham Rd., SW10 (tel. 352 0651). There's a soda-shop feel to this large airy restaurant, where the pasta specials are huge and the burgers priced by size (£5.95-7.95). Bring your ticket stub from the nearby MGM cinema and get a free drink with your entree. Open daily noon-1am, last orders 12:30am (midnight on Su).

Il Falconiere, 84 Old Brompton Rd., SW7 (tel. 589 2401). A bit of Italy on Old Brompton Rd. Sidewalk tables feature startling wicker and white decor. A full meal proves quite expensive, but pasta entrees run only £4.50-5. Cover £1. Minimum £5.50 per person. Open M-Sa noon-11:45pm.

Vingt Quatre, 325 Fulham Rd., SW10 (tel. 376 7224). Hyper-modern brushed steel tables and chairs give a strangely space-age feel to this somewhat pricey diner. Full English breakfast £4.75 for small, £6.75 for large. Burgers £6.95. Drinks served noon-midnight. Cover charge varies between 50p-£1. Open 24hr.

Hip Bagel, 323 Fulham Rd., SW10 (tel. 376 8984). This New York-style deli and patisserie is open early and late to satisfy your cravings. More than dill pickles, fresh sandwiches, and salads. Challah french toast £3.50. Open daily 7:30am-2am.

Canadian Muffin Co., 353 Fulham Rd. (tel. 351 0015). A veritable U.N. of muffins, featuring everything from traditional blueberry to spinach feta to Rocky Road, all for just £1.10 each. 7 for £6. Double espresso £1.10. Open daily 8am-8pm.

HIGH STREET KENSINGTON

There are few affordable, non-fast-food options on this tony drag. If you've got more time than money, walk uphill to Notting Hill Gate, where the range of food options is noticeably wider and less expensive. **Tube: High Street Kensington,** unless otherwise noted.

Apadna, 351 Kensington High St., W8 (tel. 603 3696). A 10min. walk from the tube and an escape from the street's commercial banality. Apadna offers savory kebabs in fresh-baked *naan* (minced lamb kebab £2.80). Watch them roll and bake the *naan* over a stone fire. Open daily 11am-11pm.

Sticky Fingers Cafe, 1a Phillimore Gdns., W8 (tel. 938 5338). Turn left onto Kensington High St. Phillimore Gdns. is a couple of blocks down on the right. Former Rolling Stone Bill Wyman operates this memorabilia-crammed diner. Those fearing a Hard Rock experience shouldn't worry; the crowd is here for the burgers, consistently rated the best in London. Burger and fries £7.25. Sticky Cake (chocolate cake with fudge topping) satisfies for £3.50. Open daily noon-11:30pm. AmEx, MC, Visa.

Wodka, 12 St. Alban's Grove, W8 (tel. 937 6513). Tube: Gloucester Rd. Although not exactly budget fare, this swank Polish restaurant serves delicious gourmet cuisine at affordable prices. *Blinis* (crepe-like pancakes filled with various goodies) come with several different toppings, including smoked salmon (£6.90) and aubergine mousse (£5.50). Fifteen odd vodkas "on tap" wash it all down. Open M-F 12:30-2pm and 7-11:15pm, Sa-Su 7-11:15pm. AmEx, DC, MC, Visa.

CHELSEA

When hunger pangs strike in gentile Chelsea, you can either sate your desires on **King's Road,** or jaunt down a neighboring thoroughfare, where affordable restaurants abound. Most destinations along King's Rd. require a bus ride or a considerable walk. Buses #11, 19, 22, 211, and 319 run the length of King's Rd. from the Victoria or Sloane Sq. tube stations. If King's Rd. doesn't whet your appetite, turn right onto Sydney St. or Edith Grove and head towards **Fulham Road,** which runs parallel to King's Rd., to access South Kensington's cornucopia of culinary delights (see p. 108).

Chelsea Kitchen, 98 King's Rd., SW3 (tel. 589 1330). 7min. walk from the tube. Locals rave about the eclectic menu of cheap, filling, and tasty food: turkey and mushroom pie, spaghetti bolognese, and a Spanish omelette are each £2.80 or less. Cozy booth seating. When the weather is amenable, grab one of the front tables and watch the Sloane Rangers pass you by. Set menu £5. Breakfast served 8-11:25am. Open M-Sa 8am-11:30pm, Su 9am-11:30pm.

SWTen, 488 King's Rd., SW10 (tel. 352 4227), near the World's End. A hike from the tube. Cosmopolitan, sun-filled French atmosphere at budget prices. Tremendously sized portions despite the chic atmosphere. Huge sandwiches on crusty bread £1.20-3. Salads £2.80-3.50. Specials (around £3) are a phenomenal value. Take-away discount. Open M-F 8am-4pm.

The Stockpot, 273 King's Rd., SW3 (tel. 823 3175). Basic brasserie fare for low prices. Minimum per person is £2.50, but most meals won't cost more than that. Simple, filling food (spaghetti bolognese £2.30, omelettes from £2.80), and cozy atmosphere. Open M-Sa 8am-midnight, Su noon-midnight.

New Culture Revolution, 305 King's Rd., SW3 (tel. 342 9281). Also at 43 Parkway, NW1 (tel. 267 2700; tube: Camden Town). China's cultural revolution finally hits Chelsea with this clean, friendly restaurant that is a favorite among locals. Highlights include the vegetarian *guo tei* (dumplings filled with vegetables and noodles, £4.90). Healthy, large portions leave you satisfied. Open daily noon-11pm.

Chelsea Deli, Chelsea Farmer's Market, Sydney St., SW3 (tel. 351 1875). Take a right off King's Cross onto Sydney St. This French deli serves *un melange* of English brasserie food in calming surroundings. All homemade and delicious. Sandwiches, quiche, and pies £1.70-2.50. Open daily 10am-8pm.

Chelsea Bun Diner, 9a Limerston St., SW10 (tel. 352 3635), just off King's Rd. near World's End. Variety of sandwiches overflowing with gourmet fillings; smoked salmon and avocado, £2.85. In summer, the glass windows open out into the street for delightful *al fresco* dining. Special includes soup, entree, and tea or coffee, £3.90. Breakfast special £3.35 (2 eggs, bacon, sausage, tomato, beans and toast, and tea or coffee); £2.30 from 7-10:30am. Open daily 7am-midnight.

Henry J. Bean's Bar and Grill, 195-97 King's Rd., SW3 (tel. 352 9255). This large, pseudo-American frontier tavern offers a huge, glorious beer garden outside, the nicest place to relax on King's Rd. Luncheon special includes main course, salad, and "fries" (served M-F noon-3pm; £5). Happy hour 6-8pm, 2 pint pitcher of cocktails for £9.50. Open M-Sa 10:45am-11pm, Su noon-10:30pm. AmEx, MC, Visa.

My Old Dutch Pancake House, 221 King's Rd., SW3 (tel. 376 5650). Saturated with things Dutch, the restaurant is fun. Hubcap-sized pancakes (more like crepes than flapjacks), both sweet and savory, served on huge Delph windmill dishes. Stick to simple ingredients—the more elaborate combinations are sometimes less than successful—and plan on becoming very, very full. Set lunch menu (served weekdays noon-4pm) offers a pancake with your choice of three toppings, a waffle with whipped cream and sauce, and tea or coffee (£6). Open M-Th noon-11:30pm, F-Sa noon-midnight, Su noon-11pm. AmEx, DC, MC, Visa.

Earl's Court

Earl's Court and **Gloucester Road** cater generously to their tourist traffic. Earl's Ct., with many take-away eateries, revolves around cheap, palatable food. Groceries charge reasonable prices; shops stay open late at night and on Sunday (some are open 24hr., a rarity in Britain). The closer you get to the high-rise hotels around Gloucester Rd. Station, the more expensive restaurants become. Look for the scores of coffee shops and Indian restaurants on Gloucester Rd. north of Cromwell Rd. (especially near Elvaston Pl.). **Tube: Earl's Court,** unless otherwise noted.

Troubador Coffee House, 265 Old Brompton Rd., SW5 (tel. 370 1434), near Earl's Ct. and Old Brompton Rd. junction. Copper pots, pitchforks, and mandolins are suspended from the ceiling, and whirring espresso machines steam up the windows in this enjoyable community cafe. Live music (see **Entertainment,** p. 239). Assorted snacks, soups, and sandwiches under £4. Special breakfasts £3-4. Liquor available with food orders. Vast selection of coffee drinks. Check *Time Out* or call for who's performing. Open M-Sa 9:30am-12:30am, Su 9:30am-11pm.

Perry's Bakery, 151 Earl's Court Rd., SW5 (tel. 370 4825). Amiable Bulgarian-Israeli management prides itself on a somewhat eclectic menu and phenomenal fresh baked goods. Jazz always playing in the background. Flaky *borekas* (pastry filled with cheese) make a filling snack (with spinach £1.40). Straight from Israel come Mitzli juices (60p) and falafel (£2.50) with know-how. For breakfast, enjoy their croissant plus all-you-can-drink tea or coffee for £2. Challah loaves £1.50. For dinner enjoy a combo plate of the day's special for less than £3. Min. charge £2 to eat in. Open daily 5:30am-midnight.

The Hi-Tide Fish and Chips Restaurant, 7 Kenway Rd., SW5 (tel. 373 9170). Classic British fish and chips. Don't know the difference between cod, rock, plaice, and haddock? Read the back of the menu, which tells all. A simple restaurant with a row of 5 booths and a little more space downstairs. Large chunk of cod and chips £4.20, cheaper take-away. Take-away only 9:30pm-close. Open M-Sa noon-midnight, Su 5-11pm.

Benjy's, 157 Earl's Court Rd., SW5 (tel. 373 0245). Crowded with hungry hostelers who weren't sated by their included "breakfast." Simple decor and great all-day breakfast specials. Load up for the day (or night) with the "Builder Breakfast" (bacon, egg, chips, beans, toast, 2 sausages; £3.60). The "vegetarian" suits smaller appetites (toast, 2 eggs, baked beans; £3.20). All fixed breakfasts come with all-you-can-drink tea or coffee. Open daily 7am-9:30pm. Cash only.

Bistro Benito, 166 Earl's Court Rd., SW5 (tel. 373 6646). 20 yr. old, family Italian bistro serves good cheer and hearty food in equal helpings. Most pastas £3.95. *Escalope Milanese* with Spaghetti £7.75. Lamb casserole with rice £5.75. Open M-Sa noon-11:30pm, Su noon-11pm. AmEx, DC, MC, Visa.

Café Deco, 62 Gloucester Rd., SW7 (tel. 225 3286). Tube: Gloucester Rd. Small French cafe with chic Art Deco decor. Delicate fresh fruit tarts (apple, peach, and pear £1.25; raspberry or strawberry £2.35) and croissants (60p) are the *spécialités de la maison.* Cappuccino £1.18, take-away 80p. Open daily 8am-8pm.

Nando's, 204 Earl's Court Rd., SW5 (tel. 259 2544). Also in Camden (tel. 424 9040) and Ealing Common (tel. 992 2290). A cut above the usual fast-food outlet. South African-born Portuguese chain that serves spicy budget-oriented chicken dishes to those tired of burgers. Don't worry that it's quick-serve—you can watch your chicken being grilled right in front of you. Half chicken and chips £5.20. Beer and wine also available. Open daily 11:45am-11:45pm.

Kramps Crêperie, 6 Kenway Rd., SW5 (tel. 244 8759). Crepes cooked right in front of you amidst a cosmopolitan Spanish and French atmosphere. Cheese, tomato, oregano crepe £4.40. Homemade sangría £5.90 per liter. 3-course set menu £6.95. 10% service charge included. Open daily noon-11pm.

Delice de France, 1 Kynance Pl. (tel. 581 5884) off Gloucester Rd. Tube: Gloucester Rd. Left out of station, cross Cromwell Rd. Kynance Pl. will be on your left. A pseudo-Parisian cafe nestled on a quiet street, with fresh bread and hefty sandwiches. Dine *al fresco* on filled baguettes (£2.10-2.50). Open M-F 7:30am-7pm, Sa-Su 7:30am-6pm.

■ Notting Hill and Ladbroke Grove

The many restaurants dotting the streets that radiate out from the Notting Hill Gate and Ladbroke Grove stations are extraordinarily cosmopolitan. Dishes from around the globe can be found in the area's hearty, reasonably priced eateries. Stylish coffeehouses and pastry shops cluster near the Ladbroke Grove station, while Portobello Road bursts at the seams with a multi-ethnic myriad of budget eateries.

Manzara, 24 Pembridge Rd., W11 (tel. 727 3062). Tube: Notting Hill Gate. Ostensibly a take-away shop, Manzara actually seats 40 people. A wonderfully cheap place to get your grub after a stroll through the Portobello market. In the afternoon, pizzas are £3.50, sandwiches £2. In the evenings, they offer a £6 all-you-can-eat array of Greek and Turkish specialties, including grilled-while-you-watch kebabs. Vegetarians should try the mixed *meze* (£4.25). Take-away discount. Open daily 7:30am-midnight.

The Grain Shop, 269a Portobello Rd., W11 (tel. 229 5571). Tube: Ladbroke Grove. Step inside this take-away shop and you'll be amazed by the surprisingly large array of tasty foods, as well as the line of customers that often reaches halfway into the streets. Organic whole grain breads baked daily on the premises (80p-£1.40 per loaf), as well as excellent sourdough loaves (£1.80). Try any combination of the 6 hot vegetarian dishes—large £4.10, medium £3, small £2. Delicious pastries made from organic flour and free-range eggs. Huge vegan brownies £1. Groceries also available, many organic. Open M-Sa 9:30am-6pm.

Makan, 270 Portobello Rd., W10 (tel. (0181) 960 5169). Exotic and delightful smells waft out of this bustling Malaysian joint. A wide variety of dishes, from chicken curry to *sambul* prepared with squid or spicy eggplant, around £4. Take-away discount 80p. Open M-Sa 11:30am-7:30pm.

O'Porto Patisserie, 62a Golborne Rd., W10 (tel. (0181) 968 8839). Tube: Ladbroke Grove. A thriving enclave of Portuguese culture, this *pastelaria* serves delectable pastries crafted from Iberian ingredients. Locals of Portuguese and North African descent mingle with city kids and Portobello strays around crowded tables. Impossibly hearty chicken, fish, or parma ham sandwiches sold on traditional Portuguese breads and rolls for only £1.40-1.75. Portugese specialities such as *Pasteis de Bacalbau* (cod fish cakes) cost only 75p. Open daily 8am-8pm.

Gallery Café, 74 Tavistock Rd., W11 (tel. 221 5844). Tube: Ladbroke Grove. A mellow vegetarian cafe just off 269 Portobello Rd. Lunch specials include Moroccan stew and *moussaka* for £4.80, small £3.80. Now features a new range of macrobiotic dishes for vegans. Enjoy your lunch with the young, pierced locals who dine here daily. Take-away discount 20-30p. Open daily 8am-6:30pm.

Coconut Grove (formerly The Bel Air), 23 All Saints Rd., W11 (tel. 229 7961). Tube: Westbourne Park or Ladbroke Grove. Behind a rust-red exterior, this candlelit restaurant serves well-prepared jerk chicken £6.50. Fried plantains £1.80. Take-away available at slightly cheaper prices. Open M-Sa 11:30am-11:30pm.

Cockney's, 314 Portobello Rd., W10 (tel. (0181) 960 9409). Tube: Ladbroke Grove. After streets of varied ethnic eateries, this stalwart of English cuisine seems downright exotic. "Traditional pie, mash, and eels," says the sign above the door, and they aren't joking. Cheap, no-nonsense pie and mash (£1.60), with portions of eel for a mere £2 (eels available F-Sa). And don't forget the cups of liquor for only 30p. Open M-Th and Sa 11:30am-5:30pm, F 11:30am-6pm.

Lisboa Patisserie, 57 Golborne Rd., W10 (tel. (0181) 968 5242). Tube: Ladbroke Grove. Join the energetic, nicotine-infused locals sitting in this marble-floored Portuguese patisserie, or if the weather is nice, position yourself at the tables outside and watch the world go by. All food prepared in the kitchen below. Loads of traditional Portuguese pastels; *pastel nata* (custard tart) melts in your mouth (55p). Glass of coffee 75p. Open daily 8am-8pm.

Geale's, 2 Farmer St., W8 (tel. 727 7969). Tube: Notting Hill Gate. Spirited locals crowd this reputable wood-paneled restaurant. Geale's has won various awards for their consistently crisp fish and chips. Fresh haddock, cod, and plaice from Grimsby in the North are house specialties. Market price usually from £5.50. Look for the £3.50 summer lunch special. Cover charge 15p per person, but take-away available. Open Tu-Sa noon-3pm and 6-11pm. Amex, MC, Visa.

Baalbak Lebanese Restaurant, 91 Golborne Rd., W10 (tel. (0181) 960 0136). Tube: Ladbroke Grove. Variety of interesting Lebanese cuisine, including the expected *tabouleh* and kebabs, as well as more unusual items such as *fattoush* (mixed vegetables with herbs and toasted Lebanese bread, £2.50). Take-away is even cheaper. Free home delivery for those spending more than £8. Open M-Su 8am-11:30pm.

FOOD AND DRINK

Bayswater and Queensway

The culinary options in this area tend to be less scintillating than those in neighboring Notting Hill/Ladbroke Grove, but Westbourne Grove has spawned a bewildering array of excellent South and East Asian restaurants as well as a growing number of Portugese and Brazilian cafes. **Tube: Bayswater or Royal Oak.**

Royal China, 13 Queens Way, W2 (tel. 221 2535). Tube: Bayswater or Queensway. The best and most exotic *dim sum* served outside of Chinatown. A huge meal of freshly made dumplings averages £10 per person, but one can easily get by on less. Try the steamed duck's tongue (£1.80) or the marinated chicken feet (£1.80). Entrees £10-15. Open daily noon-11pm. AmEx, DC, MC, Visa.

Khan's, 13-15 Westbourne Grove, W2 (tel. 727 5240). Tube: Bayswater. Cavernous, noisy, and crowded, Khan's remains a great bargain for delicious Indian cuisine. The menu explains that the distinctive flavor of each dish "cannot come from the rancid ambiguity called curry powder," but only from "spices separately prepared each day." They're not kidding—the chicken *saag* (chicken cooked with spinach, £3.20) contains piquant spices that are well complemented by flat *naan* bread or rice. Beware—dip into one of the chutneys sitting expectantly on your table when you arrive and you will be charged 35p per person. Uses only *halal* meats. Though most entrees are still under £4, ascent to budget heaven is now hampered by a £6 per person minimum. Look out for lunch specials. Open daily noon-3pm and 6pm-midnight. AmEx, DC, MC, Visa.

Mandola Cafe and Restaurant, 139 Westbourne Grove, W2 (tel. 229 4734). Tube: Bayswater. The owner claims that this is the only Sudanese restaurant in Europe, and who are we to doubt him? Beautifully decorated with African artifacts (some of which are for sale), Mandola offers a range of intriguing dishes cooked with

Sudanese spices at very reasonable prices. The salads are a particularly good value at £3, and other vegetarian delights include *filfilia* (exotic vegetables in a spicy tomato sauce), for £4. To finish your meal, try the date mousse (£2.40) and Sudanese coffee, sold in a traditional pot for £3.50 (serves two). Bring your own alcohol for a corkage fee of £1. Take-away available. Open M-Sa noon-11pm. No credit cards.

Penang, 41 Hereford Rd., W2 (tel. 229 2982). Tube: Bayswater (Hereford Rd. runs off Westbourne Grove). The standard interior hides magnificent Malaysian and Thai cuisine. Tangy lemon chicken £4. *Sayor lodeh* (mixed vegetables cooked in savory coconut milk gravy, £3) has a well-deserved reputation. Beef, pork, seafood, and curry dishes also available. Home delivery available; minimum £10. Open M-Sa 6-11:30pm, Su 6-11pm. AmEx, DC, MC, Visa.

Jewel of Siam, 39 Hereford Rd., W2 (tel. 229 4363). Tube: Bayswater. Well-prepared Thai food in a contrived yet endearing setting. Entrees are pricey (£5-6), but sumptuous appetizers (£3.50-4.50) and noodle specials (under £5 for both lunch and dinner) are quite satisfying. Take it away to one of the nearby parks for a 10% discount, or duck downstairs to dodge the upstairs cover charge (£1 per person, only applies in the evening). Open M-F noon-2:30pm and 6-11pm, Sa 6-11pm, Su 6-10:30pm. AmEx, MC, Visa.

Mr. Wu, 63 Westbourne Grove, W2 (tel. 229 0675). Tube: Bayswater. Also at 54 Queensway, W2. Part of a chain, Mr. Wu's offers only one culinary option: an all-you-can-eat Chinese buffet (£4.50). It is not necessarily the best Chinese you'll ever have—the food is a fairly standard range of spring rolls, noodles, soups, etc.—but there's plenty of it, and that makes it a great bargain. Open daily noon-11:30pm. No credit cards.

The City of London

Restaurants in this area tend to cater exclusively either to businessmen or the construction workers who build and renovate their offices. Benches and stools filled with suits are generally bad signs for budget travelers. These blokes have no time, but money to burn. Cheap lunch-time haunts line **Whitecross Street,** which is accessed by following Beech St. east from the Barbican. Sandwich shops blossom on **Bow Street** (tube: Mansion House), and bohemian (i.e. cheap) cafes somehow flourish on **Cowcross Street** (tube: Farringdon). The best way to have a cheap dinner here is to bring it yourself—the City is traditionally a ghost-town after office hours, and the nightspots springing up here are strictly executive class. And there is always, of course, McDonald's. (Just kidding.)

The Place Below (tel. 329 0789), in St. Mary-le-Bow Church crypt, Cheapside, EC2. Tube: St. Paul's. Attractive, generous vegetarian dishes served to the hippest of City executives in an impressive church basement. Second dining room moonlights as an ecclesiastical court, where the Archbishop of Canterbury still settles cases pertaining to Anglican law and swears in new bishops a few times a year. Menu changes daily. Quiche and salad £6, take-away £3. £2 discount when you sit in from 11:30am-noon. Serves as a cafe with a doughy collection of muffins, scones, etc. until lunch at 11:30am. Take-away discount. Open M-F 7:30am-2:30pm.

Futures!, 8 Botolph Alley, EC3 (tel. 623 4529). Tube: Monument. Off Botolph Ln. Fresh take-away vegetarian breakfast and lunch prepared in a petite kitchen open to view! Daily main dishes, like quiche, £3.40! Spinach pizza £1.85! Open M-F 7:30-10am and 11:30am-3pm! If you're in the mood for Futures! food and want to sit down, stop by their snazzy, more expensive Futures! branch in Exchange Sq. (behind Liverpool Station)!

St. John, 26 St. John St., EC1 (tel. 251 0849). Tube: Farringdon. This airy, classically designed establishment is a strange hybrid of restaurant, bar and bakery. There is an idiosyncratic, but nonetheless excellent, selection of food available, including smoked eel (£6.70) and winkles and *samphire* (£4). Bar menu. Fresh bread from the bakery is £1.20. Restaurant open M-F noon-3pm and 6-11:30pm, Sa 6-11:30pm. Bar open M-F 11am-11pm, Sa 6-11pm.

Saints Cafe & Photo Lab, 1 Clerkenwell Rd., EC1 (tel. 490 4199). Tube: Farringdon. Take a right onto Farringdon, left onto Clerkenwell (don't be fooled by the counter-intuitive street numbering; whatever your head might tell you, don't turn right). Think pub food with an international twist: Sri Lankan fish cakes served with chutney and Thai dressed salad (£4.25). Ratatouille and mozzarella pie, with chips (£4.25). Special "Heaven" deal: 80p per breakfast item (bacon, sausage, egg, etc.), except between noon and 3pm. After your meal, you can develop your pictures at Saints photo lab. Cafe open M-F 8am-6pm, hot meals served until 4pm.

Al's Café Bar, 11-13 Exmouth Market, EC1 (tel. 837 4821). Tube: Farringdon. Exit right from station, Al's is on the corner of Farringdon St. and Exmouth Market (5 min. walk). This stylish cafe/bar is a favorite hangout for trendy magazine journalists, and young, brooding intellectuals. Wide selection of Belgian beers and excellent diner cuisine. Salads £5-6, main courses £7-8. English breakfast £5.50. W-Th, Sa jazz and F hip-hop music in the adjoining club. W-Sa £2 cover after 10pm. Open Su-Tu 8am-midnight, W-Sa 8am-2am. (Last orders 1hr. before close.) MC, Visa.

The Nosherie, 12 Greville St., EC1 (tel. 242 1591). Tube: Chancery Ln. Set among the jewellers of Hatton Garden, this unassuming eatery serves a rather eccentric mixture of classic New York-style deli food and exotic international dishes. Specializes in hot salt beef (corned beef) from £3.70. Fish and chips £2.50. Jacket potatoes from £1.50. Min. charge £5 to eat in. Open M-F 6:30am-5pm, Sa 8:30am-4pm.

Tinseltown 24 Hour Diner, 44/46 St. John St., EC1 (tel. 689 2424; fax 689 7860). Tube: Clerkenwell. The interior of this restaurant features pictures of movie stars and 15 TV screens. The food selection is eclectic and titled with puns: "The Breakfast Club" offers a breakfast from £2, and "Full Metal Jackets," or potatoes, start at £3. All beer £1.50, house wine £5. Best of all, it's open 24hr.

Barbican Grill, 117 Whitecross St., EC1 (tel. 256 6842). Tube: Moorgate. This pleasantly managed, unassuming cafe serves up amazing bargains to its budget-minded student and workingman crowd. Chicken and chips £3.10. Sandwiches with everything from chicken to salmon, around £1.30. Minimum charge £2 from noon-2pm. Open M-F 6am-4pm, Sa 6am-11pm.

Field's Sandwiches, 5 St. John St., EC1 (tel. 608 2235). Tube: Barbican. The wooden shelves packed with bric-a-brac lend this sandwich shop a charm its brethren lack, while high ceilings prevent take-away claustrophobia. Quiche £1.20, sandwiches £1-3, *samosas* 70p. Open M-F 6am-3pm.

Sushi & Sozai, 51a Queen Victoria St., EC4 (tel. 332 0108). Tube: Mansion House. Cheap sushi stand in the City. Medium sushi (tuna, prawn, salmon, squid, mackerel and egg sushi, plus 2 *makizushi*) £4. Large sushi £5. Heated Japanese entrees, including deep-fried pork cutlet and egg on rice, £3. Open M-F 11am-3pm.

Choristers, 36 Carter Ln., EC4 (tel. 329 3811). Tube: St. Paul's. Located in the City of London Youth Hostel. Not for the gourmet, but this homemade food eatery will give you a cheap, decent meal in a smoke-free zone. 3-course dinner £4.40. Lunch served noon-2pm, dinner 5-8pm.

The East End

It's easy to feel as if one were lost in the streets of Bangladesh or Ireland when moseying around the East End. One wildly popular Indian-Bangledeshi style is **Balti,** which means that the portion you order is brought to you in the individual vessel (the Balti) in which it was cooked. **Brick Lane** is home to a suburb collection of Bangledeshi restaurants, probably the longest string outside of Dhaka.

Lahore Kebab House, 2 Umberston St., E1 (tel. 481 9738). Tube: Whitechapel or Shadwell DLR. Off Commercial Rd. The glass-topped tables here play host to some of the best, cheapest Indian and Pakistani cuisine in the city. The *seekh* kebab (50p) is delicious wrapped in freshly baked *roti* (50p) and dipped in a surprisingly spicy yoghurt dip. There's no dish over £4.50 and, if you're thirsty, feel free to bring your own beer. Open daily noon-midnight.

The Cherry Orchard Café, 247 Globe Rd., E2 (tel. (0181) 980 6678). Tube: Bethnal Green. Walk down Roman Rd., then turn left onto Globe. A fabulous restaurant run by Buddhists. Walls in the pleasant interior are a shocking orange and turquoise; the outdoor garden is lovely in warm weather. The strictly vegetarian menu changes daily. Delicious hot entrees (spinach lasagne £4) served in large portions. Hot food served from noon. Open M 11am-3pm, Tu-F 11am-7pm.

Brick Lane Beigel Bake, 159 Brick Ln., E1 (tel. 729 0616). Tube: Aldgate East. At the top of Brick Ln. perches a lonely vestige of the Jewish East End of yore. But this inexpensive, authentic bakery tries to pick up the slack in the wake of the exodus, not only by offering perfect bagels (60p for 6), but by staying open all the time. Open daily 24hr.

Shampan, 79 Brick Ln., E1 (tel. 375 0475). Tube: Aldgate East. A tad more expensive and with an interior a touch more quiet and refined than its neighbors, but still very reasonable. A favorite of food critics and city office workers in the know. Balti lamb from £3.95, seafood dishes from £5. Open daily noon-3pm and 6pm-midnight. AmEx, MC, Visa.

Nazrul, 130 Brick Ln., E1 (tel. 247 2505). Tube: Aldgate East. The rapid service in this foliage-decorated restaurant means that you don't have to linger long if you're pressed for time. Considering the size of the portions, prices are terrifically cheap; Balti menu £3.10-6. No bar, but BYOB. Open M-Th noon-3pm and 5:30pm-midnight, F-Sa noon-3pm and 5:30pm-1am, Su noon-midnight.

Sheraz, 13 Brick Ln., E1 (tel. 247 5755). Tube: Aldgate East. One of the gateways into Brick Ln., this upscale restaurant now cooks Kashmiri food as well as Balti specialties. Generically elegant interior makes for quieter atmosphere than in other Bangladeshi restaurants up the street. Entrees average £5-6, although a 10% student discount is given if the meal is paid for in cash. Fully stocked bar. Min. charge £6.50. Open daily noon-3pm and 6pm-midnight. AmEx, DC, MC, Visa.

Aladin Balti House, 132 Brick Ln., E1 (tel. 247 8210). Must be good if it's the hangout for the local Bangladeshi mayor, his cronies, and the Prince of Wales. Owner Toimus Ali once fed the future king at an East End community meeting, and if you are nice to Mr. Ali, he'll play you an LBC recording of Prince Charles mentioning the restaurant. Big mark of distinction for this unpretentious joint. Balti dishes from £3. Open noon-11:30pm, F-Sa nights until midnight.

Eastern Eye, 63a Brick Ln., E1 (tel. 375 1696). Tube: Aldgate East. Plain on the outside and pretty on the inside, this Tandoori restaurant specializes in Balti dishes (from £5.95). The dense foliage inside makes this the Bangledeshi equivalent of an 80s fern bar. Chicken or lamb *tikka* £5.95. Halal food available. Open daily noon-3pm, 6pm-midnight. AmEx, MC, Visa.

Muhib, 73 Brick Lane E1 (tel. 247 7122). Tube: Aldgate East. Billed as the cheapest food on the street, the chef will prepare anything not on menu, though given that document's extensive length, you're going to have to be pretty creative. Moderately sized portions begin as low as £3.15. Take-away available. Open M-Sa noon–3pm and 6pm-midnight, Su noon-midnight. MC, Visa.

Islington

Dress smartly for a meal in one of the many bistros that line Upper St., which runs to the right as you exit the tube station (tube: Angel). Be careful when seeking specific addresses, though, since Upper St. numbers ascend on one side of the street and descend on the other. Unfortunately, few budget restaurants can be found in this cutting-edge area; candle-lit tables and expensive menus, not budget fares, have become uniform for Islington's trendy restaurants. However, lunch specials and early evening dinner deals frequently offer a way to enjoy the pomp of Islington without the wallet-depleting circumstance. Cheaper nosh lurks in the take-away sandwich shops, bakeries, and chip shops of the less upscale Chapel Market (the 1st left off Liverpool Rd.) which also plays host to a food market from Tuesday to Sunday.

Café Olé, 119 Upper St., N1 (tel. 226 6991). A hip Italian/Spanish bar/cafe adorned with colorful playbills and painted floral borders on the salmon walls. Bustling with Islington trendies of all ages, the atmosphere remains comfortable. Endless breakfast £4.20. Variety of generously sized paellas £4.20-4.95. Lunch menu offers pasta (£3.80-4.80) and salads (£4-4.70), in addition to sandwiches (£1-2.50). Prices and options expand in the evening with dinner specials around £6. Open M-Sa 8am-11pm. MC, Visa.

LeMercury, 140a Upper St., N1 (tel. 354 4088; fax 359 7186). Tube: Angel or Highbury and Islington. This French restaurant has the quintessential Islington candle-lit effect, with outstanding prices to boot. All main courses, including honey-roasted breast of duck, £5.85. Lunch and dinner 3-course *prix fixe* 11am-7:15pm, £5.50. Kids eat Sunday Roast free. Open M-Sa 11am-1am, Su noon-11:30pm. MC, Visa.

Indian Veg Bhelpoori House, 92-93 Chapel Market, N1 (tel. 837 4607 or 833 1167). One of the best bargains in London. All-you-can-eat lunch (£3.25) or dinner buffet (£3.50) of 30 vegetarian dishes and chutneys. Open daily noon-11:30pm. MC, Visa.

La Piragua, 176 Upper St., N1 (tel. 354 2843). Tube: Angel or Highbury and Islington. Welcome to South America—all of it! Colombian, Chilean, Venezuelan, and Argentine dishes complement an extensive Latin American wine list. Low-key beige walls with pictures of the owner's hometown Patagonia make this an intimate gathering place for food or wine. Main courses £6-9. Open daily noon-1am.

Trattoria Aquilino, 31 Camden Passage, N1 (tel. 226 5454). Turn right off Upper St. onto Charlton Pl. Camden Passage is the 1st left. This intimate, authentic restaurant features an extensive menu of homemade pasta. The native Italian staff is very attentive. Pastas £3.20-4.95. Pollo parmigiana £4.85. 10% service charge. Open M-Sa 12:30-2:30pm and 6:30-11:30pm. Cash only.

Upper St. Fish Shop, 324 Upper St., N1 (tel. 359 1401). A well-known upscale fish and chips joint offering specials based on the day's catch. An energetic staff serves all things battered inside a comfortable wood-paneled interior. £5 min. for eating in. Fish and chips £7.50. Non-fried fish £7-9. Everything homemade, from the soup to the ice cream. Open M 6-10:15pm, Tu-Th noon-2:15pm and 6-10:15pm, F noon-2:15pm and 5:30-10:15pm, Sa noon-3pm and 5:30-10:15pm.

Tuk Tuk, 330 Upper St., N1 (tel. 266 0837). Bright blue exterior hides a sleek Thai restaurant with black metal chairs and speckled red tables. A moped taxi sticks its nose out of a ceiling corner. Abundant veggie options. *Pad Thai* £5.25. Noodle or rice dishes £4.75-5.95. Open M-F noon-3pm and 6-11pm, Sa 6-11pm, Su 6-10pm. AmEx, MC, Visa.

Nam Bistro, 326 Upper St., N1 (tel. 354 0851). This joint offers savory Vietnamese specialties like *banh xeo* (£4.50), a crepe stuffed with beanshoots and prawns, and delicious *goi* salad (3.50). For the less adventurous, a delicious bowl of *pho* (£5) infused with fresh herbs and hearty stock should more than suffice. Open Tu-Su noon-3pm and 6-11pm. AmEx, MC, Visa.

Gallipoli, 102 Upper St., N1 (tel. 359 0630). Turkish delights abound at this loud and comfy local cafe. Most dishes under £5, from grilled meatball *Kofte* (£3.95) to falafel sandwiches (£2.35). Finish off your meal with a powerful and generous cup of java. Open daily 10am-11:30pm.

Patisserie Bliss, 428 St. John St., N1 (tel. 837 3720). Patisserie Bliss sends the taste-buds to a flaky and buttery heaven. Homemade quiche, croissant sandwiches, and fresh fruit tarts all under £1.75. Open M-Sa 8am-6pm, Su 8am-3pm.

Camden Town

Camden Town can be a bit grotty, especially in the wake of the weekend markets. Glamorous cafes and international restaurants, however, are interspersed along the main drag, **Camden High Street,** which runs south from the Camden Town tube station to Mornington Crescent and north to Chalk Farm, becoming **Chalk Farm Road. Tube: Camden Town,** unless otherwise noted.

Le Petit Prince, 5 Holmes Rd., NW5 (tel. 267 0752). Tube: Kentish Town. French/Algerian cuisine served in a whimsically decorated cafe/bar/restaurant. Illustrations from Saint-Exupéry's *Le Petit Prince* dot the walls, which are painted to simulate a cartoon-purple night sky. Generous plantain sauté starter £3.45, vegetarian couscous £5.45. Lamb, chicken, and fish dishes are slightly more expensive, but come with unlimited couscous and vegetable broth. Open daily 5:30pm-late.

Captain Nemo, 171 Kentish Town Rd., NW1 (tel. 485 3658). Tube: Kentish Town. Just remember that *Let's Go* would not blithely send you all the way to Kentish Town for "good chips." This seemingly unassuming Chinese/chippie take-away combo rocks your world with their tangy, delicious, great chips in curry sauce (£1.40). Open M-F noon-2:45pm and 5:30-11:30pm, Sa-Su 5:30-11:30pm.

The New Cultural Revolution, 43 Parkway, NW1 (tel. 267 2700). This modern and petite noodle bar boasts a wide variety of steaming soups and sautes. *Tong Mein* (noodle soup) £4.20, sauteed chicken, mushrooms, and chinese leaves £5. A cheap, quick, and comfortable break from the bustle of the markets. Open M-Th noon-3:30pm and 5:30-11pm, F noon-11pm, Sa-Su 1:30-11pm.

Nontas, 14-16 Camden High St., NW1 (tel. 387 4579). Tube: Mornington Crescent or Camden Town. This intimate restaurant is one of the best Greek venues in the city. The incomparable *meze* (£8.75) offers a seemingly endless selection of dips, meats, and cheeses. Other Hellenic fare includes kebabs (£5.40-5.70). Ouzerie in front serves luscious pastries, like *baklava* (£1.05) and Turkish coffee (85p). If the weather seems nice, ask the friendly owners to sit in the back garden. Open M-Sa noon-2:45pm and 6-11:30pm. Ouzerie open M-Sa 8am-11:30pm. AmEx, MC, Visa.

Parkway Pizzeria, 64 Parkway, NW1 (tel. 485 0678). Exit the station to the right, then head left along Camden High St. Parkway is the immediate right. Off the main thoroughfare, a pizzeria that local food critics routinely and aptly praise. Parquet floor and cool Art Deco mirrors. A basic pizza costs £3.80; the sublime *veneto* (£4.40) has exotic toppings like pine nuts, leeks, olives, anchovies, and capers. £3 min. when restaurant is full. Take-away available. Open daily noon-midnight. Visa.

Bar Gansa, 2 Inverness St., NW1 (tel. 267 8909). Exit the station to the right and head right; Inverness is the 1st left. A small tapas bar with bright walls, festive Spanish candles, and Mediterranean ornaments. Happy, glossy people of all ages linger over their food, coffee, and wine, both indoors and out. Ham, eggs, and chips (£3.95) and other breakfast fare available as late as 1:30pm. Tapas £2-3.95. Limited outdoor seating. Open daily 10am-late.

The Raj Vegetarian, 19 Camden High St., NW1 (tel. 388 6663). Experience the best of South Indian vegetarian cuisine for ridiculous prices. All you can eat lunch buffet £3.50. If that doesn't tempt your fancy, main dishes run a measly £2-3.50. Open M-F noon-3pm and 6-11:30pm, Sa-Su noon-11:30pm.

Ruby in the Dust, 102 Camden High St., NW1 (tel. 485 2744). Also at 70 Upper St., Islington. The young crowd here is drawn to the bright decor and jazzy milieu—floppy butterflies and flowers hang from every free inch of plaster. Burgers £6.30, daily specials £5-7.50. Wide vegetarian selection. Open M-F 10am-11pm, Sa 10am-11:30pm, Su 10am-10:30pm. MC, Visa.

Bharat, 23 Camden High St., NW1 (tel. 388 4553 or 387 0349). If on Sunday morning you yearn for spicy Tandoori food, the all-you-can-eat buffet (£5, children £3.95) is your bit o' heaven. Of notable value are the set lunches, which range from £3.50-4.50, and the fully loaded bar. Open M-Th noon-3pm and 6pm-midnight, F-Sa noon-3pm and 6pm-12:30am, Su noon-midnight. AmEx, DC, MC, Visa.

Marine Ices, 8 Haverstock Hill, NW3 (tel. 482 9003). Tube: Chalk Farm. Head left from the station. Superb Italian ice cream (£1.25 for a single, £1 each additional scoop) and sundaes. Also proffers an array of epic concoctions like Vesuvius (£5.85). Ice-cream counter open M-Sa 10:30am-11pm, Su 11am-10pm. Attached restaurant offers pizza (£5.20-6.60) and other entrees (£7-9). Open M-F noon-3pm and 5:30-11pm, Sa noon-11pm, Su noon-10pm. MC, Visa.

Hampstead

While this affluent district in northern London has an artsy bent, traditional teahouses for lunching ladies still do well, and a number of pricey brasseries, cafes and new restaurants dot the landscape. The food served in local restaurants is almost as important as the show-off space they provide for the ritzy young crowd. Many of these nosheries offer *al fresco* dining; you can see and be seen as you enjoy the slightly fresher air of nearby **Hampstead Heath.** The station is on the corner of Heath St. and Hampstead High St., unless otherwise noted. **Tube: Hampstead.**

Le Crêperie de Hampstead, 77 Hampstead High St., NW3. Outside the King William IV pub (see p. 130). This Hampstead institution is guaranteed nirvana. Paper-thin Brittany crepes made in front of your eyes by a real French crepe-maker in the tiniest van imaginable. Both sweet fillings (including Belgian chocolate, bananas, and Grand Marnier) and savory (spinach and garlic cream, mushroom, and cheese) £2-3. Open M-Th 11:45am-11pm, F-Su 11:45am-11:30pm.

Paris-London Cafe, 3 Junction Rd., NW3 (tel. 561 0330). Tube: Archway. Right across the street from the station, this *petit restaurant* serves gourmet French fare straight from *belle Paris*. Main dishes hover around £5. French staples like *moules marinieres* (£3.95), *escargots en beurre d'ail* (£5.25), or *soupe a l'oignon* (£2.10) will trick you into thinking you are on the Champs-Elysees. The low prices are a reminder that you're in Archway. 3-course *prix fixe* £9.95. Well worth the trip. Open M-Sa 9am-10:30pm.

Calzone, 66 Heath St., NW3 (tel. 794 6775). Turn right from the tube station. Petite bistro serves quality pizza, calzones, and a great view of the beautiful people strolling along Heath St. The simple entrees (from £4.75) are longtime Hampstead favorites. Open daily 10am-midnight. Three new locations: in Chelsea at 335 Fulham Rd. SW10 (tel. 352 9797); in Notting Hill at 2a/26 Kensington Park Rd. W11 (tel. 243 2003); in Islington at 35 Upper St. N1 (tel. 359 9191). AmEx, MC, Visa.

Coffee Cup, 74 Hampstead High St., NW3 (tel. 435 7565). A convenient place to take in the Hampstead scene. Marble tables on the sidewalk are packed by noon and stay that way until midnight. Not surprisingly, menu items are uniformly small and tasty (omelettes £3). Open M-Sa 8am-midnight, Su 9am-midnight.

The Pasta Place, 42 Heath St., NW3 (tel. 431 0018). This Hampstead pasta shop and Italian deli serves delicious take-away treats at East End prices. They'll microwave your food at no extra charge. Grab a pizza (£1.49), quiche (£1.39), or, if you can manage it, a plate of spaghetti (£2-3) and head to the Heath. Open M-F 10am-8pm, Sa-Su 11am-6pm.

Rumbold's Bakery, 45 South End Rd., NW3 (tel. 794 2344), across from the BR Hampstead Heath station. Handy for visitors to Keats House (see **Sights,** p. 191), just around the corner. First-rate pastries, often still warm from the oven. Chocolate croissant drizzled with chocolate and dusted with powdered sugar 90p. Apricot danish 85p. Gourmet sandwiches too. Open M-F 8am-5pm.

Polly's Cafe/Tea Room, 55 South End Rd., NW3 (tel. 431 7947), next door to Rumbold's. This cozy tea room offers cheap sandwiches (£2.20-2.85), a huge breakfast with bacon, sausage, and mushrooms with eggs and toast (£5.95), and, of course, tea (£1.10 per pot). Open daily 8am-7:30pm. MC, Visa.

Al's Deli, down the alley of the Hampstead Market fruit stall next to 78 Hampstead High St., NW3. Cheap and cheerful, a Hampstead institution. One of the most inexpensive and fresh lunches offered in this ritzy suburb. The three working-class residents of Hampstead lunch on the benches across from the counter. Sandwiches and pastries under £1. Open M-Sa 7am-2pm.

South of the Thames

Currently the locus of massive new economic, cultural, and transportation projects, the regions south of the Thames are experiencing a new vibrancy and vivacity. Unfortunately for the budget diner, the upscale nature of the development means that while exciting eateries abound, few are affordable, especially those by Butler's Wharf. Nonetheless, **Lower Marsh,** just inland from the river and west off Waterloo Rd., has managed to dodge the tide of progress, and has several tasty greasy spoons to fill you up for around £3. The **Gabriel's Wharf** complex has an energetic, if touristy feel and can be a good place to grab a light lunch or a snack. **Tube: Waterloo** or **Embankment.** From Embankment, cross the Hungerford footbridge.

The Fire Station, 150 Waterloo Rd., SE1 (tel. 620 2226). A converted Edwardian fire station (and former rave venue) houses a cavernous and exquisite restaurant. Delectable dishes crafted from seasonal ingredients without use of microwaves or freezers. Chalkboard menu changes twice daily. Main dishes, from pork and leek sausages to salmon steaks, are delectable but pricey (£7-9). Come from 12:30-2:30pm or 5:30-8pm for your choice of any two courses for £9.95. Full menu served M-Sa 12:30-11pm, Su 12:30-3:30pm. The excellent bar serves a wide variety of drinks including flavored vodka shots (£1.85). Open M-Sa noon-11pm, Su noon-10:30pm. AmEx, MC, Visa.

Freshly Maid Café, 79 Lower Marsh (tel. 928 5426). One of the cheapest cafes in the city, with fresh and tasty food. The specialty is the *moussaka,* served with chips and Greek salad £2.60. Also a huge grill selection—chicken burgers from £1.35. Small seating area. Open M-F 6am-7pm.

Marie's Café, 90 Lower Marsh (tel. 928 1050). Join the regulars who queue to get into this tiny English/Thai cafe. Sit at one of the tiny red diner booths and enjoy one of 3 different daily Thai entrees (£3). Traditional English dishes and breakfasts. Open M-F 7am-5pm, Sa 7am-3pm.

Gourmet Pizza Company, Gabriel's Wharf, Upper Ground, SE1 (tel. 928 3188). A slightly pricey chain restaurant with fabulous views of bustling Gabriel's Wharf. Outdoor seating on the waterfront during summer. Crazy pizza flavors, including English breakfast, Chinese duck, Thai chicken, and smoked salmon (£6.50-8.35). Choked with office workers at lunchtime. Open M-Sa noon-11pm, Su noon-10:30pm. AmEx, MC, Visa.

Brixton

The area within a three-block radius of the Brixton tube station has a wealth of budget dining options. **Brixton Market** is a perfect place to purchase fruits and vegetables, but you don't have to stray far from the action in the marketplace to enjoy an affordable sit-down meal. **Brixton Wholefoods,** 59 Atlantic Rd. (tel. 737 2210), sells a potpourri of grains, coffees, spices, juices, candies, and nuts, and has a large bulletin board chock full of community info (open M and F 9:30am-6pm, Tu-Th and Sa 9:30am-5:30pm). **Tube: Brixton.**

Café, Bar, and Juice Bar, 407 Coldharbour Ln., Brixton SW5 (tel./fax 738 4141). Wonderful secondhand bookshop and stylish cafe combination, specializing in Black and gay issues. Excellent selection of African, Caribbean, and African-American literature is complemented by comfy armchairs. F live poetry, Su jazz performances. Open M-Sa 11am-9pm. No credit cards.

Bah Humbug, the Crypt, St. Matthew's Church, Brixton Hill, SW2 (tel. 738 3184). Located in the atmospheric basement of St. Matthew's Church, and attached to the fashionable Bug Bar (see **Entertainment,** p. 247), this is a stylish restaurant serving an eclectic mixture of food. The savory crepes are particularly tasty: one filled with refried beans will set you back £6. Open M-F 5pm-11pm, Sa-Su 11am-11pm.

Satay Bar, 447-450 Coldharbour Ln., SW9 (tel. 326 5001). Cavernous Indonesian restaurant and bar. Try the smashing *kari ikan* (moderately spicy salmon curry; £4.95) which, like all of its main course compatriots, comes with large helpings of rice and salad. Or check out the live music, Su 7-10pm, M 6-9pm. Lunch menu served noon-3pm. Open M-Sa 1pm-11pm, Su noon-10:30pm.

Asmara Restaurant, 386 Coldharbour Ln., SW9 (tel. 737 4144). This chandeliered restaurant projects an atmosphere of slightly decayed elegance, and serves an eclectic mix of Ethiopian and Italian dishes. *Rigatoni alla carbonara* £3.50. Lamb stew with *injera* (Ethiopian sponge bread) £4.50. Open M-Th 5pm-midnight, F-Su 5pm-12:30am. AmEx, MC, Visa.

Nyam's, 423 Coldharbour Ln., SW9 (tel. 737 3581). Cheap grub, low prices, and central location make this take-away joint a perfect place to sate your hunger, however late it strikes. Fried chicken £2. Guinness punch £2.50. Open daily 24hr.

Phoenix, 441 Coldharbour Ln., SW9 (tel. 733 4430). Simple dishes and friendly management make a good place to lunch. Straightforward diner ambience, but with hip fellow diners. All sandwiches under £2, and come loaded on thick, hard dough bread from area bakeries. Sizeable breakfasts £2.70 (served 6:30am-12:30pm). Open M-Sa 6:30am-5pm.

Monsieur Tom's, 14d Market Row, SW9 (tel. 274 4747). Formerly Thompson's Bakery. This tiny, simple bakery smells divine and sells bread which manages to be soft and dense at once. Buy a loaf of the sweet hard dough bread with raisins and sink your teeth into heaven (£1). Pick up a huge, round loaf of the plain hard dough and you'll be fed for days (£1.20). Open M-Tu and Th-Sa 9am-5:30pm, W 9am-1pm.

Café Pushkar, Brixton Market, 16c Market Row, SW9 (tel. 738 6161). A great vegetarian staple amid the Brixton Market. Not *haute* cuisine, but daily hot specials are cheap and filling. Casserole of the day with two salads £4, students and UB40s £3.50 (served from 2-5pm). Open M-Tu and Th-Sa 9:30am-5pm, W 9:30am-1pm.

Kim's Café, Brixton Market, 15 Market Row, SW9 (tel. 978 8515). Casual cafe garishly decked in red and green—looks like an old American diner. Affable management and crowd of regulars makes you feel right at home. Breakfast special £3.40. Open daily 8:30am-5pm.

Stop Gap, 500a Brighton Terrace, SW9 (tel. 737 5204). Right behind Red Records on Brixton Rd. Affordable sandwich bar 75p-£2.75. Jerk chicken and other hot dinners with choice of sides £4.89. Large salads £3.20. Stools, but no tables. No smoking. Open daily M-Th 7:30am-midnight, F-Sa 24hr.

Docklands

The Docklands plays host to hundreds of thousands of hungry corporate types during the weekdays. Naturally, it has a great number of the somewhat bland, though not quite cheap, sandwich shops which follow downtown corporate centers around the world, as well as a smattering of more expensive watering-holes catering to those expense-account execs requiring a three-martini lunch or post office round of gin & tonics. The area around **Canary Wharf** (DLR: Canary Wharf) is a good spot to pick up a quick bite. In the bowels of the complex is a **slick modern grocery store** featuring ready-to-eat meals at reasonable prices. Also see the pub listings for Docklands, these riverside establishments (many are hundreds of years old) offer grub in less sterile surroundings than the newer section of Docklands.

FOOD AND DRINK

St. George's of Mayfair Sandwich Shop, Turnberry Quay, E14 (tel. 537 4679). DLR: Crossharbour. Across the path from London Arena. Follow the bouncing suits to a cheap, delicious alternative to Docklands' more pricey restaurants. Fresh display of exotic salads, meats, and desserts will make choosing a sandwich pleasurably difficult. Tandoori chicken slices in sandwich £1.90. Open M-F 8am-5pm.

Farmer's Kitchen, Pier St., E14 (tel. 515 5901). DLR: Crossharbour or Mudchute. Located next to Mudchute Farm stables. Offers cheap food for hungry visitors. Breakfast items for less than £1. Open daily 10am-4:30pm.

The Pier Tavern, 299 Manchester Rd., E14 (tel. 515 9258). Tube: DLR Island Gardens. Exit right from the station and follow Manchester St. as it curves around until corner of Pier St. Or, from the main entrance of Mudchute Farm, it's about 1 block down the street. Inexpensive bar food in a quasi-upscale atmosphere. Wheelchair accessible. Open Mon.-Fri. 11:30am-11pm, Sat. noon-11pm, Sun. noon-10:30pm. Serves food M-F noon-2:30pm and 7-9:30pm, Sa-Su noon-5pm. MC, Visa.

Windsor and Eton

The Waterman's Arms, just over the bridge into Eton and to the left at Brocas St. next to the Eton College Boat House (tel. (01753) 861 001). A traditional public house (circa 1542) and a favorite of the locals. Delicious cod, chips, and salad £4.15. Guinness £2.05 per pint. Open M-Sa noon-2:30pm and 6-11pm, Su noon-3pm and 7-10pm.

Michael's The Eton Bakery, 43 Eton High St. (tel. (01753) 864 725). Eton High St. is the continuation of the bridge from Windsor. An old-time, neighborhood bakery selling fresh n' cheap baked goods. Large loaves of farmhouse bread £1.02. Mixed fruit pies £1.50, tarts 26p. Buy stale bread to feed the ducks (10p). Take-away only. Open M-F 7:30am-5pm, Sa 7:30am-4:30pm, Su 11am-4:30pm.

The Courtyard Coffee Shop, 8 King George V Pl. (tel. (01753) 858 338), turn left out of the Riverside station. A little place in Royal Windsor. Homemade scones, soup, and quiche. Fresh sandwiches £1.75-2.90. Sit in the outdoor courtyard or inside for English cream tea (£3.50). Open daily 8am-5:30pm.

The Two Brewers, 34 Park St. (tel. (01753) 855 426). Pub just outside of the entrance to the Great Park—a perfect place to pick up a delicious take-away ploughman's lunch (£4.50) or sandwich (£2.50 and up). Open M-Sa 10:30am-11pm, Su noon-10:30pm.

Castle Café, 4 River St. (tel. (01753) 830 254). Burgers, meat (£1.70) and veggie (£2). Spicy kebab rolls £2. Cheap, filling food. Sit on the river's bank or lounge on the spacious patio in front. Open Su-Th 8am-8pm, F-Sa 8am-midnight.

Golders Green

Patrons of the Hampstead Heath hostel will be hard pressed to find cheap eats in this suburb of London. However, the Jewish residents have made Golders Green the best place for kosher and Israeli cuisine in the city. Though many Jewish establishments close for the Sabbath on Friday evenings, during the summer, when the Jewish sabbath terminates past sunset at 10:30pm, many restaurants remain open on Saturday nights until 4am, making Golders Green a popular place for starving late-night teens. Most restaurants are located up a few blocks on **Golders Green Road.** Also on Golder's Green Rd. are stores selling "Elite" and "Osem" brand foodstuffs imported from Israel—this is the place to find Bazooka gum with Hebrew cartoons. **Tube: Golders Green.**

Daniel's Bagel Company, 12-13 Hallswelle Parade, Finchley Rd. (tel. (0181) 455 5826). Walk under the tube's bridge and continue straight for about 20 minutes. The bakery is on the right. The walk is long, but worth it. Best bagels in the world (25p). Open Su-Th 7am-9pm, F 7am-1 hr. before sunset.

Blooms Restaurant, 130 Golders Green Rd. (tel. (0181) 455 3033). "Think Tradition! Remember—Kosher!" admonishes Bloom's motto. Neil Diamond, Bob Dylan, Golda Meir, and various royals have sampled *kneidlach* soup, latkes, and gefilte fish at this *fleischig* (non-dairy) haven. Fried gefilte fish £3.80. Open Su-Th noon-midnight, F noon-3pm (winter until 2pm), Sa after Sabbath (around 10pm)-4am.

Dizengoff, 118 Golders Green Rd. (tel. (0181) 458 7003). Gourmet kosher Israeli cuisine. As upscale as chopped liver can get. Open Su-Th noon-11:30pm, F noon-3pm.

Carmelli's Bagel Bakery, 126-128 Golders Green Rd., is a late-night wonderland of delicious kosher sweets and bagels. Scrumptious cinnamon yeast cake £3.50. Open daily 7am-1am.

FOOD AND DRINK

NOTABLE CHAINS

Nowadays much of the cheapest urban cuisine is to be found at chains. McDonald's and Burger King do not hold the world franchise market hostage. As prices rise in London's central areas, the high streets are becoming congested with inexpensive, somewhat gourmet franchises. So, before you order another Big Mac Meal, *Let's Go* recommends you check out the following chains. The establishments listed have locations all over the city, but hours and prices may vary.

Pret a Manger. In ten short years, this bustling chrome and metal sandwich shop has grown to dominate the London franchise scene. And no wonder: despite its increasing size, the chain remains dedicated to quality. Everything Pret serves is made of the freshest, most organic ingredients. Both sandwiches and salads are nicely balanced. The chicken breast and avocado (£2.35) and hummos, pepper, and onion sandwich (£1.85) will both sate the most discerning palates. The deluxe sushi pack (£4.95) is inexpensive and satisfying. For dessert, try the freshly baked *pain au chocolat* or almond croissant (85p) and wash it all down with a cappucino, mocha, or hot chocolate (99p). Eat-in prices are slighly more expensive (the few pence aren't worth the ambience). Located at 100 Tottenham Ct. Rd (tel. 631 0014), among other branches. Many branches are closed for dinner.

The Dome Brasserie. A brasserie straight from Paris. The star of this chain is its 3-course *prix fixe* for £4.99, which changes daily. On the day it was reviewed, the *prix fixe* started with a parmesan and artichoke filo, continued with grilled smoked mackerel and mussels with seasonal vegetables marinated in a tomato and Rosemary oil, and concluded with white chocolate cheesecake. *C'est magnifique!* Fresh salads £4.95-6.95. Branches include 2 Long Acre location (tel. 379 8650).

Cafe Pasta. Generally found in rather ritzy areas, this chain serves healthy portions of Italian food at reasonable prices to and from the beautiful people. The atmosphere matches the fresh, light fare. Pastas start around £5. Soho branch at 184 Shaftesbury Ave. (tel 379 0198).

Marks & Spencer. This chain department store and supermarket always has a wide selection of sandwiches and salads from which to choose. The chicken *tikka* (£1.85) is a popular favorite. Cola is only 19p. Fresh orange juice (69p) and lemonade (43p) are also notably inexpensive. Chocolate mousse 35p. And if you can't find what you want at the sandwich shop, you are in a supermarket after all. Kensington branch at 99 Kensington High St. (tel. 938 3711). (See **Shopping,** p. 255.)

Pierre Victoire. Popular brasserie chain offers inexpensive Parisian fare in expensive London neighborhoods. French staples like seafood *pot au feu* and smoked mackerel pâté. Menu changes daily. *Prix fixe* 2 course lunch £4.90. Branch at 19 Notting Hill Gate (tel. 460 4488). MC, Visa.

Pizza Express. Gourmet pizza establishment serves pastas and pizzas throughout London. All pizzas are thin crust and covered in fresh fancy ingredients, like prosciutto, artichoke, and cherry tomato. Prices range from £5-10. Branch at 10 Dean St. (tel. 437 9595). MC, Visa.

GROCERIES AND SUPERMARKETS

Tesco and **Sainsbury's** are the two largest chains of supermarkets. Tesco branch at 21 Bedford St. (tel. 853 7500); Sainsbury's branch at 158a Cromwell Rd. (tel. 373 8313). Larger branches come complete with bakery, cafe, and housewares. Other chains include **Europa, Spar, Budgens, Safeway,** and **Asda**. If you're willing to spend a bit more, then you might consider **Marks and Spencer**, which introduced Britain to the concept of baby tomatoes, potatoes, and more cute produce. If you're up all night, **Hart's** is open 24hr. And if you're willing to splurge, the foodhalls of **Harrods, Harvey Nichols,** and **Fortnum and Mason's** are attractions in their own right.

PUBS AND BARS

> *"Did you ever taste beer?"*
> *"I had a sip of it once," said the small servant.*
> *"Here's a state of things!" cried Mr. Swiveller, "She never tasted it—it can't be tasted in a sip!"*
>
> —Charles Dickens, *The Old Curiosity Shop*

London, like much else in life, is far more fun after a few beers. In recognition of this phenomenon, the social institution that is the English pub was created centuries ago, coddling tipplers of all affiliations with mahogany paneling, soft velvet stools, and brass accents. Sir William Harcourt observed that, "As much of the history of England has been brought about in public houses as in the House of Commons," and this historic import has waned little through the centuries. While taverns and inns no longer serve as staging posts for coaches and horses, pubs remain meeting-places, signposts, and bastions of Britannia. And even if you don't see or make history, pubs provide an excellent place to get bloody pissed.

British pubs continue to evolve, as they are now beginning to offer a full bar selection, though most still specialize in beverages of the beer family. If you thirst for cocktails, martinis, or mixed drinks, you're better off visiting a **bar.** London bars offer later hours, less traditional decor, and higher prices—visit them during happy hour (around 5:30-7:30pm) for the best drink deals. The listings below include both bars and pubs; names alone should indicate which is which.

Let crowd and atmosphere, rather than price, be your guide in selecting a pub. The difference (per pint) between drinking like a lord (in a classy, "expensive" pub) and drinking like a pauper (in a sleazy dive) is seldom more than 40p—by the time you save up enough to afford that sandwich, you'll have forgotten you wanted it. Pubs closely reflect their neighborhoods: touristy (and overpriced) near the inner-city train stations (Paddington, Victoria, etc.), stylish and trendy in the West End, gritty and cheap in the East, and suit-packed in the City. Once you've found a good pub, don't be afraid to leave—making a circuit, or **pub crawl,** is fun, and lets you experience the diversity of a neighborhood's nightlife.

The "last order" bells that ring through the streets of London at 10:50pm testify to the lamentable truth that British pubs close miserably early. Don't let these bells ring your evening's death knell, however. Take a tip from the locals and begin drinking when the pubs open at 11am. Or hustle to a bar or a club before 11pm, after which they begin to charge a cover (or raise an existing one). Though liquor laws, especially on Sundays, continue to relax, most pubs are open only 11-12 hours per day. The pubs around **Smithfield Market** are a notable exception, opening at *7:30am* for English breakfast. Your average pub serves from 11am-11pm Monday through Saturday in order to get lunchtime and afternoon business. Sundays, most pubs are open from noon to 10:30pm.

Beer is the standard pub drink. Many pubs are "tied" to a particular brewery and only sell that brewery's ales. **Free houses** sell a wider range of brands. In either case, beer is "pulled" from the tap in a dizzying variety of ways. All draughts, ales, and stouts are served "warm"—at room temperature—and by the pint or half-pint. Beware this so-called "half-pint"—though it costs half as much as a full pint, it mysteriously contains less than half the volume. **Bitter** is the staple of English beer, named for the sharp hoppy aftertaste. **"Real ale,"** naturally carbonated (unlike most beer) and drawn from a barrel, retains its full flavor. Brown, mild, pale, and India pale ale all have a relatively heavy flavor with noticeable hop. **Stout** is rich, dark, creamy, and virtually synonymous with the Irish superstout, **Guinness.** If you can't stand the heat, try a **lager,** the European equivalent of American beer. Bottled beer is always more expensive than draft, and American beers are unusually expensive (e.g. in the bizarro utopia of English drinking, Budweiser costs more than Foster's, which in turn costs more than Heineken which in turn costs more than Guiness). **Cider,** English wine, is a potent apple drink. Among the more complex liquids appearing at a pub near you are the **shandy,** a refreshing combination of beer and fizzy lemonade; **black and tan,** beer and stout layered like a parfait; **black velvet,** a mating of Guinness and champagne; and **snakebite,** a murky mix of lager and cider, with two drops of grenadine.

Those who don't drink alcohol should savor the pub experience all the same; fruit juices, colas, and sometimes low-alcohol beers are served. Buy all drinks at the bar—pub barkeeps are not usually tipped, unless you're trying to chat them up. Prices vary greatly with area and even clientele. Generally, a pint will set you back £1.80-2.50. Along with food and drink, pubs often host traditional games, including darts, pool, and bar billiards, an ingenious derivative of billiards played from only one end of the table. More recently, a brash and bewildering proliferation of video games, fruit (slot) machines, and extortionary CD jukeboxes have invaded pubs.

Look before you buy pub food. Pubs now serve anything from Thai food to burgers, some of which can be quite good. Quality and prices vary greatly, with virtually no relation between the two. **Steak and kidney pie** or **pudding** is a mixture of steak and kidney, mushrooms, and pastry or pudding crust. A **cornish pasty** is filled with potato, onion, and often meat. **Shepherd's pie** consists of minced beef or lamb with onion, saddled with mashed potatoes, and baked. A **ploughman's lunch** means portions of bread, cheese, and pickled onions. **Mash** is British for "mashed potatoes." It comes coated with "liquor," (a parsley-flavored green sauce), with sausages **(bangers and mash),** or with cabbage **(bubble and squeak).**

For a selection of gay pubs, see **Bisexual, Gay, and Lesbian London**, p. 264.

Of Dogs and Ducks

Pubs are an aspect of the London cityscape that is impossible to miss—there's a place to stop and tipple on virtually every street corner. With titles like "The Doghouse," pub names, however, appear to be mysteriously unrelated to the offerings inside. But occasionally there are explanations behind these otherwise random strings of words. Many pub names are actually imbued with religious meaning: monks were among the first to brew beer in England (until Henry VIII abolished the monasteries entirely in 1534). Pub names with the word "bell" in them often referred to nearby church or monastery ringers; Christian religious icons such as lambs and doves soon found their way onto pub signs, then into the names themselves. Even the unlikely name "The Bull" has a religious derivative, "bull" being a corruption of the Latin word for monastery. Pubs also tried to align themselves with nobility; some, like the "King William IV" pub, are named after individual royal figures. It was often to impractical, however, to constantly shift names with the political tides, so many pubs adopted general terms associated with the monarchy, such as "The Crown" and "The King's Head." To align themselves with noble families, pubs often took the names of the creatures that appeared on a family coat-of-arms; the lion was a popular example of this phenomenon. Yet not all pubs named for animals are derived from the rich and powerful. Some, like the "Dog and Duck" refer to the sport of duck hunting; others, such as "The Nag's Head," announced that horses were stabled nearby. "The Water Rats" referred to neither water nor rats—actors and theater workers were members of "The Royal Order of the Water Rat," and would often enjoy a pint there.

Soho and Piccadilly

The Dog and Duck, 8 Bateman St., W1 (tel. 437 4447). Tube: Tottenham Ct. Rd. Frequent winner of the Best Pub in Soho award, its size keeps the crowd down (or at least out on the street). Local professionals crowd in at lunch for the conscientious staff's cheap pints (£1.95-2.20). Evenings bring locals, actors on the way home, and, yes, some tourists. Why dog and duck? Look closely at the tiles that line the walls. Open M-F noon-11pm, Sa 6-11pm, Su 7-10:30pm.

The Three Greyhounds, 25 Greek St., W1 (tel. 287 0754). Tube: Leicester Sq. This tiny, medieval-styled pub provides personality and a welcome respite from the endless posturing of Soho. 1996 winner of the Best Pub in Soho award. Good food as well. Open M-Sa 11am-11pm, Su noon-10:30pm.

The Coach and Horses, 29 Greek St., W1 (tel. 437 5920). Tube: Leicester Sq. Tiny and cheap, this is the way pubs used to be. Filled with locals. Bitter is £1.35 all day, sandwiches £1. Open M-Sa 11am-11pm, Su noon-10:30pm.

The Porcupine, 48 Charing Cross Rd., WC2 (tel. 836 0054). Tube: Leicester Sq. The West End's most diverse pub: young folks on the 1st floor generate smoke and noise against a background of clubby dance music. Meanwhile their parents peck at tasty pre-theater pub meals (£4.50-5.50) upstairs. Live music on Sundays. Pints: lager £2.45-2.80, bitter £2.25. Food available M-F noon-3pm and 6-9pm, Sa-Su noon-6pm. Open M-Sa noon-11pm, Su noon-10:30pm. MC, Visa (restaurant only).

Riki Tik, 23-24 Bateman St., W1 (tel. 437 1977). Tube: Leicester Square, Tottenham Ct. Rd., or Piccadilly Circus. A hyped, hip, and tremendously swinging bar specializing in flavored vodka shots; chocolate is a house favorite (£2.60). The decor is George Jetson on acid, the crowd is swish, and the drink prices are eye-popping. But come during happy hour (W-Sa noon-8pm) and the deliciously fruity cocktails are a near-bargain at £6.50 per pitcher. Sandwich bar upstairs is open noon-5:30pm. Open M-Sa noon-1am. £3 cover after 11pm. MC, Visa.

The Salisbury, 90 St. Martin's Ln., WC2 (tel. 836 5863). Tube: Leicester Sq. A dramatically decorated pub in the heart of the theater district; ornate glass and gilt bewilder as the beers slip down. Business people and tourists by day, a younger crowd by night sits amongst the velvet folds and frosted glass. Pints of Theakston's Bitter £2.18, Calder's Ale (new on tap) £2.51. Open M-Sa noon-11pm, Su noon-10:30pm.

Sherlock Holmes, 10 Northumberland St., WC2 (tel. 930 2644). Tube: Charing Cross. Upstairs replicates Holmes' 221b Baker St. den. Hosts relics to thrill tourists as well as Holmes fiends—tobacco in the slipper, correspondence affixed to the mantelpiece with a dagger, and the Hound of the Baskervilles's head. Sherlock Holmes Ale £2 per pint. Open M-Sa 11am-11pm, Su noon-10:30pm.

Covent Garden

Crown and Anchor, 22 Neal St., WC2 (tel. 836 5649). Tube: Covent Garden. One of Covent Garden's most popular pubs. The crowd, a young mix of the down-and-out and the up-and-coming, perches on kegs or sits on the cobblestones outside, forming a mellow oasis in the midst of Neal St.'s bustling pedestrian zone. Open M-Sa 11am-11pm, Su noon-10:30pm.

Walkabout Inn, 11 Henrietta St. and 33 Maiden Ln., WC2 (tel. 379 5555). A block long, 2½ stories deep, this outback watering hole packs in fun-loving backpackers from the land down under every night. Weekday nights feature 2 for the price of 1 Steinlugers (£2.30). Also serves up Aussie specialties such as crocodile steak (£5.50) and Aussie burger with fresh emu (£4.50). Open daily 11am-11pm.

Belushi's, 9 Russell St., WC2 (tel. 240 3411). Tube: Covent Garden. More of a bar than a pub, and now a restaurant as well. Upbeat Aussie and Kiwi barmen and barmaids serve Budweiser and dance to 80s pop music, making for an unrepentantly cheesy, but howlingly good time for their young Oceanic and American clientele. Watch out for the 2min. specials; they've been known to call Jäger shots for 50p. Happy hour M-Sa 5-8pm and all day Su. Open daily 11am-midnight.

Freud Café Bar Gallery, 198 Shaftesbury Ave., WC2 (tel. 240 9933). Tube: Tottenham Ct. Rd. or Covent Garden. Invigorate your psyche in this downstairs cafe-bar-gallery. You'll be surrounded by old concrete-slab walls, slate tables, and month-long art shows (bar has its own curator). The music is ambient—lots of soothing, funky tunes. Home of famous Freud's lemonade (£1.95). By night Freud's gracefully morphs from cafe to bar. Cheaper than an hour on the couch, a beer here (£2-3) is better than therapy. Open M-Sa 11am-11pm, Su noon-10:30pm.

The Detroit, 35 Earlham St., WC2 (tel. 240 2662). Hidden away at the bottom of a flight of stairs, this dimly lit bar with Gothic vaults is a great place to finish off an evening out drinking; cocktails are a pricey £4-6.50. Live DJ nightly makes it worth the trip, and Sunday nights the bar often becomes a dance club (cover £4-8). Open daily 5pm-12am—call on the weekends for extended hours and club themes.

Maple Leaf, 41 Maiden Ln., WC2 (tel. 240 2843). Tube: Covent Garden. Maiden Lane is 1 block away from the Strand and runs parallel to it. "The only place outside of North America with Molson on tap" (£2.65 per pint) says it all, eh? Start a rousing chorus of "O Canada" or "Tom Sawyer" or "It's All Coming Back to Me" and make some new friends and/or foes. Food available noon-9:30pm. Open M-F 11am-11pm, Sa noon-11pm, Su noon-10:30pm.

The White Hart, 191 Drury Ln., WC2 (tel. 242 3135). Established in 1201, this is the oldest licensed pub in England. Traditional pub fare is served along with hand-pulled ales, as you recline in the plush red seats framed by wine-dark wood. Pool tables and big screen TV to boot! Open M-Sa 11am-11pm.

Roundhouse, 1 Garrick St., WC2 (tel. 836 9838). Tube: Leicester Sq. or Covent Garden. This horseshoe-shaped pub is pleasant in the afternoons and late evenings, but beware the 5pm rush. In summer, the crowd spills outside. Pints £2.05-2.50. Open M-Sa 11am-11pm, Su noon-10:30pm.

Lamb and Flag, 33 Rose St., WC2, (tel. 497 9504), off Garrick St. Tube: Covent Garden or Leicester Sq. Rose St. is off Long Acre, which runs between the 2 tube stops. Traditional old English pub, with no music and still separated into 2 sections—the public bar for the working class, and the saloon bar for the businessmen, though today the classes mix. Filled with regulars who have been coming 'ere for years. Look for their names on the brass plaques on the bar. Live jazz upstairs Su from 7:30pm. Open M-Th 11am-11pm, F-Sa 11am-10:45pm, Su noon-10:30pm.

Nag's Head, 10 James St., WC2 (tel. 836 4678). Tube: Covent Garden. A favorite of London's theater crowd. Always busy, you may need a partner to get in—sometimes they'll call "couples only." The round, light beige booths recall airport lounges. Open M-Sa 11am-11pm, Su noon-11pm. Credit cards for food only (traditional English lunches offered noon-2:30pm).

Kensington and Chelsea

The Scarsdale, 23a Edward Sq., W8 (tel. 937 1811). Tube: High St. Kensington. Walk down High St. and turn left onto residential Edward Sq. When you see people sitting outside in a sea of flowers and ivy, contentedly throwing back a few pints, well, you've found it. Don't be thrown off by the fact that it looks like a house. Good food during meal times. Open M-Sa noon-11pm, Su noon-10:30pm.

World's End Distillery, 459 King's Rd. (tel. 376 8946), near World's End Pass before Edith Grove. Tube: Sloane Sq. This classy pub dates back to 1689 when it became renowned for its tea garden. Now a variety of ages enjoy pints in the comfy bookshelf-lined booths. Comedy every Sunday night at 8pm, £3.50 for adults, £2 concessions. Open M-Sa 11am-11pm, Su noon-10:30pm.

The Chelsea Potter, 119 King's Rd., SW3 (tel. 589 0262). Tube: Sloane Sq. Walk up Kings Rd. At the Safeway, turn onto Tryon St. and walk up a few blocks. This pub's name reflects its history as a haven for ramshackle Chelsea artists throwing pots and living on their trust funds. Noisy outdoor tables. Pints of Foster's £2.15. Open M-Sa 11am-11pm, Su noon-10:30pm.

The Goat in Boots, 333 Fulham Rd. Tube: South Kensington. Take Onslow to Fulham and walk for about 20min. Multi-level bar attracts a young, fun-lovin' crowd. Drink specials each night (W £1 vodka shots, M and Tu half-price cocktails). Foosball! Open M-Sa 11:30am-11pm, Su noon-10:30pm.

Cadogan Arms, 218 King's Rd., SW3 (tel. 352 1645), near Old Church St. Tube: Sloane Sq. or Victoria, then Bus #11 or 22. Low timbers taken from an old church mixed with various colorful flags and videogames give this pub a bipolar personality. Nonetheless, the artificial but effective country feel is a retreat from the trendiness and business that is King's Rd. Swell TV setup and pool table. Large burgers under £3. Open M-Sa 11am-11pm, Su noon-10:30pm.

The King's Head and Eight Bells, 50 Cheyne Walk, SW3 (tel. 352 1820). Tube: Sloane Sq. or South Kensington. Take any bus down King's Rd., get off at Oakley St., walk toward the river, and turn right on Cheyne Walk. Richly textured 16th-century pub where Thomas More would have a jar with his dangerous friend Henry VIII. Carlyle's house is just around the corner. Offers wide selection of beers on tap, including heavenly Hoegaarden (£3.30 per delicious pint). Open M-Sa 11am-11pm, Su noon-10:30pm.

Bar Central, 316 King's Rd. (tel. 352 0025). Tube: Sloane Sq. An electric blue facade with yellow, neo-Doric columns welcomes the thirsty to this cosmopolitan full bar and brasserie. Open M-Sa 11am-11pm, Su 11am-10:30pm.

Earl's Court

The King's Head, 17 Hogarth Pl., SW5 (tel. 244 6722). Tube: Earl's Ct. From Earl's Ct. Rd., head east on Childs Walk or Hogarth Pl. The place to get loose. Tourists pack into this classic, smoky pub. Real ale (pint £2), and a passable wine list. Open M-Sa 11am-11pm, Su noon-10:30pm.

The Prince of Teck, 161 Earl's Ct. Rd., SW5 (tel. 373 3107). Tube: Earl's Ct. Aussie headquarters. Door sign says it all: "G'day and welcome to the land of Oz." Some love it, some hate it. Restaurant and lounge bar upstairs serves a passable lunch from 11am-3pm. Pint of Fosters £2.15. Open M-Sa 11am-11pm, Su noon-3pm and 7-10:30pm.

Bloomsbury

The Old Crown, 33 New Oxford St., WC1 (tel. 836 9121). Tube: Tottenham Ct. Rd. A thoroughly untraditional pub. Cream-colored walls, faded pine-green bar, green plants, and funky brass crowns that suspend light fixtures from the ceiling. The lively crowd spills out into the outdoor seating, creating a babble of voices above the cool jazz playing in the background; quieter upstairs. Homemade food from £2.75. Open M-Sa 10am-11pm.

Cittie of Yorke, 22 High Holborn, WC1 (tel. 242 7670). Tube: Holborn. Built in 1430, the clock and half-timbered facade of this watering hole conceal a cavernous interior replete with enormous ale casks and intimate booths. Standard pub fare from £4.25. Open M-Sa 11:30am-11pm. AmEx, MC, Visa.

Lord John Russell Pub, 91 Marchmont St., WC1 (tel. 388 0500). Tube: Russell Sq. The exact point where the bustle of Marchmont St. flows into the residential calm of nearby Cartwright Gardens. Calm and pleasant. Drink a well-drawn pint of Director's bitter (£2.20) under the watchful eye of the former Lord John Russell football club. Ploughman's lunch £3.75. Open M-Sa 11:30am-11pm, Su noon-11pm.

The Lamb, 94 Lamb's Conduit St., WC1 (tel. 405 0713). Tube: Russell Sq. E.M. Forster and other Bloomsbury luminaries used to tipple here. Discreet cut-glass "snob screens" (holdovers from Victorian times) remain. Limited outdoor seating and a no-smoking room tastefully decorated with old *Vanity Fair* caricatures. Food served noon-5pm. Open M-Sa 11am-11pm, Su noon-10:30pm. MC, Visa.

Princess Louise, 208 High Holborn, WC1 (tel. 405 8816). Tube: Holborn. This big pub isn't big enough to contain the jovial crowd that assembles after office hours. Built in 1872 and refurbished in 1891, the pub retains its ornate Victorian grandeur—beautiful tiles and etched mirrors line the walls. Fancy plasterwork columns support a decadent scarlet ceiling trimmed in gold. 8-10 real ales at all times. Pint of bitter £1.90-2.10. Open M-F 11am-11pm, Sa noon-11pm, Su noon-7pm.

The Water Rats, 328 Grays Inn Rd., WC1 (tel. 837 7269). Tube: King's Cross/St. Pancras. Ordinary appearance belies radical historical connections—this used to be one of Marx and Engels' favorite haunts. Tu-F nights a venue for indie rock, punk, and occasional acoustic gigs. 3 bands per night. Cover £5, concessions £3.50. Bands start at 9pm. Closed from 7:30-8:30pm during music nights. Open daily 8:30am-midnight.

Museum Tavern, 49 Great Russell St., WC1 (tel. 242 8987). Tube: Tottenham Ct. Rd. High coffered ceiling; spacious, plush atmosphere. Karl Marx sipped *Bier* here after banging out *Das Kapital* across the street in the British Museum reading room. The Star Tavern, which formerly occupied this site, was one of Cassanova's rendezvous spots. Open M-Sa 11am-11pm, Su noon-10:30pm.

Grafton Arms, 72 Grafton Way, W1 (tel. 387 7923). Tube: Warren St. Off the tourist trail, near Regent's Park. One of the best central London pubs for a relaxed pint. Caters to a lively London University student crowd. Eight real ales. Standard pub fare sold all day. Wine bar upstairs and rooftop patio. Open M-Sa 10am-11pm, Su 11am-3pm and 7-10:30pm. MC, Visa.

The City of London

Black Friar, 174 Queen Victoria St., EC4 (tel. 236 5650). Tube: Blackfriars. Directly across from the station. One of the most exquisite and fascinating pubs in all of London. The edifice's past purpose as a 12th-century Dominican friary is celebrated not only in the pub's name but in the intriguing arches, mosaics, and reliefs that line the pub's walls. Each relief describes some aspect of the daily life of the "merry monks," but the real treasure is found in the "side chapel" (located in back), where candles hang from monk-shaped brass holders against arches and mini-columns. Prices unfortunately reflect pub's popularity. Average pint £2.10. Lunch 11:30am-2:30pm. Open M-W 11:30am-10pm, Th-F 11:30am-11pm.

Ye Olde Cheshire Cheese, Wine Office Ct. by 145 Fleet St., EC4 (tel. 353 6170). Tube: Blackfriars or St. Paul's. On Fleet St., watch out for Wine Office Ct. on the right; small sign indicates the alley. Classic 1600s bar where Dr. Johnson and Dickens, as well as little-known Americans Mark Twain and Theodore Roosevelt, hung out. Today it's hot among businessmen and theater-goers. One of the few London pubs with the original wood interior intact. Note "Gentlemen Only" sign over first room on right, where famed Polly the Parrot insulted female drinkers in 3 languages. Open M-Sa 11:30am-11pm, Su noon-3pm.

The Shakespeare, 2 Goswell Rd., EC1 (tel. 253 6166). Tube: Barbican. Upstairs flooded with hip student crowd and businesspeople getting soused during and after work. Lunch served 11:30am-2:45pm, dinner 6:30-10pm. Pint of Bard's Brew £1.60. Open M-F 11am-11pm, Sa 11am-3pm. MC, Visa.

Fuego Bar y Tapas, 1 Pudding Ln., EC3 (tel. 929 3366). Tube: Monument. Turn right on Eastcheap St., then another right onto Pudding Ln. This snazzy executive watering hole compensates for lack of windowspace and cavernous basement location with neat lighting and lively evening events. Elevated walkway makes for great, smoky disco experience. Spanish music M nights, Th-F disco nights. Tapas £2-4. Dinner main course £6.90-10. Open M-F 11:30am-2am.

La Baguette at the Kings Head, 49 Chiswell St., EC1 (tel. 606 9158). Tube: Barbican. Head straight from tube exit through the tunnel. A cross between a Las Vegas casino and an airport executive lounge, Kings Head is distinguished from all the other slot machine-filled city pubs by its outstanding baguette shop in the rear of the pub. French bread baked daily on premises. Most popular sandwiches include brie and turkey (£2.95). Open M-Sa 11am-11pm, Su noon-10:30pm.

The East End

The Blind Beggar, 337 Whitechapel Rd., E1 (tel. 247 6195). Tube: Whitechapel. You may be sitting where George Cornell sat when he was gunned down by rival Bethnal Green gangster Ronnie Kray in 1966. Keep your head low. Spacious pub with conservatory and garden. Open M-Sa 11am-11pm, Su noon-10:30pm.

The Old Blue Anchor, 133 Whitechapel Rd., E1 (tel. 247 4926). A local bar replete with a ship's helm on the wall, velvet chairs, and twangy stuff comin' o'er the speakers. Big screen TV. Open M-Sa 11am-11pm, Su noon-10:30pm.

The Black Bull, 199 Whitechapel Rd., E1 (tel. 247-6707). A woody place with real East End flavor, as well as something of a sports mecca (a Newcastle sign hangs in the corner so Arsenal fans had best steer clear). Open M-F 11am-11pm.

Camden Town

The Engineer, 65 Gloucester Ave., NW1 (tel. 722 0950; fax 483 0592). Tube: Chalk Farm. Classic pub design with bright, flowery atmosphere and a sumptuous back garden that makes everybody feel relaxed. Pints £2.25. Open daily noon-11pm. Wheelchair accessible. MC, Visa.

Lock Tavern, 35 Chalk Farm Rd., NW1 (tel. 485 0909). Tube: Chalk Farm or Camden Town. A high-vaulted pub decorated with theater bills. Roof patio offers a view of the action at Camden Market and hosts the occasional summer BBQ. Beer £2.20. Wednesday night comedy club £3.50. Open M-Sa noon-11pm, Su noon-10:30pm.

The Buck's Head, 202 Camden High St., NW1 (tel. 284 1513). Tube: Camden Town. The huge windows are a less chaotic way to experience the markets. A clean and wholesome pub, open mornings for breakfast. Pints £2.20-2.40. Open M-Sa 9am-11pm, Su 9am-10:30pm.

Edinboro Castle, 57 Mornington Terr., NW1 (tel. 387 8916). Tube: Camden Town. Exit to the right and head left down Camden High St. Turn right on Delancey St. and follow it until it intersects with Mornington Terr. Friendly neighborhood place tucked away from the bustle of Camden's main drag. Pool table. Pints £2.20. Traditional Sunday lunch £4.95. Open M-Sa 11am-11pm, Su noon-10:30pm. MC, Visa.

The Good Mixer, 30 Iverness St., NW1 (tel. 916 6176). Tube Camden Town. A very untraditional pub that looks more like a warehouse from outside. The clientele is young and hip—no starched British lords here. 2 big pool tables. Pints £2.20. Open M-Sa 11am-11pm, Su 10:30pm.

Arizona, 2 Jamestown Rd., NW1 (tel. 284 4730). Tube: Camden Town or Chalk Farm. Medieval decor still lingers from its previous owners, but the new Southwestern motif is present in its spicy (and pricey) food and bottled beers. Happy hour (M-Th 4-7:30pm, F 3-6pm) offers 2 for 1 drink specials. Live DJ F-Sa nights. Open Su-Th 10am-midnight, F-Su 10am-1am.

Islington

Filthy MacNasty's Whiskey Café, 68 Amwell St. (tel. 837 6067). Tube: Angel. Exit the station left, then right onto Pentonville Rd., and turn left at Claremont Sq., which turns into Amwell. "O' lord make me pure but not just yet," sits above the patrons of this famously small Irish pub, providing the necessary excuse. Celtic drawings line the fire-colored walls; former Pogues singer Shane MacGowan frequently appears for last call. Renowned location for traditional Irish music on Sunday nights. A pint of Guinness £2.10. Runner-up in the Time Out 1997 Best Bar in London Award. Wheelchair accessible. Open daily noon-11pm.

Slug and Lettuce, 1 Islington Green, N1 (tel. 226 3864). Tube: Angel. Follow Upper St. Serves pretty elaborate food for a pub (linguine with spinach, mushrooms, and cream for £5.25) but this is Islington. Large and glossy, this has more of a bar feel than a pub. Open M-Sa 11:30am-11pm, Su noon-10:30pm. AmEx, MC, Visa.

The Tup, 80 Liverpool Rd., N1 (tel. 354 4440). Tube: Angel. Liverpool branches left off Upper St. directly across from the station. This pub recently traded in its Irish decor for smooth cream walls and large rustic pine tables. A young professional crowd frequents this colossal pub, often crowded for its occasional DJs. Open daily 11am-11pm. AmEx, MC, Visa.

Finnegan's Wake, 2 Essex Rd., N1 (tel. 226 1483). Tube: Angel. Essex Rd. splits off from Essex by Islington Green. People come here less for the faux-Irish atmosphere than for the comedy club downstairs Friday and Saturday nights. New material by local professionals, but beware: humor takes many forms. Show gets going about 9pm. Also hosts the "Big Word" poetry club with readings every Thursday night. Open daily 11am-11pm.

The Mitre, 130 Upper St., N1 (tel. 704 7641). Tube: Angel. Large and colorful, this fun pub caters to students and backpackers with its wide range of drink specials and theme nights. All night on Thursday and Sunday, and daily from 3-8pm, beers are £1.50 and tequila shots are £1. Monday night is pint for a pound night. The huge beer garden is popular on Monday and Thursday DJ nights. Open M-Sa 11am-11pm, Su 11am-10:30pm.

Camden Head, 2 Camden Walk, N1 (tel. 359 0851). Tube: Angel. Just past the tip of the Islington Green. A beautiful pub with cut-glass windows and plush, lived-in seats, founded in 1749. Wednesday and Saturday the outdoor patio bustles with thirsty visitors taking a break from bargain-hunting at the market. Beer £2.20. Comedy routines F-Sa night. Open M-Sa 11am-11pm, Su noon-10:30pm.

All-Bar-One, 1 Liverpool St., N1 (tel. 278 5906). Tube: Angel. Only the wood floors testify to this trendy, smooth pub's previous existence as a powerhouse indie dance club. A popular, slightly expensive chain with a surprising wine selection. Beer from £2.30. Open M-Sa 11:30am-11pm, Su noon-10:30pm. MC, Visa.

Hampstead and Highgate

King of Bohemia, 10 Hampstead High St., NW3 (tel. (0181) 435 6513). Tube: Hampstead. Traditional-looking pub serves up techno music to a young, upscale clientele that swarms to the outdoor seating in summer. The quieter back room, with skylights, vintage ads, and posters, is a pleasant place to down a pint and read one of the newspapers offered. Open M-Sa 11am-11pm, Su noon-10:30pm.

Bar Room Bar, 48 Rossyln Hill, NW3 (tel. (0181) 435 0808). Tube: Hampstead. Hampstead High St. turns into Rossyln Hill. The funky exotic paintings and sculptures for sale in this "art gallery bar" are complemented by the trendy, artsy clientele. Mellow coffee-house atmosphere by day; the menu features fresh pizza made in their wood-burning stove (£3.60-6.90). The rear garden, also lined with exquisite murals and shadowed by the Gothic church next door, makes for wonderful, quiet evening drinking. By night, the music pumps and the interior is candle-lit; don't miss the incredible chandelier. Open M-Sa 11am-11pm, Su 11am-10:30pm. MC, Visa.

The Holly Bush, 22 Holly Mount, NW3 (tel. (0181) 435 2892). Tube: Hampstead. From the tube climb Holly Hill and watch for the sharp right turn. The quintessential snug Hampstead pub in a quaint cul-de-sac. A maze of glass and wood serving pints from £1.55. Open M-F noon-3pm and 5:30-11pm, Sa noon-4pm and 6-11pm, Su noon-10:30pm. MC, Visa.

The Flask Tavern, 77 Highgate West Hill, N6 (tel. (0181) 340 7260). Tube: Archway. Near the hostel. Enormously popular on summer evenings and Sunday noon for its vast terrace seating. One of few cheap eateries in Highgate. Lunch served noon-2:30pm. Dinner served 6-9:15pm. Open M-Sa 11am-11pm, Su noon-10:30pm.

King William IV, 77 Hampstead High St., NW3 (tel. (0181) 435 5747). Tube: Hampstead. Famous gay pub (and parking spot of Crêperie de Hampstead, see **Restaurants,** p. 117) that attracts a mixed clientele. Hearty Sunday lunch served noon-4pm (£5.50). Open M-Sa noon-11pm, Su noon-10:30pm.

Spaniards Inn, Spaniards End, NW3 (tel. (0181) 731 6571). Tube: Archway, then Bus 210 along Spaniards Rd. Upscale pub on north edge of Hampstead Heath that has provided huge garden in summer and hearth in winter since 1585. Infamous patrons have included highwayman Dick Turpin and the Gordon rioters—drink carefully. Open M-Sa 11am-11pm, Su noon-10:30pm.

Hammersmith and Putney

There is reason to travel to Hammersmith or Putney for a drink: the pubs listed here are all on the waterfront and have outdoor seating with expansive views of the Thames. The Victorian bridges arching across the river are often lit beautifully at night, making this area a popular evening destination. To get to any of the pubs on Upper Mall, come out of the station and head left on Blacks Rd. Walk for five minutes, take any left (Angel Walk, Bridge Ave.), and you'll hit the river. To reach **Lower Richmond Road** pubs, take the tube to Putney Bridge (District Line) and cross the Putney Bridge. After you cross, Lower Richmond is on your right.

The Dove, 19 Upper Mall, SW6 (tel. (0181) 748 5405). Tube: Hammersmith. Make the trip to the 300-year-old tavern for a delicious lunch overlooking the Thames. Lovely vine-covered conservatory brings elegance to a couple of pints. Beers around £2.20. Open M-Sa 11am-11pm, Su noon-10:30pm. MC, Visa.

The Rutland Ale House, 15 Upper Mall, SW6 (tel. (0181) 748 5586). Tube: Hammersmith. Red neon sign reflects onto the Thames. Crowded with younger locals who spill out to the picnic tables on the river walk. Lots of pub food served 'til 9pm. Mushroom quiche £4. Open M-Sa 11am-11pm, Su noon-10:30pm.

Half Moon, 93 Lower Richmond Rd., SW15 (tel. (0181) 780 9383). Tube: Putney Bridge. Slightly trendy pub with bright blue and cherry wood walls about a block off the Thames. Known for daily live tunes in the back room (cover £2-7) and great DJs. W cover £2 for Ministry of Sound DJ. Live Jazz Su 1-4pm. Bitter £1.80. Open M-Sa noon-11pm, Su noon-10:30pm.

M Bar, 4 Lower Richmond Rd., SW15 (tel. (0181) 788 0345), in the Star and Garter. Tube: Putney Bridge. A monument of a riverside pub. Cavernous lounge with even larger windows is nearly always full of students and under-25s. If you exchange your glass for a plastic cup, you can take your ale for a walk along the Thames. Open M-Sa 11am-11pm, Su noon-10:30pm.

South of the Thames

George Inn, 77 Borough High St., SE1 (tel. 407 2056; fax 403 6613). Tube: London Bridge. A fine 17th-century galleried inn with multiple bars; the older equivalent of Victoria coach station. Now it's the last stop of the day for the suits of the South Bank, not to mention a major tourist haven. But still neat for a walk through history. Open M-Sa 11am-11pm, Su noon–10:30pm. MC, Visa.

Docklands

These riverside pubs have seen almost two millennia. Located away from Canary Wharf, they are reminders that the Docklands once served as the entry point to the city Joseph Chamberlain declared the "clearing-house of the world."

Prospect of Whitby, 57 Wapping Wall, E1, London Docks (tel. 481 1095). Tube: Wapping. 600-year-old pub with a truly sweet riverside terrace. Open ceilings and a rustic flagstone bar pale next to glorious Thamescape. Rather touristy. Open M-Sa 11:30am-3pm and 5:30-11pm, Su noon-3pm and 7-10:30pm.

The Dickens Inn, St. Katherine's Way, E1 (tel. 488-2208). Tube: London Tower or DLR: Tower Gateway. From the Tube, follow St. Katherine's Way to the river, then cut left through the Tower Thistle Hotel parking structure. Before entering the Dickens to have a drink, imagine 18th-century spice traders milling about on one of the Inn's 3-story balconies. Today, it's at once a busy and peaceful place to stop if you're checking out the Crown Jewels nearby. Bar food £2.95-4.55. Open M-Sa 11am-11pm, Su noon-10:30pm. AmEx, DC, MC, Visa.

Grapes, 76 Narrow St. (tel. 987 4396). Tube: Limehouse or Westferry. Another famous river pub that has seen the ebb and flow of Docklands activity for 500 years. Dickens wrote about it in *My Mutual Friend.* Upstairs dining room is quite expensive. Open M-F noon-3pm, Sat. 7-11pm, Su noon-4pm and 7-10:30pm.

The House They Left Behind (tel. 538 5102), across from the Grapes. Tube: Limehouse or Westferry. This welcoming pub is reputed to have been a haunt of Joseph Conrad's. Real East End flavor, offering half a pint of Courage ale for 90p, scrumptious ham, cheese, and pickle sandwich for £1.80. Open M-Sa noon-11pm.

TEA

One should always eat muffins quite calmly. It is the only way to eat them.
—Oscar Wilde, *The Importance of Being Earnest*

English "tea" refers to both a drink and a social ritual. Tea, the drink, is the preferred remedy for exhaustion, ennui, a row with one's partner, a rainy morning, or a slow afternoon. English tea is served strong and milky; if you want it any other way, say so. (Aficionados always pour the milk before the tea so as not to scald it.)

Tea, the social ritual, centers around a meal. Afternoon **high tea** includes cooked meats, salad, sandwiches, and pastries. "Tea," in the north of England, refers to the evening meal, often served with a huge pot of tea. **Cream tea,** a specialty of Cornwall and Devon, includes toast, shortbread, crumpets (a much tastier sort of English muffin), scones, and jam, accompanied by delicious clotted cream (a cross between whipped cream and butter). Most Brits take short tea breaks each day, mornings ("elevenses") and afternoons (around 4pm).

London hotels serve afternoon set teas, often hybrids of cream and high tea, which are expensive and sometimes disappointing. You might order single items from the menu instead of the full set to avoid a sugar overdose. Cafes often serve a simpler tea (pot of tea, scone, preserves, and butter) for a lower price.

Louis Patisserie, 32 Heath St., NW3 (tel. 435 9908). Tube: Hampstead. This intimate Hungarian confectionary and tea room thrills with a heavenly aroma and finger-licking Florentines (a candy conglomerate of almonds, cherries, and chocolate; £1.80). A variety of cakes, tarts, and teas are also available. Open daily 9am-6pm.

Georgian Restaurant, Harrods, Knightsbridge, SW1 (tel. 225 6800). Tube: Knightsbridge. A carefully staged event. Revel in bourgeois satisfaction as you enjoy your expensive repast inside or on the terrace (£15.50). Beautiful view of downtown Knightsbridge. Tea served M-Sa 3:45-5:15pm.

The Muffin Man, 12 Wrights Ln., W8 (tel 937 6652). Tube: High St. Kensington. Everything you dreamed a tearoom could be. Set cream tea £4.50. Min. £1.50 from noon-3:30pm. Open M-Sa 8am-5:30pm.

St. James Restaurant, at Fortnum & Mason's (see **Department Stores,** p. 255). Floors below, the madding crowd scrambles to purchase some of London's most famous teas, while you sip in this splendid enclave of glass and porcelain. Set tea £13.50, with champagne £18.95. Open M-Sa 3-5:15pm. AmEx, DC, MC, Visa.

The Orangery Tea Room, Kensington Palace, Kensington Gardens, W8 (tel. 376 0239). Tube: High St. Kensington. Light meals and tea served in the marvelously airy Orangery built for Queen Anne in 1705. Two fruit scones with clotted cream and jam £3.75. Pot of tea £1.70. Trundle through the gardens afterward, smacking your lips. Open daily 10am-6pm. MC, Visa.

The Ritz, Piccadilly, W1 (tel. 493 8181). Tube: Green Park. Universally known as *the* tea experience. Set tea: £23.50. Daily 3:30-5pm seatings. AmEx, DC, MC, Visa.

The Savoy, Strand, WC2 (tel. 836 4343). The elegance of this music-accompanied tea is well worth the splurge. Starve yourself before you go, then graciously wolf down the delicious tarts, scones, and sandwiches as the bemused waitstaff refills your tray time after time. Strict dress code—no jeans or shorts. If gentlemen "forget" their jacket, they'll be forced to borrow a garish red number from the cloakroom (necktie also preferred for gentlemen). Set tea £18.50. Tea served daily 3-5pm. Sa and Su book ahead. AmEx, DC, MC, Visa.

WINE BARS

John Mortimer's fictional barrister Horace Rumpole, who drinks every afternoon at Pommeroy's Wine Bar, habitually orders a bottle of "Château Thames Embankment." Unlike Rumpole's brand, much of the wine served in London's sleek wine bars lives up to neither its price nor its pedigree, and such establishments are, in the main, ghastly and pretentious. Nevertheless, we'd be remiss not to mention some stalwarts of the City-based wine bar scene. **Simpson's,** Ball Court, off 38½ Cornhill, EC3 (tel. 626 9985; tube: Bank) allows you to rub elbows with sharp-dressed banking brass, but make sure not to step on their briefcases, piled high at each entrance. Wine of the day costs £2.30 per glass. (Open M-F 11am-4pm, restaurant open M-F 11:30am-3pm.) At **Ball's Brother's,** Cheapside EC2 (tel. 248 2708; tube: St. Paul's), the dignified interior matches the plush, elegant taste of its red wines (from £3.20; open M-F 11:30am-9:30pm). To savor the true horror of wine bar culture, however, head over to **Dôme Bar and Café,** Ludgate Hill, EC3, a new establishment with gleaming gold surfaces and an unhealthy number of French affectations. *Un peu* pretentious? Ladies and gentlemen of the jury, you be the judge. Dôme also serves a *prix fixe* meal from noon-11pm for £5.95 (open M-F 8am-11:30pm, Sa-Su 11am-7pm). For more of the same, take a stroll down Carter Ln., and be bowled over by the number of similar upscale establishments. If you still hanker for more, try **La Reina** (tel. 248 2700) on Blackfriars Ln., EC1, a wine pub and tapas bar, with glasses of wine from £2.10 (open M-F 11am-8pm).

Sights

Those who journey to London in expectation of friendly, rosy-cheeked, frumpy, tea-drinking, Queen-loving gardeners may be astounded to find that London is equally the province of slinkily dressed, buff young things who spend their nights lounging around murky Soho cafes. London is an irrepressibly international city, where the first rumblings of rave culture, the Britpop explosion, and countless other movements began, and which still move swingers the world over. At the same time, those expecting non-stop hedonism may run headlong into an exquisitely British sense of propriety, morality, and culture. Pubs close at 11pm, Di in a bathing suit makes headlines, MPs resign over the smallest sexual peccadillos, and some of the hottest pick-up scenes are at the bookstores. Drunken revelers decked out in platform shoes and clubwear returning from a late night may stumble pass fur-hatted guards wearing the same traditional scarlet coats they have for centuries. Despite an off-and-on embrace of the avant-garde, change comes slowly to London.

7,000,000 citizens have created many Londons, various of which will appeal to differently-minded visitors. Those seeking **Royal London** will be busy bees indeed. If visions of stiff guards, flashy heraldry, burnished armor, and the like make your engine race we recommend the **Changing of the Guard** at **Buckingham Palace** (p. 149), **Hampton Court Palace** (p. 212), **Windsor Castle** (p. 215), and the **Tower of London** (p. 167). For an account of the Royal Family's recent struggles see p. 9.

No visit would be complete without time spent luxuriating in **Green London:** London's glorious parks and gardens. **Hyde Park and Kensington Gardens** (p. 174), **Kew Gardens** (p. 209), **St. James's Park** (p. 148), the **Hampstead Heath** (p. 191), and the gardens at **Hampton Court Palace** (p. 212) deserve special mention. For a complete list of the more notable gardens and parks see the listings beginning on p. 217.

England is remarkable for its homegrown religion and remarkable churches—architecture buffs will not want to miss the glorious places of worship which make up **Anglican London.** The oldest district—the City—is dotted with a number of churches open to visitors. A lovely day may be spent walking from church to church (see **The City of London** p. 159). Any tour of the City churches should include Wren's favorite, **St. Stephen Walbrook.** The two most famous houses of worship—gargantuan **St. Paul's** (p. 165) and ancient **Westminster Abbey** (p. 140)—showcase two completely different eras of English Christianity.

Historic London has spanned almost three millennia. History buffs should begin their travels at the **Museum of London** (p. 227) which gives an engaging account of the city's past. The **Tower of London's** walls have borne witness to much of the City's, and country's, turbulent past—from Guinivere's flight from an oversexed Mordred to the murder of the young Princes (p. 167). **Westminster Abbey** (p. 140) is the national repository of famous British corpses, the closest you may ever be to the great men of history. Today power has shifted from the Royals to the common folk—**Whitehall** (p. 146) and **Parliament** (p. 145) contain the literal seats of power. The **Docklands** (p. 196) and **South Bank** (p. 199) are both massive new building projects; both are designed to represent the London of the Future.

Cultural London may sound forbidding and boring, but it need not be. **Dickens** and **Keats** buffs will want to visit the museums which occupy their idols' former domiciles (see p. 191 for Keats and p. 187 for Dickens). The **British Library's** new digs will showcase rare manuscripts and fascinating exhibits—though completion won't be until March 1998, so the Library will remain in the **British Museum** (p. 186). London is a world famous **theater** venue (see p. 234). Students especially should take advantage of the many theater discounts.

Finally, London is a mecca for swingers everywhere. In the 1960s, *Time* magazine dubbed **"Swingin' London"** the center of a debaucherous new youth movement. Today's city guards this hedonistic flame—rave culture began here and London's clubs are second to none. Though pubs close absurdly early, there is more fun to be had after 11pm here than almost anywhere on earth (see **Nightclubbing** p. 246). **Soho** (p. 153) is center of the night scene—cafes and nightclubs swing all night and all day, attracting night owls and early risers. **Camden** (p. 183) and **Brixton** (p. 203) rage as well.

SUGGESTED ITINERARIES

- **Here's a brief overview of the major sights to take in depending on the length of your stay:**
- **One Day**—Take in the Houses of Parliament and Westminster Abbey. Tour Buckingham Palace, then stroll down the Mall toward Trafalgar Square to visit the National Gallery. Wander around Picadilly Circus, sip a pint at a nearby pub, and enjoy a late dinner in Soho or Chinatown.
- **Three Days**—first day as above. The second day, see the City of London: climb St. Paul's Cathedral for a stunning view, then take a Beefeater tour of the Tower of London. Dine in the East End for some of the best Indian food in the city. On the third day, head over to Bloomsbury and visit the British Museum, followed by the British Library and Madame Tussaud's. Stroll through Regent's Park and dine in chic Islington. Finish off the evening with theater and coffee in Covent Garden.
- **One Week**—first three days as above. Spend a day exploring the museums of Kensington and Knightsbridge. Head over to Harrods' department store and take-away a picnic meal to Hyde Park and Kensington Gardens. Visit the Tate Gallery, the Wallace Collection, and the Courtauld Gallery. Stroll through the greenery of Hampstead Heath and see Highgate Cemetery. Explore the South Bank: visit the HMS Belfast, Southwark Cathedral, and the London Dungeon and enjoy a show at Shakespeare's Globe Theatre. To learn more about the history of Britain and London itself, tour the Museum of London, the London Transport Museum, and the Imperial War Museum. Don't miss the vibrant ethnic neighborhoods of London, including Brixton, Golders Green, and the East End. Though it's impossible to see everything in London, don't hesitate to try.

TOURING

The characteristic of London is that you never go where you wish nor do what you wish, and that you always wish to be somewhere else than where you are.

—Sydney Smith, 1818

You can begin to familiarize yourself with the eclectic wonders of London through a good city tour. Most tour buses stop at Marble Arch and do not require reservations. The **Original London Sightseeing Tour** (tel. (0181) 877 1722) provides a convenient, albeit cursory, overview of London's attractions from a double-decker bus. *(Tours daily in summer 9am-7pm, winter 9:30am-5:30pm; £12, under 16 £6.)* Two hour tours depart from Baker St., Haymarket (near Piccadilly Circus), Marble Arch, Embankment, and near Victoria Station. Route includes views of Buckingham Palace, the Houses of Parliament, Westminster Abbey, the Tower of London, St. Paul's, and Piccadilly Circus. A ticket allows you to ride the buses for a 24-hour period—permitting visitors to hop off at major sights and hop on a later bus to finish the tour. Other companies have a hop-on hop-off policy, but be sure to ask how often buses circle through the route—Original London coaches come every five to 10 minutes.

Walking tours can fill in the specifics of London that bus tours run right over. With a good guide, a tour can be as entertaining as it is informative. Among the best are **The Original London Walks** (tel. 624 3978) which cover a specific topic such as Legal London, Jack the Ripper, or Spies and Spycatchers. *(Tours £4.50, students £3.50, accompanied children under 15 free.)* The two-hour tours are led by well regarded guides;

many consider this company to be the best in London. **Historical Tours of London** (tel. (0181) 668 4019; £4.50, concessions £3.50) also leads popular tours. Leaflets for these and others are available in hotels and tourist information centers. For meeting times, see the "Around Town" section of *Time Out* magazine. If you want to walk on your own, the *Time Out Book of Country Walks* (£9.99) is a wonderful collection of idyllic ramblings which includes a schedule for self-organizing groups.

If glancing at London from the top of a bus is unsatisfactory and hoofing it seems daunting, a tour led by **The London Bicycle Tour Company** (tel. 928 6838) may be the happy medium. They offer a Saturday tour of the East End and a Sunday tour of Middle London and Royal West. *(Easter-Oct. Sa-Su 2pm. Approximately 3½hr. £10; independent bike £2 per hour, £10 per day, £30 per week. Tube: Blackfriars or Waterloo. Tours depart from Gabriel's Wharf, 56 Upper Ground, SE1.)*

The double-decker Bus #11 (which is free to Travelcard holders, otherwise standard bus fare) cruises between the city's main sights. It is a very affordable alternative to the commercial tour buses, though it doesn't feature the commercial tour guides' somewhat engaging chatter. The #11 chugs between Chelsea, Sloane Sq., Victoria Station, Westminster Abbey and Houses of Parliament, Whitehall, Trafalgar Sq., St. Paul's, and various stops in the City.

CENTRAL LONDON

Westminster

The old city of Westminster, now a borough of London, once served as haven to a seething nest of criminals seeking sanctuary in the Abbey. A slum clearance program during Victoria's reign transformed the region into the array of brick and marble it is today. For the past 1000 years, Westminster has been the center of political and religious power in England. On weekdays, the streets still bear the traffic of civil service workers who desert the high-rise canyons on weekends, leaving it to the crowds of tourists who flock here to see some of London's more monumental architecture.

In the literal shadow of Westminster Abbey, **St. Margaret's** is the church that tourists point to and say "Is that the Abbey?" in surprised tones, until the more imposing Abbey which sits behind becomes visible. *(Open daily 9:30am-5pm when services are not being held.)* St. Margaret's has served as the parish church of the House of Commons since 1614, when Protestant MPs feared Westminster Abbey was about to become Catholic. John Milton, Samuel Pepys, and Winston Churchill were married here. The stained-glass window to the north of the entrance depicts a blind Milton dictating *Paradise Lost* to one of his dutiful daughters, while the stunning east window, made in Holland in 1501, honors the marriage of Catherine of Aragon to Prince Arthur. The post-WWII John Piper windows on the south side provide a marked contrast; entitled "Spring in London," they are appropriately composed in shades of gray. Beneath the high altar lies the headless body of Sir Walter Raleigh, who was executed across the street in 1618. The inscription on his memorial respectfully asks readers not to "reflect on his errors."

On the south side of the abbey cluster the buildings of the hoity-toity **Westminster School,** founded as a part of the Abbey. References to the school date as far back as the 14th century, but Queen Elizabeth officially founded it in 1560. The arch in Dean's Yard is pitted with the carved initials of England's most privileged schoolboys, among them Ben Jonson, John Dryden, John Locke, and Christopher Wren.

The 14th-century **Jewel Tower,** a surviving tower of the medieval Westminster Palace, stands by the southeastern end of the Abbey, across from the Houses of Parliament. *(Open daily Apr.-Sept. 10am-1pm and 2-6pm; Oct.-Mar. 10am-1pm and 2-4pm. Admission £1.50, concessions £1.10.)* Formerly Parliament's outsized filing cabinet and later the Weights and Measures office, it now contains eclectic exhibits ranging from bits of the original Westminster Hall to a Norman sword dredged from the moat. The

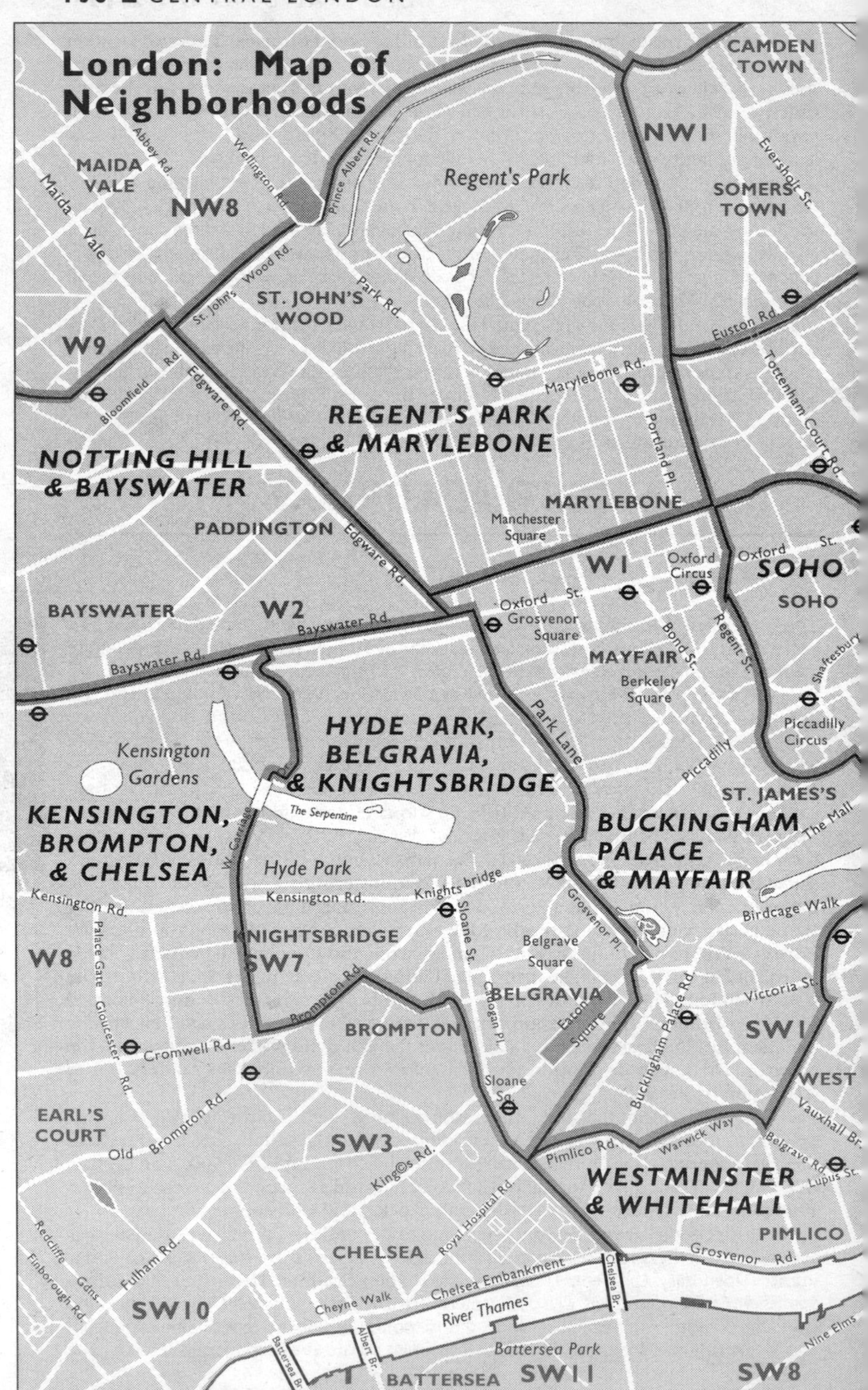
London: Map of Neighborhoods
CAMDEN TOWN
NW1
Regent's Park
SOMERS TOWN
MAIDA VALE
NW8
ST. JOHN'S WOOD
W9
REGENT'S PARK & MARYLEBONE
NOTTING HILL & BAYSWATER
MARYLEBONE
Manchester Square
PADDINGTON
W1
Oxford Circus
SOHO
BAYSWATER
W2
Grosvenor Square
MAYFAIR
Berkeley Square
HYDE PARK, BELGRAVIA, & KNIGHTSBRIDGE
Piccadilly Circus
Kensington Gardens
The Serpentine
ST. JAMES'S
KENSINGTON, BROMPTON, & CHELSEA
BUCKINGHAM PALACE & MAYFAIR
Hyde Park
KNIGHTSBRIDGE
W8
SW7
Belgrave Square
BELGRAVIA
Eaton Square
BROMPTON
SW1
Sloane Sq.
EARL'S COURT
SW3
WESTMINSTER & WHITEHALL
PIMLICO
CHELSEA
SW10
River Thames
Battersea Park
BATTERSEA
SW11
SW8
Abbey Rd.
Wellington Rd.
Prince Albert Rd.
Maida Vale
St. John's Wood Rd.
Park Rd.
Eversholt St.
Euston Rd.
Tottenham Court Rd.
Marylebone Rd.
Portland Pl.
Bloomfield Rd.
Edgware Rd.
Oxford St.
Bond St.
Regent St.
Shaftesbury
Bayswater Rd.
Park Lane
Piccadilly
The Mall
W. Carriage
Knightsbridge
Kensington Rd.
Sloane St.
Grosvenor Pl.
Birdcage Walk
Palace Gate
Gloucester Rd.
Brompton Rd.
Cadogan Pl.
Victoria St.
Buckingham Palace Rd.
Cromwell Rd.
Old Brompton Rd.
King@s Rd.
Royal Hospital Rd.
Pimlico Rd.
Warwick Way
Vauxhall Br.
Belgrave Rd.
Lupus St.
Redcliffe Gdns.
Finborough Rd.
Fulham Rd.
Grosvenor Rd.
Chelsea Br.
Chelsea Embankment
Cheyne Walk
Albert Br.
Battersea Br.
Nine Elms

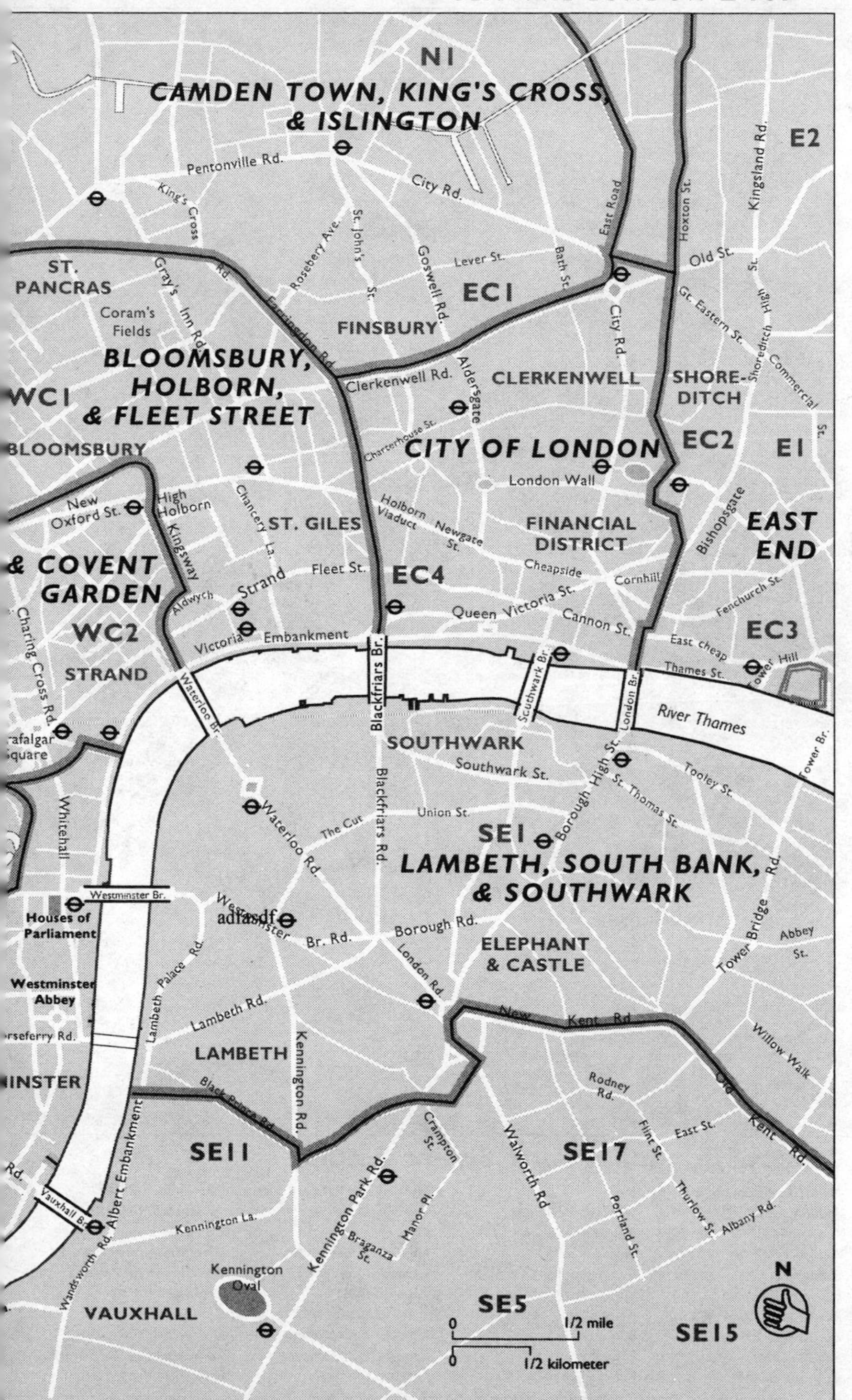
N1
CAMDEN TOWN, KING'S CROSS, & ISLINGTON
E2
Pentonville Rd.
City Rd.
King's Cross Rd.
St. John's St.
Goswell Rd.
Rosebery Ave.
East Road
Hoxton St.
Kingsland Rd.
Lever St.
Bath St.
Old St.
ST. PANCRAS
Gray's Inn Rd.
Farringdon Rd.
Coram's Fields
EC1
FINSBURY
City Rd.
Gt. Eastern St.
Shoreditch High St.
Commercial St.
BLOOMSBURY, HOLBORN, & FLEET STREET
WC1
Clerkenwell Rd.
Aldersgate
CLERKENWELL
SHORE-DITCH
Charterhouse St.
CITY OF LONDON
EC2
E1
BLOOMSBURY
London Wall
New Oxford St.
High Holborn
Chancery La.
Kingsway
ST. GILES
Holborn Viaduct
Newgate St.
FINANCIAL DISTRICT
Bishopsgate
EAST END
& COVENT GARDEN
Fleet St.
Strand
Aldwych
EC4
Cheapside
Cornhill
Fenchurch St.
Queen Victoria St.
Cannon St.
WC2
Victoria Embankment
East cheap
EC3
Charing Cross Rd.
STRAND
Blackfriars Br.
Southwark Br.
London Br.
Thames St.
Tower Hill
Waterloo Br.
River Thames
Tower Br.
Trafalgar Square
SOUTHWARK
Southwark St.
Borough High St.
Tooley St.
St. Thomas St.
Whitehall
Waterloo Rd.
Blackfriars Rd.
Union St.
The Cut
SE1
LAMBETH, SOUTH BANK, & SOUTHWARK
Westminster Br.
Houses of Parliament
Westminster Br. Rd.
adfasdf
Borough Rd.
London Rd.
ELEPHANT & CASTLE
Tower Bridge Rd.
Abbey St.
Westminster Abbey
Lambeth Palace Rd.
Lambeth Rd.
New Kent Rd.
Horseferry Rd.
LAMBETH
Kennington Rd.
Willow Walk
MINSTER
Black Prince Rd.
Rodney Rd.
Old Kent Rd.
Albert Embankment
Crampton St.
Flint St.
East St.
SE11
SE17
Walworth Rd.
Kennington Park Rd.
Manor Pl.
Portland St.
Thurlow St.
Albany Rd.
Vauxhall Br.
Kennington La.
Braganza St.
Wandsworth Rd.
Kennington Oval
N
VAUXHALL
SE5
0
1/2 mile
1/2 kilometer
SE15

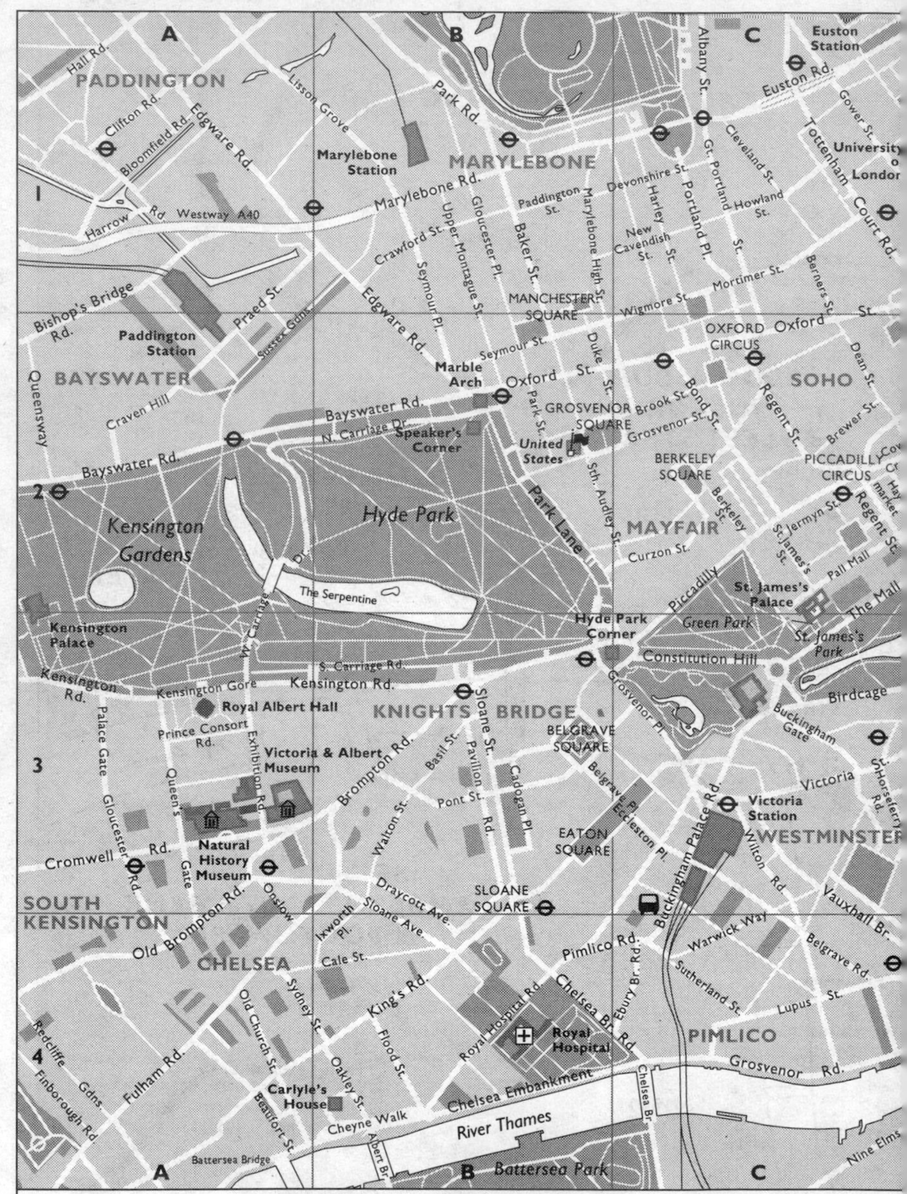

Central London: Major Street Finder

Albert Embankment **D4**
Aldersgate **E1**
Aldwych **D2**
Audley(N&S) **B2**
Baker St **B1**
Bayswater Rd **A2**
Beech St/Chiswell St **E1**
Belgrave Pl **B3**
Beaufort **A4**
Belgrave Rd **C4**
Berkeley St **C2**
Birdcage Walk **C3**
Bishops Br. Rd **A1**
Bishopsgate **F1**
Blackfriars Rd **E2**
Bloomsbury Way **D1**
Bond St (New&Old) **C2**
Bow St/Lancaster Pl **D2**
Brompton Rd **B3**
Buckingham Gate **C3**
Buckingham Palace Rd **C3**
Cannon St **F2**
Chancery Ln **D1**
Charing Cross Rd **D2**
Charterhouse St **E1**
Cheapside **E2**
Chelsea Br. Rd **B4**
Chelsea Embankment **B4**
Cheyne Walk **B4**
City Rd **F1**
Clerkenwell Rd **E1**
Constitution Hill **C3**
Cornhill/Leadenhall St **F2**
Coventry/Cranbourne **D2**
Craven Hill Rd/Praed St **A2**
Cromwell Rd **A3**
Curzon St **C2**
Drury Ln **D2**
Eastcheap/Great Tower **F2**
Eccleston Pl **C3**

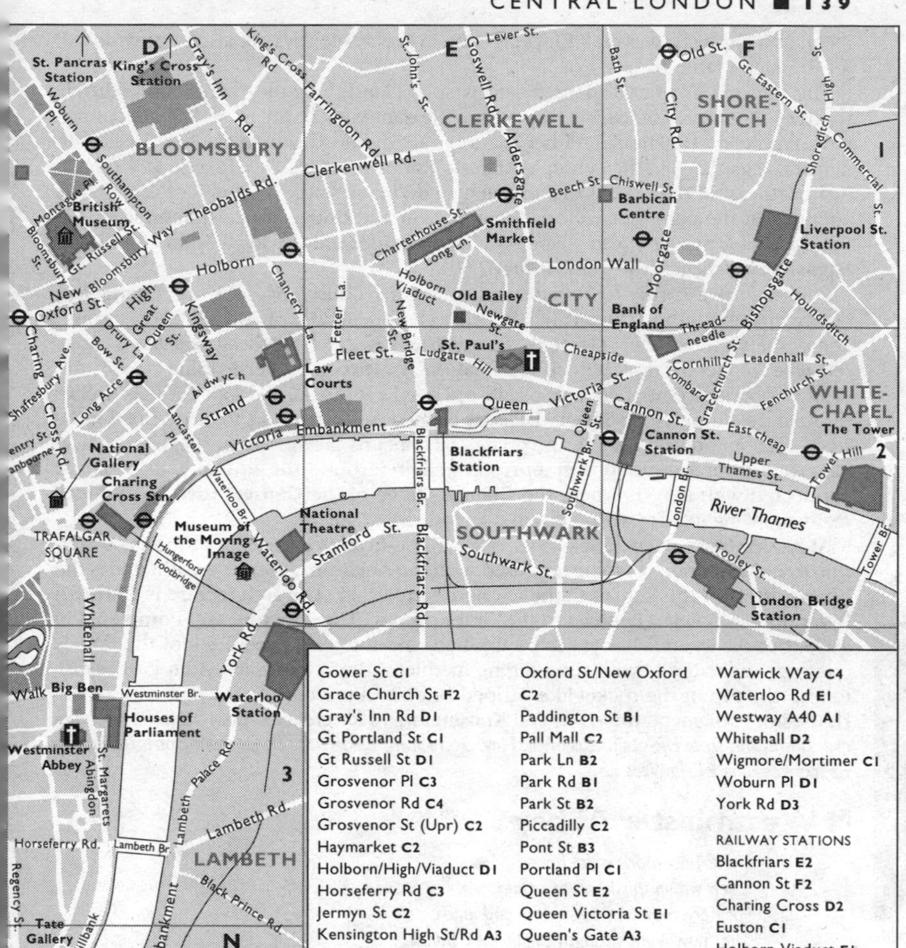

Edgware Rd **A1**
Euston Rd **C1**
Exhibition Rd **A3**
Farringdon Rd **E1**
Fenchurch/Aldgate **F2**
Fleet St **E2**
Fulham Rd **A4**
Gloucester Pl **B1**
Gloucester Rd **A3**
Goswell Rd **E1**
Gower St **C1**
Grace Church St **F2**
Gray's Inn Rd **D1**
Gt Portland St **C1**
Gt Russell St **D1**
Grosvenor Pl **C3**
Grosvenor Rd **C4**
Grosvenor St (Upr) **C2**
Haymarket **C2**
Holborn/High/Viaduct **D1**
Horseferry Rd **C3**
Jermyn St **C2**
Kensington High St/Rd **A3**
King's Cross Rd **D1**
King's Rd **B4**
Kingsway **D2**
Knightsbridge **B3**
Lambeth Palace Rd **D3**
Lisson Grove **A1**
Lombard St **F2**
London Wall **E1**
Long Acre/Grt Queen **D2**
Long Ln **E1**
Ludgate Hill **E2**
Marylebone High St **B1**
Marylebone Rd **B1**
Millbank **D4**
Montague Pl **D1**
Moorgate **F1**
New Bridge St **E2**
New Cavendish **C1**
Newgate St **E1**
Nine Elms Ln **C4**
Oakley St **B4**
Old St **F1**
Old Brompton Rd **A4**
Onslow Sq/St **A3**
Oxford St/New Oxford **C2**
Paddington St **B1**
Pall Mall **C2**
Park Ln **B2**
Park Rd **B1**
Park St **B2**
Piccadilly **C2**
Pont St **B3**
Portland Pl **C1**
Queen St **E2**
Queen Victoria St **E1**
Queen's Gate **A3**
Queensway **A2**
Redcliffe Gdns **A4**
Regent St **C2**
Royal Hospital Rd **B4**
St. James's St **C2**
Seymour Pl **A1**
Seymour St **A2**
Shaftesbury Ave **C2**
Sloane/Lwr Sloane **B3**
Southampton Row **D1**
Southwark Bridge Rd **E2**
Southwark Rd **E2**
St. Margarets/Abingdon **D3**
Stamford St **E2**
Strand **D2**
Sydney St **A4**
Thames St(Upr&Lwr) **F2**
The Mall **C2**
Theobald's Rd **D1**
Threadneedle St **F2**
Tottenham Ct Rd **C1**
Vauxhall Br. Rd **C4**
Victoria Embankment **D2**
Victoria St **C3**
Warwick Way **C4**
Waterloo Rd **E1**
Westway A40 **A1**
Whitehall **D2**
Wigmore/Mortimer **C1**
Woburn Pl **D1**
York Rd **D3**

RAILWAY STATIONS

Blackfriars **E2**
Cannon St **F2**
Charing Cross **D2**
Euston **C1**
Holborn Viaduct **E1**
King's Cross **D1**
Liverpool St **F1**
London Bridge **F2**
Marylebone **B1**
Paddington **A2**
St Pancras **D1**
Victoria **C3**
Waterloo East **E3**
Waterloo **D3**

BRIDGES

Albert **B4**
Battersea **A4**
Blackfriars **E2**
Chelsea **C4**
Hungerford Footbridge **D2**
Lambeth **D3**
London Bridge **F2**
Southwark **E2**
Tower Bridge **F2**
Waterloo **D2**
Westminster **D3**

moat, as it happens, was built for protection in less stable days but also to provide fish for the king's table.

The **Victoria Tower Gardens,** a narrow spit of land along the Thames immediately south of the Houses of Parliament, offers a pleasant view of the river. Militant suffragettes Emmeline Pankhurst and her daughter are memorialized in the northwest corner of the gardens. In the center is Auguste Rodin's famous *The Burghers of Calais.* Just northeast of the Houses of Parliament, a dramatic statue of Boudicca commands attention at the corner of Victoria Embankment and Bridge Street. Immortalized for your viewing pleasure, the valiant Queen Boudicca led the local Iceni tribe in an English revolt against the Romans in AD 60.

Four assertive corner towers distinguish former church **St. John the Evangelist,** now a chamber music concert hall in nearby Smith Square, off Millbank at the south end of the Victoria Tower Gardens. *(Box office tel. 222 1061; call ahead for details and concert times.)* Queen Anne, whose imagination was taxed by her leading role in the design of 50 new churches, supposedly upended a footstool and told Thomas Archer to build the church in its image. Dickens likened Archer's effort to a "petrified monster." Chamber music, choral, and orchestral concerts take place most evenings; tickets range from £6 to £20. Any flurry of activity around the square is likely to be connected with no. 31, where the **Central Office of the Conservative Party** lurks, ready to swing into (re)action down the road in Parliament.

At Ashley Place, a few blocks down Victoria St. from Westminster proper, is **Westminster Cathedral.** Not to be confused with the Anglican abbey, the Cathedral is the headquarters of the Roman Catholic church in Britain. The architecture is Christian Byzantine, in pointed contrast to the Gothic abbey. The structure was completed in 1903, but the interior has yet to be finished, and the blackened brick of the domes contrasts dramatically with the swirling marble of the lower walls. A lift carries visitors to the top of the rocket-like, striped brick bell tower for a decent view of the Houses of Parliament, the river, and Kensington. *(Cathedral open daily 7am-7pm. Cathedral admission free. Lift open daily Apr.-Nov. 9am-5pm; Dec.-Mar. Th-Su 9am-5pm. Admission £2, concessions £1, families £5.)*

■ Westminster Abbey

Think how many royal bones
Sleep within this heap of stones;
For here they lie, had realms and lands,
That now want strength to stir their hands.

—Francis Beaumont

Tel. *222 5152.* **Tube:** *Westminster.* **Open** *M-F 9am-4:45pm, last admission 3:45pm, some Wednesdays until 7:45pm (call 222 7110), Sa 9am-2:45pm.* **Admission** *£5, concessions £3, ages 11-18 £2, family £10, children under 11 free.* **Photography** *permitted Wednesday 6-7:45pm only.* **Tours** *(tel. 222 7110) last 1½hr. £3. Depart from the Enquiry Desk in the nave. Apr.-Oct. M-F 10, 10:30, 11am, 2, 2:30, and 3pm, F no 3pm tour, Sa 10, 11am, and 12:30pm. Nov.-Mar. M-F 10, 11am, 2, and 3pm, F no 3pm tour, Sa 10, 11am, and 12:30pm. Book tours by calling or inquiring at the Abbey desk. Portable,* **tape-recorded tours** *in assorted languages £2.*

Neither a cathedral nor a parish church, **Westminster Abbey** is a "royal peculiar," controlled directly by the Crown and outside the jurisdiction of the **Church of England.** As both the site of every royal coronation since 1066 and the final resting place for an imposing assortment of sovereigns, politicians, poets, and artists, the Abbey's significance extends far beyond the religious. Westminster today functions as a hybrid national church and honor roll (as well as an important magnet for tourism). Burial in the abbey is the greatest and rarest of honors in Britain—over the last 200 years, space has become so limited that many coffins stand upright under the pavement.

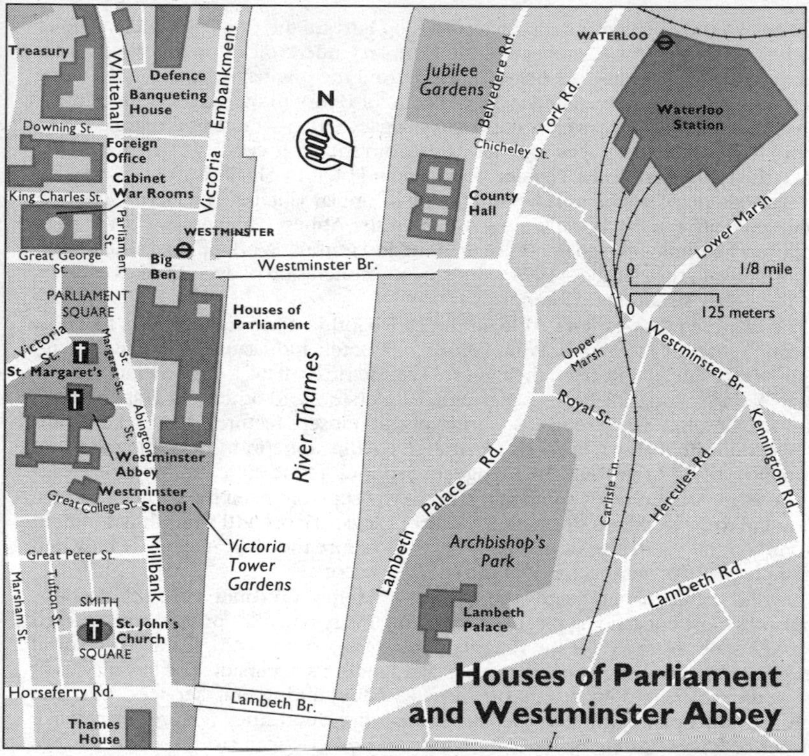
Houses of Parliament and Westminster Abbey
Treasury
Whitehall
Defence
Banqueting House
Downing St.
Foreign Office
Cabinet War Rooms
King Charles St.
Parliament St.
Victoria Embankment
N
Jubilee Gardens
Belvedere Rd.
York Rd.
WATERLOO
Waterloo Station
Chicheley St.
County Hall
WESTMINSTER
Great George St.
Big Ben
Westminster Br.
Lower Marsh
0
1/8 mile
0
125 meters
PARLIAMENT SQUARE
Houses of Parliament
Victoria St.
St. Margaret's
Margaret St.
Abingdon St.
Upper Marsh
Westminster Br.
Royal St.
Kennington Rd.
Westminster Abbey
River Thames
Palace Rd.
Lambeth
Carlisle Ln.
Hercules Rd.
Westminster School
Great College St.
Victoria Tower Gardens
Millbank
Archbishop's Park
Great Peter St.
Marsham St.
Tufton St.
SMITH SQUARE
St. John's Church
Lambeth Palace
Lambeth Rd.
Horseferry Rd.
Lambeth Br.
Thames House

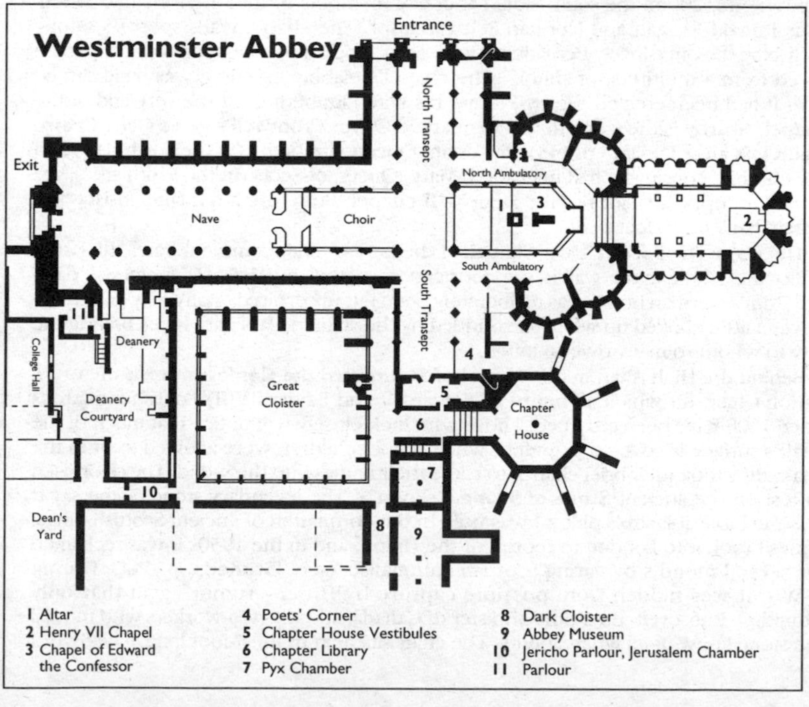
Westminster Abbey
Entrance
North Transept
Exit
North Ambulatory
Nave
Choir
South Ambulatory
South Transept
Deanery
College Hall
Great Cloister
Chapter House
Deanery Courtyard
Dean's Yard
1 Altar
2 Henry VII Chapel
3 Chapel of Edward the Confessor
4 Poets' Corner
5 Chapter House Vestibules
6 Chapter Library
7 Pyx Chamber
8 Dark Cloister
9 Abbey Museum
10 Jericho Parlour, Jerusalem Chamber
11 Parlour

Although the Abbey was consecrated by King Edward the Confessor on December 28, 1065, only the Pyx Chamber and the Norman Undercroft (now the Westminster Abbey Treasure Museum; see below) survive from the original structure. Most of the present Abbey was erected under the direction of Henry III during the 13th century. What we see today, however, is not Henry's legacy either—most of the stone visible in the Abbey is actually refacing that dates from the 18th century. The stones that make the two **West Front Towers,** designed and built by Sir Christopher Wren and his Baroque pupil, Nicholas Hawksmoor, are of similar vintage. The North Entrance, completed after 1850, is the youngest part of the Abbey. The entrance's Victorian stonework includes carved figures of dragons and griffins. Work on the cathedral has continued into this decade—1995 witnessed the conclusion of over 22 years of cleaning the Abbey's soot-stained stones.

The cluttered **Statesmen's Aisle,** in the early Gothic north transept, has the most eclectic group of memorials. Prime Ministers Disraeli and Gladstone couldn't stand each other in life, but in death their figures symmetrically flank a large memorial to Sir Peter Warren, alongside Peel, Castlereagh, Palmerston, and others. Sir Francis Vere's Elizabethan tomb in the southeast corner of the transept features the cracked shells of his armor held above his body. A strange paving stone in front of the memorial bears no exalted name, only the strange inscription, "Stone coffin underneath."

The **High Altar,** directly south of the north transept, has been the scene of coronations and royal weddings since 1066. Anne of Cleves, Henry VIII's fourth wife, lies in a tomb on the south side of the sanctuary, just before the altar. A series of crowded choir chapels fills the space east of the north transept.

Beyond these chapels stands the **Chapel of Henry VII** (built 1503-12), perhaps England's most outstanding piece of the period. Every one of its magnificently carved wooden stalls, reserved for the Knights of the Order of the Bath, features a colorful headpiece bearing the chosen personal statement of its occupant. The lower sides of the seats, which fold up to support those standing during long services, were the only part of the design left to the carpenters' discretion; they feature cartoon-like images of wives beating up their husbands and other pagan stories. Lord Nelson's stall was no. 20, on the south side. Latter-day members of the order include Americans Ronald Reagan and Norman Schwarzkopf. The chapel walls sport 95 saints, including the once-lovely Bernadette, who grew a beard overnight after praying to be saved from a multitude of suitors. The chapel's elaborate ceiling was hand-carved after it had been erected. Henry VII and his wife Elizabeth lie at the very end of the chapel. Nearby is the stone that once marked Oliver Cromwell's grave (see **"Cromwell's Life after Death,"** p. 143). Protestant Queen Elizabeth I (in the north aisle) and the Catholic cousin she had beheaded, Mary, Queen of Scots (in the south aisle), are buried on opposite sides of the Henry VII chapel. Both, the attendants insist, "put Britain back on its feet again."

The **Royal Air Force (RAF) Chapel,** at the far east end, commemorates the Battle of Britain. A hole in the wall in the northeast corner of the Air Force memorial, damage from a German bomb, has deliberately been left unrepaired. Many may find themselves a little choked up when surrounded by the stained glass panels celebrating the few to whom so many owe so much.

Behind the High Altar, in the **Chapel of St. Edward the Confessor,** rests the Coronation Chair, on which all but two (Edward V and Edward VIII) English monarchs since 1308 have been crowned. Those who look closely will notice that much of the chair's surface is covered in graffiti; when school children were allowed to sit in the chair, they took their brief chance to carve their names into the wood. The chair used to rest on the ancient **Stone of Scone** ("skoon"). The legendary stone (some say it was the biblical Jacob's pillow) was used in the coronation of ancient Scottish kings; James I took it to London to represent the Union, and in the 1950s it was reclaimed for several months by daring Scottish nationalists (see **"Stoned,"** p. 144). During WWII, it was hidden from possible capture by Hitler—rumor has it that only Churchill, Roosevelt, the Prime Minister of Canada, and the two workers who moved the stone knew of its whereabouts. The chair sits next to the 7-foot long State Sword

Cromwell's Life After Death

Oliver Cromwell's job as Lord Protectorate ended when he died of tuberculosis. His body was secretly embalmed and interred in Westminster Abbey on November 10, 1658, two weeks before his official funeral which was to cost £60,000 (an enormous sum both then and now). His eternal rest, however, did not last long. When the monarchy ousted Cromwell's son, King Charles II was unhappy with Cromwell's body lying next to the kings and queens of England. On January 30, 1661, the anniversary of the execution of Charles I, Cromwell's body was exhumed and taken to Tyburn. The procession was greeted by the "the universal outcry and curses of the people." The corpse was hanged from the gallows for a day, the body drawn and quartered, and the head taken to Westminster Hall, where it was exhibited on a pole until some time near the end of Charles II's reign in 1685. The fate of Cromwell's head is unclear, though most of the former Lord Protector still lies somewhere under what is now Connaught Square. Don't worry—he has not been forgotten. A stone in Westminster Abbey still marks his preliminary, if temporary, resting place.

and the shield of Edward III. On July 4, 1996 Prime Minister Major announced that—700 years after being taken from Scotland—the stone would return home and visit the Abbey only for coronations.

Numerous monarchs are interred in the chapel, from Henry III (d. 1272) to George II (d. 1760). Edward I had himself placed in an unsealed crypt here, in case he was needed again to fight the Scots; his mummy was carried as a standard by the English army as it tried to conquer Scotland. An engraving by William Blake commemorates the moment in 1774 when the Royal Society of Antiquaries opened this coffin in order to assess the body's state of preservation. Sick persons hoping to be cured would spend nights at the base of the Shrine of St. Edward the Confessor, at the center of the chapel. The king purportedly wielded healing powers during his life and dispensed free medical care to hundreds.

Visitors uninterested in the graves of English monarchs may find the names on the graves and plaques in the **Poets' Corner** more compelling. This shrine celebrates those who have died, been canonized, and later anthologized. It begins with Geoffrey Chaucer, who was originally buried in the abbey in 1400—the short Gothic tomb you see today in the east wall of the transept was not erected until 1556. The lower classes of the dead poets' society, and those leading "unconventional" life-styles, often had to wait a while before getting a permanent spot in the Abbey; even the Bard remained on the waiting list until 125 years after his mortal coil was shuffled off. Oscar Wilde was honored with a long overdue monument in Poets' Corner in 1995, the centenary of his conviction for homosexual activities. Floor panels commemorate Tennyson, T.S. Eliot, Dylan Thomas, Henry James, Lewis Carroll, Lord Byron, W.H. Auden, and WWI poets, all at the foot of Chaucer's tomb. Each one bears an appropriate description or image for puzzle solvers: D.H. Lawrence's publishing mark (a phoenix) or T.S. Eliot's symbol of death.

The south wall bears tributes to Edmund Spenser and John Milton. A partition wall divides the south transept, its east side graced with the graves of Samuel Johnson and actor David Garrick, its west side with busts of William Wordsworth, Samuel Taylor Coleridge, and Robert Burns, in addition to a full-length William Shakespeare that overshadows the tiny plaques memorializing the Brontë sisters. On the west wall of the transept, Händel's massive memorial looms over his grave next to the resting place of prolific Charles Dickens. On this side of the wall, you'll also find the grave of Rudyard Kipling and a memorial to that morbid Dorset farm boy, Thomas Hardy. Among the writers and poets lie two outsiders: Old Parr, who reportedly lived to the age of 152, and "Spot" Ward, who once healed George II of a thumb injury.

At the foot of the **Organ Loft,** found in the crossing, a memorial to Sir Isaac Newton sits next to the grave of Lord Kelvin. Franklin Roosevelt, David Lloyd George, Lord and Lady Baden-Powell of Boy Scout fame, the presumptive David Livingstone,

Stoned

On Christmas Day, 1950, daring Scottish patriot Ian Hamilton—posing as a visitor—hid himself in Westminster Abbey until it closed. He meant to steal the 200 kg Stone of Scone and return it to Scotland. As he approached the door near Poet's Corner to let in his three accomplices, a night watchman detected his presence inside the Abbey. Hamilton (now a prominent Scottish MP) talked fast enough to convince the watchman that he had been locked in involuntarily.

That same night the foursome forcibly entered the Abbey and pulled the stone out of its wooden container. In removing it, they inadvertently broke the famed rock into two uneven pieces. Hamilton sent his girlfriend, Kay, driving off to Scotland with the smaller piece, while he returned to deal with the larger piece. The remaining two accomplices had been instructed to drag the larger piece toward the cars, but when he returned Hamilton found only the stone and no sign of his buddies. He lugged the piece to his car, and, while driving out of London, happened across his wayward accomplices.

Unfortunately, the car's engine could not handle the weight, and the three were forced to ditch the stone in a field. Returning two weeks later to recover the stone, Hamilton found the site guarded by gypsies. To take the stone across the border into Scotland, he agreed to join the gypsy troupe.

The stone was repaired in a Glasgow workyard, but the patriots were frustrated that they could not display their nationalistic symbol in a public place. On April 11, 1951, Hamilton & Co. carried the stone to the altar at Arbroath Abbey where it was discovered and returned to England.

The final chapter of the story is that now-deceased Glasgow councilor Bertie Gray claimed, before he died, that the stone was copied and that the stone currently in Westminster Abbey is a fake. The British authorities dispute his claim.

and the heretical Charles Darwin are remembered in the nave. "Rare Ben Jonson" is buried upright; on his deathbed he proclaimed, "Six feet long by two feet wide is too much for me. Two feet by two feet will do for all I want."

Musicians' Aisle, just before the gate to the north aisle of the nave, contains the Abbey's most accomplished organists, John Blow and Henry Purcell, as well as memorials to Elgar, Britten, Vaughan Williams, and William Walton.

The Abbey's tranquil **cloister** reposes in a special peace of its own. The entrance in the northeast corner dates from the 13th century, the rest of it from the 14th century. The **Chapter House,** east down a passageway off the cloister, has one of the best-preserved medieval tile floors in Europe. *(Open daily Apr.-Oct. 10am-5:30pm; Nov.-Mar. 10am-4pm. Admission £1 with Abbey Ticket, concessions £2.80; without ticket £2.50, concessions £1.90.)* The windows in the ceiling depict scenes from the Abbey's history. The King's Great Council used the room as its chamber in 1257 and the House of Commons used it as a meeting place in the 16th century. Even today, the government, and not the abbey, administers the Chapter House and the adjacent **Pyx Chamber,** once the Royal Treasury and now a plate museum (open daily 10:30am-4pm).

Royal effigies (used instead of actual corpses for lying-in-state ceremonies) rest in the **Westminster Abbey Treasure Museum** (open daily 10:30am-4pm). The oldest, that of Edward III, has a lip permanently warped by the stroke that killed him. Those who knew Admiral Nelson found his effigy almost supernaturally accurate, perhaps because his mistress arranged his hair. The museum also includes an exhibit on the history of the Abbey as well as some historical oddities, including a Middle English lease to Chaucer and the much-abused sword of Henry V.

Enter through the cloisters on Great College St. to visit the 900-year-old **College Garden,** the oldest garden in England. *(Open Apr.-Sept. Tu and Th 10am-6pm; Oct.-Mar. Tu and Th 10am-4pm. Admission 20p. July-Aug. concerts Th 12:30-2pm.)*

Past the cloisters, in the Abbey's narrow **nave,** the highest in all of England, a slab of black Belgian marble marks the **Grave of the Unknown Warrior.** Here the body of a World War I soldier is buried in soil from the bloody battlefields of France, with an oration written in letters made from melted bullets. A piece of green marble engraved with the words "Remember Winston Churchill" sits nearby, rather than among fellow prime ministers in Statesmen's Aisle. Parliament placed it here 25 years after the Battle of Britain, perhaps prompted by pangs of regret that Churchill's body lay buried in Bladon and not in the Abbey's hall of fame.

Music lovers can catch **Evensong,** which is sung at 5pm on weekdays (except Wednesday when it is spoken) and 3pm on weekends. Organ recitals are given on Tuesday during the summer at 6:30pm. *(Admission £6, concessions £5; call 222-5152 or write the Concert Secretary, 20 Dean's Yard, SW1P 3PA.)*

■ The Houses of Parliament

The Houses of Parliament (tube: Westminster), oft-imagined in foggy silhouette against the Thames, have become London's visual trademark. For the classic view captured by Claude Monet, walk about halfway over Westminster Bridge, preferably at dusk. Like the government offices along Whitehall, the Houses of Parliament occupy the former site of a royal palace. Only Jewel Tower (see **Westminster,** p. 135) and Westminster Hall (to the left of St. Stephen's entrance on St. Margaret St.) survive from the original palace, which was destroyed by a fire on October 16, 1834. **Sir Charles Barry** and **A.W.N. Pugin** won a competition for the design of the new houses. From 1840 to 1888, Barry built a hulking, symmetrical block that Pugin ornamented with tortured imitations of late medieval decoration—"Tudor details on a classic body," Pugin later sneered, before dying of insanity.

The immense complex blankets eight acres and includes more than 1000 rooms and 100 staircases. Space is nevertheless so inadequate that Members of Parliament (MPs) cannot have private offices or staff, and the archives—the original copies of every Act of Parliament passed since 1497—are stuffed into **Victoria Tower,** the large tower to the south. A flag flown from the tower (a signal light after dusk) indicates that Parliament is in session.

Although you can hear **Big Ben,** you can't see him; he's actually neither the northernmost tower nor the clock but the 14-ton bell that tolls the hours. Ben is most likely named after the robustly proportioned Sir Benjamin Hall, who served as Commissioner of Works when the bell was cast and hung in 1858. Over the years Big Ben (the bell) has developed a crack. Each of the Roman numerals on the clock face measures 2 ft. in length; the minute hands, 14 ft. The mechanism moving the hands is still wound manually. The familiar 16-note tune that precedes the top-of-the-hour toll is a selection from Handel's *Messiah.*

Unfortunately, access to Westminster Hall and the Houses of Parliament has been restricted since a bomb killed an MP in 1979. To get a **guided tour** (M-Th) or a seat at **Question Time** when the Prime Minister attends (W 3-3:30pm), you need to obtain tickets—available on a limited basis from your embassy—or an introduction from an MP. Because demand for these tickets is extremely high, the most likely way of getting into the building is to queue for a seat at a debate when Parliament is in session. As a rough guide, the Houses are not in session during Easter week, summer recess (late July to mid-Oct.), and a three-week winter recess during Christmas time.

Tours for overseas visitors can be arranged by sending a written request to the Public Information Office, 1 Derby Gate, Westminster, SW1. The **House of Commons Visitors' Gallery** (for "Distinguished and Ordinary Strangers") holds extraordinary hours. *(Open M-Tu and Th 2:30-10pm, W 9:30am-2pm, F 9:30am-3pm.)* The **House of Lords Visitors' Gallery** is often easier to access, though the Lords perform less important work for the country. *(Open M-W 2:30pm-late, Th 3pm-late, occasionally F 11am-4pm.)* These hours are very rough guidelines—the MPs leave when they're done with business and begin when they feel like it. Visitors should arrive early and be prepared to wait by St. Stephen's Gate (on the left for Commons, on the right for Lords; free). Crowds thin out considerably after 6pm for both Houses. Those willing to sacrifice the roar of the debate for smaller, more focused business can attend meetings of any of the various committees by jumping the queue and going straight up to the entrance. For times of committee meetings each week, call the **House of Commons Information Office** (tel. 219 4272). Both houses' business is announced daily in the major newspapers and in a weekly schedule by St. Stephen's Gate.

After entering St. Stephen's Gate and submitting to an elaborate security check, you will be standing in **St. Stephen's Hall.** This chapel is where the House of Commons used to sit. In the floor are four brass markers where the Speaker's Chair stood. Charles I, in his ill-fated attempt to arrest five MPs, sat here in the place of the Speaker in 1641. No sovereign has entered the Commons since.

To the left from the Central Lobby are the **Chambers of the House of Commons.** Destroyed during the Blitz, the rebuilt chamber is modest, even anticlimactic. Most traditional features still remain, such as two red lines fixed two sword-lengths apart, which (for safety's sake) debating members may not cross. The Government party (the party with the most MPs in the House) sits to the Speaker's right, and the Opposition sits to his left. There are not enough benches in the chamber to seat all 650 members, which adds a sense of huddled drama to the few occasions when all are present. Members vote by filing into **division lobbies** parallel to the chamber: ayes to the west, nays to the east.

To enter the Lords' Gallery, go back through the Central Lobby and pass through the Peers' corridor—never passing up a chance to gloat, the MPs have bedecked the passage with scenes of Charles I's downfall. The ostentation of the **House of Lords,** dominated by the sovereign's Throne of State under a gilt canopy, contrasts with the sober, green-upholstered Commons' Chamber. Elaborate wall carvings divert attention from the speakers on the floor. The Lord Chancellor presides over the House from his seat on the **Woolsack,** stuffed with wool from all nations of the Kingdom and Commonwealth—harking back to a time when wool, like the Lords, was more vital to Britain. The woolsack may first appear to be a small white pillow on the throne where no one sits, but actually it's the red behemoth the size of a Volkswagen bug. The poor Lord Chancellor looks lost on this huge wash of red, propped up only by a small, insufficient pillow. Next to him rests the almost 6 ft. **Mace,** which is brought in to open the House each morning.

Outside the Houses is the **Old Palace Yard,** site of the untimely demises of Sir Walter Raleigh and the Gunpowder Plotter Guy Fawkes (the palace's cellars are still ceremonially searched before every opening of Parliament). To the north squats **Westminster Hall** (rebuilt around 1400), where high treason trials, including those of Thomas More, Fawkes, and Charles I, were held until 1825. The **New Palace Yard** is a good place to espy your favorite MPs as they enter the complex through the Members' entrance just north of Westminster Hall. For more detailed information about the English government, see **Politics,** p. 6.

SIGHTS

Whitehall

Whitehall was born in 1245 as York Place, residence for the Archbishops of York. Cardinal Wolsey enlarged York Place into a palace he thought fit for a king. Henry VIII agreed and later moved into his new London apartments of state, rechristened Whitehall, in 1530. This gargantuan palace stretched all the way to Somerset House on the Strand, but William II resented an unnamed diplomat's description of Whitehall as "the biggest, most hideous place in all Europe," and relocated to a shiny new Kensington Palace. The rejected palace burned in 1698, and since then "Whitehall" (tube: Westminster or Charing Cross), stretching from Parliament St. to Trafalgar Sq., has become the home and a synonym for the British civil service.

Conveniently enough, **10 Downing Street,** which serves as the Prime Minister's headquarters, lies just steps up Parliament St. from the Houses. Sir George Downing, ex-Ambassador to The Hague (and the 2nd person to graduate from Harvard College in Cambridge, Massachusetts), built this house in 1681. Prime Minister Sir Robert Walpole, who is best remembered for his role in a series of vicious political satires, made it his official residence in 1732. The exterior of "Number Ten" is decidedly unimpressive, especially from a distance, but behind the famous door spreads an extensive political network. The Chancellor of the Exchequer generally forecasts economic recovery from No. 11 Downing St., and the Chief Whip of the House of Commons plans Party campaigns at No. 12. However, Tony Blair's family is too big for 10 Downing St., so he's moved in next door to 11 Downing St. Visitors have long been banned from entering Downing St.

The **Cabinet War Rooms** lurk at the end of King Charles St., near Horse Guards Rd. (see **Museums,** p. 229). The formal **Cenotaph,** which honors the war dead, usually decked with wreaths, stands where Parliament St. turns into Whitehall.

Just off Whitehall, at 6 Derby Gate, **New Scotland Yard** will probably fall short of crime-hounds' expectations. The second of three incarnations of the lair of those unimaginative detectives humbled by Sherlock Holmes and Hercule Poirot is nothing more than two buildings, connected by an arch, that currently contain government offices. The original Yard was at the top of Whitehall, on Great Scotland Yard, and the current New Scotland Yard is on Victoria St.

Henry VIII's **wine cellar** was one of the few parts of the palace spared in the fire of 1698. In 1953, the government erected the massive **Ministry of Defense Building** (nicknamed the Quadragon) just to the north, over Henry's cache. The cellar had to be relocated deeper into the ground to accommodate the new structure. Technically visitors may view the cellar, but permission is dauntingly difficult to obtain (apply in writing to the Department of the Environment or the Ministry of Defense with a compelling story). Near the statue of General Gordon in the gardens behind the Ministry of Defense Building, you'll find the remnants of Queen Mary's terrace, built for Queen Mary II. The bottom of the steps leading from the terrace mark the 17th-century water level, reminding observers of the extent to which river transport determined the locations of 16th- and 17th-century buildings.

The 1622 **Banqueting House** (tel. 930 4179), at the corner of Horse Guards Ave. and Whitehall, opposite Horse Guards Hall, is one of the few intact masterpieces of Inigo Jones, dripping with beauty and irony that recall the tumultuous times of the Stuart monarchy. *(Open M-Sa 10am-5pm, last admission 4pm. Closed for government functions. Admission £3.50, concessions £2.70, children £2.30.)* James I and Charles I held feasts and staged elaborate masques (thinly-disguised pieces of theatrical propaganda) in the main hall. The 60 ft. high ceiling was commissioned by Charles I; the scenes Rubens painted are allegorical representations of the divine strength of the English monarch. But not even the hall's considerable beauty could quell the crics of Cromwell's men. The party ended on January 27, 1649, when King Charles I, draped in black velvet, stepped out of a first floor window to the scaffold where he was beheaded. The weather vane on the roof tells another tale of Stuart misfortune—James II placed it there to see if the wind was favorable for his rival to the throne William of Orange's voyage from the Netherlands. From 1724 to 1890, the Banqueting House served as a Chapel Royal. These days the hall sees no executions, just harmless state dinners (behind bulletproof glass) and the occasional concert.

For folks who can't get enough of mounted, betassled guards, another battery of the **Queen's Life Guard** mark time on the west side of Whitehall north of Downing St. Monday to Saturday at 11am and Sunday at 10am. The arrival of more mounted troops, and lots of barking in incoherent English mark Whitehall's **Changing of the Guard,** a less crowded and impressive version of the Buckingham Palace spectacle (see **Buckingham Palace,** p. 149). The barking occurs again daily at 4pm, this time accompanied by dismounting and strutting, and is called the **Inspection of the Guard.** The Changing and Inspection don't occur on June Saturdays, when the Guard is gearing up for Trooping the Colour (see p. 151). Note that many of the guards now wear UN medals after having served in Bosnia in 1995; the Queen's Cavalry serve six-month tours of duty with UN peace-keeping forces. Through the gates lies Horse Guards Parade, a large court (opening onto St. James's Park) from which the bureaucratic array of different architectural styles that make up Whitehall can be seen. The **Armistice Day Parade** (closest Sunday to Nov. 11) and the **Belgian Army Veteran's Parade** (closest Sunday to July 15) are launched annually from this sight. In addition, **Beating the Retreat,** a must for lovers of pomp and circumstance, takes place here at the beginning of June (call 414 2271 for dates and ticket information). Beating the Retreat is merely a warm-up for **Trooping the Colour,** in which the Queen gives the royal salute to the Root Guards. The ceremony takes place in the middle of June and is preceeded by two rehearsals open to the public (without the Queen).

The Mall and St. James's

Just north of Buckingham Palace and the Mall, up Stable Yard or Marlborough Rd., stands **St. James's Palace,** the residence of the monarchy from 1660 to 1668 and again from 1715 to 1837 (tube: Green Park). The scene of many a three-volume novel and Regency romance, over the years this palace has hosted tens of thousands of the young girls whose families "presented" them at Court. Ambassadors and the elite set of barristers known as "Queen's Counsel" are still received "into the Court of St. James's." Only Henry VIII's gateway and clock tower and a pair of parading guards at the foot of St. James's St. still hark back to the Tudor palace; the guards' bayoneted rifles are a little too modern for comfort.

Today the **Queen Mum** inhabits St. James, where she can keep a motherly eye on her daughter, the Queen, who bunks just down the road at Buckingham. St. James's Palace is closed to the public, except for Inigo Jones's **Queen's Chapel,** built in 1626, which is open for Sunday services at 8:30 and 11am (Oct.-July). King Charles I slept for four hours in the palace's guardroom before crossing St. James's Park to be executed at the Banqueting House (see **Whitehall,** p. 140).

Henry VIII declared **St. James's Park** London's first royal park in 1532. The fenced-off peninsula at the east end of the park's pond, **Duck Island,** is the mating ground for thousands of waterfowl. St. James's is also a good place to discover that lawn chairs in England are not free—chairs have been hired out here since the 18th century (rental 70p for a 4hr. sit—don't find the attendants, just sit and they'll find you). For a nice view of the guards who change at Buckingham Palace, wait between the Victoria Memorial and St. James's Palace from about 10:40 to 11:25am. You might miss the band (it usually travels down Birdcage walk from Wellington Barracks), but you will also avoid the swarm of tourists.

The high-rent district around the palace has also taken the moniker St. James's. Bordered by St. James's Park and Green Park to the south and Piccadilly to the north, it begins at an equestrian statue of notorious madman George III on Cockspur St. off Trafalgar Sq. **St. James's Street,** next to St. James's Palace, runs into stately **Pall Mall** (both rhyme with "pal"). The name derives from "pail-mail," a 17th-century predecessor of croquet. Until Buckingham Palace was built, today's Mall was merely an endless playing field for the King. Lined with double rows of plane trees, the Mall grandly traverses the space from Trafalgar Sq. to Buckingham Palace (tube: Charing Cross). Two monuments to Queen Victoria contribute to the Mall's grandeur: the golden horses of the **Queen Victoria Memorial,** near Buckingham Palace, and the massive **Admiralty Arch** opening onto Trafalgar Sq.

Along the north side of the Mall lie the imposing facades of grand houses, starting with **Carlton House Terrace,** demolished, rebuilt, and remodeled since John Nash erected it along the Mall as part of the 18th-century Regent's Park route; the statue on the terrace memorializes the "Grand Old Duke of York." The building became the office of the Free French Forces from 1940 to 1945 under the leadership of General Charles de Gaulle. It now contains the Royal Society of Distinguished Scientists and, the area's newest and most attention-grabbing neighbor, the avant-garde **Institute of Contemporary Arts** (ICA), (see **Museums,** p. 231, **Film,** p. 240, and **Theater,** p. 234). The hipper-than-thou ICA was established in 1947 to provide British artists with the kinds of resources and facilities then available only at the Museum of Modern Art in New York and has been located in Carlton House since 1968.

Pall Mall and St. James's St., together with **Jermyn Street,** parallel to Pall Mall to the north, flank the traditional stomping grounds of the upper-class English clubman. At 70-72 Jermyn he will buy his shirts from Turnbull and Asser (one of Churchill's custom-made "siren suits" is on display). His bowler will be from Lock & Co. Hatters (ask politely to see their sinister-looking head measuring device), and his bespoke shoes will be the craft of John Lobb. Berry & Co. wine merchants supply the madeira, and Cuban cigars should really be purchased at Robert Lewis, where Churchill indulged his habit for 60 years. "I am the sort of man easily pleased by the best of everything," claimed Sir Winston. Revel in the patrician solemnity of the area at the quintessential men's store **Alfred Dunhill,** 30 Duke Street (tel. 838 8000; entrance on Jermyn)—lurking upstairs above the staid merchandise is a riotously sublime collection of smoking vessels from the world over (open M-F 9am-6pm).

These Regency storefronts rub elbows with a number of famous London coffeehouses-turned-clubs. The coffeehouses of the early 18th century, whose political life was painted vividly by Addison and Steele in their journal *The Spectator,* were transformed by the 19th century into exclusive clubs for political and literary men of a particular social station. The chief Tory club, the **Carlton,** at 69 St. James's St., was bombed by the IRA not long ago. The chief Liberal club, the **Reform,** at 104 Pall Mall, served as a social center of Parliamentary power. In 1823, a Prime Minister and the presidents of the Royal Academy and the Royal Society founded the **Athenaeum,** on Waterloo Pl., for scientific, literary, and artistic men. Gibbon, Hume, and Garrick belonged to the **Whig Brooks,** at 60 St. James's St., founded in 1764.

Around the corner from St. James's Palace stand royal medalists Spink's, and Christie, Manson, and Wodds Fine Art Auctioneers—better known as **Christie's,** 8 King St. (tel. 839 9060; tube: Green Park). The pamphlets describing the furniture, historical documents, and artworks being auctioned are lovely but cost £6-27. Auctions, open to the public, are held most weekdays at 10:30am. Amuse yourself on a rainy afternoon by watching the dealers do their bidding.

Between aristocratic Jermyn St. and Piccadilly, you can enter **St. James's Church** (tube: Green Park or Piccadilly Circus), a postwar reconstruction by Sir Albert Richardson of what Wren considered his best parish church. The work of Grinling Gibbons, Wren's master-carver, can be seen in the delightful flowers, garlands, and cherubs. Blake was baptized here, which will delight fans of innocence and experience alike. A small market flourishes here Thursday through Saturday, 10am to 6pm.

■ Buckingham Palace

> *I must say, notwithstanding the expense which has been incurred in building the palace, no sovereign in Europe, I may even add, perhaps no private gentleman, is so ill-lodged as the king of this country.*
>
> —Duke of Wellington, 1828

Tel. *799 2331; www.royal.gov.uk.* ***Tube:*** *Victoria, and walk up Buckingham Palace Rd.; Green Park and St. James's Park are also convenient.* ***Open*** *daily Aug.-Sept.* ***Admission*** *£9.50, seniors £7, under 17 £5.* ***Tours*** *may be available; call for details.*

When a freshly crowned Victoria moved from St. James's Palace in 1837, Buckingham Palace, built in 1825 by John Nash, had faulty drains and a host of other leaky difficulties. Home improvements were made, and now, when the flag is flying, the Queen is at home—and you can visit her home.

After a recent debate about the proper way to subsidize the monarchy's senselessly posh existence (spurred by the need for funds to rebuild Windsor castle, which went up in flames in November 1992), Buckingham Palace finally opened to the public. Sort of. The doors have been open for the past couple years—at press time it was unknown as to the exact opening dates for 1999. Not all of the Palace is laid open; the tour is well roped off from the State Rooms, the principal rooms used for ceremonies and official entertaining. But visitors are able to stroll through the Blue Drawing Room, the Throne Room, the Picture Gallery (filled with pictures by Rubens, Rembrandt, and Van Dyck), and the Music Room (where Mendelsohn played for Queen Victoria), as well as other stately rooms.

In the opulent **White Drawing Room,** notice the large mirror to the left of the fireplace; it conceals a door used by the Royal Family to make a grand appearance before formal dinners. Critics of the palace suggest it looks less like the home or even the office of the Queen and more like a museum, thus diminishing much of the excitement of seeing a monarch's digs. Indeed, the monarch scuttles off to Balmoral to avoid the plague of tourists descending upon her immaculate residence.

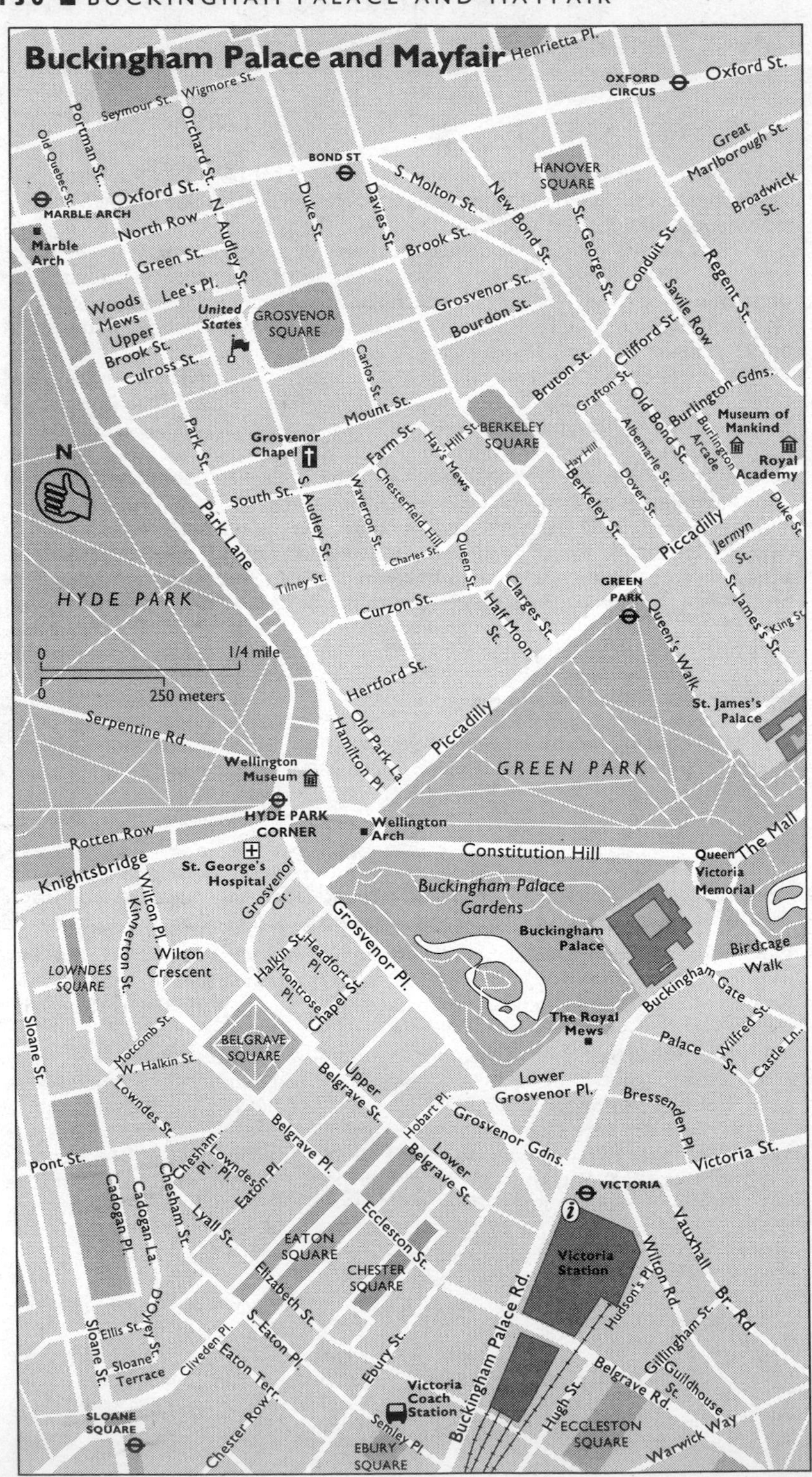
Buckingham Palace and Mayfair
Oxford St.
OXFORD CIRCUS
BOND ST
MARBLE ARCH
Marble Arch
HANOVER SQUARE
GROSVENOR SQUARE
United States
Grosvenor Chapel
BERKELEY SQUARE
Museum of Mankind
Royal Academy
HYDE PARK
GREEN PARK
Piccadilly
Park Lane
Wellington Museum
HYDE PARK CORNER
Wellington Arch
Constitution Hill
Buckingham Palace Gardens
Buckingham Palace
Queen Victoria Memorial
The Mall
St. James's Palace
The Royal Mews
St. George's Hospital
BELGRAVE SQUARE
LOWNDES SQUARE
EATON SQUARE
CHESTER SQUARE
VICTORIA
Victoria Station
Victoria Coach Station
ECCLESTON SQUARE
EBURY SQUARE
SLOANE SQUARE
0 1/4 mile
0 250 meters
N

The 20th-century facade on the Mall is only big, not beautiful—the Palace's best side, the garden front, is seldom seen by ordinary visitors as it is protected by the 40-acre spread where the Queen holds garden parties. The most visible facade is patrolled by a set of very recognizable guards. Their fur hats look as if they were designed for guards with heads four times bigger; but no teasing, the guards carry modern assault rifles with bayonets.

If you happen to visit the palace during an off month, try to catch the chart-topping Kodak Moment for London tourists—the **Changing of the Guard,** which takes place daily from April to late August, and only on alternate days from September to March. This cutback in the winter spectacle is attributed to budget constraints, but is generally interpreted as an attempt on the army's part to manipulate public opinion in favor of increased spending on the military. The "Old Guard" marches from St. James's Palace down the Mall to Buckingham Palace, leaving at approximately 11:10am. The "New Guard" begins marching as early as 10:20am. When they meet at the central gates of the palace, the officers of the regiments then touch hands, symbolically exchanging keys, *et voilà,* the guard is officially changed. The soldiers gradually split up to relieve the guards currently protecting the palace. The ceremony moves to the beat of royal band music and the menacing clicks of thousands of cameras. In wet weather or on pressing state holidays, the Changing of the Guard does not occur. To witness the spectacle, show up well before 11:30am and stand directly in front of the palace. You can also watch along the routes of the troops prior to their arrival at the palace (10:40-11:25am) between the Victoria Memorial and St. James's Palace or along Birdcage Walk.

In the extravagant **Trooping the Colour** ceremony, held on the Queen's official birthday in the middle of June, the colors of a chosen regiment are paraded ceremonially before her and her family. The parade in honor of the Queen brings out luminaries mounted on horses while somewhat less influential types putter about in limousines with little golden crowns on top. The actual ceremony takes place at Horse Guards Parade, followed by a procession down the Mall to the palace, where she reviews her Household Cavalry and appears on the balcony for a Royal Air Force fly-by. The best view of all this is on TV, but you might catch a glimpse of the Queen in person as she rides down the Mall. Tickets for the event must be obtained through the mail. Write well in advance to the Household Division HQ, Horse Guards, SW1. If you don't get a ticket for the event, you should ask for tickets to one of the rehearsals on the two preceding Saturdays. Since the Queen does not need to rehearse, these tend to be noticeably less crowded.

Down the left side of the palace, off Buckingham Gate, an enclosed passageway leads to the **Queen's Gallery.** *(Open daily 9:30am-4:30pm, last admission 4pm. Admission £4, seniors £3, under 17 £2.)* Selected treasures from the royal collection fill the rooms of this modern suite. The exhibition changes every few months, but you can usually catch a few of Charles I's Italian masters, George IV's Dutch still-lifes, Prince Albert's primitives, and occasionally a couple of Leonardo da Vinci drawings from Windsor. An excellent show featuring "Raphael and his Circle" will be on display from May to October 1999. Other planned exhibits include 18th-century nature drawings.

Also off Buckingham Gate stands the curious **Royal Mews Museum,** which houses the royal coaches and other historic royal riding implements. *(Open Oct.-Mar. W noon-4pm; Apr.-July Tu-Th noon-4pm; Aug.-Sept. M 10:30am-4:30pm, Tu-Th noon-4pm. Admission £4, seniors £3, under 17 £2, family of 4 £10.)* A combined pass for the Gallery and Mews may be purchased (admission £6.50, seniors £4.50, under 17 £3.50).

Nearby, you can drop in on the **Guards Museum** at Wellington Barracks on Birdcage Walk, off Buckingham Gate. *(Open M-Th and Sa-Su 10am-4pm; admission £2, concessions £1.)* This museum features, among other things, the history of those famous red coats. The courtyard outside Wellington Barracks is probably the only place where you'll ever see the Guards at relative ease. Go around 10 or 10:30am and you're likely to see them hanging around preparing for the Changing.

Trafalgar Square and Charing Cross

Unlike many squares in London, **Trafalgar Square** (tube: Charing Cross), which slopes down from the National Gallery into the center of a vicious traffic roundabout, has been public land ever since the razing of several hundred houses made way for its construction in the 1830s. **Nelson's Column,** a fluted granite pillar, commands the square, with four majestic, beloved lions guarding the base. The monument and square commemorate Admiral Horatio Nelson, killed during his triumph over Napoleon's navy off of Trafalgar (the monument's reliefs were cast from French cannons). Now, streams of tourists mingle amongst the legions of pigeons that have become tame enough to sit upon the most unwilling of shoulders. Floodlights bathe the square after dark, when it fills up with eager tourists and club kids trying to catch the right night bus home. Enthusiastic, rambunctious New Year's celebrations take place here, featuring universal indiscriminate kissing.

At the head of the square squats the ordering façade of the **National Gallery,** Britain's collection of Old Masters (see **Museums,** p. 215). A competition to design a new extension to the gallery ended in Prince Charles' denouncing the winning entry as a "monstrous carbuncle" on the face of London and the subsequent selection of a new architect. Philadelphian Robert Venturi's wing to the west of the main building is now open; the mock columns and pillars that echo the old building and even Nelson's Column are much discussed and generally liked.

The church of **St. Martin-in-the-Fields,** on the northeastern corner of the square opposite the National Gallery, dates from the 1720s. Designer James Gibbs topped its templar classicism with a Gothic steeple. The interior, despite the gilded and chubby cherubim, is simple, its walls relatively uncluttered with monuments. St. Martin, which has its own world-renowned chamber orchestra, sponsors lunchtime and evening concerts, as well as a summer festival in mid-July *(Lunchtime concerts M-Tu and F 1:05pm. Box office in the bookshop open M-W 10am-6pm and Th-Sa 10am-7:30pm. Phone bookings (tel. 839 8362) M-F 10am-4pm.)* The crypt has been cleared of all those dreary coffins to make room for a gallery, the book shop, a brass rubbing center (where you can actually do your own rubbing), and a cafe that serves cappuccino (95p) and yummy deserts with baroque flair (crème brulee £2.10). (Open M-Sa 10am-8pm, Su noon-6pm). Across the street from St. Martin's, half obscured by the mammoth buildings that ring Trafalgar Square, sits the **National Portrait Gallery,** wherein lie busts, caricatures, photos, and paintings of everyone who is or was anyone in the U.K. (p. 216).

The original **Charing Cross,** last of 13 crosses set up to mark the stages of Queen Eleanor's royal funeral procession in 1291 ("charing" comes from "beloved queen" in French), was actually located at the top of Whitehall, immediately south of the present Trafalgar Square. Like many things, it was destroyed by Cromwell, and a replica now stands outside Charing Cross Station, just uphill from the Victoria Embankment. While the spot is still the geographical center of the city (all distances to London are measured from it), it is no longer the pulsing heart of London life it once was. "Why, Sir, Fleet Street has a very animated appearance," Samuel Johnson once remarked, "but I think the full tide of human existence is at Charing Cross." An overfull tide of traffic now engulfs the place, and the bronze statue of King Charles drowns in the ebb and flow of automobiles. The statue escaped the cross's fate with the aid of one wily John Rivett. He bought the statue "for scrap" and did a roaring trade in brass souvenirs supposedly made from the melted-down figure; it was in fact hidden and later sold, at a tidy profit, to Charles II.

Piccadilly

All of the West End's major arteries—Piccadilly, Regent St., Shaftesbury Ave., and The Haymarket—merge and swirl around **Piccadilly Circus,** the bright, gaudy hub of Nash's 19th-century London. Today, the Circus earns its place on postcards with lurid neon signs, hordes of tourists, and a fountain topped by a statue everyone calls

"Eros," though it was intended to be the Angel of Christian Charity in memory of the Earl of Shaftesbury. Akin to New York's Times Square, Piccadilly overflows with glam, glitz, and commerce, and, like its Gotham sibling, is undergoing a high-profile incursion by American corporations.

The Circus was ground zero for Victorian popular entertainment, but only the facades of the great music halls remain, propped up against contemporary tourist traps. **London Pavilion,** 1 Piccadilly Circus, is a historic theater recently converted into a mall (across the street from the Lillywhite's and Sogo stores). Inside the Pavilion lurks **Madame Tussaud's Rock Circus** (tel. 734 7203), an ultra-cheesy waxwork museum and revolving theatre dedicated to the history of rock 'n' roll. *(Open Su-M and W-Th 11am-9pm, Tu noon-9pm, F-Sa 11am-10pm; July 9-Sept. 3 Tu 11am-10pm, Su-M and W-Sa 10am-10pm. Admission £7.95, students and seniors £6.95, children £6.50, family £19.95.)* Elvis, the Beatles, James Brown, and more recently, Lenny Kravitz and Jon Bon Jovi stand among the 50 rock and pop artists eerily re-created as wax effigies. Infrared headsets pick up a CD soundtrack as you wander past each display. The massive, laser-decorated arcade and mall **Trocadero,** 13 Coventry Street (tel. 439 1791), specializes in charging tourists exorbitant sums for contrived entertainments. Trocadero now also holds the entrance to Segaworld, a "virtual amusement park," in which access to each new floor of "rides" costs £3 and video games range from 30p-£1. Featured alongside the Trocadero's other many delights is an IMAX theatre (tel. 494 4153) where tickets will run you £6.95, concessions £5.50.

For an escape from the world of the gaudy and the touristy, check out **Piccadilly,** a broad, mile-long avenue once lined with aristocratic mansions stretching from Regent St. in the east to Hyde Park Corner in the west. The name derives from Piccadilly Hall, the 17th-century home of Robert Baker, an affluent tailor who did brisk business in the sale of "pickadills," frilly lace collars that were then in fashion. The only remnant of Piccadilly's stately past is the showy **Burlington House** (across from 185 Piccadilly), built in 1665 for the Earls of Burlington and redesigned in the 18th century by Colin Campbell to accommodate the burgeoning **Royal Academy of Arts.** Founded in 1768, the Academy consists of 40 academicians and 30 associates who administer the exhibition galleries and a massive annual summer show, and maintain a free school of art (see **Museums**, p. 227).

An easily overlooked courtyard next to the Academy opens onto the **Albany,** an 18th-century apartment block renowned as one of London's most prestigious addresses. Built in 1771 and remodeled in 1812 to serve as "residential chambers for bachelor gentlemen," the Albany evolved into an exclusive enclave of literary repute. Lord Byron wrote his epic "Childe Harold" here. Other past residents include Macaulay, Gladstone, Canning, "Monk" Lewis, and J.B. Priestley.

Piccadilly continues past imperious Bond St., the Ritz Hotel and its distinctive light-bulb sign, the Green Park tube station, and a string of privileged men's clubs on the rim of Green Park. At the gateway of the **Wellington Museum** in **Apsley House,** described by its first owner as "No. 1, London," the avenue merges into the impenetrable Hyde Park corner traffic nightmare. Apsley House was built by Robert Adam in the 1780s as the home of the Duke of Wellington.

Running north from Piccadilly Circus are the grand facades of (upper) **Regent Street,** leading to Oxford Circus. The buildings and street were built by John Nash in the early 19th century as part of a processional route for the Prince Regent to follow from St. James's Park through Oxford Circus to his house in Regent's Park. The facades have changed since Nash's time, and today the street is known for the crisp cuts of Burberry raincoats and Aquascutum suits.

Soho, Leicester Square, and Chinatown

For centuries, **Soho** was London's red-light district of prostitutes and sex shows. Though most of the prostitutes were forced off the streets by legislation in 1959, the peep shows and porn shops concentrated along Brewer St. and Greek St. honor this licentious tradition. Far from defining its flavor, however, the sex industry adds merely one small ingredient to the cosmopolitan stew that is today's Soho. It's a young and vibrant area with narrow streets lined by cool cafes, classic pubs, unpretentious shops, and theaters. Many Londoners agree that some of the city's best cafes and restaurants (especially for those on a budget) are to be found here.

Loosely bounded by Oxford St. to the north, Shaftesbury Ave. to the south, Charing Cross Rd. to the east, and Regent St. to the west (tube: Leicester Sq., Piccadilly Circus, or Tottenham Ct. Rd.), Soho first emerged as a discrete area in 1681 with the laying out of **Soho Square,** originally King's Square (tube: Tottenham Ct. Rd., just off Oxford St.). Grand mansions quickly sprang up as the area became popular with the fashionable set, famous for throwing extravagant parties. By the end of the 18th century, however, the leisure classes had moved out, replaced by the leisure industries. Today, the square is a center of the film-making industry.

A statue of Charles II (1681), blurred by weather and cracked with age, presides over the **Soho Square Gardens** (tel. 798 2064; open daily 10am-dusk). His illegitimate son, the Duke of Monmouth, who rebelled against (and was beheaded by) uncle James II, once commissioned a palatial house on this site; according to legend, the district's current name comes from his rallying cry at the battle of Sedgemoor, *"Soe-hoe!"* Today, the gardens attract a panoply of Londoners young and otherwise.

Soho has a history of welcoming all colors and creeds to its streets. The district was first settled by French Huguenots fleeing religious persecution after the revocation of the Edict of Nantes in 1685. In more recent years, an influx of settlers from the New Territories of Hong Kong have built London's Chinatown south of Soho. A strong Mediterranean influence can also be detected in the aromas of espresso, garlic, and sizzling meats wafting through the area's maze of streets.

Perhaps contemporary Soho's most salient feature, especially on sunny days, is its vibrant **sidewalk cafe culture,** a recent development marking an intentional departure from the pornographic past. An *al fresco* mecca, today's Soho overflows with media types (mostly in the film and TV industries), artists, writers, club kids, and posers. The area has a significant and visible gay presence; a concentration of gay-owned restaurants and bars has turned **Old Compton Street** into the gay heart of London.

Like the other SoHo in New York, Soho has become almost too stylish for its own good. Attracted by the scent of money, large corporations and chains are moving in for the kill, threatening to destroy the area's distinct character and turn it into another Covent Garden. Nevertheless, today's Soho manages to skillfully tread the line between sleazy grit and boring corporate sanitization. For a long time, the ruins of **St. Anne's Church** (tel. 437 5006) provided an eerie backdrop to Wardour St., which runs north through the offices of Britain's film industry from Shaftesbury Ave. Leveled by German bombers in 1940, only Wren's anomalous tower of 1685 and the ungainly, bottle-shaped steeple added by Cockerell in 1803 emerged unscathed, but a new building was constructed around it in 1991. The author William Hazlitt is buried in the Churchyard. *(Church gardens open M-Sa 8am-dusk, Su 9am-dusk.)*

Since the 1840s, **Berwick Street Market** (parallel to the north end of Wardour St.) has rumbled with trade and far-flung Cockney accents (open M-Sa 9am-6pm). Famous for the widest and cheapest selection of fruits and vegetables in central London, the market has expanded to include cheap electrical appliances and a small selection of clothes. The street also boasts an impressive array of shops and cafes. Nearby **Meard Street** offers up an impression of Soho in its earlier, more residential days.

Running parallel to Regent St. is **Carnaby Street,** a notorious hotbed of 1960s sex, fashion, and Mods. It witnessed the rise of youth culture and became the heart of what *Time* magazine termed "Swingin' London." Many of the chic boutiques and parading celebrities of the mid-1960s have long since left the area, which has lapsed into a lurid tourist trap crammed with stalls of junky souvenirs. However, some of its more traditional denizens (like **Luderwicks,** the oldest pipe-makers in London), have weathered storms of fads and tourists alike.

Soho also has a rich literary past: Blake and Defoe lived on Broadwick St. (off Wardour St.), and Thomas de Quincey *(Confessions of an English Opium Eater)* ate dope in his houses on Greek and Tavistock St. To the north, a blue plaque above the

Quo Vadis restaurant at **28 Dean Street** locates the austere two-room flat where the impoverished Karl Marx lived with his wife, maid, and five children while writing *Das Kapital.* The fact that this house is next door to a strip joint is one of history's little ironies.

Leicester Square, just south of Shaftesbury Ave., between Piccadilly Circus and Charing Cross Rd. (the pedestrian-only streets perpendicular to Charing Cross Rd. all lead to the square itself) is an entertainment nexus. Amusements range from very expensive, mammoth cinemas to the free performances provided by the street entertainers, to the glockenspiel of the **Swiss Centre.** Its 25 bells ring M-F at noon, 6, 7, and 8pm, Sa-Su at noon, 2, 4, 5, 6, 7, and 8pm; the ringing is accompanied by a moving model of herdsmen leading their cattle through the Alps. If that's not enough, there's always a constant cacophony of tourists and locals to keep the eye and ear occupied. Though there's safety in crowds and plenty of police, watch out—the square is a notorious hotbed of bag snatchers and drug addicts.

On the north side of the square, at Leicester Pl., the French presence in Soho manifests itself in **Notre-Dame de France** (tel. 437 9363). This church may not be architecturally distinguished, but those who venture inside will be rewarded with the exquisite Aubusson tapestry lining the inner walls. The tiny chapel built into the western wall features an arresting 1960 Jean Cocteau mural. On the south side of the square, a large queue marks the **half-price ticket booth,** where theater tickets are sold for half price on the day of the show (see **Theater,** p. 227).

Cantonese immigrants first arrived in Britain as cooks on British ships, and London's first Chinese community formed around the docks near Limehouse. Today, however, London's primary **Chinatown** (known in Chinese as *Tong Yan Kai,* "Chinese Street") lies off the north side of Leicester Sq. Chinatown swelled with immigrants from Hong Kong in the 1950s; a smaller influx has arrived since the colony changed hands in 1997. Between Shaftesbury Ave.'s theaters and Leicester Sq.'s cinemas, the streets sprout Chinese language signs and pagoda-capped telephone booths. **Gerrard Street,** the main thoroughfare, runs closest to the Leicester Sq. tube station. This street, where poet John Dryden once lived, is now a pedestrian avenue framed by scroll-worked dragon gates.

Chinatown is most vibrant during the year's two major festivals: the **Mid-Autumn Festival,** at the end of September, and the **Chinese New Year Festival,** during the beginning of February. For further information on festivals or Chinatown call the **Chinese Community Centre,** 44 Gerrard St., 2nd floor (tel. 439 3822; open M-Th and Sa-Su 11am-5pm). Those thirsty for eastern newspapers (in English or Chinese) should check out the bustling bookshop **Guanghwa,** 7 Newport Pl. (see **Bookstores,** p. 255). The church of St. Martin-in-the-Fields in Trafalgar Sq. conducts a Chinese service every Sunday afternoon at 2:45pm.

Covent Garden

The outdoor cafes, upscale shops, and slick crowds animating Covent Garden today belie the square's medieval beginnings as a literal "convent garden" where the monks of Westminster Abbey grew their vegetables. When Henry VIII abolished the monasteries in 1536, he granted the land to John Russell, first Earl of Bedford. The Earl's descendants developed it into a fashionable *piazza* (designed by Inigo Jones) in the 1630s, giving London its first planned square.

Today Covent Garden is filled with street performers who swallow swords, juggle flaming torches, or sketch other street performers as they perform. With lots of pubs, cafes, and trendy shops, Covent Garden attracts all kinds, but especially the young and vibrant. The streets are constantly bustling—Friday and Saturday nights are downright hectic, as theater crowds converge with pub crawlers.

Jones's **St. Paul's Church** now stands as the sole remnant of the original square, although the interior had to be rebuilt after bring gutted by a fire in 1795. *(Open M 10am-2:30pm, Tu 9am-4pm, W 9:30am-4pm, Th 8:30am-4pm, F 9:30am-4pm, Su 9am-12:30pm. Services M 8:30am. Holy Communion services Su 11am, W 1:10pm, and Th 8:30am.*

Evensong sung on the 2nd Su of each month at 4pm.) Known as "the actor's church," St. Paul's is filled with plaques commemorating the achievements of Boris Karloff, Vivien Leigh, Noel Coward, and Tony Simpson ("inspired player of small parts"), among others. The connection to the theater dates back to the mid-17th century when this was the center of London's theatrical culture. The placid back flower garden serves as a lunchtime retreat for an appealing cross-section of Londoners.

The misleading east portico facing the Covent Garden Piazza never served as a door, but rather as a stage; an inscription marks it as the site of the first known performance of a Punch and Judy puppet show, recorded by Samuel Pepys in 1662.

During the 1800s, a glass and iron roof was built to shelter the fruit, vegetable, and flower market centered in the Piazza. Though the wholesalers' carts left Covent Garden in 1974 for Nine Elms, south of the Thames, the Victorian architecture has remained to house the fashionable shops and expensive restaurants that sprouted during a tourist-oriented redevelopment. The Victorian Flower Market building in the southeast corner of the piazza now contains the **London Transport Museum** (see **Museums**, p. 226). Markets selling crafts and antiques, madding crowds, and omnipresent street performers reenact the jostling marketplace of yore.

Two of London's most venerable venues, the **Theatre Royal** and the **Royal Opera House,** lend a feeling of civility to the area, adding pre-theater and pre-concert-goers to the throng of visitors. These venues represent a long tradition of theater in the Covent Garden area. The Theatre Royal (entrance on Catherine St.) was first built in 1663 as one of two legal theatrical venues in London. Four previous incarnations burnt down; the present building dates from 1812. The Royal Opera House (on Bow St.) began as a theater for concerts and plays in 1732 and currently houses the Royal Opera and Royal Ballet companies, as well as scores of workmen, who are currently refurbishing the outside of the building and will be until late 1999. For information on how to see performances, see **Entertainment**, p. 243.

Right across the street from the Royal Opera House stands **Bow Street Magistrates' Court** (which closed in 1992), the oldest of London's 12 magistrates' courts and home of the Bow Street Runners, predecessors of the city's present-day police. In the courthouse, novelist Henry Fielding and his brother Sir John presided over a bench famed for its compassion (in a time when compassion meant sentencing petty thieves to 14 years deportation to Australia rather than hanging).

The **Theatre Museum** sits to the south, on the corner of Russell and Wellington streets (see **Museums**, p. 232). Nearby, a blue plaque at 8 Russell St. marks the site of James Boswell's home, where he first met Dr. Johnson in 1763.

Even outside the renovated central market area, Covent Garden buzzes with activity. Curious stage-design shops cluster near the Opera House, and moss-covered artisans' studios stud the surrounding streets, interspersed with an odd assortment of theatre-related businesses. Rose St. (between Garrick and Floral streets) leads to the notorious **Lamb and Flag** (see **Pubs**, p. 122), supposedly the only timber building left in the West End. In this lively pub, Dryden was attacked and nearly murdered by an angry mob hired by the Duchess of Portsmouth (Louise de Keroualle, Mistress of Charles II) who held him responsible for "certain scurrilous verses and lampoons then published concerning her behavior." This attempted murder is commemorated each December 19th (called **Dryden Night**).

On Great Newport St. to the west, **The Photographers' Gallery** holds its reputation as one of London's major venues for contemporary photographic exhibitions. Long Acre and Neal St. bustle with diverse specialty shops, similar only in their high prices. But many of these stores are great for browsing.

Further along, Neal St. leads to **Neal's Yard,** where the adventurous can come face to face with wild vegetarians and peruse their stores and restaurants, which sell wholesome foods, cheeses and yogurts, herbs, fresh-baked breads, and homeopathic remedies. At the northern section of St. Martin's Lane, six streets converge at the **Seven Dials** monument (the 7th dial is the monument itself, a sundial).

Holborn and the Inns of Court

There's no law like English law. The historical center of English law lies in an area straddling the precincts of Westminster and the City and surrounding long and litigious precincts of High Holborn, Chancery Lane, and Fleet Street. The Strand and Fleet St. meet at the **Royal Courts of Justice** (tel. 936 6000; tube: Temple), a wonderfully elaborate Gothic structure—easily mistaken for a cathedral—designed in 1874 by architect G.E. Street for the Supreme Court of Judicature. At the Strand entrance there are a helpful set of displays explaining the court system. Today's not the day to wear that plated Mercedes medallion—security is tight, metal detectors are highly sensitive. The biggest draw for tourists who sit in on proceedings are the **wigs** the justices and barristers wear. On hot days the judge may allow everyone to remove their wigs, but newer weaves have made this indecorous allowance rare. (Courts and galleries open to the public Mon.-Fri. 9am-4:30pm. Court cases start at 10-10:30am, but they break for lunch 1-2pm.) The first floor contains an otherwise dreary cafeteria which permits patrons to determine the size of their own orders of chips (90p)—some daredevils test the bounds of self-service by emptying the pan onto a tray. Rules are rules, *and barristers know this,* so let your appetite guide you.

Barristers in the City are affiliated with one of the famous **Inns of Court** (Middle Temple, Inner Temple, Lincoln's Inn, and Gray's Inn), four ancient legal institutions that provide lectures and apprenticeships for law students and regulate admission to the bar. The tiny gates and narrow alleyways that lead to the Inns are invisible to most passersby. Inside, the Inns are organized like colleges at Oxford, each with its own gardens (great for sunbathing or picnicking), chapel, library, dining hall, common rooms, and chambers. Most were founded in the 13th century when a royal decree barred the clergy from the courts of justice, giving rise to a new class of professional legal advocates. Today, students may seek their legal training outside of the Inns, but to be considered for membership they must "keep term" by dining regularly in one of the halls. Most inns do not allow visitors but are still worth seeing from the outside.

South of Fleet St., the labyrinth of the **Temple** (tube: Temple) encloses the prestigious and stately Middle and Inner Temple Inns. They derive their name from the clandestine, crusading Order of the Knights Templar, who embraced this site as their English seat in the 12th century. The secretive order dissolved in 1312 (although some claim it still exists in the form of the Masons and Skull &Bones) and this property was eventually passed on to the Knights Hospitallers of St. John, who leased it to a community of common-law scholars in 1338. Virtually leveled by the Germans in the early 1940s, only the church, crypt, and buttery of the Inner Temple survive intact from the Middle Ages.

Held in common by both the Middle and Inner Temples, the **Temple Church** is made of an older round church (1185 AD) and a newer addition of a rectangular nave (1240 AD). The older portion is the finest of the few round churches left in England. It contains gorgeous stained-glass windows, a handsome 12th-century Norman doorway, an altar screen by Wren (1682), and 10 arresting, armor-clad stone effigies of sinister Knights Templar dating from the 12th and 14th centuries. Be sure to note the grotesque heads lining the circular wall surrounding the effigies.

According to Shakespeare *(Henry VI),* the red and white roses that served as emblems throughout the War of the Roses were plucked from the Middle Temple Garden. On Groundhog Day in 1601, Shakespeare himself supposedly appeared in a performance of *Twelfth Night* in **Middle Temple Hall,** a grand Elizabethan dining room in a building on Middle Temple Ln., just past Brick Ct. (not open to the public). **Fountain Court** contains its 1681 namesake, restored in 1919. Nearby, a handful of London's last functioning gas lamps illuminate Middle Temple Lane.

Back across Fleet St., on the other side of the Royal Courts, **Lincoln's Inn** (tube: Holborn) was the only Inn to emerge unscathed from the Blitz. The lawyers of Lincoln's Inn were mocked by John Donne's rhyming couplets in his *Satire: On Lawyers.* **New Square** and its cloistered churchyard (to the right as you enter from Lincoln's Inn Fields) appear today much as they did in the 1680s. The **Old Hall,** east of New Sq., dates from 1492; here the Lord High Chancellor presided over the High Court of Chancery from 1733 to 1873. The best-known chancery case is that of Jarndyce and Jarndyce, whose life-sapping machinations are played out in the many pages of *Bleak House.* Dickens knew well what he described, having worked as a lawyer's clerk in New Court just across the yard. To the west, Tudor-style **New Hall** houses a 19th-century mural by G.F. Watts and a collection of lugubrious, legal portraits. Built in 1497, the adjacent library is London's oldest. John Donne, William Pitt, Horace Walpole, and Benjamin Disraeli number among the many luminaries associated with Lincoln's Inn. The only portion of the grounds open to visitors is the grassy quadrangle and the **New Chapel,** which features a spectacular red roof (open Mon.-Fri. noon-2:30pm). **Sir John Soane's Museum** sits on the north side of Lincoln's Inn Fields, London's largest square; it's the house bedecked with sculpture amidst a row of plain buildings (see **Museums,** p. 228).

Gray's Inn (tube: Chancery Ln.), dubbed "that stronghold of melancholy" by Dickens, stands at the northern end of Fulwood Pl., off High Holborn. Reduced to ashes by German bombers in 1941, Gray's Inn was restored during the 1950s. The **Hall,** to your right as you pass through the archway, retains its original stained glass (1580) and most of its ornate screen. The first performance of Shakespeare's *Comedy of Errors* took place here in 1594. Francis Bacon maintained chambers here from 1577 until his death in 1626, and is the purported designer of the gardens.

Of the nine Inns of Chancery, only **Staple Inn's** building survives (located where Gray's Inn Rd. meets High Holborn; tube: Chancery Ln.). The half-timbered Elizabethan front, with its easily recognized vertical striping, dates from 1586. Devoted son Samuel Johnson wrote "Rasselas" here in one week to pay for his mother's funeral. For those who can't get enough of the fascinating Inns of Court, "Legal London" **walking tours** are held every Monday at 2pm and Wednesday at 11am departing from the Holborn tube station. Call for details (tel. 624 3978; £4.50, students £3.50).

The Strand

Hugging the embankment of the River Thames, **The Strand** (tube: Charing Cross or Temple) has fared ill throughout London's growth. The street was built to connect the City with Westminster Palace and Parliament. Once lined with fine Tudor houses, today this major thoroughfare curves from Trafalgar Sq. through a jumbled assortment of dull commercial buildings. All of the sights are at the Aldwych and Temple end of the street.

Somerset House, a magnificent Palladian structure built by Sir William Chambers in 1776, stands on the site of the 16th-century palace where Elizabeth I resided during the brief reign of her sister Mary. Formerly the administrative center of the Royal Navy, the building now houses the exquisite and intimately-housed **Courtauld Collection** (see **Museums,** p. 226).

Just east of the Courtauld, **St. Mary-le-Strand's** (tel. 836 3205), slender steeple and elegant portico rise above an island of decaying steps in the middle of the modern roadway (open M-F 11am-3:30pm). Designed by James Gibbs and consecrated in 1724, the church overlooks the site of the original Maypole, where London's first hackney cabs assembled in 1634. Parishioner Isaac Newton laid claim to the pole for a telescope stand. Inside, the baroque barrel vault and altar walls reflect not only the glory of God but also Gibbs' architectural training in Rome. The mesmerizing blue windows are another reminder of things more temporal; they are replacements of those blown out in WWII. Across the street, newsreaders intone "This is London" every hour from Bush House, the nerve center of the BBC's radio services.

To the east stands handsome **St. Clement Danes** (tel. 242 8282), whose melodious bells get their 15 seconds of fame in the nursery rhyme "Oranges and lemons, say the bells of St. Clement's" (open daily 8am-5pm). Children get their 15 minutes of fruit when oranges and lemons are distributed in a ceremony near the end of March. (The bells still ring at 9am, noon, 3, and 6pm every day.) Designed by Wren in 1682, the church was built over the ruins of an older Norman structure reputed to be the tomb of Harold Harefoot, leader of a colony of Danes who settled the area in the 9th century. In 1720, Gibbs replaced Wren's original truncated tower with a slimmer spire. Although German firebombs gutted the church in 1941, the ornately molded white stucco and gilt interior has been restored. Today it is the official church of the Royal Air Force—evident in the many plaques and monuments which honor these bold airmen. A crypt-cum-prayer-chapel houses an eerie collection of 17th-century funerary monuments. Samuel Johnson worshipped here—a statue of the Doctor strikes a bizarre pose outside the church. The good doctor looks like a portly high school football coach urging the team on to victory.

The nearby Gothic giant houses the Royal Courts of Justice (see **Holborn and Inns of Court,** p. 157). **Twining's Teas,** 216 The Strand (tel. 353 3511), near the Fleet St. end of the road, honors the leaf which started a war (open M-F 9:30am-4:30pm). After nine generations of Mr. Twining, it is both the oldest business in Britain still on original premises and the narrowest shop in London. Because of fire regulations they can't brew tea on premises, but they still sell the dry leaves. Just east stands the only Strand building to avoid the Great Fire, the **Wig and Pen Club,** 229-230 The Strand, which was constructed over Roman ruins in 1625. Frequented by the best-known barristers and journalists in London, the Wig and Pen is the ultimate old-boys hangout, although women of the legal and newspaper professions are now permitted to join. The club is open to members only, though an overseas traveler dressed in a coat and tie may be able to peek upstairs. If you have the nerve, walk up the ancient, crooked staircase—the only remnant of the original 17th-century house—and take note of the photographs of Prince Charles dining at the club, as well as signed photos of Nixon, Reagan, and former Chief Justice Burger. Backpackers beware—the doorman will haughtily reject denim-clad budget travelers.

As you stroll away from the Courts of Justice, two of London's top educational institutions heave into view. **King's College,** an unremarkable concrete building, is on the left; straight across the road stands the **London School of Economics,** the setting for feisty student radicalism in the 1960s, now newly installed as Prime Minister Tony Blair's favorite generator of political ideas.

The **Temple Bar Monument** stands where The Strand meets Fleet St., marking the boundary between Westminster and the City. The Sovereign must obtain ceremonial permission from the Lord Mayor to enter the City here.

To the south, the **Embankment** (tube: Charing Cross or Embankment) runs along the Thames, parallel to The Strand. The **Victoria Embankment Gardens** (tel. 641 5264), sit next to the Embankment tube station and offer a pleasant location to sit on the well-kept lawns and have a bite of lunch (open 7:30am-dusk). Between the Hungerford and Waterloo Bridges stands London's oldest (though not indigenous) landmark, **Cleopatra's Needle,** an Egyptian obelisk from 1450 BC, stolen by the Viceroy of Egypt in 1878. A sister stone stands in Central Park in New York. Fairly near Trafalgar Sq., the **Queen's Chapel of the Savoy** (tel. 836 7221), on Savoy Hill—an appendage of Savoy Palace, inhabited after 1268 by John of Gaunt—provides a respite from the traffic and sensationalistic journalism of Fleet St. (open Tu-F 11:30am-3pm, services Su 11am).

The City of London

Until the 18th century, the **City of London** was London; all other boroughs and neighborhoods now swallowed up by "London" were neighboring towns or outlying villages. Enclosed by Roman and medieval walls, the City had six gates: Aldersgate, Aldgate, Bishopsgate, Cripplegate, Newgate, and Ludgate.

Today, the one-square-mile City of London is the financial center of Europe. Each weekday 350,000 people surge in at 9am and rush out again unfailingly at 5pm, leaving behind a resident population of only 6000. Today's City hums with activity during the weekdays, is dead on Saturdays, and seems downright ghostly on Sundays. At the center of the City, the massive **Bank of England** controls the country's finances, and the **Stock Exchange** makes (or breaks) the nation's fortune (see **City: Bank to Tower,** p. 163). International banks proliferate around them, bowing in homage to these great temples of mammon. Towering cranes, office building sites, and rising share indices bore witness to the British "economic resurgence" of the late 1980s. Panic in such City stalwarts as Lloyd's of London is testimony to the precariousness of the early 1990s. Terrorist attacks in the recent past have prompted the government to regulate traffic into the City. Roadblocks are no longer manned, and Londoners hope that recent negotiations in Northern Ireland may make them altogether redundant. However, security measures have exacerbated the traffic congestion, which was already considered horrendous by most City dwellers. London's air quality is among the poorest in the world, and many Londoners hope that the roadblocks, or other public measures, will be used as a weapon against excessive traffic and pollution.

Behind this array of modern chaos rest pieces of another city: old London. Aged churches, friaries, and pubs, many of them still in use, dwell behind small alleys and above the roofs of steel office buildings. **St. Paul's Cathedral,** the most glorious and significant of these structures, anchors London's memory to its colorful past (see **St. Paul's Cathedral,** p. 165). The City owes much of its graceful appearance to Sir Christopher Wren, who was the chief architect working after the **Great Fire of 1666** almost completely razed the area. In his diary, Samuel Pepys gives a moving firsthand account of the fire that started in a bakery in Pudding Lane, and leapt between the overhanging houses to bring destruction upon the City. In a classic case of locking the barn door after the barn has burned down, Charles II issued a proclamation afterwards that City buildings should be rebuilt in brick and stone, rather than highly flammable wood and thatch. Wren's studio designed 52 churches to replace the 89 destroyed in the fire, and the surviving 24 churches are some of the only buildings in the City from the period immediately following the Great Fire. A host of variations on a theme, they gave Wren a valuable chance to work out design problems that would come up as he rebuilt **St. Paul's Cathedral** (see p. 165). The original effect of a forest of steeples surrounding the great dome of St. Paul's is perhaps his greatest contribution to London's cityscape; unfortunately, modern skyscrapers now obscure that effect. Some churches and old buildings have not withstood the collision with modernity. Many old structures were totally gutted by the German Blitz in 1941, while others have taken on a bombed-out and blackened appearance as a result of coal fires during the 1960s and today's thickening air pollution.

The Lord Mayor

The Lord Mayor's position has not always been entirely ceremonial, nor has it always been lordly. The job originally consisted of running the affairs of the City 900 years ago. The wily merchants of the City used their financial leverage to win increasing amounts of autonomy from the monarchy throughout the years, culminating in the construction of Guildhall—the Lord Mayor's official worshipping site—and the move from just plain Mayorship to Lord Mayorship. While the position today is ceremonial, it retains its pomp and grandeur. The Lord Mayor is the Chief Magistrate, Chairman of the Court of Aldermen and the Court of Common Council. In the City, he is second only to the Queen, although the Queen—and only the Queen—has to ask his permission before entering the city gates.

Perhaps the most important secular structures of the City are the buildings of the **Livery Companies.** The companies began as medieval guilds representing specific trades and occupations, such as the Drapers and the Fishmongers. New guilds, such as the Information Technologists, have formed to keep up with changing times. The 84 **livery halls** are scattered around the square mile. Most halls do not open to the public; those that do require tickets. The City of London Information Centre (see below) receives a batch of tickets in February, but they disappear rapidly. Some halls sponsor spring celebrations, and a few hold fascinating exhibits—for example, a showing of the finest products of London's goldsmiths.

The **City of London Information Centre,** St. Paul's Churchyard, EC4 (tel. 332 1456; tube: St. Paul's), specializes in information about the City of London, but answers questions on all of London. *(Open Apr.-Sept. daily 9:30am-5pm; Oct.-Mar. M-F 9:30am-5pm, Sa 9:30am-12:30pm.)* The helpful, knowledgeable staff is worth speaking to before exploring this part of the city. The oldest part of London, the City is home to many municipal traditions. One of the largest is the **Lord Mayor's Show,** on the second Saturday of November—a glittering parade of pomp and red velvet to the Royal Courts of Justice in celebration of London citizens' right to elect their Lord Mayor. Information and street plans are available from the City of London Information Centre starting in mid-October. One of the newer traditions is July's **City of London Festival,** which jam-packs the churches, halls, squares, and sidewalks of the area with music and theater (see **Entertainment,** p. 242).

The area is filled with architecturally stunning churches—beware, opening times are often changed without notice due to the small staffs in many of these financially strapped houses of worship. The sights in the City area are helpfully marked by distinctive brown signs which direct you from tube stations.

CITY (WESTERN SECTION): BANK TO ST. PAUL'S

The few remaining stones of the Roman **Temple of Mithras,** Queen Victoria St. (tube: Bank or Mansion House), dwell incongruously in the shadow of the Temple Court building. Discovered during construction work, and shifted a few yards from its original location, what remains are two-feet-tall walls in the shape of the original temple. Down Queen Victoria St., **St. Mary Aldermary** (tel. 248 4906), so named because it is older than any other St. Mary's church in the City, towers over its surroundings (open W-F 11am-3pm). A rare Gothic Wren creation, it is especially notable for its delicate fan vaulting. The bells that recalled Mayor Dick Whittington to London rang out from St. Marie de Arcubus, replaced by Wren's **St. Mary-le-Bow** (tel. 248 5139) Cheapside, in 1683 (open M-Th 6:30am-6pm, F 6:30am-4pm). The range of the Bow bells' toll is supposed to define the extent of true-blue Cockney London.

St. James Garlickhythe (tel. 236 1719), on Upper Thames St., gets its name from the garlic once sold nearby (open M-F 10am-4pm). Its modest Hawksmoor steeple is dwarfed by the huge Vintners Place development across the street. To the west on Queen Victoria St. stands a rare red-brick Wren church with an elegant cupola, **St. Benet's.** Just across the street, the **College of Arms** (tel. 248 2762) rests on its heraldic authority behind ornate gates (open M-F 10am-4pm). The College regulates the granting and recognition of coats of arms, and is directed by the Earl Marshal, the Duke of Norfolk. The officer-in-waiting can assess your claim to a British family coat of arms. Farther west, **St. Andrew-by-the-Wardrobe,** 146 Queen Victoria (tel. 248 7546; tube: Blackfriars), was originally built next to Edward III's Royal Stores (open Sept.-July M-F 8:30am-6pm). Now the church cowers beneath the Faraday building, the first building allowed to exceed the City's previously strict height limit.

Queen Victoria St. meets New Bridge St. in the area known as **Blackfriars,** named in reference to the darkly-clad Dominican brothers who built a monastery there in the Middle Ages. Shakespeare acted in James Burbage's theatre here in the late 1500s. Ludgate Circus, to the north, has recently received a major facelift. A peaceful haven is offered by **St. Martin Ludgate** (tel. 248 6054), a Wren church on Ludgate Hill untouched by the Blitz (open M-F 11am-3pm). The square interior boasts some fine Grinling Gibbons woodwork, and the slim spire still pierces the dome of St. Paul's when seen from Ludgate Circus, just as Wren intended.

If you begin to tire of churches, the **Old Bailey** (tel. 248 3277; tube: St. Paul's) is just around the corner. *(Open M-F 10am-1pm and 2-5pm; entrance in Warwick Passage off Old Bailey.)* Technically the Central Criminal Courts, but infamous as the site of Britain's grimiest prison, it crouches under a copper dome and a wide-eyed figure of justice on the corner of Old Bailey and Newgate St. Trial-watching persists as a favorite occupation, and the Old Bailey fills up whenever a gruesome or scandalous case is in progress. You can enter the public Visitors' Gallery and watch bewigged barristers at work. Even women wear wigs so that they too may look like wise old men (although plans are afoot to modernize the British legal system, so catch the wigs while you can). Cameras and large bags may not be taken inside, but in exchange for a pint, you can leave them at the Irish pub across the street. The Chief Post Office building, off Newgate to the north, envelops the stimulating **National Postal Museum** (see **Museums,** p. 232). **Postman's Park,** nestled behind obscuring gates and church walls, provides wonderful space for a quick snooze or picnic. The park was once the churchyard of St. Leonard's Cathedral and the graveyard for Christ Church; crumbling gravestones still line its southern perimeter. Toward the back of the park rests a 19th-century memorial to firefighters, police officers, and good samaritans killed in the line of duty.

Further east on Angel and Gresham St., going left up Aldermanbury, huddles the **Guildhall** (tel. 606 3030), a cavernous space where dignitaries were once tried for treason. *(Open daily May-Sept. 10am-5pm; Oct.-Apr. closed Sunday.)* An improbable mix of high Gothic and modish 1960s concrete, the building currently serves as the City's administrative center and houses the town clerk, a library, offices, and the **Guildhall Clock Museum** (see **Museums,** p. 230). Its **Great Hall,** lined with monuments to national figures like Nelson and Wellington, hosts monthly city council meetings and banquets. On the balcony stand the nine-foot gilded statues of the ancient giants **Gog** and **Magog.** Visitors are welcome every third Thursday to watch the Lord Mayor of London, bedecked in traditional robes and followed by a sword-wielding entourage, preside over council meetings. He ranks above the Queen when she enters the City. The **Guildhall Library** on Aldermanbury St. specializes in the history of London—holdings include City church manuscripts, family genealogies, and early maps (open M-Sa 9:30am-5pm). Visitors are free to browse through the collection of books as well as to visit the library's quadrennial exhibitions in the Print Room. Visitors are not permitted to take books out of the library. For a quick respite after the Guildhall, visit **Finsbury Park** (on Finsbury Circus around the corner from Moorgate Tube). Surrounded by round-faced Georgian office buildings, this circular park's colorful flower bed and jungle-green bowling area offer delightful spots for picnics, free summer concerts, and bowling, British style.

Next to the Guildhall is the Wren-designed **St. Lawrence Jewry** (tel. 600 9478), the official church of the Corporation of London (open M-F 7:30am-2pm). This seemingly absurd title reflects the fact that the church was, in days of yore, the sole Christian house in a predominantly Jewish area. It was rebuilt after the war, due to damage from what the sign outside formally refers to as "action by the King's Enemies," namely, a German bomb.

CITY: BARBICAN AND NORTHERN SECTION

Housing some of England's greatest cultural treasures, at times the **Barbican Centre** (tube: Barbican or Moorgate) seems like a shopping mall that never ends. A 35-acre brutalist masterpiece, the Barbican is a maze of apartment buildings, restaurants, gardens, and exhibition halls, described at its 1982 opening as "the city's gift to the nation." **The Royal Shakespeare Company,** the **London Symphony Orchestra,** the **Museum of London,** the **Guildhall School for Music and Drama,** and the **Barbican Art Gallery** (see **Entertainment,** p. 234, and **Museums,** p. 220) call this complex home, as do the many politicians and actors who reside in the Barbican's distinctive apartment buildings. St. Giles Church and the City of London School for Girls stand in the complex's unexpectedly verdant central courtyard, whose artificial lakes and planned gardens temper the Barbican's relentless urbanity.

Most visitors enter the Centre through the Silk St. entrance, where statues of nine golden Muses exemplify the Barbican's dazzling elegance. Once inside, though, the Barbican can be daunting. To help visitors successfully navigate the Centre's labyrinthine walkways and vast interior, a reception desk has been installed at the front entrance. In addition, Barbican's floors have been renumbered, so that the ground floor is now called Level 0, not Level 5. Pick up a free pocket guide by the Lakeside Terrace to find your way through the Barbican's wonders, including the Centre's third-floor conservatory, second-floor **library,** and ground-floor foyers, where free concerts are held daily. *(Library open M and W-F 9:30am-5:30pm, Tu 9:30am-7:30pm, Sa 9:30am-12:30pm.)* The Barbican has recently commissioned another redesign—expect more big, friendly signs telling you where you are in the confusing layout.

In order to reach **St. Bartholomew the Great** (tel. 606 5171), continue past the Barbican tube on Beech St. and make a left on Little Britain. *(Open M-F 8:30am-5pm, Sa 10:30am-1:30pm, Su 8am-8pm.)* One must enter through an exceedingly narrow Tudor house to reach this architectural jewel. Parts of the church date from 1123, although 800 years of alteration have much embellished it. The tomb near the central main altar belongs to Rahere, who allegedly founded the church after he was cured of malaria through prayer. Party people anxious to begin a day of drinking should try one of the pubs around **Smithfield Market,** an ancient meat and poultry trade market—the pubs around here are licensed to ale starting at 7am. Smithfield's associations with butchery antedate the meat market. Scotsman William Wallace (recently depicted by Mel Gibson in *Braveheart*) and rebel Wat Tyler rank among those executed here in the Middle Ages. It was also among the tolerant Queen Mary's favorite Protestant-burning sites.

Charterhouse (tel. 253 3260), a peculiar institution first established as a priory and converted in 1611 to a school and hospital for poor gentlemen, stands on the edge of Charterhouse Sq. *(Tours Apr.-July W 2:15pm; a small donation is expected.)* The school has moved, but the fine group of 15th- to 17th-century buildings still houses around 40 residents, who are required to be bachelors or widowers over 60.

Just north of the square, up St. John's St. and off Clerkenwell Rd., **St. John's Gate** (tel. 253 6644), holds the headquarters of the British Order of the Hospital of St. John, the last vestiges of the medieval crusading order of Knights Hospitallers. *(Open M-F 10am-5pm, Sa 10am-4pm. 1-hr. tours Tu and F-Sa 11am and 2:30pm; £2.50 donation.)* Exhibits relate the order's tumultuous history, from their rise as healers (their 12th-century priory was one of Europe's first hospitals), through their crusading and subsequent dissolution under Henry VIII, and their reemergence in the 19th century as a volunteer community service organization chartered by Queen Victoria.

CITY (EASTERN SECTION): BANK TO THE TOWER

The massive windowless walls and foreboding doors of the **Bank of England** enclose four full acres (tube: Bank). The present building dates from 1925, but the 8-ft.-thick outer wall is the same one built by eccentric architect Sir John Soane in 1788. The only part open to the public is the plush **Bank of England Museum** (see **Museums,** p. 220). Its neighbors, the Greek-columned Royal Exchange, Stock Exchange, and Lloyd's financial building remain, relics of the days when this block stood as the financial capital of the world. After recent terrorist attacks, the three were closed to visitors, but there is not much to see in them anyway. The grand trading pit of the Royal Exchange has been vacated by traders who now use office-based computers. The room is so empty, in fact, that the government has considered turning it into a gymnasium for local employees. (Head to the Futures Market on Cannon St. to see frenetic traders in brightly colored jackets continue the Exchange's bustling tradition.) Wren's penultimate church, **St. Margaret Lothbury** (tel. 606 8330), down Throgmorton St., was built in 1689 and contains a sumptuous carved wood screen (open M-F 8am-5pm). Most of the church's furnishings have been conglomerated from demolished City churches. A couple of blocks north, the **National Westminster Tower** hovers at over 600 ft. Until recently, it was Britain's tallest skyscraper, now displaced by the distant Canary Wharf.

The 1986 **Lloyd's** building and **Leadenhall Market,** off Leadenhall St., supply the most startling architectural clash in the City. The ducts, lifts, and chutes of Lloyd's are straight out of the 21st century. As one commentator put it, it is not so much a building as a vertical street. This futuristic setting houses the **Lutine Bell,** which is still occasionally rung—once for bad insurance news, twice for good. In contrast, across a narrow alley behind Lloyd's stretch the ornate red canopies and dazzling gargoyles of Victorian **Leadenhall Market.**

Behind the imposing **Mansion House,** home of the Lord Mayor, stands **St. Stephen Walbrook** (tel 283 4444), on Walbrook St. *(Open M-Th 10am-4pm, F 10am-3pm.)* Arguably Wren's finest, and allegedly his personal favorite, the church combines four major styles: the old-fashioned English church characterized by nave and chancel; the Puritan hall church, which lacks any separation between priest and congregation; the Greek Cross-plan church; and the domed church, a study for St. Paul's. The Samaritans, a social service group that advises the suicidal and severely depressed, was founded here in 1953 by rector Chad Varah. In one corner you can see the phone he used while in another is an honorary phone given to him by British Telecom. The mysterious cheese-like object ringed by the psychedelic lime, orange, purple, and pink cushion in the center is actually the altar. Sculpted by Henry Moore, it is as controversial as you think it is.

The church of **St. Mary Woolnoth** (tel. 626 7901), at King William and Lombard St., may look odd without a spire, but the interior proportions and the black and gilt reredos confirm the talents of Wren's pupil Nicholas Hawksmoor (open M-F 7:45am-5pm). It appears almost wider than it is long. The upper reaches are light and airy; lower portions are filled with dark wood. The only City church untouched by the Blitz, it "kept the hours" in T.S. Eliot's *The Waste Land.* **St. Mary Abchurch** (tel. 626 0306), off Abchurch Ln., provides a neat domed comparison to St. Stephen's—its mellow, dark wood and Baroque paintings contrast with St. Stephen's bright, airy interior (open M-Th 10am-2pm).

Before even the most basic rebuilding of the city, Wren designed a tall Doric pillar. Completed in 1677, the simply-named **Monument** (tube: Monument) lies at the bottom of Monument St. *(Open Apr.-Sept. M-F 10am-5:40pm, Sa-Su 2-5:40pm; Oct.-Mar. M-Sa 10am-5:40pm.)* Supposedly, the 202 ft. pillar stands exactly that many feet from where the Great Fire broke out in Pudding Lane on September 2, 1666, and "rushed devastating through every quarter with astonishing swiftness and worse." In 1681, a small addition was made to the inscription on the monument: "but Popish frenzy, which wrought such horrors, is not yet quenched." For some reason, this charming sentiment was deleted in 1830. High on Fish Street Hill, the column offers an expansive view of London. Bring stern resolution and £1.50 (child 50p) to climb its 311 steps. Upon successfully descending the tower, you'll be given a free certificate announcing your feat, signed by the City Secretary.

Over the river near the Monument, the current **London Bridge** succeeds a slew of ancestors. The famed version crowded with houses stood from 1176 until it burned in 1758. The most recent predecessor didn't fall down; in 1973 it was sold to an American millionaire for £1.03 million and shipped, block by block, to Lake Havasu City, Arizona. **St. Magnus Martyr** (tel. 626 4481), on Lower Thames St., stands next to the path to the 12th-century London Bridge, and proudly displays a chunk of wood from a Roman jetty (open Tu-F 10am-4pm, Su 10am-1pm). According to Eliot, the walls of the church "hold inexplicable splendor of Ionian white and gold," a soothing contrast to the forlorn (and former) Billingsgate fish market next door.

St. Mary-at-Hill (tel. 626 4184), Lovat Ln., is a typical Wren church with a surprisingly convincing reworking of the old interior by early Victorian craftsmen, and an even more convincing contemporary reconstruction project (open M-F 10am-3pm). **St. Dunstan-in-the-East,** St. Dunstan's Hill, suffered severe damage in the Blitz; only Wren's amazing spire remains. The ruins have been converted into a gorgeous little garden that makes a fine picnic spot. Covered in green, the remaining walls demarcate a secluded oasis in the middle of the City.

Pepys witnessed the spread of the Great Fire from atop **All Hallows by the Tower,** at the end of Great Tower St. Just inside the south entrance is an arch from the 7th-century Saxon church, discovered in 1960. To the left, the baptistry contains a striking wood font cover by Grinling Gibbons. For those wishing to take some Anglican church home, brass rubbings cost a mere £1.20. At the tiny **St. Olave's** on Hart St., an annual memorial service is held for Pepys, who is buried here with his wife (open M-F 9am-5pm). According to a 1586 entry in the church's Burial Register, Mother Goose is also interred here.

■ St. Paul's Cathedral

Tube: *St. Paul's.* **Open** *M-Sa 8:30am-4pm. Galleries and ambulatory open M-Sa 8:45am-4:15pm.* **Admission** *to cathedral, ambulatory, and crypt £4.50, students £3.50, children £2; with galleries £7.50, £6.50, £3.50.* **Tours** *depart at 11, 11:30am, 1:30, and 2pm; £3, students £2.* **Audio tours** *(45min.) £3, students £2.50, families £7; available from opening until 3pm in various languages.*

An extraordinary Anglican spinoff of the Vatican, **St. Paul's** is arguably the most stunning architectural sight in London. It dominates its surroundings, even as modern usurpers sneak up around it. St. Paul's has become a physical and spiritual symbol of London. Prince Charles and Lady Diana broke a 200-year tradition of holding royal weddings in Westminster Abbey so they could celebrate their ill-fated nuptials here. The current edifice is the third cathedral to stand on the site; the first was founded in 604 and destroyed by fire in 1089. The second and most massive cathedral was a medieval structure, one of the largest in Europe, topped by a spire ascending 489 ft. Falling into almost complete neglect in the 16th century, the cathedral became more of a marketplace than a church, and plans for its reconstruction were in the works well before the Great Fire. Wren had already started drawing up his grand scheme in 1666, when the conflagration demolished the cathedral, along with most of London, and gave him the opportunity to build from scratch.

Both the design and the building of the cathedral were dogged by controversy. Like his Renaissance predecessors, Wren preferred an equal-armed Greek Cross plan, while ecclesiastical authorities insisted upon a traditional medieval design with a long nave and choir for services. Wren's final design compromised by translating a Gothic cathedral into Baroque and Classical terms: a Greek Cross floor plan with medieval detailing. Wren's second model received the King's warrant of approval (and is thus known as the "Warrant Model"), but still differed from today's St. Paul's. The shrewd architect won permission to make necessary alterations as building proceeded and, behind the scaffolding, Wren had his way. The cathedral was topped off in 1710; at 365 ft. above the ground, the huge classical dome is the second largest free-standing dome in Europe (St. Peter's in the Vatican is the largest). Queen Victoria, believing the cathedral's cream and wooden interior to be too dull, flooded it with gold before her death in 1901.

In December 1940, London burned once again. On the night of the 29th, at the height of the Blitz, St. Paul's was engulfed by a sea of fire. This time it survived. Fifty-one firebombs landed on the cathedral, all swiftly put out by the heroic volunteer St. Paul's Fire Watch; a small monument in the floor at the end of the nave honors them. Two of the four high-explosive bombs that landed did explode, wrecking the north transept; the clear glass there bears silent testimony. Today, St. Paul's serves as a center for state functions, including Winston Churchill's funeral in 1965 (a plaque marks the spot in front of the choir where the coffin stood) and VE-Day ceremonies in 1994.

Dotted with sculptures, bronzes, and mosaics, St. Paul's makes a rewarding place for a wander. Above the choir, three neo-Byzantine glass mosaics by William Richmond, done in 1904, tell the story of Creation. The stalls in the **Choir,** carved by Grinling Gibbons, narrowly escaped a bomb, but the old altar did not. It was replaced with the current marble **High Altar,** covered by a St. Peter's-like *baldacchino* of oak, splendidly gilded. Above looms the crowning glory, the ceiling mosaic of Christ Seated in Majesty. A trial mosaic adorns the east wall of **St. Dunstan's Chapel,** on the left by the entrance. On the other side of the nave in the **Chapel of St. Michael and St. George** sits a richly carved throne by Grinling Gibbons, made for the coronation of William and Mary in 1710. Along the south aisle hangs Holman Hunt's third version of *The Light of the World,* allegedly the most well-traveled picture in the world. Monuments to the mighty abound—Wellington, Nelson, Kitchener, and Samuel Johnson are all remembered here.

The **ambulatory** contains a statue of poet John Donne (Dean of the Cathedral 1621-1631) in shrouds, one of the few monuments to survive from old St. Paul's. Also in the ambulatory is a modern, abstract sculpture of the Virgin Mary and Baby Jesus

St. Paul's Cathedral

SELECTED MONUMENTS AND TOMBS

1 Duke of Wellington
2 Sir Joshua Reynolds
3 Dr. Samuel Johnson
4 General Gordon
5 Lord Leighton
6 Earl Kitchener
7 General Abercromby
8 Sir John Moore
9 Lord Nelson
10 J.M.W. Turner
11 Admiral Collingwood
12 Admiral Earl Howe
13 John Howard
14 John Donne

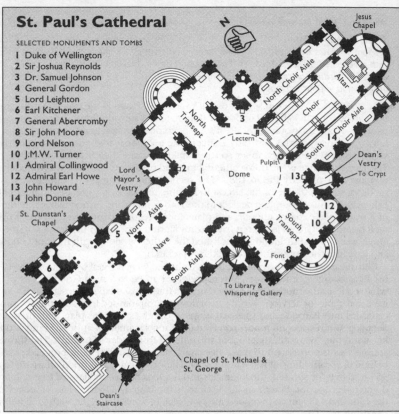

N
Jesus Chapel
Altar
North Choir Aisle
Choir
South Choir Aisle
North Transept
Lectern
Pulpit
Dome
Dean's Vestry
To Crypt
Lord Mayor's Vestry
St. Dunstan's Chapel
North Aisle
Nave
South Aisle
South Transept
Font
To Library & Whispering Gallery
Chapel of St. Michael & St. George
Dean's Staircase

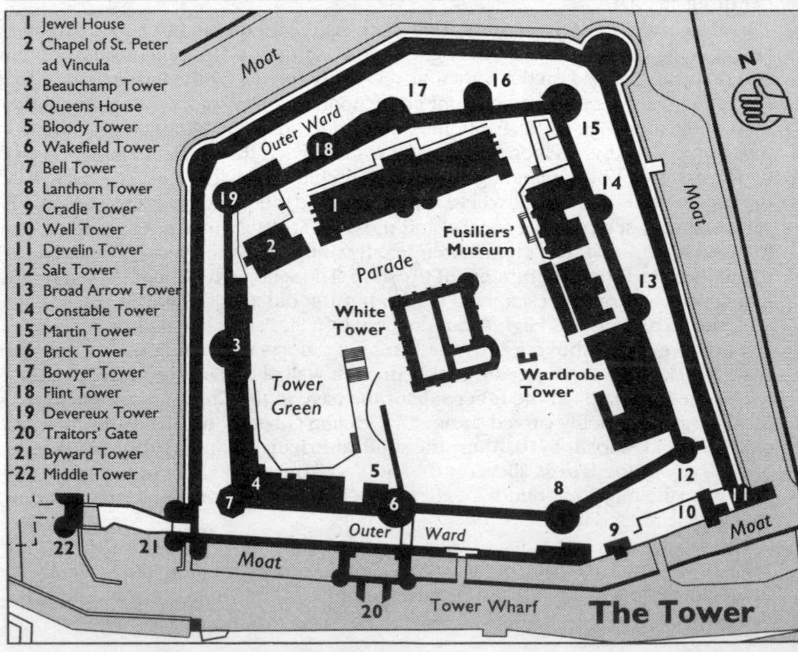

by Henry Moore. One month after the arrival of Moore's sculpture, entitled *Mother and Child,* guides insisted a name plaque be affixed to the base, as no one knew what it was meant to represent. Britain restored the former **Jesus Chapel** after the Blitz and dedicated it to U.S. soldiers who died during WWII. The graceful and intricate choir gates were executed by Jean Tijou early in the 18th century.

The **crypt,** saturated with tombs and monuments, forms a catalogue of Britain's officially "great" figures of the last two centuries, including Florence Nightingale and sculptor Henry Moore. (A few remnants made it through the Great Fire, including a memorial to Francis Bacon's father Nicolas.) The massive tombs of the Duke of Wellington and Nelson command attention; Nelson's coffin, placed directly beneath the dome, was originally intended for Cardinal Wolsey. A bust of George Washington stands opposite a memorial to Lawrence of Arabia. Around the corner lounges Rodin's fine bust of poet W.F. Henley (1849-1903). **Painter's Corner** holds the tombs of Sir Joshua Reynolds, Sir Lawrence Alma-Tadema, and J.M.W. Turner, along with memorials to John Constable and the revolutionary William Blake. Nearby, a black slab in the floor marks Wren's grave, with his son's famous epitaph close by: *Lector, si monumentum requiris circumspice* (roughly, "If you seek his monument, just look around you"). Outside the entrance to the crypt you will find a former **"Loo of the Year,"** as judged by the British Tourist Authority. Sure enough, the W.C. is sparkly clean and, best of all, free.

The display of **models** of St. Paul's details the history of the cathedral in all of its incarnations. Creating the great model of 1674, the star exhibit, cost as much as constructing a small house. In these models you can see how the upper parts of the exterior walls are mere facades, concealing the flying buttresses which support the nave roof. *(Audiovisual presentations every 30min. 10:30am-3pm; crypt open M-Sa 8:45am-4:45pm; last admission at 4pm.)*

The best place to head in St. Paul's is straight up. A visitor may ascend to whichever of three different levels in the dome his legs, heart, and courage will allow. Going up St. Paul's proves more challenging than going down: 259 steps lead to the vertiginous **Whispering Gallery,** on the inside base of the dome. During your ascent, look for the 18th-century grafitti carved into the stairwell. Words whispered against the wall whizz round the sides. A further 119 steps up, the first external view glitters from the **Stone Gallery,** only to be eclipsed by the uninterrupted and incomparable panorama from the **Golden Gallery,** 152 steps higher at the top of the dome. Before descending, take a peek down into the cathedral through the glass peephole in the floor; Nelson lies buried more than 400 ft. directly below.

Evensong is performed Monday through Saturday at around 5pm (precise time varies). This lovely Anglican ceremony celebrates Christ's assumption of mortal form, and gives visitors a chance to hear the cathedral's superb choir. Five minutes before the singing begins, worshippers will be allowed to sit in the choir, a few feet from the singers, though this means that you must stay for the duration (about 40min.). **St. Paul's Churchyard,** a fine picnic spot popular since Shakespeare's day, is surrounded by railings of mostly unappreciated interest; they were one of the first applications of cast iron. The modern St. Paul's Cross marks the spot where the papal pronouncement condemning Martin Luther was read to the public.

■ The Tower of London

***Tel.** 709 0765. **Tube:** Tower Hill. **Open** M-Sa 9am-5pm, Su 10am-5pm (last ticket sold at 4pm). **Admission** £9.50, students and seniors £7.15, children £6.25, families £28.40. Yeomen lead 1hr. **tours** every 30min. For tickets to the **Ceremony of the Keys,** the nightly ritual locking of the gates, write six weeks in advance to the Ceremony of the Keys, Waterloo Block, HM Tower of London, EC3 N4AB, with the number and date of tickets and enclosing a stamped addressed envelope or coupon-response international.*

The **Tower of London,** palace and prison of English monarchs for over 500 years, is soaked in blood and history. Its intriguing past and striking buildings attract over two million visitors per year. The oldest continuously occupied fortress in Europe, "The

Tower" was founded by William the Conqueror in 1066 to provide protection for and from his subjects. Not one but 20 towers stand behind its walls, though many associate the image of the **White Tower,** the oldest one, with the Tower of London. Completed in 1097, it overpowers all the fortifications that were built around it in the following centuries. Originally a royal residence, the last monarch it housed was James I. Since then it has served as a wardrobe, storehouse, public records office, mint, armory, and prison.

The various towers are connected by massive walls and gateways, forming fortifications disheartening to visitors even today. Richard I, the Lionheart, began the construction of defenses around the White Tower in 1189. Subsequent work by Henry III and Edward I brought the Tower close to its present condition.

Two rings of defenses surround the White Tower. On the first floor of the White Tower nests the **Chapel of St. John,** dating from 1080, the finest Norman chapel in London. Stark and pristine, it is the only chapel in the world with an "aisled nave and encircling ambulatory," a balcony where women were allowed to join the otherwise men-only chapel services. Failed arsonist Guy Fawkes of the Gunpowder Plot was tortured beneath this chapel. Currently under renovation and open only by Yeoman tour, the chapel will likely be closed to the public when the renovations are completed. The White Tower also houses an expansive display from the **Royal Armouries** and a display of **Instruments of Torture.** Don't expect an extensive collection; there are only a couple of instruments of torture on display, the scariest of which is the extremely long line. If all this won't slake your thirst for violence, visit the **New Armouries** to the east to gorge on even more armor and weaponry.

On the **Inner Ward,** the **Bell Tower** squats on the southwest corner. Since the 1190s, this tower has sounded the curfew bell each night. Sir Thomas More, "the king's good servant but God's first," spent some time here, courtesy of his former friend Henry VIII, before he was executed on **Tower Hill,** the scaffold site just northwest of the fortress where thousands gathered to watch the axe fall.

SIGHTS

Along the curtain wall hovers the **Bloody Tower,** arguably the most famous, and certainly the most infamous, part of the fortress. Once pleasantly named the Garden Tower, due to the officers' garden nearby, the Bloody Tower supposedly saw the murder of the Little Princes, the uncrowned King Edward V and his brother (aged 13 and 10), by agents of Richard III. The murder remains one of history's great mysteries; some believe that Richard was innocent and that Henry VII arranged the murders to ease his own ascent. Two children's remains found in the grounds in 1674 (and buried in Westminster Abbey) have never been conclusively identified as those of the Princes. Sir Walter Raleigh did some time in the prison here off and on for 13 years and occupied himself by writing a voluminous *History of the World Part I.* Before he got around to writing Part II, James I had him beheaded.

Henry III lived in the adjacent **Wakefield Tower,** largest after the White Tower. The crown kept its public records and its jewels here until 1856 and 1967 respectively, although Wakefield also has its own gruesome past. Lancastrian Henry VI was imprisoned by Yorkist Edward IV during the Wars of the Roses and was murdered on May 21, 1471, while praying here. Students from King's College, Cambridge—founded by Henry—annually place lilies on the spot of the murder.

Counterclockwise around the inner **Wall Walk** come the **Lanthorn, Salt, Broad Arrow, Constable,** and **Martin** towers. In 1671, the self-styled "Colonel" Thomas Blood nearly pulled off the heist of the millennium. Blood befriended the ward of Martin tower, where the crown jewels were kept, and visited him late at night with some "friends." They subdued the guard and stuffed their trousers with booty, only to be caught at the nearby docks. Surprisingly, Blood wasn't executed, and was later awarded a privileged spot in the court of Charles II, the moral being, of course, that crime does pay (*Let's Go* does not endorse the theft of state treasures). The inner ring comes full circle, completed by the **Brick, Bowyer, Flint, Devereux,** and **Beauchamp** towers.

Within the inner ring adjoining the Bell Tower lurks the Tudor **Queen's House** (which will become the King's House when Prince Charles ascends the throne). The house has served time as a prison for some of the Tower's most notable guests: both

Anne Boleyn and Catherine Howard were incarcerated here by charming hubby Henry VIII; Guy Fawkes was interrogated in the Council Chamber on the upper floor; and in 1941, Hitler's henchman Rudolf Hess was brought here after parachuting into Scotland. The only prisoners remaining today are the clipped **ravens** hopping around on the grass outside the White Tower. Legend has it that without the ravens the Tower would crumble and a great disaster would befall the monarchy; the ravens even have a tomb and gravestone of their own.

Although more famous for the prisoners who languished and died here, the Tower has seen a handful of spectacular escape attempts. The Bishop of Durham escaped from Henry I out a window and down a rope. The Welsh Prince Gruffydd ap Llewelyn, prisoner of Henry III in 1244, had a less successful escape attempt—his rope of knotted sheets broke and he fell to his death.

Prisoners of special privilege sometimes received the honor of a private execution, particularly when their public execution risked escape or riot. A block on the Tower Green, inside the Inner Ward, marks the spot where the axe fell on Queen Catherine Howard, Lady Jane Grey, Anne Boleyn, and the Earl of Essex, Queen Elizabeth's rejected suitor. All these and More (Sir Thomas) were treated to unconsecrated burial in the nearby **Chapel of St. Peter ad Vincula** (St. Peter in Chains; entrance to the chapel by Yeoman tour only).

For many, a visit to the Tower climaxes with a glimpse of the **Crown Jewels.** The queue at the **Jewel House** (about 15-30min.) is a miracle of crowd management—as tourists file past room after room of rope barriers, video projections on the walls show larger-than-life depictions of the Jewels in action, including stirring footage of Queen Elizabeth II's coronation. Finally, the crowd is ushered into the vault and onto "people-movers" which whisk them past the dazzling crowns and insure no awe-struck gazers hold up the queue. Oliver Cromwell melted down much of the original royal booty; most of the collection dates from after Charles II's Restoration in 1660. The **Imperial State Crown** and the **Sceptre with the Cross** feature the Stars of Africa, cut from the Cullinan Diamond. Scotland Yard mailed the precious stone third class from the Transvaal in an unmarked brown paper parcel, a scheme they believed was the safest way of getting it to London. **St. Edward's Crown,** made for Charles II in 1661, is only worn by the monarch during coronation.

The Tower is still guarded by the **Yeomen** of the Guard Extraordinary, popularly known as the "Beefeaters," who live in the fortress. The name does actually derive from "eaters of beef"—well-nourished domestic servants. To be eligible for Beefeater-hood, a candidate must have at least 22 years honorable service in the armed forces, as well as a strong appetite for flash photography.

Visitors enter the Tower through the **Byward Tower** on the southwest of the **Outer Ward,** which sports a precariously hung portcullis. The password, required for entry here after hours, has been changed every day since 1327. German spies were executed in the Outer Ward during WWII. Along the outer wall, **St. Thomas's Tower** (after Thomas à Becket) tops the evocative **Traitors' Gate,** through which boats once brought new captives. The whole castle used to be surrounded by a broad **moat** dug by Edward I. Cholera epidemics forced the Duke of Wellington to drain the stagnant pond in 1843. The filled land became a vegetable garden during World War II but has since sprouted a tennis court and bowling green for the Yeomen who live and work in the Tower. Yeomen **tours** provide an amusing and dramatic introduction to the Tower, but are by no means comprehensive. Signs are posted inside the tower for similar free tours highlighting other points of interest. Come early (the biggest crowds come in the afternoon, particularly on Sundays) and stay long; the Tower is one of London's priciest sights, so don't go if you're pressed for time.

Tower Bridge, a granite-and-steel structure reminiscent of a castle with a drawbridge, is a familiar sight. The **Tower Bridge Experience** (tel. 403 3761), an exhibition nearly as technologically elaborate as the bridge itself, explains the bridge's genesis through the eyes of its painters, designers, and ghosts in cute but expensive 75-minute tours. *(Open Apr.-Oct. daily 10am-6:30pm; Nov.-Mar. 9:30am-6pm. Last entry 1¼ hr. before closing. Admission £5.70, children £3.90.)* The view from the upper level, hampered by steel bars, is far less panoramic than it seems from below.

SIGHTS

Fleet Street

Named for the one-time river (now a sewer) that flows from Hampstead to the Thames, **Fleet Street** (tube: Blackfriars or St. Paul's) was until recently the hub of British journalism. Nowadays, Fleet St. is just a celebrated name and a few (vacated) famous buildings. Following a standoff with the printing unions in 1986, *The Times,* under the command of infamous media mogul Rupert Murdoch, moved to cheaper land at Wapping, Docklands, initiating a mass exodus from the street. The *Daily Telegraph* soon abandoned its startling Greek and Egyptian Revival building, in favor of the delights of Canary Wharf. The *Daily Express,* once the occupant of an Art Deco manse of chrome and black glass on Fleet St., now resides in Blackfriars. *The Sun,* also under the command of Murdoch, followed its sister paper to Wapping. (When looking for addresses of the following sights, beware that, like many English streets, Fleet St. is numbered up one side and down the other.)

The tiered spire of Wren's **St. Bride's** (1675), near 89 Fleet St., became the inspiration for countless wedding cakes thanks to an ingenious local baker. *(Open M-F 8am-6pm, Sa 9am-5pm.)* Dubbed "the printers' cathedral" because the first printing press with moveable type was housed here in 1500, it has long had a connection with newspapermen. In fact, church officials seem to have taken a lesson from the tabloids in creating their sign board, covered with catchy (and somewhat misleading) "Did you know?" facts about the church. One listing asks (paraphrasing): Did you know that a German bomb falling in 1940 caused the discovery of ancient ruins below the church? The full story is that in 1952, 12 years after the bomb fell, during foundation inspections made before rebuilding the church, a set of skeletons were found below the church. The bodies had been buried in a sealed-off crypt during a 19th-century cholera epidemic. The current church is sparklingly clean and quite beautiful inside. Next to St. Bride's stands *Reuters,* one of the last remaining media powerhouses left on Fleet St.

A few blocks down the street, opposite 54 Fleet St., a large white sign labels the alleyway entrance (through Hind Ct.) to Johnson's Ct. Inside the alley, more discreet signs point the way to **Samuel Johnson's House,** 17 Gough Sq. (tel. 353 3745), a self-described "shrine to the English language" that was Dr. Johnson's abode from 1748-1759. *(Open May-Sept. M-Sa 11am-5:30pm; Oct.-Apr. M-Sa 11am-5pm. Admission £3, concessions £2, children £1. Audio tour 50p.)* Follow the signs carefully; Carlyle got lost on his way to this dark brick house in 1832. Here Johnson completed his *Dictionary,* the first definitive English lexicon, even though rumor falsely insists that he omitted "sausage." He compiled this amazing document by reading all the great books of the age and marking the words he wanted included in the Dictionary with black pen. He was assisted by six clerks—the books he used were unreadable by the project's end. The knowledgeable curator is eager to supplement your visit with anecdotes about the **Great Cham** and his hyperbolic biographer, James Boswell.

A few more blocks down Fleet St., the neo-Gothic **St. Dunstan-in-the-West** (tel. 405 1929) holds its magnificent lantern tower high above the banks surrounding it. *(Open Tu and F 9:30am-3pm, Su 10am-4pm.)* The chimes of its curious 17th-century clock are sounded on the quarter hour by a pair of hammer-wielding mechanical giants. A statue of Elizabeth I (one of the few contemporary likenesses of the Queen) rises above the vestry door. The three 16th-century effigies leaning against the porch may represent King Lud, the mythical founder of London, and his sons. For an example of more recent London architecture, take a look at the Goldman Sachs UK Headquarters on 133 Fleet St. Located behind the old *Daily Telegraph* Building, this New York-style corporate powerhouse introduces a bit of postmodern glass and stainless steel to the Fleet St. skyline. The results are not unimpressive, and offer an instance of London's present, dynamic architectural developments.

WEST LONDON

Mayfair

The center of London's blue-blooded *beau monde* was—in a delightful twist of fate—named for the 17th-century May Fair, held on the site of Shepherd's Market, a notorious haunt of prostitutes. Modern Mayfair has a distinctly patrician atmosphere; it is the most expensive property in the British version of *Monopoly*. In the 18th and 19th centuries, the aristocracy kept houses in Mayfair where they lived during "the season" (the season for opera and balls), retiring to their country estates in the summer. Mayfair is bordered by Oxford St. to the north, Piccadilly to the south, Park Lane to the west, and Regent St. to the east. *(Tube: Green Park, Bond St., or Piccadilly Circus.)*

Near what is now the Bond St. tube station, Blake saw mystical visions for 17 years on South Molton St. On busy Brook St., home to the ritzy **Claridge's Hotel** (tel. 629 8860), Handel wrote the *Messiah. (Singles £255; 2-bedroom penthouse £2450; no student discounts.)* The reigning queen was born in a house (recently demolished) at no. 17 Bruton St. Laurence Sterne ended his life on haughty Bond St. (no. 39). Back in the 60s, on Davies Mews, **Vidal Sassoon** revolutionized hair styles at his first salon (now the **Vidal Sassoon School;** see **Entertainment,** p. 242).

Bond Street itself is the traditional address for the oldest and most prestigious shops, art dealers, auction houses, and hair salons in the city. It is divided into Old and New Bond St. Not surprisingly—in this most historically snobbish of cities—Old Bond is the locale of choice for the area's most expensive shops. Cartier, Armani, Brioni, Bally, and Chanel exhibit their lavish wares in elaborately prepared window displays. Alongside these Continental extravagances, long-established homegrown shops—sporting crests indicating royal patronage—sell everything from handmade shotguns to emerald tiaras to antique furniture to *objets d'art*. Every store is watched over by one or several bored, white-shirted guards. Art dealers and auctioneers with public galleries frequently offer special shows of exceptional quality.

Starting at the New Bond St. end, **Sotheby's,** 34 Bond St. (tel. 493 5000), displays everything from Dutch masters to the world's oldest condom before they're put on the auction block. *(Open for viewing M-F 9am-4:30pm, Su noon-4pm.)* Dress smartly—not too smartly, though, as real art dealers affect a slightly shabby appearance—and spend a wonderful (and free) hour perusing the collections that you can't afford. The pieces up for bids are displayed in the honeycomb of galleries. A typical collection will include originals by artists like Picasso, Miro, Chagall, Warhol, and other luminaries you thought you'd only see in museums. And yes, the tag on some of the pieces *does* say that bids begin at £1,000,000. The cafe (tel. 293 5077) offers a non-astronomically priced tea (£4.50) from 3-5pm during the week (make reservations for lunch) and allows you to eavesdrop on the even more interesting hushed bargain debates on the opposite couches. Keep in mind that, unlike most items here, the price of scones is non-negotiable. You can get a catalog with high quality pictures of the pieces in a particular offering for £5-20, or pick up old catalogs for half price.

Modern art aficionados should note the rugged Henry Moore frieze high up on the crest of the **Time/Life Building,** corner of Bruton St. At the **Marlborough Fine Arts** (tel. 629 5161), the biggest contemporary names are sold (entrance by Albemarle St.); **Agnew's,** 43 Old Bond St (tel. 629 6176), and **Colnaghi's,** 14 Old Bond St. (tel. 491 7408), deal in Old Masters.

Running west off Bond St., Grosvenor St. ends at **Grosvenor Square,** one of the largest in central London. The square, occasionally called "little America," has gradually evolved into a U.S. military and political enclave since future President John Adams lived at no. 9 while serving as the first American ambassador to England in 1785. Almost two centuries later, General Eisenhower established his wartime headquarters at no. 20, and memory of his stay persists in the area's postwar nickname, "Eisenhowerplatz." From here you can see the humorless and top-heavy **U.S.**

Embassy rising to the west. The metal eagle atop the building is as long as a double-decker bus. West of Grosvenor Sq., a walk down **Park Lane,** the western border of Mayfair at Hyde Park, will take you past the legendary hotels of yesteryear.

In the opposite (northeast) corner of Mayfair (tube: Oxford Circus), tiny Hanover Square provides a gracious residential setting for **St. George's Hanover Church,** where the *crème de la crème* of London society have been married. Percy Bysshe Shelley, George Eliot, Benjamin Disraeli, and the soft-speaking Teddy Roosevelt came here to tie the bonds of holy matrimony beneath the radiant barrel vault. To the south, off Conduit St., you may window-shop the finest in men's threads. The name **Savile Row** is synonymous with the elegant and expensive "bespoke" tailoring that has prospered there for centuries.

At 28 Bond St. you'll find the oldest chocolate shop in London, opened in 1875 by request of Kind Edward VII (then Prince of Wales). He encouraged Mme. Charbonnel to leave her Parisian chocolate house and to join Mrs. Walker in opening a shop on Bond St. Chocolate lovers will swoon inside **Charbonnel et Walker** (tel. 491 0939). *(Open M-F 9am-6pm, Sa 10am-5pm.)* The delicious smell of truffles being crafted of fresh cream, based on the same recipe Mme. Charbonnel once used, is overwhelming. An expensive sampler of these delectable treats will tell you why the Queen herself nibbles on this chocolatier's magical yummies. A delicate (tiny) truffle will run you a decadent 50p.

Kensington, Knightsbridge, & Belgravia

Kensington, a gracious, sheltered residential area, reposes between multi-ethnic Notting Hill to the north and chic Chelsea to the south. **Kensington High Street,** which pierces the area, has become a locus for shopping and scoping. Obscure specialty and antique shops fill the area along Kensington Church St. to the north, Victorian museums and colleges dominate South Kensington, and the area around Earl's Court has become something of a tourist colony, yet retains a substantial gay population.

Take the tube to High St. Kensington, Notting Hill Gate, or Holland Park to reach **Holland Park,** a peacock-peppered swath of green full of small pleasures. **Holland House** (see **Accommodations,** p. 74), a Jacobean mansion built in 1607, lies on the park's grounds. Destroyed in WWII, the house has since been restored and turned into a youth hostel. Holland Park also contains rose gardens, an open-air amphitheater (box office tel. 602 7856), an ecology center, and a number of playgrounds, as well as cricket pitches, public tennis courts, and traditional Japanese Kyoto Gardens (open daily 7:30am-9:30pm).

Two petite exhibition galleries, the **Ice House** and the **Orangery** (tel. 361 3204) blossom in the middle of the park (open daily 11am-7pm; free). They mount free displays of contemporary painting and ceramics by local artists. The flag-ridden **Commonwealth Institute** stands by the park's southern entrance on the High St. (see **Museums,** p. 223).

The curious **Leighton House,** 12 Holland Park Rd. (tel. 602 3316), lies a block west of the Institute (open M-Sa 11am-5:30pm; free). Devised by the imaginative painter Lord Leighton in the 19th century, the house is a presumptuous yet pleasant pastiche. The thoroughly blue Arab Hall, with inlaid tiles, a pool, and a dome, is an attempt to recreate the wonders of the Orient in thoroughly Occidental Kensington. Now a center for the arts, Leighton House features concerts, receptions, and other events in the evenings, as well as frequent contemporary art exhibitions and competitions.

To reach the grandiose South Kensington museums, take the tube to the South Kensington station or Bus 49 from Kensington High St. The **Victoria and Albert Museum**, the **Natural History Museum** (both on Cromwell Rd.), and the **Science Museum** (on Exhibition Rd.) all testify on a grand scale to the Victorian mania for collecting, codifying, and cataloging. The Great Exhibition of 1851 funded many of these monumental buildings, built between 1867 and 1935.

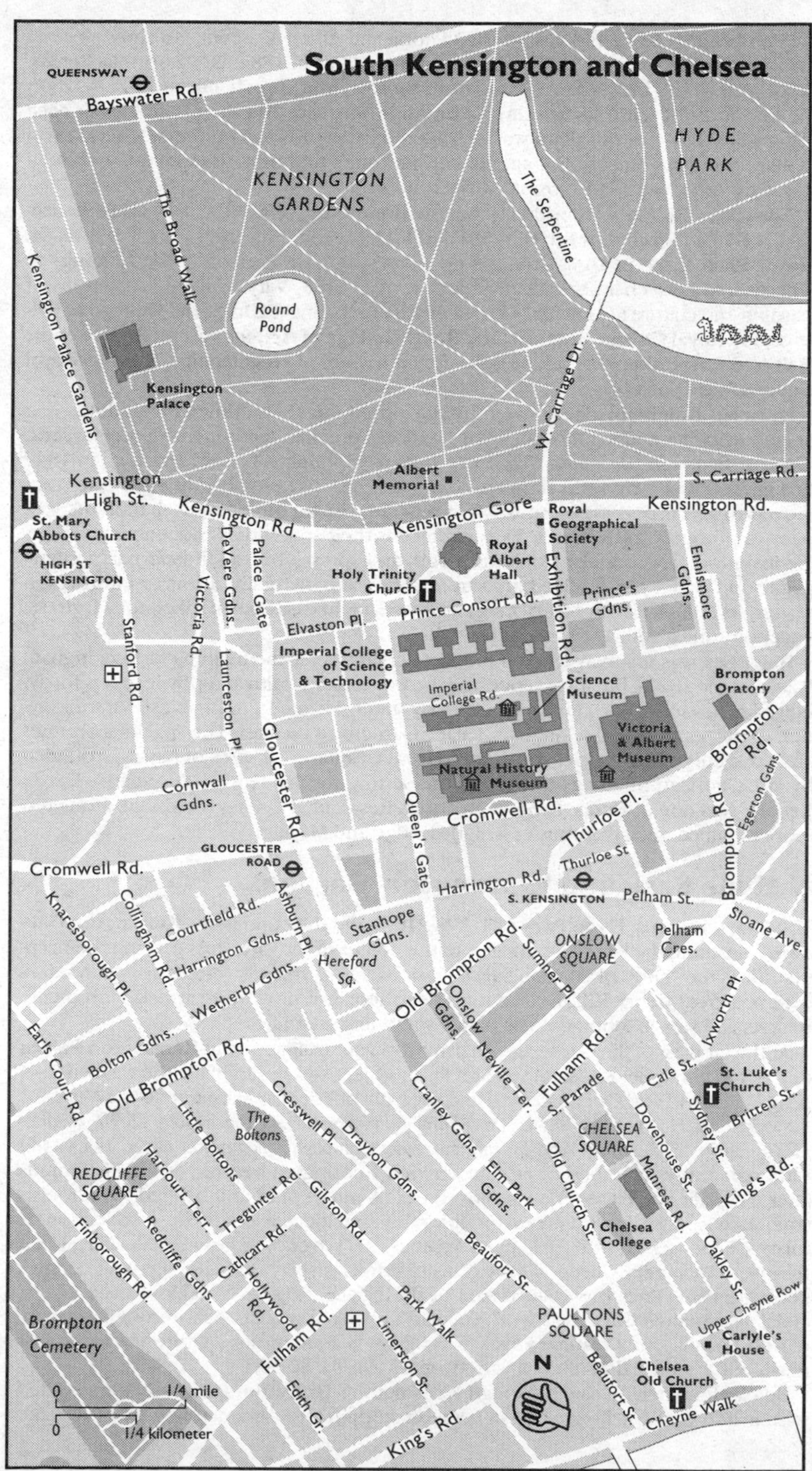
South Kensington and Chelsea
QUEENSWAY
Bayswater Rd.
HYDE PARK
KENSINGTON GARDENS
The Serpentine
The Broad Walk
Kensington Palace Gardens
Round Pond
Kensington Palace
W. Carriage Dr.
Albert Memorial
S. Carriage Rd.
Kensington High St.
Kensington Rd.
Kensington Gore
Royal Geographical Society
Kensington Rd.
St. Mary Abbots Church
HIGH ST KENSINGTON
DeVere Gdns.
Palace Gate
Royal Albert Hall
Exhibition Rd.
Ennismore Gdns.
Victoria Rd.
Holy Trinity Church
Prince Consort Rd.
Prince's Gdns.
Stanford Rd.
Launceston Pl.
Elvaston Pl.
Imperial College of Science & Technology
Imperial College Rd.
Science Museum
Brompton Oratory
Victoria & Albert Museum
Gloucester Rd.
Natural History Museum
Brompton Rd.
Cornwall Gdns.
Queen's Gate
Cromwell Rd.
Thurloe Pl.
Egerton Gdns.
GLOUCESTER ROAD
Cromwell Rd.
Thurloe St.
Brompton Rd.
Harrington Rd.
S. KENSINGTON
Pelham St.
Ashburn Pl.
Courtfield Rd.
Collingham Rd.
Knaresborough Pl.
Stanhope Gdns.
Sloane Ave.
Pelham Cres.
Harrington Gdns.
Hereford Sq.
Old Brompton Rd.
Sumner Pl.
ONSLOW SQUARE
Wetherby Gdns.
Onslow Gdns.
Ixworth Pl.
Earls Court Rd.
Bolton Gdns.
Old Brompton Rd.
Neville Ter.
Fulham Rd.
Cale St.
St. Luke's Church
Cresswell Pl.
Cranley Gdns.
S. Parade
Britten St.
Little Boltons
The Boltons
Drayton Gdns.
Sydney St.
CHELSEA SQUARE
Dovehouse St.
REDCLIFFE SQUARE
Harcourt Terr.
Elm Park Gdns.
Old Church St.
King's Rd.
Tregunter Rd.
Gilston Rd.
Manresa Rd.
Redcliffe Gdns.
Finborough Rd.
Cathcart Rd.
Chelsea College
Oakley St.
Hollywood Rd.
Beaufort St.
Upper Cheyne Row
Park Walk
Brompton Cemetery
Fulham Rd.
Limerston St.
PAULTONS SQUARE
Carlyle's House
N
Chelsea Old Church
0 1/4 mile
0 1/4 kilometer
Edith Gr.
Beaufort St.
Cheyne Walk
King's Rd.

SIGHTS

Brompton Oratory, just east of the Victoria and Albert Museum, is a showpiece of Italian art and architecture. H. Gribble built the edifice in 1884; the enormous Renaissance altar in the Lady Chapel came from Brescia. The church affirms its reputation for fine music during its **Sunday Latin High Masses.** *(Masses 11am. Church open 6:30am-8pm.)* One of the altars was considered by the KGB to be the best dead drop in all of London—until 1985, agents left microfilm and other documents behind a statue for other agents to surreptitiously requisition.

Christie's, the internationally famous auction house, sells off its less valuable trinkets at 85 Old Brompton Rd. (tel. 581 7611), its second branch. (Its first is near **St. James Palace;** see p. 143.) Still, it's no "Everything's a Pound!!!"; the bidding for objects sold here characteristically starts at over £100. Various royal institutions of learning and culture lie north of Cromwell Rd., including the **Imperial College of Science,** the **Royal College of Music,** the **Royal College of Art,** the rotund **Royal Albert Hall** (see **Entertainment,** p. 234), the **Royal School of Needlepoint,** and the **Royal Geographical Society.**

Patrician **Knightsbridge** is wealthy, groomed, and sometimes forbidding. The neighborhood is defined most of all by London's premier department store, **Harrods.** *(Open M-Tu and Sa 10am-6pm, W-F 10am-7pm; see* **Shopping,** *p. 249.)* Founded in 1849 as a grocery store, by 1880 Harrods employed over 100 workers. In 1905, the store moved to its current location; today it requires 5000 employees to handle its vast array of products and services. Extravagance is their specialty. Besides an encyclopedic inventory, Harrods also contains a pub, an espresso bar, a salt beef bar, a champagne and oyster bar, a juice bar, a fromagerie, and, naturally, a tourist information center. Its dominating five-story megastructure might easily be mistaken for a fortress, except for the giant flag proclaiming "sale."

Belgravia was first constructed to billet servants after the building of Buckingham Palace in the 1820s, but it soon became the bastion of wealth and privilege it is today. Belgravia lies south of Hyde Park, ringed by stately Sloane St. to the west, Victoria Station to the south, and Buckingham Palace Gardens to the east. The spacious avenues and crescents of the district surround **Belgrave Square,** 10 acres of park surrounded by late-Georgian buildings that were the setting for *My Fair Lady.* Nearby **Eaton Square** was one of Henry James's favorites. Residential Belgravia exhibits a quieter, more dignified mien than busier Knightsbridge and Mayfair.

■ Hyde Park and Kensington Gardens

Totalling 630 acres, **Hyde Park** (tel. 298 2100) and the contiguous **Kensington Gardens** constitute the largest open area in the center of the city, thus earning their reputation as the "lungs of London." *(Park open daily 5am-midnight; gardens open daily dawn-dusk; both free.)* Henry VIII used to hunt deer here, but now those armed with picnic baskets and suntan lotion dot the park's sprawling green fields.

At the far west of the Gardens, you can drop your calling card at **Kensington Palace** (tel. 376 0198; tube: Kensington High St. or Queensway), originally the residence of King William III and Queen Mary II and recently of Princess Margaret. *(Open May-Sept for tours only. Hourly tours M-Sa 10am-5pm. Admission £7.50, concessions £5.90, children £5.35, families £23. Allow 1¼hr. for the tour; reserve through Ticketmaster at tel. 344 4444.)* Although always a hotbed of tabloid activity, Kensington became especially famous after a certain heir to the throne moved out. A museum of uninhabited royal rooms (the State Apartments) and regal memorabilia includes a Court dress collection. A former centerpiece of the display, Princess Di's wedding gown, has since been removed. **Orangery Gardens,** an exquisite flower display studded by young couples getting mushy, lines the eastern side of the palace. Be sure to seek out the lovely, cloistered **Sunken Garden** as well. You can't go in but you can peer through the manicured foliage. The **Orangery** (tel. 376 0239) is a sumptuous white tea room just north of the palace that offers a variety of set teas for £6.50.

Be careful when crossing through Kensington's pathways—the park is now filled with in-line skaters who are not so keen on stopping for camera-toting tourists. Skate

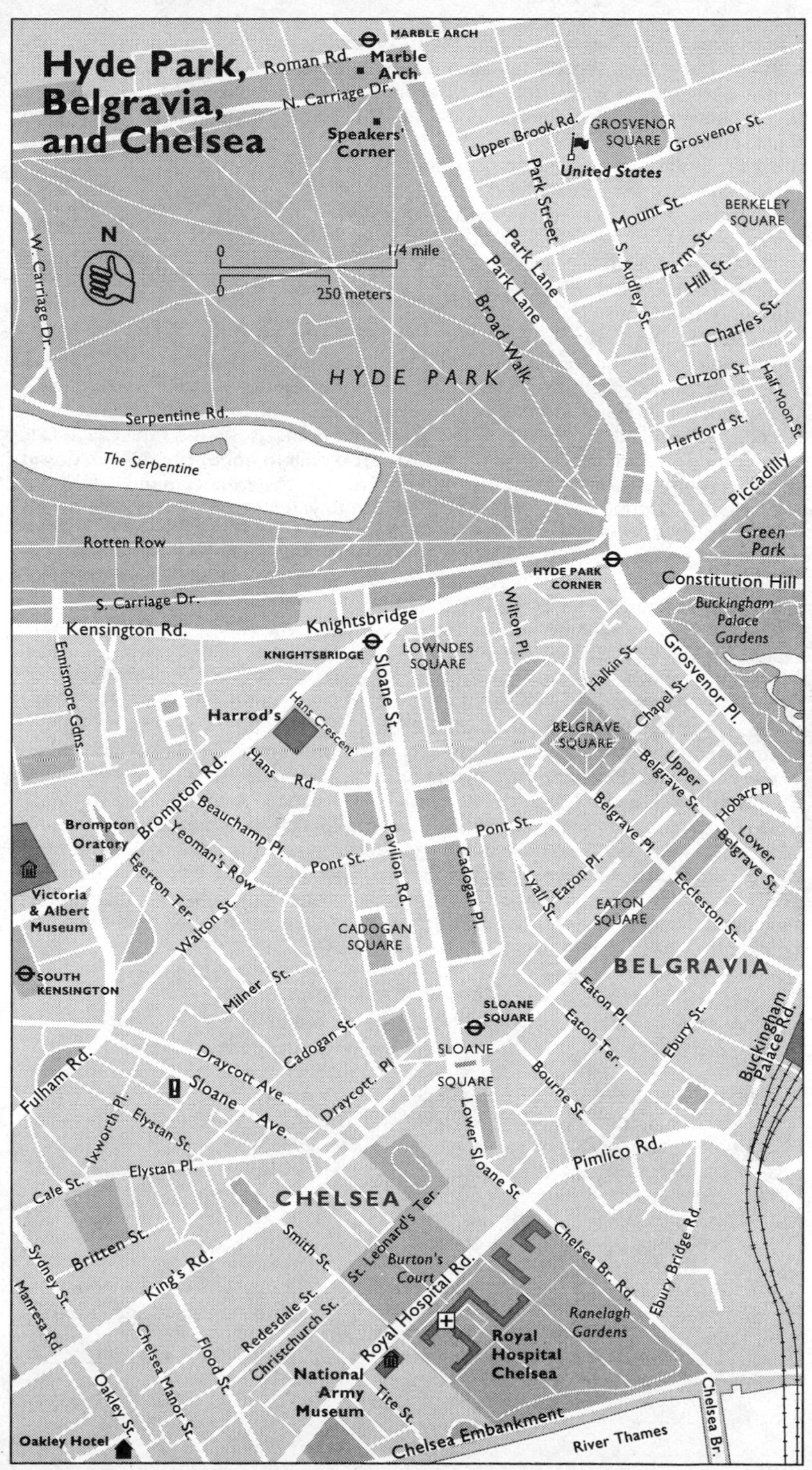
Hyde Park, Belgravia, and Chelsea
MARBLE ARCH
Marble Arch
Roman Rd.
N. Carriage Dr.
Speakers' Corner
Upper Brook Rd.
GROSVENOR SQUARE
Grosvenor St.
United States
Park Street
Mount St.
BERKELEY SQUARE
N
0
1/4 mile
0
250 meters
W. Carriage Dr.
Park Lane
Park Lane
Broad Walk
S. Audley St.
Farm St.
Hill St.
Charles St.
HYDE PARK
Curzon St.
Half Moon St.
Serpentine Rd.
The Serpentine
Hertford St.
Piccadilly
Green Park
Rotten Row
HYDE PARK CORNER
Constitution Hill
S. Carriage Dr.
Kensington Rd.
Knightsbridge
Wilton Pl.
Buckingham Palace Gardens
KNIGHTSBRIDGE
Sloane St.
LOWNDES SQUARE
Halkin St.
Grosvenor Pl.
Ennismore Gdns.
Harrod's
Hans Crescent
Chapel St.
BELGRAVE SQUARE
Hans Rd.
Upper Belgrave St.
Brompton Rd.
Hobart Pl.
Beauchamp Pl.
Belgrave Pl.
Brompton Oratory
Yeoman's Row
Pont St.
Pont St.
Pavilion Rd.
Cadogan Pl.
Lower Belgrave St.
Victoria & Albert Museum
Egerton Ter.
Eaton Pl.
Lyall St.
Eccleston St.
EATON SQUARE
Walton St.
CADOGAN SQUARE
SOUTH KENSINGTON
BELGRAVIA
Milner St.
SLOANE SQUARE
Eaton Pl.
Eaton Ter.
Ebury St.
Buckingham Palace Rd.
Cadogan St.
SLOANE SQUARE
Fulham Rd.
Draycott Ave.
Draycott Pl.
Sloane Ave.
Bourne St.
Ixworth Pl.
Elystan St.
Lower Sloane St.
Elystan Pl.
Pimlico Rd.
Cale St.
CHELSEA
St. Leonard's Ter.
Smith St.
Chelsea Br. Rd.
Britten St.
Burton's Court
Ebury Bridge Rd.
Sydney St.
King's Rd.
Royal Hospital Rd.
Ranelagh Gardens
Manresa Rd.
Redesdale St.
Christchurch St.
Royal Hospital Chelsea
Chelsea Manor St.
Flood St.
National Army Museum
Oakley St.
Tite St.
Chelsea Br.
Chelsea Embankment
River Thames
Oakley Hotel

rentals park themselves on the main pathways if you want to try a pair yourself. The statue of **Peter Pan,** actually modeled from a girl, stands near the **Italian Fountains** on the Serpentine's west bank. The **Serpentine,** a lake carved in 1730, runs from these fountains in the north, near Bayswater Rd., south toward Knightsbridge. From the number of people who pay the £6.50 per hour to row in the pond, one would think the water was the fountain of youth. Perhaps not—Harriet Westbrook, Percy Bysshe Shelley's first wife, numbers among the famous people who have drowned in this human-made "pond." A bone-white arch derived from a Henry Moore sculpture stands on the northwest bank, but the best view is from across the water.

The **Serpentine Gallery** (tel. 402 6075), in Kensington Gardens, hosts interesting exhibitions of contemporary works and art workshops (open daily during exhibitions only 10am-6pm).

On the southern edge of Kensington Gardens, the Lord Mayor had the **Albert Memorial** built to honor Victoria's beloved husband. Considered a great artistic achievement when first unveiled in 1869, the extravagant monument has now spent years under scaffolding and had yet to be unveiled as of summer 1998. Across the street, the **Royal Albert Hall,** with its ornate oval dome, hosts the Promenade Concerts (Proms) in summer (see **Music,** p. 234). Also built to honor the Prince Consort, the hall is simpler than the memorial, and features a frieze of the "Triumph of the Arts and Sciences" around its circumference. **Rotten Row** (a corruption of Route du Roi, "king's road") was the first English thoroughfare to be lighted to prevent crime. However, this east-west path through southern Hyde Park, like the rest of the park, remains dangerous at night. There is a police station about 300 yards north of the Serpentine. (Constabulary tel. 298 2076.)

The **Marble Arch** is built on the exact site where the public gallows of Tyburn rested until 1783. Hangings here drew immense crowds, who jeered and threw stones and rotting food at the unfortunate criminals (some of whom had done as little as steal a shilling's worth of goods) as they rolled in carts to the "Triple Tree," which stood at the present corner of Bayswater Rd. and Edgware Rd. Nowadays, on summer evenings and Sundays from late morning to dusk, proselytizers, politicos, and flat-out crazies assemble to dispense the fruits of their knowledge to whoever's biting at **Speakers' Corner,** in the northeast corner of Hyde Park (tube: Marble Arch, not Hyde Park Corner), the finest example of free speech in action anywhere in the world. At the southern end of Hyde Park clusters a group of statues: a Diana fountain, the "family of man," a likeness of Lord Byron, and a fig-leafed Achilles dedicated to Wellington. Royal park band performances occasionally take place in the summertime at the bandstand 200 yards from Hyde Park Corner, in the direction of the Serpentine (call 298 2100 for details).

Beefcake Wellington

Before television, film, and Hugh Grant, British women culled their sex symbols from the military, and few soldiers set pulses racing faster than Arthur Wellesley, Duke of Wellington. Charlotte Brontë fancied the victor at Waterloo so much as a child that she modeled Jane Eyre's Rochester after him. Countess Lavinia Spencer showed her affection in another way, by launching a women-only public subscription to raise funds for a memorial statue. The result was the "Ladies' Trophy," Hyde Park's nude statue of Achilles, cheekily referred to as the ladies' fancy. The statue, London's first nude, was embroiled in controversy from its creation. Lady Holland wrote saucily: "A difficulty has arisen, and the artist had submitted to the female subscribers whether this colossal figure should preserve its antique nudity or should be garnished with a fig leaf. It was carried for the leaf by a majority...The names of the *minority* have not transpired." Those eager to accuse British women of prudery should be advised that it was in fact the gentleman head of the statue committee who insisted on the fig leaf.

Chelsea

Now quiet and expensive, **Chelsea** has historically been one of London's flashiest districts—Thomas More, Oscar Wilde, and the Sex Pistols have all been residents at one time or another. It used to be that few streets in London screamed louder for a visit than **King's Road.** Mohawked UB40s (a reference to the unemployed: it's the form they must fill out to get benefits) and pearl-necklaced Sloane Rangers (the awfully loose English equivalent of preppies) gazed at trendy window displays and at each other. While the hordes still flock here on Saturday afternoons to see and be seen, the ambience is drastically muted; most current scenesters look like they are desperately trying to recapture a past they have only read about.

Symbolic of the street's recent metamorphosis from the center of a dynamic youth culture into a respectable shopping district is the chameleonic storefront at 430 King's Rd., **World's End.** In the 70s, impressario Malcolm McLaren and designer Vivienne Westwood masterminded a series of trendy boutiques at this address that capitalized on the subcultural fashions then in vogue, like the Teddy Boy look. Let it Rock, Too Young To Live Too Fast To Die, and Seditionaries were some of the shop's various inventions; its most important incarnation was Sex, the punk clothing store in which the Sex Pistols (and, some would argue, punk rock) were born. Ripped clothing, safety pins, and bondage gear as fashion originated here. While Westwood still displays her designs in a boutique at this address, she now sells fabulously expensive couture garments. Ironically, the boutique's current neighbor is the Chelsea Conservative Club.

Any proper exploration of Chelsea begins at **Sloane Square.** The square takes its name from Sir Hans Sloane (1660-1753), whose collection comprised the whole of the first British Museum. The nearby **Royal Court Theatre** debuted many of George Bernard Shaw's plays. Until 1829, King's Rd., stretching southwest from Sloane Sq., served as a private royal thoroughfare from Hampton Court to Whitehall. Today the street is a commercial thoroughfare where overpriced restaurants, historic pubs, and antique stores lurk amid many boutiques. The recent presence of three supermodeling agencies in the square fills many of the boutiques with London's most fashionable women. Be aware that the tube is practically nonexistent around here, so you'll have to rely on **buses** (#11, 19, 22, 211, and 319).

Off King's Rd., Chelsea becomes cozier, the closest thing to a village that central London now possesses. Totally immune to the ever-changing world of King's Rd. are the commandingly militaresque buildings of Wren's **Royal Hospital,** founded in 1691 by Charles II for retired soldiers and still inhabited by 400 army pensioners. *(Grounds open daily Apr.-Sept., 10am-8pm. Museum open daily Apr.-Sept. 10am-noon and 2-4pm. Call ahead.)* Former soldiers in Royal Hospital uniform welcome visitors to the spacious, well-groomed grounds and splendid buildings. The hospital museum features the war medals of deceased veterans. The North wing of the hospital has borne war's scars quite directly in the last century. In 1918 a German 500 lb. bomb destroyed the wing, killing five residents. After the war it was rebuilt only to be destroyed toward the end of WWII by a German V-2 rocket, again killing five retired soldiers.

East of the Hospital lie the **Ranelagh Gardens** (usually open until dusk; free). Here 18th-century pleasure-seekers spent their evenings watching pageants and fireworks and imbibing to excess. The **Chelsea Flower Show** blooms here during the third week in May (Tu-F), but even Royal Horticultural Society members have trouble procuring tickets for the first two days. The lovely **Chelsea Physic Garden** (tel. 352-5646) is next door. *(Open W 2-5pm, Su 2-6pm. Admission £3.50, concessions £1.80. Wheelchair accessible.)*

Cheyne (pronounced "CHAY-nee") **Walk, Cheyne Row,** and **Tite Street** formed the heart of Chelsea's artist colony at the turn of the century. Watch for the blue plaques on the houses; J.M.W. Turner moved into a house in Cheyne Walk, and Edgar Allan Poe lived nearby. Mary Ann Evans (a.k.a. George Eliot) moved into No. 4 just before her death. Dante Gabriel Rossetti kept his disreputable *ménage* (which included peacocks and a kangaroo) in No. 16, where he doused himself with chloral hydrate. Nos. 19 to 26 cover the ground that used to be Chelsea Manor, where Queen

Elizabeth I once lived. Both Mick Jagger and Keith Richards got satisfaction on the Walk in the 1960s. The area's arbiter of the aesthetic, Oscar Wilde, reposed stylishly at 34 Tite St. from 1884-1895 and was arrested for homosexual activity at Chelsea's best-known hotel, the Cadogan (75 Sloane St.). John Singer Sargent, James MacNeill Whistler, Radclyffe Hall, and Bertrand Russell also lived on Tite St. Today, fashionable artists' and designers' homes line the street, though the area is too expensive to remain a true bastion of bohemian culture.

At the west end of Cheyne Walk lies the **Chelsea Old Church,** partially designed by Sir Thomas More. Henry VIII is reported to have married his third wife here before the official wedding took place. The friendly verger will point out **Crosby Hall** down the street, a 15th-century hall that was More's residence in Bishopsgate before it was moved, stone by stone, to its present position in 1910.

Chelsea's famed resident Thomas Carlyle crafted his magnificent prose on Cheyne Row. On this miraculously quiet street colored by flowers and tidy houses, **Carlyle's House,** 24 Cheyne Row (tel. 352 7087), has remained virtually unchanged since the Sage of Chelsea expired in his armchair. *(Open Apr.-Oct. W-Su 11am-5pm. Last admission 4:30pm. Admission £3.20, children £1.60.)* Family portraits and sketches ornament the walls—which he had doubled in thickness, vainly hoping to keep out noise. Be sure to read the letters between Disraeli and Carlyle which are displayed in the upstairs study. Disraeli wanted to give Carlyle the Grand Cross of the Bath—heretofore reserved only for those in direct service of the state—as well as a sizable pension. Carlyle replied that he would always cherish such a compliment from a man as great as Disraeli, but declined, saying that the rest of such an honor would be pure "sorrow."

Notting Hill and Ladbroke Grove

Notting Hill is one of London's most diverse neighborhoods—a variety of racial, ethnic, and socioeconomic groups call this area home. On the lively streets, trendy places to eat and shop ply their trade among dilapidated stores, wafts of incense, and Bob Marley posters, while MPs mingle cautiously with hipsters. Fans of MTV's *The Real World* will recognize this as the neighborhood where the company-assembled group of roommates lived. The region explodes with exuberant festivity every summer during the **Notting Hill Carnival,** Europe's biggest outdoor festival (every Aug. bank holiday weekend). Around 500,000 people line Portobello Rd. to watch and walk in a parade of steel drummers, fantastic costumes, entranced followers, and dancing policemen, while Afro-Caribbean music reverberates through the streets.

The scenery that surrounded the village of Notting Hill in the mid-19th century (a few cornfields, a meadow, an occasional lane) changed drastically when the **Great Western Railway** opened up North Kensington to development in 1838. The Ladbroke family commissioned high-society architects to develop the area, whereupon upper-middle-class families quickly took up residence in spacious Neoclassical mansion townhouses.

Commercial Portobello Rd., the area's lively main thoroughfare, runs parallel to Ladbroke Grove. Starting on the southern end near Notting Hill Gate, it is lined with various antique stores and thriving galleries. As the idler meanders north, antiquarians give way to fresh produce and baked goods stalls. Near Lancaster Rd. and the Westway (the overhead highway), stalls vend secondhand clothing, collector's vinyl, and various desirable trinkets. Finally, Golborne Rd. offers its own lively street scene, marked by dirt-cheap, bohemian, delicious Portuguese patisseries. The **Portobello Market** (see p. 257) makes this already lively commercial district downright vivacious every Saturday. The name "Portobello" may evoke childhood memories, even if you've never been to London—one of the market's most famed patrons is **Paddington Bear,** whose purchases here always landed his paws in a pot of trouble. Portobello has hosted freakshows, fortune-tellers, conjurers, and charlatans selling miracle elixirs since the early Victorian age. A look at the tattoo parlors or juice bars hawking Gusto herbal drink today should convince cynics that some things never change.

The area has a checkered past of racial conflict that it is gradually putting to rest. Irish and Jewish immigrants were the first to occupy the poor areas of "Notting Dale"

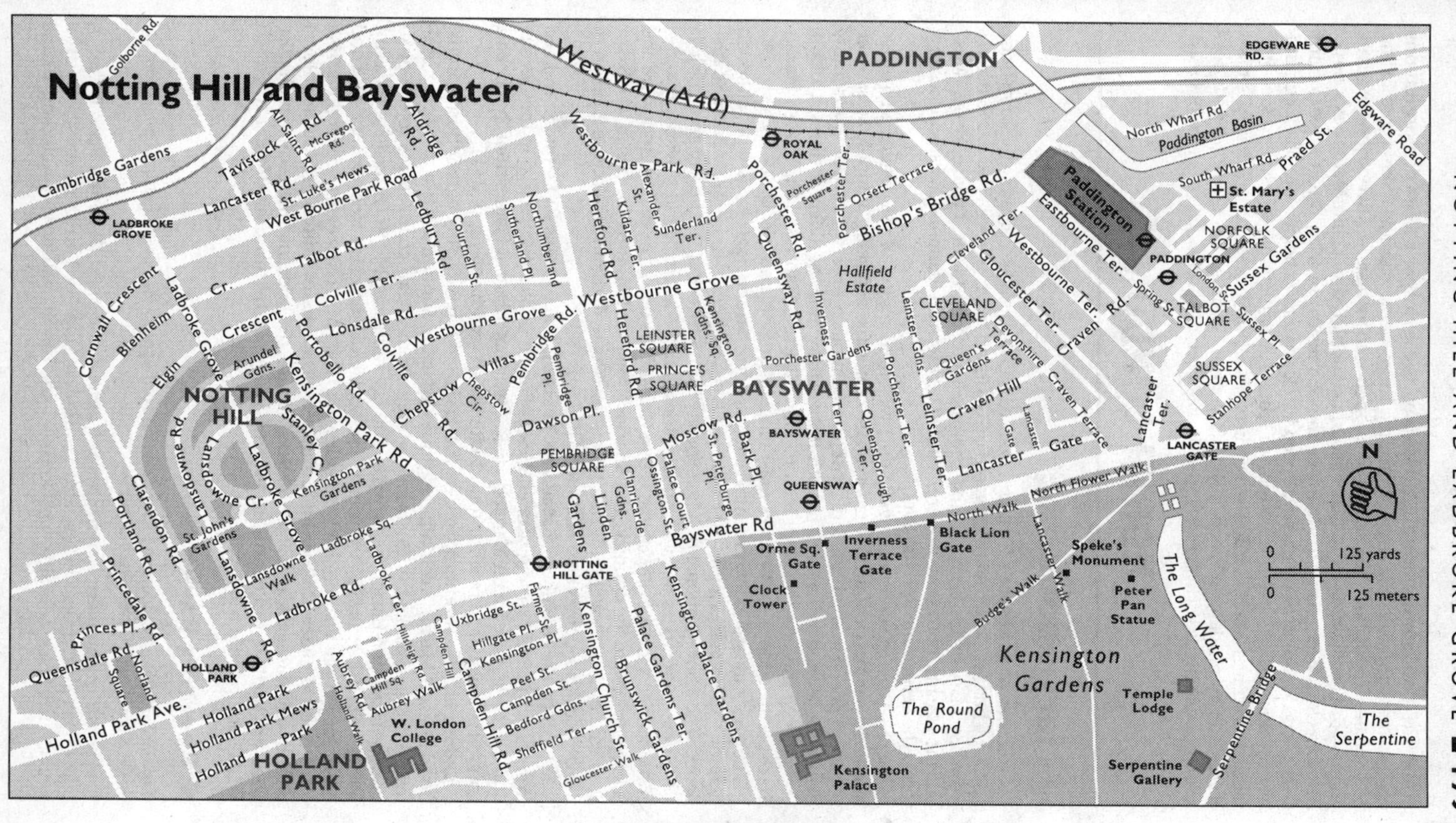
Notting Hill and Bayswater
PADDINGTON
BAYSWATER
NOTTING HILL
HOLLAND PARK
Westway (A40)
EDGEWARE RD.
ROYAL OAK
PADDINGTON
LADBROKE GROVE
BAYSWATER
QUEENSWAY
LANCASTER GATE
NOTTING HILL GATE
HOLLAND PARK
Paddington Station
Paddington Basin
North Wharf Rd.
South Wharf Rd.
Praed St.
Edgware Road
St. Mary's Estate
NORFOLK SQUARE
TALBOT SQUARE
SUSSEX SQUARE
Sussex Gardens
Sussex Pl.
London St.
Spring St.
Stanhope Terrace
Eastbourne Ter.
Westbourne Ter.
Gloucester Ter.
Craven Rd.
Cleveland Ter.
Bishop's Bridge Rd.
Orsett Terrace
Porchester Ter.
Porchester Square
Porchester Rd.
Queensway Rd.
Hallfield Estate
CLEVELAND SQUARE
Devonshire Terrace
Queen's Gardens
Craven Hill
Craven Terrace
Lancaster Ter.
Lancaster Gate
Leinster Gdns.
Leinster Ter.
Porchester Ter.
Porchester Gardens
Inverness Terr
Queensborough Ter.
Westbourne Park Rd.
Alexander St.
Sunderland Ter.
Kildare Ter.
Hereford Rd.
Kensington Gdns. Sq.
LEINSTER SQUARE
PRINCE'S SQUARE
Westbourne Grove
Moscow Rd.
St. Peterburg Pl.
Bark Pl.
Pembridge Rd.
Pembridge Pl.
Dawson Pl.
PEMBRIDGE SQUARE
Clanricarde Gdns.
Ossington St.
Palace Court
Linden Gardens
Bayswater Rd
North Walk
North Flower Walk
Northumberland
Sutherland Pl.
Courtnell St.
Ledbury Rd.
Aldridge Rd.
McGregor Rd.
All Saints Rd.
Tavistock Rd.
Cambridge Gardens
Golborne Rd.
Lancaster Rd.
St. Luke's Mews
West Bourne Park Road
Talbot Rd.
Colville Ter.
Lonsdale Rd.
Colville Rd.
Chepstow Villas
Chepstow Cir.
Portobello Rd.
Kensington Park Rd.
Ladbroke Grove
Cornwall Crescent
Blenheim Cr.
Elgin Crescent
Arundel Gdns.
Stanley Cr.
Kensington Park Gardens
Lansdowne Rd.
Lansdowne Cr.
Clarendon Rd.
Portland Rd.
St. John's Gardens
Lansdowne Walk
Ladbroke Sq.
Ladbroke Rd.
Ladbroke Ter.
Lansdowne Rd.
Princedale Rd.
Princes Pl.
Queensdale Rd.
Norland Square
Holland Park Ave.
Holland Park
Holland Park Mews
Holland Walk
Aubrey Rd.
Campden Hill Sq.
Aubrey Walk
Hillsleigh Rd.
Campden Hill
W. London College
Uxbridge St.
Farmer St.
Hillgate Pl.
Kensington Pl.
Peel St.
Campden St.
Bedford Gdns.
Sheffield Ter.
Campden Hill Rd.
Kensington Church St.
Gloucester Walk
Brunswick Gardens
Palace Gardens Ter.
Kensington Palace Gardens
Orme Sq. Gate
Inverness Terrace Gate
Black Lion Gate
Clock Tower
Lancaster Walk
Speke's Monument
Peter Pan Statue
Budge's Walk
Kensington Gardens
The Long Water
The Round Pond
Kensington Palace
Temple Lodge
Serpentine Gallery
Serpentine Bridge
The Serpentine
N
0
125 yards
0
125 meters

in the late-19th century, but the 1930s saw the arrival of Fascist demonstrations against Jews and local immigrant groups. Inter-ethnic tension re-emerged in the 1950s when Teddy-Boy gangs engaged in open warfare against Afro-Caribbean immigrants—the devastating riots that ensued are depicted in Colin MacInnes's novel *Absolute Beginners* (later made into a movie musical starring David Bowie). Amy Garvey (widow of Marcus Garvey, famed black separatist) helped the black community on Notting Hill survive various onslaughts. Today the multi-ethnic area sees little racial animosity, a fact London's novelists have not overlooked. The area's most recent literary resident—dartsman Keith Talent of Martin Amis's *London Fields* does not engage in bigotry. He cheats and swindles everyone, regardless of color or creed.

NORTH LONDON

Marylebone

Located between Regent's Park and Oxford St., the grid-like district of **Marylebone** (MAR-lee-bun) is dotted with elegant late-Georgian town houses. The name derives from "St. Mary-by-the-bourne," the "bourne" referring to the Tyburn or the Westbourne stream, both now underground. The eternally dammed Westbourne now forms the Serpentine in Hyde Park.

There's little to see in this well-kept, well-bred region of residences and office buildings, but Marylebone has had its share of notable denizens. Wimpole St. saw the reclusive poet Elizabeth Barrett write the fabulous *Sonnets from the Portuguese* before she eloped and moved in with Robert Browning. At different times, 19 York St. has been the home of John Milton, John Stuart Mill, and William Hazlitt. **Harley Street** is the address for Britain's most eminent doctors and specialists.

SIGHTS

The area's most fondly remembered resident is **Sherlock Holmes** who, although fictitious, still receives about 50 letters per week addressed to his 221b Baker St. residence. The Abbey National Building Society currently occupies the site and employs a full-time secretary to answer requests for Holmes's assistance in solving mysteries around the world. The official line is that Holmes has retired from detective work and is keeping bees in the country. The **Sherlock Holmes Museum,** located at 239 Baker St. (marked "221b") will thrill Holmes enthusiasts with the meticulous re-creation of the detective's lodgings (see **Museums,** p. 220).

Ever since the redoubtable **Madame Tussaud,** one of Louis XVI's tutors, trekked from Paris in 1802 carrying wax effigies of French nobles decapitated in the Revolution, her eerie museum on Marylebone Rd. (with an adjacent Planetarium) has been a London landmark and popular tourist attraction (see **Museums,** p. 231).

Oxford St., the southern border of Marylebone, passes through Oxford Circus, Bond St., and Marble Arch tube stations. Arguably London's major shopping boulevard, it's jam-packed with shops (ranging from cheap chain stores to the posh boutiques around Bond St.), crowds, and fast-food stands. Off Oxford St., pleasant **James's St.** (tube: Bond St.) lures passersby with one cafe after another—a good place for people-watching from a sidewalk table. Manchester Sq. holds the lavish (and free) **Wallace Collection,** a must-see for fans of Dutch art and medieval armor (see **Museums,** p. 228). **Hertford House,** the ancestral mansion which contains the Wallace Collection, is worth a visit even by those indifferent to Dutch art, if such people truly exist.

Regent's Park

***Tel.** 486 7905; constabulary 935 1259. **Tube:** Regent's Pk., Great Portland St., Baker St., or Camden Town. **Open** 6am-dusk.*

Just south of Camden Town, the 500-acre, wide-open **Regent's Park** is full of lakes, gardens, promenades, and Londoners. One of London's most beautiful spaces, the park contains well-kept lawns, broad walkways (including **Broad**

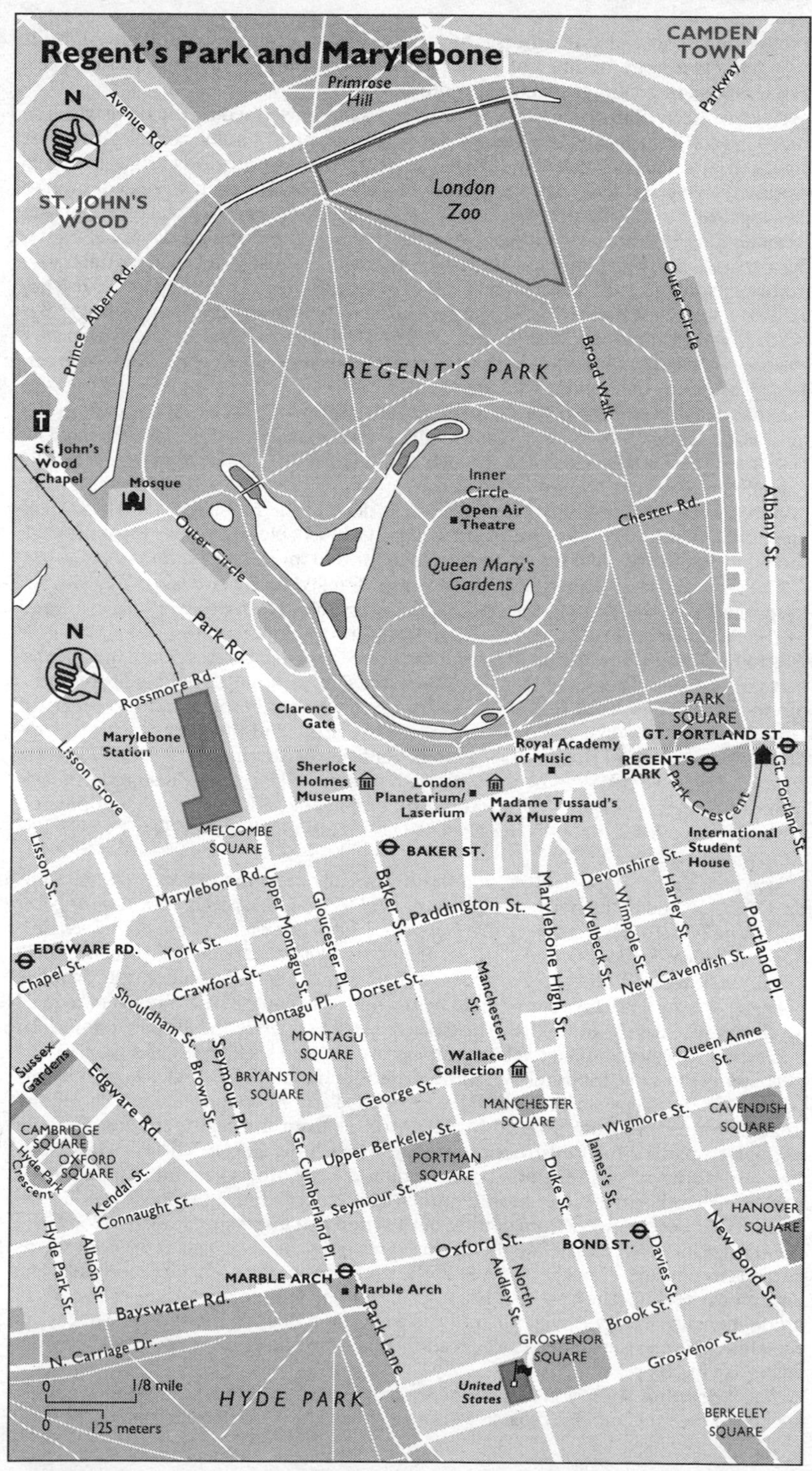
Regent's Park and Marylebone
CAMDEN TOWN
Primrose Hill
Parkway
Avenue Rd.
N
London Zoo
ST. JOHN'S WOOD
Prince Albert Rd.
Outer Circle
Broad Walk
REGENT'S PARK
St. John's Wood Chapel
Mosque
Inner Circle
Open Air Theatre
Chester Rd.
Albany St.
Outer Circle
Queen Mary's Gardens
Park Rd.
N
Rossmore Rd.
Clarence Gate
PARK SQUARE
Marylebone Station
GT. PORTLAND ST.
Royal Academy of Music
REGENT'S PARK
Lisson Grove
Sherlock Holmes Museum
London Planetarium/ Laserium
Madame Tussaud's Wax Museum
Park Crescent
Gt. Portland St.
MELCOMBE SQUARE
BAKER ST.
International Student House
Lisson St.
Marylebone Rd.
Upper Montagu St.
Gloucester Pl.
Baker St.
Marylebone High St.
Devonshire St.
Welbeck St.
Wimpole St.
Harley St.
Portland Pl.
Paddington St.
EDGWARE RD.
York St.
Chapel St.
Crawford St.
Dorset St.
Manchester St.
New Cavendish St.
Shouldham St.
Montagu Pl.
MONTAGU SQUARE
Wallace Collection
Queen Anne St.
Sussex Gardens
Seymour Pl.
Brown St.
Edgware Rd.
BRYANSTON SQUARE
George St.
MANCHESTER SQUARE
CAVENDISH SQUARE
Wigmore St.
CAMBRIDGE SQUARE
OXFORD SQUARE
Hyde Park Crescent
Gt. Cumberland Pl.
Upper Berkeley St.
PORTMAN SQUARE
Duke St.
James's St.
Kendal St.
Connaught St.
Seymour St.
HANOVER SQUARE
New Bond St.
Hyde Park St.
Albion St.
Oxford St.
BOND ST.
Davies St.
North Audley St.
MARBLE ARCH
Marble Arch
Bayswater Rd.
Park Lane
Brook St.
GROSVENOR SQUARE
N. Carriage Dr.
Grosvenor St.
0
1/8 mile
United States
HYDE PARK
0
125 meters
BERKELEY SQUARE

SIGHTS

Walk), and scores of sunbathers. During the mid-morning and early afternoon it also attracts a large number of senior citizens—battalions of retired crumb dispensers sustain a vibrant pigeon community.

The true heart of the park is the 30 or so acres circumscribed by the drive with the veddy, veddy British title, the **Inner Circle.** This area plays home to the park's best lawns in a town (and country for that matter) with a notorious fetish for well-groomed greenery. Within are the **Queen Mary's Gardens,** which were dedicated to this royal lady in 1938 simply because she liked them. Be sure to stroll by the ornate fountain at the center, which pales in comparison to the stunning display of exotic flora that flanks it. On Sundays from June through August you can hear tubas and trumpets honking away at the bandstand or see performances in the **Open Air Theatre** (tel. 486 2431) near Queen Mary's Gardens (see **Entertainment,** p. 231). *(Box office open M-Sa 10am-8pm. Ticketmaster (tel. 344 4444) also sells tickets and adds a maddeningly steep surcharge.)* This outdoor theater puts on Shakespearean plays every summer, as well as more contemporary theater.

Just outside of the Inner Circle is the park's largest lake. Take a boat ride on the motorized barge (£1.50), or if you're feeling hale, navigate your own. *(Rowboat for max. 4 people £7.50 plus £5 deposit. Available daily 10am-dusk.)* Children and the vertically challenged may toot around in small rowboats (£5 per hr.) or pedalboats (£3 per 30min.) in a miniature, calmer lake right next door to the full-sized lake. These lakes were designed for the pleasure of the self-consciously elegant upper crust; indeed, the whole park was once envisioned as a playground for the well-born.

The area was cleared in 1650 when Cromwell felled 16,000 trees to raise cash for his cavalry's payroll. In 1812 the scrappy architect **John Nash** drew up plans ordered by the Prince Regent (the future George IV) for a park dotted with 40 luxury villas. It was to be a project for "the wealthy and the good" which would separate the fine districts from the less-fashionable ones to the east. Due to some admirable liberal sentiments, this plan was not realized. Parliament was concerned that too much of London would become the province of the wealthy, and the park was, in stages, opened to the public. The 40 villas were never built. Nash's mark is still evident—the park is edged on three sides by majestic Nash terraces. The recently restored Regency terraces present a magnificent facade. The cream-colored, porticoed, and pillared buildings have been home to the likes of H.G. Wells (17 Hanover Terr.) and Wallis Simpson (7 Hanover Terr.).

The park's most popular attraction has historically been the privately owned **London Zoo,** located in the northeast quadrant. *(Tel. 722 3333; tube: Camden Town or Baker St.; Bus #274 from either station or City Hopper C2 takes you almost to the door. Open daily Apr.-Sept. 10am-5:30pm; Oct.-Mar. 10am-4pm. Last admission 1hr. before close. Admission £8.50, concessions £7, under 15 £6, families £26.)* Despite a long period of near financial collapse, the zoo, Britain's largest, survived, and today you can see rare tigers, as well as elephants, snakes, and more. The 36-acre park was once the storage ground for zoological specimens collected by members of a learned society; Charles Darwin was perhaps its most illustrious fellow. **Jumbo the Elephant** was the park's biggest attraction in 1882, until cynical Yankee showman P.T. Barnum bought him and carted the big-eared celebrity from burg to burg. Proceeds from the sale were considerable enough to pay for the construction of an entire reptile house. The **Charles Clore Pavilion** displays "small mammals," including a large, underground, nocturnal display. This dank, cave-like exhibit is pitch-black except for lighted arrows that are intended to keep viewers from getting disoriented and lost. Many walk headlong into the hard stone walls that define the narrow, twisted passage. A sign at the door warns patrons to beware of pickpockets. Still, the creatures o' the night are eerily arresting and worth seeing. The zoo also has a snake house which, according to the £2.25 guide, contains a freezer with an antidote to every resident's venom. The snakes are nice little critters; the guide assures readers that only one snakekeeper has died from snakebite in 163 years.

The **Snowdon Aviary** is a striking structure, reminiscent of a nylon stocking stretched over a giant child's jack. Various other exhibits are architecturally notable as well. The **Aquarium** houses a fairly mundane bunch of fish that still seems to enchant the kiddies. Ominous posted warnings at the entrance talk of biting squirrels. **Regent's Park Canal,** part of the Grand Union Canal, flows though the zoo. The **London Waterbus Company** offers canal rides April through October between Camden Lock and "Little Venice." *(Tel. 482 2550 or 482 2660; tube: Warwick Avenue. Single £3.80, concessions £2.40; return £5, £3. Open daily 10am-5pm.)*

Camden Town

In the 18th century, **Camden Town** was still only farmland and cattle fields owned by the Lord Chancellor Charles Pratt, Earl of Camden. Although he began some minor building projects in the area around Camden High Street, the town really started to develop with the opening of the Regent's Canal in 1820, bringing with it timber and coal wharves, family-run breweries, saddlers, picture-framers, and the like. By the 19th century, Camden Town was a solid working-class district spliced with railways and covered in soot. Charles Dickens spent his childhood here, crowded in a four-room tenement with his extended family at 16 (now 141) Bayham St. The experience served as the model for the Cratchit family in *A Christmas Carol.* Poet Dylan Thomas found inspiration on Delancey St. Waves of Irish, Cypriot, Greek, Italian, and Portuguese immigrants brought a diversity to the area that persists to this day.

Contemporary Camden Town is a stomping ground for trendy youth of all subcultural affiliations. Every Sunday thousands of merchants set up stands offering everything from vintage pornography to antique sewing machines at the **Camden Markets,** drawing swarms of bargain-seeking Londoners and curious, often bewildered, tourists each weekend (tube: Camden Town; see **Shopping,** p. 257). The market has become fertile ground for new-age religions to distribute literature, incense sellers to be worshipped by wide-eyed teens, and tattoo artists to find willing patients for experimentation. Opened in 1974 with only four stall holders, the market now crams in hundreds of bohemian vendors catering to an international youth culture. On Sundays, almost anything can be found here. One tip is to head toward the stalls at the back of the market, off Camden High Street. Here students of popular culture will find crates of yesterday's toys, books, lighters, and other unfamiliar knick-knacks. Other stores offer truly bizarre devices, including exotic instruments such as the Russian theremin. Straggly-haired neo-hippies, black-clad goths, pierced punks, clean-cut preppies, and 30-something couples (little kids in tow) all add to the madness.

On weekdays, you can avoid the elbows and boots of your fellow shoppers. Strung-out beggars and equally strung-out students are the worst you'll have to contend with. Although the markets will be closed, the area's restaurants, cafes, and specialty shops, including one of London's best left-wing bookstores, a gay sex and fetish-wear shop, a healthy collection of (ahem) tobacco paraphernalia boutiques, and London's only store dedicated to folk music still offer plenty of fodder for more relaxed browsing. A visitor may find Camden High Street dominated by a series of almost identical shops: each offers a few flavors of Dr. Martens, a few cheap leather jackets, some well-worn corduroy and velvet blazers, and a selection of fruit-print shirts (or whatever is sweeping the club scene). In front of the shop will invariably stand several salesmen wearing bored expressions. After visiting a few of these shops you may find yourself wearing a similar expression. But for those who just can't get enough, **Camden Lock Market,** which lies exactly where Camden High Street turns into Chalk Farm Rd., offers a pseudo-Camden Market every day of the week.

Camden is connected to nearby Regent's Park and Little Venice by a series of canals and locks. Camden High St., near its intersection with Chalk Farm Rd., crosses over the main canal. From this bridge one can see the occasional barge being lowered or raised in the lock.

Although parts of Camden Town have turned into genteel residential enclaves, the area has for the most part resisted gentrification, as the scruffy storefronts on High St. and dilapidated warehouses along Regent's Canal will attest. But there is a growing sense that the scruffiness itself is chic, as trendy cafes that pride themselves on not

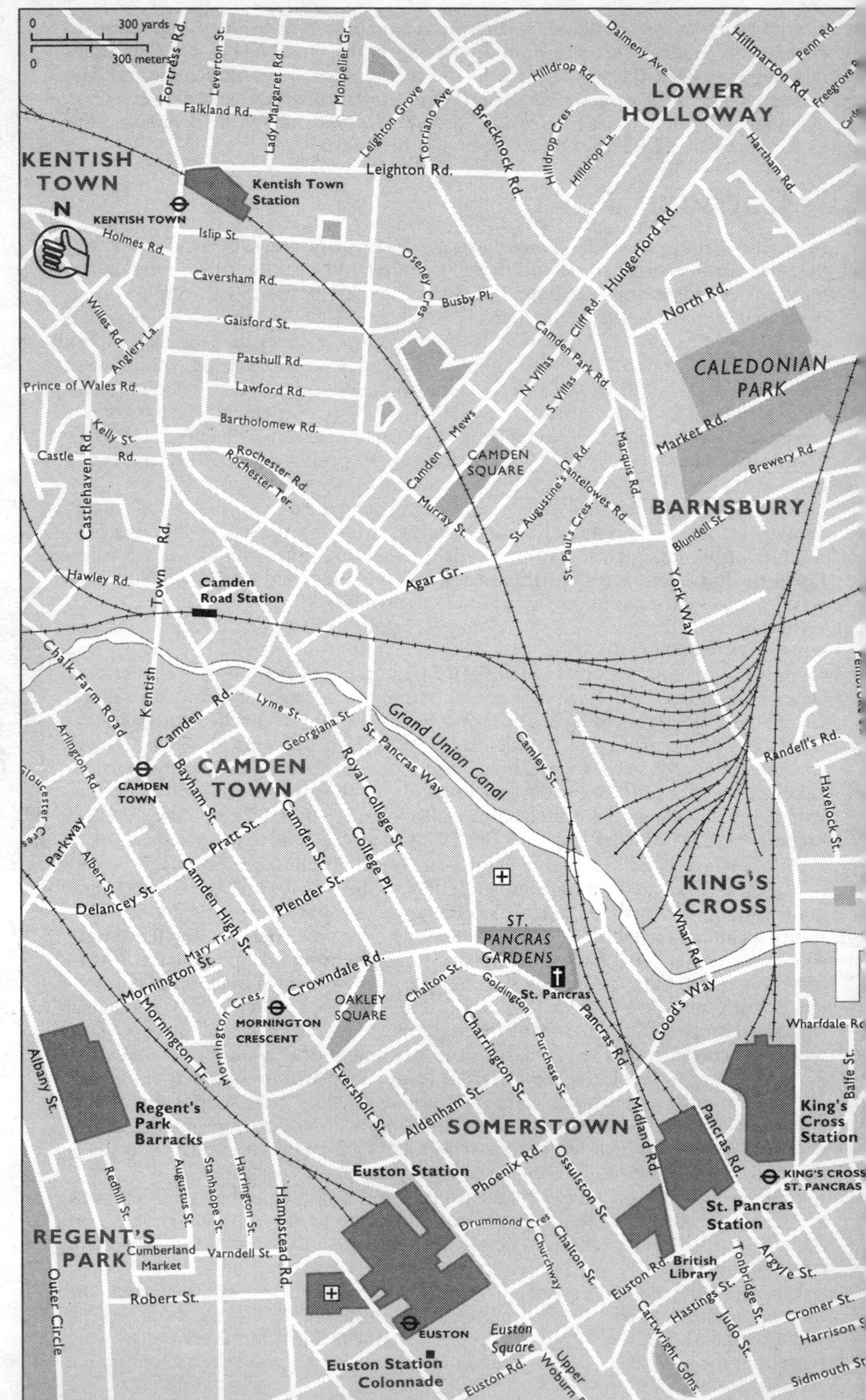

0 300 yards
0 300 meters
KENTISH TOWN
LOWER HOLLOWAY
CAMDEN TOWN
CAMDEN SQUARE
BARNSBURY
CALEDONIAN PARK
KING'S CROSS
SOMERSTOWN
REGENT'S PARK
ST. PANCRAS GARDENS
OAKLEY SQUARE
Kentish Town Station
Camden Road Station
Euston Station
St. Pancras Station
King's Cross Station
Regent's Park Barracks
British Library
Euston Station Colonnade
Grand Union Canal
KENTISH TOWN
CAMDEN TOWN
MORNINGTON CRESCENT
EUSTON
KING'S CROSS ST. PANCRAS
St. Pancras

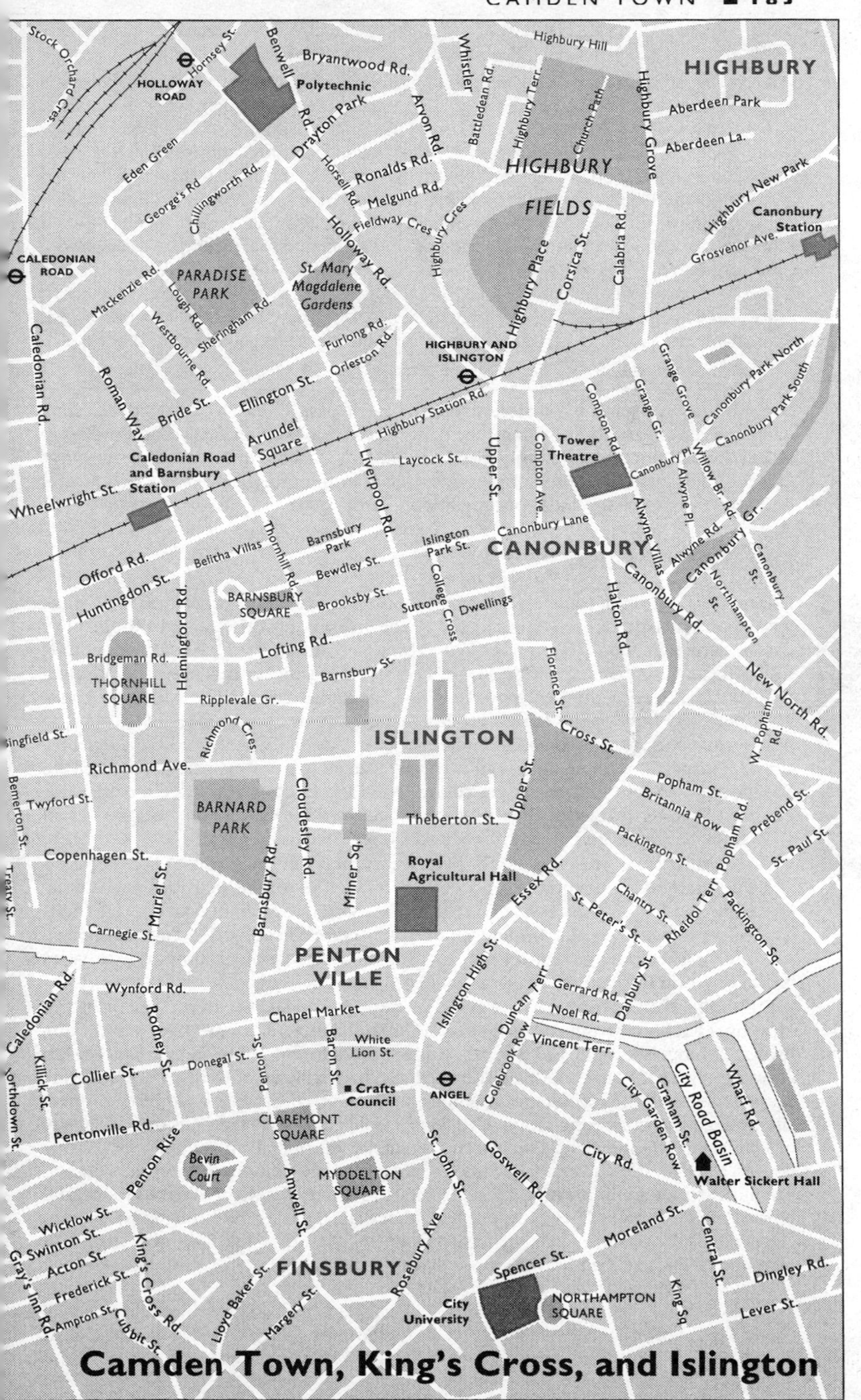

Camden Town, King's Cross, and Islington

Jeremy Bentham's "Auto-Icon"

Jeremy Bentham's utilitarianism and religious iconoclasm have resulted in a truly bizarre last request. His organs were donated to science, a highly controversial move in a world dominated by notions of Christians rising from the grave, bodies and all. He hoped for a similarly utilitarian use of his body, and ordered it to be dressed in his customary suit and favorite cane. Bentham hoped that such "auto-icons" of himself and other inspiring individuals might be put on display as encouragement to their successors. He even suggested that famous bodies could be used as lawn ornaments. After the body was donated to University College and put on display, its head corroded to such a state that it was removed from the body and placed between his legs. Eventually, the powers that be realized just how creepy this was (check the picture to see for yourself) and finally removed it to a University safe. It is rumored that the Auto-Icon sits in on board meetings, always noted as "present, but abstaining."

being trendy grow in the off-streets. For the most part, Camden Town's restaurants and pubs remain attractively dingy gathering places for rising indie stars and rock sensations. Sweat-laden band members and drunk fans stumble into local hangouts after gigs for a last taste of Saturday night fever; even in the grungiest places you can still find stars like Morrissey and Björk mellowing out.

Bloomsbury

During the first half of the 20th century, Bloomsbury gained its reputation as an intellectual and artistic center, due largely to the presence of the famed Bloomsbury Group, which included biographer Lytton Strachey, novelist E.M. Forster, economist John Maynard Keynes, art critic Roger Fry, painter Vanessa Bell (sister of Virginia Woolf), and hovering on the fringe, T.S. Eliot, the eminent British poet from St. Louis. Although very little of the famed intellectual gossip and high modernist argot currently emanates from 51 Gordon Square, where Virginia Woolf lived with her husband Leonard, the area maintains an earnestly intellectual atmosphere. Even after the Bloomsbury Group's disintegration, young artists and radicals populated the area, giving rise to the term "Bloomsbury bluestockings" to describe modern young women who smoked, drank, and defied the period's restrictive rules.

Today, the British Museum, the British Library, and the University of London guarantee a continued concentration of cerebral, as well as tourist, activities in the area. The streets of Bloomsbury are lined with B&Bs as well as student housing. The **British Museum** makes an appropriate Bloomsbury centerpiece; forbidding on the outside but quirky and amazing within, it contains the remains of thousands of years worth of world history and civilization.

Buildings of the **University of London** pepper the streets to the north of the Museum. Excluded from the Anglican-dominated universities at Oxford and Cambridge, Jeremy Bentham and a group of dissenters founded **University College** on Gower St. in 1828. They modeled the curriculum after those of German research universities, banned the teaching of theology, and admitted Catholics and Jews. University College was chartered (along with King's College in The Strand) as the University of London in 1836, making London the last major European capital to acquire a university. In 1878, the university became the first to admit women to its degree courses. The university's administrative headquarters and library reside in **Senate House,** the white concrete tower (1933) dominating Malet St. (open M-F 8:30am–5pm). Just up Gower St. across from the University Hospital at Chadwick Building, the eerie **remains of Jeremy Bentham** sit proudly in the South Wing. The entrance is in the southwest corner of the quad as you enter from Gower St.

To the north, close by Strachey and Keynes's former homes, stands the **Percival David Foundation of Chinese Art,** 53 Gordon Sq. (tel. 387 3909; tube: Russell Sq. or Goodge St.), a connoisseur's hoard of fabulously rare ceramics (open M-F

10:30am-5pm; admission free). Sir David presented his ceramics collection to the University of London in 1950; it is currently administered by **SOAS** (School of Oriental and African Studies). The ground floor of the museum resembles a high school trophy case, but the top floors offer more eccentric delights. The museum most recently showcased a collection of rare Oriental snuffboxes.

To the northeast, along Euston Rd., **St. Pancras Station** (tube: King's Cross/St. Pancras) is a monument to Victorian prosperity rising over a currently shabby neighborhood. This red-brick Neo-Gothic fantasy, completed in 1867, opened in 1874 as the Midland Grand Hotel. In 1890 the hotel opened the first smoking room for women in London. After serving as an office building from 1935 until the early 1980s, the now abandoned building faces an uncertain future. Next door, the sprawling new (and controversially ugly) **British Library** is Bloomsbury's latest addition; the library is home to thousands of books and manuscripts of the past millennia. Exhibition spaces are open to the public, while reading rooms are not.

Up St. Pancras Rd., past the station's red brick effluvia, **St. Pancras Old Church** sits serenely in its large and leafy garden. Parts of the church date from the 11th century. Mary Godwin first met Shelley here in 1813 by the grave of her mother, Mary Wollstonecraft. Rumor has it that believing her mum died during her birth, Godwin insisted that Shelley make love with her on the grave. Moving right along, directly northeast of the British museum, **Russell Square** squares off as central London's second-largest, after Lincoln's Inn Fields. T.S. Eliot, the "Pope of Russell Square," hid from his emotionally ailing first wife at no. 24 while he worked as an editor and later director of Faber and Faber, the famed publishing house.

Bernard St. leads east to Brunswick Sq., sight of the **Thomas Coram Foundation for Children,** 40 Brunswick Sq. (tel. 278 2424; tube: Russell Square). Thomas Coram, a retired sea captain, established the Foundling Hospital for abandoned children here in 1747. In order to raise funds, he sought the help of prominent artists, including William Hogarth, who, in addition to serving as a governor of the hospital, donated paintings and persuaded his friends to do the same. The composer Händel also lent a hand, giving the hospital an organ and performing in a number of benefit concerts. Although the hospital was torn down in 1926, its art treasures remain, displayed in a suite of splendidly restored 18th-century rooms. Unfortunately the museum is to be closed for refurbishment until 1999 (call for information).

Across from the Foundation lies **Coram's Fields** (93 Guilford St.; tel. 837 6138), seven acres of old Foundling Hospital grounds that have been preserved as a children's park, complete with a menagerie of petting animals, an aviary, and a paddling pool for tykes under five. *(Open daily Easter-Oct. 9am-dusk; Nov.-March 9am-5pm. Admission free.)* No dogs allowed—no adults, either, unless accompanied by a child. Although there are no sheep to pet, the adjacent parks are open to the public.

Charles Dickens lived at 48 Doughty St. (east of Russell Sq., parallel to Gray's Inn Rd.) from 1837 to 1839, scribbling parts of *The Pickwick Papers, Nicholas Nickleby, Barnaby Rudge,* and *Oliver Twist.* Now a four-floor museum and library of Dickens paraphernalia, the **Dickens House** (tel. 405 2127; tube: Russell Sq. or Chancery Ln.) holds an array of prints, photographs, manuscripts, letters, and personal effects. *(Open M-Sa 10am-5pm, last entry 4:30pm. Admission £3.50, students £2.50, children £1.50, families £7.)* What it lacks in pizazz, it makes up for by being extremely informative. The rusty iron grill mounted on a basement wall was salvaged by the author from the Marshalsea Jail, a notorious debtor's prison where Dickens's father did time for three months in 1824 while his young son labored in a shoeblack factory.

To the south of the British museum, the shrapnel-scarred Corinthian portico of Hawksmoor's 18th-century church, **St. George's, Bloomsbury** looms in Bloomsbury Way (open M-Sa 9:30am-5:30pm). Completed in 1730 according to Nicholas Hawksmoor's design, a statue of George I crowns the heavy steeple, which was modeled on the tomb of King Mansolos in Turkey. Inside, novelist Anthony Trollope was baptized before the gilded mahogany altar, where Dickens set his "Bloomsbury Christening" in *Sketches by Boz.*

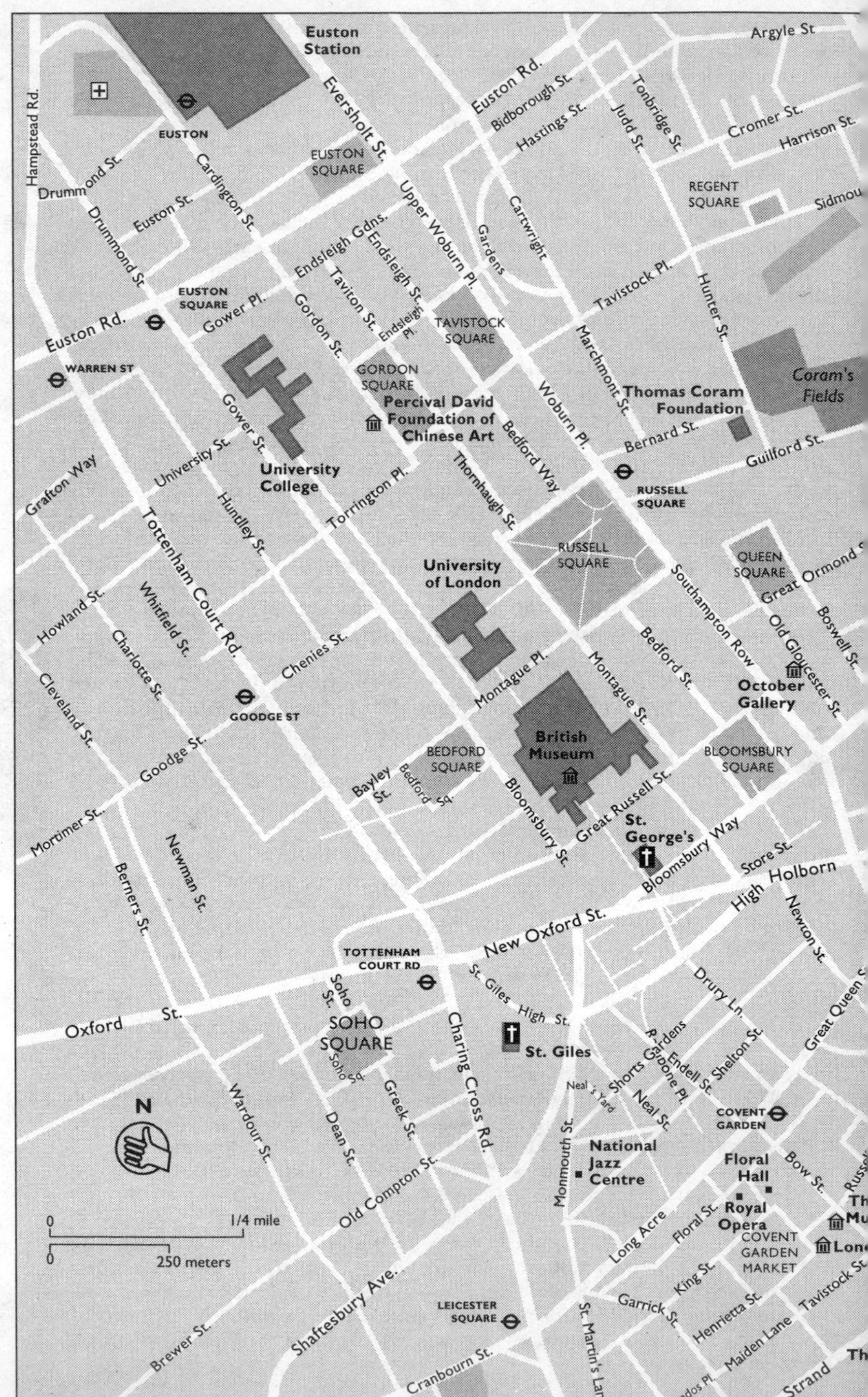
Euston Station
EUSTON
EUSTON SQUARE
Argyle St
Euston Rd.
Eversholt St.
Bidborough St.
Hastings St.
Tonbridge St.
Judd St.
Cromer St.
Harrison St.
Hampstead Rd.
Drummond St.
Cardington St.
Euston St.
Upper Woburn Pl.
Cartwright Gardens
REGENT SQUARE
Sidmou
Endsleigh Gdns.
Endsleigh St.
Endsleigh Pl.
Tavistock Pl.
Hunter St.
EUSTON SQUARE
Gower Pl.
Gordon St.
Taviton St.
TAVISTOCK SQUARE
Euston Rd.
WARREN ST
GORDON SQUARE
Marchmont St.
Woburn Pl.
Thomas Coram Foundation
Coram's Fields
Percival David Foundation of Chinese Art
Gower St.
University St.
Bedford Way
Bernard St.
Guilford St.
Grafton Way
University College
Torrington Pl.
Thornhaugh St.
RUSSELL SQUARE
Tottenham Court Rd.
Huntley St.
RUSSELL SQUARE
QUEEN SQUARE
Great Ormond St.
University of London
Southampton Row
Howland St.
Whitfield St.
Old Gloucester St.
Boswell St.
Charlotte St.
Chenies St.
Bedford St.
Montague St.
Cleveland St.
Montague Pl.
October Gallery
GOODGE ST
British Museum
BEDFORD SQUARE
BLOOMSBURY SQUARE
Goodge St.
Bayley St.
Bedford Sq.
Bloomsbury St.
Great Russell St.
St. George's
Mortimer St.
Newman St.
Bloomsbury Way
Store St.
Berners St.
High Holborn
Newton St.
New Oxford St.
TOTTENHAM COURT RD
Soho St.
St. Giles High St.
Drury Ln.
Great Queen St.
Oxford St.
SOHO SQUARE
Soho Sq.
Charing Cross Rd.
St. Giles
Shorts Gardens
Endell St.
Shelton St.
Earlham St.
Neal's Yard
Neal St.
Greek St.
Wardour St.
Dean St.
N
COVENT GARDEN
Monmouth St.
National Jazz Centre
Floral Hall
Bow St.
Old Compton St.
0
1/4 mile
0
250 meters
Long Acre
Floral St.
Royal Opera
COVENT GARDEN MARKET
Shaftesbury Ave.
King St.
Garrick St.
Henrietta St.
Tavistock St.
LEICESTER SQUARE
St. Martin's Lane
Maiden Lane
Brewer St.
Cranbourn St.
Chandos Pl.
Strand

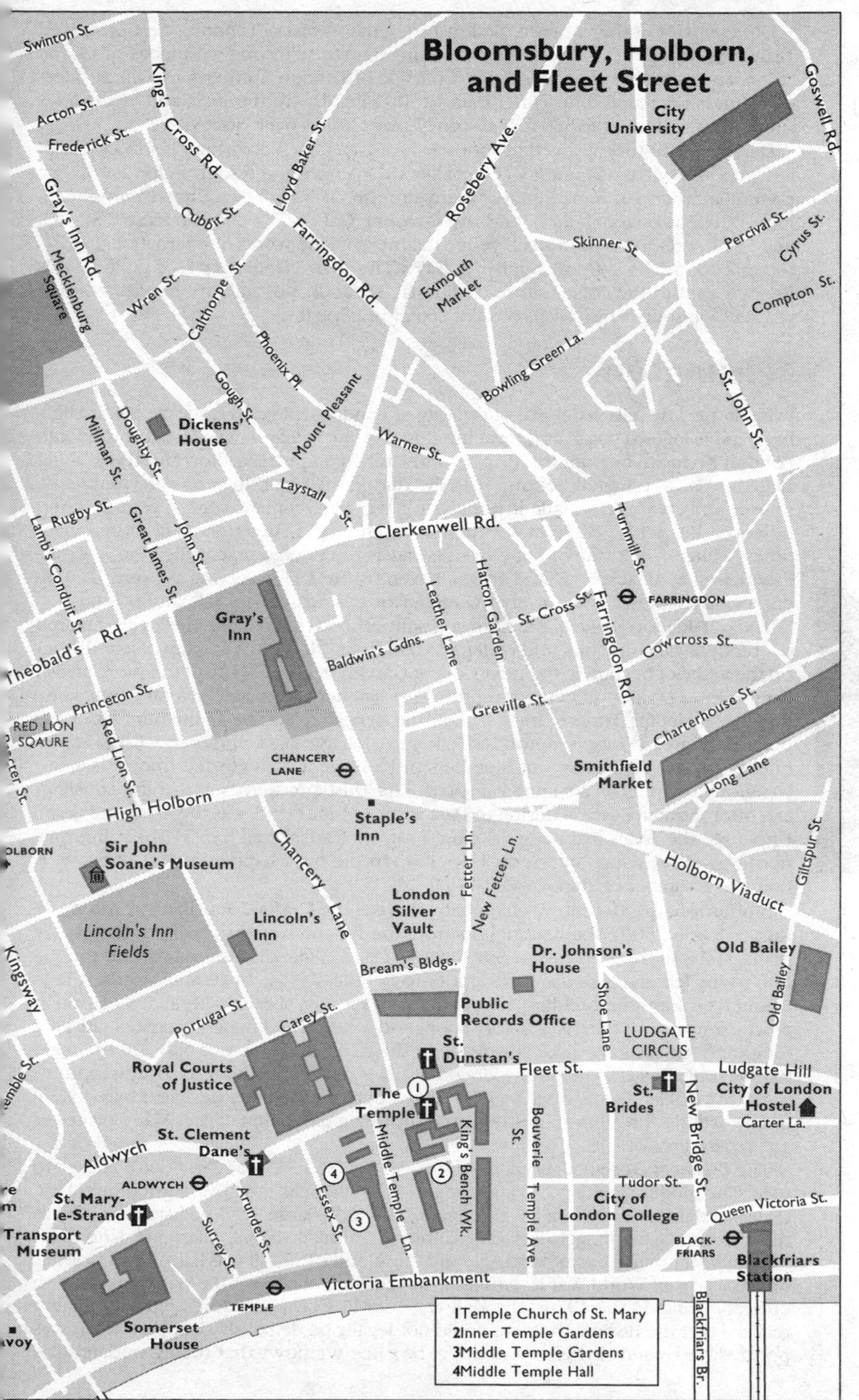
Bloomsbury, Holborn, and Fleet Street
City University
Dickens' House
Gray's Inn
Staple's Inn
Sir John Soane's Museum
Lincoln's Inn Fields
Lincoln's Inn
London Silver Vault
Dr. Johnson's House
Public Records Office
Smithfield Market
Old Bailey
Royal Courts of Justice
St. Dunstan's
The Temple
St. Brides
City of London Hostel
St. Clement Dane's
St. Mary-le-Strand
Transport Museum
City of London College
Blackfriars Station
Somerset House
RED LION SQAURE
CHANCERY LANE
FARRINGDON
ALDWYCH
TEMPLE
BLACK-FRIARS
LUDGATE CIRCUS
1Temple Church of St. Mary
2Inner Temple Gardens
3Middle Temple Gardens
4Middle Temple Hall

Directly west of the museum, Bedford Sq. remains one of London's best-preserved 18th-century squares. All the doorways are framed with original pieces of Coade Stone, an artificial stone manufactured outside of London. Farther west, the residential calm is interrupted by Tottenham Ct. Rd., lined with furniture and electronics shops. To the north, the 580-ft. **Telecom Tower** looms over Fitzrovia.

Despite the historical aura that suffuses the area today, Bloomsbury is still a locus of innovation. Several community centers provide venues and resources for alternative cultural activity. Particularly noteworthy are the **Drill Hall** (see **Entertainment,** p. 239), **The Place** (see p. 243), and the **October Gallery,** 24 Old Gloucester St. (tel. 242 7367), off Queen St., a small venue that mounts the works of international artists (open Tu-Sa 12:30-5:30pm). Similarly, **Gay's The Word Bookshop** (see p. 266) adds its own slant to the collection of traditional, secondhand, and rare bookstores that recall Bloomsbury's historical role as a center of book trade.

Islington

Lying in the low hills just north of the City of London, **Islington** (tube: Angel or Highbury and Islington) began as a royal hunting ground. Islington was first absorbed into London by fugitives from the Plague, and later by industrialization and trade along Regent's Canal. Islington became "trendy" during the late 17th century, when its ale houses and cream teas made it popular for wealthy scene-makers. A century later, however, the rich began to move out, leaving the area to deteriorate. In more recent times, Islington was one of London's first areas to undergo regentrification; it established itself as an academic and artistic haven by the 1930s, serving as home to writers such as George Orwell, Evelyn Waugh, Douglas Adams, and Salman Rushdie.

Today, Islington is one of the hottest neighborhoods in London. The area is favored by trendy, style-conscious, and well-to-do Londoners. It is often spoken of as a district on the verge of becoming the next Covent Garden or Soho. Many of the more stylish University of London students and professors live here, alongside several ethnic communities including Turkish, Irish, Italian, and Bengali residents. As the number of gay pubs in the area attests, Islington is also home to a large gay community. (Chris Smith, one of the few voluntarily out Members of Parliament, was elected from this area.) Islington now puts on a summer display of its artistic resources in the annual **Islington International Festival** during the last week of June (1995 was the inaugural year). Upper St., the area's main drag, is closed for the festival (call 833 3131 for information). Angel St., which intersects Upper St., in the most happenin' part of town, is home to a number of quirky, mod shops.

A refurbished 19th-century chapel now houses the **Crafts Council,** 44a Pentonville Rd., (tel. 806 2500), the national organization for the promotion of contemporary crafts. *(Tube: Angel. Open Tu-Sa 11am-6pm, Su 2-6pm. Wheelchair accessible.)* Exit the station to the left and take the first right onto Pentonville Rd. In addition to the Crafts Council Gallery, the building also contains a picture library with slides of British works, a reference library, a gallery shop, and a cafe. The council sponsors fantastic temporary exhibitions. Take advantage of the free admission; not only are the main exhibition galleries wonderfully air-conditioned, but the building's lighting fixtures, furniture, clocks, floors, door handles, and lettering have been designed by contemporary artisans, creating an aesthetically appealing exhibition space. Many pieces of art are also for sale.

The **Business Design Centre,** 52 Upper St. (tel. 359 3535 or 288 8666), is hard to miss. The modern-looking glass facade belies its origin as the Royal Agricultural Hall, completed in 1861. Known as "the Aggie," the Hall's large, enclosed space served as the site for a wide range of crafts exhibitions, animal shows, meetings, Christmas fêtes, military tournaments, circuses, and the World's Fair. All was happy and glorious until the start of World War II, when the government took over the Hall to use it as an office building. In the 1970s, the Hall was sold to a property developer who hadn't realized that the historic building could not legally be demolished; apparently it was permissible to add skylights and huge, box-like windows that totally updated the building's appearance. Annual exhibits include Fresh Art, a showcase for recent fine arts graduates, and New Designers, a springboard for commercial and consumer design students. Many exhibitions charge admission—call for details.

Hampstead and Highgate

Foliage in London traditionally pulls in well-heeled and artistic residents, and the twin villages of "Ham and High," surrounding the gorgeous Hampstead Heath, are no exception. Keats, Dickens, and more recently, Emma Thompson and Kenneth Branagh have all called the area home. The tidy streets lined with Jaguars, boutiques, and Georgian townhouses provide a window on the theory and practice of being idly rich, which may explain Karl Marx's, Jinnah's (the founder of Pakistan), and former Labour leader Michael Foot's past residences. Such affluence gives rise to curiosities, making the area worth a visit—even the McDonald's has slick, Italian, black-lacquered chairs. *(To get to Hampstead, take the tube to Hampstead or British Rail to Hampstead Heath. To reach Highgate, take the tube to Archway, then Bus #210 to Highgate Village. Either trip takes around 30 min. from the center of London.)*

This dual legacy of art and wealth shines through in the area's many restored houses, most notably the **Keats House,** Keats Grove (tel. 435 2062), one of London's finest literary shrines. *(Open Apr.-Oct. M-F 10am-1pm and 2-6pm, Sa 10am-1pm and 2-5pm, Su 2-5pm; Nov.-Mar. M-F 1-5pm, Sa 10am-1pm and 2-5pm, Su 2-5pm. Free.)* To get there from the Hampstead tube station, head left down High St. for several blocks, turn left down Downshire Hill, and then take the first right onto Keats Grove. (The BR Hampstead Heath station is much closer.) Before dashing off to Italy to breathe his last consumptive breath in true Romantic style, John Keats pined here for his next-door fiancee, Fanny Brawne. He allegedly composed "Ode to a Nightingale" under a plum tree here; one wonders what the Romantic would have made of the "keep off the grass" signs in the garden today. The decor and furnishings stay true to the Regency style of the early 19th century, providing an evocative showcase for manuscripts, letters, and contemporary pans of Keats' works by critics dead and forgotten. The **Keats Memorial Library** (tel. 794 6829) next door contains 8500 books on the poet's life, family, and friends (open by appointment to accredited researchers only).

Among the delicate china, furniture, and early keyboard instruments exhibited in the **Fenton House,** Hampstead Grove (tel. 435 3471), sits a prototype 18th-century "double guitar," proving that Britain's fascination with excessively stringed instruments predates the meaty guitar hooks of the young Jimmy Page. *(Open Apr.-Nov. W-F 2-5pm, Sa-Su 11am-5pm. Admission £4, children £2.)* If you're lucky, area musicians will be strumming, plucking, and tickling as you stroll through. If you fancy yourself a musical type, you may audition with the curator to play them yourself. For permission, apply in writing to Mimi Waitzman, 11 Sprowston Rd., Forest Gate, London E7 9AD. You can see the walled garden and orchard free of charge. Note the boarded windows of Fenton House—the revenue man tried to levy a tax upon the number of windows in people's homes, leading people like the Fentons to board up their glass, setting a fine example of tax evasion for the area's well-heeled denizens to emulate. To get there, cross the street onto Holly Bush Hill, then bear right at the fork onto Hampstead Grove.

Farther up Hampstead Grove, a left turn onto Admiral's Walk takes visitors to the **Admiral's House.** The house failed in its attempt to simulate a steam ship, but earned celluloid immortality as the home of the nutty admiral in *Mary Poppins.*

The idyllic walk to the **Burgh House,** New End Sq. (tel. 431 0144), is much more satisfying than the exhibitions of the **Hampstead Museum** inside (open W-Su 11am-5:30pm). Just a few narrow streets and cobblestone sidewalks away from High St., the town is transformed into a country village with flowers everywhere and birds chirping in the boughs of commandingly large trees. Stop for a peaceful cup of tea at **The Buttery** in the basement. Head left from the Hampstead tube on Hampstead High St. and take the first left onto Flask Walk.

Church Row, off Heath St., assiduously guards its 18th-century style and dignified terraces. The narrow alleyways off the Row hark back to the days of Mary Poppins, complete with small, overflowing secret gardens. The painter John Constable lies buried in St. John's Churchyard down the row.

Hampstead Heath (tube: Hampstead or BR Hampstead Heath) separates Hampstead and Highgate from the rest of London. Stroll through acres of lush greenery and forget the hustle and bustle of the city among the care-free picnickers, kite flyers, and anglers. But don't stay too late—it's inadvisable to wander the heath alone at night.

The southeastern tip of the heath is called **Parliament Hill,** but rather deceptively—no Parliament, no hill. It was toward this "hill" that Guy Fawkes and his accomplices fled after planting explosives under the House of Commons in 1605, hoping for a good view of the explosion. He was later caught and tortured in the Tower of London (see p. 167). Visitors who journey here for the same view may be similarly disappointed; the heath is worth a visit for other reasons, but the view is overrated. What little elevation exists reputedly owes much to the piles of corpses left here during the Plague. The bones of Queen Boudicca—who after a flogging by the Romans raised an army and sacked London—reputedly lie here too.

On a hot day, take a dip in the murky waters of **Kenwood Ladies' Pond, Highgate Men's Pond,** or the *outré* **Mixed Bathing Pond.** The ponds are a refreshing, free way to escape the rare, sunny London days. In July 1994, gay protestors held a "strip-off" demonstration at the men's pond to protest the Corporation of London's introduction of a **trunks-on policy.** In all, the heath boasts six ponds.

Kenwood House, Hampstead Ln., a picture-perfect example of an 18th-century country estate, presides over the heath. *(Grounds open daily 8am-8:30pm or dusk, whichever comes first.)* This airy mansion now houses the **Iveagh Bequest** (see **Museums,** p. 231). Chief justice Lord Mansfield, the original owner of Kenwood, decreed an end to slavery on English soil. Mansfield's progressive policies did not win him universal popularity and after destroying his abandoned townhouse in Bloomsbury, the Gordon Rioters pursued him north to Hampstead. Luckily for him (and for Kenwood House), his pursuers stopped for a drink at the **Spaniards Inn** on Spaniards Rd. (see **Pubs,** p. 122), where a responsible publican plied them with drink until the militia could seize them. In summer, Kenwood hosts a hugely popular series of **outdoor concerts** (see **Music,** p. 241) in which top-flight orchestras play from a bandshell across the lake (tube: Archway or Golders Green, then bus #210 to Kenwood). From Hampstead High St., bus #268 goes to Golders Green.

SIGHTS

To get from Hampstead to Highgate, walk across the heath (an easy way to get lost, but very scenic) or up Hampstead Ln. Both take about 45 minutes. You can also take Bus #210 from Jack Straw's Castle junction, or take the tube to Archway.

Highgate Village stands 424 ft. above the River Thames. You can climb Highgate Hill for a view of London. From Archway tube station, exit onto Highgate Hill, which goes up.75km to the village, or wait there for bus #210.

Once in **Highgate Village,** turn left onto South Grove at the triangular bus depot. Here hides **The Grove,** an avenue of late 17th-century houses secluded behind magnificent elms. Poet and critic Samuel Taylor Coleridge lived at No. 3 for the last 11 years of his life, entertaining Carlyle, Emerson, and other literary luminaries.

Highgate Cemetery (tel. (0181) 340 1834), on Swains Ln., is a remarkable monument to the Victorian fascination with death. Curiously, the most famous resident of this deathbed of Victoriana is Karl Marx, buried in the **Eastern Cemetery** in 1883. *(Open M-F 10am-6pm, Sa-Su 11am-6pm; Admission £1.)* The larger-than-life bust placed above his grave in 1956 is hard to miss, though the number of visits to Marx's tomb has declined noticeably in recent years. Death and politics make strange bedfellows—Herbert Spencer, who vehemently opposed socialism, shares Highgate with socialism's most influential proponent, Marx. On a more harmonious note, Spencer's bones lie near those of his reputed lover, the novelist George Eliot (Mary Ann Evans, buried in the western section). Resist the temptation to dance on the grave of Communism—this is, after all, a private cemetery. Be aware that the cemetery closes its gates to visitors during funerals. Though its guest list lacks the same notoriety, the western section, appropriately termed the **Western Cemetery,** provides rest for Michael Faraday, the Dickens family, and ornate tombs and mausolea worth seeing regardless of their occupants. The guided tour visits such sepulchral wonders as the **Egyptian Avenue,** constructed with lotus blossom columns and Cleopatra's needles, in the exotic *mode du jour* of the Victorian era. *(Access by guided tour only M-F noon, 2, and 4pm, Sa-Su every hr. 11am-4pm. Admission around £3. Camera permit £1, valid in both sections.)*

Golders Green

Located north of Hampstead, **Golders Green** seems a bland suburb at first, but a walk along its main street reveals a richer texture. Here is the center of London's Jewish community. Kosher restaurants, men in black hats, and yarmulke-bedecked youths dot the wide sidewalks of this neighborhood. Though it is some distance from the city center, the tube to Golders Green, Bus #13 from Oxford Circus, bus #268 from Hampstead High St., bus #28 through Kensington High St., and bus #210 from Archway tube all deposit visitors at the intersection of North End Way and Golders Green Rd. This wide shopping strip houses some mundane stores and a surprising number of Chinese restaurants. Jewish eateries and Hebrew/English signs begin to appear several blocks away from the station. The **Jewish Chronicle** (tel. 415 1500), the world's oldest Jewish newspaper, provides information on local Jewish events (50p).

The ashes of Freud, in his favorite Greek vase, rest near those of ballerina Anna Pavlova at the **Golders Green Crematorium,** 62 Hoop Ln., NW11 (tel. (0181) 455 2374; open daily 8am-6pm; free). Spanning several acres of pastoral land, Golders Green was the first legal crematorium in England. Other celeb ashes and memorials include five prime ministers, Marks and Spencer founder and Zionist Lord Sieff, Marc Bolan of T-Rex and "Get It On" fame, famed composer Gustav Holst, science fiction writer H.G. Wells, and Dracula creator Bram Stoker. To pay your respects, walk under the tube's bridge, then turn right at the first traffic light (at the church) onto Hoop Lane Rd. To prevent disgruntled psychology students' vandalism, the good doctor's ashes are locked away in the Ernest George Columbarium—ask an attendant to let you in on weekdays.

The grassy collection of fields, intricate gardens (including a Japanese display), and exotic zoo of **Golders Hill Park** rest on the other side of the tube station (off North End Rd.). A horticulturist's dreamland, the park attracts both avid plant watchers and young kite-flyers looking for green space in suburbia (open daily 8am-dusk).

EAST LONDON

The East End

Today's East End eludes the simple characterization that earlier times would have allowed. Once it was the Jewish center of London, then the Huguenot center, and later the center for a number of more recent immigrant groups—Irish, Somalis, Chinese, and Muslim Bangladeshi. Though its traditional working-class character is being slowly eroded by corporate culture oozing in from the City, you still get a "neighborhood" feel walking through this area.

Marked today by an invisible line across Bishops Gate St., London's East End nonetheless continues to serve, as it always has, as a refuge for both those who aren't welcome in the City and those who don't want to be subject to the City's jurisdiction. During the 17th century, this included political dissenters, religious orders, and the French Huguenots (Protestants fleeing religious persecution in France). By 1687, 13,000 Huguenots had settled in Spitalfields, the area northeast of the City of London (which takes its name from a long-gone medieval priory, St. Mary Spital). The silk-weaving Huguenots soon built a reputation for high-quality cloth—but as they attracted rich customers, they also attracted resentment. A large working-class English population moved into the district during the Industrial Revolution, followed by a wave of Jewish immigrants fleeing persecution in Eastern Europe who settled around **Whitechapel.** Jewish success in the rag trade drew the attention of the British Union of Fascists, who instigated anti-Semitic violence that culminated in the "Battle of Cable Street" in 1936. A mural on **St. George's Town Hall,** 236 Cable St. (tube: Shadwell), commemorates the victory against bigotry won in the streets that day.

In 1978, the latest immigration wave brought a large Muslim Bangladeshi community to the East End. At the heart of this community is Brick Lane (tube: Aldgate East), a street lined with Indian and Bangladeshi restaurants (see **Food and Drink,** p. 96), colorful textile shops, and grocers stocking ethnic foods. (To reach Brick Ln., head left up Whitechapel as you exit the tube station; turn left onto Osbourne St., which turns into Brick Ln.) On Sundays, vibrant market stalls selling books, bric-a-brac, leather jackets, and salt beef sandwiches flank this street and Middlesex St., better known as **Petticoat Lane**—its original name, drawn from the street's historical role as a center of the clothing trade (see **Shopping,** p. 263). A prudish Queen Victoria gave the street the more respectable, official name it bears today. Along with great bargains, these markets draw a diverse crowd from throughout London. At Fournier St., a former church now holds a mosque; it is not uncommon to hear the Islamic call to prayer, bellowed from the loudspeakers of numerous local mosques, compete with honking cars. The **East London Mosque,** 82-92 Whitechapel Rd. (tel. 247 1357; tube: Aldgate East), was London's first to have its own building. Its towering minarets, grand scale, and large congregation testify to the size of London's Muslim community.

Even the communities that have since moved out of the East End have not vanished without leaving some trace behind. **Christ Church,** Commercial St., E1 (tel. 247 7202; tube: Aldgate East; left on leaving the station, left again onto Commercial St.), in any other London neighborhood would be just another ancient building; here it is an island of Anglicanism amid a diverse spectrum of other traditions (open to visitors M-F noon-2:30pm). The church was begun by Hawksmoor in 1714 as part of Parliament's Fifty New Churches Act of 1711 and is currently undergoing a massive restoration of its tower and spire in an effort to return them to Hawksmoor's original design. The church also sponsors the **Spitalfields Festival** of classical music during the last three weeks of June (box office tel. 377 1362; tickets free-£25), and the church's crypt also serves as a rehabilitation center for alcoholics.

Most of the Jewish community has moved on to suburbs to the north and west of central London, like Stamford Hill and Golders Green (see **Greater London,** p. 193), taking along even such landmarks as the renowned kosher restaurant **Bloom's.** The city's oldest standing synagogue, **Bevis Marks Synagogue,** Bevis Marks and Heneage Ln., EC3 (tel. 626 1274; fax 283 8825; tube: Aldgate; from Aldgate High St. turn right onto Houndsditch; Creechurch Ln. on the left leads to Bevis Marks), remains and is well worth a visit. *(Organized tours Su-W and F noon; call in advance. Building open Su-M, W, and F 11:30am-1pm, Tu 10:30am-4pm. Entrance donation £1.)* Bevis Marks prides itself upon being situated in the heart of London, but its congregants undoubtedly came from the outcast East End neighborhood. The congregation traces its roots back to Spanish and Portuguese Jews who inhabited the area as early as 1657. Rabbi Menashe Ben Israel founded the synagogue in 1701, 435 years after the Jews were first expelled from England. Oliver Cromwell allowed the Jews to return because he wanted to be prepared for the millennium and believed that the sudden conversion of the Jews would be one of the surest signs of its approach. Recently, the Archbishop of Canterbury and several major politicians attended VE-Day ceremonies in this ancient synagogue, whose distinguished congregation has included Rothschilds, Montefiores, and Disraelis. Another major synagogue on Fieldgate St., marked by the remaining Hebrew letters above its entrance, has been amalgamated into the East London Mosque, underscoring the religious layering of this area.

The most recent wave of immigrants to join this cultural milieu consists of City artists. In today's East End, scattered deserted warehouse spaces and airy studios house

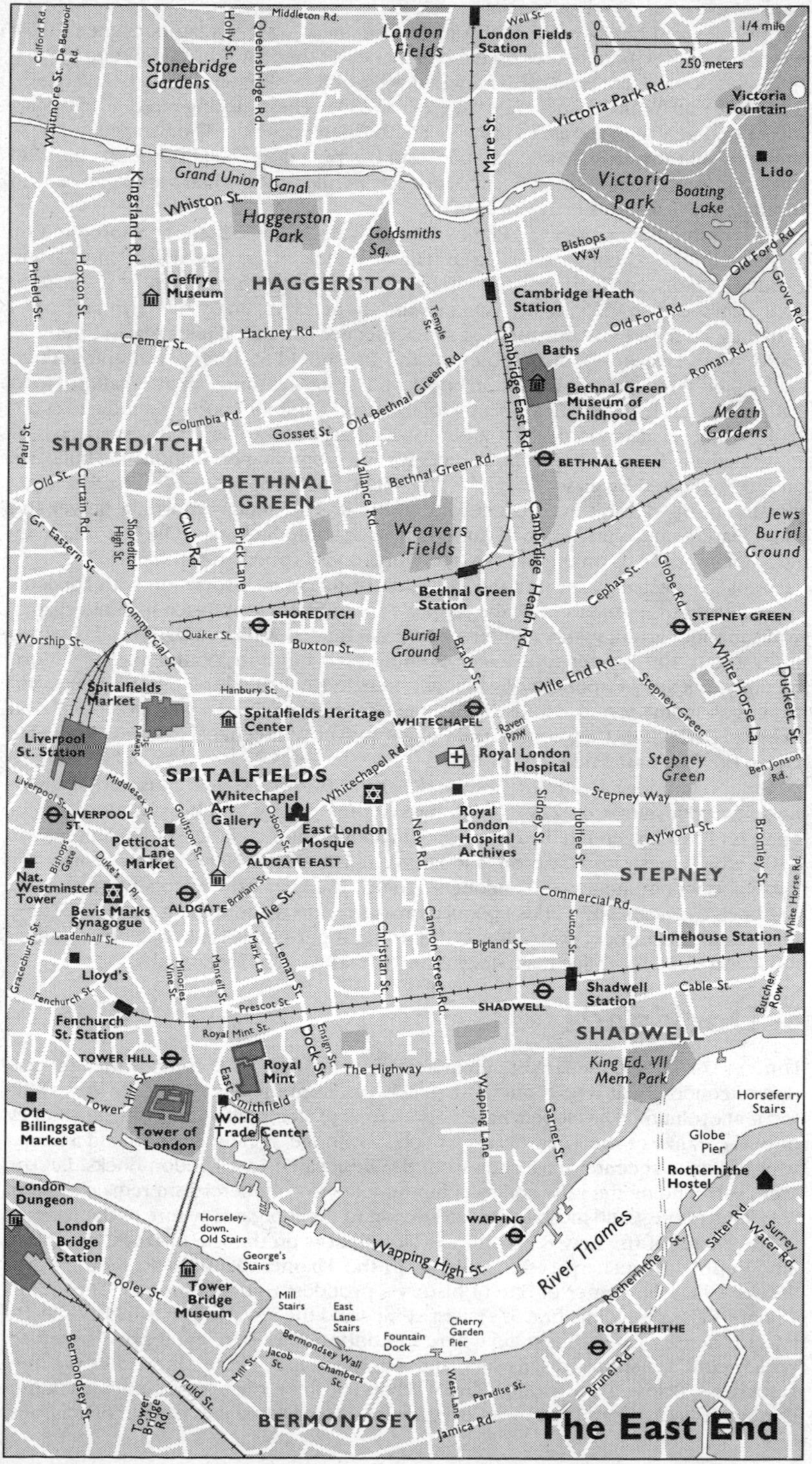

The East End

Middleton Rd.
London Fields
London Fields Station
Well St.
0 1/4 mile
0 250 meters
Culford Rd.
De Beauvoir Rd.
Whitmore St.
Holly St.
Queensbridge Rd.
Stonebridge Gardens
Victoria Park Rd.
Victoria Fountain
Lido
Mare St.
Grand Union Canal
Kingsland Rd.
Whiston St.
Haggerston Park
Goldsmiths Sq.
Victoria Park
Boating Lake
Bishops Way
Old Ford Rd.
Grove Rd.
Pitfield St.
Hoxton St.
Geffrye Museum
HAGGERSTON
Cambridge Heath Station
Temple St.
Old Ford Rd.
Cremer St.
Hackney Rd.
Baths
Roman Rd.
Old Bethnal Green Rd.
Cambridge East Rd.
Bethnal Green Museum of Childhood
Columbia Rd.
Gosset St.
Meath Gardens
Paul St.
SHOREDITCH
BETHNAL GREEN
Bethnal Green Rd.
Vallance Rd.
Old St.
Curtain Rd.
BETHNAL GREEN
Jews Burial Ground
Shoreditch High St.
Club Rd.
Brick Lane
Weavers Fields
Cambridge Heath Rd.
Gr. Eastern St.
Cephas St.
Globe Rd.
Bethnal Green Station
Commercial St.
SHOREDITCH
STEPNEY GREEN
Worship St.
Quaker St.
Buxton St.
Burial Ground
Brady St.
White Horse La.
Duckett St.
Mile End Rd.
Stepney Green
Spitalfields Market
Hanbury St.
Spitalfields Heritage Center
WHITECHAPEL
Raven Row
Liverpool St. Station
Steward St.
Royal London Hospital
Stepney Green
Ben Jonson Rd.
SPITALFIELDS
Whitechapel Rd.
Liverpool St.
Middlesex St.
Stepney Way
Whitechapel Art Gallery
LIVERPOOL ST.
Goulston St.
Osborn St.
East London Mosque
Royal London Hospital Archives
Sidney St.
Jubilee St.
Aylword St.
Bromley St.
Bishops Gate
Petticoat Lane Market
ALDGATE EAST
New Rd.
Duke's Pl.
Nat. Westminster Tower
Braham St.
STEPNEY
White Horse Rd.
Bevis Marks Synagogue
ALDGATE
Alie St.
Commercial Rd.
Leadenhall St.
Christian St.
Cannon Street Rd.
Sutton St.
Gracechurch St.
Mark La.
Leman St.
Bigland St.
Limehouse Station
Lloyd's
Minories
Vine St.
Mansell St.
Shadwell Station
Cable St.
Fenchurch St.
Prescot St.
SHADWELL
Butcher Row
Fenchurch St. Station
Royal Mint St.
Ensign St.
Dock St.
SHADWELL
TOWER HILL
Royal Mint
The Highway
King Ed. VII Mem. Park
Hill St.
East Smithfield
Wapping Lane
Garnet St.
Horseferry Stairs
Old Billingsgate Market
Tower
Tower of London
World Trade Center
Globe Pier
Rotherhithe Hostel
London Dungeon
Horseley-down. Old Stairs
WAPPING
River Thames
Salter Rd.
Surrey Water Rd.
London Bridge Station
George's Stairs
Wapping High St.
Rotherhithe St.
Tooley St.
Tower Bridge Museum
Mill Stairs
East Lane Stairs
Cherry Garden Pier
ROTHERHITHE
Fountain Dock
Bermondsey Wall
Bermondsey St.
Mill St.
Jacob St.
Chambers St.
Brunel Rd.
Druid St.
West Lane
Paradise St.
Tower Bridge Rd.
BERMONDSEY
Jamica Rd.

SIGHTS

the brushes and oils of over 6000 painters and "new wave" creators. Some of their work, much of which focuses on the experience of the East End's nonwhite population, occasionally hangs on the high white walls of the **Whitechapel Art Gallery** (tel. 522 7888) on Whitechapel High St. (see p. 233). Their cutting-edge, urban tone mixes strangely with the area's growing South Asian presence. The Bangladeshi community's shift towards Islamic traditionalism has pulled the neighborhood culturally further from the neighboring financial districts, while the East End's artists are slowly forging new ties with the City of London.

Spitalfields Farm, Weaver/Pedley St., E1 (tel. 247 8762; tube: Shoreditch or Whitechapel), is a genuine working farm in the middle of the city, where one can buy produce, plants, and manure—fill your own bag for a mere 50p. *(Open Tu-Su 10:30am-5pm; admission free.)* During the summer and on Sundays, enjoy the farm and crafts activities, go for a pony ride, or feast at a barbecue. The **Spitalfields Market** (tel. 247 6590; tube: Liverpool), at Commercial and Brushfield St. offers craft and antique stalls, special retail shops like "Roughneck and Thug" clothing, an international food hall (including London's first organic food market), indoor sports (including basketball), a large-scale train display, and changing art exhibits in a bizarre space best described as a large parking lot built under some crumbling brick industrial buildings and then encased by glass. *(Open M-F 11am-2pm, Su 9am-5pm; Su is the best time to go.)* "Postmodern" doesn't even begin to describe it. The Sunday morning flower and plant market on **Columbia Road** (tube: Old St. or Shoreditch; take Old St. to Hackney Rd., Columbia Rd. is on the right) is also worth a visit (open Su 8am-2pm).

An overdramatized aspect of the East End's history is its association with London's most notorious criminals. Jack the Ripper's six murders took place in Whitechapel; you can tour his trail with a number of different guided walk companies, all of which offer a Jack the Ripper tour every evening (see **London Walks,** p. 134). More recently, cockney Capone twins Ron and Reggie Kray ruled the 1960s underworld from their mum's terraced house in Bethnal Green. Ron wiped out an ale-sipping rival in broad daylight in 1966 at the **Blind Beggar** pub at Whitechapel Rd. and Cambridge Heath Rd. (see **East End Pubs,** p. 122).

Along Cambridge Heath Rd. lies the delightful **Bethnal Green Museum of Childhood** (see **Museums,** p. 229). North past Bethnal Green and beyond the wafts of curry on Brick Ln. stretch the expanses of **Hackney** (home of the Geffrye Museum, p. 230), which mesh into **Clapton,** and farther north, **Stoke Newington.** Traditionally known as a community of "Londoners' stock," Hackney now adapts to its growing Caribbean, African, and Turkish populations—Brixton without the hype and the tube line. West Indian beef patty shops, thumping night clubs, and discount clothing, food, and shoe stores line main drags Mare St. and Lower Clapton Rd.

Docklands

London Docklands, the largest commercial development in Europe, is the only section of London built wholly anew—a total break from the city's typically slow architectural evolution. Developers have poured tons of steel, reflective glass, and money onto the banks of the Thames east of London Bridge. A new Fleet St. and a heavyweight financial center have risen from the desiccated East London docks. But the areas surrounding the glass and steel monuments to commercialism remain some of London's poorest and most isolated, testifying to the inorganic nature of the project.

The center of the new 8.5-sq.-mi. development is on the **Isle of Dogs,** the spit of land defined by a sharp U-shaped bend in the Thames. To the east lie the **Royal Docks,** once the center of one of history's proudest trading empires. The 800 ft. **Canary Wharf** building, Britain's tallest edifice and the jewel of the Docklands, is visible to the east from almost anywhere in London. The pyramid-topped structure, which contains shops, restaurants, and a concert hall, is the emblem of the new Docklands. Below the towering Canary Wharf sprouts a huge fountain which during the lunch hour is carpeted by an expanse of conservative colors, starched fabrics, power ties, and tightly-pulled-back hair—anyone not kitted out in office wear will stick out like a sore thumb.

Docklands proper covers a huge expanse (55 mi. of waterfront to be exact), from the Tower of London to Greenwich. The best way to see the region is via the **Docklands Light Railway (DLR),** a driverless, totally automatic elevated rail system (tel. 918 4000 or 363 9700). The DLR's smooth ride affords a panoramic view that helps you put the huge expanse of the Docklands into perspective. All tickets, Travelcards, and passes issued by London Transport, London Underground, and Britrail are valid on the DLR, provided they cover the correct zones.

The **Docklands Visitor Centre** (tel. 512 1111; DLR: Crossharbour, then left up the road) should be the first stop for any tour of the Docklands (open M-F 8:30am-6pm, Sa-Su 9:30am-5pm). Loads of brochures hide behind the reception, the most useful being the *DLR Tourist Guide,* which includes a map, points of interest, and DLR info. A huge room is devoted to informing visitors about the history of the Docklands and its future, using photos, charts, maps, architects' plans, and a gushy propaganda video. Other Docklands information desks are at the Tower Hill/Gateway and Island Gardens stops. A separate **Museum of Docklands** is still in the works; until then, a section in the Museum of London counts as the Docklands museum (call the **Museum of Docklands Project,** tel. 515 1162, for an update).

London has a long history as a maritime gateway—Londinium was already a prominent port in Roman times—and by the Middle Ages the city's wharves and quays had creeped east from the City. The **Royal Dockyards** were established at Deptford and Woolwich in 1515. As London grew in importance, the docks grew with it, stretching miles down the Thames, until they had become the powerful trading center of the British Empire. During World War II, the Blitz obliterated much of the dock area, and the war itself seriously diminished Britain's world influence. Though the sun had set on the empire, the docks continued to do brisk business until the early 1960s, when the advent of container transport and modern shipping methods rendered them obsolete. By 1982, all had closed, leaving swaths of desperate dereliction.

As part of the Thatcher government's privatization program, redevelopment of the area was handed over to the private sector—in the form of the **London Docklands Development Corporation (LDDC)**—along with a generous helping of public funds. Since then, the LDDC has been at the helm of what it calls "the most significant urban regeneration program in the world." The all-powerful company is accountable only to Parliament and the Department of the Environment; however, local councils retain responsibility for housing, highway, and education decisions.

The LDDC's first mission was to convince Londoners that this blossoming area was an organic part of the city and not a distant, capitalistic wasteland. The Docklands' original investors, Olympia and York Co. of Toronto, poured millions of pounds into British Telecom to ensure that the Docklands received coveted city area codes and not suburban numbers, despite the area's peripheral location.

Since then, building has taken place on a phenomenal scale, but the task of populating new office space with businesses initially lagged behind. Hesitantly at first but now more steadily, big businesses have begun to take up residence in the area, filling in the previously empty floors of shiny new skyscrapers. In 1993, when Canary Wharf remained largely unoccupied due to the recession, Spiral Tribe, an underground rave-coordinating organization, attempted to use the building as a rave venue but were thwarted by the police. After a disastrous recession slump, the Docklands are poised for a new housing boom. Low-cost housing communities are springing up all over the southern bank, especially on the Isle of Dogs, which local residents hope will benefit them as well. Whatever recent successes they may have had, however, the new Docklands and the LDDC remain a sort of Disneyland Paris of urban renewal, resented by some and disregarded by more. Even the locals who are supposed to have been rescued by the new developments often seem little more than bemused by the sudden appearance of skyscrapers and monorails in their midst.

On the southern end of the Isle of Dogs, the pastoral expanses of **Mudchute Park** (DLR: Crossharbour or Mudchute), come as a relief after the human-made modernity of Canary Wharf. At **Mudchute City Farm,** Pier St., E14 (tel. 515 5901) there are 32 acres of grassy heath, plus horses to ride and farm animals to pet (open daily 9am-5pm, Tu and Th later—call for details). Note the round stone pathways leading into the park from West Ferry St. These odd markings run parallel to the Prime Meridian, which is defined by the green-domed observatory just visible across the river. Also note the cement walls and ditches at the entrance to the park. These were WWII anti-aircraft gun sites installed just before the Battle of Britain. For a sweeping view of Greenwich, follow the DLR southern line to its endpoint at Island Gardens. You can walk through the chilly foot tunnel (the steps at either end are quicker than waiting for the lift) and take in some of the sights (see **Greenwich and Blackheath,** p. 204).

Getting off at **Shadwell** station, you'll see an old, working class, dock community—drab brick housing, dusty streets, traditional pubs, cafes, and pie-and-mash shops—in the throes of a major transformation through an infusion of Bengali immigrants. Southwest of the station, down Cable Rd., left onto Cannon St. Rd., and right onto The Highway, is the turreted **St. George in the East** (tel. 481 1345), built 714-26, whose plain facade and tower can be seen from afar (open daily 9am-5pm). Designed by Wren's disciple Nicholas Hawksmoor, it was bombed and, in 1964, restored with a modern interior.

From the **Westferry** stop, turn left onto West India Dock Rd., then left onto Three Colt St. for another, now sadly grafitti-ridden, Hawksmoor church. **St. Anne's** (tel. 987 1502), built 1712-24, presides over a leafy churchyard and some barely legible but still engrossing Victorian headstones (open M-F 2-4pm, Sa 2-5pm, Su 2:30-5:30pm). The sister church of St. George in the East, its clock face comes from the workshop that made Big Ben's. The church's Victorian organ won the organ prize at the Great Exhibition of 1851.

The Limehouse and Westferry stops cover the historic **Limehouse** area, where dock and factory workers once lived. The legacy of Limehouse's 19th-century Chinese community can be seen in the Chinese restaurants along West India Dock Rd. The famous **Narrow Street** along the Thames is an official conservation area, where many Georgian houses and ancient pubs can be seen. At 76 Narrow St., **The Grapes,** the pub Dickens described in *Our Mutual Friend* maintains its original ambience. Just across from The Grapes, on Ropemaker's Fields, lies **The House They Left Behind,** a pub famed as a Joseph Conrad haunt (for more on both pubs, see p. 122).

Many of the ancient Dockland wharfs have now been turned into major leisure spots. Six sailing centers, three pools, a go-karting racetrack, and an artificial ski mountain currently stand where ships and toxic waste used to rest. For general information and bookings for all of the above activities, call 476 2134. The Docklands Visitor Centre also has a list of all sport and leisure facilities.

The year-round **Beckton Alps Ski Centre** (tel. 511 0351; DLR: Beckton, zone 4), is a one-run hillock rising 45m above the surrounding supermarkets and electronics superstores. *(Admission £6 per 3hr. weekdays, £7 per 3hr. including equipment rental.)* It is covered with a specially designed carpet upon which water is sprayed to make it slippery. The carpet is similar to white astroturf; you definitely don't want to fall, as it would be truly unpleasant at any speed. The 200meter-long run is served by a rope tow. Amateurs may not have much luck turning heads, but the regulars who pay £300 per season manage to look like Tomba. The center is owned and operated by a former Austrian olympic skier, he bills it as "London's Premiere Ski Centre," which, by force of logic, it is. The slope is open most days, but call to check on conditions—cold rainy days are the best. Pants, long sleeves, and gloves are required.

SOUTH LONDON

South Bank and Lambeth

A hulk of worn concrete and futuristic slate, the **South Bank** gestures defiantly at the center of London from across the Thames. Housing the British terminus of the Channel Tunnel, this region is currently becoming one of London's most dynamic, as major commercial development is currently underway. Waterloo station is the London exit from the "Chunnel," and Nicholas Grimshaw's spectacular new blue and silver international terminal has become many visitors' introduction to Britain. Nonetheless, to the untutored eye, this area initially appears confusing and dismal, especially on the average cloudy London day. The massive **South Bank Centre** is the predominant architectural eyesore; yet behind this hulking facade lurks London's most concentrated campus of artistic and cultural activity (tube: Waterloo, then follow signs for York Rd.; or Embankment and cross the Hungerford footbridge).

The region south of the Thames has long been home to entertainment, much of it bawdy—until the English Civil Wars, most of this area fell under the legal jurisdiction of the Bishop of Winchester, and was thus protected from London censors. The region stayed almost entirely rural until the 18th-century Westminster and Blackfriars bridges were built. Until post-WWII development began, the area was a den of working-class neighborhoods, dark breweries, smoky industry, and murky wharves through which suburbanites passed on their way into the city.

Contemporary development began in 1951 during the Festival of Britain, the centenary of the Great Exhibition of 1851, when the **Royal Festival Hall** was built. A veritable eruption of construction ensued, producing the many concrete blocks that comprise the South Bank Centre: the **National Film Theatre,** the **Hayward Gallery** and **Queen Elizabeth Hall** complex, and the **Royal National Theatre.** Recent calls for the demolition and replacement of the Queen Elizabeth Hall and the Hayward Gallery have prompted many to declare their fondness for the complex. More recent additions to the South Bank landscape include the **Jubilee Gardens,** planted for the Queen's Silver Jubilee in 1977, which stretch along the Embankment.

The 3000-seat **Royal Festival Hall** and its three auditoriums (Olivier, Lyttleton, and Cottlesoe) are home to the Philharmonia and London Philharmonic orchestras, the English National Ballet, and host to countless others; its chamber-musical sibling is the **Queen Elizabeth Hall** (see p. 235). **The National Theatre** (see p. 227), opened by Lord Olivier in 1978, promotes "art for the people" through convivial platform performances, foyer concerts, lectures, tours, and workshops. The **Hayward Gallery** (see p. 223), on Belvedere Rd., houses imaginative contemporary art exhibitions. Multicolored posters displaying Russian titles and Asian warriors distinguish the entrance to the **National Film Theatre** (see p. 234), directly on the South Bank. The Film Theatre also operates the stupendous **Museum of the Moving Image** (see p. 220).

The most colorful recent changes in the South Bank landscape result from the unflagging efforts of a non-profit development company, **Coin Street Community Builders (CSCB).** Since 1984 CSCB has converted 13 previously derelict acres into a park and riverside walkway, seven housing cooperatives, and a designer crafts market at Gabriel's Wharf. **Gabriel's Wharf** (tel. 401 3610), is a great place to watch original crafts being fashioned while grabbing a snack after a visit to the National Theatre. During the summer, take advantage of sporadic free festivals. *(Crafts workshops Tu-Su 11am-6pm; call the Wharf for information on festivals.)*

CSCB's next renovation project, the **OXO Tower,** is adjacent to Gabriel's Wharf. Formerly the headquarters of a company that produced meat extract, the Art Deco tower is notable for its clever subversion of rules prohibiting permanent advertising on buildings—architects built the tower's distinct windows in the shape of the company's logo. CSCB boasts that the meticulously planned potpourri of rooftop cafes,

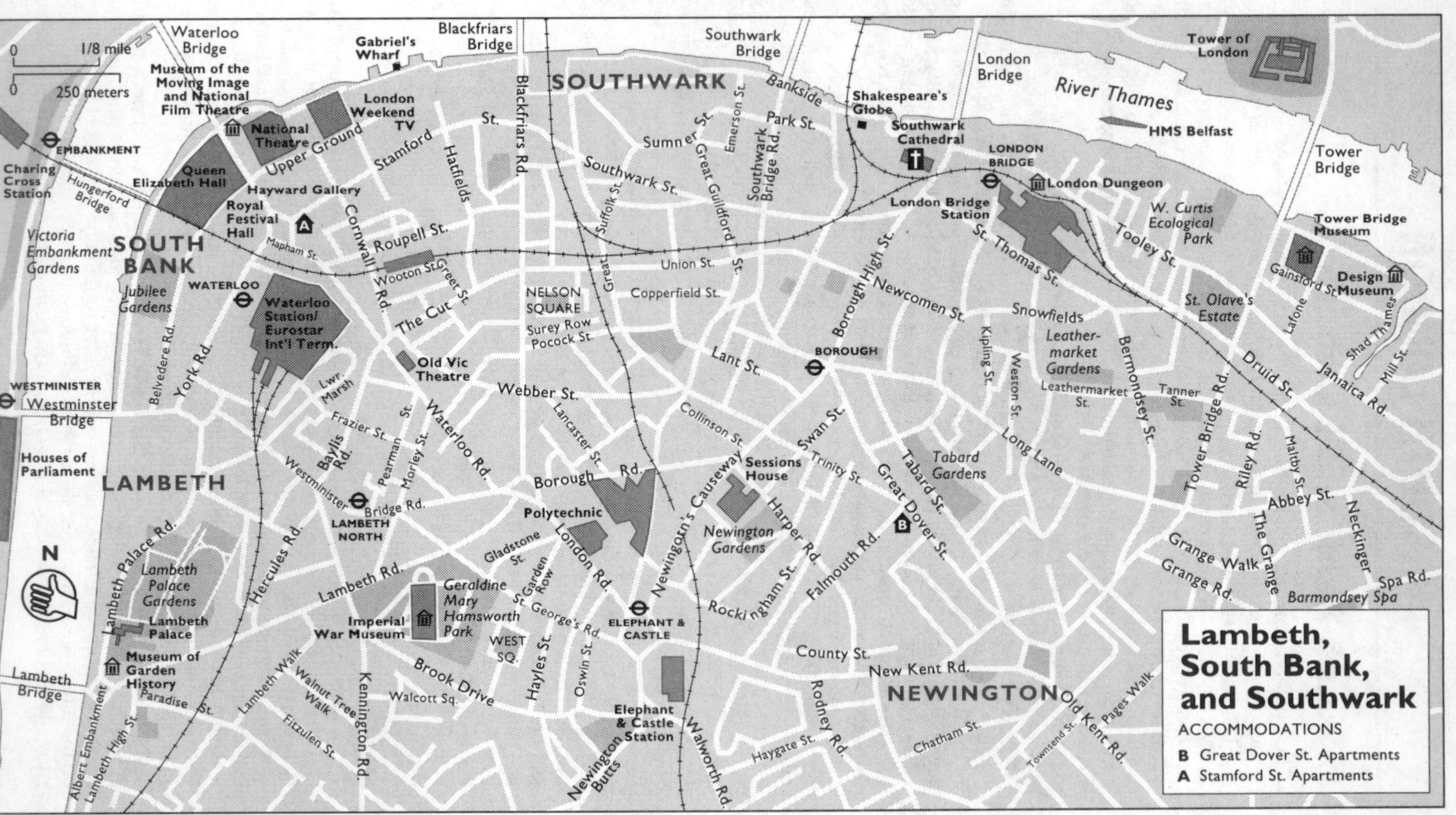

Lambeth, South Bank, and Southwark
ACCOMMODATIONS
B Great Dover St. Apartments
A Stamford St. Apartments
0 1/8 mile
0 250 meters
Waterloo Bridge
Gabriel's Wharf
Blackfriars Bridge
Southwark Bridge
London Bridge
River Thames
Tower of London
HMS Belfast
Tower Bridge
Museum of the Moving Image and National Film Theatre
London Weekend TV
National Theatre
SOUTHWARK
Shakespeare's Globe
Southwark Cathedral
LONDON BRIDGE
London Dungeon
London Bridge Station
EMBANKMENT
Charing Cross Station
Hungerford Bridge
Queen Elizabeth Hall
Hayward Gallery
Royal Festival Hall
Victoria Embankment Gardens
SOUTH BANK
WATERLOO
Jubilee Gardens
Waterloo Station/ Eurostar Int'l Term.
W. Curtis Ecological Park
Tower Bridge Museum
Design Museum
St. Olave's Estate
NELSON SQUARE
Old Vic Theatre
BOROUGH
Leather-market Gardens
WESTMINISTER
Westminster Bridge
Houses of Parliament
LAMBETH
Tabard Gardens
Sessions House
Newington Gardens
Polytechnic
LAMBETH NORTH
N
Lambeth Palace Gardens
Lambeth Palace
Geraldine Mary Hamsworth Park
Imperial War Museum
WEST SQ.
ELEPHANT & CASTLE
Museum of Garden History
Lambeth Bridge
Elephant & Castle Station
NEWINGTON
Newington Butts
Upper Ground
Stamford St.
Hatfields
Blackfriars Rd.
Southwark St.
Sumner St.
Great Guildford St.
Emerson St.
Southwark Bridge Rd.
Park St.
Bankside
Suffolk St.
Cornwall Rd.
Roupell St.
Mapham St.
Wooton St.
Greet St.
Union St.
Great Suffolk St.
Copperfield St.
Borough High St.
Newcomen St.
St. Thomas St.
Tooley St.
The Cut
Surey Row
Pocock St.
Lant St.
Snowfields
Kipling St.
Weston St.
Leathermarket St.
Bermondsey St.
Tanner St.
Tower Bridge Rd.
Druid St.
Jamaica Rd.
Gainsford St.
Lafone
Shad Thames
Mill St.
Belvedere Rd.
York Rd.
Lwr. Marsh
Webber St.
Lancaster St.
Collinson St.
Swan St.
Long Lane
Frazier St.
Baylis Rd.
Pearman St.
Morley St.
Waterloo Rd.
Westminster Bridge Rd.
Borough Rd.
Newington's Causeway
Trinity St.
Great Dover St.
Tabard St.
Harper Rd.
Falmouth Rd.
Riley Rd.
Maltby St.
Abbey St.
Neckinger
The Grange
Grange Walk
Grange Rd.
Spa Rd.
Barmondsey Spa
Lambeth Palace Rd.
Hercules Rd.
Lambeth Rd.
Gladstone St.
Garden Row
London Rd.
St. George's Rd.
Rockingham St.
County St.
New Kent Rd.
Old Kent Rd.
Pages Walk
Lambeth Walk
Walnut Tree Walk
Kennington Rd.
Brook Drive
Walcott Sq.
Hayles St.
Oswin St.
Walworth Rd.
Rodney Rd.
Haygate St.
Chatham St.
Townsend St.
Paradise St.
Fitzulen St.
Albert Embankment
Lambeth High St.

retail outlets, designer workshops, performance spaces, and flats that opened two summers ago at the OXO Tower Wharf will make it a hub of London activity.

Numerous pedestrian pathways are being planned for the region, which will make it easier to get to the jumbled stalls of the **Cut Street Market** near Waterloo station. The market's old character has waned as ambitious development projects consume more of the area's residential neighborhoods, but prices have stayed low, and used-book sellers and curiosity stands have maintained the district's flavor.

Farther along Waterloo Rd., the magnificently restored **Old Vic,** former home of Olivier's National Repertory Theatre, now hosts popular seasons of lesser-known classics and worthy revivals. The smaller, quirkier **Young Vic** is just a bit farther down the road (for more information, see **Theater,** p. 233).

The **Christ Church Tower** of 1876 rises above a mundane block of office buildings at the corner of Kennington Rd., directly across from Lambeth North tube station. **Lambeth Palace,** on the Embankment opposite the Lambeth Bridge in Archbishops Park, has been the Archbishop of Canterbury's London residence for seven centuries. *(Tube: Lambeth North. Open by prior arrangement only; contact Lambeth Palace, Lambeth Palace Road, SE1.)* Although Archbishop Langton founded it in the early 13th century, most of the palace dates from the 19th century. The palace's notable exterior includes the entrance at the 15th-century brick Morton's Tower, and Lollard's Tower, where John Wyclif's followers were thought to be imprisoned. Next door to the Palace's southernmost entrance stands the **Museum of Garden History** (tel. 401 8865), complete with a replica of a 17th-century garden. *(Open mid-Mar. to mid-Dec. M-F 10:30am-4pm, Su 10:30am-5pm. Free.)* East on Lambeth Rd. is the **Imperial War Museum** (see **Museums,** p. 224).

Southwark and Bankside

Historically a hotbed of prostitution, incarceration, and bear-baiting, **Southwark** (across London Bridge from the city) seems an unlikely location for a new cradle of London high culture (tube: London Bridge). The area around the **Borough High Street,** "the Borough," has survived—with a few minor changes—for nearly 2000 years. Until 1750, London Bridge was the only bridge over the Thames in London, and the inns along the highway leading to it hosted many travelers. The neighborhood has also been associated with entertainment from the days of the frost fairs (the old London Bridge used to cause the Thames to freeze over during the winter) to the more vicious pleasures of Defoe's *Moll Flanders.* Located along the Thames's bank, **Bear Gardens** received its name from the bear-baiting arena that stood there in Elizabethan times, when bears and bulls were pitted against mastiffs for sport.

But Southwark's greatest "vice" has always been theater. Shakespeare's and Marlowe's plays were performed at the **Rose Theatre,** built in 1587 and rediscovered during construction in 1989. The remnants are to be preserved and displayed underneath a new *Financial Times* office block at Park St. and Rose Alley. The remains of Shakespeare's **Globe Theatre** were discovered just months after those of the Rose.

A project spearheaded by the late actor/director Sam Wanamaker built a "new" Globe (tel. 902 1400) on the riverbank. The theater held its first full season in the summer of 1997 (see **Entertainment,** p. 236), featuring Shakespeare's *The Winter's Tale* and *Henry V,* as well the Womad Acoustic Concert and other non-Bardic performances. *(1hr. tours available May-Sept. M 9am-4pm, Tu-Sa 9am-12:30pm, Su 9am-2:30pm; Oct.-Apr. daily 10am-5pm. Admission £5, seniors and students £4, under 15 £3, families £14.)* The space itself is not only a wonderful reconstruction, but a unique opportunity in theater-going, allowing the audience (both seated and "groundling") a sort of contact with and perspective on the actors unavailable in most modern venues. The replica is also part of the **International Shakespeare Globe Centre,** which will ultimately contain a second theatre, an exhibition gallery, an archival library, an auditorium, and various shops; it's scheduled for completion in 2000 (see p. 228).

An awesome architectural monolith looms menacingly over the new Globe. The huge, terrible **CEGB Power Station's** windowless tower rises to the height of 325 ft.

Closed due to its obsolescence in 1980, the tower will become the new home of the Tate Gallery's **Modern Art Museum,** housing the foreign works of the Tate collection. To date, the Tate has poured over £100 million into the project, and expects it to be completed around 2000. Around the corner from the Globe, the new **Golden Hinde** offers landlubbers the chance to board a rebuilt 16th-century galleon. *(Open daily 10am-4pm. Admission £2.30, children £1.50, seniors £1.90, families £6.)* Attendants clad as pirates lead tours through the five levels of the vessel, seemingly geared especially toward the kiddies. Yar.

Before the "hoose-gow," the "big house," and "Club Fed," there was "the Clink," testament to Southwark's less than rosy past. The **Liberty of the Clink** comprised 70 acres of bankside land, under the jurisdiction of the Bishop of Winchester's Court. "The Clink" itself, which was in operation for more than six centuries, was the Bishop's private prison for London's criminals. Henry Barrowe and John Greenwood, early Separatists, were imprisoned here before being hanged. The **Clink Prison Museum,** 1 Clink St. (tel. 378 1558), recreates the "glory days" of the prison with an eerie choral soundtrack and hands-on restraining and torture devices. *(Open June-Sept. M-F 10am-6pm, Sa-Su 10am-9pm; Oct.-May daily 10am-6pm. Admission £4, concessions £3, children £3, families £9.)*

The **Southwark Cathedral** (tel. 407 2939) is a more endearing remnant of ecclesiatical power. *(Open M-F 9am-6pm. Evensong is Su 3pm. Admission free. Photo permit £1, video permit £5.)* Probably the most striking Gothic church in the city after Westminster Abbey, it is certainly the oldest—having been the site of a nunnery as early as 606. Mostly rebuilt in the 1890s, only the church's 1207 choir and retro-choir survive. The glorious altar screen is Tudor, with 20th-century statues. The cathedral is dotted with interesting stone and wood effigies, which have explanatory notes. Edmund Shakespeare, brother of Bill, was buried in the church in 1607 and lies beneath a stained-glass window depicting many of his talented sibling's characters. Medieval poet John Gower is also buried here in a colorful tomb. Furthermore, Southwark was the parish church of the Harvard family, and a chapel was dedicated in 1907 to the memory of John Harvard, benefactor (but not founder) of Harvard College, who was baptized here 300 years earlier.

Just a couple of blocks southeast, your hair will rise and your spine will chill at the **Old Operating Theatre, Museum, and Herb Garret,** 9a St. Thomas St. (tel. 955 4791), a carefully preserved 19th-century surgical hospital. *(Open Tu-Su 10am-4pm and "frequent Mondays." Admission £3, concessions £2, families £7.)* Rediscovered in 1956, it is the only known example of a pre-Victorian operating theatre. See the wooden table where unanesthetized patients endured excruciatingly painful surgery, or travel through the herb garret and museum to learn the properties of mugwort and why John Keats never finished his medical training. On the first Sunday of every month, the museum offers special lectures at 2:30pm.

If your appetite for the macabre is not sated by the minutiae of early medicine, the **London Dungeon** awaits buried beneath the London Bridge Station at 28 Tooley St. (see **Museums,** p. 224). Not for the squeamish, this dark maze of more than 40 exhibits recreates horrifying historical scenarios of execution, torture, and plague.

Moored on the south bank of the Thames, just upstream from Tower Bridge, the WWII warship **HMS Belfast** (tel. 407 6434) once led the bombardment of the French coast during D-Day landings and still looks as if it would enjoy nothing better than blowing 100 Golden Hindes to smithereens. *(Open daily Mar. 1-Oct. 31 10am-6pm, last admission 5:15pm; Nov. 1-Feb. 28 10am-5pm, last admission 4:15pm. Admission £4.70, children £2.40, students and seniors £3.60. Pool of London ferries run between five destinations along the river including the HMS Belfast; all-day pass adults £2, concessions £1.)* The labyrinth of the engine house and the whopping great guns make it a fun place to play sailor. Mind your head, matey. You can take the ferry that runs from Tower Pier on the north bank to the Belfast whenever the ship is open, or take the tube to London Bridge. Follow Tooley St. from London Bridge, past the London Dungeon, and look for the signs. East of Tower Bridge, the bleached Bauhaus box perching on the Thames is the

Design Museum (see **Museums,** p. 223), around the corner from which hides the **Bramah Tea and Coffee Museum** (see **Museums,** p. 222).

Hundreds of stalls selling antiques have been located at **Bermondsey Market** on Bermondsey St. since 1949. Go early (the serious traders arrive at 5am) on Friday morning to catch the best bargains. **Hay's Galleria,** bankside between Hay's Ln., Battlebridge Ln. and Tooley St. (tube: London Bridge), occupies the reconstructed Hay's Wharf. Underneath the glass and steel, the galleria houses restaurants, shops, and a giant kinetic sculpture by David Kemp called *The Navigators,* which combines water jets and all of the accoutrements of Britain's nautical past. The **Southwark Tourist Information Centre** (tel. 403 8299), in the lower level of Hay's Galleria, Tooley St., SE1, books rooms and provides information on the area's sights (open M-Sa 10am-5pm, Su 11am-5pm). Ask for the handy list of conveniently located accommodation. Galleria also inexplicably possesses a free petanque court—ask for rules and boules inside Balls Brothers Wine Bar. Across Tooley St. from the Galleria lies **Winston Churchill's Britain At War Museum** (see **Museums,** p. 226).

Brixton

The genteel Victorian shopping and residential district of SW9 (tube: Brixton) became the center of the London Caribbean and African community following large-scale Commonwealth immigration in the 1950s and 60s. Brixton gained notoriety in mid-April 1981, when fierce riots broke out pitting locals against police. Headlines screamed about "The Battle of Brixton," and alarmist copy spoke of "Bloody Saturday"—simmering fires, charred buildings, Molotov cocktails, and widespread looting. The desperation of those times was captured in The Clash's anthem "The Guns of Brixton," as well as Hanif Kureishi's film *Sammie and Rosie Get Laid.*

There has been much ex post speculation as to the cause of the riots. Some locals argue that as the black population in Brixton grew, so did police harassment, and boiling resentment finally turned into aggression. Many compare the Brixton riots to the race-related riots that rocked major American cities in the 1960s.

One optimistic theory asserted that a vibrant commercial sector would emerge from the post-riot shambles. Brixton has certainly revived since 26 of its buildings were destroyed by fire that April. The firms "Backing Brixton" on the railway bridge testify to this revitalization. Another good omen is a growing influx of the young and hip into the area's restaurants, shops, and burgeoning club scene, a visible testament to the area's newfound "up and coming" status.

Nonetheless radicalism and poverty still thrive in Brixton, and tourists should be duly careful, especially at night. Outside the tube station, revolutionaries distribute a thousand different militant newspapers. If political activism is your cup of tea, then Brixton is a good place to take up your cudgels. Meetings of black Muslims, neo-Marxists, Rastafarians and countless other groups are easily found—just take a look at the many flyposters around the station.

Most of the activity in Brixton centers around the **Brixton Market** at Electric Ave., Popes Rd., and Brixton Station Rd. (see **Shopping,** p. 257). Step out of the station and you're practically at the market's heart. One of the market's main arteries inspired Eddie Grant to "take it higher" in the early-1980s techno-reggae hit, "Electric Avenue." Shoppers from all over London mix with local crowds among vendors of food, clothing, and junk. Street preachers preach, performers busk, and waves of music pour out of the record shops. Choose from among the stalls of fresh fish, vegetables, and West Indian cuisine, or browse through the stalls of African crafts and discount clothing. And don't miss the delicious hard dough breads and tropical pastries produced by the abundant local bakeries.

Nearby, on the corner of Coldharbour and Atlantic, stand the **Black Cultural Archives,** 378 Coldharbour Ln., SW9 (tel. 738 4591; fax 738 7168). Begun by black parents who were concerned that their children's history curriculum in school taught them nothing about blacks' achievements, the Archives mounts small, but informative exhibits on black history and local issues in a downstairs gallery (open M-

SIGHTS

Sa 10am-6pm). Upstairs, books, documents, clippings, and photographs relating to the black presence in Britain are catalogued and stored (open M-F 10am-4pm and 1st Sa of each month 10am-3pm).

Strolling further up Brixton Rd. leads to a rewarding, and increasingly trendy part of town. The dramatic spire of **St. Matthew's Church** is surrounded by the **St. Matthew's Peace Garden,** a pleasant park that includes a memorial to the Sharpeville Massacre. Just opposite the Church are some of the bigger nightclubs in the area, as well as the arresting **Lambeth Town Hall,** located at Brixton Hill and Coldharbour Ln. (open M-F 9am-5pm). Stop by here for information on upcoming concerts and festivals in the Brixton area. It also compiles a list of community groups' meetings.

GREATER LONDON

Lo, where huge London, huger day by day,
O'er six fair counties spreads its hideous sway.

—Jane Austen, *The Golden Age*

London is the world's largest capital in area, but what is popularly considered part of this city changes quickly. Far-flung villages, once thought of as distinct, separate cities, are being swallowed up by London's creeping spread. Once serene hamlets like Hampstead are now mainstream night spots, and don't even think about finding a cheap, quiet drink in distant Richmond. This growth, however, has been met by iron resolve among outlying burgs to maintain their own identities amidst sheets of mundane commuter housing. London Transport and British Rail cover Greater London thoroughly; most areas are accessible without a car. If you plan to discover Greater London—and it would be a shame not to—a Travelcard covering the appropriate areas will save you a great deal of money. Keep in mind that within the correct zones, Travelcards are valid on British Rail.

Greenwich and Blackheath

London's love affair with the Thames and Britain's love affair with the sea climax in **Greenwich** (GREN-idge), at a point where the Thames runs wide and deep. Although the village functioned historically as the eastern water approach to London, Greenwich is synonymous with time in modern-day minds. After Charles II authorized the establishment of a small observatory here in 1675 "for perfecting navigation and astronomy," successive royal astronomers perfected their craft to such a degree that they were blessed with the Prime Meridian in 1884.

When industrialization hit Britain in the 18th century, Greenwich managed to hover above the fracas. As a result, the streets around the pier feel quaint (if somewhat touristy), with their tiny storefronts, pubs, and cafes. Greenwich also offers numerous corner markets. On summer Sundays, the village streets are taken over by the young, old, bold, and beautiful seeking the ultimate bargain at the **Greenwich Market** (tel. (0181) 293 3110), at Greenwich Church St. and College Approach. (Open Th-Su 9am-6pm.) Thursdays are set aside for the sale of antiques and collectibles, while the other days offer the traditional range of arts and crafts. In addition to this covered crafts market, Greenwich boasts an **Antique Market** on Burney St., where peddlers hawk antiques, books, and various bric-a-brac (open Sa-Su 8am-4pm). Come in the summer—the number of stalls and bargains dwindle during the winter months.

The splendid **Greenwich Park,** used as a burial ground during the 1353 plague, contains most of the major sights. The shriveled trunk of the **Queen Elizabeth Oak** on the east side of the park (now fenced off and covered in ivy) marks the spot where Henry VIII frolicked with an 11-fingered Anne Boleyn. The garden in the southeast corner of the park combines English garden and fairy tale, with a wild deer park thrown in for good measure. In summer, bands perform at Greenwich Park as a part

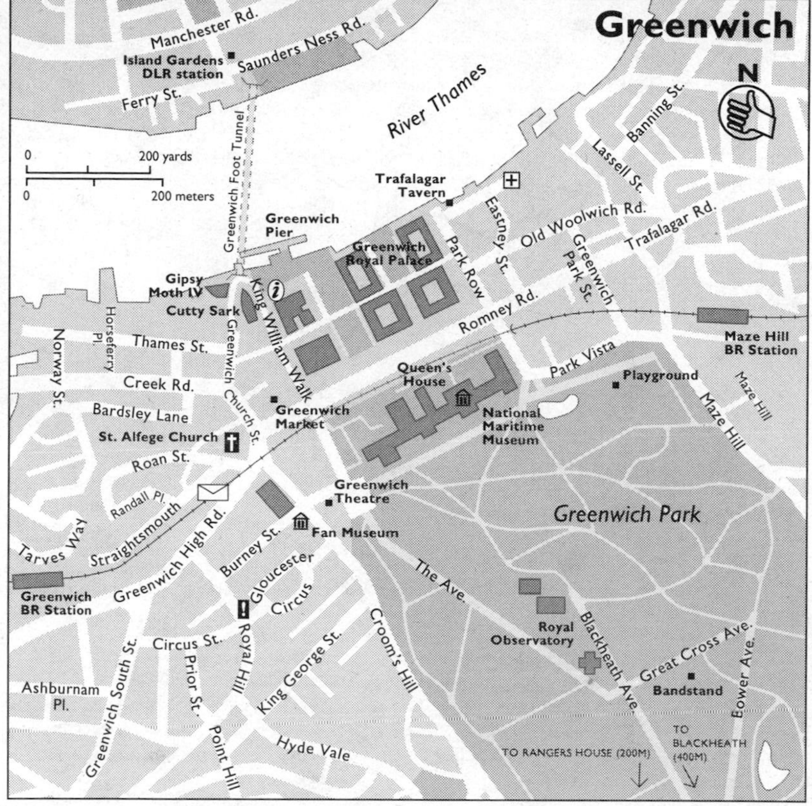

of the **Royal Park Band** performance series. Free shows begin at 3 and 6pm (June-Aug. every Sunday) in the bandstand north of the gardens. The **Children's Boating Pool** next to the playground gives kids a chance to unleash pent-up seafaring energy accumulated in the nearby museums. *(Open Apr.-Oct. daily 9am-dusk; £1.50 per person for 20min., or £2.50 per 2-3 child boat for 20min.)*

At the top of the hill in the middle of the park stands the **Old Royal Observatory** (tel. (0181) 312 6565), designed by Sir Christopher Wren. *(Open daily 10am-5pm; last admission 4:30pm. Admission to the Old Royal Observatory, National Maritime Museum, and the Queen's House: adults £5, concessions £4, children (5-16) £2.50, family £15. Admission to the Observatory alone: adults £4, concessions £3, children £2, family £12. Planetarium usually features a show M-Sa every ½hr. 11:30am-4pm; tickets £2, concessions and children £1.50. 45min. audio guide to the observatory £2.)* Only select parts are open to the public. Flamsteed House, remarkable for its unique, octagonal top room, contains Britain's largest refracting telescope and an excellent collection of early astronomical instruments displayed with nearly comprehensible explanations. The **Prime Meridian** is marked by a brass strip in the observatory courtyard and a laser beam inside; play the "now I'm west, now I'm east" game for as long as you're amused. Greenwich Mean Time, still the standard for international communications and navigation, is displayed on a clock over 120 years old. The red time ball, used since 1833 to indicate time to ships on the Thames, drops, quite unspectacularly, daily at 1pm. In 1894, an anarchist blew himself up while trying to destroy the observatory, and Polish sailor Joseph Conrad used the bizarre event as the seed for his novel The Secret Agent. Just outside of the observatory, you can share a splendid view of the Thames with a statue of General Wolfe

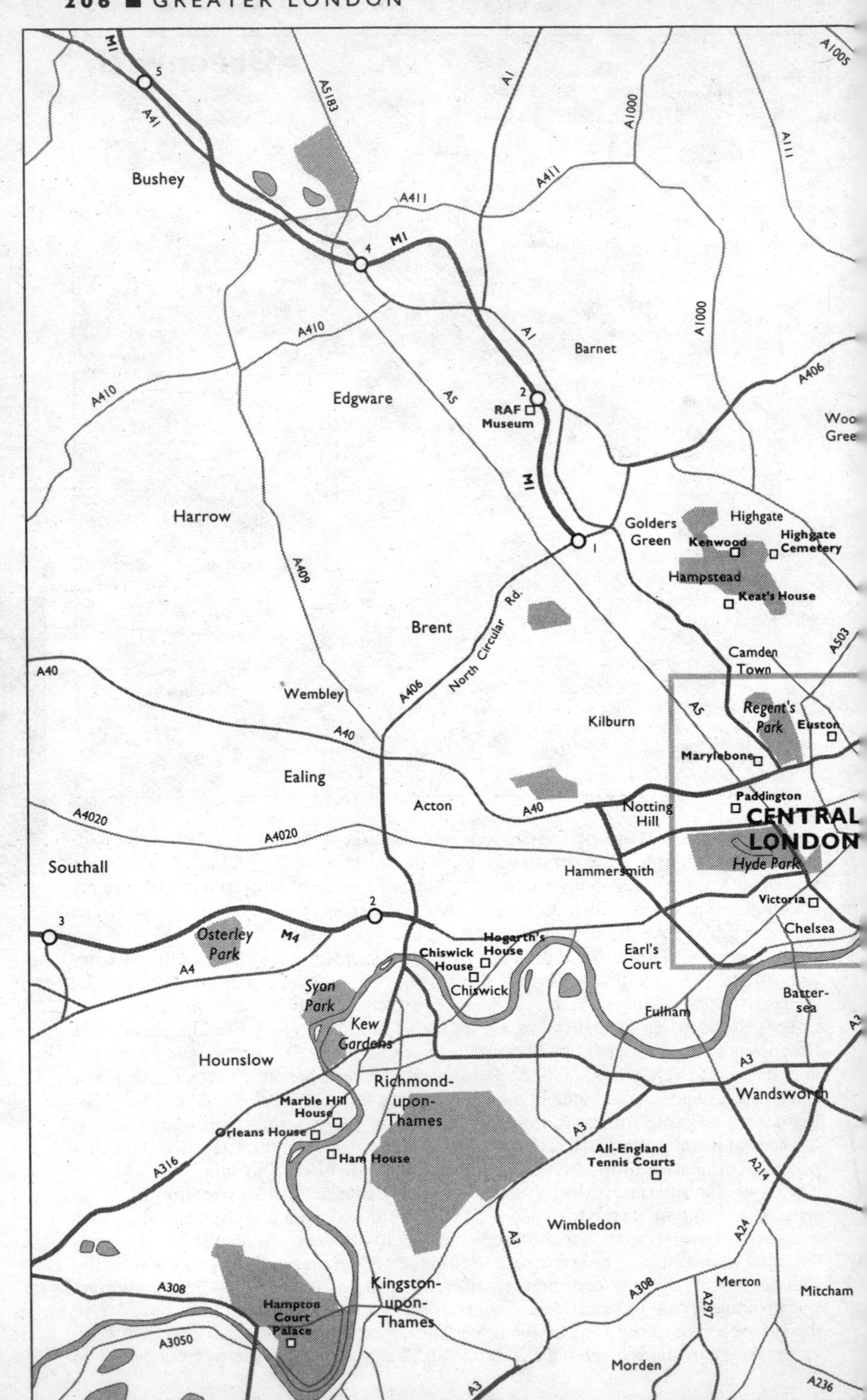
M1
5
A41
A5183
A1
A1000
A1005
A111
Bushey
A411
A411
4
M1
A410
A1
Barnet
A1000
A406
A410
Edgware
A5
2
RAF Museum
Woo
Gree
M1
Harrow
Golders Green
Highgate
Kenwood
Highgate Cemetery
1
Hampstead
A409
Keat's House
North Circular Rd.
Brent
Camden Town
A503
A40
Wembley
A406
A5
Regent's Park
Euston
Kilburn
A40
Marylebone
Ealing
Paddington
Acton
A40
Notting Hill
CENTRAL LONDON
A4020
A4020
Hyde Park
Southall
Hammersmith
Victoria
3
2
Osterley Park
M4
Hogarth's House
Chelsea
Chiswick House
Earl's Court
A4
Syon Park
Chiswick
Fulham
Batter-sea
Kew Gardens
Hounslow
A3
Richmond-upon-Thames
Wandsworth
Marble Hill House
Orleans House
A3
Ham House
All-England Tennis Courts
A316
A214
Wimbledon
A3
A24
A308
Kingston-upon-Thames
A308
Merton
Mitcham
Hampton Court Palace
A297
A3050
Morden
A3
A236

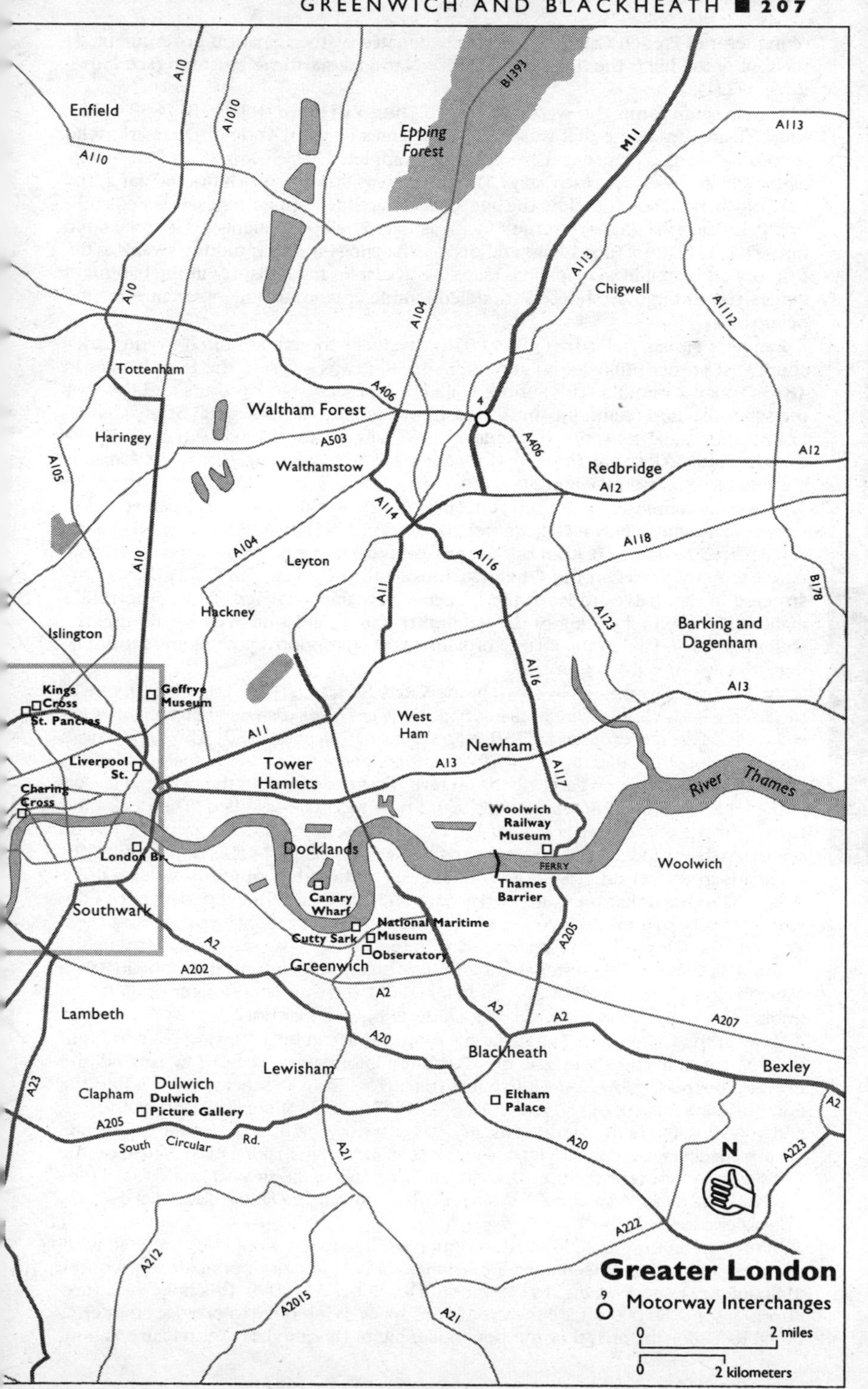
Enfield
Epping Forest
Chigwell
Tottenham
Waltham Forest
Haringey
Walthamstow
Redbridge
Leyton
Hackney
Islington
Barking and Dagenham
Kings Cross
St. Pancras
Geffrye Museum
West Ham
Newham
Liverpool St.
Tower Hamlets
Charing Cross
River Thames
Woolwich Railway Museum
Docklands
London Br.
FERRY
Woolwich
Thames Barrier
Canary Wharf
Southwark
National Maritime Museum
Cutty Sark
Observatory
Greenwich
Lambeth
Blackheath
Lewisham
Bexley
Dulwich
Clapham
Dulwich Picture Gallery
Eltham Palace
South Circular Rd.
N
Greater London
Motorway Interchanges
0 2 miles
0 2 kilometers

(conqueror of French Canada) generously donated by the Canadian government. At the foot of the hill is the highly-informative **National Maritime Museum** (see **Museums,** p. 221).

The museum forms the west addition to **Queen's House** (tel. (0181) 858 4422), the 17th-century home that was started for James I's wife, Anne of Denmark, who unfortunately died before construction was completed. *(Open daily 10am-5pm; no separate entry, see prices for observatory.)* The house was finished for Henrietta Maria, the wife of Charles I. Designed by the age's master architect, Inigo Jones, it is England's first Palladian villa, known to the Queen as her "house of delights." The renovated house's 17th-century furnishings and rich silk hangings are sumptuously swank as the featured art is stolidly stately. Free maps are available, and a display in the basement guides you through the house's muddled jumble of commissioners, architects, and occupants.

Ranger's House (tel. (0181) 853 0035) overlooks the cricket pitch in the park's southwest corner. Built for an admiral in 1688, it was given to the Park Ranger in 1815. Today it contains the Suffolk Collection of Jacobean portraits and the Dolmetsch Collection of antique musical instruments. The **Architectural Study Centre** holds a substantial collection of architectural details from 18th- and 19th-century London dwellings. *(Open Apr.-Oct. daily 10am-6pm; Nov.-Mar. W-Su only, 10am-4pm. Admission and taped tour £2, concessions £1.50, children £1.)*

Charles II commissioned Wren to tear down the Royal Palace of Placentia and to construct the **Royal Naval College** (tel. (0181) 858 2154) in its place. *(Open daily 2:30-4:30pm. Free. Services Su 8:30am holy communion, 11am sung eucharist.)* Because it was situated directly between the Queen's House and the river, the College was constructed in two halves to leave the Queen's view unobstructed. James Thornhill's elaborately frescoed ceiling in the Painted Hall and Benjamin West's painting of a shipwrecked St. Paul in the chapel provide excellent opportunity to view breathtaking art in its original location.

SIGHTS

By the River Thames in Greenwich, the **Cutty Sark** (tel. (0181) 858 2698), one of the last great tea clippers, anchors in dry dock. *(Open M-Sa 10am-6pm, Su noon-6pm; last entry ½hr. before close. Admission £3.50, concessions £2.50, families £8.50.)* The ship (whose name, meaning "short shift," comes from Burns's poem "Tam O'Shanter") carried 1.3 million pounds of tea on each 120-day return trip from China. In the prime of its sea-going days, between 1869 and 1938, it set new records for speed. The decks and crews' quarters have been restored, and exhibits describing the history of the Pacific trade have been added. The vessel is also filled with the largest collection of ships' figureheads in the world. Those who hanker after the whiff of gunpowder will be delighted to learn that the Cutty Sark's cannon is fired at 1pm every day, but as the large, friendly sign informs you, it is very loud indeed. Don't say you haven't been warned. The **Gipsy Moth IV** rests nearby. In this rather cozy 54-ft.-long craft, the 66-year-old Sir Francis Chichester spent 226 days sailing solo around the globe in 1966-67, covering a grand total of 29 630 miles. Sadly, the ship is no longer open to the public, so you'll have to make do by looking at its sleek exterior.

A show at the **Greenwich Theatre,** on Croom's Hill, can be a relaxing conclusion to a day spent traipsing about galleries. For more information, see **Off West End and Fringe Theaters,** p. 232. At 12 Crooms Hill, across from the theater, you'll find the **Fan Museum** (tel. (0181) 305 1441 or 858 7879), which opened in 1991 as the first and only museum in the world dedicated to the history, craft, and coquetry of the fan. Do-it-yourselfers can emulate what they've seen in the fan-making classes held on the first Saturday of every month. *(Open Tu-Sa 11am-5pm in the summer and Tu-Sa. 11am-4.30pm in the winter. Admission £3, children £2; Tu 2-4:30pm free for the disabled and seniors. Wheelchair accessible.)*

In the run up to year 2000, no description of Greenwich would be complete without mentioning **The Millennium Experience,** or as it is more popularly known, the Millennium Dome. Not due to open until December 31, 1999, this huge structure, covering some 80 000 square meters of floor space, is intended to provide an international focus for the arrival of the new millennium. Designed by Tony Blair's Labour administration to reflect the vibrancy of modern Britain, the dome has become something of a running joke in the media, criticized both because of its cost and the organizers' vagueness about the content of the Experience (it's theme is "Time to Make a Difference", whatever that's supposed to mean). The Dome itself has now been erected so you can catch a glimpse of its exterior in the distance (the site of the Experience is pretty inaccessible at the moment, although that will change soon - see transport information below). For further information on the plans for the Experience, you can visit the Millennium Experience Visitor Centre (tel. (0181) 305 3456), which is located just opposite the Cutty Sark. (Open M-F 11am-7pm, Sa-Su 10am-6pm.)

The most picturesque (and appropriate) passage to Greenwich is by boat. Cruises to Greenwich pier depart from the Westminster (tel. 930 4097), Charing Cross, and Tower (tel. 987 1185 for both) piers (see **Boats,** p. 69, for times and prices). Make sure you choose a boat with running commentary on the river's major sights. Trains leave from Charing Cross, Waterloo East, and London Bridge for Greenwich (less than 20min., day return £3). The DLR whizzes from Tower Gateway to Island Gardens (16min.). From there, Greenwich is just a 7-minute walk through a foot tunnel under the Thames. When the DLR is not in service, Bus D9 runs from the Island Gardens station to Bank Station. Bus 188 runs between Euston and Greenwich, stopping at Kingsway and Waterloo. Even more exciting, however, is the news that the extension of the Underground's Jubilee Line should be completed in 1999, which will open a new station right next to the site of the Millennium Experience, allowing visitors to take a look at the notorious dome (see above). The friendly **Greenwich Tourist Information Centre,** 46 Greenwich Church St., SE10 (tel. (0181) 858 6376) will go out of their way to arrange a variety of afternoon tours. *(Open daily 10:15am-5pm; Winter usually 11am-4pm. Tours £4, concessions £3, under 14 free; 1-1½hr.; call (0181) 858 6169 for info.)*

Just south of Greenwich Park, the sloping fields of **Blackheath** offer a checkered history of love, rebellion, and golf. Wat Tyler and his fellow peasants revolting over a poll tax congregated on the heath in 1381. Henry VII fought Cornish rebels here, while Henry VIII had a similarly unfortunate experience—it was here that he meet his betrothed Ann, the "mare of Cleves." Henry chose his bride, sight unseen, based on a flattering portrait by Holbein, but repeatedly commented on her equine features when life failed to imitate art. The **Royal Blackheath Golf Club** was founded on the common—James I was known to take an occasional bash here with his three wood. A traditional site for celebrations, Blackheath still holds fairs on Bank Holidays, and serves as the starting point for the **London Marathon,** the world's largest.

A bit farther down the river, the steel and concrete **Thames Barrier,** 1 Unity Way, Woolwich SE18 (tel. (0181) 305 4188), the world's largest movable flood barrier, is the reason that London no longer enjoys the exciting high tides of yesteryear. *(Open M-F 10am-5pm, Sa-Su 10:30am-5:30pm. Admission £3.40, seniors and children £2, families £7.50.)* Constructed during the 1970s, the barrier spans 520m and consists of 10 separate movable steel gates; when raised, the main gates stand as high as a five-story building. A visitors centre has a working model of the barrier, in addition to exhibits explaining its history. From Charing Cross take BR to Charlton Station; from there it's a 15-minute walk. Alternatively take the boat from Greenwich pier (25min.; 75min. from Westminster pier). Call 930 3373 for details of Westminster service; (0181) 305 0300 for Greenwich.

Kew Gardens

***Tel.** (0181) 940 1171. **Tube:** Kew Gardens (zone 3). **BR North London line:** Kew Gardens. **Boats** travel daily between Kew and Westminster pier. From Westminster 10:15, 10:30, 11:15am, noon, 2pm; from Kew 3:30, 4:30, and 5:30pm; call 930 2062 beforehand, as trip times may vary according to fluctuations in the Thames. £6, return £10, discounts for seniors and children. **Parking** available outside of the gardens. **Open** M-F 9:30am-6:30pm, last admission 6pm, Sa-Su and bank holidays 9:30am-7:30pm, last admission 7pm. Conservato-*

SIGHTS

ries close at 5:30pm. Call to confirm closing times, as they may vary by season. ***Admission*** *£5, students and seniors £3.50, ages 5-16 £2.50, under 5 free, late admission from 4:45pm £3.50.* ***Tours*** *leave Victoria Gate daily at 11am and 2pm, £1; sign up early as tours fill quickly. Kew also hosts* ***summer jazz concerts****—tickets run £18-25. Call Ticketmaster at 344 4444 for details.*

The perfect complement or antidote to days of sightseeing in central London, the **Royal Botanic Gardens** at Kew provide a restorative breath of fresh air. Yet another example of the Empire's collecting frenzy, the Gardens were originally intended to recreate Eden by bringing together plants from all over the world. Today the park displays thousands of flowers, plants, bushes, fruits, trees, and vegetables from throughout the globe, spread over 300 perfectly maintained acres. Founded in 1759 by Princess Augusta, Kew gradually grew in size until it became a royal park in 1841.

The wonders of the gardens comprise several buildings and sections, and demand several hours to be viewed properly. The steamy, tropical **Palm House,** a unique masterpiece of Victorian engineering built in 1848, will stun you with the revelation that bananas are in fact giant herbs. Still reeling from this blow, one may then visit *Encephalartos Altensteinii,* "The Oldest Pot Plant In The World," which is not at all what it sounds like, but interesting nonetheless. Downstairs, the beautifully lit aquariums of the **Marine Display** let you watch batfish and porcupine puffer fish interact with colorful sea kelp.

Although replete with voluptuous fronds, the Palm House is dwarfed by its younger Victorian sibling, the **Temperate House.** The cooler climate here nurtures 3000 species, arranged over 50,000 square feet according to geographical origins. Across from the Temperate House, the **Evolution House** leads you through 3.5 billion years of floracentric history, from the primordial ooze (recreated with relish) to the exciting moment when flowering plants appeared. Its misty waterfalls and dinosaur footprints play like a cross between "Land of the Lost" and Biosphere II.

On the opposite side of the park from William Chambers's 1762 **pagoda,** the **Princess of Wales Conservatory** allows a browse through 10 different tropical climates; it's just a few steps from a rainforest to an arid desert. Its award-winning pyramidal design allows it to both remain innocuous among the foliage and conserve energy. While the pineapple family displayed within is quite amiable, the gargantuan lilypads inspire a holy terror of the absent frogs that must roost here.

In the northeastern section of the gardens stands **Kew Palace.** Built in 1631 but leased as a royal residence since 1730, this inconspicuous summer home of King George III and Queen Charlotte is closed until further notice. Instead, visitors may wish to visit **Queen Charlotte's Cottage,** a small, picturesque structure given by George to Charlotte as a picnic site. *(Open Sa-Su and holidays 10:30am-4pm.)* The cottage's distinctly Bavarian feel may speak to the King's Teutonic roots.

Other points of interest at the gardens include the **Marianne North Gallery,** a small but interesting collection of 19th-century paintings, the **Rhododendron Dell** (built by Capability Brown), and the **Waterlily House.**

Syon Park

Syon Park, just across the Thames from Kew in Brentford, was originally founded as part of a religious order—hence the phonetic reference to Zion in the Holy Land. *(BR: Syon Lane or tube: Gunnersbury (zone 3), then bus #237 or 267 to Brentlea Gate. Cross Kew Bridge and walk left along London Rd.)* Stately **Syon House** (tel. (0181) 560 0881), in the Park, was built on the site of a medieval abbey dissolved by Henry VIII. *(Open Apr.-Oct. W-Su 11am-5pm; Nov.-Mar. Su 11am-dusk; last admission 4:15pm. Gardens open daily 10am-6pm or dusk. Admission for both £5.50, concessions £4; garden only £2.50, concessions £2.)* The exterior of the house is Tudor, built to incorporate the buildings of a monastery where Queen Catherine Howard was imprisoned before her execution in 1542. In 1553 ownership of the house passed to the Duke of Northumberland, who offered the crown to his daughter-in-law Lady Jane Grey here. Not a week later, Mary Tudor took back the house, and the Duke's head. The house reverted to the Northumberlands in 1594, and they still own it today, making this the last mansion left in London still under its original hereditary ownership. The 11th Duke of Northumberland calls this 200-acre parkland home, and many of the rooms open for viewing serve as private entertaining areas at night.

The mansion's exquisite interior was created by Robert Adam in 1766. The Anteroom, a green marble and gilt extravaganza, is dazzling; the Long Gallery is imbued with a simpler elegance. The highlight of the stately gardens around Syon House is the six-acre rose garden, landscaped by Capability Brown.

Though the rarefied delights of Syon House appeal to almost every eye, most other aspects of the Syon Park complex cater to the younger set. This is where Londoners take their little 'uns on the weekends. At **London Butterfly House** (tel. (0181) 560 7272), over 1000 butterflies fly "free," and the tykes can pet "giant spiders and other creepy crawlies." *(Open Apr.-Oct. 10am-5:30pm; Nov.-Mar. 10am-3:30pm. Admission £2.90, children £1.85.)* The **London Aquatic Experience** (tel. (0181) 847 4730) next door purveys critters of a more amphibious sort, which the children won't be permitted to touch—piranhas, snakes, frogs, and the like. *(Open daily Apr.-Sept. 10am-6pm; Oct.-Mar. 10am-5pm. Admission £3.50, concessions £2.50.)* Outside the main gate and to the left, toddlers will squeal at **Snakes and Ladders** (tel. (0181) 847 0946), a warehouse full of kids' toys, battery-operated kiddy cars, and a three-tiered adventure playground with a special area for toddlers. *(Open daily 10am-6pm; last entry 5:15pm. Admission £3.65, under 5 £2.65; weekends £4.25, £3.25; after 4:30pm £3, £2. Note that some activities have a height requirement of 4 ft. 8 in.)*

Richmond

Getting to Richmond

Tube or BR: Richmond. Richmond can also be reached by a boat from Westminster (see Boats, p. 69) which stops at Richmond on its way to Hampton Court. Boats leave Westminster Pier (tel. 930 4721) at 10:15, 10:30, 11, 11:15am, noon, 2 and 2:30pm but depend largely on the water level of the Thames; last boat returns at 5pm (2-3hr.; adult £7, return £11).

Ever since Henry I came up the Thames in the 12th century, **Richmond** has preened its royal pedigree. Although Henry VII's Richmond Palace, built in 1500, was demolished during Cromwell's Commonwealth, the town has not lost its dignified sheen—the sprawling grounds of the 18th-century riverside houses and pathways beneath Richmond Hill make this area possibly the most serene in or around London. Richmond is where the banks along the Thames become rural, with trendy shops giving way to luscious fields and forests along the river.

The **Richmond Tourist Information Centre** (tel. (0181) 940 9125), in the old Town Hall on Whittaker Ave., has complete information on Richmond and surrounding areas. *(Open June-Sept. M-F 10am-6pm, Sa 10am-5pm, Su 10:15am-4:15pm; Oct.-May same hours, but closed Sundays.)* The **Museum of Richmond** (tel. (0181) 332 1141), located in the same building, is an excellent local museum with exhibits on famous inhabitants, from actor Edmund Kean to writers George Eliot and Virginia Woolf. *(Open daily Sept.-Apr. Tu-Sa 11am-5pm; May-Oct. 1-4pm. Admission £2, children £1.)* Mondays are Kids Club days, with cartooning workshops and t-shirt making geared towards kids from 5-14yrs; call for details. The **Richmond Festival** (tel. (0181) 831 6138), in the first two weeks of July, explodes with music, dance, and children's activities, much of it free.

Most of Richmond's sights are scattered around the actual village. The town itself is perched above the river valley. **Richmond Hill** provides an extraordinary view of the snake-like Thames and its bankside 18th-century Georgian mansions. So many English paintings have copied this view that Parliament declared it a protected site. The road leads up to more beautiful parkland before descending Thamesward. **Richmond**

Park, atop Richmond Hill, is Europe's largest city park. A former royal hunting ground, its 2500 acres are still home to several hundred nervous deer who share the grounds with tourists and the **Royal Ballet School,** housed in the **Palladian White Lodge.** The **Isabella Plantation** woodland garden, deep inside the park, bursts with color in the spring, when its azaleas and rhododendrons bloom.

Descend Richmond Hill and follow Bridge St. across the Thames. The **Marble Hill House** (tel. (0181) 892 5115; bus #33, 90B, 290, H22, R68, or R70 from the station) is a 10-minute walk left along the river (follow the signs and the tourists) from here. *(Open daily Apr.-Oct. 10am-6pm; Nov.-Mar. W-Su 10am-4pm. Admission £3, concessions £2.30.)* Perched on the Thames amid vast trimmed lawns, this Palladian house was built in 1729 for Henrietta Howard, George II's mistress. The Great Room, on the first floor, is lavishly decorated with gilt and carvings by James Richards and original Panini paintings of ancient Rome. Alexander Pope, the famed satirist and Howard's close friend, designed some of the gardens. During the summer, a series of outdoor concerts are held on the grounds (see **Entertainment,** p. 235).

Exit left from Marble Hill House along the path until a brick wall across the road. Turn left, then find the remains of the 18th-century **Orleans House** (tel. (0181) 892 0221) through a gated entrance concealed in the wall. *(Open Apr.-Sept. Tu-Sa 1-5:30pm, Su 2-5:30pm; Oct.-Mar. Tu-Sa 1-4:30pm, Su 2-4:30pm. Grounds open daily 9am-dusk. Admission £1.)* This Georgian, geometrically intriguing house holds a gallery of art and artifacts of local history. Only the Octagon Room survives from the original building, which put up with the Duc D'Orleans (the future King Louis Philippe) for three years in the 19th century. The grounds surrounding the house remain untrimmed wildland.

A small passenger ferry (tel. (0181) 892 9620) runs between **Marble Hill Park** (next to Orleans House) and **Ham House** (tel. (0181) 940 1950; Bus #65 or 371 from Richmond station), on Ham Street. *(Open Apr.-Oct. M-W 1-5pm, Sa-Su noon-5:30pm; Nov. to mid-Dec. Sa-Su 1-4pm. Admission £5, children £3. Ferry runs Feb.-Oct. Sa-Su 10am-6:30pm, M-F 10am-6pm; 40p, kids 20p)* Built in 1610, this house boasts artwork and room designs that are almost as beautiful as the grounds outside. The Duke of Lauderdale inherited the house from his wife's father, Charles I's "whipping boy." (As part of his "reward" for taking all the future king's punishments whenever he misbehaved, he received the lease to the Ham estate when he became an adult.) Rooms filled with family portraits of royalty, including Charles II and his loyal servants, overlook Ham House's recently restored gardens and sprawling riverfront fields. *(Gardens open M-W and Sa-Su 10:30am-dusk. Admission free.)* Don't be too surprised to see some recent touch-ups, however; the house was lavishly "modernized" during the 1960s. Have tea (95p) and scones (70p) in the Orangery and enjoy the surrounding meadows. On Sundays from May through September, visitors can catch a match at the Ham Polo Club west of the house (beginning around 3-3:30pm).

Hampton Court Palace

Getting to Hampton Court

By tube, take the district line to Richmond (zone 3); Bus #R68 runs from the station to Hampton court (80p). BR runs trains from Waterloo to Hampton Court every 30min. (day return £4). From the first Monday before Easter until the end of September, a boat runs from Westminster Pier (See **Boats,** p. 71) to Hampton Court, leaving in the morning at 10:30, 11:15am, and noon, and returning from Hampton Court at 3, 4, and 5pm (adult one-way £8, return £12; duration 3-4hrs.). Times sometimes vary—call in advance.

Open *Mar. to late Oct. M 10:15am-6pm, Tu-Su 9:30am-6pm; late Oct. to Mar. M 10:15am-4:30pm, Tu-Su 9:30am-4:30pm; last admission 45min. before closing. Privy gardens and maze open and close with palace. Gardens open at the same time as the palace, but close at 9pm or dusk, whichever comes first (admission free). All-encompassing* ***admission*** *£9.25, concessions £7, under 15 £6.10, under 5 free, families £27.65; only to maze or Privy Garden £2.10, under 16 £1.30; only to tennis court 50p, children 20p. Wheelchair accessible.*

SIGHTS

Although a monarch hasn't lived here since George II packed it in over 200 years ago, **Hampton Court Palace** (tel. (0181) 781 9500) continues to exude regal charm. Located 6 mi. down the Thames from Richmond, the brown-bricked palace housed over 1500 court members at its height. Cardinal Wolsey built it in 1514, showing Henry VIII by his example how to act the part of a splendid and all-powerful ruler. Henry learned the lesson well—he confiscated the Court in 1525 when Wolsey fell out of favor. Today, the palace stands in three distinct parts, each bearing the mark of one of its strong-willed inhabitants.

To help tourists make sense of the chaos of the chaotic and schizophrenic arrangement of the palace, it is divided into six "routes" through which tourists may meander. Fans of Henry VIII have a myriad options for discovering how the king lived, reigned, and ate his way to a size 54 waist. **Henry VIII's State Apartments,** the first of the palace routes, allows would-be sycophants a chance to reenact some Tudor brown-nosing. Every morning, courtiers would gather in the **Great Watching Chamber,** clamoring for a chance to kiss some royal tuckus as Henry proceeded to morning services in the Chapel Royal (currently held at 8:30am). A nine-minute video starring Sir Ian McKellen describes the origin and function of each room of the apartments, down to the Chapel's remarkably preserved Tudor ceiling.

For those curious as to how Henry acquired his massive girth in the days before the deep-fat fryer, the **Tudor Kitchens,** another palace route, provide the answer. The numerous vast rooms demonstrate, with the aid of fake animal carcasses, pies, and a bubbling cauldron, how one of England's most colorful kings got his grub.

If the style of Henry's rooms strikes you as a bit vulgar, you're not alone. When William III (of William and Mary fame) sailed up from the Netherlands to ascend to the throne with his wife, he declared the palace a "gothic monstrosity," and commissioned Wren to demolish the entire structure and build a palace to rival Louis XIV's Versailles. Though lack of funds and the death of his queen sapped William's energy and the project was never completed, Wren's work can be seen in the opulent **King's and Queen's Apartments,** two complementary palace routes. Newly restored after a 1986 fire, the King's Apartments held courtiers who watched in rapture as William III publicly dressed, dined, and took the occasional powder. Along the ceiling of the **King's Guard Chamber,** almost 3000 guns and weapons arranged in six repeating patterns along the upper wall reminded visitors that the man they were about to see, no matter which throne they found him on, was not to be trifled with. As you pass through the public and private bedchambers and down the stairs, don't miss the plush **velvet-covered toilet** in a small enclave on your left. This petite chamber served as the "office" for the **Groom of the Stool,** William's most trusted servant, who received a royal sum for attending the king's toilet.

George II was the last monarch to rule from Hampton Court. **The Georgian Rooms** are made significantly more exciting with the audio guide which aids in recreating a tumultuous day in his scandal-ridden court.

The legacies of all the palace's past residents can be felt in the **Wolsey Rooms.** Chambers that housed Cardinal Wolsey before he fell from favor now house some of the finest treasures of the Royal Collection, including **tapestries** woven from the Raphael cartoons in the Victoria and Albert Museum (p. 224), and a roomful of grisaille work originally by Mantegna but poorly repainted in the 18th century.

The walls of the palace are steeped in more royal lore and anecdotes than can possibly be discovered during a quick stroll through. If you do pay the hefty admission fee, allow yourself plenty of time. Stop by the information center to pick up **free audio guides** for the Georgian Rooms, Kitchens, and King's apartments. The free **costumed guided tours** of Henry's Apartments and the King's Apartments, given by guards and courtiers in period costumes, teach you Stuart drinking toasts and explain how the English attained world renown for **poor dental hygiene.**

The exterior of the palace holds nearly as many delights, mostly free. Note the black, spiked steel railings along the Clock Court; these were installed in 1850 to keep **public urinators** from defacing palace walls. Sixty marvelous acres of Palace gardens are open and free, and contain some highly celebrated amusements, including the **maze** (open Mar.-Oct.), a hedgerow labyrinth first planted in 1714 that inspired the hedges a crazed Jack Nicholson dashed through at Stanley Kubrick's Overlook Hotel. "Solve" the maze by getting to the benches in the middle, and back.

By following the signs on the grounds to the Tudor Tennis Court, you may be lucky enough to catch a match of **"Real Tennis"** in progress on the indoor tennis court (1529). The rules, including playing off the terraces and the baffling "chases" are posted for all to see, but make cricket seem downright comprehensible. According to legend, Henry VIII was chasing lobs on this court whilst the executioner lopped off the head of Anne Boleyn. Henry's is one of only four courts of its kind left in England (open Mar.-Oct.). Also note the exhibit of Tijou's ironwork gates, left freestanding for the most part, and admirable from all sides.

Chiswick

Six miles west of central London, the riverside village of Chiswick was long ago engulfed by London's suburban sprawl. Today, two houses of great historical and artistic interest stand off from the undistinguished dwellings of this busy village.

Chiswick House (tel. (0181) 995 0508; BR: Chiswick, or tube: Turnham Green, Gunnersbury, or Chiswick Park; from Turnham Green take bus #E3), built by Lord Burlington in 1729, studs the heart of Chiswick with 68 acres of luscious gardens, ponds, and wild forests. *(Call (0181) 577 6969 for information. House open daily 10am-6pm; Oct.-Apr. W-Su 10am-4pm. Grounds open daily 8am-dusk. Admission £3, concessions £2.30, children £1.50.)* Heavily influenced by Andrea Palladio's ancient Italian forms, architect William Kent took English society by storm with his creation. Lord Harvey, a contemporary free-lance critic, sneered, "You call it a house? Why? It is too small to live in, and too large to hang from one's watch." But the day's notables were more than happy to see and be seen when Burlington entertained at Chiswick.

As exquisite as Chiswick's architecture are the 67 acres of gardens and manicured fields surrounding the house itself. The sixth Duke of Devonshire—an eccentric fond of horticulture and exotic animals—built up the mansion's grounds in order to house his pet elephant, giraffe, and kangaroo. Next to the house are an Italian garden as well as a conservatory. The house has played host to two tsars, Queen Victoria, Alexander Pope, and the King of Prussia. The beautiful fields provide perfect staging grounds for annual summer Shakespeare plays hosted by the National Heritage.

Just northeast of the Chiswick House grounds, on Hogarth Ln., the modest abode of artist and social critic William Hogarth stands as a subtle jab to Lord Burlington's extravagance. Rumor has it that the two hated each other. Hogarth, the great moralist, saw Lord Burlington as a sycophant who imported "foreign" trends to England. **Hogarth's House** (tel. (0181) 994 6757; follow Burlington Ln. north to Chiswick Sq. and go left at the Hogarth Roundabout; the house is about 200 yards down Hogarth Ln., next to a very busy road), which Hogarth called his "country box by the Thames," has recently been renovated and focuses on the historical and biographical detail of Hogarth's prints. Perhaps most famous for his six part, pictorial satire, "Marriage a la Mode," Hogarth spent his time in this country house with Henry Fielding, author of *Tom Jones* and other fellow Freemasons. His work and life lives on in this small but impressive museum. Die-hard fans can avenge Hogarth by skipping the fabulously ornate Chiswick House and enjoying this house's simple subtlety. Either way, these two contemporary abodes are a fascinating study in contrasts. *(Open Tu-F 1-5pm, Sa-Su 1-6pm, closes 1hr. earlier Nov.-Mar.; admission free.)*

Nearby, the remains of Alexander Pope's summer house reside on the site of London's oldest brewery. Quench your thirst at **Fuller, Smith & Turner's Brewery** (tel. (0181) 996 2000; fax (0181) 995 0230; tube: Turnham Green; take a left onto Chiswick High Rd. and a right onto Chiswick Ln.; gain access via the pedestrian tunnel under the A4). Beer connoisseurs will recognize Fuller's London Ale, Chiswick Bitter, London Pride, and ESB, all four of which are popular in the city's pubs. Tours (1½hr.) are offered of the facilities and end with a tasting. *(Tours M and W-F at 10,*

11am, 1, and 2pm. Adults £5, children £2.50.) Learn about such appetizing products as "wort," and sneak a peek at the bins of yeast to be made into that unual British delicacy, Marmite. But be warned—you may hear the ghostly meowing of the Brewery cat who, in the 19 century, fell into the boiling sugar dissolving vessel. Unfortunately, **Cat Ale** was not as successful as their beer consultants had predicted.

Windsor and Eton

Getting to Windsor and Eton

British Rail (tel. 262 6767) serves Windsor and Eton Central station and Windsor and Eton Riverside station, both of which are near Windsor Castle (follow the signs). Trains leaving Victoria or Paddington go via a change in Slough to Windsor and Eton Central Station. Trains for Waterloo go directly to Windsor and Eton Riverside station (every 30min., 50min., day return £5.70). Green Line **coaches** (tel. (0181) 668 7261) #700 and 702 also make the trip from their station on Eccleston Bridge, behind Victoria Station (50min.-1½hr., day return £4.35-5.50).

Windsor Castle

***Tel.** (01753) 868 286 or (01753) 831 118 for 24hr. information. **Open** daily Apr.-Oct. 10am-5:30pm, last entry 4pm; Nov.-Mar. 10am-4pm; last entry 3pm. **Admission** £8.80, over 60 £6.20, under 17 £4.60, families £20.50. Most of the castle is wheelchair accessible—call (01753) 868 286, ext. 2235 for details.*

Windsor Castle proves beyond a doubt that, to borrow from Mel Brooks, it's good to be the Queen. Within these ancient stone walls lie some of the most sumptuous rooms in Europe and some of the rarest artworks in the Western world. But beyond the velvet and fine art, this castle's essence is its strategic location high in the hills above the Thames and the thousands of hauberks, swords, pistols, rifles, and suits of armor that bedeck its walls. The castle now dominates this cutesy river town of cobbled lanes and tea shops surrounded by the 4800-acre Great Park, far away from London in the farming country of Surrey. Built by William the Conqueror as a fortress rather than as a residence, it has grown over nine centuries into the world's largest inhabited castle. Saunter blithely in and out of its labyrinthine terraces and enjoy dreamlike views of the Thames Valley.

Be aware that Windsor is a working castle, which may sound a little strange in this day and age, but only means that various members of the Royal Family reside here on weekends and for various special ceremonies. The practical consequence of the Royals' residence is that, often without warning, large areas of the castle will be unavailable to visitors. The steep admission prices will be lowered, but it is wise to call before visiting to check that the areas you want to see are open.

The 13 acres covered by the castle are organized into the lower, middle, and upper wards. The **Round Tower** dominates the middle ward. The **Moat Garden,** filled not with water but with roses and well-attended grass, surrounds the tower.

On passing through Norman Tower and Gate (built by Edward III from 1359-1360) you enter the upper ward, where many of the rooms are open to the public. You can visit the elegantly furnished **state apartments,** which are mostly used for ceremonial occasions and official entertainment. The rooms are richly decorated with artwork from the massive Royal Collection, including works by Holbein, Rubens, Rembrandt, and an entire room of Van Dycks. Instruments of war cover the walls, bearing witness to the more savage side of the Royal history. In the same wing is **Queen Mary's Doll House,** an exact replica of a palace on a tiny scale. Sadly, the room displaying the house is kept very dark, which makes viewing difficult. The Queen's collection of 20,000 drawings and 10,000 watercolors includes works by da Vinci, Michelangelo, and more recent artists.

A stroll down to the lower ward will bring you to **St. George's Chapel,** a sumptuous 15th-century building with delicate fan vaulting and an amazing wall of stained glass dedicated to the Order of the Garter. Here, Henry VIII rests in a surprisingly modest tomb near George V, Edward IV, Charles I, and Henry VI. A ceremonial procession of the Knights of the Garter, led by the Queen, takes place here in June. Windsor's **Changing of the Guard** takes place in front of the Guard Room at 11am (summer M-Sa, winter alternate days M-Sa).

Windsor is notorious to contemporary visitors as the site of a fire that helped make 1992 an *annus horribilis* for the royal family. The fierce conflagration blazed for nine hours on November 20, 1992, and was only extinguished through the efforts of 225 firefighters and 39 fire engines. Six rooms and three towers were destroyed or badly damaged by smoke and flames, although 80% of the state rooms escaped harm. Refurbishments following the fire are now completed, and the redesigned St. Gearge's Hall, Lantern Lobby, and Grand Reception Room are all now available for viewing. To see Queen Mary's doll house, pay an extra pound, which, according to Queen Mary's original 1924 request, is still donated to charity.

Follow the road that bears left around royal grounds to reach the entrance to **Windsor Great Park,** a huge expanse of parkland where deer graze and royals ride. The park follows the three-mile **Long Walk,** which passes by a couple of former hunting lodges, one of which houses the Queen Mum (on weekends). The town of Royal Windsor is directly across the road from the castle gate. Built up around the castle during the Middle Ages, it is filled with specialty shops, tea houses, and pubs.

Eton College

***Tel.** (01753) 671 177. **Located** 10min. down Thames St., across the river. **Open** daily July-Aug. and late-Mar. to mid-Apr. 10:30am-4:30pm; other times 2-4:30pm. **Admission** £2.50, under 16 £2; tours £3.50, under 16 £3. **Tours** depart daily 2:15pm and 3:30pm.*

Eton College is still England's preeminent public (which is to say, private) school, founded by Henry VI in 1440. Eton boys still wear tailcoats to every class and solemnly raise one finger in greeting to any teacher on the street. Wellington claimed that the Battle of Waterloo was "won on the playing fields of Eton"—catch a glimpse of the uniquely brutal "Wall Game" and see why. Despite its position at the apex of the British class system, Eton has molded some notable dissidents and revolutionaries—Percy Bysshe Shelley, Aldous Huxley, George Orwell, and even former Liberal Party leader Jeremy Thorpe. The Queen is the sole (honorary) female Old Etonian.

Wander around the schoolyard, a central quad where Eton boys have frolicked for centuries. A statue of Henry VI and the school's chapel, an unfinished cathedral, occupy this space. The central area is surrounded by the 25 houses that shelter approximately 1250 students. Under the school's harsh but admirably meritocratic code, King's Scholars, students selected for full scholarship based on their exam scores, live in the house known as "College," in the courtyard of College Chapel.

Legoland Windsor

***Tel.** (0990) 040 404. **Open** daily Mar. 14-Nov. 1 and Oct. weekends 10am-6pm; July 18-Aug. 31 10am-8pm. **Admission** £16, children £13, seniors £10; additional £1 for the shuttle from the BR: Windsor and Eton Riverside stations.*

The **Legoland Windsor** is a recent (1996), whimsical, and expensive addition to the area. This high class amusement park is directed mainly at the 13-and-under set, but adults will be amazed by **Miniland,** which 100 workers spent 3 years and 25 million blocks to build. The replica of the City of London includes a six-foot high St. Paul's, as well as every other major building or landmark in the city. The Lego buses that motor along the city's streets without hitting a car or building are a marvel. The rest of Miniland offers superbly detailed buildings and sights from other European cities.

VIEWS, PARKS, AND GARDENS

Great Views

"Your architects were madmen, your builders sane but drunk," Shane MacGowan sang of London's "planners." The best way to experience the strange appeal of this aged city's disheveled *mien* and endless sprawl is from above. The following are roosts which permit a comprehensive view of this oddly beautiful muddle.

Monument, King William St. Tube: Monument. A fantastic 332-step view of the Thames, Tower of London, and St. Paul's from one of Wren's most famously ramrod buildings. Right in the middle of the Bank District. £1 (see **City (Western Section): Bank to St.Paul's,** p. 161).

St. Paul's. Tube: St. Paul's. Set in the heart of the City of London, this cathedral's inner elegance can only be matched by the view from its 271-step dome. Unrivalled views of ye olde City, the modern financial district, the distant weirdness of the Docklands, and the chic West End (p. 159).

Primrose Hill, Regent's Park. Tube: Camden Town, Great Portland Baker Street and Baker Street. You're up to your head in urban slime, and suddenly, by the grace of Primrose Hill's grassy surroundings, you rise above the city to a wonderful view of London. On a good day you can see past the Surrey Downs (p. 180).

Anywhere along the South bank of the Thames at night. Tube: Tower Hill or Tower Gateway. Cross Tower Bridge and look upon the city's skyscrapers floodlit in evening colors. A wonderful place for dinner or an evening walk.

Parks

> *The tulip-beds across the road flamed like throbbing rings of fire. A white dust, tremulous cloud of orris-root it seemed, hung in the panting air. The brightly-coloured parasols danced and dipped like monstrous butterflies.*
>
> —Oscar Wilde on Hyde Park

London's parks have always been the refuge of the happy and sad. There is no better place to luxuriate in the sun or stroll away a languid evening. And the splendor of flaming gardens and unmovable trunks cannot fail to comfort the weary and heavy-hearted.

During the mid-morning the unoccupied—chiefly the very young, the very old, and, of course, travelers—enjoy the park's early glory. By lunchtime the green fields are dotted with office workers enjoying a take-away lunch. In the summer evenings Londoners flock to the curving walks to stroll, blade, and revel in the open-air performances put on in these graceful collections of lawns and gardens. With the exception of Hyde Park's midnight closing, London's parks are generally open from 7am-dusk, which comes to London extraordinarily late in the summer.

Battersea Park. Tube: Sloane Sq., then a walk to the Thames and over the Chelsea or Albert Bridge. On the south bank of the Thames, across from Chelsea, this lovely park is one of the city's best kept secrets. Don't miss the small walled garden in the center of the park.

Green Park. Tube: Green Park. Green Park is an expanse of grounds which would suit a palace—which is fitting because it forms Buckingham Palace's back yard. This set of well-kept lawns and open walks is located between the southeast corner of Hyde Park and the northwest corner of St. James.

Hampstead Heath. Tube: Hampstead, Belsize Park. BR: Hampstead Heath. A delightfully vast sprawl of wilderness sandwiched between two tony neighborhoods. Hampstead Heath boasts over 6 ponds (you can swim in 3 of them), the Iveagh Bequest (see p. 191), summer concerts (see **Music: Kenwood,** p. 242), and acres of lush hiking ground. This gorgeous area is more rustic than other city parks; the term city sanctuary is perhaps more *a propos.*

Hyde Park and Kensington Gardens. Tube: South Kensington, Hyde Park Corner, Lancaster Gate, Queensway. This park's luscious 600 acres make up the "lungs of London." Skaters streak past the park's art gallery, huge man-made pond, and Princess Di's Kensington Palace. **Speaker's Corner** invites the lunatic and loquacious to practice their art in the northeast corner of Hyde Park (tube: Marble Arch). More citified than other parks but still exquisite (see p. 174).

Mudchute. DLR: Mudchute. Escape the Docklands' futuristic weirdness in this classic London park. Contains a "city farm" (p. 248) and locals' veggie gardens.

Postman's Park. Tube: St. Paul's. Peaceful old men's hangout and sanctuary for local businessmen. This petite park dwells across the street from the Central Post Office, surrounded by church walls on one side and a graveyard on the other.

St. James's Park. Tube: St. James's Park. Many think that this is London's most beautiful park. Weeping willows bend over mirror-surfaced ponds; lush greenery and immaculate lawns makes this a welcome respite from the nearby offices. During lunch hour London's workers lose their office pallor here (see p. 148).

Regent's Park. Tube: Camden Town, Great Portland St., Regent's Park, Baker St. The largest of London's parks (though the contiguous Ken. Gardens/Hyde Park space is larger), Regent's Park boasts vast football and cricket fields for its adoring Sunday visitors. It is also the home of the London Zoo and beautiful Primrose Hill, and it shelters the gorgeous Queen Mary's gardens (p. 180).

Richmond Park. Tube: Richmond. Standing on this vast, hilly garden spot overlooking a splendid view of the Thames below, one feels like the king of England. Particularly if you're Henry VIII, who used to hunt deer in this vast park (see p. 211).

Waterlow Park. Tube: Archway. Sweetly donated by Sidney Waterlow to the people of London to provide "a garden for the gardenless." This park's sloping hills provide a splendid vista of the city below. Towering trees and duck-dotted ponds line the path. Highgate Cemetery, Marx's resting place, lies nearby (see p. 192)

Notable Gardens

Gardening is the English national obsession in the hinterlands and the capital alike. It is no surprise then that London has some of the world's most lovingly manicured lawn and best trimmed topiary. Here are short descriptions of the best. Refer to the longer write-ups in previous sections for more information.

Chelsea Physic Garden. Tube: Sloane Sq. A beautiful patch of green near the Chelsea bank of the Thames. The smallish garden is filled with glorious wispy fauna, making it a perfect place for a Wednesday or Sunday afternoon stroll. Open Apr.-Oct. W 2-5pm, Su 2-6pm. Admission £3.50, concessions £1.80 (see p. 177).

Hampton Court Palace. A palace this impressive needs a helluva backyard to match, and King William's gorgeous Privy Gardens turn the trick. Also the site of a well-known and well-loved hedge maze and the world's oldest vine (p. 213).

Kew Gardens. A 300-acre wonderland that takes us to a place beyond lush. Field after greenhouse after pond of botanical treasures from around the world. London's most famous garden (p. 209).

The Orangery Gardens in Kensington Gardens. Tube: Bayswater or Queensway. The gorgeous gardens outside Lady Di's window are open for commoners to stroll about, though the prettiest part is walled off and may be seen only by peeking through the hedge in a few niches designed for such a purpose. Next door is a field covered with what appear to be scampering squirrels—on closer examination they reveal themselves to be a fleet of pet rabbits. Free (p. 174).

Queen Mary's Gardens at Regent's Park. Tube: Baker St. The area of Regent's Park within the Inner Circle is a symphony in color. The roses are famous. Nearby one may rent a rowboat or lawn chair. Free (see p. 180).

Ranleagh Gardens at the Royal Hospital. Tube: Sloane Sq. Here 18th-century pleasure seekers spent their evenings watching pageants and fireworks and imbibing to excess. Today aging army veterans from the nearby hospital seek peace of mind here, and no wonder. The site of the Chelsea Flower Show during the third week of May. Free (p. 177).

Syon Park. The name is a phonetic reference to Zion, and the foliage, including a rose garden designed by Capability Brown, is appropriately divine (p. 210).

Museums

A couple of centuries as capital of one of the world's richest and most powerful countries, focus of an empire upon which the sun never set, advanced navigation combined with something of a wanderlust and a decidedly English penchant for collecting have given London a spectacular set of museums. Art lovers, history buffs, and amateur ethnologists will not know which way to turn when they land. London will inevitably frustrate those who vow to see all that is displayed—the city suffers from an embarrassment of riches. It would be impossible, in less than a year, to see everything in the British Museum, let alone view the whole of this city's varied and excellent collections.

Museums tend to be the most peaceful on weekday mornings. Admission to major collections is usually free, but many museums, no longer heavily subsidized by the government, now charge or request a £1-5 donation. Most charge for special exhibits and offer student and senior citizen discounts **("concessions").** The last few years have witnessed the birth of a number of expensive theme museums, with elaborate sound systems and computers supplementing more traditional exhibits.

The **London White Card** is a discount card that allows unlimited access to 13 participating museums for a period of three or seven days. The card can be purchased at any of the participating museums, including the V&A, the Science Museum, the Natural History Museum, the Royal Academy of Arts, the Hayward Gallery, the Design Museum, the London Transport Museum, the Museum of London, the Museum of the Moving Image, and the Courtauld Institute. The card will only afford you substantial discounts if you plan to visit *many* museums, or if you plan to visit a particularly expensive museum more than once (3-day card £15, families £30; 7-day card £25, families £50).

British Museum

Located *at Great Russell St., WC1.* ***Tel.*** *323 8299 for information desk.* ***Tube:*** *Tottenham Ct. Rd., Goodge St., Russell Sq., or Holborn.* ***Open*** *M-Sa 10am-5pm, Su 2:30-6pm.* ***Admission*** *free; suggested donation £2.* ***Guided tours*** *depart M-Sa 10:30, 11am, 1:30, 2:30pm; Su 3, 3:20, 3:45pm; £7, students £4, under 16 £3; 1½hr.* ***Highlights*** *of the Museum tour departs M-Sa 1pm from upstairs, 3pm downstairs; cost £5, students £3; 1hr. Larger,* ***special exhibits*** *cost £4, concessions £3. Rear entrance on Montague St. Visually-impaired should enquire about tactile exhibits; a* ***touch tour*** *of Roman and Egyptian sculpture is offered in room 84 in the basement—ask at the main information desk for details.*

The sheer volume of the **British Museum's** collections is a fascinating document of the political, military, and economic power of the British Empire. Founded in 1753, the museum began with the personal collection of the physician Sir Hans Sloane. In the following decades, the museum became so swollen with gifts, purchases, and imperialist spoils that a new building had to be commissioned. Robert Smirke drew up the design in 1824. Constructed over the next 30 years, his Neoclassical building is still home to the museum today.

The British Museum's national archaeological collections recapitulate the glory days of Egypt, Asia, Greece, Rome, and prehistoric and medieval Europe. The museum also houses superb temporary exhibitions of its coin and medal and its print and drawing collections.

The outstanding **ancient Egypt** collection occupies rooms on the ground and upper floors. Entering the ground floor gallery, one is greeted by two of the many imposing statues of Amenophis III. To the left rests the **Rosetta Stone,** discovered in 1799 by French soldiers. Its Greek text enabled Champollion finally to crack the hieroglyphic code. The head of Ramses II, famed for his arrogance towards Joseph and higher beings in Exodus, dominates the northern section of Room 25. Among the sculptures, the sublime royal head in green schist (1490 BC) stands out. The asexual representation of the latter has left scholars to debate whether it represents dominatrix Queen Hatshepsut or her successor, King Tuthmosis. In the side gallery 25a, don't miss three of the finest and best-known Theban tomb paintings. While famed as one of the most "human" of the daunting sculptures in the collection, the black granite Sesostris III remains more noteworthy for its ears than its warmth. To the right of the virile Ramses (reputed father of 150), in a side gallery, glistens the gold of the inner coffin of priestess Henutmehit. The central gallery is filled with tributes to the animal world, including a tiny blue hippo. The upstairs Egyptian gallery, known for its extensive collection of grisly mummies, also contains brilliant sarcophagi, an ancient body "desiccated by the dry, hot sand," and delicate papyri include the *Book of the Dead of Ani.*

The **Assyrian galleries,** wedged between Egypt and Greece, are renowned for the reliefs from Nineveh (704-668 BC), illustrating a campaign in southern Iraq. Room 16's entrance is guarded by the enormous, five-legged, human-headed bulls, made to look stationary from the front, mobile from the side.

The **Greek antiquities** exhibits are dominated by the **Elgin Marbles,** 5th-century BC reliefs from the Parthenon, now residing in the spacious Duveen Gallery. In 1810, Lord Elgin procured the statues and pieces of the Parthenon frieze while serving as ambassador to Constantinople. The museum claims that Elgin's "agents removed many sculptures from the Parthenon with the approval" of unnamed "authorities" for the price of £75,000. Later, for reasons of financial necessity, he sold them to Britain for £35,000. Every so often, the Greeks renew their efforts to convince the British government to return the marbles. Carved under the direction of ancient Greece's greatest sculptor, Phidias, the marbles comprise three main groups: the frieze, which portrays the most important Athenian civic festivals; the metopes, which depict incidents from the battle of the Lapiths and Centaurs (symbolizing the triumph of "civilization" over "barbarism"); and the remains of large statues that stood in the east and west pediments of the building. Recently opened are two new galleries devoted to the Elgin marbles, complete with a miniature model of the Acropolis.

Other Greek highlights include the complete Ionic facade of the **Nereid Monument,** one of the female caryatid columns from the Acropolis, and two of the Seven Wonders of the Ancient World. Once crowded by a four-horse chariot, the **Mausoleum at Halicarnassus** gained such fame in antiquity that it coined the word "mausoleum" in many European languages. Frieze slabs and some free-standing sculpture commemorate the second wonder—the **Temple of Artemis,** built to replace the one buried by Herostratus in 356 BC in order to perpetuate his name in history.

Among the many sculptures of the **Roman antiquities,** the dark blue glass of the **Portland Vase** stands out. The inspiration for ceramic designer Josiah Wedgwood, the vase has tenaciously survived a series of mishaps and reconstructive operations that took place even before the vase was dug up in 1582. When it was discovered, the base had already been broken and replaced. In 1845, it was shattered by a drunken museum-goer; when it was put back together, 37 small chips were left over. Since then, the vase has been beautifully reconstructed twice, with more left-over chips being reincorporated each time—don't touch! The scene depicted is an enigma; controversy still rages among experts over a Ph.D. student's recent interpretation of it as the depiction of an ancient poem.

The **Roman-Britain** section includes the **Mindenhall Treasure,** a magnificent collection of 4th-century silver tableware. With a diameter of almost two feet and weighing over 18 lb., the aptly named Great Dish impresses with its size and elaborate decorations. Nearby crouches **Lindow Man,** an Iron Age Celt supposedly sacrificed in a gruesome ritual and preserved by peat bog. The **Money Gallery** is next door, tracing finance from cowrie shells to credit cards; check out the 500,000,000,000 Yugoslav dinar note. The **Sutton Hoo Ship Burial,** an Anglo-Saxon ship buried (and subsequently dug up) in Suffolk complete with an unknown king, is the centerpiece of the **Medieval** galleries. Other fascinating highlights of these allegedly dark ages include a display of elaborate clocks, and the **Lewis Chessmen,** an 800-year-old ivory set more elaborately carved than anything offered by Franklin Mint.

The majority of the museum's **Oriental Collections** reside in the recently refurbished Gallery 33. The gallery's eastern half is dedicated to the Chinese collection, renowned for its ancient Shang bronzes and fine porcelains, and the western half is filled by Indian and Southeast Asian exhibits, which include the largest collection of Indian religious sculpture outside of India. Upstairs, the collection continues with a series of three galleries displaying Japanese artifacts, paintings, and calligraphy.

The most recent gallery additions are **Renaissance to the 20th Century,** featuring housewares from Bach to *Bauhaus,* and the **Mexican Gallery,** highlighted by exquisite masks, weapons, and ornaments coated with a mosaic of turquoise.

In addition to their prodigious permanent collections, the British Museum puts on a number of temporary exhibits. You also might get lucky and be able to catch one of the occasional free tours or gallery talks offered by the museum (call for info or pick up a "Current Events" leaflet at the information desk). Wandering through 2½ mi. of galleries may frustrate even the most die-hard museum-goer. To catch the main attractions, buy the £3 short guide; for a more in-depth look, introductory books on specific parts of the collection are available for about £5. The museum is always busy, but to avoid suffocation go during the week. Sundays and holidays are deadly.

■ National Gallery

Located in Trafalgar Sq., WC2. ***Tel.*** *839 3321 or 747 2885.* ***Tube:*** *Charing Cross, Leicester Sq., Embankment, or Piccadilly Circus.* ***Open*** *M-Tu and F-Sa 10am-6pm, W 10am-8pm, Su noon-6pm.* ***Admission*** *free.* ***Tours*** *depart from the Sainsbury Wing M-F 11:30am and 2:30pm, evening tour W 6:30pm, Sa 2 and 3:30pm; tours also in sign language the 1st Saturday of each month 11:30am. The Orange St. and Sainsbury Wing entrances are* ***wheelchair accessible.***
The **National Gallery** maintains one of the world's finest collections of Western painting, especially strong in works by Rembrandt, Rubens, and Renaissance Italian painters. The Tate Gallery (see p. 224) has joint custody of the British Collection, and is a better bet if you are more interested in 20th-century works.

You can spend days in this maze of galleries, renovated and rehung in 1992. A helpful guide is the **Micro Gallery,** a computerized, easy-to-use illustrated catalogue that cross references works by artist, title, subject, and school, and prints out (at £1 per 5 pages) a personal tour, mapping out the locations of the paintings you want to see. *(Open M-Tu and F-Sa 10am-5:30pm, W 10am-7:30pm, Su noon-5:30pm.)*

The National Gallery's collection is chronologically divided into four color-coded wings; paintings within these sections are arranged by school or artist. The collection starts in the new Sainsbury Wing, to the west of the main building, designed by post-modernist Philadelphian Robert Venturi. Amid fake ceiling supports and false perspectives hang works painted from 1260 to 1510. Early Italian paintings such as Botticelli's *Venus and Mars,* Raphael's *Crucifixion,* and da Vinci's famous *Virgin of the Rocks* are framed by the arches and columns of the new building. Although Van Eyck's *Arnolfini Marriage* appears to be a depiction of a medieval "shotgun wedding," the bride is merely holding up the hem of her dress as per the style of the day. More mystery surrounds the mysterious figures reflected in the mirror—many believe one of them to be Van Eyck himself.

Paintings from 1510 to 1600 are found in the West Wing, to the left of the Trafalgar Sq. entrance. Titian's *Bacchus* and *Ariadne* displays his mastery of contrast. Stormy El Grecos are featured here as well. Holbein's *The Ambassadors* contains a cunning blob that resolves itself into a skull when viewed from the right. Strong Rembrandt and Rubens collections adorn the North Wing (devoted to works from the 17th century)—Rembrandt's young and old self-portraits make a fascinating contrast. Placid Claude and Poussin landscapes are routed by the unabashed romanticism of Caravaggio and Velázquez. Van Dyck's *Equestrian Portrait of Charles I* headlines the State Portrait room.

The East Wing, to the right of the main entrance, is devoted to painting from 1700 to 1920, including a strong English collection. The natural light provides the perfect setting for viewing the paintings; many, such as Turner's *Rain, Steam, and Speed* (note the tiny jackrabbit running alongside the train), seem to acquire a special luminosity. Gainsborough's tight *Mr. and Mrs. Andrews* and Constable's rustic *The Hay Wain* whet the appetite before the Impressionists clamor for attention. Impressionist works include a number of Monet's near-abstract water lilies, Cézanne's *Old Woman with Roses,* and Rousseau's rainswept *Tropical Storm with a Tiger.* Picasso's *Fruit Dish, Bottle, and Violin* (1914), the National Gallery's initial foray into the abstract, has since been joined by another room of Picasso's work.

The National Gallery holds frequent special exhibitions in the basement galleries of the Sainsbury Wing, which sometimes cost up to £6 but are often free. In 1999, look for "Luca Signorelli in British Collections" (Nov. 11, 1998-Jan. 31, 1999), "Portraits by Ingres" (Jan. 27, 1998-Apr. 25, 1999), and "Rembrandt Self Portraits" (June 9-Sept. 5, 1999), among others. The National shows free films about art every Monday at 1pm in the Sainsbury Wing, and lectures take place in the afternoons (Tu-F at 1pm, Sa at noon; for more info, call 747 2885). Linger on Wednesday nights and admire the musuem's treasures against music performed by students of the Royal College of Music in the Sainsbury Wing Foyer (free).

■ National Portrait Gallery

Located at St. Martin's Pl., WC2, just opposite St.-Martin's-in-the-Fields. ***Tel.*** *306 0055.* ***Tube:*** *Charing Cross, Leicester Sq., Piccadilly Circus, or Embankment.* ***Open*** *M-Sa 10am-6pm, Su noon-6pm.* ***Admission*** *free, excluding temporary exhibits. Informative 1hr. lectures, Tu and Th 1:10pm, Sa-Su 3pm. Check the monthly schedule for topics and locations. Orange St. entrance is* ***wheelchair accessible*** *and there is a lift to all floors. For more information, call ext. 216.*

This unofficial Who's Who in Britain began in 1856 as "the fulfillment of a patriotic and moral ideal"—namely to showcase Britain's most officially noteworthy citizens. The museum's declared principle of looking "to the celebrity of the person represented, rather than to the merit of the artist" does not seem to have affected the quality of the works displayed—portraits by Reynolds, Lawrence, Holbein, Sargent, and Gainsborough that have stared up from countless history books segue easily into Warhol's depictions of Queen Elizabeth II and Elizabeth Taylor, Annie Leibovitz's classic photos of John Lennon and Yoko Ono, and Lucien Freud's compellingly tweaked self-portrait.

Over 9000 works have been arranged more or less chronologically. The earliest portraits hang in the top story—solemn Thomas More, maligned Richard III, venerated Elizabeth I, and canny Henry VII. Charles II is here, surrounded by his wife and mistresses. Follow the flow of British history through the galleries: from the War of the Roses (Yorks and Lancasters), to the Civil War (Cromwell and his buddies), to the American Revolution (George Washington), to imperial days (Florence Nightingale), and on to modern times (Margaret Thatcher).

Level four, dedicated to Henry VIII and predecessors, cherishes the Holbein cartoon of the king. Famous geologists, politicians, reformers, and fops populate the Victorian section, along with literary figures such as Tennyson, Thackeray, and Dickens. Charming "informal" portraits of the royal family are displayed on the mezzanine.

The first floor is jammed with displays of the 20th century, from Churchill to Peter Gabriel; the modern works take more amusing liberties with their likenesses (but then again, we never saw the old guys).

The gallery often mounts temporary displays and has planned exhibits of "British Sporting Heroes" (Oct. 16, 1998-Jan. 24 1999), the Raeburn (Jan.-Feb. 1999), the "John Kobal Photographic Portrait Award 1998 (Oct. 30, 1998-Feb. 14, 1999), and "Millias: Portraits" (Feb. 19-June 6, 1999), in addition to others. Admission to special exhibits averages £4, concessions £3. The annual British Petroleum Portrait Award brings out a selection of works from England's most promising portrait artists (June-Oct.).

Tate Gallery

***Located** at Millbank, SW1. **Tel.** 887 8000 for recorded information or tel. 887 8725 for personal assistance. **Tube:** Pimlico. **Open** daily 10am-5:50pm. **Admission** free. **Tours** run M-F 11am for British Old Masters: Van Dyck to the Pre-Raphaelites, noon for the Turner Collection, 2pm for Early Modern Art, 3pm for Conceptual Art, and only Sa 3pm for the General Tour: The Essential Tate. **Audio guides** (£3, concessions £2, for the main collection, the Clore galleries, or the Turner galleries; £4, concessions £3, for 2; £5, concessions £4 for all 3) feature a 5-10min. discussion on major works.*

The **Tate Gallery** opened in 1897 expressly to display contemporary British art, though a modern visitor could hardly divine this original intent from today's collection. Since then, the gallery has widened its scope, obtaining a superb collection of British works from the 16th century to the present and a distinguished ensemble of international modern art. The exhibits in the main galleries change frequently. Each room contains related works, either by the same artist or by members of similar movements. About 10-15% of the collection is displayed at any one time.

The Tate's **British collection** starts with a room at the far end of the gallery devoted to 16th- and 17th-century painting. The parade of Constables includes the famous views of Salisbury Cathedral, and a number of Hampstead scenes dotted with the requisite red saddle splashes. George Stubbs's enlivening landscapes and sporting scenes lead to Gainsborough's landscapes and Sir Joshua Reynolds's portraits. Don't miss the visionary works of poet, philosopher, and painter William Blake, or the haunting images of Sir John Everett Millais, one of the three founding members of the Pre-Raphaelite Brotherhood.

The paintings in each of the 30 rooms of the main gallery are organized chronologically and grouped by theme, offering a clear perspective on the development of British art, from early landscapes and portraits through Victorian, Pre-Raphaelite, and Impressionist paintings. At this point, the rooms begin to emphasize the relationship between British and foreign art movements, thus providing the perfect segue into the Tate's outstanding **modern collection** of international 20th-century art. Sculptures by Henry Moore, Epstein, Eric Gill, and Barbara Hepworth, in addition to Rodin's **The Kiss,** are found in the **Duveen Sculpture Galleries,** the central hall of which leads to the start of the British collection. Modern paintings and sculptures are displayed in subsequent rooms: the works of Monet, Degas, Van Gogh, Beardsley, Matisse, and the Camden Town Group (Sickert, Bevan) hang to the left of the entrance. Paintings by members of the Bloomsbury Group, Picasso, Dalí, and Francis Bacon, sculptures by Modigliani and Giacometti, and samples of the styles that have dominated since the 1950s—Constructivism, Minimalism, Pop, Super-realism, and Process Art—lie to the right of the central hall.

The Tate's 300-work J.M.W. Turner collection resides in the **Clore Gallery.** Architect James Stirling designed the annex to allow natural light to illuminate both the serenity of *Peace—Burial at Sea* and the raging brushstrokes of gale-swept ocean scenes. The collection covers all of Turner's career, from early, dreamy landscapes such as *Chevening Park* to the later visionary works, in which the subject is lost in a sublime array of light and color.

The Tate hosts a series of temporary exhibits in the downstairs galleries. In 1999 the Tate will host exhibitions on Jackson Pollack (Mar. 11-June 6), and the Bloomsbury group (Nov. 1999-Jan. 2000). Admission varies.

Victoria and Albert Museum

*The V&A is located on Cromwell Rd., SW7. Tel. 938 8500, 938 8441 for 24hr. recorded info, or 938 8349 for current exhibitions. **Tube:** South Kensington. **Buses** C1, 14, and 74. **Open** M noon-5:50pm, Tu-Su 10am-5:50pm. **Admission** £5, concessions £3, students and those under 18 free. Admissions free 4:30-6pm. Most of the museum is **wheelchair accessible**; wheelchair users are advised to use the side entrance on Exhibition Rd. and to* *call ahead at 938 8638. Gallery tours and taped tours are available for the visually impaired. One-hour introductory* ***museum tours*** *meet at the Cromwell entrance information desk daily 12:30, 1:30, 2:30 and 3:30pm, Tu-Su additional 10:30 and 11:30am tours. On Wednesday evenings during the summer, the V&A hires a few musicians, sets up a wine bar, and opens a few galleries for museum patrons from 6:30-9:30pm (£3). Experts give* ***lectures*** *on select pieces during these open gallery evenings (£5). Call 938 8500 for more info or to make (required)* ***reservations.*** *The V&A also offers scores of special events. Free gallery talks on a wide array of topics are given throughout the summer Tu-Sa 2pm.*

Housing the best collection of Italian Renaissance sculpture outside of Italy, the greatest collection of Indian art outside of India, and an abundant collection of John Constable studies, the mind-bogglingly inclusive V&A has practically perfected the display of fine and applied arts. Founded in 1899 by Queen Victoria, the museum took on its eclectic contours when the original curators were deluged with objects donated for exhibition from every epoch and region of the world. One of the most enchanting museums in London, the V&A (a.k.a. "the British Museum's attic") lets you saunter through the histories of art, design, and style in its 12 acres of galleries.

The vast scope of the museum's permanent collection does not stop the V&A from constantly creating **temporary exhibitions.** Displays include Grinling Gibbons's cascading flower woodcarvings (Oct. 22, 1998-Jan. 24, 1999), a collection of Henri Cartier Bresson photographs of the Americas and Asia (Nov 26, 1998-Apr. 12, 1999) and 300-year-old treasures from Northern India in "The Arts of the Sikh Kingdoms" exhibit (Mar. 25-July 25, 1999).

After gazing at the comics, the visitor may turn to the recently reopened **Raphael Cartoons** (from the Italian *cartone,* meaning "large pieces of paper"). Seven of the 10 huge, full-color sketches (scenes from the Acts of the Apostles) were done by Raphael and his apprentices as tapestry patterns for the Sistine Chapel. The many galleries of Italian sculpture include Donatello's *Ascension* and *Madonna and Child.* The **Medieval Treasury,** in the center of the ground floor, features vestments, plates, stained glass, and illuminations.

Plaster cast reproductions of European sculpture and architecture (the 80 ft. Trojan column from Rome; the facade of the Santiago Cathedral in Spain; Michelangelo's *Moses, Dying Slave, Rebellious Slave,* and *David*) occupy rooms 46A-B on the ground floor. These are the remnants of an abandoned movement, popular in the 1800s, to place casts of the great works of Western art in the major European cities in order to enlighten those masses who could not afford jaunts to Italy. Next door, test the knowledge you've gained here to distinguish impostors from the real things in the **Fakes and Forgeries Gallery.**

The **dress collection,** also on the ground floor, traces popular and elite clothing fashions from 17th-century shoes to the latest John Galliano confection. Focused primarily on Western women's garb, this exhibit documents the vagaries of sartorial design and textile technology—and implicitly documents changing gender roles. Women can count their fully intact ribs in thankful glee that they are no longer subject to the corsets and stays of 200 years ago; however, both genders may shed a tear for the demise of the 1920s.

The V&A's formidable **Asian collections** have recently been supplemented by the Nehru Gallery of Indian Art and the T.T. Tsui Gallery of Chinese Art. The **Nehru Gallery** contains splendid examples of textiles, painting, Mughal jewelry and decor, and revealing displays on European imperial conduct. You can see Tippoo's Tiger, a life-sized wooden musical automaton that simulates groans and roars while consuming a European gentleman, alluded to by John Keats in his poem "The Cap and Bells." The elegant **Tsui gallery** divides its 5000-year span of Chinese art into six areas of life—Eating and Drinking, Living, Worship, Ruling, Collecting, and Burial. Creative display techniques abound, including placing the decapitated head of a giant Buddha at the height it would occupy were the rest of the statue there with it. The **Toshiba Gallery of Japanese Art** next door contains engrossingly elaborate traditional armor and intriguing contemporary sculpture, as the **Samsung Gallery of Korean Art** recognizes the depth and longevity of Korean culture while refusing to recognize the current split between North and South. The V&A's displays of **Islamic Art** are punctuated by the intricacies of Persian carpets and Moroccan rugs. The collection's largest and most breathtaking piece is the Persian Ardabil carpet.

The first floor holds the collection of **British art and design.** Shakespeare immortalized the immense Great Bed of Ware (room 54) in *Twelfth Night*. Cool, dim room 74 exhibits modern British design, including works by Wyndham Lewis, Charles Rennie Mackintosh, and Eric Gill. International design classics—mostly chairs—grace "Twentieth Century Design." Unfortunately, the British Galleries are expected to close for renovations in July or August of 1998 and will reopen in 2001.

The **jewelry collection** (rooms 91-93—actually a pilfer-proof vault!), so unwieldy that it has been annotated in bound catalogues instead of posted descriptions, includes pieces dating from 2000 BC.

The new **Frank Lloyd Wright gallery,** on the second floor of the Henry Cole Wing, illustrates Wright's philosophy of Organic Architecture. The Wright-designed interior of the Kauffmann Office, originally commissioned for a Pittsburgh department store, is the V&A's first 20th-century period room.

The exquisitely redesigned **Glass Gallery** recently reopened in room C-131. Vases, bowls, pipes, and brandy bottles provide a colorful and shiny assault on visitors' eyes. A sophisticated electronic labeling system allows visitors to retrieve extensive details about any piece in the gallery by entering a code into a computer.

John Constable's prodigious collection of weather studies resides on the sixth floor of the Henry Cole Wing. For those whose tastes run smaller, room 406 showcases English and Continental **portrait miniatures** (including Holbein's *Anne of Cleves* and *Elizabeth I*).

The **New Restaurant,** on the ground floor of the Henry Cole Wing, serves tired museum-goers. (*Open M noon-5pm, Tu-Su 10am-5pm.*) On Sunday mornings, the restaurant hosts a jazz brunch featuring live music and an English breakfast or lunch (served 11am-3pm. £8.50).

Recommended Collections

These collections are the few that, in addition to the five heavyweights mentioned above, simply must be seen.

The Courtauld Gallery, Somerset House, the Strand, WC2 (tel. 873 2526), across from the corner of Aldwych and the Strand. Tube: Temple, Embankment, Charing Cross, or Covent Garden. The gallery is open again after a year long refurbishment. This intimate 11-room gallery in Somerset House is an ideal place to see some world-famous masterpieces. Mostly Impressionist and post-Impressionist works, including pieces by Cézanne, Degas, Gauguin, Seurat, and Renoir, plus Van Gogh's *Portrait of the Artist with a Bandaged Ear,* and Manet's *Bar aux Folies Bergère.* The Institute's other collections include early Italian religious paintings—key works by Botticelli, Rubens (*Descent from the Cross*), Bruegel, Cranach (*Adam and Eve*), and Modigliani. Frequent special free student exhibitions. Lectures about the exhibits are offered throughout the year (call 873 2526 for info). Open M-Sa 10am-6pm. Admission £4, concessions £2. M ½-price. Free for UK students, under 18. Wheelchair accessible.

London Transport Museum, Covent Garden, WC2 (tel. 379 6344, recorded info 565 7299). Tube: Covent Garden. On the east side of the Covent Garden plaza. Wildly revamped in 1993, the museum now boasts 2 new mezzanine floors, 2 new air-conditioned galleries, and a variety of interactive video displays. Although much of the ground floor traffic flows through a maze of historic trains, trams, and buses, the museum offers much more than a history of London's public transport vehicles. Low-tech exhibits provide a thought-provoking cultural history: see how the expansion of the transportation system fed the growth of suburbs. High-tech simulators allow you to recklessly endanger the lives of scores of cyber-commuters as you take the helm of a subway train. A fabulous place for kids and superb disabled access. First-class museum shop sells London Transport posters and postcards, as well as "Mind The Gap" t-shirts. Open M-Th and Sa-Su 10am-6pm, F 11am-6pm, last admission 5:15pm. Admission £4.95, concessions £2.95, families (2 adults, 2 kids) £12.85, under 5 free. Wheelchair accessible. MC, Visa.

Museum of London, 150 London Wall, EC2 (tel. 600 3699, 24hr. info tel. 600 0807; email info@museum-london.org.uk). Tube: St. Paul's or Barbican. Comprehensive is an understatement: this fabulously engrossing museum tells the story of the metropolis from the beginning of time, from its origins as Londinium up through the 1996 European Soccer Championships hosted here. Exhibits including reconstructed industrial-age streets and 17th-century royal carriages outline London's domestic, political, religious, cultural, industrial, sartorial, and natural histories. At the museum's center, the Nursery Garden flourishes—a living history of the flora trade in London (garden closes at 5:20pm). The new fast-changing Capital Concerns gallery displays a series of short exhibits looking at what's new in London. W-F free historical lectures; check for times. Open Tu-Sa 10am-5:50pm, Su noon-5:50pm, last entry 5:30pm. Admission £4, concessions £2, families £9.50, free after 4:30pm. Wheelchair accessible.

Museum of the Moving Image (MOMI), South Bank Centre, SE1 (tel. 401 2636, or 24hr. info 401 2636). Tube: Waterloo; or Embankment (cross the Hungerford footbridge). MOMI and the National Film Theatre, both appendages of the British Film Institute, are housed in a phenomenal building on the South Bank. The entertaining museum charts the development of image-making with light, from shadow puppets to film and telly. Costumed actor-guides are stationed at interactive exhibits—act out your favorite western, read the TV news, or watch your own superimposed image fly over the River Thames. The camera-shy will enjoy countless clips and props, from silent movie slapstick to the gaudy days of "Dr. Who." Open daily 10am-6pm; last entry 5pm, but allow around 2hr. Admission £6.25, students £5.25, handicapped, seniors, and children £4.50, families £17. MC, Visa.

National Maritime Museum, Romney Rd., Greenwich, SE10 (tel. (0181) 858 4422, recorded info (0181) 312 6565; fax (0181) 312 6632). BR: Greenwich or DLR: Island Gardens and use the pedestrian foot tunnel under the Thames. Set in picturesque Greenwich, the museum's loving documentation of the history of British sea power can have even the staunchest land-lubber swearing allegiance to the deified Admiral Nelson and longing to sail the bounding main. The highlight is the hands-on gallery, where visitors can play modern sailor, tracking and destroying enemy ships using sophisticated radar. But drink too much grog on shore-leave, and it's into the scuppers with a hose-pipe for ye! Arrr! Admission £5, concessions £4, ages 5-16 £2.50, families £15. Open 10am-5pm, last admission 4:30. (includes **Old Royal Observatory and Queen's House,** see p. 204).

Royal Academy, Piccadilly, W1 (tel. 439 7438, fax 434 0837), across from no. 185. Tube: Green Park or Piccadilly Circus. The academy hosts traveling exhibits of the highest order. Space for these shows has recently been enlarged by high-tech architect Norman Foster. The whopping annual summer exhibition (June-Aug.) is a London institution—the works of established and unknown contemporary artists festoon every square inch of wall space and are for sale (at non-budget prices). The architectural models offered are often spectacular. Monet (January 1999) Open daily M-Sa 10am-6pm, Su 10am-8:30pm. Admission varies by exhibition; average £6, concessions £4. Advance tickets often necessary for popular exhibitions.

Royal Air Force Museum, Grahame Park Way, NW9 (tel. (0181) 205 6867 or (0181) 205 2266 for 24hr. information). Tube: Colindale. Exit left and head straight for about 15min. until the giant missile battery and Spitfires inform you of your arrival at the museum, or take the Bus #303 from the tube station. Even those uninterested in aerial combat will have a tough time being bored in Britain's Smithsonian-like national museum of aviation. The RAF has converted this former WWI airbase into a hangarful of the country's aeronautic greatest hits. WWI Bristols, Korean War submarine hunters, and Falkland War Tornados display the dignified history of the RAF, while Gulf War footage and high-tech weapons exhibits hint at the future of Britain's air defense. Glance inside the cockpit of an F-4 or test fly a flight simulator (£1.50) in the cavernous Main Aircraft Hall, then prepare to be awed by the Bomber Command Hall, where nuclear bombers appear hauntingly poised for take-off. Open daily 10am-6pm, last admission 5:30pm. Admission £6.50, students £3.25, family £16.60. Wheelchair accessible.

Science Museum, Exhibition Rd., SW7 (tel. 938 8008 or 938 8080). Tube: South Kensington. Closet science geeks will be outed by their ecstatic cries as they enter this wonderland of diagrammed motors, springs, and spaceships. The museum's introductory exhibit romps through a "synopsis" of science since 6000 BC, lingering (a bit self-indulgently) over the steam-powered Industrial Revolution that vaulted Britain to world domination. Other permanent exhibits include "Food for Thought," which demonstrates the impact of technology on food and offers the foreign visitor startling insights into the British diet, and the excellent Flight Gallery of aeronautics, where you can help launch a rocket in the "Flight Lab." The 3-floor Wellcome Museum of Medical History confronts visitors with a glut of fascinating information, as well as a dried, dissected human head (see **The Wellcome Center,** p. 226). Perfect place for the kiddies to run free, with numerous exhibits geared toward the under 12 sector. The "Science Line" answers all those "scientific" questions (why do apples go brown?) at tel. (0345) 600 444. Open daily 10am-6pm. Admission £6.50, concessions £3.50, under 5 and people with disabilities free. Free daily 4:30-6pm.

Sir John Soane's Museum, 13 Lincoln's Inn Fields, WC2 (tel. 405 2107). Tube: Holborn. Soane was an architect's architect, but the idiosyncratic home he designed for himself will intrigue even laypersons. Window-sized, inset, and convex mirrors placed strategically throughout the house for lighting effects create skewed angles and weird distortions. The columns in the Colonnade room support a room-within-a-room above. Artifacts on display include Hogarth paintings, the massive sarcophagus of Seti I, and casts of famous buildings and sculptures from around the world. Look for the little numbers on the objects and art works; Soane catalogued everything himself. Open Tu-Sa 10am-5pm. Admission free. Tours (restricted to 22 people) leave Sa 2:30pm; tickets sold from 2pm on day of tour.

The Wallace Collection, Hertford House, Manchester Sq., W1 (tel. 935 0687). Tube: Bond St. Founded by various Marquises of Hertford and the illegitimate son of the 4th Marquis, Sir Richard Wallace, this unassuming mansion defines the adjective "sumptuous." The wall of much of the first floor is covered in red-velvet-patterned wallpaper, ceilings and mouldings are drizzled with gold, and shelf space is cluttered with porcelain and miniature paintings. Outstanding works include Hals's *The Laughing Cavalier,* Delacroix's *Execution of Marino Faliero,* Fragnard's *The Swing,* and Rubens's *Christ on the Cross.* Landscapes, interiors, portraits, and genre scenes from the major Dutch Golden Age artists hang near a number of Rubens oil sketches (drafts of some of his most famous works). Alongside paintings are beautiful pieces of furniture and ornamental art. Also home to the largest armor and weaponry collection outside of the Tower of London (see **Sights,** p. 183). This is perhaps the best free collection in London outside of the British Museum (see **Museums,** p. 213). Open M-Sa 10am-5pm, Su 11am-5pm. Guided tours M-Tu 1pm, W 11:30am and 1pm, Th-F 1pm, Sa 11:30am, Su 3pm. Free.

Other Outstanding Collections

Bank of England Museum, Threadneedle St., EC2 (tel. 601 5545). Tube: Bank. Entrance on Bartholomew Ln., left off Threadneedle St. Housed in the Bank of England itself, this museum traces the Bank's history from its foundation in 1694 right up to its recently acquired status as an independent central bank. Includes all sorts of banknotes, gold bars, and even some muskets once used to defend the bank. Also affords you the opportunity of sitting at a replica dealing desk, complete with up-to-date charts and graphs about market movements. Should you (for whatever bizarre reasons) wish to purchase Bank of England memorabilia, there is also a shop. Open M-F 10am-5pm. Free.

Barbican Galleries, Barbican Centre, EC2 (tel. 638 8891). Tube: Barbican. A community arts center, the Barbican hosts free concerts, art exhibitions, and library displays in its labyrinthine network of foyers. Open M and Th-Sa 10am-6:45pm, Tu 10am-5:45pm, W 10am-7:45pm, Su and bank holidays noon-6:45pm. Admission £6, concessions £4, M-F after 5pm £4.

Bethnal Green Museum of Childhood, Cambridge Heath Rd., E2 (tel. (0181) 980 3204 or info line (0181) 980 2415). Tube: Bethnal Green. Colorful toy store entrance leads into elegant Victorian warehouse full of toys, dolls, board games, and puppets that provide endless fun for the kiddies and a fascinating romp through social history for the adults. Displays also include children's books, costumes, and nursery furniture. Pay 20p to activate an automaton that graphically displays "what little boys are made of" and recount what follows years later in therapy. Open M-Th and Sa 10am-5:50pm, Su 2:30-5:50pm. Free.

Bramah Tea and Coffee Museum, The Clove Building, Maguire St., Butlers Wharf, SE1 (tel. 378 0222; fax 378 0219). Tube: Tower Hill or London Bridge, or DLR: Tower Gateway. Follow Design Museum directions and turn right on Maguire St. Appropriately located in the spot on Butlers Wharf that used to see 6000 chests of tea unloaded each day. A highly educational, refreshingly straightforward collection whose holdings include many tea and coffee plants themselves, some elegant espresso machines, and an alarmingly engrossing collection of novelty teapots. The jasmine aroma steaming around the entrance leaves you thirsting for a drink at the teashop on premises (pot of tea or coffee £1 per person). Admission £3.50, concessions £2, families £8. Group discounts. Open daily 10am-6pm.

British Library, 96 Euston Rd., NW1 (tel. 412 7332). Tube: King's Cross/St. Pancras or Euston. This red brick building beside St. Pancras station is a modern, airy home to Britain's national literature collection of over 180 million works. While the reading rooms are not available to the public, you can still enjoy the excellent exhibits downstairs. The **Ritblat Gallery** is home to many of the manuscripts that used to be in the British museum, and showcases scrawling from Lenin to Lennon—and that's just the 20th-century offerings. In the manuscript area, the English Literature displays contain the bane of the high school English student: manuscripts from *Beowulf* (c. 1000) and the *Canterbury Tales* (1410), as well as works by Jonson, Jane Austen, Elizabeth Barrett Browning, James Joyce, Virginia Woolf, Philip Larkin, and more. Biblical displays include ravishing illuminated texts and some of the oldest surviving fragments (the *Codex Sinaiticus* and the *Codex Alexandrius*), 3rd-century Greek gospels, and the Celtic Lindesfarne Gospels. The Historical Documents section proffers epistles by Henry VIII, Elizabeth I, Churchill, Napoleon, and Jeremy Bentham, among others. Two copies of the Magna Carta get their very own cases. Music displays show off works by Handel, Beethoven, and Stravinsky, as well as lyric drafts by Lennon and McCartney. The workshop of words and sounds follows the history of book production from medieval times to the present-day computer lay-outs.Open M and W-F 9:30am-6pm, Tu 9:30am-8pm, Sa 9:30am-5pm, Su 11am-5pm. Tours cost £3, concessions £2 and depart M, W, F, and Su 3pm, Sa 10:30am, 3pm. Book in advance.

Cabinet War Rooms, Clive Steps, King Charles St., SW1 (tel. 930 6961). Tube: Westminster. Follow the signs from Whitehall. Churchill and his cabinet ran a nation at war from this secret warren of underground rooms. Free cassette guides lead you through the room where Churchill made his famous wartime broadcasts and point out the transatlantic hotline disguised as a loo. Open daily Apr.-Sept. 9:30am-6pm; Oct.-Mar. 10am-6pm. Last entrance 5:15pm. Admission £4.40, concession £3.30, under 16 £2.40, disabled half-price.

Commonwealth Institute, Kensington High St., W8 (tel. 603 4535 or 371 3530; http://www.commonwealth.org.uk). Tube: High St. Kensington. Right by Holland Park. This organization of the 53 Commonwealth states has a well-regarded gallery celebrating the member states' culture and resources, from Indian musical instruments to Asian film. Newly renovated in 1997, it now also features a video immersion "Heliride" over Malaysia and an increased number of interactive exhibits. Open daily 10am-5pm. Admission £4.45, child £2.95, concession £3.45, family (2 adults and 2 children) £11.95. MC, Visa.

Crystal Palace Museum, Anerly Hill, SE19 (tel (0181) 676 0700). BR: Crystal Palace. Originally located in Hyde Park, the all-glass Crystal Palace was moved to Sydenham at the end of the Great Exhibition in 1851. Sadly, in 1836, the Crystal Palace was destroyed by fire. This museum is located in the old engineering school and chronicles the story of the Palace. Check out the very funky model dinosaurs. Open bank holidays and Su 11am-5pm.

The Design Museum, Butlers Wharf, Shad Thames, SE1 (tel. 403 6933 or 407 6261, exhibition hotline 378 6055; http://www.virtual/guide/london/gallery/Design-m.htm). Tube: London Bridge, then follow signs on Tooley St; Tower Hill (cross the Tower Bridge). Housed in an appropriately Bauhaus-like box on the river, this museum is dedicated to mass-produced classics of culture and industry. Young, artsy visitors peruse exhibits of modern art and suburban history and sit in some of the century's most influential chairs. About half of the space is devoted to excellent changing exhibitions—"Modern Britain" runs from January 19-July 18, 1999. Open M-F 11:30am-6pm. Admission £5.25, concessions £4, families £12.

Dulwich Picture Gallery, College Rd., SE21 (tel. (0181) 693 5254 or (0181) 693 8000 for recorded information). BR: West Dulwich (10min. from Victoria, day return £1.80), then right from the station and follow the signs (15min.), or tube: Brixton and take the P4 bus to the door. English Portraiture and Dutch landscapes, including Gainsborough, Reynolds, and Rembrandt fix here. Thieves fancied Rembrandt's *Jacob III de Gheyn* so much that it was stolen on 4 separate occasions (it has since been recovered). Afterwards, sit outside in the pleasant gardens. Open Tu-F 10am-5pm, Sa 11am-5pm, Su 2-5pm. Admission free Fridays, otherwise £3, concessions £1.50, children free.

Freud Museum, 20 Maresfield Gdns., NW3 (tel. 435 2002). Tube: Finchley Rd. Head right from the tube station down Finchley Rd. Take the 5th left onto Trinity Walk; Maresfield Gdns. is at the end of the street. A re-creation of the home where Freud spent a year after escaping Nazi Vienna in 1938. The museum includes the library, study, and, of course, couch, where he completed some of his most influential works. Open W-Su noon-5pm. Admission £3, students £1.50.

Geffrye Museum, Kingsland Road, E2 (tel 739 9893). Tube: Liverpool St., then Bus #242 or 149 from Bishops Gate exit. Set in a large former poorhouse founded and funded by the rags-to-riches Sir Geffrye, the current incarnation of this building traces the history of English interior design. Outside are a large courtyard and a lovely herb garden. The Geffrye meticulously chronicles the English home interior, from the well-appointed formalities of the 1600s to the height of the Linoleum and Bakelite Age in the 1950s. Excellent temporary exhibits. Open Tu-Sa 10am-5pm, Su 2-5pm. Wheelchair accessible. Free.

Guildhall Clock Museum, in the Guildhall Library, Aldermanbury, EC2 (tel. 260 1858). Tube: Bank, St. Paul's, or Moorgate. "The Worshipful Company of Clockmakers" presents a well-labeled collection of pocket watches, jeweled watch keys, and a few curiosities. A macabre, silver, skull-shaped watch, suspected to belong to Mary Queen of Scots, is notable—she checked the time by opening the jaw and looking inside its mouth. The watch Sir Edmund Hilary wore on the 1st ascent of Everest now rests here in a less dramatic setting. Open M-F 9:30am-4:45pm. Free.

Hayward Gallery, at Royal Festival Hall, Belvedere Rd., SE1 (tel. 928 3144, or recorded info 261 0127). Tube: Waterloo. A fixture of the South Bank Centre, this 6-room gallery hosts high-powered exhibitions of 20th-century art. On tap for 1999: works by Francis Bacon (Feb.-Apr.), Anish Kapoor (May-June 21), and Bruce Nauman (July 16-Sept. 6). Gallery talks and events correspond with current exhibits—call for information. Open daily 10am-6pm, Tu-W until 8pm. Admission £5, concessions £3.50, families £12, children under 12 free with adult.

Horniman Museum, London Rd., SE23 (tel. (0181) 699 1872). BR: Dulwich. An extraordinary collection of anything you can think of, brought together by the kleptomania of 19th-century tea merchant Frederick Horniman. Features an impressive and eclectic mixture of ethnographic exhibits. An aquarium and small zoo are attached. Open M-Sa 10:30am-5:30pm, Su 2-5:30pm.

Imperial War Museum, Lambeth Rd., SE1 (tel. 416 5000). Tube: Lambeth North or Elephant and Castle. Don't be misled by the jingoistic resonance of the name; this museum is a moving reminder of the brutal human cost of war. The atrium is filled with tanks and planes; the eloquent testimony to the horror of war is downstairs. Gripping exhibits illuminate every aspect of two world wars, in every possible medium. The Blitz and Trench Experiences recreate every detail (even smells); veterans and victims speak through telephone handsets. The powerful Bergen-Belsen exhibit documents the genocide of the concentration camps and the story of the rescue and rehabilitation of survivors. Don't miss the "peace in our time" agree-

ment Neville Chamberlain triumphantly brought back from Munich in 1938, or Adolf Hitler's "political testament," dictated in the chancellory bunker. Upstairs, the art galleries keep fine examples of war painting, such as Sargent's *Gassed,* 1918. Also features large temporary exhibits; notable in 1998 was Princess Diana's campaign against landmines. Open daily 10am-6pm. Admission £5, students £4, ages 5-16 £2.50. Free daily 4:30-6pm. Wheelchair accessible.

Institute of Contemporary Arts (ICA), the Mall, SW1 (tel. 930 3647, or for 24hr. recorded info, 930 6393). Tube: Charing Cross. Entrance is located on the Mall at the foot of the Duke of York steps. Vigorous, hipper-than-thou outpost of the avant garde of visual and performance art. 3 temporary galleries, a cinema featuring 1st-run independent films (£6.50, concessions £5), experimental space for film and video, and a theater. Films vary from classics like *Animal Farm* to the more current and artsy (£6.50, concessions £5). Open Su-Th noon-7:30pm, F noon-7:30pm. Box office (tel. 930 3647) is open daily noon-8:30pm. M-F admission £1.50, concessions £1; Sa-Su £2.50, £1.50.

The Iveagh Bequest, Kenwood House, Hampstead La., NW3 (tel. (0181) 348 1286). Tube: Archway or Golders Green, then Bus 210 to Kenwood. An impeccable recreation of an 18th-century Neoclassical villa, beautifully located on the Kenwood Estate overlooking Hampstead Heath. Fine works by Dutch masters, including Vermeer's *Guitar Player* and the last of Rembrandt's self-portraits. Plenty of Sir Joshua Reynolds for his fans. Open daily 10am-6pm; Oct. to mid-April 10am-4pm. Free. Admission charged for special visiting exhibitions.

Jewish Museum, 129-31 Albert St., NW1 (tel. 284 1997). Tube: Camden Town. Exit the station to the right and head left. Take the 1st right onto Parkway; Albert St. will be on the left. A collection of antiques, manuscripts, and paintings documenting Jewish history, set inside an elegant museum with Jerusalem-stone walkways. Intimate setup focuses on the history of Jews in London from 1066 to the present. Impressive collection of silver. Open Su-Th 10am-4pm. Admission £3, concessions £1.50, families (up to 4) £7.50. MC, Visa.

London Dungeon, 28-34 Tooley St., SE1 (tel. 403 0606). Tube: London Bridge. An expensive and popular spectacle. The terrifying groans that accompany scenes of drowning, disembowelment, head crushing, and body stretching scare adults and children alike. Plague, decomposition, and anything else remotely connected to horror and British history thrown in for effect. Even the Pizza Hut and ice cream shop at the end of the museum can't make the chills go away. Reserve at least 2hr., not including the queue to get in. Open daily Apr.-Sept. 10am-6:30pm, last entrance 5:30pm; Nov.-Feb. 10am-5:30pm, last entrance 4:30pm. Admission £9.50, students £7.95, under 14 £6.25, seniors £6.25. Group discounts.

Madame Tussaud's, Marylebone Rd., NW1 (tel. 935 6861). Tube: Baker St. The classic waxwork museum, founded by an *emigré* aristocrat who manufactured life-size models of French nobility who met their demise at the guillotine. Figures are disconcertingly lifelike, with a tendency towards being flattering (see Bogart) with some exceptions (see Prince Charles). Sarah Ferguson has been effaced. The more macabre exhibits, like the display of famous psychopaths and wife-murderers from English history, are eerie and powerful. Be warned: this is one of London's most popular attractions, which translates into huge lines and high prices—visitors should think carefully about whether the museum is worth 9 quid and an hour-long wait. Madame Tussaud's is best visited in the morning to get a good view of the most popular collections. To avoid the horrific queues, form a group with at least 9 fellow sufferers and use the group entrance, or go either when they first open or in the late afternoon. Open M-F 9am-5:30pm (last admission, actually stays open later), Sa-Su 9:30am-5:30pm. Winter M-F opens 1hr. later. A distinctive green dome shelters the adjacent **Planetarium.** Ride the Space Trail through a model universe and watch a Star Show. Admission to Madame Tussaud's £9.75, children £6.60, seniors £7.45. Planetarium £5.85, children £3.85, seniors £4.50. Both museum and planetarium £12, children £8, seniors £9.25.

National Army Museum, Royal Hospital Rd., SW3 (tel. 730 0717). Tube: Sloane Sq. Set next to the dignified buildings of the Royal Hospital for army pensioners, this 4-story concrete block ironically presents the more personal side of serving in the Royal Majesty's army. Not the slickest museum, but clean, efficient, and decent—

much as a good armed force should be. Includes weapons (2 centuries of swords in the chillingly titled **Cut, Thrust, Swagger** room), uniforms, and medals, huge war paintings and battle drums of Britain's cleanly shaven, beefeating soldiers (they had to shave daily, even on the beaches of Normandy), as well as random artifacts like the skeleton of Napolean's horse at Waterloo. Open daily 10am-5:30pm. Free.

National Postal Museum, London Chief Post Office, King Edward Building, King Edward St., EC1 (tel. 600 8914). Tube: St. Paul's. A stamptastic array of postal memorabilia sure to delight dedicated post fiends and Johnny-come-philatelies alike. See everything from the "Penny Black," the world's 1st adhesive postage stamp, to the ludicrous 5-wheeled bikes used by Victorian postmen. The astute visitor will learn about the legendary connection between the Post Office and military service, and the untutored will be initiated into the mysteries of pneumatic postage and stamp security. No disabled access. Open M-F 9:30am-4:30pm. Free.

Natural History Museum, Cromwell Rd., SW7 (tel. 938 9123). Tube: South Kensington. See whales, volcanos, and dinosaurs all in one day in this former Victorian cathedral. The museum's personality is split between glorious, encyclopedic explanations and high-tech, more hands-on exhibits (buttons, levers, and microscopes galore). Permanent exhibits include "Creepy Crawlies," "Ecology," "Human Biology—An Exhibition of Ourselves," and the superb dinosaur and fossil exhibits, with tantalizing computer displays and relatively realistic life-size models. Also houses the British Geological Survey (tel. 589 4090). Open M-Sa 10am-5:50pm, Su 11am-5:50pm. Admission £6, concessions £3.20, families (up to 2 adults and 4 children) £16, ages 5-17 £3. Free M-F 4:30-6pm, Sa-Su, and Bank holidays 5-5:50pm. Wheelchair accessible. AmEx, MC, Visa.

Pollock's Toy Museum, 1 Scala St. (entrance on Whitfield St.), W1 (tel. 636 3452). Tube: Goodge St.; head west on Goodge St. then right onto Whitfield St. Housed above a modern toy shop in a maze of tiny, 18th-century rooms congested with antique playthings of every size and description. Highlights include Eric, the oldest known teddy bear (b. 1905), and German "saucy Fraulines," who expose their britches at the tug of a string. Elaborate toy theaters take center stage in one room. The histories and anecdotes which accompany the collection often astound—did you know "Chutes and Ladders" was originally a tool for Hindu religious instruction? Open M-Sa 10am-5pm, last admission 4:30pm. Admission £2.50, under 18 £1.

Royal Festival Hall Galleries, Royal Festival Hall, South Bank Centre, SE1 (tel. 960 4242). Tube: Waterloo, or Embankment and cross the Hungerford footbridge. In what is essentially the lobby of the Royal Festival Hall (see p. 241), a creative display space for contemporary art exhibits. Photography and architecture are this gallery's primary art forms. A necessary part of any stroll along the South Bank. Open daily 10am-10:30pm. Free.

Saatchi Gallery, 98a Boundary Rd., NW8 (tel. 624 8299). Tube: Swiss Cottage. Bus 139 stops outside gallery. This is art. *This* is beauty! The holdings of enormously influential art-collector Charles Saatchi (he of the eponymous advertising firm). Hot modern art! Closed Aug. Open Th-Su noon-6pm. Admission £3.50, Th free.

The Sherlock Holmes Museum, 239 Baker St. (marked "221b"), W1 (tel. 935 8866). Tube: Baker St. Sir Arthur Conan Doyle actually occupied this small house in the late 1800s. Students of Holmes' deductive method will be intrigued by the museum's meticulous re-creation of his storied lodgings. Upstairs is a display of "artifacts" from the stories. Leaf through a hilarious selection of letters Holmes has received in the last few years. You are encouraged to try on the deerstalker cap and cloak; a museum employee will snap a picture if you'd like. Open daily 10am-6pm (last admission). Admission £5, under 17 £3.

Theatre Museum, 1E Tavistock St., WC2E 7PA (tel. 836 7891, box office 836 2330). Tube: Covent Garden. Public entrance on Russell St., off the east end of the Covent Garden plaza. This branch of the V&A contains Britain's richest holding of theatrical memorabilia; see numerous 19th-century Shakespearean daggers before you. Theater models are exhibited, and other stage-related arts such as bullet, opera, puppetry, the circus and rock music play supporting roles. Guided tours, theatrical make-up demos (watch a bullet wound made while you wait), and costume workshops are free with admission. Eccentric temporary exhibits. Box office just inside the door sells tickets to West End plays, musicals, and concerts with negligible

mark-up in most cases. Box office and museum open Tu-Su 11am-7pm, last admission 6:30pm. Admission £3.50, concessions £2, families £8, groups of 10 or more £2.50 per person. AmEx, MC, Visa.

The Wellcome Center, 183 Euston Rd., NW1(tel. 611 7211). Tube: Euston. Across the street from the station. This huge center plays host to **Science for Life,** a permanent exhibit on medicine and the body. Fun and informative interactive displays abound providing creative instruction on topics ranging from organ size to research methods. Upstairs, the small History of Medicine Gallery offers changing exhibitions. Across the street, the **Two10 Gallery** hosts rotating art exhibitions which pertain specifically to the medical world. Open M-F 9:45am-5pm, Sa 9:45am-1pm. Admission free.

Wellington Museum, Apsley House, on the north side of Hyde Park Corner at 149 Piccadilly, W1 (tel. 499 5676). Tube: Hyde Park Corner. Following a 3-year renovation, this 19th-century mansion built for the First Duke of Wellington has been restored to its original glory and glitz. Built between 1771 and 1778, the Apsley House is popularly known as Number One, London, as it is just past the toll gate into the capital when approached from the west. The Duke's collection of paintings, silver, porcelain, sculpture, and furniture is housed here, and is displayed in its full and wholly ostentatious splendor. Open Tu-Su 11am-5pm. Last admission 4:30pm. Admission £4.50, concessions £3. Guided audio tour coming soon. Limited disabled access.

Whitechapel Art Gallery, Whitechapel High St., E1 (tel. 377 7888). Tube: Aldgate East. The high-ceilinged and sunny galleries of the Whitechapel contain no permanent collection, but host some of Britain's (and the Continent's) most daring exhibitions of contemporary art. Exhibits are informal, sometimes downright weird, and often aim to reflect the East End community. In 1999, look for a show from German Rosemarie Trockel, which includes her "Bridgette Bardot Room" (Sept. 4 1999-Feb. 7 2000), among others. The gallery's appropriately hip cafe is open Tu and Th-Su 11am-4:30pm, W 11am-6:30pm. Gallery open Tu and Th-Su 11am-5pm, W 11am-8pm. Free. Wheelchair accessible.

Winston Churchill's Britain at War, 64-66 Tooley St., SE1 (tel. 403 3171; fax 403 5104). Tube: London Bridge. Across from Hay's Galleria. Macabre reconstruction of underground life in London during the Blitz with all the "sights, sounds and sights." Jitterbug with mannequin GIs in the "Rainbow Corner" club, then step into a bombed-out street with bodies flung all over. Open daily 10am-7pm; Apr.-Sept. last admission 5:30pm; Oct.-Mar. last admission 4:30pm. Admission £5.95, concessions £3.95, under 16 £2.95, families £14.

Entertainment

When a man is tired of London, he is tired of life; for there is in London all that life can afford.

—Samuel Johnson, 1777

On any given day or night, Londoners and visitors can choose from the widest range of entertainment a city can offer. Suffering competition only from Broadway, the West End is the world's theater capital, supplemented by an adventurous "fringe" and a surprisingly experimental, well-financed National Theatre. Music scenes range from the black ties of the Royal Opera House to Wembley mobs and nightclub raves. The work of British filmmakers like Derek Jarman, Sally Potter, and Mike Leigh—often available in the States only on video—is shown in cinemas all over the city. Dance, comedy, sports, and countless unclassifiable happenings can leave you poring in bewilderment over the listings in *Time Out* (£1.80) and *What's On* (£1.30). Their recommendations are usually dead on. **Kidsline** (tel. 222 8070) answers queries on children's events (M-F 4-6pm). **Artsline** (tel. 388 2227) provides information about disabled access at entertainment venues across London (M-F 9:30am-5:30pm).

Theater

The stage for a national dramatic tradition dating from Shakespeare, London maintains unrivaled standards in theater. The renowned Royal Academy for the Dramatic Arts draws students from around the globe. Playwrights such as Tom Stoppard and Alan Ayckbourn premier their works in the West End, class-conscious political dramas, younger writers, and performance artists sustain a vibrant fringe theater scene, and classic tragedies are revived everywhere. The cheapest seats in most theaters cost about £8, progressing upward to £30 for orchestra seats. Previews and matinees cost a few pounds less, and many theaters offer dirt-cheap **student/senior standbys** (indicated by "concs," "concessions," or "S" in newspaper and *Time Out* listings)—around £7-10 shortly before curtain (come two hours beforehand to be sure of a seat and bring ID). **Day seats** are sold to the public from 9 or 10am on the day of the performance at a reduced price, but you must queue up earlier to snag one. If a show is sold out, returned tickets may be sold (at full price) just before curtain. Most theaters also offer senior citizen discounts on advance ticket purchases for weekday matinees. For the latest on standbys for West End shows, call the **Student Theatreline** (tel. 379 8900; updated from 2pm daily).

Stalls are orchestra seats. **Upper Circle** and **Dress Circle** refer to balcony seats above the stalls. **Slips** are seats along the top edges of the theater; usually the cheapest, they often have restricted views of the stage. The **interval** is the intermission. Programs are never free; these large, glossy booklets cost £1.50-2. Matinees are on weekdays and Saturday between 2-3pm. Evening performances start between 7:15 and 8pm.

The **Leicester Square Half Price Ticket Booth** sells tickets at half-price (plus booking fee) on the day of the performance, but carries only tickets for the West End, Barbican (and Pit), and National Theatres. Tickets are sold from the top of the pile, which means you can't choose a seat and the most expensive seats are sold first. Lines are the worst on Saturday (open M-Sa 11am-6:30pm; credit cards accepted, but with a £2 service charge; max. 4 per person). Accept no imitations: the peculiar structure with the small tower on the south side of Leicester Sq. is the only discount booth sanctioned by the **Society of London Theatre,** but doesn't offer tickets to the huge musicals (Cats, Phantom, etc.). Keep in mind that, if a student, you will still save more by purchasing student rush tickets. If you do get burned by bogus vendors, or have other problems with ticket vendors, contact the Society (tel. 836 0971, open M-F 9am-6pm). Your next best bet for the lowest prices is to schlep to a box office in per-

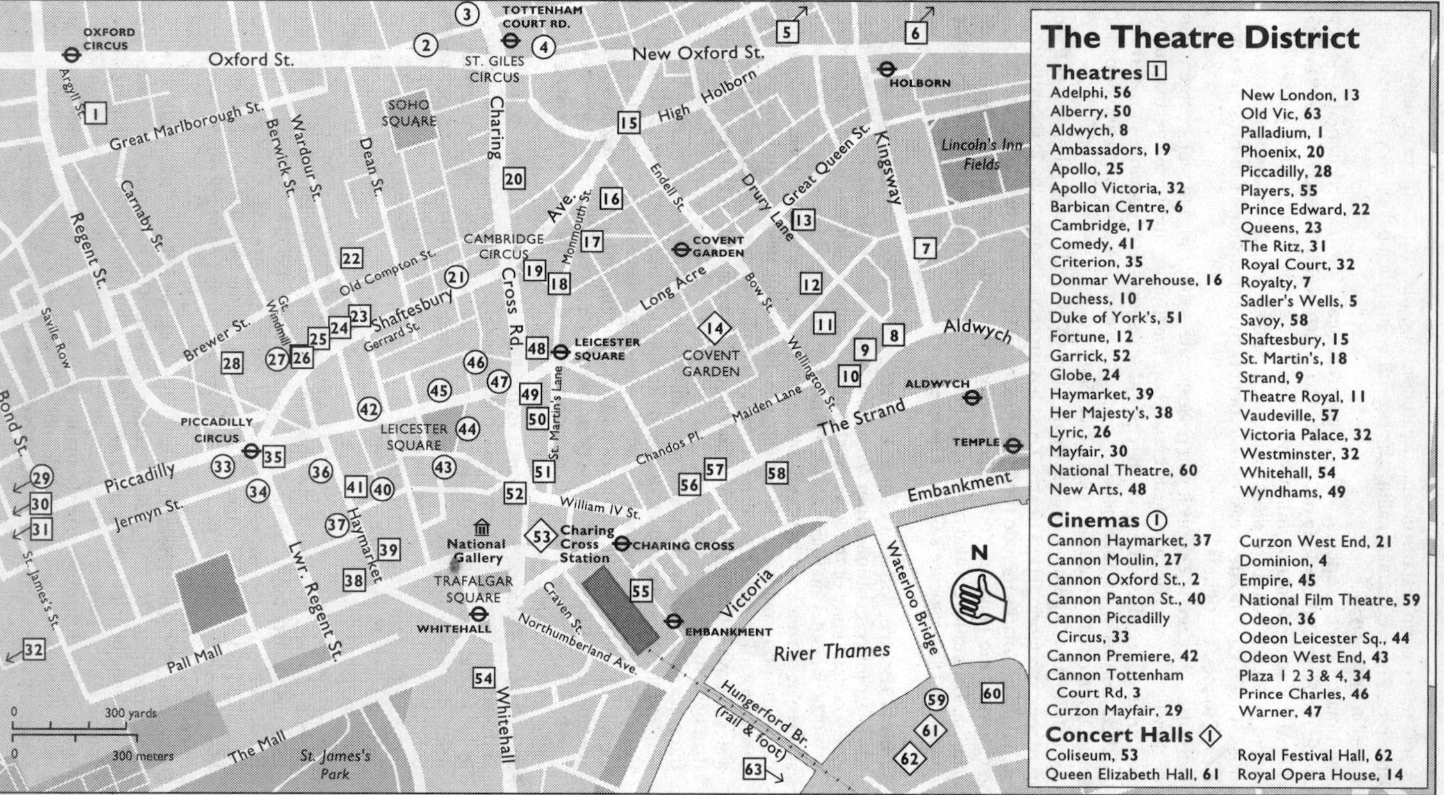

ENTERTAINMENT

son and select your seats from the theater seating plan (box offices usually open 10am-8pm). Reserve seats by calling the box office and then paying by post or in person within three days.

Legitimate ticket agencies will get you real seats but no real bargains—they include the **First Call booking office** (tel. 420 0000), **Keith Prowse** (tel. (0181) 795 1111; M-F 9am-5:30pm), London's largest ticket agency, and **Ticketmaster** (tel. 344 4444). All sell tickets to most major West End shows, as well as larger concert venues. Credit card holders can charge tickets over the phone but must produce the card to pick up tickets.

Patronize ticket agencies only if you're desperate—they can, and will, charge whatever they like. Avoid package deals cooked up for tourists, and be aware that many shows around Piccadilly are tawdry farces and sex shows. For big-name shows, try to get tickets months in advance or go to the theaters early in the morning and hope for returns. Write or call the theater box office first.

Aside from what's going on inside them, many West End theaters themselves form part of the city's fabric. The **Theatre Trust** has protected many historic theaters from demolition; landmarks include the Theatre Royal, Haymarket, the Albery, the Palace, the Criterion, the Duke of York, Her Majesty's, the Shaftesbury, the Savoy, and the Palladium. Theater-lovers also now finally have the chance to see performances in the reconstructed Shakespeare's **Globe Theatre.**

Barbican Theatre, Barbican Centre, EC2 (tel. 382 7272 for 24hr. information or call 638 8891 for reservations; http://www.barbican.org.uk). Tube: Barbican or Moorgate. London home of the Royal Shakespeare Company. Tickets for the main stage £7.50-24; weekday matinees £6-13; Saturday matinees and previews £8-18. Student and senior citizen standbys bookable in person or by telephone from 9am on the day of the performance, £6 (1 per person). Fascinating futuristic auditorium showcases the Bard's work in style; each row of seats has its own side door (there are no aisles). Forward-leaning balconies guarantee that none of the 1100 seats sit farther than 65 ft. from center stage, and every seat gives a clear view. Stick around at the interval to watch the shiny metal safety curtain seal off the stage. The Pit—the 200-seat 2nd theater—showcases Jacobean, Restoration, and experimental contemporary works in a more intimate setting. Evenings and Saturday matinees £14-17; previews £11-13; midweek matinees £13-16. Student and senior citizen standbys available from 9am the day of the performance for £6.50. There are always several sign language and audio-described performances during the run of each show. Box office (Level 0 of the Centre) open daily 9am-8pm. AmEx, MC, Visa.

Royal National Theatre, South Bank Centre, SE1 (tel. 452 3400). Tube: Waterloo, or Embankment (cross the Hungerford footbridge). The brilliant repertory companies in the Olivier and Lyttleton theaters (£10-27) put on classics from Shakespeare to Ibsen, as well as mainstream contemporary drama. The smaller Cottesloe theater (£12 or 18) plays with more experimental works, like Kushner's *Angels in America.* All 3 theaters are well-ranked and have widely spaced rows, so even the rear balcony seats offer an unobstructed view of the stage. 40 day seats in each of the 3 theaters reduced to £10-12 at 10am on day of performance. General standby seats sold 2hr. before performance (£10-14); student and senior standby 45min. before show £7.50; senior citizens can book any show in advance for £10.50. The complex features live music, exhibitions, and other activities. The National's outstanding bookshop has the widest selection in London for plays and books about theater (tel. 452 3456; open M-Sa 10am-10:45pm; ask for the bookstore). Backstage tours M-Sa £4, concessions £3.50. Book in advance; call 452 3400 for times. Box office open M-Sa 10am-8pm.

Shakespeare's Globe Theatre, New Globe Walk, Bankside, SE1 (tel. 401 9919 or Ticketmaster at 316 4703). Tube: London Bridge. This meticulous reconstruction of the Globe began its inaugural 1997 season with *Henry V* and *The Winter's Tale,* among others. Patrons may either purchase spots on the benches in the 3-tier space or stand through a performance as "groundlings." The groundling option may actually be the preferable one, not only because it costs less and allows a historical communion with the Elizabethan peasantry, but because it puts you much

closer to both the stage and the roaming wine vendors. However, groundlings should prepare for the possibility of rain without the use of umbrellas (which impede sight lines). For information on educational workshops and "walkshops," call 902 1400. Groundling tickets for any performance £5. Box office open M-Sa 10am-8pm, 'til 6pm by phone.

WEST END THEATERS

In a country where Andrew Lloyd Webber is a Lord, it's not surprising that *Phantom of the Opera* remains the hardest show in town to get seats for. Similar fare dominates the theaters of the West End, the London theater district that out-Broadways Broadway. To guarantee a seat for the big musicals, comedies, and thrillers that constitute West End fare, book a week or two ahead.

Adelphi Theatre, The Strand, WC2R (tel. 379 8884). Tube: Charing Cross. Musicals, both new and revivals. Now showing *Chicago*. £12.50-32.50.

Albery Theatre, St. Martin's La., WC2N (tel. 369 1730). Tube: Leicester Sq. Comedies and dramas, old and new, seats £12.50-27.50. Standby for conc. £12.50 ½hr. before performance.

Aldwych Theatre, The Strand, WC2B (tel. 416 6003). Tube: Covent Garden. Sir Andrew Lloyd Webber's *Whistle Down the Wind,* £10-32.50.

Apollo Shaftesbury, Shaftesbury Ave., W1 (tel. 494 5070). Tube: Piccadilly Circus. New comedies and musicals. £6.50-23.50.

Apollo Victoria Theatre, Wilton Rd., SW1 (tel. 416 6070). Tube: Victoria. Venue for *Starlight Express,* Lloyd Webber on roller skates, is in its 15th year. £12.50-30. Concessions 1hr. before performance.

Arts Theatre, 6-7 Great Newport St., WC2 (tel. 836 2132). Tube: Leicester Sq. New Dramas and musicals. £15. Children's shows Sept.-May £5-£9.

Cambridge Theatre, Earlham St., WC2 (tel. 494 5080). Tube: Covent Garden. *Grease* is the word. £10-27.50, Sa £12.50-£30. Student stand-bys M-Th 1hr. before performance.

Criterion Theatre, Piccadilly Circus, W1 (tel. 369 1747). Tube: Piccadilly Circus. *The Complete Works of William Shakespeare (Abridged)*. Tu *The Complete History of America (Abridged)*. £5.50-22.50. Standby for concessions £12.50.

Dominion Theatre, Tottenham Ct. Rd., W1 (tel. 656 1888). Tube: Tottenham Ct. Rd. *Beauty and the Beast*. Booking from now until the apocalypse. £18.50-35.

Drury Lane Theatre Royal, Catherine St., WC2B (tel. 494 5000). Tube: Covent Garden. *Miss Saigon*. £5.75-35. Student standbys £15, M-Th 1hr. before performance.

Duke of York's Theatre, St. Martin's Ln., WC2 (tel. 836 5122). Tube: Leicester Sq. New experimental dramas. £10-19.50.

Duchess Theatre, Catherine St., WC2 (tel. 494 5075). Tube: Covent Garden. New dramas and musicals. £10.50-22.50. Standby for concessions. £10.

Fortune Theatre, Russell St., WC2 (tel. 836 2238). Tube: Covent Garden. *The Woman in Black*—never screamed in a theater? You will. In its ninth year. £8.50-23.50. Standby for conc. £9.

Garrick Theatre, Charing Cross Rd., WC2 (tel. 494 5085). Tube: Leicester Sq. Revivals of dramas and musicals. £10.50-25. Standby for conc. £9.

Gielgud Theatre, 33 Shaftesbury Ave., W1 (tel. 494 5065). Tube: Piccadilly Circus. Straight plays, mainly comedies. £10.50-27.50. Student Standbys ½price.

Her Majesty's Theatre, Haymarket, SW1 (tel. 494 5400). Tube: Piccadilly Circus. *Phantom of the Opera*—The most incredible musical ever written; also, a chandelier falls on the audience. £10-35. Book before you arrive, at least a month ahead if you want Sa night tickets.

London Palladium Theatre, Argyll St., W1 (tel. 494 5020). Tube: Oxford Circus. *Saturday Night Fever*. £10-32.50. Student standbys for W matinee £10-£15.

Lyceum Theatre, Wellington St., WC2 (tel. 656 1803). Tube: Charing Cross. Musicals—call for information. £15-32.50. Conc. £15 1hr. before performance.

Lyric Hammersmith, King St., W6 (tel. (0181) 741 2311). Tube: Hammersmith. High-quality repertory comedies and drama from Ibsen to Coward. More experimental fringe-type doings in the Studio Theatre. £10-18. Mon. all seats £5.

Lyric Shaftesbury Theatre, Shaftesbury Ave., W1 (tel. 494 5045). Tube: Piccadilly Circus. *Rent.* Incredible rock 'n' roll theater. £7.50-26.

New London Theatre, Pirker St., WC2 (tel. 405 0072). Tube: Covent Garden. *Cats.* Singing, dancing cats, because hey, that's how T.S. Eliot would've wanted it. £12.50-32.50.

Old Vic, Waterloo Rd., SE1 (tel. 928 7616). Tube: Waterloo. Historic, famed repertory company in one of the most beautiful performance spaces in London. *Waiting for Godot, The Seagull,* and other high-brow theater. £13.50-30.

Open Air Theatre, Inner Circle, Regent's Park, NW1 (tel. 486 2431, 481 1933). Tube: Baker St. or Regent's Park. A musical, 2 Shakespeares, and a kids' show every summer; sit in the front to catch every word. 2:30pm matinees on Wed.-Thurs. and Sat. Bring a blanket and a bottle of wine. £8-20. Concessions 1hr. before showtime £6; kids' and late night shows £5.

Palace Theatre, Shaftesbury Ave., W1 (tel. 434 0909). Tube: Leicester Sq. *Les Miserables.* Singing, dancing French peasants, because hey, that's how Victor Hugo would've wanted it. £7-32.50.

Phoenix Theatre, Charing Cross Rd., WC2 (tel. 369 1733). Tube: Leicester Sq. *Blood Brothers;* a play loaded with sentimentality and frighteningly catchy tunes. £10.50-29.50, concessions £12.50.

Prince Edward Theatre, Old Compton St., W1 (tel. 447 5400). Tube: Leicester Sq. *West Side Story* through Jan. '98; *Ragtime* through spring. £16.50-32.50.

Prince of Wales Theatre, Coventry St., W1 (tel. 839 5987). Tube: Piccadilly Circus. *Smokey Joe's Café* through Apr. '99. F occasional ½-price matinee. £10-33.50. Student standbys £12.50.

St. Martin's Theatre, West St., WC2 (tel. 836 1443). Tube: Leicester Sq. Agatha Christie's *The Mousetrap* in its 5th decade. Not the original cast. £9-23.

Savoy Theatre, The Strand, WC2 (tel. 836 8888). Tube: Charing Cross. Varied—plays, musicals, and some ballets, mostly contemporary. £12.50-25.

Victoria Palace Theatre, Victoria St., SW1 (tel. 834 1317). Tube: Victoria. *Annie,* the irresistible orphan who sings and dances her way through depression-era New York. £15-30. Student standby £15.

Wyndham's Theatre, Charing Cross Rd., WC2 (tel. 369 1746). Tube: Leicester Sq. *Art* through October. £9.50-27.50.

OFF-WEST END AND FRINGE THEATERS

"The fringe" is what Londoners dub the dozens of smaller, less commercial theaters that nurture unrefined talents and stage the city's most cutting-edge productions. Born in the avant-garde late 1960s, the fringe today runs the gamut from amateur community productions to top notch experimental dramas. Ticket prices are lower than the West End (£4.50-10). All offer student and senior citizen's discounts in advance or at the door—no standby necessary. Off-West End theaters tend to be larger than the fringe performance spaces, but smaller than the grand West End spaces.

Lunchtime theater productions are generally less serious than evening performances, but at £2-4 they're a great way to start the afternoon. (Most productions start around 1:15pm.) Check the lunchtime listings at the end of *Time Out*'s theater section. The **King's Head** (see below) is probably the most successful at daytime shows. **St. Paul's Church,** at the central marketplace in Covent Garden, often has free lunchtime theater on its steps.

Almeida Theatre, Almeida St., N1 (tel. 359 4404). Tube: Angel or Highbury & Islington. A highly notable theater. The summer new opera series generates rave reviews from critics. Box office open M-Sa 10am-6pm.

Trinity Arts Center London, 17 Gloucester Terr., W2. Tube: Paddington, then Bus #27. Also served by Buses #7, 23, 36. Community theater based in Paddington—local kid's productions to guest companies. Student discounts. £2.50-7.

Battersea Arts Centre (BAC), Old Town Hall, 176 Lavender Hill, SW11 (tel. 223 2223). BR: Clapham Junction. One of the top fringe venues, with innovative productions and talented new playwrights. Main and 2 studio stages with "main-

stream" (radical corruptions of Shakespeare and other canonical texts) and experimental works, plus improv in the Arts Café. In Oct. holds British Festival of Visual Theatre. £6-8.50. Tu pay what you can.

The Bush, Bush Hotel, Shepherd's Bush Green, W12 (tel. (0181) 743 3388). Tube: Goldhawk Rd. or Shepherd's Bush. Above a busy old English pub. Well-known for producing innovative plays by new writers. 50p membership fee. Telephone booking M-Sa 10am-6pm. Box office open M-F from 6:30pm, Sa from 6:30pm. £10, concessions £7.

Donmar Warehouse, Earlham St., WC2 (tel. 369 1732). Tube: Covent Garden. Mainstream contemporary works. £12-18, concessions £8 1hr. before show.

Drill Hall, 16 Chenies St., WC1 (tel. 637 8270). Tube: Goodge St. Politically active productions, often with a gay slant. Vegetarian restaurant downstairs. Also workshops, darkroom, bar.

Etcetera Theatre, Oxford Arms, 265 Camden High St., NW1 (tel. 482 4857). Tube: Camden Town. Don't expect a lot of seating room in this super-small theater, but do look forward to frequent presentations of inventive, experimental plays by new playwrights. £5-7. Box office open M-Sa 10am-8pm.

The Gate, The Prince Albert, 11 Pembridge Rd., W11 (tel. 229 0706). Tube: Notting Hill Gate. Pub-theater with a big reputation hosts an international array of mostly new plays. £10, conc. £5. Box office open M-F 10am-½ hr. before performance.

Greenwich Theatre, Croom's Hill, SE18 (tel. (0181) 858 7755). BR: Greenwich. This friendly 423-seat venue mixes West End quality with fringe adventurousness. £9.25-15.50, concessions £5.50-6.50. Call ahead for wheelchair access.

Hampstead Theatre, Avenue Rd., Swiss Cottage Centre, NW3 (tel. 722 9301). Tube: Swiss Cottage. One of London's oldest small theaters: notable alumni like John "Mr. Sunshine" Malkovich. Much new writing. Shows change every 6-8 weeks. £8-13.50. Box office open M-Sa 10am-7:30pm. Concessions £5.

Holland Park Open Air Theatre, Holland Park, W8 (tel. 602 7856). Tube: Holland Park or High St. Kensington. Open-air stage with opera and ballet in the summer. £20, concessions £14.50.

King's Head, 115 Upper St., N1 (tel. 226 1916). Tube: Highbury & Islington or Angel. A Very Big Deal. The slightly ramshackle atmosphere of this pub theater is well known among dedicated London theater-goers as the first dinner-theater since Shakespeare's time. Kenneth Branagh and Ben Kingsley are alumni. Occasional lunchtime performances. £9-10, concessions £7.50.

Man in the Moon, 392 Kings Rd., SW3 (tel. 351 2876). A small pub-theater on its way to greatness. Last year's performances included the British premiere of *Oh What a Bloody Circus*. Open 6 nights a week, with 2 shows every night.

New End Theatre, 27 New End, NW3 (tel. 794 0022). Tube: Hampstead. New and classic works presented by local and touring companies. £5-10, students £7.

Old Red Lion, St. John's St., N1 (tel. 837 7816). Tube: Angel. Yet another of Islington's gems, the Lion is one of the top fringe theaters and usually presents intriguing plays by new writers. Box office open daily 10am-11pm.

Oval House, 52-54 Kennington Oval, SE11 (tel. 582 7680). Tube: Oval. Flamboyant, provocative productions by Black, Asian, lesbian, and gay playwrights. £6.50, conc. £3. Box office open M-F 5-8:30pm.

Theatre Royal Stratford East, Gerry Raffles Sq., E15 (tel. (0181) 534 0310). Tube: Stratford. Closed for refurbishment—call for details. £5-15. Box office open M-F 9:30am-6pm.

Tricycle Theatre, 269 Kilburn High Rd., NW6 (tel. 328 1000). Tube: Kilburn. A local favorite—some good avant-garde performances. Best known for new Black, Jewish, and Irish playwrights. £7.50-13. Box office open Mon.-Sat. 10am-8pm.

Young Vic, 66 The Cut, SE1 (tel. 928 6363). Tube: Waterloo. Inland from the actual river bank, across from the Old Vic. One of London's favorite and most acclaimed Off-West End venues. Presents theater in the round. £6-18. Box office open M-Sa 10am-6pm (by telephone) or curtain (in person).

Film

London's film scene offers everything from Arnold Schwarzenegger to French existentialism, from Hollywood dramas to Asian documentaries. The degenerate heart of the celluloid monster is **Leicester Square,** where the most recent hits premiere a day before hitting the chains around the city. West End first-run screens include the Empire (tel. 437 1234), Odeon Leicester Sq. (tel. (0181) 315 4215), and the Warner West End (tel. 437 4347), all at Leicester Sq. tube, as well as the Odeon Haymarket (tel. (0181) 315 4215; tube: Piccadilly Circus).

Thousands of films pass through the capital every year, old and new. Newspapers have listings, while *Time Out* covers both commercial films and the vast range of cheaper alternatives: late-night films, free films, "serious" films, and repertory cinema clubs. Also worth perusing are the ICA and NFT monthly schedules, available on-site (see listings below). Cinema clubs charge a small membership fee. This fee (usually 30p-£1.50) entitles cardholders and one guest to reduced admission. Some cards work at more than one cinema. Fees and cards make cinemas "clubs," and "clubs" can legally serve liquor, so most cinemas have bars and many have restaurants. For evening performances buy your ticket early or book in advance, especially on weekends. Many cinemas have assigned seating; ushers will help you find your place. Big theaters often charge different prices for different seats. Most London moviehouses charge £5-9, but many charge £3 all day Monday and for first shows Tuesday through Friday. Repertory and other cinemas include:

The Prince Charles, Leicester Pl., WC2 (tel. 437 8181). Tube: Leicester Sq. A Soho institution: 4 shows per day (cheerily deconstructed on the recorded phone message), generally second runs and a sprinkling of classics for only £2-2.50. Has a lively bar, and patrons may take their drinks into the cinema with them. Every Friday features the *Rocky Horror Picture Show,* complete with a live troupe for £6, concessions £3.

Everyman Cinema, Hollybush Vale, Hampstead, NW3 (tel. 435 1525). Tube: Hampstead. Double and triple bills based on themes and classic movie stars. Set to reopen this year with a coffee shop, and bookstore. Call for information.

Gate Cinema, Notting Hill Gate, W11 (tel. 727 4043). Tube: Notting Hill Gate. Art house films, with a repertory on Sun. Featured directors include Wim Wenders, Jane Campion, and Derek Jarman. £6.50, M-F before 6pm and late shows £3.50, Su matinee £4, concessions £3.

Goethe Institute, 50 Prince's Gate, Exhibition Rd., SW7 (tel. 411 3400). Tube: South Kensington. German classics and a sprinkling of U.S. favorites. £2.50.

Institute of Contemporary Arts (ICA) Cinema, Nash House, The Mall, W1 (tel. 930 3647). Tube: Piccadilly Circus or Charing Cross. Cutting-edge contemporary cinema, plus an extensive list of classics. Frequent special programs celebrating the work of a single director; recent tributes have lauded Rainer Fassbinder and Peter Greenaway. £6.50, concessions, M screenings, and first screenings Tu-F £5. Experimental films and classics in the *cinémathèque* £5.

ABC Swiss Centre, Leicester Sq., WC2 (tel. 439 4470). Tube: Leicester Sq. or Piccadilly Circus. New French films with subtitles, as well as artsy films not shown in other theaters. Hidden around the left side of the Centre. £6.50, concessions £4.

Minema, 45 Knightsbridge, W1 (tel. 369 1723). Tube: Knightsbridge or Hyde Park Corner. Small screen behind a tiny door, showing reborn art classics and popular foreign films as well as "commercial art." £7.50, M-F before 5pm £5.50.

National Film Theatre (NFT), South Bank Centre, SE1 (tel. 928 3232 for box office). Tube: Waterloo, or Embankment and cross the Hungerford footbridge. One of the world's leading cinemas, with a mind-boggling array of film, TV, and video in its three auditoria. Program changes daily but is arranged in seasonal series. Home of the London Film Festival, held in Nov. For ticket availability, call 633 0274. Annual membership gives discounted tickets, mailings, and priority bookings (£11.95, concs. £8). Most main screenings £5, members and concessions £3.50.

Phoenix, 52 High Rd., N2 (tel. (0181) 883 2233, 444 6789). Tube: East Finchley. Double bills mix and match European, American, and Asian mainstream hits and

classics. Children's cinema club on Sa mornings. £4.50, all day M and afternoons £3, students (except Sa night) £3, children £2, seniors £2.50.

The Ritzy Cinema, Brixton Oval, Coldharbour Ln., SW2 (tel. 737 2121, reservations 733 2229). Tube: Brixton. This classy old-style picture house shows a combination of artsy and mainstream films. Tickets £6, concessions £3.

Music

Gustav Holst, the Beatles, and the Sex Pistols are all reflected in the diversity of London's current music scene. Unparalleled classical resources include five world-class orchestras, two opera houses, two huge arts centers, and countless concert halls. Additionally, London serves as the port of call for popular music: any rocker hoping to storm the British Isles, or conquer the world from Liverpool, Dublin, or Manchester, must first gig successfully in one of the capital's numerous clubs.

Check the listings in *Time Out.* Keep your eyes open for special festivals or gigs posted on most of the city's surfaces and for discounts posted on student union bulletin boards. Keep in mind that many troupes take the summer off.

CLASSICAL

London's world-class orchestras provide only a fraction of the notes that fill its major music centers. London has been the professional home of some of the greatest conductors of the century—Sir Thomas Beecham, Otto Klemperer, and Andre Previn.

Barbican Hall, Barbican Centre (tel. 638 4141 or 638 8891 for box office; internet: www.barbican.org.uk). Tube: Barbican or Moorgate. Houses the venerable London Symphony Orchestra. Also welcomes a number of guest artists. Concerts £6-30, student and senior standby tickets sold shortly before the performance £6-8.

Blackheath Concert Halls, 23 Lee Rd., Blackheath, SE3 (tel. (0181) 463 0100). BR (from Charing Cross): Blackheath, then left from the station. Attracts top performers year-round, and serves as a venue for the Greenwich and Docklands Festival (see below). £3.50-20.

Royal Albert Hall, Kensington Gore, SW7 (tel. 589 8212). Tube: South Kensington. Exuberant and skilled, the Proms (BBC Henry Wood Promenade Concerts) never fail to enliven London summers. Every day for 8 weeks between the end of July and mid-Sept., an impressive roster of musicians performs outstanding programs, including annually commissioned new works. Camaraderie and craziness develop in the long lines for standing room outside. The last night of the Proms traditionally steals the show, with the massed singing of "Land of Hope and Glory" and "Jerusalem." Don't expect to show up at the last minute and get in. A lottery of thousands determines who will be allowed to paint their faces as Union Jacks and "air-conduct" in person. Gallery £2 (the tippy-top of the theatre), arena £3 (the floor of the hall, best seats in the house but you gotta stand)—join the queue around 6pm; £4-18, sometimes £4-23 or £4-30 for special performances. Box office open daily 9am-9pm, or try Ticketmaster (tel. 379 4444).

South Bank Centre (tel. 960 4242). Tube: Waterloo, or Embankment and cross the Hungerford footbridge. 3 venues here host classical shows. The 2500-seat **Royal Festival Hall** often houses the **London Philharmonic** and the **Philharmonia Orchestra.** The 2 other venues in the South Bank Centre, the **Queen Elizabeth Hall** and the **Purcell Room,** also host some classical shows. Summer season booking begins in early May. Tickets for the RFH £5-35, for the QEH and PR £8-12. Students, seniors, and children receive a discount of around £2 for advance tickets, and can queue for standbys (usually a little over ½-price) from 5pm on the night of performances. Box office open daily 10am-9pm.

St. John's, Smith Square, converted church just off Millbank (tel. 222 1061). Tube: Westminster. A schedule weighted toward chamber groups and soloists. £6-20, occasional concessions for students and seniors.

Wigmore Hall, 36 Wigmore St., W1 (tel. 935 2141). Tube: Bond St. or Oxford Circus. Small, elegant, and Victorian. Many young artists debut here. Master concerts and chamber music series. Tickets £6-35. 1hr. standbys at lowest price. In summer,

Su morning coffee concerts begin at 11:30am; £8, coffee free. Closed end of July through Aug. Box office open 10am-7pm, until 8:30pm in person.

The two main locations of the Barbican and the Royal Festival Hall, as well as the South Bank's smaller halls, the **Queen Elizabeth Hall** and the **Purcell Room,** play host to a superb lineup of groups, including the **Academy of St. Martin-in-the-Fields,** the **London Festival Orchestra,** the **London Chamber Orchestra,** the **London Soloists Chamber Orchestra,** the **London Classical Players,** and the **London Mozart Players,** as well as diverse national and international orchestras. Vladimir Ashkenazy's **Royal Philharmonic Orchestra** performs at both the Barbican and the South Bank, and the **BBC Symphony Orchestra** pops up around town as well. Although the regular season ends in mid-July, a series of festivals on the South Bank in July and August take up the slack admirably, offering traditional orchestral music along with more exotic tidbits (tickets £3-20). Festivals include:

City of London Festival (tel. 638 8891; email cityfest@dircon.co.uk). Tube: St. Paul's. Explosion of activity around the city's grandest monuments: music in the livery halls and churches, plays at various venues, grand opera, art exhibitions, and a trail of dance winding among the monuments. June 22-July 15, 1999. Box office (Barbican Centre, Silk St. entrance) open daily 9am-8pm. Many events free, most others £10-30. Call for information from early May.

Greenwich and Docklands International Festival (tel. (0181) 305 1818). Opening night ceremonies culminate in a fireworks show so big it shuts down the river. Other events include free concerts in Greenwich Park (see **Greenwich and Blackheath,** p. 204) and other area venues. '99 dates: July 9-18. Free-£14.

Kenwood Lakeside Concerts, at Kenwood, on Hampstead Heath (tel. 973 3427, 344 4444 for Ticketmaster booking with an unpleasant £1 service charge). Tube: Golders Green or Archway, then bus #210; or East Finchley, then take a free shuttle bus to Kenwood (5-7:50pm, and after concerts until 10:45pm). The concerts are on the North side of Hampstead Heath. The National Symphony Orchestra, the English National Opera, and others offer top-notch outdoor performances, often graced by firework displays and laser shows. Every summer (mid-June to Aug. 30) at 7:30pm, music floats to the audience from a performance shell across the lake. Reserved deck chairs £12-16.50, concs. £9-13. Grass admission £9-13, concs. £7.50-11.50. If "outdoor" is more important than "concert," you can listen from afar for free. Limited free parking available.

Lufthansa Festival of Baroque Music, main site at St. James's Church, Piccadilly (tel. 437 5053). Tube: Piccadilly Circus. One of the top period music festivals in the world. Held yearly in Jun.-July. Baroque tunes from throughout Europe. £5-15.

Marble Hill House (tel. 413 1443 for booking). Tube/BR: Richmond, then Bus R70. Hosts outdoor concerts in summer Su at 7:30pm. Bring a blanket and picnic on the grounds of this stately house (mid- July to late Aug.). £12, concs. £10.50.

Medieval and Renaissance music still commands a following in England; many London churches offer performances, often at lunchtime. Premier among them are **St. Martin-in-the-Fields,** Trafalgar Sq. (tel. 839 8362; tube: Charing Cross); **St. James's Piccadilly** (see above); and **St. Bride's,** Fleet St. (tel. 353 1301; tube: Blackfriars). **St. Paul's boys' choir** sings at the Sunday 5pm service. Concerts are usually free. Watch for the **Academy of Ancient Music,** the **Early Music Consort of London,** and the **Praetorius Ensemble.**

Artists from the **Royal College of Music,** Prince Consort Rd., SW7 (tel. 589 3643) and the **Royal Academy of Music,** Marylebone Rd., NW1 (tel. 935 5461) play at their home institutions and at the main city halls. Concerts at these schools are often free—call for details. Check with the **University of London Union,** 1 Malet St., WC1 (tel. 580 9551; tube: Goodge St.) for on-campus music there.

OPERA AND BALLET

Victoria Embankment Gardens. Tube: Embankment. Popular, free *al fresco* opera in the Victoria Embankment gardens summer W-Sa at 6pm.

Holland Park Theatre, box office in the Visitor Centre (tel. 602 7856). Tube: Holland Park. Open-air opera from a number of companies early June to late Aug., in both English and the original languages. Some dance and classical music, too. £24, children, seniors, and students £18.50.

London Coliseum, St. Martin's La., WC2 (tel. 632 8300; fax 379 1264). Tube: Charing Cross or Leicester Sq. The English National Opera's (ENO) repertoire leans toward the contemporary, and all works are sung in English. Seats reserved in advance range £6.50-55. The Half-Price Ticket Booth sells tickets the day of the show if available (see p. 227), or you can show up at the box office weekdays (and Sa matinees) from 10am to claim the 100 day seats in the balcony for £5. Standby seats also available 3hr. before the performance; the best seats go first. Weekdays, students and seniors get the best seats available (1 per person, £18). Saturday, anyone can get standby tickets for £28. If all of these tickets are sold out, they will also sell a few standing room tickets on the day of performance for £5. From mid-July to September, when the ENO is off, various visiting ballet companies perform, including the Kirov Ballet, American Ballet Theatre, and Royal Swedish Ballet.

Peacock Theatre, Portugal St. WC2 (tel. 314 8800, 305 1818). Tube: Holborn. The Sadler's Wells organization currently occupies this space as their theatre is being rebuilt. Hosts modern and contemporary dance troupes. Box office open daily 8am-8pm.

The Place, 17 Duke's Rd., WC1 (tel. 387 0031). Tube: Euston. Britain's national contemporary dance center. Four seasons showcasing new/experimental dance, independent British dance, Continental and Oriental dance. Put on your boogie shoes for the evening dance classes (around £5, concessions £3; call 388 8430 for details). Performances £4-10.

Royal Festival Hall, see South Bank Centre, above. Visiting ballet companies and the English National Ballet grace the stage year-round. £10-35.

Royal Opera House, at Covent Garden, Box St.; box office at 48 Floral St., WC2 (tel. 304 4000; fax 497 1256). Tube: Covent Garden. The Royal Opera House is going to be closed for refurbishment until November 1999, but both the opera and ballet will be touring around London. Ticket prices at this grand old venue do much to keep ballet and opera an amusement of the idle rich. Tickets for the resident companies, the **Royal Opera** and the **Royal Ballet,** come in a bewildering variety of prices and flavors. Since both companies are touring, it's best to call the box office for ticket prices. Box office open M-Sa 10am-7pm.

ROCK, POP, JAZZ, AND FOLK

London generates and attracts almost every type of performer under the sun. The clubs and pubs of the capital offer a wide, strange, and satisfying variety of musical entertainment. Often, thrash metallists play the same venue as Gaelic folk singers, so check weekly listings carefully. *Time Out* and *What's On* have extensive listings and information about bookings and festivals. Also try the Friday *Evening Standard's* insert *Hot Tickets.* You can make credit card reservations for major events by calling **Ticketmaster** (tel. 344 4444). If you do not buy your tickets directly from the venue's box office, you may be charged a booking fee.

Rock and Pop

Major venues for rock concerts include the indoor **Wembley Arena** and the huge outdoor **Wembley Stadium** (tel. (0181) 900 1234; tube: Wembley Park or Wembley Central), the **Royal Albert Hall** (see **Classical Music,** p. 241), and the **Forum** (see below). In the summer, many outdoor arenas such as **Finsbury Park** become venues for major concerts and festivals.

Apollo Hammersmith, Queen Caroline St., W6 (tel. 416 6080). Tube: Hammersmith. Mainstream rock. Tickets £17.50, 22.50, 27.50, or 32.50. Box office phones answered M-Sa 8am-9:30pm, Su 10am-8pm.

Astoria, 157 Charing Cross Rd., WC2 (tel. 434 0403). Tube: Tottenham Ct. Rd. Hot and sweaty hard rock, but the patrons don't seem to mind. Capacity 1800. £7-16. Open M-Sa 10:30am-5:30pm.

Borderline, Orange Yard, off Manette St., WC2 (tel. 734 2095). Tube: Tottenham Ct. Rd. British record companies test new rock and pop talent in this basement club. £5-9, student discount £5. Music nights range from indie to industrial.

Brixton Academy, 211 Stockwell Rd., SW9 (tel. 924 9999). Tube: Brixton. Time-honored, rowdy venue for a wide variety of music, including rock, reggae, rap, and alternative. 4300 capacity. £8-25. Box office takes cash only—book ahead with a credit card. MC, Visa.

Dublin Castle, 94 Parkway St. (tel. 485 1773). Tube: Camden Town. Irish pub facade hides one of London's most legendary indie clubs. A no-holds-barred joint. 3-4 bands a night, usually starting at 9pm. £3.50-9.

Forum, 9-17 Highgate Rd., NW5 (Ticketmaster 344 0044). Tube: Kentish Town. Night bus #N2. Top-notch audio system in a popular venue that was formerly the Town-and-Country Club. Open Su-Th 7-11pm, F-Sa 7pm-2am. £7.50-17.50.

Garage, 20-24 Highbury Corner, N5 (tel. 607 1818). Tube: Highbury and Islington. Night bus #N92 or N65. Club/performance space with decent views. Rock, pop, and indie bands most nights. £4-12.50. Music starts 8:30pm.

Hackney Empire, 291 Mare St., E8 (tel. (0181) 985 2424). Tube: Bethnal Green then Bus #253 north or BR: Hackney Central. Comedy theater hosts popular routines like the Caribbean duo Bello and Blacka. £3-12. Prices and hours vary by show.

Half Moon Putney, 93 Lower Richmond Rd., SW15 (tel. (0181) 780 9383). Tube: Putney Bridge. Rocking pub with a mix of rock, jazz, and folk. £3-7. Music starts at 8:30-9:45pm (see **Hammersmith and Putney,** p. 130).

London Palladium, 8 Argyll St., W1 (tel. 494 5020). Tube: Oxford Circus. They've hosted Lou Reed. Serves primarily as a theater venue. Music usually starts at 7:30pm. Capacity 2312. £10-32.50. W 2:30 matinees £6.

Mean Fiddler, 24-28 Harlesden High St., NW10 (tel. (0181) 963 0940). Tube: Willesden Junction. Night Bus #N18. Cavernous club with good bars, mixing country & western, folk, and indie. Tu-Th 8pm-2am, F-Sa 8:30pm-3am, Su 8pm-1am. £10-15.

Rock Garden, The Piazza, Covent Garden, WC2 (tel. 240 3961). Tube: Covent Garden. A variety of great new bands play nightly £5—rock, indie, acid jazz, soul. Happy hour daily 5-8pm, cover £2, all drinks £1. Th pop, F live music, Su '70s disco. Open M-Th 5pm-3am, F 5pm-6am, Sa 4pm-4am, Su 7-3am.

Royal Albert Hall, Kensington Gore, SW7 (tel. 589 8212). Tube: South Kensington. Elton John, Elvis Costello, Eric Clapton, and others. Box office open daily 9am-9pm. (See **Royal Albert Hall,** p. 241.)

Shepherd's Bush Empire, Shepherds Bush Green, W12 (tel. (0181) 740 7474). Tube: Shepherds Bush. Hosts dorky cool musicians like David Byrne, the Proclaimers, and Boy George. 2000 capacity, with 6 bars. Concerts £6-20.

Wembley Stadium and **Wembley Arena,** Empire Way, Wembley (tel. (0181) 902 0902). Tube: Wembley Park or Wembley Central. A football (soccer) stadium. Take a pair of binoculars. Open M-Sa 8am-9pm, Su 9am-8pm. £25-65. The **Arena** is the largest indoor venue in London, serving high-priced refreshments. Open 6:30-11pm selected nights. £16-30.

The Venue, 2A Clifton Rise, New Cross, SE14 (tel. (0181) 692 4077). Tube: New Cross, Night Bus #N77. Getting to be a big indie scene. Dancing goes late into the night. Open F-Sa 8pm-4am; music starts 8pm. £5-6, £3 before 9pm.

Jazz

In the summer, hundreds of jazz festivals appear in the city and its outskirts, including July's **City of London Festival** (tel. 377 0540) and the **JVC Capital Radio Jazz, Funk, and Soul Festival** (Royal Albert Hall box office tel. 589 8212). Ronnie Scott's, Bass Clef, and Jazz Café are the most popular clubs. Jazz clubs often stay open much later than pubs.

100 Club, 100 Oxford St., W1 (tel. 636 0933). Tube: Tottenham Ct. Rd. A melange of traditional modern jazz, swing, and blues hidden behind a battered doorway. Staged one of the Sex Pistols' 1st London gigs. Fridays are indie dance nights and Saturdays welcomes big band jazz. Discount for groups of 5 or more. £5-8. Open Su-Th 7:30pm-midnight, F 7:30pm-3am, Sa 7:30pm-1am.

606 Club, 90 Lots Rd., SW10 (tel. 352 5953). Tube: Fulham Broadway. Blossoming talent along with household names in diverse styles. Open M-Sa 8:30pm-2am, Su 8:30pm-midnight. Music begins M-W 9:30pm, Th-Sa 10pm, Su 9:30pm. Non-members are not allowed on the weekend without eating dinner. Cover Su-Th £4, F-Sa £4.50.

Blue Note, 1 Hoxton Sq., N1 (tel. 837 6900). Tube: Old St., Night Bus N96. New ownership of one of London's most P-funkified jazz houses has maintained the club's soulful reputation. Tu-W modern funk jazz. M and Th-Sa dance club nights (see p. 247). Hours vary with shows but usually are Tu 10pm-3am for jazz. £3-8, concession prices available for some shows.

Bull's Head, Barnes Bridge, SW13 (tel. (0181) 876 5241). Tube: Hammersmith, then Bus 9. A waterside pub renowned for good food and modern jazz and funk. £3-8. Open M-Sa 11am-11pm, Su noon-10:30pm. Music starts at 8:30pm and Su 2-5.

Jazz Café, 5 Parkway, Camden Town, NW1 (tel. 344 0044). Tube: Camden Town. Night Bus #N93. Top new venue in a converted bank. Classic and experimental jazz with threads of Latin, soul, and African. Tickets for shows £6-18, cover £3. Open M-Th 7pm-midnight, F-Sa 7pm-2am, Su noon-5pm and 7-11pm.

Jazz at Pizza Express, 10 Dean St., W1 (tel. 439 8722). Tube: Tottenham Ct. Rd. or Leicester Sq. Packed, dark club hiding behind a pizzeria. Fantastic groups and occasional greats; get there early. Cover £10-20. Music daily 9pm-midnight; doors open at 7:45pm. Restaurant open daily 11:30am-12:30am.

Pizza on the Park, 11 Knightsbridge, Hyde Park Corner, SW1 (tel. 235 5273). Tube: Hyde Park Corner. Another Pizza Express branch that hosts mainstream jazz musicians. Music starts 9:15pm. £18. Restaurant open daily 8am-midnight.

Ronnie Scott's, 47 Frith St., W1 (tel. 439 0747; fax 437 5081). Tube: Leicester Sq. or Piccadilly Circus. The most famous jazz club in London and one of the oldest in the world; saw the likes of Ella Fitzgerald and Dizzy Gillespie. Expensive food (but don't overlook the various starters; £2.75-5.25) and great music. Waiters masterfully keep noisy clients from ruining the music by politely telling them to shut up. Open fabulously late—the music just keeps going. Cover £15, 26 and under £8. Book ahead or arrive by 9:30pm. Box office open M-F 11am-6pm, Sa 12:30pm-6pm. Music 9:30pm-2am. Open M-Sa 8:30pm-3am.

Folk and Roots

To a large extent, folk music in London means Irish music. But aside from the Celtic variety, the term "folk" covers a whole host of musical hybrids including acoustic folk rock, political tunes, folky blues, and even English country & western. Some of the best are free, but welcome donations.

Africa Centre, 38 King St., WC2 (tel. 836 1973). Tube: Covent Garden. African music and dance. More of a cultural center than a club. African music Friday nights 9pm-3am. Cover £7. (See **Nightclubs,** p. 246.)

Bunjie's, 27 Litchfield St., WC2 (tel. 240 1796). Tube: Covent Garden. Packed vegetarian restaurant with folk and almost-folk groups; lively, dancing audience. Cover £3-3.50, students £2. Open M-Sa noon-11pm. Intimate venue for folk music, featured M-W and Sa 8:30-11pm. Poetry night F 8-11pm. Comedy Th 8-11pm.

Cecil Sharpe House, 2 Regent's Park Rd., NW1 (tel. 485 2206). Tube: Camden Town. Night Bus #N2, N29, or N93. Regents canal-side view. Happening folk scene with singing and dancing. £3-5. Open Tu 7-11pm, Th-Sa 7:30pm-11pm, but events take place throughout the week.

Halfway House, 142 The Broadway, West Ealing, W13 (tel. (0181) 567 0236). Tube: Ealing Broadway. Irish, Cajun, and blues. Open M-Sa 11am-midnight, Su noon-10:30pm. Free.

The Mean Fiddler, 22-28 Harlesden Hight St., NW10 (tel. (0181) 961 5490). Tube: Willesden Junction. Superb performers, with a decidedly "alternative" slant. Open daily 8pm-midnight. Box office 9:15am-7pm. £4-8.

Troubadour Coffee House, 265 Old Brompton Rd., SW5 (tel. 370 1434). Tube: Earl's Ct. Acoustic entertainment served up in a warm cafe. Bob Dylan and Paul Simon played here early in their careers. W cafe becomes "Institute for Acoustic Research"; M attracts some of the best poets around. F-Sa folk and jazz. Now offers classical music—call for info. Cover £4.50, concessions £3.50. Open 8pm-11pm.

Weavers, 98 Newington Green Rd., N1 (tel. 354 9501). Tube: Highbury and Islington. Head straight along St. Pauls, left on Newington Green, or take Bus #70 or 277 to Newington Green. Well-respected folk and country acts. £2-6. Open M-Sa 8:30pm-midnight, Su 8-10:30.

Nightclubs

London pounds to 100% Groovy Liverpool tunes, ecstatic Manchester rave, hometown soul and house, imported U.S. hip-hop, and Jamaican reggae. Fashion evolves and revolves, but **black** (and simple) **is always in,** and dress codes (denoted in listings as DC), when they exist, are rarely more elaborate than standard London wear.

In a scene striving to exude effortless extravagance, budget clubbing is a bit difficult. If you must go out with the rest of the city on Friday and Saturday, **show up before the pubs close**—perverse things happen to cover charges after 11pm. Though it's always cooler to slide in fashionably late, earlier's cheaper and the beautiful people will glare enviously at your table when they slink in after midnight.

Take advantage of your tourist status and **party during the week**—though there are fewer options, London has enough tourists, slackers, and devoted party people to pack a few clubs even on Sunday through Wednesday. On these nights, covers rarely top £4, and drink specials abound. Many clubs host a variety of provocative weekly, fortnightly, or monthly one-nighters (e.g. "Horny"), where the club is rented out to independent DJs and promoters. Travelers with fewer scruples than pounds will often call clubs during the day and try to weasel their way onto the guest list, often by expressing a desire to hire the club for such purposes. If you see a cover price prefixed by "NUS (National Union of Students)," an ISIC card or halfway legit-looking college ID should fetch a discount.

For the discriminating clubber, planning is important—**look before you leap, and especially before you drink.** Wandering around drunk after the pubs close looking for a disco is the surest way to end up paying £10 to drink £5 beers and dance the Macarena with prepubescent Essex kids in some glitzy tourist trap. It is best to avoid the bright glitzy clubs in Leicester Square. These tend to be tourist traps saturated with a clientele more interested in pawing then dancing. *Time Out* is the undisputed scene cop, their starred picks of the day are usually a safe bet, and will inevitably be crowded with *Time Out* readers (a generally young, hip, and slightly spendy crowd). Don't let bouncers sweat you. If they tell you "members and regulars only," they don't think you'll fit in, but if you persist you may be able to talk your way in (the clientele are on average much less pretentious than the doorman). If there's no queue and it's less than two hours before closing, you may not have to pay full cover, so try to strike a deal. Remember that the tube shuts down two or three hours before most clubs and that taxis can be hard to find in the wee hours of the morning. Some late-night frolickers catch "minicabs," little unmarked cars that sometimes wait outside clubs (see **Essentials**, p. 69). Arrange transportation in advance or acquaint yourself with the extensive network of night buses (tel. 222 1234 for information). Listings include some of the night bus routes that connect to venues outside of central London, but routes change and a quick double-check is recommended. **Call ahead** for times, prices, and special events as they often change.

For gay and lesbian clubs, see **Bisexual, Gay, and Lesbian London**, p. 264.

Africa Centre, 38 King St., WC2 (tel. 836 1973). Tube: Covent Garden. Art center by day, psychedelic, blacklit den of funk by night. Live African music at the "Limpopo

Club" most Fridays, but Saturday's "Funkin' Pussy" lets Funkateers shake booty to vintage funk and hip-hop. Spontaneous breakdancing. F 9pm-3am, cover £5 in advance, £6 at the door; Sa 9pm-3am, cover before 11pm £3, after 11pm £7, concessions £5. (See **Folk and Roots,** p. 239.)

Bar Rumba, 36 Shaftesbury Ave., W1 (tel. 287 6933). Tube: Piccadilly Circus. ¡Muy caliente! The legion of industrial fans aren't enough to keep things cool at this basement bar and dance floor. At Tuesday's excellent "Salsa Pa'Ti," a seemingly random crowd of all ages and nationalities are fused into one nation under a salsa groove. The dancing is somewhat formal, so if you can't tango, cha-cha, or pachanga, arrive at 7pm for instruction (£6, cover included), or look forlorn and one of the fledgling Latin lovers will volunteer to "teach you." Dancing is informal other nights, but the Latin flavor persists, the bar serves 'til 3am, and the cover's low. Cover goes up each hour after 9pm on busy nights, so come early or pay anywhere from £6-12. Open most nights 5pm-3:30am, Fridays 'til 4am, Saturdays 'til 6am. Call ahead.

Blue Note, 1 Hoxton Sq., N1 (tel. 837 6900). Tube: Old St. A new club on the cutting edge of the London dance scene, where DJs searching for the perfect beat nightly perfect genres most Americans have never heard of, taking dub, drum 'n' bass, house, and garage to other levels. £8-10. Open M-Th 9pm-3am, F-Sa 10pm-5am, Su 6pm-2am.

The Bug Bar, The Crypt, St. Matthew's Church, Brixton Hill, SW2 (tel. 738 3184). Tube: Brixton. Trendy Brixton hangout in the basement of St. Matthew's church. Decked out with fantastically comfortable velvet sofas and a sizeable dance floor. Different DJs every night. Cover varies. Open M-F 5pm-late, Sa-Su 11am-late (closing times vary according to events).

The Camden Palace, 1a Camden High St. NW1 (tel. 387 0428). Tube: Camden Town. Night Bus #N2, N29, or N90. Huge and hugely popular with tourists and Brits alike. Friday's "Peach" packs 'em in with house and garage, while Tuesday's "Feet First" does the same with indie, Britpop, and the occasional live act. £2-10. Open Tu 10pm-2am, F-Sa 10pm-6am.

Club 414, 414 Coldharbour Ln., SW2 (tel. 924 9322 or (0802) 774 699). Tube: Brixton. Groove to melodic deep house, underground, and garage at this lesser-known dance venue. Downstairs offers laser lights; upstairs is "melo melo" chill-out floor. £7 entry, members £5. Bar open until 2am, juice bar open all night. Open Th-Sa 10pm-6am, Su 6pm-2am.

The Electric Ballroom, 184 Camden High St., NW1 (tel. 485 9006). Tube: Camden Town. Night Bus N2, N29, N90, or N93. Cheap and fun. "Saturday Night Fever" offers free admission to those bedecked in suitable 70s attire. Most of the clientele refuse to wear natural fibers. Cover £7, members £5-6.

The Fridge, Town Hall Parade, Brixton Hill, SW2 (tel. 326 5100). Tube: Brixton. "Love Muscle" on Saturday is one of the biggest, most popular 1-nighters in all of London. Totally packed; get there early or get ready to queue. Mixed crowd. Open Sa 10pm-6am. Cover £8 before 11pm, £10 before midnight or after 3am; £12 otherwise. Cafe open Su 6am-11am for chill out session and breakfast.

The Hanover Grand, 6 Hanover St., W1 (tel. 499 7977). Tube: Oxford Circus. Big, big fun in large, loud funkified atmosphere. Where the swingers go to get down to underground garage and hip-hop. Don't be afraid to dress all out. £5-15. On Wednesdays before 11pm only £3. Open Tuesday for venues only, W-F 10:30pm-4am, Sa 10:30pm-5am.

Iceni, 11 White Horse St., W1 (tel. 495 5333). Tube: Green Park. Off Curzon St. 3 beautiful floors of deep funk entertainment in this stylish Mayfair hotspot. Often wildly different beats between floors, from Swing to 80s to techno. £10-12. Open F 11pm-3am, Sa 10pm-3am.

Jazz Bistro, 340 Farringdon St., EC1 (tel. 236 8112). Tube: Farringdon. With a handle like "Jazz Bistro" it's amazing how unpretentious this place is. A refreshing enclave of Farringdon bohemian on the fringe of the decidedly un-boho City, this joint serves up the freshest beats in town, both live and canned. On weekends, Bright Young People pack into the basement and intimate dance floor to boogie among the trippy visual projections. Cover never tops £4. Open nightly 10pm-3am.

Legends, 29 Old Burlington St., W1 (tel. 437 9933). Tube: Green Park, Piccadilly Circus, or Oxford Circus. Excellent one-nighters in this dark, chrome-lined dance

club. Thursday is "Horny" with garage grooves and a "devilish, wicked, and horny" dress code. Bring your pheromones and bump and grind with the sleek Beautiful People of Mayfair. £7-15. Open Th 10pm-3:30am, F-Sa 10pm-4am.

Ministry of Sound, 103 Gaunt St., SE1 (tel. 378 6528). Tube: Elephant and Castle. Night buses #N12, N62, N65, N72, N77, or N78. Mega-club with long queues, beefy covers, beautiful people, and pumping house tunes, but beware—bouncers concoct the "most appropriate" crowd, so without the right look you'll be eternally stuck in the queue. One of the first major rave spots. Cover F £10, Sa £15. Open F 10:30pm-6:30am, Sa midnight-9am.

The Roadhouse, Jubilee Hull, 35 The Piazza, WC2 (tel. 240-6001). Tube: Covent Garden. Mix with the natives at this lively club in the middle of Covent Garden. Excellent live cover bands every night (2 bands on Saturday) spice up the place and let you know that everyone is getting what they want, what they really really want—a good time. Cover £3-10. Open M-Th 5:30pm-3am, F 4:30pm-3am, Sa 6:30pm-3am.

Subterania, 12 Acklam Rd., W10 (tel. (0181) 960 4590). Tube: Ladbroke Grove. This is where it's at—directly beneath the Westway flyover. Relaxed, multi-ethnic crowd comes to dance to wicked house and garage music. Club classics and "90s disco." Cover £5-10. Open M-Sa 9pm-3:30am.

The Underworld, 174 Camden High St., NW1 (tel. 482 1932). Tube: Camden Town. Across the street from the tube. Huge, fire station-like pub leads into soul center and techno training camp downstairs. Thursday night is "Stardust County," with indie DJ and moshers. Cover £2-5.

Velvet Underground, 143 Charing Cross Rd. (tel. 439 4655). Tube: Tottenham Ct. Rd. Velvet-soaked bar and leisure lounge combined with pumping house and techno dance club after 10pm. Particularly cheap and juicy during the week; various promotions attract the young and foreign. F-Sa free before 10pm. Cover varies from £6-10. Open M-Th 5pm-3am, F 5pm-4am, Sa 8pm-4am.

The Wag Club, 35 Wardour St., W1 (tel. 437 5534). Tube: Piccadilly Circus. Known just as "The Wag," this funky, multi-level complex features bars and an eatery among the carefully coifed clientele. Two dance floors and a wild variety of beats guarantee some groove for everyone's taste. M-Th £4, F £9, Sa £10; £1 less with flier before 11pm. Open M-Th 10pm-3:30am, F 10:30pm-4am, Sa 10:30pm-5am.

Off the Beaten Path

London, that great cesspool into which all the loungers and idlers of the Empire are irresistibly drained.

—Sir Arthur Conan Doyle, *A Study in Scarlet*

If you've got the cash, you can indulge in luxuries like rowing boats in the pond at Regent's Park or being wrapped by beauty consultants in the latest combination of mud, seaweed, and turtle spit. If you haven't, there are other options for entertainment that won't break the budget traveler's bank.

City Farms: Goats, ducks, sheep, poultry, and sometimes cattle, horses, and donkeys bleat, quack, baa, moo, and cluck at **Kentish Town,** 1 Cressfield Close, off Grafton Rd., NW5 (tel. 916 5420; tube: Kentish Town; open Tu-Su 9:30am-5:30pm; **pony rides** Su from 1pm); **Freightliners,** Sheringham Rd., N7 (tel. 609 0467; tube: Highbury & Islington; open Tu-Su 9am-1pm and 2-5pm); **Hackney,** 1a Goldsmith's Row, E2 (tel. 729 6381; tube: Bethnal Green; open Tu-Su 10am-4:30pm); **Muchute City Farm,** Pier St., E14 (tel. 515 5901; open daily 8am-5pm, sometimes later on Tu and Th); **Stepping Stones,** Stepney Way, E1 (tel. 790 8204; tube: Stepney Green; open Tu-Su 10am-6pm); and **Surrey Docks,** Rotherhithe St., SE16 (tel. 231 1010; tube: Surrey Quays; open Tu-Th and Sa-Su 10am-1pm and 2-5pm). Call to confirm times. All are free.

The College of Psychic Studies, 16 Queensberry Pl., SW7 (tel. 589 3292). Tube: South Kensington. Increase your psychic sensitivity through lectures (£4), musical events (free-£7), and evening courses (£39-70) dealing with healing and spiritual awareness. Open M-Th 10am-7:30pm, F 10am-5pm.

Daily Mail and **Evening Standard.** Tour the plants of one of these tabloids. Witness an actual press run, and finally get your chance to (ineffectually) yell "Stop the presses!" For information write at least a month in advance to Managing Director John Bird, Harmsworth Quays Printers Ltd., Surrey Quays Rd., SE16 1PI.

Islington Arts Factory, 2 Parkhurst Rd., N7 (tel. 607 0561). Tube: Holloway Rd. Exit left onto Holloway Rd. Turn left onto Camden Rd., which leads to the corner of Camden and Parkhurst. Music, art, and dance studios available for hire. The Factory itself offers classes and sponsors small free exhibitions. For £4-6.50 per hr. (in the daytime) you can rent a music room fully equipped with a drum set, P.A., and mikes. (£10 annual membership fee required to enroll in classes.) Open M-Th 10am-10pm, F 10am-7:30pm, Sa 2-5pm.

London College of Fashion, 20 John Princes St., W1 (tel. 514 7400). Tube: Oxford Circus. If you want some pampering and have a few quid and a few hours to spare, offer yourself to the students at the LCF's beauty-therapy department, where they learn how to give everything from cathiodermie to pedicures. Prices (to cover the cost of products used) start from £3 for a haircut. Open Oct.-June M-F 9am-5pm, but call to make an appointment—no walk-ins.

Old Bailey (tel. 248 3277), at the corner of Old Bailey and Newgate St. Tube: St. Paul's. Technically the Central Criminal Courts, but infamous as the site of Britain's grimiest prison, Old Bailey crouches under a copper dome and a wide-eyed figure of Justice. Trial-watching persists as a favorite diversion, and the Old Bailey fills up whenever a gruesome or scandalous case is in progress. Enter the public Visitors' Gallery and watch bewigged barristers at work. Cameras, phones, drinks, food, large bags, and backpacks may not be taken inside. If you order a pint at the pub across the street, they may offer to keep an eye on your stuff. Open M-F 10:30am-1pm and 2-4:30pm; entrance in Warwick Passage, off Old Bailey.

Porchester Spa (tel. 792 3980), Queensway, W2. Tube: Bayswater or Royal Oak. In the Porchester Centre. A Turkish bath with steam and dry heat rooms and a swimming pool. Built in 1929, the baths are a newly refurbished Art Deco masterpiece of gold and marble. Rates are high (£17.95), but devoted fans keep taking the plunge. Open daily 10am-10pm. Men bathe M, W, and Sa; women bathe Th and F. On Tuesday and Sunday women may bathe from 10am-4pm, and couples may bathe together from 4-10pm at the special rate of £25 per couple (for 3hr.). Swimwear required for mixed couples night. Last admission 8pm.

Speakers' Corner, in the northeast corner of Hyde Park. Tube: Marble Arch. Bring a soapbox and join the crackpots, evangelists, political activists, and more crackpots who speak their minds every Su 11am-dusk. (See **Hyde Park,** p. 174.)

Radio and TV Shows. Become part of a live studio audience. Get free tickets for the endless variations on "Master Mind." Write to the **BBC Ticket Unit,** Broadcasting House, Portland Pl., W1; **Thames TV Ticket Unit,** 306 Euston Rd., NW1; or **London Weekend Television,** Kent House, Upper Ground, SE1.

The Rocky Horror Picture Show, at the Prince Charles Cinema (see p. 240). This ain't *Cats* anymore, boys. Witness the legend in its hometown, complete with a live troupe, pelvic thrusting, and Meatloaf. F 11:30pm. £6, concessions £3.

Shri Swaminarayan Mandir, 105/115 Brentfield Rd., Neasden N10 (tel. (0181) 965 2651; fax (0181) 961 2444). Tube: Stonebridge Park or Neasden. This is a stunning Hindu temple, located right next to one of London's most run-down estates. Carved in intricate detail out of imported marble and limestone, it serves as a religious, social, and cultural center for London's Hindus. Visitors are welcome, and a restaurant and shop are attached. A permanent exhibition on the meaning of Hinduism runs in the basement. Viewing of the icons that form the centerpiece of the temple daily 7:15am-noon and 4pm-7:30pm.

Vidal Sassoon School of Hairdressing, 56 Davies Mews, W1 (tel. 318 5205). Tube: Bond St. Become your own offbeat entertainment. Cuts, perms, and colorings at the hand of *un petit Sassoony.* Cut and blow dry £15 (concessions £7.50), which includes lengthy consultations with an experienced stylist before the students do their worst. Actually most "students" have spent time styling at lesser studios before even being allowed to study with the maestro. Make sure you have about 2-3hr. to spare. Book at least a week in advance. Open M-F 8:30am-6pm.

Sports

SPECTATOR SPORTS

Association Football

Many evils may arise which God forbid.

—King Edward II, banning football in London, 1314

Football (soccer) draws huge crowds—over half a million people attend professional matches in Britain every Saturday. Each club's fans dress with fierce loyalty in team colors and make themselves heard with eerily synchronized cheering. Mass violence and vandalism at stadiums have dogged the game for years. Ninety-five people were crushed to death in Sheffield in 1989 after a surge of fans tried to push their way into the grounds. The atmosphere in the stands has become a bit tamer now that most stadiums sell only seats rather than spaces in the once infamous "terraces." In 1996, during England's turn at hosting the European Championships, a small-scale riot broke out in Trafalgar Square.

The season runs from mid-August to May. Most games take place on Saturday, kicking off at 3pm. Allow time to wander through the crowds milling around the stadium. London has been blessed with 13 of the 92 professional teams in England. The big two are **Arsenal,** Arsenal Stadium, Avenell Rd., N5 (tel. 704 4000; tube: Arsenal) and **Tottenham Hotspur,** White Hart Lane, 748 High Rd., W17 (tel. (0181) 365 5000; BR: White Hart Lane). But the football scene is very partisan and favorites vary from neighborhood to neighborhood. Tickets are available in advance from each club's box office; many have a credit card telephone booking system. Seats cost £10-35. England plays occasional international matches at Wembley Stadium, usually on Wednesday evenings (tel. (0181) 900 1234; tube: Wembley Park).

Rugby

The game was spontaneously created when a Rugby College student picked up a soccer ball and ran it into the goal. Rugby has since evolved into a complex and subtle game. **Rugby League,** a professional sport played by teams of 13, has traditionally been a northern game. Wembley Stadium (tel. (0181) 900 1234) stages some of the championship matches in May. A random *melee* of blood, mud, and drinking songs, "rugger" can be incomprehensible to the outsider, yet aesthetically exciting nonetheless. The season runs from September to May. The most significant contests, including the Oxford vs. Cambridge varsity match in December and the springtime five nations championship (featuring England, Scotland, Wales, Ireland, and France) are played at **Twickenham** (tel. (0181) 892 2000; BR: Twickenham). First-rate games can be seen in relaxed surroundings at one of London's premiere clubs such as **Saracens,** Vicarage Road Stadium, Watford WD1 (tel. (01923) 496 200; BR: Watford High Street), and **Rosslyn Park,** Priory Ln., Upper Richmond Rd., SW15 (tel. (0181) 876 1879; BR: Barnes).

Cricket

Cricket remains a confusing spectacle to most North Americans. The impossibility of explaining its rules to an American has virtually become a national in-joke in England (see below). Once a synonym for civility, cricket's image has been dulled. While purists disdain one-day matches, novices find these the most exciting. "First class" matches amble on rather ambiguously for days, often ending in "draws."

London's two grounds stage both county and international matches. **Lord's,** St. John's Wood Rd., NW8 (tel. 289 1300 for Middlesex, 289 1611 for Marylebone; tube: St. John's Wood), is *the* cricket ground, home turf of the Marylebone Cricket Club, the established governing body of cricket. Archaic stuffiness pervades the MCC; women have yet to see the pavilion's interior. **Middlesex** plays its games here (tickets £7 for summer matches). Tickets to international matches cost £24-36 (booking

required for major matches). **Foster's Oval,** Kennington Oval, SE11 (tel. 582 6660; tube: Oval), home to **Surrey** cricket club (tickets £7-8), also fields Test Matches (tickets for internationals £21-36, book ahead).

Rowing

The **Henley Royal Regatta,** the most famous annual crew race in the world, conducts itself both as a proper hobnob social affair (like Ascot) and as a popular corporate social event (like Wimbledon). The rowing is graceful, though laypeople are often unable to divine what on earth is going on. The event transpires from July 1-5 in 1998. Saturday is the most popular and busiest day, but some of the best races are the finals on Sunday. Public enclosure tickets (£5 for the first three days, £6 for the last two) are available by the river (the side opposite the train station) or write to the Secretary's Office, Regatta Headquarters, Henley-on-Thames, Oxfordshire, England RG9 2LY (tel. (01491) 572 153).

The **Boat Race,** between eights from Oxford and Cambridge Universities, enacts the traditional rivalry between the schools. The course runs from Putney to Mortlake on Saturday, April 3, 1999. Old-money alums, fortified by strawberries and champagne, sport their crested blazers and college ties to cheer the teams on. Bumptious crowds line the Thames and fill the pubs (tube: Putney Bridge or Hammersmith; BR: Barnes Bridge or Mortlake). Call 379 3234 for info.

Tennis

From June 21-July 4, 1999, tennis buffs all over the world will focus their attention on **Wimbledon.** This village-like suburb annually converts itself into a tennis lovefest where top tennis stars are gently applauded by the toffs (English slang meaning upper crust). If you want to get in, arrive early (6am); the gate opens at 10:30am (get off the tube at Southfields or take buses #39, 93 or 200 from central London, which run frequently during the season). Though details were not available at press time, you can expect the following prices to be slightly higher in 1999. Entrance to the grounds (including lesser matches) costs £7-8, £5-6 after 5pm. If you arrive in the queue early enough, you can buy one of the few show court tickets that were not sold months before. Depending on the day, center court tickets cost £21-47, No.1 court tickets £12-33, No.2 court tickets £14-22. Other courts have first-come, first-served seats or standing room only. Get a copy of the order of play on each court, printed in most newspapers. If you fail to get center or No. 1 court tickets in the morning, try to find the resale booth (usually in Aorangi Park), which sells tickets handed in by those who leave early (open from 2:30pm; tickets £5 before 5pm, £3 after). Also, on the first Saturday of the championships, 2000 extra center court tickets are put up for sale at the "bargain" price of £25. Call (0181) 971 2473 for ticket information.

For details on the 1999 championships send a self-addressed stamped envelope from Sept. 1-Dec. 31, 1998 to **The All England Lawn Tennis and Croquet Club,** P.O. Box 98, Church Rd., Wimbledon SW19 5AE. Overseas fans should also send an international reply coupon to cover postage. Top-spin lob fans mustn't miss the **Wimbledon Lawn Tennis Museum** (tel. (0181) 946 6131), located right on the grounds. *(Open Tu-Sa 10am-5pm, Su 2-5pm; during the tournament daily 10:30am-7pm for ticketholders only.)*

Horses

The **Royal Gold Cup Meeting** at **Ascot** takes place each summer in the second half of June. An "important" society event, it is essentially an excuse for Brits of all strata to indulge in the twin pastimes of drinking and gambling while wearing silly hats. The Queen takes up residence at Windsor Castle in order to lavish her full attentions on this socio-political vaudeville act. (The enclosure is open only by invitation; grandstand tickets £26-34, Silver Ring £7; tel. (01344) 622 211). In July, the popular George VI and Queen Elizabeth Diamond Stakes are run here, and during the winter Ascot hosts excellent steeplechase meetings (BR from Waterloo to Ascot). Top hats, gyp-

sies, and Pimms also distinguish the **Derby** ("darby"), run on June 5, 1999 at **Epsom** Racecourse, Epsom, Surrey (tel. (01372) 726 311; grandstand tickets £10-20). More accessible, less expensive summer evening races are run at **Royal Windsor Racecourse,** Berkshire (tel. (01753) 865 234; BR: Windsor Riverside; admission to tattersalls and paddock £10), and **Kempton Park Racecourse,** Sunbury-on-Thames (tel. (01932) 782 292; BR: Kempton Park; grandstand £12, Silver Ring £6).

In late June, **polo** aficionados flock to the **Royal Windsor Cup,** The Guards Polo Club, Smiths Lawn, Windsor Great Park (tel. (01784) 437 797; BR: Windsor & Eton Central; admission £10 per car). You can stand on the "wrong" side of the field for free, or hobnob in the clubhouse (one-day membership £10).

Greyhound Racing

Greyhound racing—a.k.a. "the dogs"—is the second most popular spectator sport in Britain, after football. It's a quick and easy way to lose money—races last all of 20 seconds. Almost all races start at 7:30pm. Races are held year-round at **Walthamstow** (tel. (0181) 531 4255), and **Wembley** (tel. (0181) 902 8833). In late June, Wimbledon hosts the **Greyhound Derby,** nephew to its horseracing uncle (tel. (0181) 944 1066; Admission starts at £2.50).

The Lottery

George Orwell's apocalyptic vision of the future, *1984,* predicted that the Lottery would be the one event which would continue to delight the masses even when all else had been eradicated by Big Brother.

Following the introduction of the National Lottery many fear that Orwell has been proven right. The choosing of the winning numbers has become the highest rated television program, and Britain is indeed in Lottery fever. The first multi-million pound pay-outs first brought joy, and then ruined many families not able to bear the full glare of tabloid intrusion and the stress that large undeserved bounty induces.

The lottery has created a furor not just because it's brash and American, but also because it represents a radical departure from how taxes used to be raised in Britain. Surplus funds are to go to the *Millennium Fund* which is supposed to oversee a program of beautification and public works to prepare Britain for the year 2000. The administration of the funds, however, has also been controversial, with some suggesting that subsidies to the Opera are unwarranted when evidence suggests that it is the poorest and least educated Britons who are contributing most to this *fin-de-siècle* project.

PARTICIPATORY SPORTS

Time Out's section on Sports, Mind, and Body can give you more complete information on the sports listed below. Another outstanding resource is **The Sportsline** which answers queries M-F from 10am-6pm (tel. 222 8000). A live operator can give information on an unbelievable range of sporting opportunities in your area.

For general fitness during your visit, **London Central YMCA,** 112 Great Russell St., WC1 (tel. 637 8131; tube: Tottenham Ct. Rd.), has a pool, gym, weights, and offers weekly membership for £32. (Open M-F 7am-10pm.)

Swimming

Dive into the **Britannia Leisure Centre,** 40 Hyde Rd., N1 (tel. 729 4485; tube: Old Street), a sensational aquatic playground replete with a towering flume, fountains, and monstrous inflatables (open M-F 9am-10pm, Sa-Su 9am-6pm; admission £2.60, children £1.30). The Britannia also offers various women-only swimming times. Outdoor bathers may prefer the popular **Serpentine Lido** (tube: Knightsbridge or Hyde Park Corner), a chlorinated section of the Serpentine Lake in Hyde Park with surprisingly luxurious changing rooms and a kiddie pool and sandpit for children (open May-Sept. daily 10am-5pm; admission £2, concs. £1, sunloungers £3). The pool at the

University of London Union, Malet St., WC1 (tel. 664 2000, ext. 200), is closer to the center of town; a £30 Community user membership will enable you to use the pool and other fitness facilities for a small surcharge. Also see the sports centers listed below, most of which have pools.

Tennis

Public courts vary in quality; all cost about £3-6 per hour. Courts generally cost more for non-members, so if you're planning on playing frequently, you may want to invest in a membership card. You can call ahead and book in advance, though walk-ons are sometimes available. Hard courts include **Battersea Park** (tel. (0181) 871 7542; BR: Battersea Park); **Hyde Park** (tel. 262 3474; tube: Hyde Park Corner or Knightsbridge); **Lincoln's Inn Fields** (tel. 580 2403; tube: Holborn); and **Regent's Park** (tel. 486 7905; tube: Regent's Park).

Squash

While London is honeycombed with squash courts, the vast majority reside within private health and racket clubs that charge £200-400 for membership plus steep court fees. Visitors and casual players can, however, use the courts maintained by the city's numerous sports centers on a "pay as you play" basis; most charge around £6 per hour. Call the **Chelsea Sports Centre,** Chelsea Manor St., SW3 (tel. 352 6985); the **Queen Mother's Sports Centre,** 223 Vauxhall St., SW1 (tel. 630 5522); and the **Saddlers Sports Centre** (for details, see **Health and Fitness Centers** below).

Health and Fitness Centers

London is blessed with over 200 public sports and fitness centers; consult the yellow pages under "Leisure Centers" for more exhaustive listings or call the local borough council for a list of centers near you.

Barbican YMCA, 2 Fann St., EC2 (tel. 628 0697; fax 638 2420). Tube: Barbican. Spacious fitness center with free weights, Nautilus machines, treadmills and bikes. Annual membership £55, £3.50 per use.

Chelsea Sports Centre, (tel. 352 6985), Chelsea Manor St., off Kings Rd., SW3. Tube: Sloane Sq. or South Kensington. Activities: aerobics, badminton, basketball, bowling, canoeing, dance, football, lacrosse, martial arts, racquetball, roller skating, swimming, tennis, volleyball, weight training, and yoga. Solarium and spa baths. No membership or admission charge. Gym card £15.50 annually for use of weights, with a fee of £4.50 per use. Swimming £2.30. Classes £3.60. Open M-F 7am-10pm, Sa 8am-10pm, Su 8am-6:30pm. Closing hours may vary—call ahead.

Jubilee Hall Recreation Centre, 30 The Piazza, WC2 (tel. 836 4835), on the south side of Covent Garden. Tube: Covent Garden. Regular classes and activities include weight lifting, yoga, martial arts, gymnastics, dance, badminton, and aerobics. Special facilities include a sauna, solarium, and an alternative sports medicine clinic. Crowded with West End office workers at lunchtime. Monthly membership £49.50. Admission free to members; day membership £6.50. Open M-F 7am-10pm, Sa-Su 10am-5pm. Major credit cards.

Queen Mother Sports Centre, 223 Vauxhall Bridge Rd., SW1 (tel. 630 5522). Tube: Victoria. Over 14 sports and activities. Equipment rental. Activities and classes (£4.20-6.30 per hour) and full use of facilities on a pay-per-use basis are open to non-members, but membership (£39 per year) entitles one to lower prices. Use of weight gym requires completion of a 1-hr. course (£27.40) on the weights, and costs £6.30 per use thereafter for non-members. Pool £2.25 per use, £1.70 for members (open M-Tu 6:30am-8pm, W-F 6:30am-7:30pm, Sa-Su 8am-5:30pm). Open M-F 6:30am-10pm, Sa 8am-8pm.

Shopping

London Transport's handy *Shoppers' Bus Wheel* instructs Routemaster shoppers on the routes between shopping areas (available free from any London Transport Information Centre). *Nicholson's Shopping Guide and Streetfinder* (£3) should suit bargain hunters seeking further guidance. Serious shoppers should read *Time Out*'s massive *Directory to London's Shops and Services* (£8) cover to cover.

Budget shoppers should keep a keen eye out for the London **sales.** These anxiously awaited affairs involve substantial discounts on large portions of the merchandise as well as extended shopping hours. Most stores have both a winter and a summer sale, usually around January and July. This is the time to pick up designer fashions at almost reasonable prices. The London sales reward the shopper who begins early and wades through rack after rack looking for the diamond in the rough. *Time Out*'s "Sell Out" section has listings of stores offering markdowns.

Tourists who have purchased anything over £50 should ask about getting a refund on the 17.5% VAT (see p. 30). Another option is to save receipts and to send off for a refund at the airport. Each shopping area has a late night of shopping. Kings Rd. and Kensington High St., for example, stay open late on Wednesday, while the West End shops close late on Thursday. Many stores may be closed on Sunday.

Shopping Districts

Certain areas of the city will offer exciting threads even if one or two shops have missed the mark—the best way to shop may be by strolling along the main boulevards and checking out what's in the windows. Keep in mind that trendy stores, even during sales, are still trendy. The discounts offered might not be all that enormous.

Oxford St. Tube: Bond St., Oxford Circus, or Tottenham Ct. Rd. This dirty, bustling thoroughfare may be the busiest pedestrian street in all of London. Venerable department stores like **Selfridges,** discount chains, and trendy boutiques offer options for every shopper. The districts to the south of Oxford St. (**Bond St.** and **Regent St.**) feature absurdly expensive couture while the areas to the north offer pretty dismal wares.

Regent St. Tube: Oxford Circus or Piccadilly Circus. This elegant, Nash-designed street intersects Oxford St. at the Oxford Circus tube. The section south of Oxford St. is the home of some of the city's oldest and best-known stores, including **Liberty's of London.** Elegance compensates for a lack in affordability.

Jermyn St. Tube: Piccadilly Circus or Green Park. The last refuge of the English gentleman. This street also offers conservative ties, well-turned shoes, expensive cigars, and fine spirits. Running parallel to Jermyn St., just north, is Piccadilly St.—the home of **Fortnum & Mason** as well as several other luxury shops.

Knightsbridge. Tube: Knightsbridge. This famous shopping area is anchored by the city's most celebrated department stores, **Harvey Nichols** and **Harrods.** Sloane St., Knightsbridge, and Brompton Rd. radiate outward from the tube station.

Kensington High St. Tube: High St. Kensington. A fairly heterogeneous district at the southwest corner of Kensington Gardens offering a couple of camping outfitters, a few boutiques, and a wealth of trendy chains. This is another of London's busiest streets.

Covent Garden. Tube: Covent Garden. Emerging as the hottest proving ground for new designers, Covent Garden is filled with small boutiques vending off-the-wall fashion, as well as massive chains posing as small boutiques. The tamer clothing is what everyone will be wearing in a few years.

Bond St. Tube: Bond St. The heart of couture and unjustifiable excess. Old and New Bond St., extending south of Oxford St., are the most prestigious shop addresses in all of London. Old Bond street is particularly glitzy—a cloudy Rodeo Drive. For more on Bond St. and its Mayfair surroundings, see **Mayfair,** p. 171.

King's Rd. Tube: Sloane Sq. Extending west of Sloane Sq., this busy Chelsea street is lined with small stores offering everything from high fashion to cheap knockoffs of so-called American fashion (mostly jeans, Hawaiian prints, and bowling shirts). The stores here are generously interspersed with pubs and cafes, making it a less concentrated dose for true shopaholics.

Camden High St. Tube: Camden Town. Filled with shoe stores, the shops here are geared to the Sunday market crowds looking for cheap used jeans and leather jackets. Some stores sell trend-conscious new clothes as well, making it a good place to pick up clubwear at reasonable prices. Still, it's a good policy to compare the prices here with those at the chain stores found along Oxford St. and Covent Garden before buying anything.

Department Stores

Fortnum & Mason, 181 Piccadilly, W1 (tel. 734 8040). Tube: Green Park or Piccadilly Circus. Liveried clerks vend expensive foods in red-carpeted and chandeliered halls at this renowned establishment. Queen Victoria naturally turned to Fortnum & Mason when she wanted to send Florence Nightingale 250 lbs. of beef tea for the Crimean field hospitals. The upper floors carry clothing, jewelry, shoes, etc., in a posh and sophisticated setting. The St. James Restaurant on the 4th floor serves a mean high tea (see **Tea,** p. 129). Expensive but fun to sniff around. Pick a souvenir gift from their phenomenal selection of preserves (£2.25). Open M-Sa 9:30am-6pm.

Harrods, 87-135 Brompton Rd., SW3 (tel. 730 1234). Tube: Knightsbridge. Simply put, this is *the* store in London, perhaps in the world—English gentlemen keeping a stiff upper lip elsewhere dream of the Harrods food court. Their humble motto, "Omnia Omnibus Ubique" (All things for all people, everywhere), says it all. They can do everything from fitting a saddle for your thoroughbred to selling you a Bosendorfer grand piano (£70,000) or a 75-CD jukebox (£5995). They also stock more than 450 kinds of cheese and pour an elegant afternoon tea. Harrods' sales (mid-July and after Christmas) get so crazy that the police bring out a whole detail to deal with the shoppers. Shorts, ripped clothing, and backpacks are forbidden in this quasi-museum of luxury. Nevertheless, the downstairs seems like a tourist convention at times. Security cameras in the ceiling follow suspicious-looking shoppers. Luxury washrooms (£1) aren't as exciting from the inside—spend the pound on a truffle in the food court. Open M-Tu and Sa 10am-6pm, W-F 10am-7pm.

Harvey Nichols, 109-125 Knightsbridge, SW3 (tel. 235 5000). Tube: Knightsbridge. The trendiest of London's huge department stores; also one of the most expensive. Cellular phones ring just as often as the registers. Known for interesting and avant-garde window displays that change frequently. Stupendous sale in early July. Outrageous prices at downstairs bar Foundations (tel. 201 8000; cocktails £6-7.25) and the chic, well-known 5th-floor cafe (entrees from £10) cater to the deep pockets of Harvey Nichols shoppers. Now, they (and you!) can also spend scads to beautify themselves at the 4th-floor Urban Retreat Aveda Concept Salon (tel. 201 8610). Clothing is priced as one might expect. Open M-Tu and Th-Sa 10am-7pm, W 10am-8pm, Su noon-6pm.

John Lewis, 278-306 Oxford St. (tel. 629 7711). Tube: Oxford Circus. Giant department store offering merchandise in various price ranges. Open M-W and F 9:30am-6pm, Th 10am-8pm, Sa 9am-6pm. Sister shop **Peter Jones** (tel. 730 3434) at Sloane Square is equally wide-ranging (tube: Sloane Sq.). Both have a price guarantee similar to Selfridges. Open M-Tu and Th-Sa 9:30am-6pm, W 9:30am-7pm. Only accepts its own credit card.

Liberty's of London (tel. 734 1234), south of Oxford Circus on Regent St. and Great Marlborough St. Tube: Oxford Circus. A prime exponent of the 19th-century arts and crafts movement, this is the home of the famous Liberty prints, ranging from entire bolts of fabric to silk ties. Playing dress up in the hat department is much more acceptable here than at fayre Harrods and is just as good. Giant, store-altering sales in early July and December. Open M-W and F-Sa 10am-6:30pm, Th 10am-7:30pm, Su noon-6pm. Major credit cards.

Marks & Spencer, 458 Oxford St., W1 (tel. 935 7954). Tube: Bond St. Also at 113 Kensington High St. (tel. 938 3711), 85 Kings Rd. (tel. 376 5634; tube: Sloane Sq.),

and literally hundreds of other locations. Brits know it as Marks & Sparks or M & S. Sells British staples in a classy but value-conscious manner. The clothes err on the conservative side. Everyone British, including Margaret Thatcher, buys their underwear here. Also features a food department with large offerings of ready made items. Open M-F 9am-8pm, Sa 9am-7pm, Su noon-6pm (weekend hours vary slightly). Major credit cards.

Selfridges, 400 Oxford St. (tel. 629 1234). Tube: Bond St. An enormous pseudo-Renaissance building with a vast array of fashions, homewares, and foods in addition to services like dry cleaning, a bureau de change and a tourist office. The incredible food hall offers cheeses, meats, beautifully displayed produce, a deli, a bakery, and even an oyster bar. Look out for free samples. The kind folks at Selfridges will refund the difference on any item found for less elsewhere. Huge mid-July sale. Open M-W 10am-7pm and Th-F 10am-8pm, Sa 9:30am-7pm, Su noon-6pm. Major credit cards.

Clothing

Smaller stores in London also cluster around the main shopping districts. Some of the most revolutionary new styles are first offered in these boutiques, and some of the best bargains are to be found here.

Big Apple, 96 Kensington High St., W8 (tel. 376 1404). Tube: High St. Kensington. Also at 70 Neal St., WC2 (tel. 497 0165; tube: Covent Garden). Sale racks of tiny tees and daring spandex items, some for a mere £5. Open M-Sa 10am-7:30pm, Su 11am-7pm.

Cornucopia, 12 Upper Tachbrook St., SW1 (tel. 828 5752). Tube: Victoria. The grande dame of period clothing shops, selling women's attire from 1910-1960. Ball gowns start at £35. Open M-Sa 11am-6pm.

Hennes & Mauritz, 261-271 Regent St., W1 (tel. 495 4003). Tube: Oxford Circus. At the intersection of Oxford and Regent St. Also known as H&M or Hennes. This discount chain sells fairly fashion-conscious, inexpensive women's wear. Somewhere on these 2 floors is an inexpensive piece to suit every taste. Also sells children's ware and men's clothing. Open M-W and F-Sa 10am-6:30pm, Th 10am-8pm, Su noon-6pm.

Kensington Market, 49-53 Kensington High St., W8. Tube: High St. Kensington. An alternashopper's bazaar—3 crowded floors of stalls selling cheap threads and trinkets in every countercultural style from punk to camo to rave. Open M-Sa 10am-6pm.

Miss Moneypenny, 30 Chapel Market, N1 (tel. 833 2445). Tube: Angel. The place for ladies' wear small and tight enough for any dance club floor. Colorful £5 rack offers items worth grabbing at such a discount. Open M-Sa 10am-6pm.

Top Shop/Top Man, 214 Oxford St., W1 (tel. 636 7700). Tube: Oxford Circus. An absolute must visit for the wannabe club kid on a budget. The Top Shop multi-story megastore at Oxford Circus offers the trendiest of inexpensive fashions for women—there's something to suit everyone's flamboyant side. Aspiring Topmen *must* be sure to spend some time perusing the sale racks in the new addition's ground floor next door. Aspiring Topwomen *must* also check out the less inspiring, but no less colorful, sale racks in the basement. Open M-W and F-Sa 10am-7pm, Th 10am-8pm, Su noon-6pm.

CHAIN STORES

These **chain stores** specialize in relatively affordable, yet very trendy, duds for lads and ladies. They appeal to a younger crowd interested in sleek, tight clothing. In truth, there is not much that is particularly English about the following stores—they take their cues from European and other trends in international fashion. We have given several of the larger locations for each of the listings; check the phone books for smaller stores which may be nearer. Beware that not all of the smaller locations have both the men's and women's lines.

Amazon, 1-22 Kensington Church St., W8 (tel. 937 9694). Tube: High St. Kensington. Gargantuan collection of designer wares includes Versace and other big names in addition to popular chain store seconds such as French Connection. Discounts

sometimes exceed 50%. Be sure about your purchases, though, because the exchange policy is extremely limited. Other branches around the city. Open M-W and F 10am-6pm, Th 10am-7pm, Sa 9am-6pm, Su noon-5pm. DC, MC, V.

Burton Menswear and Dorothy Perkins, 379 Oxford St., W1 (tel. 495 6282). Tube: Bond St. In the West One shopping center above the tube stop. Burton handles conservative casualwear and shoes for men, while Dorothy takes care of slightly less sober (but still responsible) casuals for women. Many other locations. Open M-W and F-Sa 10am-7pm, Th 10am-8pm, Su noon-5pm.

French Connection, 99-103 Long Acre, WC2 (tel. 379 6560). Tube: Covent Garden. Also at 249-251 Regent St., W1 (493 3124; tube: Oxford Circus); 140-144 King's Rd., SW3 (tel. 225 3302; tube: Sloane Sq.). An unfailingly current collection of men's and women's wear. As the name implies, the cuts and fabrics are heavily influenced by the latest Gallic fashions. Prices are a bit upscale, but there are some less expensive pieces. There is a huge sale during mid-July. Open M-W 10:30am-7pm, Th 11:30am-8pm, F-Sa 10:30am-7pm, Su 12-6pm.

Kookai, 5-7 Brompton Rd., SW3 (tel. 581 9633). Tube: Knightsbridge. Also at 360 Oxford St., W1 (tel. 499 4564; tube: Bond St.); 123 Kensington High St., W8 (tel. 938 1427); 27a Sloane Sq., SW1 (tel. 730 6903); 124 King's Rd., SW1 (tel. 589 0120; tube: Sloane Sq.); and numerous other locations. Sexy, billowy women's clothes at almost reasonable prices. Often lovely details (embroidery, beads, etc.). Stores throb with slow jams and dance tunes. Open M-Tu and Th-Sa 10am-7pm, W 10am-8pm, Su noon-5pm. Major credit cards.

Jigsaw, 31 Brompton Rd., SW3 (tel. 584 6226). Tube: Knightsbridge. Also at 21 Long Acre, WC2 (tel. 240 3855; tube: Covent Garden); 65 Kensington High St., W8 (tel. 937 3572); 126 Kings Rd., SW3 (tel. 823 7304; tube: Sloane Sq.); and numerous others. Purveyors of somewhat pricey, but very stylish women's threads in a variety of luscious fabrics (such as deliciously soft leather) and muted, subtle colors. Some stores have smallish men's departments as well. The Covent Garden location has a large men's-only store next door. Open M-Tu and Th-F 10:30am-7pm, W 10:30am-7:30pm, Sa 10am-7pm, Su noon-5pm.

Next, 33 Brompton Rd., SW3 (tel. 584 0619). Tube: Knightsbridge. Also at 323-329 Oxford St., W1 (tel. 494 3646; tube: Oxford Circus); 54 Kensington High St., W8 (tel. 938 4211). Basic yet sophisticated pieces for a wide range of ages. Fair prices for everything from office garb to beach garb. Open M-F 10:30am-7pm, Sa 10am-6pm, Su noon-6pm.

Warehouse, The Plaza, Oxford St., W1 (tel. 436 4179). Tube: Oxford Circus and Bond St. Also at 24 Long Acre, WC2 (tube: Covent Garden); 63-67 Kensington High St., W8; 96 King's Rd., SW3; and 19-21 Argyll St. Women's clothes only, serving fashion at fair prices. Everything flared, stretchy, or three-quartered sleeved. Open M-W and F-Sa 10am-7pm, Th 10am-8pm. Some branches open Su noon-5pm. AmEx, MC, Visa.

Some of the better-known British fashion designers and their ateliers:

Hype Designer Forum, 26-40 Kensington High St., W8 (tel. 938 4343). Tube: High St. Kensington. A mall of boutiques exhibiting the work of young British designers and larger brands. These garments sometimes appear in the pages of Vogue and Elle. Open M-W and F 10am-6pm, Th 10am-8pm, Sa 10am-6pm, Su noon-6pm.

Paul Smith, 23 Avery Row, W1 (tel. 493 1287), off of Brook St. Tube: Bond St. The seconds and out-of-season outlet for the witty yet elegant menswear store. Emphasis here tends toward stylish and bright casual wear, with savings of up to 70% off regular retail prices. Open M-W and F-Sa 10am-6pm, Th 10am-7pm.

Shoes

Devout shoppers come to London for shoes, where they find the coolest soles at decent prices. More hip than fashionable, platforms have recently been stuck on everything from sandals to Adidas sneakers. Shoe vendors take a cue from Henry Ford—you can get a shoe in any color so long as it's black. Actually, this a bit of an overstatement—faux black and white snakeskin, fur, and pastelly patent leather often adorn newer styles.

Dr. Marten's Dept. Store Ltd., 1-4 King St. WC2 (tel. 497 1460). Tube: Covent Garden. Tourist-packed 6-tiered mega-store; showcases watches, sunglasses, candles, a cafe, and a hair salon. Buy Docs for everyone in your family, from baby to granny. Open M-W and F-Su 10am-7pm, Th 10:30am-8pm. AmEx, MC, Visa.

Dolci's, 333 Oxford St., W1 (tel. 493 9626). Tube: Bond St. Also at 42-60 Kensington High St., W8. Almost as hip as Shelly's (see below), but also stocks more conventional styles, foul-weather footwear, and dressy pumps. Very popular with young hipsters on a budget. Open M-W and F-Sa 10am-7pm, Th 10am-8pm, Su noon-6pm. AmEx, MC, Visa.

Eternity, 46 Oxford St. (tel. 580 0890). Tube: Oxford Circus. Although difficult to find (only the "ET" remains on the store sign), this shop is worth the search, as the deals here are unbeatable. Italian leather imports go for as little as £20. Open daily 9:30am-7pm.

Office, 43 Kensington High St., W8 (tel. 937 7022). Tube: High St. Kensington. Also at 57 Neal St., WC2 (tel. 379 1896; tube: Covent Garden); women's shoes only at 59 So. Molton St., W1 (tel. 493 0051; tube: Bond St.); sale shop at 61 Martin's Ln. WC2 (tel. 497 0390; tube: Leicester Square). Ultra-trendy mid-range chain patronized by chic, black-clad types. Carries well-known designers and a hip collection of own-label stompers. Open daily 10am-6pm. Hours vary between branches.

Shelly's, 159 Oxford St., W1 (tel. 437 5842). Tube: Oxford Circus. Also at 14-18 Neal St., WC2 (tel. 240 3726; tube: Covent Garden); 40 Kensington High St., W8 (tel. 938 1082; tube: Kensington High St.); 124b King's Rd., SW3 (tel. 581 5537; tube: Sloane Sq.). Shelly's is *the* London shoe store, always displaying the most current styles. Shelly's reverses the preppie ethic of sensible shoes at outrageous prices—they offer outrageous shoes at sensible prices. Open M-W and F-Sa 9:30am-6pm, Th 9:30am-8pm, Su noon-6pm. AmEx, MC, Visa.

Swear, 61 Neal St., WC2 (tel./fax 240 5313; email swear@mail.telepac.pt; http://www.swear.pt/fashion). Tube: Covent Garden. This hipper-than-thou footwear boutique takes the high-soled sneaker to new literal and aesthetic levels. Carpeted with turf. Open M-F 11am-7pm, Sa 10:30am-7pm, Su 2:30-6:30pm.

Bookstores

In London, even the chain bookstores are wonders. An exhaustive selection of bookshops lines **Charing Cross Road** between Tottenham Ct. Rd. and Leicester Sq. and many vend secondhand paperbacks. Cecil Ct., near Leicester Sq., is a treasure trove of tiny shops with specialty bookstores for dance, Italian, travel, etc. Establishments along Great Russell St. stock esoteric and specialized books on any subject from Adorno to the Zohar. The chains can be found along most main commercial thoroughfares, like Oxford St. and Kensington High St.

You can find maps and other travel literature at **Stanford's,** 12 Long Acre (tel. 836 1321). Tube: Covent Garden. Open M 10am-6pm, Tu-F 9am-7pm, Sa 10am-7pm. Also try the travel sections at the larger bookstores (Waterstones and Dillons) and the YHA shop in Covent Garden (see p. 76).

GIANT BOOKSTORES

Dillons, Trafalgar Sq., Grand Building, WC2 (tel. 839 4411). Tube: Charing Cross or Leicester Sq. This branch is open latest; the largest is at 82 Gower St., WC2 (tel. 636 1577). Numerous branches. One of London's best. Strong on academic subjects, particularly history and politics. Fair selection of reduced-price and secondhand books, plus classical CDs and tapes. Open M-Sa 9:30am-9pm, Su noon-6pm.

Foyles, 113-119 Charing Cross Rd., WC1. Tube: Tottenham Ct. Rd. or Leicester Sq. A giant warehouse of books that sprawls over 2 large floors. You'll get lost in this labyrinth. Open M-W and F-Sa 9am-6pm, Th 9am-7pm. Major credit cards.

Hatchards, 187 Piccadilly, W1 (tel. 439 9921). Tube: Green Park. Oldest of London's bookstores. Four floors of intellectual goodies. Open M and W-Sa 9am-6pm, Tu 9:30am-6pm, Su noon-6pm. Major credit cards.

Waterstone's, 121-125 Charing Cross Rd.,WC1 (tel. 434 4291), next door to Foyles. Tube: Leicester Sq. Also at 193 Kensington High St., W8 (tel. 937 8432); 101 Old Bro-

mpton Rd., SW7 (tel. 581 8522). This rather cramped branch concentrates on non-fiction, but is literally 2 doors away from a branch at 131 Charing Cross Rd. that exclusively features fiction. Open M-Sa 9am-8pm, Su noon-6pm. Major credit cards.

ANTIQUE AND USED BOOKSTORES

Bell, Book, and Radmall, 4 Cecil Ct., WC2 (tel. 240 2161). Tube: Leicester Sq. A small antiquarian bookstore with a zippy staff, an exceptional selection of American and British first editions, and an impressive supply of sci-fi and detective novels. Open M-F 10am-5:30pm, Sa 11am-4pm. Major credit cards.

Bookmongers, 439 Coldharbour Ln., SW9 (tel. 738 4225). Tube: Brixton. Fabulous secondhand bookstore with a healthy selection of works by African and Caribbean authors. Also features a gay and lesbian novels section, and a section of modern classics by women authors. Open M-Sa 10:30am-6:30pm. No credit cards.

Maggs Brothers Ltd., 50 Berkeley Sq., W1 (tel. 493 7160). Tube: Green Park. A bibliophile's paradise housed in an allegedly haunted 18th-century mansion. Tremendous selection of 19th-century travel narratives, illuminated manuscripts, militaria, and autographs. Open M-F 9am-5pm. Major credit cards.

Southeran's of Sackville Street, 2-5 Sackville St., W1 (tel. 439 6151). Tube: Piccadilly Circus. Founded in 1761 in York, Southeran's moved to London in 1815 and established itself as a literary institution of the city. Dickens frequented these silent stacks, and the firm handled the sale of his library after his death in 1870. Strong departments include architecture and literary first editions. If you want to know how people traveled before the *Let's Go* era, check out their superb collection of antiquarian travel narratives. Open M-F 9:30am-6pm, Sa 10am-4pm.

Skoob Books, 15-17 Sicilian Ave., Southampton Row and Vernon Pl., WC1 (tel. 405 0030 or 405 0015). Tube: Holborn. The best used bookstore in Bloomsbury; academic and general interest. 10% student discount. Open M-Sa 10:30am-6:30pm. Major credit cards.

ART AND THEATRE BOOKS

Dillons Arts Bookshop, 8 Long Acre, WC2 (tel. 836 1359). Tube: Leicester Sq. or Covent Garden. This branch of Dillons carries a very browsable selection of art books. Covers the performing arts as well as poetry, art theory, art history, and design. Open M and W-Sa 9:30am-10pm, Tu 10am-10pm, Su noon-6pm.

National Theatre Bookshop, South Bank Centre, SE1 (tel. 452 3333). Tube: Waterloo. Widest selection of plays and books about theater. Open M-Sa 10am-1am.

Offstage Theatre and Film Bookstore, 37 Chalk Farm Rd. (tel. 485 4996). Tube: Chalk Farm. A converted theater that serves as an actors' hangout. Ground floor houses new theater, film, and cultural literature; downstairs offers used books and scripts. 10% off for students. Open daily 10am-6pm.

David Drummond, Theatrical Bookseller and Ephemerist, 11 Cecil Ct., WC2 (tel. 836 1142). Tube: Leicester Sq. A friendly, fascinating shop crammed with various theatrical paraphernalia, plus early children's books with exquisite color plates, adventure stories, fairy tales, antique postcards, Victorian valentines, and other vintage juvenalia. Open M-F 11am-2:30pm and 3:30-5:45pm, Sa by appointment. Major credit cards.

Samuel French's, 52 Fitzroy St., W1 (tel. 387 9373). Tube: Warren St. Has a wide selection of books on the theater. Open M-F 9:30am-5:30pm, Sa 11am-5pm. Major credit cards.

Thomas Heneage & Co., 42 Duke St., SW1 (tel. 930 9223). Tube: Green Park. A truly outstanding collection of art books and a knowledgeable staff. Close to Christie's. Open M-F 9:30am-6pm. Major credit cards.

Zwemmers, 24 Litchfield St., WC2 (tel. 379 7886). Tube: Leicester Sq. A multi-store art book empire, headquartered at Litchfield St. The store here, just east of Charing Cross Rd., specializes in books on art, architecture, and design. A stone's throw to the south at 80 Charing Cross Rd., the focus is on graphics, film, and photography. The final branch in the immediate vicinity is at 72 Charing Cross Rd., which sells diverse offerings published by the Oxford University Press. All three open M-F 10am-6:30pm, Sa 10am-6pm. Major credit cards.

SPECIAL INTERESTS

Angel Bookshop, 102 Islington High St., N1 (tel. 226 2904). Tube: Angel. A well-read staff and a nice selection make this small bookstore worth checking out if you're in Islington for the market or for dinner. Classics only £1. Open daily 9:30am-6pm. MC, Visa.

Bookshop Islington Green, 76 Upper St., N1 (tel. 359 4699). Tube: Angel. Small store with pleasant staff and excellent selection of paperbacks. Open M-Sa 10am-10pm, Su noon-6pm. AmEx, MC, Visa.

Books for Cooks, 4 Blenheim Crescent, W11 (tel. 221 1992, -8102). Tube: Ladbroke Grove. The definitive cookbook shop. Titles range from Classic Austrian Cooking to Exotic Cuisine of Mauritius. Cuisines of many countries are covered with extensive works on Italy and France. Whole food and vegan section. Budget cookery section with secondhand books. Test kitchen in the rear serves samples from different books. Small restaurant/cafe now attached to the shop. Open M-Sa 9:30am-6pm. Major credit cards.

Compendium, 234 Camden High St., NW1 (tel. 485 8944). Tube: Camden Town. A good general selection, but specializes in postmodern literature, the left, the occult, and the all-around avant-garde. "Male fiction" shelved apart from "Women's fiction." Open M-Sa 10am-6pm, Su noon-6pm.

Guanghwa, 7 Newport Pl., WC2 (tel. 437 3737). Tube: Leicester Sq. The sweet smell of incense enhances the exotic feel of this bookstore, which specializes in Eastern literature, dictionaries, and periodicals, with a good number of English offerings as well. Healthy martial arts and philosophy sections. Open M-Sa 10:30am-7pm, Su 11am-6:30pm.

Kilburn Book Shop, 8 Kilburn Bridge, Kilburn High Rd., NW6 (tel. 328 7071). Tube: Kilburn. Features ethnic studies and leftist books. Open M-Sa 10am-6pm.

Silver Moon, 64-68 Charing Cross Rd., WC2 (tel. 836 7906). Tube: Leicester Sq. A radical feminist bookstore and the largest women's bookshop in Europe. An exhaustive selection of books by and about women (fiction by women, non-fiction about women written by either sex), the largest lesbian department in Britain, a complete stock of all Virago books, and a nice travel section. Open M-W and F-Sa 10am-6:30pm, Th 10am-8pm, Su noon-6pm. AmEx, MC, Visa.

Sportspages, Caxton Walk at 94-96 Charing Cross Rd., WC2 (tel. 240 9604; http://www.sportspages.co.uk). Tube: Leicester Sq. Specializes in books for both sports fans and professionals on practically every sport imaginable. Also sports an impressive selection of soccer and rugby merchandise, from jerseys to videotapes of classic matches, and a decent sports science section. A chalkboard posts recent event results. Kicks off M-Sa 9:30am, with the final whistle at 7pm. AmEx, MC, Visa.

Timbuktu Bookshop, 378 Coldharbour Ln., SW9 (tel. 737 2770), in the Black Cultural Archives. Tube: Brixton. Features a small collection of both academic and spiritual books relating to people of African origin in the diaspora. Also carries local crafts and African clothing. Open (usually) M-Sa 10am-6pm.

Vintage Magazine Market, 39-43 Brewer St. (tel. 439 8525; http://www.vinmag.com). On the corner of Brewer and Great Windmill St. near Piccadilly Circus. Also at 55 Charing Cross Rd. (tel. 494 4064) and 247 Camden High St. (tel. 482 0527). Vintage film magazines and posters, from Bogart to Bruce Lee, along with hip postcards and t-shirts. Open M-F 10am-7pm, Sa 10am-10pm, Su noon-8pm. AmEx, MC, Visa.

Record Stores

If a record can't be found in London, it's probably not worth your listening time. London, for years the hub of the English music scene, has a record collection to match. Corporate megaliths **HMV, Virgin,** and **Tower Records** fall over each other claiming to be the world's largest record store. Don't expect any bargains or rarities, and remember that when it comes to records, "import" means "rip-off." CDs will seem expensive to Americans. The best bargains, just as in the states, are found in vinyl, although the record market is frustratingly efficient. At **Camden Town, Brixton, Ladbroke Grove,** or Soho's **Hanway Street,** record stores tempt collectors and intimi-

date browsers with rare vinyl and memorabilia at rock star prices. The shops surrounding the intersection of **D'Arblay** and **Berwick Streets** in Soho provide listening booths for DJs to sample the latest 12 inch singles. Dig deep in the bargain bins. Think about how British tastes differ from your own, and shop accordingly: early LPs and singles by British bands aren't as rare and dear here as they are elsewhere, and the enduring popularity of jazz is also reflected in the wide collections of many stores.

Black Market, 25 D'Arblay St., W1 (tel. 437 0478). Tube: Oxford Circus. This Soho institution flirts with tourist trap oblivion by hawking logoed merchandise, but if you're looking for the latest hip-hop, techno, house, or garage 12-inches, they've got the goods. Ticket agent in the back books for the hottest shows and festivals. Open M-Sa 11am-7pm, Su 11:45am-7pm.

Cheapo Cheapo Records, 53 Rupert St., W1 (tel. 437 8272). Tube: Piccadilly Circus. A warren of 70s and early 80s records at rock-bottom prices. Open M-F 11am-10pm, Sa 10:30am-10pm.

Honest Jon's, 276-8 Portobello Rd., W10 (tel. (0181) 969 9822). Tube: Ladbroke Grove. Newly refurbished but still fonkay. 276 holds an impressive jazz collection where Blakey, Parker, and Mingus are only the tip of the iceberg. 278 sports a wide selection of hip-hop LPs and some decent 12-inch singles, as well as funk holdings from A to Zappa. Open M-Sa 10am-6pm, Su 11am-5pm. Major credit cards.

Intoxica!, 231 Portobello Rd., W11 (tel. 229 8010). Tube: Ladbroke Grove. Enviable collection of surf-rock and rockabilly, with a smattering of punk and soul. Prices vary from affordable to unbelievable. All vinyl. Open M-Sa 10:30am-6:30pm, Su noon-4pm. Major credit cards.

Music and Video Exchange, 229 Camden High St., NW1 (tel. 267 1898). Tube: Camden Town. Branch at 95 Berwick St., W8 (tel. 434 2939). Dirt-cheap 70s stuff in the basement. 3 floors of strong offerings in rap, indie, garage, and jungle. The continually renovated house room is a groovy place to listen. Open daily 10am-8pm.

Out on the Floor, 10 Inverness St., NW1 (tel. 267 5989). Tube: Camden Town. A well-stocked used-CD and vinyl shop. CDs £7.50-12; vinyl from £6. Upstairs mostly jazz and funk, downstairs indie and new wave punk. Open M-F 11am-6pm, Sa-Su 11am-7pm.

Red Records, 500 Brixton Rd., SW2 (tel. 274 4476; fax 274 5896; http://www.redrecords.com). Tube: Brixton. Though it touts itself as "the Black Music Store of the 90s," Red Records' collection of jazz, hip-hop, reggae, soul, and garage will appeal to loose booties of all colors. Vinyl, cassettes, CDs, and DJ equipment. Open M-Sa 9:30am-8pm, Su 9:30am-6pm. AmEx, MC, Visa.

Rhythm Records, 281 Camden High St., NW1 (tel. 267 0123). Tube: Camden Town. Modern, clean shop offers secondhand reggae, ska, and dub; proudly offers no top 40 discs at all. Good deals on secondhand. New CDs begin around £9. Open daily 10:30am-6:30pm. MC, Visa.

Rough Trade, 130 Talbot Rd., W11 (tel. 229 8541). Tube: Ladbroke Grove. Also at 16 Neal's Yard (tel. 240 0105; tube: Covent Garden). Birthplace of the legendary independent record label. Original snapshots of Johnny Rotten are casually tacked up on the wall next to old posters advertising concerts for Rough Trade bands like The Smiths, The Raincoats, and X-Ray Spex. Open M-Sa 9:30am-6:30pm. Major credit cards.

Sister Ray, 94 Berwick St., W1 (tel. 287 8385; fax 287 1087). Tube: Piccadilly Circus or Tottenham Ct. Rd. The loud music competes with shouts from nearby Berwick St. Market. Knowledgeable staff helps guide you through their collection of 90s indie and 70s rock and punk. Open M-Sa 9:30am-8pm, Su 11am-5pm. Major credit cards.

Specialty Shops

Cadenhead's Covent Garden Whisky Shop (tel. 379 4640), corner of Wellington and Russell, next to Fifi's in Covent Garden. Tube: Covent Garden. Incomparable assemblage of scotches and whiskeys, many of them collector's items. Open M-F 11am-7pm, Sa 11am-6:30pm, Su noon-4:30pm. AmEx, DC, MC, Visa.

Declare, the Do It Yourself Computer Centre, 58 Kenway Rd., SW5 (tel. 835 0203). An alternative to expensive Internet cafes, Declare offers a wide range of computer facilities including email, Internet, word processing and desk-top publishing. Charges are by the minute, so there is no rounding up to the nearest half hour; you pay for what you use. Internet access 12p per min. (minimum 5 min.). Open M-Th 9am-9pm, F-Sa 10am-6pm.

Hamley's, 188-189 Regent St., W1 (tel. 734 3161). Tube: Oxford Circus. Even Santa and his elves do their shopping here, in a place most kids would call heaven. London's largest toy shop offers 6 floors of every conceivable toy and game, not to mention an arcade, soda fountain, and sandwich bar. Employees demonstrate the hottest toys to swarms of anxious tots. Open M-W 10am-7:30pm, Th-Sa 10am-8pm, Su noon-6pm. Hours vary. Major credit cards.

Honour, 86 Lower Marsh, SE1 (tel. 401 8220). Tube: Waterloo. One of the few places in England where rubber isn't just another word for an eraser: the 1st floor stocks wigs and all sorts of rubber and PVC gear for fetish trendies, the 2nd floor features bondage gear. Information on upcoming gothic, pagan, and fetish happenings. Open M-F 10:30am-7pm, Sa 11:30am-5pm. AmEx, MC, Visa.

Into You, 144 St. John St., EC1 (tel. 253 5085). Tattooing, body-piercing, and related literature and items. If pain is pleasure for you, and permanency doesn't bother you, then take the plunge. Open Tu-F noon-7pm, Sa noon-6pm.

Mrs. Price's Junk Shop, 2 White Conduit Rd., NW1 (tel. 833 3518). Tube: Angel. Exit station, cross street to Chapel Market, then right onto White Conduit. Even Fred and Lamont Sanford would be dismayed by this place. Piles of junk, dust and other stuff surround old bookcases and chests. You might get lucky and find something swell. Open daily noon-6pm, but hours fluctuate.

G. Smith and Sons Snuff Shop, 74 Charing Cross Rd., WC2 (tel. 836 7422). Tube: Leicester Sq. Established in 1869 by George Smith, this is the main snuff shop in London. Buy a can of snuff for £4.95. A pocket tin (only 75p) will keep you sneezin' through London. But it's not just a snuff shop: it doubles as a tobacconist and offers a host of pipes, lighters, and cigars from around the world. Open M-F 9am-6pm, Sa 9:30am-5:30pm. Major credit cards.

Rococos, 321 King's Rd., SW7 (tel. 352 5857). Tube: Victoria or Sloane Sq. Well-stocked, brightly lit chocolate store, a 5min. walk down King's Rd. Delicious chocolate in a variety of forms, from exotic chocolate bars with geranium (£2.50), to traditional truffles (50p). Open M-Sa 10am-6:30pm, Su noon-5pm.

Snow and Rock Ski and Mountain Specialists, 188 Kensington High St., W8 (tel. 937 0872). Tube: High St. Kensington. Decent collection of ropes, climbing hardware, rock shoes, tents, packs, and camping gear. Also stocks a wide selection of expensive outerwear by North Face, Patagonia, and Berghaus and skimpy holiday sunning attire. Skis and in-line skates. Small climbing wall. Open M-W and F 10am-6pm, Th 10am-7pm, Sa 9am-6pm, Su 11am-5pm.

The Tea and Coffee Plant, 170 Portobello Rd., London W8 (tel. 221 8137). Tube: Ladbroke Grove. This wonderful little shop sells a whole range of fairly traded coffee and tea, much of it organically grown. Ask the friendly staff to offer you guidance through their huge selection. The mild Guatemalan is a good place to start (£5 per lb), but cheaper varieties such as Mocha Blend (£2.80 per lb.) are also worth a look. On Saturdays, the shop has a cappucino machine and serves what is described as the best coffee in London, made from freshly roasted and drained coffee beans. Mail order available. Open Tu-Th 10:30am-6:30pm, F-Sa 9:15am-6pm.

Markets

STREET MARKETS

Time spent bopping around London's street markets means 99% perspiration and 1% inspiration. There are wonderful bargains and must-have gems thrown in with more questionable items. No matter your budget, it is likely that you can find the perfect gift or knick-knack that you didn't know you needed somewhere in the miles of stalls

which magically appear on market day. Many prices (even posted ones) are merely a first offer—a clever bargainer can shave prices down with a bit of haggling.

Many well-appointed shops lining the market streets (especially along **Portobello Rd.** and **Camden Passage**) offer extremely rare and expensive antiques. Next door, hastily constructed stalls sell to the young and penniless looking for an absurdly cheap pair of used jeans or a vintage Ronson. Still other stalls display exotic wares appealing to immigrants who have retained a taste for traditional foods, music, and languages.

Page numbers in parentheses feature comprehensive descriptions of the areas containing these markets. In all of these markets, *watch out for pickpockets.*

Brick Lane, E1. Tube: Aldgate East. Market with a South Asian flair: food, rugs, spices, bolts of fabric, and strains of sitar. Open Su 6am-1pm (p. 193).

Brixton Market, Electric Ave., Brixton Station Rd. and Popes Rd., SW2. Tube: Brixton. Halls and outdoor stalls sprawl out from the station. Wide selection of African and West Indian foods and goods make Brixton one of the most vibrant and exciting markets. Open M-Tu and Th-Sa 8:30am-5:30pm, W 8:30am-1pm (see p. 192).

Camden Markets, by Regent's Canal and along Camden High St., NW1. Tube: Camden Town. Popular and crowded place to find anything old or funky at discount prices. Visit Sundays for the best stalls. Open W-Su 9:30am-5:30pm (see p. 160).

Camden Passage, Islington High St., N1. Tube: Angel. Right from the tube, then right on narrow, pedestrian-only Islington High St. Antiques, prints and drawings. Open W and Sa 8:30am-3pm, but many start to pack up around 2pm (see p. 160).

Greenwich Market, Covered Market Sq., SE10, near the Cutty Sark. BR: Greenwich. A popular crafts market in a pastoral setting frequented by London lawyers on daytrips down the river. On Greenwich High Rd., the open-air secondhand market proffers vintage print dresses. Open Sa-Su 9am-6pm (see p. 204).

Petticoat Lane, E1. Tube: Liverpool St., Aldgate, or Aldgate East. Street after street of stalls, mostly cheap clothing and household appliances. The real action begins at about 9:30am. Open Su 9am-2pm; starts shutting down around noon (p. 193).

Portobello Road, W11. Tube: Notting Hill Gate or Ladbroke Grove. A popular and very old London market, immortalized by Paddington Bear. Antique market Sa 7am-5pm. Clothes market F-Sa 8am-3pm (p. 178).

Spitalfields Market, E1. Tube: Liverpool St. This smaller, indoor market with a soaring ceiling is the place to find a really special item at a reasonable price. Lots of fresh veggies and produce (p. 196).

TRADE MARKETS

London's fresh produce comes in through massive wholesale markets. These markets don't exactly roll out the red carpet for visitors, but they have wall-to-wall atmosphere. You won't find a more fascinating place to have a pint at 6:30am than near the trading. The new **Billingsgate** market (tel. 987 1118; DLR: Canary Wharf or Poplar; open Tu-Sa 5-9am) removed its fishy smells from the old site by St. Magnus Martyr in the City. **Smithfield,** Charterhouse St., EC1 (tel. 248 0367; tube: Farringdon or Barbican; open M-F 4-10am), allegedly the largest meat market in the world, sells wholesale only. The market's name is derived from the "smooth field" upon which cattle were sold here in the mid-1800s. Pubs in the area wake up as early as the meat mongers and serve correspondingly flesh-filled breakfasts.

Bisexual, Gay, and Lesbian London

Travelers coming to London will be delighted by the range of London's very visible gay scene, which covers everything from the flamboyant to the cruisy to the mainstream. London presents a paradoxical mix of tolerance and homophobia. On the one hand, gay culture is so visible that an entire section of the general entertainment weekly *Time Out* is dedicated to Gay Listings; on the other, queer bashings and police arrests of cruisers are not uncommon occurrences.

Britain suffers from a number of regressive laws, most notably Section 28, which prohibits local governments from "promoting" homosexuality. Another developing issue involves the National Health Secretary's recent move to ban lesbian mothers and single women from the NHS's artificial insemination treatment. In June 1998, Parliament voted to lower the age of consent law for male homosexuals from 18 to 16, the age of consent for heterosexuals.

Despite this negative political climate, gay communities thrive in London. Heavily gay-populated areas like Earl's Court, Islington, and Soho attest to the liveliness of the social scene; London also boasts an active network of political groups. Section 28 sparked an immediate call to action within the gay community, and the spirit of political activism has not died out; July 1994 witnessed the launch of London's first Lesbian Avengers branch. The Labour Party has committed itself to repealing Section 28 as soon as it returns to power. The **Gay Pride Festival** attracted over 40,000 participants in 1998 (call the Gay Pride Trust for information at tel. 738 7644.)

With so many bisexual-, gay-, and lesbian-specific **periodicals** in London, it's easy to educate yourself of the current concerns of London's many gay communities. *Capital Gay* (free) mostly caters to men. The *Pink Paper* is a free newspaper covering stories of interest to the pink community. Its bi-monthly sister publication, *Shebang,* covers all aspects of lesbian life. *Gay Times* (£3) is the British counterpart to the *Advocate; Diva* (£2) is a monthly lesbian lifestyle magazine with an excellent mix of political and entertainment features, and good listings. Also check *Time Out* each week for the latest from clubs to community groups.

The gay scene is spread throughout London. Gay pubs and bars can be found across the city and will often attract mixed crowds. However, Islington, Earl's Court, and Soho are all particularly **gay-friendly areas**. In Soho, **Old Compton Street** is the unofficial center of London's gay community.

Information and Advice Lines

Bisexual Helpline: tel. (0181) 569 7500. Tu-W 7:30-9:30pm.

Jewish Lesbian and Gay Line: tel. 706 3123. M and Th 7-10pm.

Lesbian and Gay Switchboard: tel. 837 7324. A 24hr. advice, support, and information service. Minicom facility for the deaf.

Lesbian Line: tel. 251 6911. Advice, information, and support. M 2-10pm, Tu-Th 7-10pm, F 2-10pm.

London Friend: tel.837 3337. Lesbian and gay helpline. Daily 7:30-10pm. Lesbian helpline (tel. 837 2782), Su-Th 7:30-10:30pm.

Bars, Cafes, Pubs, and Restaurants

The Box, Seven Dials, 32-34 Monmouth St., WC2 (tel. 240 5828). Tube: Covent Garden. You won't feel boxed in at this intimate and stylish gay bar and brasserie, removed from the bustle of Covent Garden. Fun, hip clientele of both genders and all races. The dance floor downstairs makes this an excellent venue for a cheap

night of dancing and drinking (lager £2.50 per pint). Open M-Sa 11am-11pm, Su 7-10:30pm.

Balans, 60 Old Compton St., W1 (tel. 437 5212). Tube: Leicester Sq. Another branch at 239 Old Brompton Rd. (tel. 244 8838; open daily 8am-2am). Fiery flower arrangements and feral zebra-print lampshades create a ruthlessly glamorous ambience for the mostly gay male clientele in this brasserie/bar. Lots of veggie options, but, as the sign says, "no pipes, cigars or herbal cigarettes." Open daily 8am-5am.

The Black Cap, 171 Camden High St., NW1 (tel. 428 2721). Tube: Camden Town. North London's best-known drag bar. Live shows every night attract a mixed male and female crowd. When the shows aren't on, a DJ plays top 40. Monday's oldies and "trash" night is a favorite. No cover before 11pm. Open M-Th 9pm-2am, F-Sa 9pm-3am, Su noon-3pm and 7pm-midnight. Cover Tu-Sa £2-4.

Brompton's Bar, 294 Old Brompton Rd. (tel. 370 1344). Tube: Earl's Court. Capacious men's bar, usually packed. Two bars and an exciting cabaret stage. Open M-Sa 4pm-2am, Su 1pm-midnight.

The Candy Bar, 4 Carlisle St., W1 (tel. 494 4041) Tube: Tottenham Ct. Rd. 3 floors of women (men welcome as guests) at London's first lesbian bar. Lesbians of all stripes sip drinks and check out the scene. Bar downstairs becomes dance floor W-Sa. Cover £5 F and Sa after 10pm.

Comptons of Soho, 53 Old Compton St., W1 (tel. 479 7461). Tube: Leicester Sq. or Piccadilly Circus. Soho's "official" gay pub is always busy, with a mostly male crowd of all ages. Horseshoe-shaped bar encourages the exchange of meaningful glances, while upstairs offers a mellower scene. Occasional specials on double drinks. Open M-Sa noon-11pm, Su noon-10:30pm.

The Coleherne, 261 Old Brompton Rd. (tel. 244 5951). Tube: Earl's Court. Take a right out of the station, then another right at Old Brompton Rd. A center of the glam, glitz, and leather scene. A bit more hard-core than other local gay bars. Open M-Sa noon-11pm, Su noon-10:30pm; upstairs bar open noon-midnight.

Drill Hall Women-Only Bar, 16 Chenies St., WC1 (tel. 631 1353). Tube: Goodge St. A much anticipated 1-nighter located in the lobby of 1 of London's biggest alternative theaters. Dim lighting and red walls. Crowded and laid back. Open M 6-11pm.

The Edge, 11 Soho Sq., W1 (tel. 439 1313). Tube: Tottenham Ct. Rd. Possibly the prime cafe/bar in which gay and straight of both sexes pose and socialize in Soho. Purple walls, plenty of metal trim, and a brassy bar decorate the 4 floors inside. Pricey food served all day. Open M-Sa noon-1am, Su noon-10:30pm.

Freedom, 60-66 Wardour St., W1 (tel. 734 0071). Tube: Piccadilly Circus or Leicester Sq. This hyper-trendy Soho haunt sports a basement disco club and a predominantly gay crowd. The pricey cocktails include the Leaving Las Vegas and the Lesbian Nun (£5). Cover £5 after 11pm. Open M-Sa 11am-3am, Su 11am-midnight. Disco club open W-Sa 9pm-3am.

Fridge Café/Bar, Town Hall Parade, Brixton Hill, SW2 (tel. 326 5100). Tube: Brixton. A refuge from the throbbing music and gyrating bodies of one of London's biggest nightclubs, this cafe's downstairs dancefloor becomes a chill out session following Sa gay night. Open M-W 10am-11pm, Th 10pm-2am, F-Sa 10am-4am.

Old Compton Café, 35 Old Compton St., W1 (tel. 439 3309). Tube: Leicester Sq. In the geographic epicenter of Soho, this is *the* gay cafe. Tables and people (predominantly 20- and 30-something males) overflow onto the street. Open daily 7am-5am.

Substation Soho, Falconberg Ct., W1 (tel. 287 9608). Tube: Tottenham Ct. Rd. For gay men who find the Old Compton St. scene too tame, a cruisy, late-night testosterone fest—one popular 1-nighter is the underwear-only grope-a-thon "Y Front" (changing rooms provided). Open M-Th 10pm-3am, Fri.-10pm-4am, Sa 10:30pm-6am. If it's Su, you can't wait for 10pm, or you live south of the Thames, **Substation South,** 9 Brighton Terr., SW9 (tel. 737 2095; tube: Brixton) provides a similar scene in Brixton, but is open at 6pm, and on Su 6pm-1am. Cover for either £2-4.

Wilde About Oscar, 30-31 Philbeach Gdns., SW5 (tel. 373 1244 before 5pm or 835 1858 after 5pm). Tube: Earl's Court. In the garden of a gay B&B. A definite splurge (entrees about £10), but manicured garden is worth it. Candles, flowers, and few tables make for an intimate dining encounter. Main courses are mostly French dishes. Open daily 7-10:30pm.

"Wow Bar," 15 Gordon Square (tel. (0956) 514 574 for info and free membership). Tube: Russell Sq. Newly transplanted "lipstick lesbian" haunt whose former guests include Martina Navratilova. Cover before 9pm and for members £3; otherwise £5. Open Sa 8pm-midnight.

Dance Clubs

Heaven, Villiers St., WC2 (tel. 930 2020), underneath The Arches. Tube: Embankment or Charing Cross (Villiers is off the Strand). Still the oldest and biggest gay disco in Europe, it has recently undergone major remodeling and will reopen shinier and newer than ever before. Call in advance for theme nights, like "Fruit Machine" (W 10pm-3:30am; cover £4, after 11:30pm £6) which sometimes features a drag bar. Bumping garage music F-Sa 10pm-3am. Cover F £6, after 11:30pm £7.50. Sa £7; after 11:30pm £8.

"G.A.Y.," at London Astoria, 157 Charing Cross Rd., WC2 (tel. 734 6963). Tube: Tottenham Ct. Rd. A 3-nights-a-week pop extravaganza amidst chrome and mirrored disco balls. Unpretentious clientele (mixed in both gender and orientation). Open Th 10:30pm-4am, F 11pm-4am, Sa 10:30pm-5am. M £3; £1 if student or with flyer. Th £3, free with flyer. Sa £6, with flyer £5.

The Fridge, Town Hall Parade, Brixton Hill, SW2 (tel. 326 5100). Tube: Brixton. For details, see **Nightclubs,** p. 246.

"Mis-shapes," Sunday at Plastic People, 37-39 Oxford St., W1 (tel. 439 0464). Tube: King's Cross/St. Pancras. Su this club turns into a haven for emphatically non-Beautiful People: "all those mis-shapen types bullied at school, and rejected by the fashion/attitude side of the gay scene." Music is a suitably non-trendy blend of indie and straight-ahead rock. Open Su 10pm-4am. Cover £4, concessions £2.

"Popstarz," Friday at the Leisure Lounge, 121 Holborn, EC1 (tel. 738 2336). Tube: Chancery Ln. This weekly gay indie 1-nighter proved so popular during its 1996 inception that it moved to this larger venue at the swank Leisure Lounge. Open F 10pm-5am. £5, after 11pm £6, concessions £4.

Turnmills, 63B Clerkenwell Rd., EC1 (tel. 250 3409). Tube: Farringdon. Walk up Turnmill St. and turn right onto Clerkenwell Rd. Sat. nights at 3am, "Trade" gets kickin' and keeps on kickin' until noon. Get there early or late to avoid long queues, or call and get an advance ticket. Open F-Sa 3am-noon. £10.

Shopping and Services

Gay's the Word, 66 Marchmont St., WC1N 1AB (tel. 278 7654). Tube: Russell Sq. Widest stock of gay and lesbian literature in England; mail order service available. Noticeboard, discussion groups, readings, coffee, and tea. Free newspapers provide info on other happenings. Lots of information on accommodations. Open M-Sa 10am-6:30pm, Su 2-6pm. AmEx, MC, Visa.

Clone Zone, 64 Old Compton St., W1 (tel. 287 3530). Tube: Piccadilly Circus or Leicester Sq. Also at 266 Old Brompton Rd. (tel. 373 0598). Well-stocked shop for gifts, cards, books, and tons of biker gear. Huge selection of super-tight clubbing shirts. Sex toys and bondage gear in the basement. Both shops open M-W 11am-8pm, Th-Sa noon-9pm, Su 1-7pm. AmEx, MC, Visa.

SH!, 46 Coronet St., N1 (tel. 613 5458). Tube: Old St. Head east on Old St. and turn left onto Pitfield St., Coronet St. will be off the right. A sex shop run by women, for women. Men cannot enter unless escorted by a lady. Open M-Sa 11:30am-6:30pm.

Soho Prowler, 3-7 Brewer St., W1 (tel. 734 4037). Tube: Piccadilly Circus. Beautiful staff and bumping music make this busy store seem almost like a packed club. A mostly male clientele shops for unique clothing, jewelry, toys and other gifts. Open M-Th 11am-10pm, F-Sa 11am-midnight, Su noon-8pm. MC, Visa.

Families with Children

London has an endless number of activities to entertain children; from parks, farms, and zoos to museums with interactive exhibits, there's always something for the little ones. The London Tourist Board publishes the brochure "Where to Take Children," filled with child-friendly sights, restaurants, and services, available at any London Tourist Centre (see p. 57). For up-to-date information on entertainment for kids, call Kidsline (tel. 222 8070) or the London Tourist Board's Children's Information line (tel. (0839) 123 404). Most sights and museums offer discounted family and child admission prices, and many offer special exhibits and events specifically for children. Below is a list of sights especially geared towards children. For more services catering to families with children, see p. 41.

In **Trafalgar Square,** children never seem to tire of feeding the pigeons, playing in the fountains, and watching red double-decker buses swirl around the square (see p. 152). When they've had enough (or you've had enough), venture toward **Picadilly Circus,** where the **Trocadero** offers older kids video games, Spice Girls paraphernalia, and bumper cars. Next door, **Madame Tussaud's Rock Circus** features waxwork incarnations of popular music artists with an accompanying sound tour (see p. 231).

Covent Garden is home to the **London Transport Museum,** which explores the history of public transport in the city through interactive video displays and a high-tech simulator (see p. 226). Don't forget to visit the incredible museum shop.

In the **City of London,** the **Tower of London** offers endless entertainment for the entire family, including the amusing and informative Beefeater tours—kids are sure to be intrigued by the sight of the Crown Jewels (see p. 159). Take a family picture in front of the **Tower Bridge** before heading inside to the **Tower Bridge Experience,** an interactive tour of the engineering and history of the Bridge (see p. 167).

Visit the **Science Museum** (see p. 228) and **Natural History Museum** (see p. 232) in Kensington, then see the Peter Pan statue in **Hyde Park** and stroll through **Kensington Gardens** (see p. 174). Picnic at the side of the picturesque Serpentine lake.

In **Marylebone,** visit the **London Planetarium** and gaze at the stars; at the adjoining **Madame Tussaud's Wax Museum,** take pictures with wax incarnations of the stars (see p. 231). Then head over to **Regent's Park,** home of the Łōńðōń Źōō the 36-acre park which once housed the real-life Jumbo the Elephant (see p. 180). Nearby **Bloomsbury** offers the **Wellcome Center,** with fun, interesting exhibits on the human body (see p. 233). Across from the **Thomas Coram Foundation for Children** in Brunswich Sq. lies **Coram's Fields,** a childrens' park with petting animals, an aviary, and a pool for children under five (see p. 187).

Along with a number of inexpensive children's clothing stores, the **East End** offers the wonderful **Bethnal Green Museum of Childhood,** devoted to displaying children's books, dolls, & more. You'll be having more fun than the kiddies (see p. 229).

While the **Docklands** are devoted mainly to business, the **Mudchute City Farm,** near Canary Wharf, offers petting animals and horseback-riding (see p. 196).

In **Greenwich, Greenwich Park** offers gardens, a wild deer park, and a children's boating pool (see p. 204). After visiting the park, you can have even more fun jumping back and forth across the Prime Meridian in the **Old Royal Observatory** before heading over to the Cutty Sark, one of the last great tea clipper ships (see p. 205).

Kew Gardens offers relaxation and sanctuary from the hustle and bustle of the city (see p. 209). The Gardens house an incredible array of plants from around the world, while the Marine Display offers a glimpse of life below sea level.

Join local London families at **Syon Park,** where children can pet creepy crawlies at the **London Butterfly House,** watch marine critters at the **London Aquatic Experience,** and play at **Snakes and Ladders,** a toy warehouse and playground (see p. 210).

After viewing the grandeur of **Windsor Castle** and strolling the grounds of the prestigious **Eton College,** head over to **Legoland Windsor** for stunning models of London and major European sights constructed from Legos (see p. 215).

Daytrips

London is a splendid place to live for those who can get out of it.
—Lord Balfour, *Observer Sayings of the Week,* Oct. 1, 1944

GETTING OUT OF LONDON

Trains and Buses

Most sites of general interest are served by both rail and bus services, though buses tend to be cheaper and slower. For information on the cheapest ways to get in and out of the city by bus or train, see **Getting In and Out of London,** p. 61. Specific information on how to reach the following destinations is described in the **Practical Information** section.

Cars

If three or four people pool resources, a car is a cheap and quick way to travel. Disadvantages include high gasoline prices, the unfamiliar laws and habits associated with foreign driving, and the heinous exhaust that results from lax British emissions standards. It's not our place to criticize cultural peculiarities, but it's pretty hard to say that Brits drive on the right side of the road. Be particularly cautious at roundabouts (rotary interchanges): give way to traffic from the right. British law requires drivers and front-seat passengers to wear seat belts; rear-seat passengers also should buckle up when belts are provided. Speed limits are always marked at the beginning of town areas; upon leaving, you'll see a circular sign with a slash through it, signaling the end of the speed restriction. Speed limits are strictly enforced, and note that many British roads are sinuous and single-track; drivers should use common sense.

Hiring (renting) an automobile is the least expensive option if you drive for a month or less. For more extended travel, you might consider **leasing.** Rental prices are £150 to £300 per week with unlimited mileage plus VAT; for insurance reasons, renters are required to be over 21 and under 70. **Europe by Car** (see below), however, will rent to younger people if the paperwork is done, in advance, in the U.S. All plans require sizable deposits unless you pay by credit card. Make sure you understand insurance before you rent; some agreements make you pay for damages you may not have caused. Expect to pay more for an automatic than for a stick.

Several U.S. firms offer rental or leasing plans for Britain; try **Kemwel Holiday Autos,** 106 Calvert St., Harrison, NY 10528-3199 (tel. (800) 678-0678), or **Europe by Car,** 1 Rockefeller Plaza, New York, NY 10020 (tel. (800) 223-1516; fax (212) 426-1458; http://www.europebycar.com; 5% student and faculty discounts available).

Brighton

In Lydia's imagination, a visit to Brighton comprised every possibility of earthly happiness.
—Jane Austen, *Pride and Prejudice*

The undisputed home of the "dirty weekend," Brighton (pop. 145,000) sparkles with a risque, tawdry luster all its own. The future King George IV allegedly sidled into Brighton for some hanky-panky around 1784. Kemp Town, among other areas of Brighton, thrives with what is collectively one of the largest gay and lesbian populations in Britain. Foreign students flock to the southern coast (ostensibly to learn English) and join an already immense student population in setting the town abuzz with mayhem and frivolity. Nab a stick of "Brighton Rock" (fluorescent hard candy) along with some naughty postcards on the seafront, and nestle down for some fun.

Daytrips from London

ORIENTATION AND PRACTICAL INFORMATION

The train stands at least 10 minutes from the town center and seafront. To reach the tourist office in Bartholomew Sq., opposite the town hall, walk south along Queen's Rd. toward the water. Turn left onto North St. (not to be confused with North Rd.) and continue until you reach Ship St.; then turn right onto Ship and proceed along to Prince Albert St., which leads right up to the tourist office.

Getting There: Trains (tel. (0345) 484950) arrive from London (1¼hr., at least 6 per hr., £13.70). **National Express** (tel. (0990) 808080) buses arrive from London (2hr., 15 per day, return £9).

Bus Station: National Express (tel. (0990) 808080) stops at Pool Valley, at the southern angle of Old Steine. Tickets and info at **I Stop Travel,** Old Steine (tel. 700406). Open M-F 8:30am-5:45pm, Sa 9am-5pm; June-Sept. also Su 11am-4:30pm.

Local Transportation: Most local buses are operated by **Brighton and Hove** (tel. 886200). The tourist office can give route and price information for most buses. All carriers in the central area charge 60p.

Bike Rental: Freedom Bikes, 108 St. James's St. (tel. 681698). £8 per day for a snazzy mountain bike. Open M-Sa 9:30am-5:30pm.

Tourist Office: 10 Bartholomew Sq. (tel. 292599). Enthusiastic staff. Books National Express tickets and beds (£1 per adult plus 10% deposit). Free street maps available. Open M-F 9am-5pm, Sa 10am-5pm, Su 10am-4pm. **Walking tours** leave the tourist office June-Aug. Th 11am (£3).

Hospital: Royal Sussex County, Eastern Rd. (tel. 696955), parallel to Marine Parade.

Emergency: Dial 999; no coins required.

Police: John St. (tel. 606744).

Postal Code: BN1 1BA.

Telephone Code: 01273.

ACCOMMODATIONS

Brighton's best bets for budget lodging are its three hostels. B&Bs and cheaper hotels begin at £18. Shabbier B&Bs and hotels collect west of West Pier and east of Palace Pier. There is a huge number of B&Bs in **Kemp Town,** the neighborhood that runs perpendicular to the sea east of Palace Pier a bit farther from town center.

Brighton Backpackers Hostel, 75-76 Middle St. (tel. 777717). An unforgettably painted independent hostel that bubbles with international flavor. *The* place to meet other backpackers in Brighton. Clean, somewhat cramped rooms overlook the ocean. Friendly Miles offers advice and tunes from his guitar against the chirp of the resident parakeets. TV lounge, jungle-colored cafe, and pool table. The quieter, newly opened annex faces the ocean. 4- to 8-bed coed and single-sex dorms. £9, less in winter. Annex £10-12.50. Inexpensive breakfast and dinner. Sheets £1. Kitchen and laundry.

Baggies Back-packers, 33 Oriental Pl. (tel. 733740), near West Pier. Go west of West Pier along King's Rd.; Oriental Pl. will be on your right. Owners spin a little jazz and take a turn on the floor in the bar with a blue mosaic floor. Exquisite murals line the walls, and a mosaic floor of world maps set the tone for this mellow, international hostel. Spacious and clean. Co-ed dorms £9, single-sex dorms £10; doubles £23. Bedding £1 for entire stay. Key deposit £5. Laundry facilities. No lockout. No curfew.

YHA Youth Hostel, Patcham Pl. (tel. 556196), 4 mi. north on the main London Rd. Take Patcham bus #5 or 5A (from stop E) from Old Steine in front of the Royal Pavilion to the Black Lion Hotel. Georgian-style country home beside a gorgeous, sloping park. Rooms (6-16 beds each) look new, though they're 400 years old. A good jumping-off point for the South Downs Way. £9.75, under 18 £6.30. Breakfast £3. Laundry facilities. Reception closed 10am-1pm. Curfew 11pm. Often full; call ahead in July-Aug. or show up around breakfast time; closed Jan.

FOOD AND PUBS

The area around the Lanes is filled with trendy and expensive places waiting to gobble up tourist dollars. For cheaper, fare try the fish and chip shops along the beach or north of the Lanes.

Food for Friends, 17a Prince Albert St. (tel. 202310). Cheap, friendly vegetarian food in a friendly atmosphere. Daily friendly specials—the salads send the taste buds straight to friendly heaven (£2-3.25). Entrees £3-6. Get the "Taster" special: £5.20 for a portion of all the day's entrees. Open daily 8am-10. Bring a friend!

Terre à Terre, 71 East St. (tel. 729051). When backpackers want to splurge, this is often the place they do it. Terre apart vegetarian dishes cheerfully dispensed. Entrees £8. Open Tu-Su noon-11pm.

Piccolo, 52 Ship St. (tel. 203701). Busy even on late Monday nights, Piccolo specializes in homemade pasta and pizza. Take-away pizza for lunch £2.50. Pastas £4-5. Open daily 11:30am-11pm. Wheelchair access.

SIGHTS AND ENTERTAINMENT

John Nash's transformation of a plain-Jane farmhouse into the **Royal Pavilion** (tel. 290900) from 1815 to 1822 brought about Brighton's rise to fashion and popularity. *(Open daily June-Sept. 10am-6pm; Oct.-May 10am-5pm. £4.50, students and seniors £3.25, children £2.50. Partially wheelchair accessible. Beach rentals £1.)* George IV (then Prince of Wales) had Nash, his favorite architect, embellish the estate in a loosely Oriental, unabashedly ornate fashion, mixing Chinese, Indian, and even Gothic decorations. "Opulence" doesn't do the place justice.

Around the corner from the Pavilion stands the **Brighton Museum and Art Gallery** (tel. 603005), Church St. It features paintings, English pottery, and Art Deco collections. Leer at Salavador Dalí's incredibly sexy, red, pursing sofa, *Mae West's Lips.* At the fine **Willett Collection of Pottery,** avant-garde art and antique Brighton relics simultaneously reflect the varied faces of this seaside escape. *(Open M-Tu and Th-Sa 10am-5pm, Su 2-5:30pm. Free. Limited wheelchair access.)*

The main attraction in Brighton is, of course, the **beach.** Those who associate the word "beach" with visions of sand and sun may be sorely disappointed—the weather can be quite nippy even in June and July, and the closest thing to sand on the beach are the fist-sized brown rocks. Even in 70°F weather with overcast skies, beach-goers gamely strip to bikinis and lifeguards don sunglasses. Hang loose just west of Brighton Marina at the **nude bathing** areas. Be sure to stay within the limits. **Telescombe Beach,** nearly 4½ mi. to the east of Palace Pier, is frequented for the most part by a gay crowd. Look for a sign before Telescombe Tavern marked "Telescombe Cliffs." Numerous sailing opportunities crop up in summer; check bulletin boards at the tourist office. After heading to the seafront, stroll through the **Lanes,** a jumble of 17th-century streets—some no wider than 3 ft.—stretching south of North St. and filled with antique jewelry shops, cafes, and overpriced knick-knack vendors. The heavily promoted **Palace Pier,** a century old and recently repainted, offers a host of amusements, including a museum of slot machines, between the piers under King's Rd. Arches.

Brighton brims with nightlife options, earning it the nickname "London-by-the-Sea." And as surely as the tide turns, clubs and venues go in and out of fashion. The local monthly, *The Punter* details evening events and can be found at pubs, newsagents, and record stores. *What's On,* a poster-sized flysheet, points the hedonist toward hot-and-happening scenes. Gay and lesbian venues can be found in the latest issues of *Gay Times* (£2.20) or *Capital Gay.*

Brighton is a student town, and where there are students there are cheap drinks somewhere. Many pubs and clubs offer fantastic drink specials during the week—some budget-minded backpackers find no reason to go out on weekends, when most places are crowded and expensive. **Fortune of War,** 157 King's Rd. Arches (tel. 205065), is always a lucky choice. *(Open M-Sa 11am-11pm, Su noon-10:30pm.)* **Cuba,** 160 King's Rd. Arches (tel. 770505), is close-by. *(Cover £3-6. Open M-Sa 11am-11pm, Su 11am-10:30pm.)* Revelers congregate in front of these two pubs and drink on the beach until about 11pm. Also popular is **Squid and Starfish,** 77 Middle St. (tel. 727114), next door to the Backpacker's Hostel. Brightly colored walls and a vodka mural make this pub a popular place to begin an evening. *(Open M-F 5-11pm, Sa noon-11pm, Su 5-10:30pm.)* Bedsteads and vodka bottle chandeliers make **Smugglers** on Ship St. a raucous place to drink. The pirate theme makes you thirst for more ale; pints go for £1.60. *(Happy Hour M-F noon-8pm.)* See what America is not at **Beider-**

beck's (tel. 326778), an "American" pub with fantastic outdoor seating flooded by Europeans in Clarence Yard, Meeting House Ln.

Most clubs open from 10pm to 2am every day except Sunday. The most technically armed and massively populated are **Paradox** (tel. 321628) and **Event II** (tel. 732627), both on West St. Paradox gets a bit dressy towards the end of the week; the monthly "Wild Fruit" gay night is popular with people of all persuasions. Event spent over £1 million adding all of the electric trimmings to its already immense dance floor. The arches of old-WWII-tunnels-turned-**Zap Club** (tel. 821588), King's Rd., provide space for dark rendezvous and dirty dancing; come here for hard-core pounding to rave and house music. The club hosts frequent gay nights and is open into the wee hours of the morn. **Gloucester,** Gloucester Plaza (tel. 699068), provides good cheap fun with music varying nightly. Slightly unsightly **Casablanca** (tel. 321817), Middle St., plays live jazz to a largely student crowd—discount for Backpackers hostelers. Get ready to sweat it again, Sam.

Gay clubbers flock to **Zanzibar,** St. James St. (tel. 622100), and **Revenge** on Old Steine, Brighton's largest gay dance club. The **Queen's Arms,** 8 George St. (tel. 696873), packs an enthusiastic gay and lesbian crowd into its Sunday night cabaret. On Wednesday and Saturday nights the disco ball also sees some action.

Oxford

Towery city and branchy between towers;
Cuckoo-echoing, bell-swarmèd, lark-charmèd, rook-racked, river-rounded...

—Gerard Manley Hopkins, "Duns Scotus's Oxford"

Originally named as the place where oxen could ford the Thames, Oxford has always inspired stories of crossings. Oxford's three favorite sons—Lewis Carroll, C.S. Lewis, and J.R.R. Tolkien—sat near the stone-bridged waters dreaming of crossings through mirrors, through wardrobes, through mountain passes. Today, the spires of the University still inspire, but are in some places black with soot; two centuries of industrial bustle have left their mark. Still, there are pockets of respite to charm and edify the academic pilgrim. Despite the crush of tourists, Oxford has an irrepressible grandeur.

ORIENTATION AND PRACTICAL INFORMATION

Queen St., High St., St. Aldates St., and Cornmarket St. meet at right angles at Carfax, the town center. The colleges lie mainly to the east of Carfax along High and **Broad Street.** The **bus** and **train** stations and **tourist information** center lie to the northwest. Past the east end of High St. over **Magdalen Bridge,** the neighborhoods of East Oxford stretch along Cowley Rd. and Iffley Rd. Abingdon Rd. leads off to South Oxford, while more upscale residential areas surround Woodstock Rd. and Banbury Rd. to the north.

Getting There: Local trains depart every 30min. from London. **Thames Trains** leave from **Paddington** (1hr., day return £11.80). The **Oxford Tube** (tel. 772250) sends buses from **Victoria** (1½hr., 1-6 per hr., next-day return £7, students, seniors, and children £6).

Train Station: Park End St. (tel. (0345) 484950, recording 794422), west of Carfax. Ticket office open M-F 6am-8pm, Sa 6:45am-8pm, Su 7:45am-8pm.

Bus Station: Gloucester Green (follow arrows from Carfax). **Oxford CityLink** (tel. 785400 or 772250 for timetable) desk open daily 6:30am-6:30pm. **National Express** (tel. (0990) 808080) office open M-F 8am-5:30pm, Sa 8am-5pm, Su 9:45am-3:15pm.

Public Transportation: The **Oxford Bus Company** (tel. 785400) and **Stagecoach** (tel. 772250) offer swift and frequent service. The Oxford Bus Company operates **Park & Ride** (mostly for commuters) and **Cityline.** Most local services board on the streets around Carfax. Fares are low (most 60p single). Day passes are available and well worth the purchase; buy them from the bus driver or at the bus station.

Taxi: Radio Taxi (tel. 242424); **ABC** (tel. 770077).

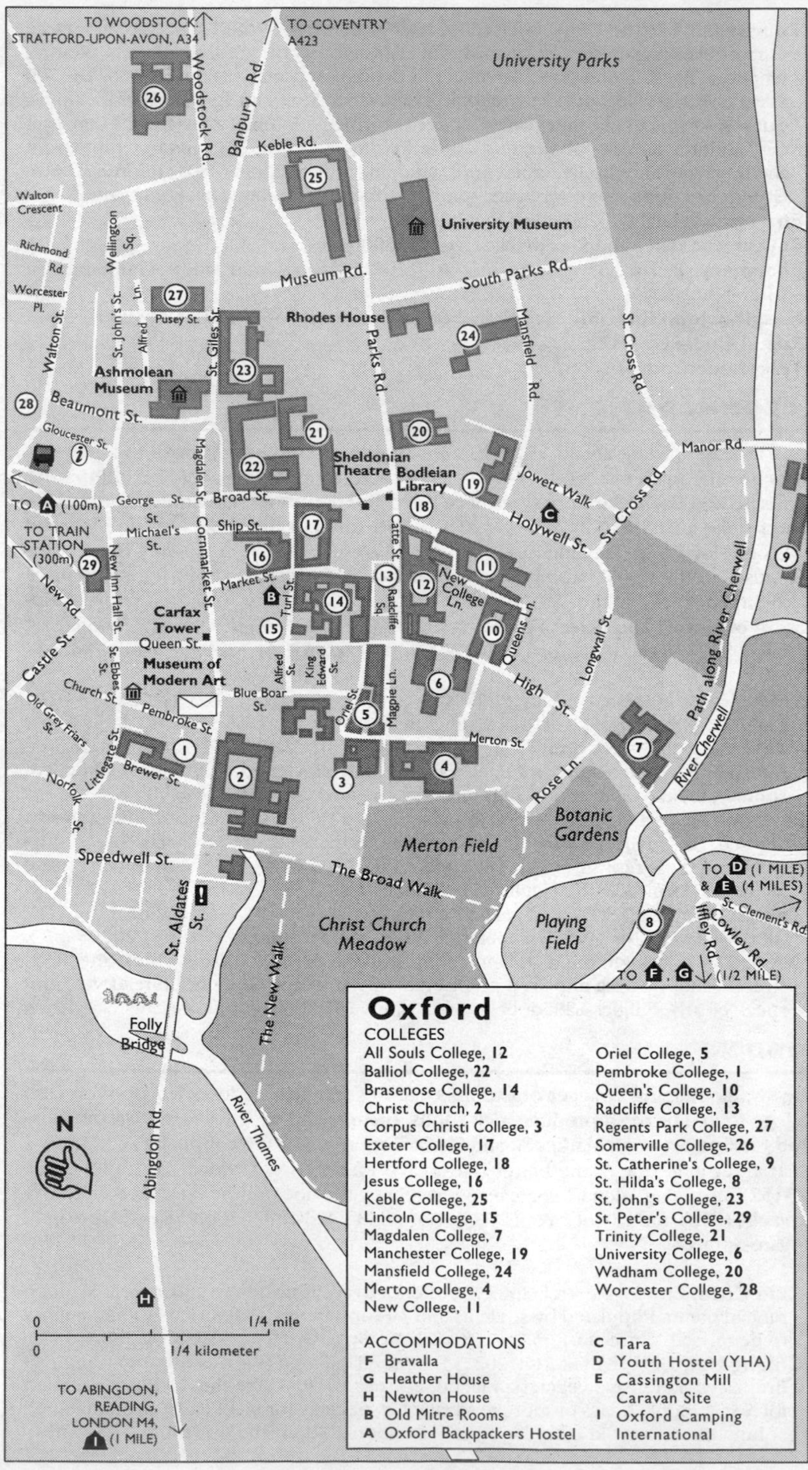

TO WOODSTOCK, STRATFORD-UPON-AVON, A34
TO COVENTRY A423
University Parks
Woodstock Rd.
Banbury Rd.
Keble Rd.
University Museum
Walton Crescent
Richmond Rd.
Wellington Sq.
Museum Rd.
South Parks Rd.
Worcester Pl.
Pusey St.
Alfred Ln.
St. John's St.
Walton St.
Rhodes House
Parks Rd.
Mansfield Rd.
St. Cross Rd.
Ashmolean Museum
St. Giles St.
Beaumont St.
Gloucester St.
Magdalen St.
Sheldonian Theatre
Bodleian Library
Manor Rd.
Jowett Walk
Holywell St.
TO A (100m)
George St.
Broad St.
TO TRAIN STATION (300m)
St Michael's St.
Ship St.
Cornmarket St.
Catte St.
New College Ln.
Market St.
Turl St.
Radcliffe Sq.
Queens Ln.
Longwall St.
Path along River Cherwell
New Rd.
New Inn Hall St.
Carfax Tower
Queen St.
Castle St.
St. Ebbes St.
Museum of Modern Art
Alfred St.
King Edward St.
Magpie Ln.
High St.
Church St.
Blue Boar St.
Oriel St.
Pembroke St.
Old Grey Friars St.
Merton St.
Littlegate St.
Brewer St.
Rose Ln.
River Cherwell
Norfolk St.
Botanic Gardens
Merton Field
Speedwell St.
The Broad Walk
TO D (1 MILE) & E (4 MILES)
St. Clement's Rd.
St. Aldates St.
Christ Church Meadow
Playing Field
Iffley Rd.
Cowley Rd.
TO F, G (1/2 MILE)
The New Walk
Folly Bridge
River Thames
Abingdon Rd.
N
0 1/4 mile
0 1/4 kilometer
TO ABINGDON, READING, LONDON M4, I (1 MILE)
Oxford
COLLEGES
All Souls College, 12
Balliol College, 22
Brasenose College, 14
Christ Church, 2
Corpus Christi College, 3
Exeter College, 17
Hertford College, 18
Jesus College, 16
Keble College, 25
Lincoln College, 15
Magdalen College, 7
Manchester College, 19
Mansfield College, 24
Merton College, 4
New College, 11
Oriel College, 5
Pembroke College, 1
Queen's College, 10
Radcliffe College, 13
Regents Park College, 27
Somerville College, 26
St. Catherine's College, 9
St. Hilda's College, 8
St. John's College, 23
St. Peter's College, 29
Trinity College, 21
University College, 6
Wadham College, 20
Worcester College, 28
ACCOMMODATIONS
F Bravalla
G Heather House
H Newton House
B Old Mitre Rooms
A Oxford Backpackers Hostel
C Tara
D Youth Hostel (YHA)
E Cassington Mill Caravan Site
I Oxford Camping International

DAYTRIPS

Tourist Office: The Old School, Gloucester Green (tel. 726871; fax 240261). From Carfax, follow signposts up Cornmarket St., left onto George St., and right into Gloucester Green. Books rooms for £2.50 and a 10% deposit. Accommodations list 50p. The 70p street map and guide includes a valuable index. Open M-Sa 9am-5pm, Su 10am-3:30pm.

Tours: A 2hr. walking tour leaves the tourist office 2-5 times daily from 11am-2pm (£4, children £2.50). Ubiquitous **Guide Friday** (tel. 790522) runs bus tours from the train station with live guides (£8, students and seniors £6.50, children £2.50). **Student groups** also offer tours, some of which offer money-back guarantees.

Emergency: Dial 999; no coins required.

Police: St. Aldates and Speedwell St. (tel. 266000).

Pharmacy: Boots, 6-8 Cornmarket St. (tel. 247461). Open M-F 8:45am-6pm, Su 11am-5pm.

Hospital: John Radcliffe Hospital, Headley Way (tel. 741166). Bus #13B or 14A.

Postal Code: OX1 1ZZ.

Telephone Code: 01865.

ACCOMMODATIONS

Book at least a week ahead, especially for singles, and expect to mail in a deposit. B&Bs line the main roads out of town, all of them a vigorous walk (15-20min.) from Carfax. The 300s on **Banbury Road,** fern-laced and domestic, stand miles north of the center (take a Cityline bus in the #20s). You'll find cheaper B&Bs in the 200s and 300s on **Iffley Road** (Cityline bus #3 or 4) and from 250-350 on **Cowley Road** (Cityline buses in the #50s). **Abingdon Road,** in South Oxford, is about the same price (take Cityline buses in the 30s). If it's late and you're homeless, call the **Oxford Association of Hotels and Guest Houses** at one of the following numbers: 774083 (East Oxford), 862138 (West Oxford), 510327 (North Oxford), or 722995 (South Oxford).

YHA Youth Hostel, 32 Jack Straw's Ln., Headington (tel. 762997; fax 769402). Catch Citylink bus #13 or 14 heading away from Carfax on High St. and ask the driver to stop at Jack Straw's Ln. (at least 4 per hr., last bus 11:10pm, single 60p, return £1). The hostel is an 8min. walk up the hill. Generous facilities: a kitchen, laundry, lockers, and a food shop all crowd in. £10.25, under 18 £7.05.

Heather House, 192 Iffley Rd. (tel./fax 249757). Walk 20min. or take the bus marked "Rose Hill" (60p) from the bus station, train station, or Carfax Tower. Vivian's matchless repository of advice will remind you why you love to travel. Private facilities. Dorms £18-20; singles £22; doubles £46.

Tara, 10 Holywell St. (call *Typetalk* (free) at (04451) 494 2022, within the U.K. (0800) 515152, or give the operator Tara's phone number (01865) 202953; fax 200297). A lark-charmed dream among the spires on Oxford's oldest medieval street. Kind, hearing-impaired proprietors Mr. and Mrs. Godwin lip-read well and speak clearly. Singles £28; doubles £46; triples £55. Reserve at least 2 weeks ahead.

FOOD

The swank, bulging swagger of Oxford's eateries seduces students fed up with fetid college food. For fresh produce, deli goods, breads, and shoe leather, visit the **Covered Market** between Market St. and Carfax (open M-Sa 8am-5:30pm).

Eat and run at one of the better take-aways: **Harvey's of Oxford,** 58 High St. (tel. 723152), near Magdalen College, recognizable by the line out the door, serves cherry flapjacks (85p) and carrot cake (£1.25). (Open M-F 8:30am-5:30pm, Sa 8:30am-6pm, Su 9am-6pm.)

Café Coco, Cowley Rd. (tel. 200232), offers a lively atmosphere and a great Mediterranean menu. Populated by students and 30-somethings, Café Coco is a bargain not to be missed. Entrees £4.65-7.50 ("Greek Messe"). Open daily 10am-11pm.

Chiang Mai, 130a High St. (tel. 202233). Spicy Thai food (we mean *spicy*). Victorian fireplaces. Extensive vegetarian menu; entrees £5.50-9. Try the sticky rice dessert for £3.50. Book 2 days or more in advance, especially for weekends. In summer, go at lunchtime to avoid crowds. Open M-Sa noon-2:30pm and 6-11pm.

Heroes, 8 Ship St. (tel. 723459). Packs in student clientele, serving sandwiches on a variety of freshly baked breads with a super selection of stuffings (£1.70-3.30). Potted home-made pâté for the adventurous. Open M-F 8am-5pm, Sa 8:30am-6pm, Su 10am-5pm.

Cherwell Boathouse, Bardwell Rd. (tel. 552746), off Banbury Rd., 1 mi. north of town; make a right at the sign for the boathouse. All Citylink Buses in the 20s go up Banbury Rd. Perched on the Cherwell, the romantic Boathouse makes a good place to propose. Book well in advance and expect to spend the entire evening. Lunch £17.50, dinner £18.50, and worth every pence. When you're finished, rent a punt next door (£8, weekends £10, deposit £40). Open Tu-Sa noon-2pm and 6-10pm, Su noon-2pm only. Call to arrange a time.

PUBS

Pubs far outnumber colleges in Oxford; many consider them the city's prime attraction. Most pubs are open all afternoon and begin to fill up around 5pm. Be ready to crawl—some pubs are so small that a single band of merry students will squeeze out other patrons. *Good Pubs of Oxford* (£3 at bookstores and tourist office) is an indispensable guide to the town's beer dungeons. Buy it, use it, keep it dry.

Turf Tavern, 4 Bath Pl. (tel. 243235), off Holywell St. Sprawling, cavernous 13th-century pub is nestled deep in an alleyway against the ruins of the city wall. Intimate and relaxed until the student crowd turns things lively. Beers, punches, ciders, and country wines—mead, elderberry, apple, and red-and-white currant. Open M-Sa 11am-11pm, Su noon-10:30pm. Hot food served noon-8pm.

The Eagle and Child, 49 St. Giles St. (tel. 310154). Known to all as the Bird and Baby, this pub moistened the tongues of C.S. Lewis and J.R.R. Tolkien for a quarter-century. Open M-Sa 11am-11pm, Su noon-10:30pm.

The Bear, Alfred St. So old (est. 1242) it's forgotten its street number. 5000 ties from England's brightest and most boastful cover every flat surface but the floor; you can buy your own "The Bear 1242-1992" tie for £9. Open M-Sa noon-11pm, Su noon-3pm.

The Perch (tel. 240386), Binsey Village. From Walton St. in Jericho, walk down Walton Well Rd. and straight through Port Meadow. Cross Rainbow Bridge and head north along the Thames Path, then follow the trail west when you see a few buildings several hundred yards across a field. This pub on the Thames will make your whole vacation worthwhile. Open M-Sa 11:30am-11pm, Su noon-10:30pm.

The Jolly Farmers, 20 Paradise St. (tel. 793759). Take Queen St. from Carfax, turn left on Castle St., then right on Paradise St. Oxfordshire's only gay and lesbian pub. Open M-Sa noon-11pm, Su 12:30-10:30pm.

SIGHTS

The tourist office guide *Welcome to Oxford* (£1) and the tourist office map (20p) list the colleges' public visiting hours (usually for a few hours in the afternoon; often curtailed without prior notice or explanation). Some colleges charge admission; others may impose mercenary fees during peak tourist times. At Christ Church, don't bother trying to sneak in (even after cleverly hiding your backpack and bright yellow *Let's Go*): elderly bouncers sporting bowler hats (porters) stationed 50 feet apart will squint at you and kick you out. Other colleges have been known to be less vigilant near the back gates. Coddle the porters or you will get nowhere.

Start your walking tour by hiking up the 99 spiral stairs of **Carfax Tower** (tel. 792653) for an overview of the city. *(Open daily Apr.-Oct. 10am-5:30pm; Nov.-Mar. 10am-3:30pm. £1.20, children 60p.)* Before hitting the heights, get a free map of the rooftops from the attendant at the bottom.

Just down St. Aldates St. stands **Christ Church** (tel. 276492), an intimidating pile of stone dwarfing the other colleges. *(Open M-Sa 9am-5pm, Su 1-5pm. Admission is a scandalous £3, concessions £2, families £6.)* "The House" has Oxford's grandest quad and its most socially distinguished (obnoxious) students. Christ Church's chapel is also Oxford's **cathedral,** the smallest in England. In AD 730, Oxford's patron saint, St. Frideswide, built a nunnery on this site in thanks for two miracles: the blinding and subsequent recovery of an annoying suitor. The cathedral contains a stained-glass

window (c. 1320) depicting Thomas à Becket kneeling in supplication, just before being hacked apart in Canterbury Cathedral.

Curiouser and curiouser, the adjoining **Tom Quad** sometimes becomes the site of undergraduate pond dunking. The quad takes its name from **Great Tom,** the seven-ton bell in Tom Tower, which has faithfully rung 101 strokes (the original number of students) at 9:05pm (the original undergraduate curfew) every evening since 1682. Nearby, the fan-vaulted **College Hall** bears imposing portraits of some of Christ Church's most famous alums—Charles "Lewis Carroll" Dodgson, John Ruskin, John Locke, and a bored-looking W.H. Auden (in the corner by the kitchen).

Through an archway (to your left as you face the cathedral) lies **Peckwater Quad,** encircled by the most elegant Palladian building in Oxford. Look here for faded rowing standings chalked on the walls and for Christ Church's library (closed to visitors). The adjoining **Canterbury Quad** houses the **Christ Church Picture Gallery** (tel. 276172; enter on Oriel Sq. and at Canterbury Gate), a fine collection of Italian, Dutch, and Flemish paintings. *(Open Apr.-Sept. M-Sa 10:30am-1pm and 2-5:30pm, Su 2-5:30pm; Oct.-Mar. closes at 4:30pm. £1, students and seniors 50p. Visitors to gallery only should enter through Canterbury Gate off Oriel St.)* The **Museum of Modern Art,** 30 Pembroke St. (tel. 722733), across St. Aldates, showcases changing exhibitions. *(Open Tu-W and F-Su 11am-6pm, Th 11am-9pm. £2.50, students and seniors £1.50, children free. Free for all W 11am-1pm and Th 6-9pm. Wheelchair access.)*

Merton College, off Merton St. (tel. 276310), features a fine garden and a 14th-century library holding the first printed Welsh Bible. The college also houses the **Mob Quad** (Oxford's oldest and least impressive), and some of the University's best gargoyles. *(College open M-F 2-4pm, Sa-Su 10am-4pm.)*

The soot-blackened **University College** (tel. 276619), on High St. up the crooked Logic Ln. from Merton St., dates from 1249 and vies with Merton for the title of oldest college, claiming Alfred the Great as its founder. *(Open July-Aug. daily 10am-6pm.)* Percy Bysshe Shelley was expelled from University for writing *The Necessity of Atheism,* but has since been immortalized in a prominent godless monument inside the college (to the right as you enter from High St.). Bill Clinton spent his Rhodes days here; his rooms at 46 Leckford Rd. are an endless source of smoked-but-didn't-inhale jokes for tour guides. Down High St. on the right lies the **Botanic Garden,** a sumptuous array of plants that have flourished for three centuries. *(Open daily Apr.-Sept. 9am-5pm; Oct.-Mar. 9am-4:30pm; glasshouses open daily 2-4pm. Late June to early Sept. £1.50, children free; free for everyone rest of year.)*

Picking up where the Botanic Garden across the street left off, extensive verdant grounds surround the flower-laced quads of **Magdalen College** (MAUD-lin; tel. 276000), traditionally considered Oxford's handsomest. *(Open daily July-Sept. noon-6pm; Oct.-June 2-5pm; Apr.-Sept. £2, students, seniors, and children £1; Oct.-Mar. free.)* The college's spiritual patron is alumnus Oscar Wilde—the place has always walked on the flamboyant side. Edward Gibbon declared the 14 months he spent here "the most idle and unprofitable of my whole career."

Just up High St. toward Carfax, a statue of Queen Caroline (wife of George II) crowns the front gate of **Queen's College** (tel. 279121). Wren and Hawksmoor went to the trouble of rebuilding Queen's in the 17th and 18th centuries with a distinctive Queen Anne style. A boar's head graces the Christmas table—supposedly commemorating an early student of the college who, attacked by a boar on the outskirts of Oxford, choked his assailant to death with a volume of Aristotle (closed to the public, except for authorized tours).

Next to Queen's stands **All Souls** (tel. 279379), a graduate college with a prodigious endowment. *(Open Apr.-Oct. M-F 2-4:30pm; Nov.-Mar. 2-4pm; closed in Aug.)* Candidates who survive the admission exams get invited to dinner, when it is ensured that they are "well-born, well-bred, and only moderately learned."

Turn up Catte St. to the **Bodleian Library** (tel. 277165), Oxford's principal reading and research library with over five million books and 50,000 manuscripts. Sir Thomas Bodley endowed the library's first wing in 1602; the institution has since grown to fill the immense **Old Library** complex, the **Radcliffe Camera** next door, and two Broad St. buildings. Admission to the reading rooms is by pass only. *(Library open M-F 9am-*

6pm, Sa 9am-1pm. Tours in summer M-F 4 per day, Sa-Su 2 per day; in winter 2 per day. £3.50. Tours leave from the Divinity School, across the street.) A student ID (and optimally a letter of introduction from your college), two passport photos (available on the spot), and the admission office will issue you a £3 two-day pass. On Broad St., across from the Bodleian, you can browse at **Blackwell's,** the famous bookstore.

The **Sheldonian Theatre** (tel. 277299), set beside the Bodleian, is a Roman-style jewel of an auditorium designed by Wren when he was a teenager. Graduation ceremonies, conducted in Latin, take place in the Sheldonian and can be witnessed with permission from one of the "bulldogs" (an "affectionate" term for porter). The cupola of the theatre affords a great view of the spires of Oxford. *(Open M-Sa 10am-12:30pm and 2-4:30pm, subject to change. £1.50, children £1.)*

The gates of **Balliol College** (tel. 277777), across Broad St., still bear scorch marks from the immolations of 16th-century Protestant martyrs. The pyres were built near the college. Look for the small cross set into Broad St. This monument is often identified to gullible tourists as Oxford's "famous sunken cathedral." Matthew Arnold, the poet Swinburne, Aldous Huxley, and Adam Smith were all sons of Balliol's spires. *(Open daily 2-5pm. £1, students and children free.)* Balliol students preserve a semblance of tradition by hurling bricks over the wall at their arch-rival, conservative **Trinity College** (tel. 279900), on Broad St. Founded in 1555, Trinity's baroque chapel features a limewood altarpiece, cedar lattices, and angel-capped pediments. *(Open daily 10:40-11:45am and 2-5pm. £2, students, seniors, and children £1.)*

DAYTRIPS

Across Catte St. from the Bodleian, New College Ln. leads inevitably to **New College** (tel. 279555). Founded by William of Wykeham in 1379, New College has become one of Oxford's most prestigious colleges. *(Open daily Easter-Oct. 11am-5pm; Nov.-Easter 2-4pm. Use the Holywell St. Gate. £1.50.)* The multiple layers of the front quad (compare the different stones of the first and second stories) reveal the architectural history of the college. Look for the exquisitely detailed misericords, carved into the pews by sympathetic carpenters to support monks' bottoms. A peaceful croquet garden is encircled by part of the **old city wall,** and every few years the mayor of the City of Oxford visits the college for a ceremonial inspection to ascertain the wall's good repair. A former head of the college, Rev. Warden Spooner, is now remembered as the unintentional inventor of the "spoonerism." This stern but befuddled academic would raise a toast to "our queer old dean" or rebuke students who had "hissed all the mystery lectures" and "tasted the whole worm." Many colleges hold sporting matches on the nearby **University Parks.**

Walk through the **University Museum** (tel. 272950), Parks Rd. *(Open M-Sa noon-5pm. Free.)* Next door the **Pitt Rivers Museum** (tel. 270949) contains a wonderfully eclectic ethnography and natural history collection that includes shrunken heads and rare butterflies. *(Open M-Sa 1-4:30pm. Free.)*

Keble College (tel. 272727), across from the University Museum, was designed by architect William Butterfield to stand out from the museum's sandstone background. *(Open daily 2-5pm.)* The intricate and multi-patterned red brick, known as "The Fair Isle Sweater," was deemed "actively ugly" by Sir Nikolaus Pevsner.

The imposing **Ashmolean Museum** (tel. 278000), Beaumont St., opened in 1683, is Britain's first public museum. Van Gogh, Michelangelo, and Monet convene in the permanent collection. *(Open Tu-Sa 10am-4pm, Su 2-4pm. Free.)* The **Cast Gallery** behind the museum stores over 250 casts of Greek sculptures. *(Open Tu-Sa 10am-4pm, Su 2-4pm. Free.)*

A few blocks up St. Giles, as the street becomes Woodstock Rd., stands **Somerville College** (tel. 270600), Oxford's most famous women's college. Somerville's alumnae include Dorothy Sayers, Indira Gandhi, and Margaret Thatcher. Women were not granted degrees until 1920, and they comprise only about 38% of today's student body. *(Open daily 2-5:30pm.)*

ENTERTAINMENT

Public transit shuts down early. For information on what's happening, check the bulletin boards at the tourist office, or pick up a copy of *This Month in Oxford.* Most colleges will provide pointers.

Oxford cherishes music; try to attend a concert or Evensong service at one of the colleges, or a performance at the **Holywell Music Rooms. City of Oxford Orchestra** (tel. 744457), the city's professional symphony orchestra, plays Sunday coffee concerts and a subscription series in the Sheldonian Theatre and college chapels throughout the summer. *(Shows at 8pm. Tickets £12-15, 25% student discount.)* **Blackwell's Music Shop,** 38 Holywell St. (tel. 261384), sells tickets. *(Open M and W-Sa 9am-6pm, Tu 9:30am-6pm, Su noon-5pm.)*

The **Apollo Theatre** (tel. 244544), George St., presents a wide range of performances, ranging from lounge-lizard jazz to the Welsh National Opera. *(Open M-Sa 10am-6pm. Tickets from £6, student and senior discounts.)* The **Oxford Playhouse,** 11-12 Beaumont St. (tel. 798600), is a venue for bands, dance troupes, and the Oxford Stage Company. *(Tickets from £6, students and seniors £4, standby tickets for students and seniors on day of show.)* The **Oxford Union,** St. Michael's St. (tel. (0171) 385 8993), shows student productions. *(Tickets £8, students, seniors, and children £5.)* **The Old Fire Station,** 40 George St. (tel. 794490), features more avant-garde work.

The **Westgate Pub,** 190 Cowley Rd. (tel. 250099), is the best option for late-night live jazz and comedy. The **Zodiac,** 193 Cowley Rd., provides the best bands around for a hefty cover of £5 and up.

A favorite pastime in Oxford is **punting** on the River Thames (known here as the Isis) or on the River Cherwell (CHAR-wul). **Oxford Boat Hire,** Folly Bridge, south of Carfax and behind the Head of the River pub, rents from June to September. *(£6-8 per hr., £15-20 deposit.)* **Riverside Boating Co.,** Folly Bridge, across St. Aldates from the Head of the River pub, rents from April to September. *(£6 per hr., £20 deposit. Open daily 10am-dusk.)* Or try **Magdalen Bridge Boat Co.** (tel. 202643), Magdalen Bridge, east of Carfax along High St. *(£10 per hr., deposit £20 plus ID. Open daily Mar.-Oct. 10am-9pm.)* Watch for **Parson's Pleasure,** a small riverside area where men sometimes sunbathe nude. Female passersby are expected to open their parasols and tip them at a discreet angle to obscure the view.

The university celebrates **Eights Week** at the end of May, when all the colleges enter crews in the bumping races and beautiful people gather on the banks to nibble strawberries and sip champagne. In early September, **St. Giles Fair** invades one of Oxford's main streets with an old-fashioned carnival, complete with Victorian roundabout and whirligigs. Daybreak on May 1 brings one of Oxford's loveliest moments: the Magdalen College Choir greets the summer by singing madrigals from the top of the tower to a crowd below, and the town indulges in morris dancing, beating the bounds, and other age-old rituals of merrymaking—pubs open at 7am.

Cambridge

The winds of change have so often weathered Cambridge that it has grown aslant, peculiar in configuration and even texture. This Roman-invaded trading town endured a series of nasty Viking raids before the Normans arrived in the 11th century. The 13th century brought Oxford's refugees, an invasion that would permanently alter the city more than any military conquest. In recent years, Cambridge has ceased to be the exclusive preserve of upper-class sons, although roughly half of its students still come from independent schools and only 40% are women.

While tradition mandates that students bedeck themselves with cravat and cane, almost none actually preserve this staid image, except during exams, when they are required to deck themselves out in full regalia. The University itself exists mainly as a bureaucracy that handles the formalities of lectures, degrees, and real estate, leaving to individual colleges the small tutorials and seminars that comprise a Cambridge education. At exams' end, Cambridge explodes with gin-soaked glee, and May Week (in mid-June, naturally) launches a dizzying schedule of cocktail parties; students down a bevy of alcoholic beverages on aptly named Suicide Sunday.

ORIENTATION AND PRACTICAL INFORMATION

Cambridge (pop. 105,000), about 60 mi. north of London, has two main avenues, both changing names. The main shopping street starts at **Magdalene Bridge** and

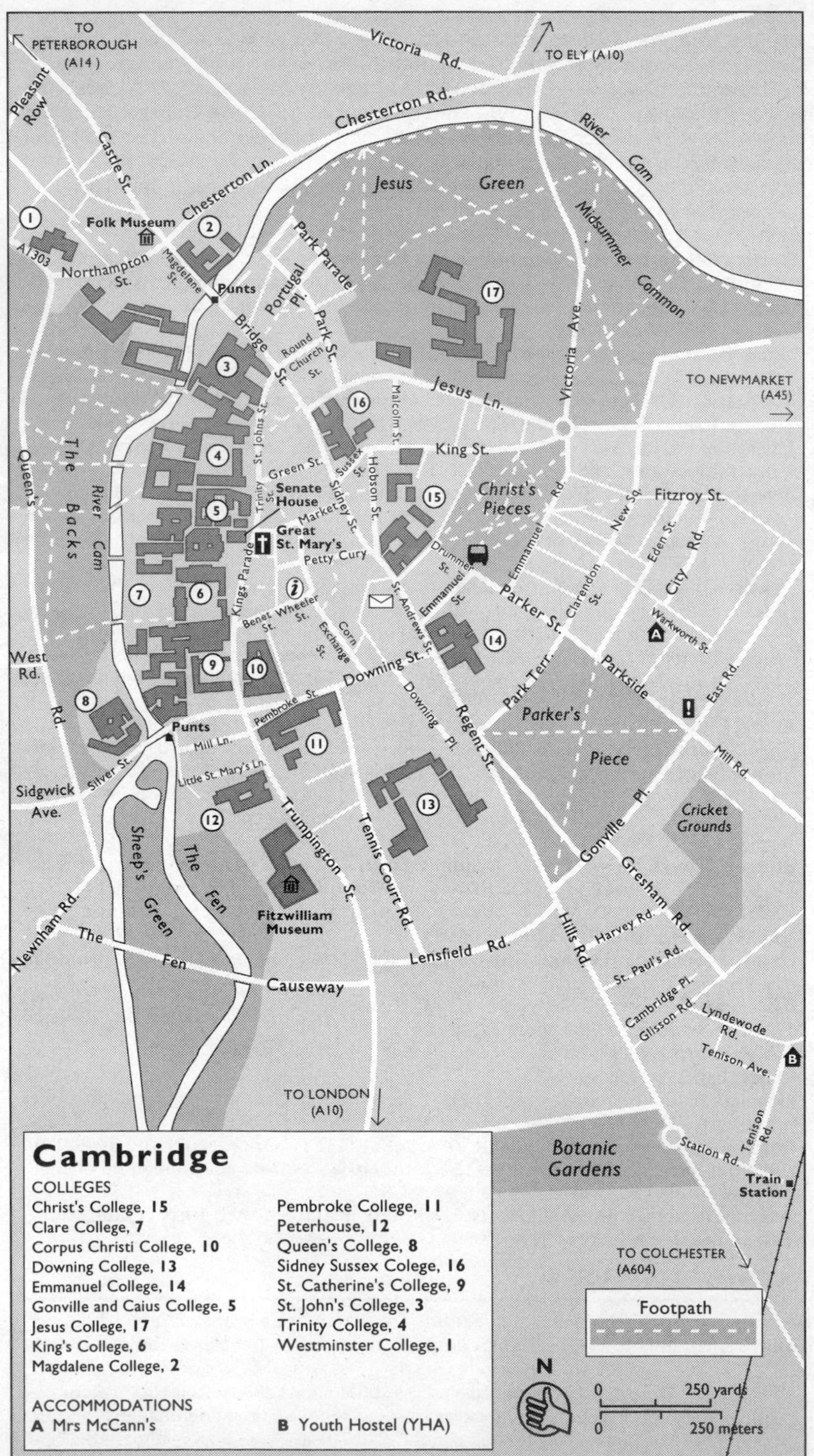

TO PETERBOROUGH (A14)
Victoria Rd.
TO ELY (A10)
Pleasant Row
Chesterton Rd.
River Cam
Castle St.
Chesterton Ln.
Jesus Green
Midsummer Common
Folk Museum
A1303
Northampton St.
Magdalene St.
Punts
Park Parade
Portugal Pl.
Bridge St.
Round Church St.
Park St.
Victoria Ave.
Jesus Ln.
TO NEWMARKET (A45)
Malcolm St.
St. Johns St.
King St.
Green St.
Sussex St.
Hobson St.
Queen's
The Backs
River Cam
Trinity St.
Senate House
Market St.
Sidney St.
Christ's Pieces
Emmanuel Rd.
New Sq.
Fitzroy St.
Eden St.
City Rd.
Great St. Mary's
Petty Cury
Kings Parade
Drummer St.
Emmanuel St.
Clarendon St.
Parker St.
Warkworth St.
Benet St.
Wheeler St.
Corn Exchange St.
St. Andrews St.
West Rd.
Downing St.
Park Terr.
Parkside
East Rd.
Pembroke St.
Downing Pl.
Regent St.
Parker's Piece
Punts
Mill Ln.
Mill Rd.
Silver St.
Little St. Mary's Ln.
Sidgwick Ave.
Trumpington St.
Tennis Court Rd.
Gonville Pl.
Cricket Grounds
Sheep's Green
The Fen
Gresham Rd.
Fitzwilliam Museum
Newnham Rd.
The Fen Causeway
Lensfield Rd.
Hills Rd.
Harvey Rd.
St. Paul's Rd.
Cambridge Pl.
Glisson Rd.
Lyndewode Rd.
Tenison Ave.
TO LONDON (A10)
Tenison Rd.
Station Rd.
Botanic Gardens
Train Station
TO COLCHESTER (A604)
Cambridge
COLLEGES
Christ's College, 15
Clare College, 7
Corpus Christi College, 10
Downing College, 13
Emmanuel College, 14
Gonville and Caius College, 5
Jesus College, 17
King's College, 6
Magdalene College, 2
Pembroke College, 11
Peterhouse, 12
Queen's College, 8
Sidney Sussex College, 16
St. Catherine's College, 9
St. John's College, 3
Trinity College, 4
Westminster College, 1
ACCOMMODATIONS
A Mrs McCann's
B Youth Hostel (YHA)
Footpath
N
0 250 yards
0 250 meters

DAYTRIPS

becomes Bridge St., Sidney St., St. Andrew's St., Regent St., and finally Hills Rd. The other—alternately St. John's St., Trinity St., King's Parade, Trumpington St., and Trumpington Rd.—is the academic thoroughfare, with several colleges lying between it and the Cam. The two streets merge at **St. John's College.** From the bus station at Drummer St., a hop-skip-and-jump down Emmanuel St. will land you right in the shopping district near the tourist office. To get to the heart of things from the train station, go west along Station Rd., turn right onto Hills Rd., and continue straight ahead.

Getting There: Trains to Cambridge run from both King's Cross and Liverpool St. stations (1hr., 1 per hr., £15.10, day return £28.70). **National Express** (tel. (0990) 808080) buses connect Victoria Station and Drummer St. Station in Cambridge (2hr., 1 per hr., from £8).

Train Station: Station Rd. (tel. (0345) 484950). Open daily 5am-11pm to purchase tickets. Help desk open M-Sa 8:30am-6:30pm, Su 11am-7pm.

Bus Station: Drummer St. Station (C3). **National Express** (tel. (0990) 808080) open M-Sa 8:15am-5:30pm. **Cambus** (tel. 423554) handles city and area service (60p-£1).

Taxis: Cabco, tel. 312444. **Camtax,** tel. 313131. Both 24hr. Or hail one at the bus and train stations, or St. Andrew's St. and Market Sq.

Bike Rental: Geoff's Bike Hike, 65 Devonshire Rd. (tel. 365629), near the railway station, behind the youth hostel. Helmets and locks available. £6 per day. Open daily 9am-6pm. **University Cycle,** 9 Victoria Ave. (tel. 355517). £7 per day; cash deposit £25. Open M-Sa 9am-5:30pm.

Tourist Office: Wheeler St. (tel. 322640; fax 457588), a block south of the marketplace. Mini-guide 40p, town maps 20p. *Cambridge: The Complete Guide* includes a street-indexed map (£1.30). Stocks maps of cycling tours around the area (£4). Books rooms for a £3 fee and a 10% deposit. Advance booking hotline (7 days or more in an advance; tel. (01223) 457581). Open Apr.-Oct. M-F 10am-6pm, Sa 10am-5pm, Su 11am-4pm; Nov.-Mar. M-F 10am-5:30pm, Sa 10am-5pm.

Tours: Informative 2hr. walking tours of the city and some colleges leave from the main tourist office. Call for times. Tours are well narrated but usually enter only one college—probably King's (£5.75, children £3.75). Special **Drama Tour** in July and Aug. Tu at 6:30pm, led by guides in period dress (£3.90). **Guide Friday** (tel. 362444) runs its familiar **bus tours** every 15 or 30min. Apr.-Oct. £7, students and seniors £5.50, children £2.

Budget Travel: STA Travel, 38 Sidney St. (tel. 366966). Open M-W and F 9am-5:30pm, Th 10am-5:30pm, Sa 10am-4pm. **Campus Travel,** 5 Emmanuel St. (tel. 324283). Open M-Tu and Th-F 9am-5:30pm, W 10am-5:30pm, Sa 10am-5pm. Also on Bridge St., same hours (tel. 360201).

Financial Services: Thomas Cook, 18 Market St. (tel. 366141). Open M-Tu and Th-Sa 9am-5:30pm, W 10am-5:30pm.

American Express: 25 Sidney St. (tel. 351636). Open M-W and F 9am-5:30pm, Th 9:30am-5:30pm, Sa 9am-5pm.

Emergency: Dial 999; no coins required.

Police: Parkside (tel. 358966).

Hospital: Addenbrookes (tel. 245151), Hills Rd. Catch Cambus #95 from Emmanuel St. (95p).

Post Office: 9-11 St. Andrew's St. (C3; tel. 323325). Open M-Tu and Th-F 9am-5:30pm, W 9:30am-5pm, Sa 9am-12:30pm. *Poste Restante* and bureau de change. **Postal Code:** CB2 3AA.

Internet Access: CBI, 32 Mill Rd. (tel. 576306), near the hostel. 10p per min., £6/hr.

Telephone Code: 01223.

ACCOMMODATIONS

Book ahead, especially in summer. Rooms are scarce, which makes prices high and quality remarkably low. Check the comprehensive list in the tourist office window after they close, or pick up their guide (50p).

YHA Youth Hostel, 97 Tenison Rd. (tel. 354601; fax 312780). Relaxed, welcoming atmosphere. TV lounge. Small lockers in some rooms. Bureau de change. Cafeteria could pass as a restaurant in its own right. £10.70, students £9.70, under 18 £7.30.

Breakfast £3, packed lunch £2.55-3.35, 3-course evening meal £4. Luggage Storage available. No curfew or lockout. Crowded Mar.-Oct.; in the summer, call a week ahead with a credit card.

Mrs. McCann, 40 Warkworth St. (tel. 314098). A jolly hostess with comfortably lived-in twin rooms in a quiet neighborhood near the bus station. £15. Discount after 3 nights. Breakfast included.

FOOD

Market Square has fruit and vegetables for the budgetarian. For vegetarian and wholefood groceries, try **Arjuna,** 12 Mill Rd. (tel. 364845; open M-F 9:30am-6pm, Sa 9am-5:30pm). Curry and Greek restaurants sate the curious tastebuds of hungry students (make sure that the Christ's College football club has not arrived on their ritual curry night out). South of town, Hills Rd. and Mill Rd. brim with good, cheap restaurants.

Rainbow's Vegetarian Bistro, 9a King's Parade (tel 321551). Duck under the rainbow sign on King's Parade. A tiny, creative burrow featuring delicious international vegan and vegetarian fare, all for £5.45. Try the Cypriot-style *moussaka.* Open daily 9am-9pm.

Nadia's, 11 St. John's St. (tel. 460961). An uncommonly good bakery at commoner's prices. Wonderful flapjacks and quiches (65p-£1). You'll get smiles from the chocolate-chocolate-chip cookie. Sandwiches and muffins that are a brunch unto themselves. Take-away only; sit outside Trinity across the street or try the branches on King's Parade and Silver St. Open June-Aug. M-Sa 8am-6pm, Su 8am-5pm.; Sept.-May M-Sa 7:30am-5:30pm, Su 7:30am-5pm.

The Little Tea Room, 1 All Saints' Passage, off Trinity St. As hopelessly precious as it sounds; tip-top teas served in a teeny basement room opposite Trinity. "Post-tutorial tea" (pot of tea, scone, cucumber sandwich, jam, and choice of cake) £5. Open M-Sa 9:30am-5:30pm, Su 11:30am-6pm.

SIGHTS

Cambridge is an architect's fantasia, packing some of the most breathtaking monuments to English aesthetics over the last 700 years into one square mile. The University has three eight-week terms: Michaelmas (Oct.-Dec.), Lent (Jan.-Mar.), and Easter (Apr.-June). Visitors can gain access to most of the college grounds from 9am-5:30pm, though many close to sightseers during the Easter term. Virtually all close during exams (mid-May to mid-June); call ahead (tel. 331100) for hours. If you're pressed for time, visit at least one chapel (preferably King's College), one garden (try Christ's), one library (Trinity's is the most interesting), and one dining hall (though many are emphatically closed to visitors).

King's College, on King's Parade, is the proud possessor of the university's most famous chapel, a spectacular Gothic monument. *(College open M-F 9:30am-4:30pm, Su 10am-5pm. £3, under 12 free with adults. Guided 45 min. tours £1.50, under 12 free. Check notices in the chapel for daily times. Chapel open term-time M-Sa 9:30am-3:30pm, Su 1:15-2:15pm and 5-5:30pm; chapel and exhibitions open college vacations 9:30am-4:30pm. Free.)* In 1441, Henry VI cleared away most of the center of medieval Cambridge for the foundation of King's College, and he intended this chapel to be England's finest. Although he wanted the inside to remain unadorned, his successors spent nearly £5000 carving an elaborate interior. If you stand at the southwest corner of the courtyard, you can see where Henry's master mason John Wastell (who also worked on the cathedrals of Peterborough and Canterbury) left off and where work under the Tudors began. The earlier stone is off-white, the later, dark. The interior consists of one huge chamber cleft by a carved wooden choir screen, one of the purest examples of the early Renaissance style in England. Wordsworth described the ceiling as a "branching roof self-poised, and scooped into ten thousand cells where light and shade repose." Windows depicting the life of Jesus were preserved from the iconoclasm of the English Civil War, allegedly because John Milton, then Cromwell's secretary, groveled on their behalf. Behind the altar hangs Rubens' magnificent *Adoration of the Magi*

(1639). Enjoy the classic view of the chapel and of the adjacent **Gibbs Building** from the river. As you picnic by the water, think of those who have gone before you: E.M. Forster was an undergraduate at King's, basing *The Longest Journey* and his posthumous novel *Maurice* on his Cambridge days.

In early June the university posts the names and final grades of every student in the Georgian **Senate House** opposite the King's College chapel, designed by Gibbs and built in the 1720s; about a week later, degree ceremonies are held there. Cambridge graduates are eligible for the world's easiest master's degrees: after spending three and one-third years out in the Real World, a graduate sends £15 to the university. Provided that said graduate is not in the custody of one of Her Majesty's Gaols, the grad receives an M.A. without further ado, making Cambridge the world's easiest correspondence school.

Trinity College (tel. 338400), on Trinity St., holds the largest purse at the University. The college's status as the wealthiest at Cambridge has become legendary—myth-mongers claim that it was once possible to walk from Cambridge to Oxford without stepping off Trinity land. Founded in 1546 by Henry VIII, Trinity specialized in literati (alums include George Herbert, John Dryden, Lord Byron, Lord Tennyson, and A.E. Housman). Inside the courtyard, in a florid fountain built in 1602, Byron used to bathe nude. The eccentric young poet lived in Nevile's Court and shared his rooms with a pet bear, whom he claimed would take his fellowship exams for him. Generations later, Prince Charles was an average anthropology student here. The expanse of Trinity's **Great Court** encompasses an area so large you can almost fail to notice its utter lack of straight lines and symmetry. What William Wordsworth called the "loquacious clock that speaks with male and female voice" still strikes 24 times each noon. Sir Isaac Newton, who lived on the first floor of E-entry for 30 years, originally measured the speed of sound by stamping his foot in the cloister along the north side of the court. Underneath the courtyards lie the well-hidden, well-stocked Trinity wine cellars. The college recently purchased over £20,000 worth of port that won't be drinkable until 2020.

Amble through the college toward the river to reach the reddish stone walls of the impressive **Wren Library.** *(£1.75. Library open M-F noon-2pm. Hall open 3-5pm; chapel and courtyard open 10am-6pm. College and library closed during exams.)* Treasures in this naturally lit building include A.A. Milne's handwritten manuscript of *Winnie the Pooh* and less momentous works such as John Milton's *Lycidas.* The collection also contains works by Byron, Tennyson, and Thackeray. German-speakers certain of the existence of books might look for Wittgenstein's journals. His phenomenal *Philosophical Investigations* was conceived here during years of intense discussion with G.E. Moore and students in his top-floor K-entry rooms.

Established in 1511 by the mother of Henry VIII, **St. John's College** (tel. 338600) is one of seven Cambridge colleges founded by women (but *for* men). *(Chapel open M-Sa 9:30am-6:30pm, Su 10:30am-6:30pm. Evensong at 6:30pm most nights. College open daily during vacation. £1.50, seniors and children 75p, families £3.)* The striking brick-and-stone gatehouse bears Lady Margaret's heraldic emblem. St. John's centers around a paved plaza rather than a grassy courtyard, and its two most interesting buildings stand across the river from the other colleges. A copy of Venice's Bridge of Sighs connects the older part of the college to the towering neo-Gothic extravagance of New Court, likened by philistines to a wedding cake in silhouette. Next door, you can see more adventurous college architecture, the modern **Cripps Building,** with clever bends that create three distinct courts under the shade of a noble willow. The12th-century **School of Pythagoras,** rumored to be the oldest complete building in Cambridge, hides in the gardens. *(Courtyard and some buildings open until 5pm.)*

Queens' College (tel. 335511), was founded not once, but twice—by painted Queen Margaret of Anjou in 1448 and again by Elizabeth Woodville in 1465. It has the only unaltered Tudor courtyard in Cambridge, housing the half-timbered President's Gallery. The **Mathematical Bridge,** just past Cloister Court, was built in 1749 without a single bolt or nail, relying only on mathematical principle. A meddling Victorian dismantled the bridge to see how it worked and the inevitable occurred—he couldn't

put it back together without using a steel rivet every two inches. *(College open daily 1:45-4:30pm; during summer vacation also 10:30am-12:45pm. Closed during exams. £1.)*

Clare College (tel. 333200), founded in 1326 by the thrice-widowed, 29-year-old Lady Elizabeth de Clare, has preserved an appropriate coat of arms: golden teardrops on a black border. *(College open daily 10am-5pm. £1.50, under 10 free.)* Across Clare Bridge (the most elegant on the Cam) lie the **Clare Gardens.** *(Open M-F 2-4:45pm; during summer vacation also 10am-4:30pm.)* Walk through Clare's **Old Court** for a view of the University Library, where 82 mi. of shelves hold books arranged according to size rather than subject. *(Old Court open during exams after 4:45pm to groups of 3 or fewer.)* George V called it "the greatest erection in Cambridge."

Christ's College (tel. 334900), founded as "God's-house" in 1448 and renamed in 1505, has won fame for its gardens and its association with the poet John Milton. *(Open summer M-F 10:30am-noon; in session M-F 10:30am-12:30pm and 2-4pm.)* To reach the gardens, walk under the lovely Neoclassical Fellows Building. Charles Darwin dallied through Christ's before informing man he was little more than a clean-shaven ape with a tie. His rooms (unmarked and closed to visitors) were on G staircase in First Court. **New Court,** on King St., is one of the most stunning modern structures in Cambridge; its symmetrical, gray concrete walls and black-curtained windows look like the whelp of an Egyptian pyramid, a Polaroid camera, and a typewriter. Bowing to pressure from aesthetically offended Cantabridgians, a new wall has been built to block the view of the building from all sides except the inner courtyard of the college. The college closes during exams, save for access to the chapel (inquire at the porter's desk).

Cloistered on a secluded site, **Jesus College** (tel. 339339) has preserved an enormous amount of unaltered medieval work, dating from 1496. Beyond the long, high-walled walk called the "Chimny" lies a three-sided court fringed with colorful gardens. Through the archway on the right sit the remains of a gloomy medieval nunnery. The Pre-Raphaelite stained glass of Burne-Jones and ceiling decorations by William "Wallpaper" Morris festoon the chapel. Sterne made a sentimental journey through Jesus, along with Malthus, Coleridge, and Alistair *"Masterpiece Theatre"* Cooke. *(Courtyard open until 6pm; closed during exams.)*

Inhabiting buildings from a 15th-century Benedictine hostel, **Magdalene College** (MAUD-lin; tel. 332100), founded in 1524, has acquired an aristocratic reputation. Don't forget to take a peek at the **Pepys Library** (ridiculously labeled **Bibliotheca Pepysiana**) in the second court; the library displays the noted statesman and prolific diarist's collection in their original cases. *(Library open Easter-Aug. 11:30am-12:30pm and 2:30-3:30pm; Sept.-Easter M-Sa 2:30-5:30pm. Free. Courtyards closed during exams.)* Pepys wrote his diaries in shorthand that took three years to decipher.

Thomas Gray wrote his *Elegy in a Country Churchyard* while staying in **Peterhouse,** on Trumpington St., the oldest and smallest college, founded in 1294. In contrast, **Robinson College,** across the river on Grange Rd., distinguishes itself by being the college's newest. Founded in 1977, this mod-medieval brick pastiche sits just behind the university library. Bronze plants writhe about the door of the college chapel, which features some fascinating stained glass.

Corpus Christi College (tel. 338000), founded in 1352 by the common people, contains the Old Court, the dreariest courtyard in Cambridge, unaltered since its enclosure. *(Courtyards open until 6pm; closed during exams; call ahead for hours.)* The library maintains the snazziest collection of Anglo-Saxon manuscripts in England, including the Parker Manuscript of the *Anglo-Saxon Chronicle.* Alums include Sir Francis Drake and Christopher Marlowe. The 1347 **Pembroke College** next door harbors the earliest architectural effort of Sir Christopher Wren and counts Edmund Spenser, Ted Hughes, and Eric Idle among grads.

A chapel designed by Sir Christopher Wren dominates the front court of **Emmanuel College** (tel. 334200). Emmanuel, founded in 1584, on St. Andrew's St. at Downing St., and **Downing College** (tel. 334800), founded in 1807, just to the south along Regent St., are both pleasantly isolated. *(Courtyards open until 6pm; chapel open when not in use.)* John Harvard, benefactor of a certain New England university, attended

Emmanuel; a stained-glass panel depicting Harvard graces the college chapel. Among alumni with more tangible accomplishments is John Cleese.

The **Round Church (Holy Sepulchre),** Bridge St. and St. John's St., one of five circular churches surviving in England, was built in 1130 (and later rebuilt) on the pattern of the Church of the Holy Sepulchre in Jerusalem. The pattern merits comparison with **St. Benet's Church,** a rough Saxon church on Benet St. The tower of St. Benet's, built in 1050, is the oldest structure in Cambridge. The tower once had a spire, but spire-building was a technology the Normans lacked, so they spitefully knocked it down: "Saxon freaks! We'll show *you!*" The tower of **Church of St. Mary the Great,** just off King's Parade, lets you ogle the mind-boggling collection of colleges in a single glance. *(And 123 steps. Tower open M-Sa 10am-5pm, Su 12:30-5pm. £1.50, children 50p).*

The **Fitzwilliam Museum** (tel. 332900), Trumpington St., a 10-minute walk down the road from King's College, dwells within an immense Roman-style building. Inside, an opulent marble foyer leads to an impressive collection including paintings by Michelangelo, Cezanne, Picasso, Degas, and Monet. Egyptian, Chinese, Japanese and Greek antiquities, and 16th-century German armor bide their time downstairs. The drawing room displays William Blake's books and woodcuts. *(Open Tu-Sa 10am-5pm, Su 2:15-5pm. Free, but suggested donation £3. Guided tours Sa at 2:30pm. £3.)*

The **Museum of Zoology** (tel. 336650), off Downing St., houses a fine assemblage of wildlife specimens in a modern, well-lit building. *(Open M-F 2:15-4:45pm. Free. Wheelchair accessible.)* Across the road, on Downing St. opposite Corn Exchange St., the **Museum of Archaeology and Anthropology** (tel. 333516) contains an excellent display of prehistoric artifacts from American, African, Pacific, and Asian cultures, as well as exhibits on Cambridge through the ages. Special exhibits change regularly. *(Open mid-June to Aug. M-F 10:30am-5pm, Sa 10am-12:30pm; Sept. to mid-June M-F 2-4pm, Sa 10am-12:30pm. Free W. Wheelchair accessible, but call ahead.)* **Kettle's Yard** (tel. 352124), at the corner of Castle and Northampton St., houses early 20th-century art. *(Gallery open year-round Tu-Sa 12:30-5:30pm, Su 2-5:30pm. Free.)* Cambridge's **Botanic Gardens** (tel. 336265; enter from Hill Rd. or Bateman St.) were ingeniously designed by Henslow, Sir Joseph Hooker's father-in-law (c. 1846). *(Open daily 10am-4pm or 6pm, depending on season; Nov.-Feb. M-F free; otherwise £1.50, seniors and under 18 £1.)* When the wind gets rolling, the scented gardens turn into a perfume factory.

Stratford-upon-Avon

It is something, I thought, to have seen the dust of Shakespeare.

—Washington Irving

Shakespeare lived here. The rest follows predictably. Knick-knack huts hawk "Will Power" t-shirts, while proprietors tout the dozen-odd properties linked, however tenuously, to William Shakespeare and his extended family. But the ghosts are here if you know where to seek them: collecting flowers by the weeping Avon, ducking into groves in the once-forest of Arden, guzzling sacks under the timbers of 16th-century inns, and appearing in the pin-drop silence before a soliloquy in the Royal Shakespeare Theatre.

PRACTICAL INFORMATION

Getting There: Trains (tel. (0345) 484950) are a fretful 2¼hr. from **Paddington** by **Thames Trains** (tel. 579453). **National Express buses** (tel. (0990) 808080) run from **Victoria** (3hr., 3 per day, return £17).

Train Station: off Alcester Rd.

Bus Station: The corner of **Waterside** and **Bridge St.,** in front of or opposite McDonald's, is as close to a bus station as Stratford gets; **Midland Red South** stops here. **National Express** stops on Bridgeway Rd. by the Leisure Centre. Local **Stratford Blue** service also stops on **Wood St.** You can buy tickets for National Express buses at the tourist office.

DAYTRIPS

Taxi: Main Taxis (tel. 414514) or **007 Taxis** (tel. 414007). Both open 24hr. **Bike Rental: Clarke's Cycle Renta** (tel. 205057), Guild St., at Union St.; look for the Esso sign. £7 per day; deposit £50. Open Tu-Sa 9:30am-5:30pm; in summer also Su 10am-1pm.

Tourist Office: Bridgefoot (tel. 293127). Cross Warwick Rd. at Bridge St. toward the waterside park. Books accommodations for £3 plus a 10% deposit. Open Apr.-Oct. M-Sa 9am-6pm, Su 11am-5pm; Nov.-Mar. M-Sa 9am-5pm.

Tours: Guide Friday, 14 Rother St. (tel. 294466), operates tours of Stratford departing daily from various spots. 4 per hr. £8, students and seniors £6.50, children under 12 £2.50.

Royal Shakespeare Theatre Box Office, Waterside (tel. 295623; 24hr. recorded information tel. 269191; fax 261974). Standby tickets for students and seniors (£11-15) available immediately before the show at the RST, the Swan, and The Other Place. Open M-Sa 9:30am-8pm, closes at 6pm when there is no performance.

Emergency: Dial 999; no coins required.

Police: Rother St. (tel. 414111).

Hospital: Stratford-upon-Avon Hospital (tel. 205831), Arden St.

Postal Code: CV37 6PU.

Telephone Code: 01789.

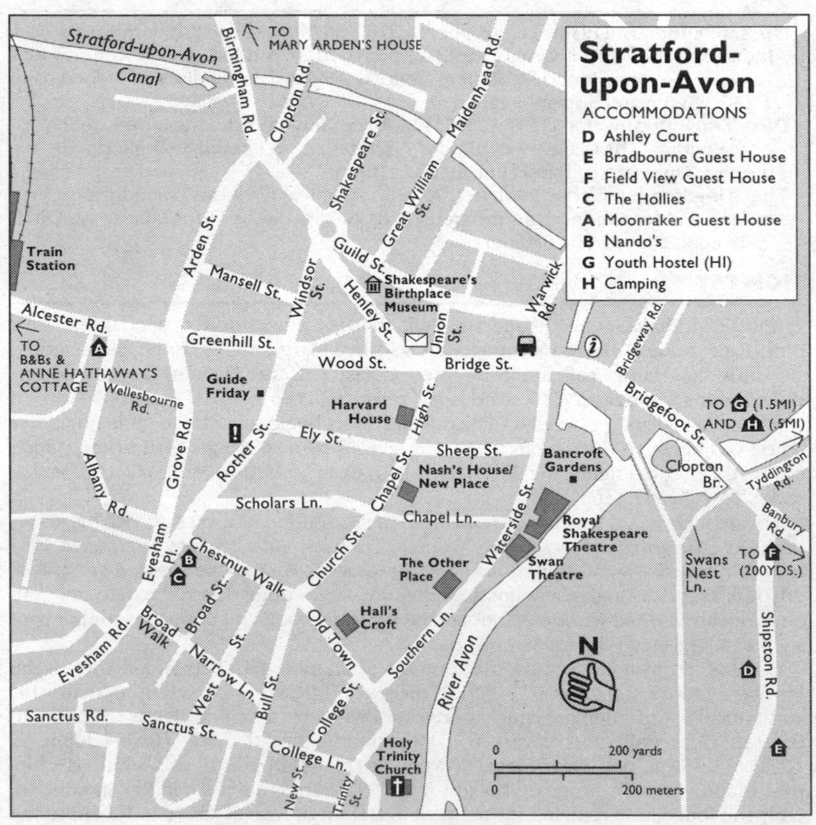

ACCOMMODATIONS

To B&B or not to B&B? This hamlet has tons of them, but singles are hard to find. In summer, 'tis nobler to make advance reservations by phone. Guest houses (£15-22) line Grove Rd., Evesham Pl., and Evesham Rd. (From the train station, walk down Alcester Rd., take a right on Grove Rd., and continue to Evesham Pl., which becomes Evesham Rd.) If these fail you, try Shipston and Banbury Rd. across the river. The nearest youth hostel is more than 2 mi. out of town, and with a return bus fare costs as much as some B&Bs. The tourist office will find and book accommodations for you, while you await what dreams may come.

Field View Guest House, 35 Banbury Rd. (tel. 292694). Quiet, peaceful rooms with a welcoming owner. Bathroom scale gives your weight in stones. Vegetarian options at breakfast. Singles £16; doubles £32.

YHA Youth Hostel, Hemmingford House, Wellesbourne Rd., Alveston (tel. 297093), 2 mi. from Stratford. Follow the B4086; take bus #18 or X18 from Bridge St., across from the McDonald's (theoretically 1 per hr., £1.50). 130 beds in rooms of 2-14. £13.45, under 18 £10.05. Breakfast included. Packed lunch £3.35. Kitchen. Reception open 7am-midnight, night guard on duty. Curfew midnight.

The Hollies, 16 Evesham Pl. (tel. 266857). Warm and attentive proprietors for whom the guest house has become a labor of love. From the mint walls to the ivy scaling the outer wall, green prevails. No singles. Spacious doubles £35, with bath £45.

DAYTRIPS

FOOD

Hussain's Indian Cuisine, 6a Chapel St. (tel. 267506). Probably Stratford's best Indian cuisine, with a slew of tandoori prepared as you like it. A favorite of Ben Kingsley. 3-course lunch £6. Entrees from £6. 15% take-away discount. Open daily 12:30-2:30pm and 5pm-midnight.

Dirty Duck Pub, Waterside (tel. 297312). River view outside, huge bust of Shakespeare within. Theater crowds abound. Traditional pub lunch £2-4.50; double for dinners. Open M-Sa 11am-11pm, Su noon-10pm.

Thai Kingdom, 11 Warwick Rd. (tel. 261103). Tropical plants and friendly staff. Vegetarian entrees £6, meat dishes around £8; 20-25% discount for take-away. Open daily noon-2pm and 6-10:45pm.

SIGHTS

Five official **Shakespeare properties** (tel. 204016) grace the town: Shakespeare's Birthplace, Anne Hathaway's cottage, the so-called Mary Arden's House and Countryside Museum, Hall's Croft, and New Place or Nash's House. Diehard fans should buy the **combination ticket.** *(£10, students and seniors £9, children £5.)* If you don't want to visit them all—dark-timbered roof beams and floors begin to look the same no matter who lived between them—buy a **Shakespeare's Town Heritage Trail ticket,** which covers the in-town sights: the Birthplace, Hall's Croft, and New Place. *(£7, students and seniors £6, children £3.50.)*

The least crowded way to pay homage to the institution himself is to visit his grave, his little, little grave in **Holy Trinity Church,** Trinity St. *(60p, students and children 40p.)* In town, begin your walking tour at **Shakespeare's Birthplace** on Henley St. (tel. 204016; enter through the adjoining museum), a combination recreation and half Shakespeare life-and-work exhibition. Sign the guestbook and enter the company of such distinguished pilgrims as Dickens.

On High St., you can see another example of humble Elizabethan lodgings in the **Harvard House** (tel. 204507). Period pieces and pewter sparsely punctuate this authentic Tudor building, vaguely connected with the man who lends his name to the American college that runs it. *(Open late May to Oct. Tu-Sa 10am-4:30pm, Su 10:30am-4:30pm. Free.)* **New Place,** down the road and opposite, was Stratford's hippest home when Shakespeare bought it in 1597 after writing some hits in London. Only the foundation remains; it can be viewed from the street above. Adjacent to the site is **Nash's House,** containing Tudor furnishings and a local history collection.

(Open Mar.-Oct. M-Sa 9:30am-5pm, Su 10am-5pm; Nov.-Feb. M-Sa 10am-4pm, Su 10:30-4pm. £3, children £1.50.) New Place is accessible through admission to Nash's House. Down Chapel Ln. from Nash's House, the **Great Garden of New Place** offers a peaceful retreat from Stratford's streets. *(Open daily dawn-dusk. Free.)*

The violets have not withered in the **Royal Shakespeare Theatre Gardens,** on the pilgrim's progress between the theater and Holy Trinity (free). The riverbank between the RST and Clopton Bridge is a sight in itself. Gazing out at the serene rowers, you'd never guess that approximately six million buses are groaning behind you. The **RST Summer House** (tel. 297671) in the gardens contains a **brass-rubbing studio,** an alternative to plastic Shakespeare memorabilia. *(Open daily Apr.-Sept. 10am-6pm; Oct.-Mar. 11am-4pm. Free, but frottage materials cost £1-10, average £3.)* The RSC offers **backstage tours** (tel. 412602) that cram camera-happy groups into the wooden "O"s of the RST and the Swan for booking. *(Tours daily at 1:30 and 5:30pm, and following performances. £4, students and seniors £3.)*

Anne Hathaway's Cottage (tel. 292100), the birthplace of Shakespeare's wife, lies about 1 mi. from Stratford in Shottery; take one of the ill-marked footpaths north. Admission entitles you to sit on a bench Will may or may not have sat on; view from outside if you've already seen the birthplace. *(Open Mar.-Oct. M-Sa 9am-5pm, Su 9:30am-5pm; Nov.-Feb. M-Sa 9:30am-4pm, Su 10am-4pm. £3.50, children £1.50.)* **Mary Arden's House,** a farmhouse restored in the style a 19th-century entrepreneur determined to be precisely that of Shakespeare's mother, stands 4 mi. from Stratford in Wilmcote; a footpath connects it to Anne Hathaway's Cottage. *(Open Mar.-Oct. M-Sa 9:30am-5pm, Su 10am-5pm; Nov.-Feb. M-Sa 10am-4pm, Su 10:30am-4pm. £4, children £2, families £11.)*

DAYTRIPS

ENTERTAINMENT

He was born on Henley St., died at New Place, and lives on at the **Royal Shakespeare Theatre,** towering eloquently over the slanting willows. One of the world's most acclaimed repertories, the **Royal Shakespeare Company** boasts such recent sons as Kenneth Branagh and Ralph Fiennes. Call or visit the **box office** (tel. 295623, 24hr. recording tel. 269191; fax 261974) in advance to reserve seats, which range in price from £5 (standing room) to £49 (superseats). Located in the foyer of the RSC Theatre, the box office is open daily 9:30am-6pm (until 8pm on performance days), and a group gathers outside about 20 minutes before opening for same-day sales. Phones open at 9am. Without payment, seats can only be held for three days. **Matinee** seats are usually available on the day of show. A happy few get customer returns and standing-room tickets later in the day for evening shows; line up 1-2 hours before curtain. **Student and senior** standbys exist in principle. *(£11; available just before curtain—be ready to pounce.)* **Disabled travelers** should call in advance to advise box office of their needs. The RSC's newly extended season lasts from November to September. The RSC also offers daily 45-minute **tours** (tel. 412602; £6.90).

The **Swan Theatre,** resembling a model of Shakespeare's Globe made from giant matchsticks, is a thrust stage designed for RSC productions of Renaissance and Restoration plays. The theatre is located down Waterside, behind the Royal Shakespeare Theatre, on the grounds of the old Memorial Theatre. *(Tickets £9-32, standing room £5.)* It's smaller and often more crowded than the RST; line up early for tickets. *(Same-day sale tickets £12-14.50.)* Standbys are rare. **The Other Place** is the RSC's newest branch, producing modern dramas, avant-garde premieres, and rarely performed plays. *(Tickets £15-19, standbys £11.)*

Astonishingly, the **Stratford Festival** (for 2 weeks in July) celebrates artistic achievement other than Shakespeare's, from music to poetry. Tickets (when required) can be purchased from the Festival box office (tel. 414513), on Rother St. The modern, well-respected **Shakespeare Centre** (tel. 204016) Henley St., hosts the annual **Poetry Festival** throughout July and August every Sunday evening. Over the past few years, Seamus Heaney, Ted Hughes, and Derek Walcott have put in appearances. *(Tickets £6-7.)* No Twelfth Night revels here—chimes at midnight in Stratford are next to nil; go to the theater or go to bed early, or what you will.

York

With a pace suitable for ambling and its tallest building a cathedral, York is as different from London as from its American namesake. Today, York beckons with its medieval thoroughfares, a Viking legacy, and Britain's largest Gothic cathedral.

ORIENTATION AND PRACTICAL INFORMATION

York's streets are winding, short, and rarely labeled, and the longer, straighter streets change names every block or so. Most attractions lie within the city walls. The thoroughfare formed by Station Rd., the **Lendal Bridge,** Museum St., and Duncombe Pl. leads from the train station to the **Minster.** The River Ouse cuts through the city, curving from the west to the south. The city center lies between the Ouse and the Minster; Coney St., Parliament St., and Stonegate are main streets.

Getting There: Trains run to **King's Cross** (2hr., 2 per hr., £54). **National Express** runs to **Victoria** (4hr., 6 per day, £17.50).

Train Station: Station Rd. (tel. (0345) 484950). Ticket and information office open M-Sa 5:45am-10:15pm, Su 7:30am-10:10pm. Travel center open M-F 8am-7:45pm, Sa 9am-5pm, Su 10am-4pm.

Bus Station: Rougier St., the train station, Exhibition Sq., and on Piccadilly.

Local Transportation: Call **Rider York** (tel. 435609) for information. Ticket office open M-Sa 9am-5pm. Buses to **Scarborough, Harrowgate,** and **Castle Howard** board at Rougier St.

Boats: Several companies along the River Ouse near Lendal, Ouse, and Skeldergate Bridges offer 1hr. cruises. **Yorkboat,** Lendel Bridge (tel. 623752). 30 trips per day. £5.50. Open Apr.-Oct. daily at 10am.

Taxis: Station Taxis (tel. 623332 or 628197).

Bike Rental: Bob Trotter, 13 Lord Mayor's Walk (tel. 622868). £9.50 per day plus £50 deposit. Open M-Sa 9am-5:30pm, Su 10am-4pm. The tourist office's *York Cycle Route Map* (behind the counter, but free!) is helpful.

Tourist Offices: Tourist Information Centre, De Grey Rooms, Exhibition Sq. (tel. 621756). Room-finding service £3 plus a 10% deposit. *York Visitor Guide* includes "Where to Stay" and "What to See" sections. *York for Less* booklet (£3.50) offers a collection of discount coupons. The *Disabled Guide to York* (£2.25) and *Snickelways of York* (£5), an off-beat self-tour guide, are also available. Open July-Aug. M-Sa 9am-7pm, Su 9am-6pm; Sept.-June daily 9am-6pm. **Smaller branch** (tel. 640316) awaits in the train station. Open Apr.-Oct. M-Sa 9am-8pm, Su 9:30am-5pm; Nov.-Mar. M-Sa 9am-5pm, Su 10am-5pm. **York Visitor and Conference Bureau,** 20 George St., by the bus station, offers similar services. Open M-Sa 9am-6pm.

Tours: Free 2hr. **walking tour** emphasizes York's architectural glories. Meet in front of the **York City Art Gallery,** directly across from the tourist office. Runs daily Apr.-Oct. 10:15am and 2:15pm; July-Aug. also 7pm. Bewildering array of **ghost tours** available; try **The Ghost Hunt of York** (tel. 608600), daily at 7:30pm; £2-3.

Financial Services: Banks are ubiquitous. Try **Thomas Cook,** 4 Nessgate (tel. 653626). Open M-W and F 9am-5:30pm, Th 10am-5:30pm.

American Express: 6 Stonegate (tel. 670030). Open M-F 9am-5:30pm, Sa 9am-5pm; in summer foreign exchange also open Su 10am-4pm.

Emergency: Dial 999; no coins required.

Police: Fulford Rd. (tel. 631321).

Hotlines: Samaritans (crisis), 89 Nunnery Ln. (tel. 655888). Open 24hr.

Pharmacy: Gillygate Pharmacy, 6 Gillygate (tel. 642557). Open M-F 9am-8pm, Sa 9am-6pm.

Hospital: York District Hospital (tel. 631313), off Wigginton Rd. Take bus #1, 2, 3, or 18 from Exhibition Sq.

Post Office: 22 Lendal (tel. 617285). Bureau de change. Open M-Sa 9am-5:30pm. **Postal Code:** YO1 2DA.

Internet Access: Impressions Gallery (tel. 654724), Castlegate. 2 computers. Open M-Tu and Th-Sa 9:30-5:30pm, W 10am-5:30pm, Su 11am-5pm. £2.50 per 30min.

Telephone Code: 01904.

ACCOMMODATIONS

Competition for inexpensive B&Bs (from £16) can be fierce during the summer. The **York Visitor and Conference Bureau** can be helpful (see p. 288). B&Bs are most concentrated on the sidestreets along **Bootham/Clifton** (Bootham becomes Clifton at Grosvenor Terr.), in the **Mount area** (past the train station and down Blossom St.), and on **Bishopsthorpe Road** (due south away from town).

Avenue Guest House, 6 The Avenue (tel. 620575), off Bootham/Clifton on a quiet, residential sidestreet. River footpath from the train station leads to the bottom of the Ave. Enthusiastic hosts provide 7 bright, immaculate rooms with soft, puffy beds. Charming view and plush towels make it a step up without the usual increase in

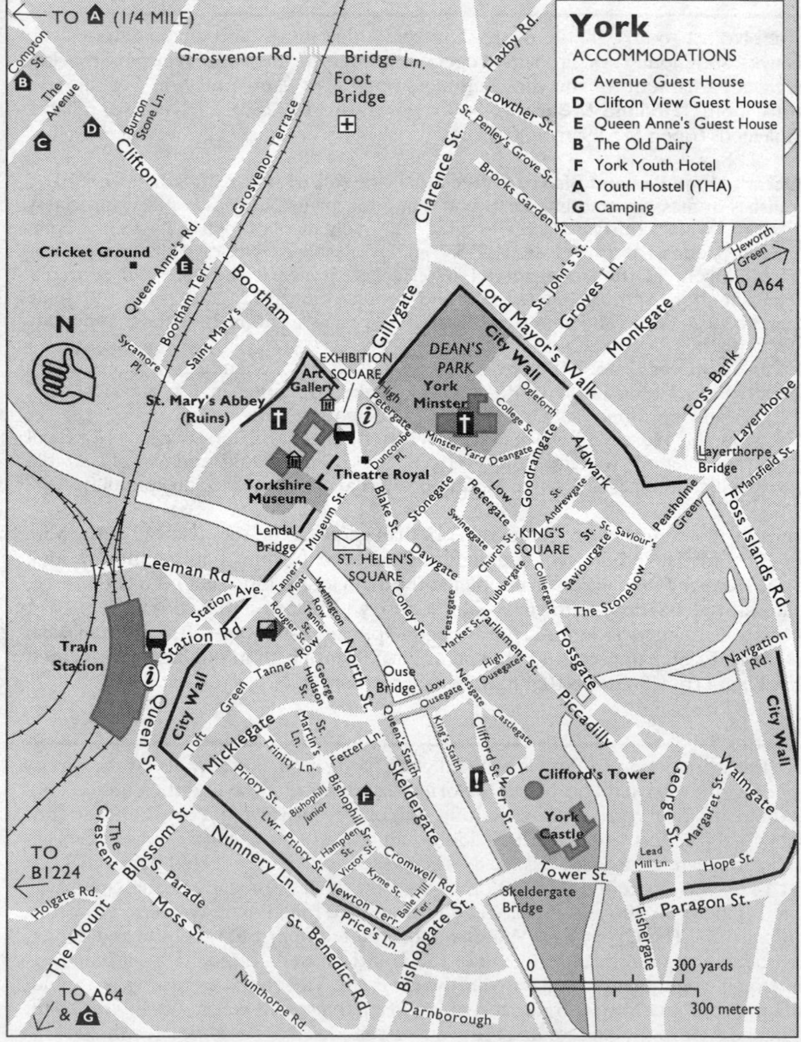

price. Some family rooms with baths available. No smoking. All rooms with TV. Singles £15-17; doubles £28-32, with bath £30-40.

Queen Anne's Guest House, 24 Queen Anne's Rd. (tel. 629389), a short walk out Bootham from Exhibition Sq. Spotless single, double, and family rooms with TV. Large bathrooms and breakfasts. No smoking. Mar.-Oct. £14-16 per person; Nov.-Feb. £13-15 per person. £11 without breakfast.

YHA Youth Hostel, Water End, Clifton (tel. 653147), 1 mi. from town center. From Exhibition Sq. tourist office, walk about ¾ mi. out Bootham/Clifton, and take a left at Water End; or take a bus to Clifton Green and walk ¼ mi. down Water End. Superior-grade hostel with excellent facilities: kitchen, TV room, hot showers, laundry. 156 beds. Dorms £14.40, under 18 £11; singles £17.50; twins £37; family rooms £52 or £78. Breakfast included (served 7:30-9:30am), packed lunch £3.35, dinner £4.40 (served 5:30-7:30pm). Snacks available 11am-10pm. Reception open 7am-11:30pm. Bedroom lockout 10am-1pm. Closed Dec. 5-Jan. 15.

FOOD AND PUBS

Expensive tea rooms, medium-range bistros, fudge shops, and cheap eateries rub elbows throughout York. Fruit and vegetable grocers peddle at the **Newgate market** between Parliament St. and the Shambles (open M-Sa 9am-5pm; Apr.-Dec. also Su 9am-4:30pm). **Holland & Barrett,** 28 Coney St. (tel. 627257), shelves ever-reliable wholefoods (open M-Sa 9am-5:30pm).

Oscar's Wine Bar and Bistro, 8 Little Stonegate (tel. 652002), off Stonegate. Hearty dishes in massive amounts keep you going for a week (£5-7). Popular and classy with a swank courtyard, varied menu, and lively mood. Open daily 11am-11pm. Happy Hour Su-M 4pm-close, Tu-F 5-7pm. Live jazz and blues on Monday nights.

The Rubicon, 5 Little Stonegate (tel. 676076), off Stonegate. Upscale vegetarian restaurant offers 2-course lunches (£5) and 3-course dinners (£12.50), both with juice and coffee. Vegan and gluten-free options. Open Tu-Sa noon-2pm and 5-10pm, Su-M 5-10pm.

Little Shambles Café, Little Shambles (tel. 627871), off Shambles. Upstairs eatery tucked in a Tudor house overlooking the market. Open for English breakfast (£2), lunch, and afternoon tea. Open M-Sa 7am-5:30pm, Su 9am-5pm.

Waggon and Horse, 48 Gillygate (tel. 654103). Mighty platters at mild prices will set your tongue a waggin'. Soup, veggies, Yorkshire pudding, and half of a sizable roast chicken for £4.75. Open M-Sa noon-2pm and 6-9pm, Su noon-2pm only.

There are more **pubs** in the center of York than gargoyles on the east wall of the Minster. Most are packed on weekend nights and all serve bar meals during the day. Pick up the *Historic Pubs of York* pamphlet at the main tourist office (£1). **Ye Old Starre,** Stonegate (tel. 623063), is the city's oldest pub, with a license that goes back to 1644 (meals £4-5; open M-Sa 11am-11pm, Su noon-3pm and 7-10:30pm). The **Roman Bath** (tel. 620455), St. Sampson's Sq., has an original Roman bath in the basement. (Open M-Sa 11am-11pm, Su noon-10:30pm. Bath admission £1, 50p if you eat there.)

SIGHTS

The best introduction to York is a 2½ mi. walk along its medieval walls. At the tourist office, ask for the useful brochure *Historic Attractions of York,* and then hit the cobbled streets. Everyone and everything in York converges at **York Minster** (tel. 639347), the largest Gothic cathedral in Britain. *(Open in summer daily 7am-8:30pm; off-season 7am-5pm. £2 donation requested.)* The present structure, erected between 1220 and 1470, was preceded by the Roman fortress where Constantine the Great was hailed emperor in 306 and the Saxon church where King Edwin converted to Christianity in 627. The **Great East Window,** constructed from 1405 to 1408 and depicting both the beginning and the end of the world in over a hundred small scenes, is the largest single medieval glass window on Earth. The choral **evensong** is a mind-blowing combination of organ and choir. *(Performances M-F 5pm, Sa-Su 4pm.)* The cathedral is currently undergoing renovations scheduled to be completed in 2000.

It's a mere 275 steps up to the top of the **Central Tower,** from which you can stare down at the red roofs of York. The Tower is open daily from 9:30am to 6:30pm (until dark in winter), but there is only a five-minute period every 30 minutes during which you may ascend, as the stairs don't allow two people to pass. *(£2, children £1.)* **The Foundations and Treasury** tell the incredible story of how the central tower began to crack apart in 1967. *(Open in summer M-Sa 9:30am-6:30pm, Su 1-6:30pm; in winter until 4:30pm. £1.80, students and seniors £1.50, children 70p.)* Also worth a look are the **crypt** and the **chapter house.** *(Both open M-F 9:30am-4:30pm, Sa 9:15am-3:30pm, Su 1-3:30pm. Crypt 60p, children 30p. Chapter house 70p, children 30p.)* The **Minster Library** guards books at the far corner of the grounds. *(Open M-Th 9am-5pm, F 9am-noon. Free.)*

The **Yorkshire Museum** (tel. 629745), hidden within the 10 gorgeous acres of the Museum Gardens (enter from Museum St. or Marygate), presents Roman, Anglo-Saxon, and Viking art galleries, as well as the £2.5 million **Middleham Jewel** (c.1450), a gold amulet engraved with the Trinity and the nativity, and holding an enormous sapphire. *(Open daily 10am-5pm; last admission 4:30pm. £3, students, seniors, and children £2; 2 adults and 2 children £9. Wheelchair accessible.)* In the museum gardens, peacocks fan themselves among the haunting ruins of **St. Mary's Abbey,** once the most influential Benedictine monastery in northern England.

Housed in a former debtor's prison, the huge York **Castle Museum** (tel. 613161), Minster Yard, by the river and Skeldergate Bridge, is billed as a museum of extraordinary objects and everyday life—for the last 300 years. *(Open Apr.-Oct. M-Sa 9:30am-5:30pm, Su 10am-5:30pm; Nov.-Mar. M-Sa 9:30am-4pm, Su 10am-4pm. £4.50, students, seniors, and children £3.15.)* Across from the museum squats the haunting **Clifford's Tower** (tel. 646940), one of the last remaining pieces of York Castle, and a reminder of the worst outbreak of anti-Semitic violence in English history. *(Tower open daily Apr.-Oct. 10am-6pm; Nov.-Mar. 10am-4pm. £1.70, students and seniors £1.30, children 90p.)* In 1190, Christian merchants tried to erase their debts to Jewish bankers by destroying York's Jewish community. On the last Sabbath before Passover, 150 Jews took refuge in a tower that previously stood on this site and, faced with the prospect of starvation or butchery, committed suicide.

Castle Howard (tel. (01653) 648333), still inhabited by the Howard family, made its TV debut in the BBC version of Evelyn Waugh's *Brideshead Revisited.* The famous hall is dubbed "one of the greatest treasure houses of England." Head to the **Orléans Room** to view the impressive art collection of a former duke or to the **chapel** for the kaleidoscopic stained glass. *(10min. services Sa-Su 5:15pm.)* More stunning than the castle itself are its 999 acres of glorious grounds; be sure to see the **Temple of the Four Winds,** whose hilltop perch offers views of water and sheep-dotted fields. *(Castle and galleries open daily mid-Mar. to Oct. at 11am, last admission 4:30pm. Grounds open at 10am. Call for winter hours. £7, students and seniors £6, children £4. 10min. chapel services Sa-Su 5:15pm. Wheelchair access.)* **York Pullman** (tel. 622992), in Bootham Tower, Exhibition Sq., offers half-day excursions to the Castle (£3.75). *(Office open M-Sa 9am-5pm, Su 9am-4pm.)* By showing your bus ticket, you can receive reduced admission at the Castle.

Canterbury

With pilgrims coming and going for nearly a millennium, the soul of Canterbury is a flighty thing, tossed somewhere between a cathedral and the open road. Archbishop Thomas à Becket met his demise after an irate Henry II asked, "Will no one rid me of this troublesome priest?" and a few of his henchmen took the hint. Subsequent healings and miracles were attributed to "the hooly blisful martir," and thus "to Canterbury they wende." Chaucer saw enough irony in tourist flocks to capture them in his ever-bawdy *Canterbury Tales.*

ORIENTATION AND PRACTICAL INFORMATION

Canterbury is roughly circular, its slowly eroding city wall ringed by a road. An unbroken street crosses the circle from west to east, taking the names St. Peter's St., High St., and St. George's St. The cathedral rises in the northeast quadrant. To reach the tourist office from East Station, cross the footbridge, take a left down the hill onto Station Rd. East, bear right into the roundabout onto Castle St., which becomes St. Margaret's St. From West Station, make a right onto Station Rd. West, turn left onto St. Dunstan's St., walk through Westgate Tower onto St. Peter's St. (which becomes High St.), and after about six blocks, make a right onto St. Margaret's St.

Getting There: A pilgrimage from London to Canterbury? How original. Trains (tel. (0345) 484950) run from Victoria Station to Canterbury East Station (the stop nearest the youth hostel), and from Charing Cross and Waterloo stations to Canterbury's West Station (1½hr., 1 per hr., £15.70, day return £15.80). **National Express** buses (tel. (0990) 808080) to Canterbury leave Victoria hourly (2hr., £6-8).

Train Station: East Station, Station Rd. East, off Castle St., southeast of town. Open M-Sa 6:10am-8pm, Su 6:30am-9pm. **West Station,** Station Rd. West, off St. Dunstan's St. Open M-F 6:15am-8pm, Sa 6:30am-8pm, Su 7:15am-9:30pm.

Bus Station: St. George's Ln. (tel. 472082). Open M-Sa 8:15am-5:15pm. Get there by 5pm to book National Express tickets.

Taxis: Longport (tel. 458885). Open daily 6am-4am.

Bike Rental: Byways Bicycle Hire, 2 Admiralty Walk (tel. 277397). Owner delivers. £10 per day, plus a £50 deposit.

Tourist Office: 34 St. Margaret's St., CT1 2TG (tel. 766567; fax 459840). Free mini-guide. Wide range of maps, guides, and walks of Canterbury. Open daily Apr.-June 9:30am-5:30pm; July-Aug. 9am-6pm; Sept.-Mar. 9:30am-5pm. **Tours:** 1½hr. depart from the tourist office Apr.-Nov. daily 2pm; additional tour July-Aug. M-Sa 11:30am. £3, students, seniors, and children £2.50, family ticket £7.50, under 14 free.

Emergency: Dial 999; no coins required.

Police: Old Dover Rd. (tel. 762055), outside the eastern city wall.

Hospital: Kent and Canterbury Hospital (tel. 766877), off Ethelbert Rd.

Post Office: 28 High St. (tel. 475280), across from Best Ln. Accepts *Poste Restante.* Open M-F 9am-5:30pm, Sa 9am-12:30pm. **Postal Code:** CT1 2BA.

Telephone Code: 01227.

ACCOMMODATIONS AND FOOD

Book ahead in summer or arrive by mid-morning to secure recently vacated rooms. B&Bs bunch by both train stations and on London and Whitstable Rd., just beyond West Station. Singles are scarce.

YHA Youth Hostel, 54 New Dover Rd. (tel. 462911; fax 470752), ¾ mi. from East Station and ½ mi. southeast of the bus station. Turn right as you leave the station and continue up the main artery, which becomes Upper Bridge St. At the 2nd rotary, turn right onto St. George's Pl., which becomes New Dover Rd. £9.75, under 18 £6.55. 86 beds. Breakfast £3, packed lunch £3.35, evening meal £4.45. Lockers £1 plus deposit. Bureau de change. Doors open 7:30-10am and 1-11pm. In summer book in advance. Open daily Feb.-Dec.; call for off-season openings.

Kingsbridge Villa, 14-15 Best Ln. (tel. 766415). Refurbished rooms a few steps off the main street; breakfast room moonlights as an Italian restaurant. Full English breakfast. £18 per person; doubles with bath £45. Rates negotiable off-season.

Request pizzas and pasta at **Ask,** 24 High St. (tel. 767617), at surprisingly decent prices (main dishes about £5; open daily 11:30am-11pm). **Marlowe's,** 55 St. Peter's St. (tel. 462194), presents an eclectic mix of vegetarian and beefy English, American, and Mexican food (open daily 11:30am-10:30pm). The **Miller's Arms,** Mill Ln. off Radigund St., offers six draught beers, while nearby **Simple Simon's,** 3-9 Church Ln. (tel. 762355), draws in students from the university (open daily 11am-11pm).

SIGHTS

Canterbury Cathedral has drawn the faithful (and the morbidly curious) since 1170, when Archbishop Thomas à Becket was beheaded here with a strike so forceful it broke the blade of the axe. Little information about the building is posted, presumably to encourage you to take a guided tour. *(Open Easter-Oct. M-Sa 8:45am-7pm, Su 11am-2:30pm and 4:30-5:30pm; Nov.-Easter daily 8:45am-5pm. £2.50, students, seniors, children £1.50. Tours 4 per day, fewer off-season. Check the nave or visitors center for times. £3, students and seniors £2, children £1.20. Self-guide booklet £1.25. Audio tour £2.50.)* The murder site today is closed off by a rail—a kind of permanent police line—around the **Altar of the Sword's Point.** The **Norman crypt** is a huge, 12th-century chapel. The **Corona Tower,** with 105 steps offers obstructed views of treetops. *(60p, children 30p.)*

The remainder of Chaucer's medieval Canterbury crowds around the branches of the River Stour on the way to the **West Gate,** through which pilgrims entered the city, and the only one of the city's seven medieval gates to survive the wartime blitz. The **West Gate Museum** (tel. 452747, ext. 129), formerly a prison, keeps armor and prison relics, and commands broad views of the city. *(Open M-Sa 11am-12:30pm and 1:30-3:30pm. 90p, students and seniors 60p, children and disabled 45p.)* For a quiet break, walk over to Stour St. and visit the riverside gardens of the **Greyfriars,** the first Franciscan friary in England. Greyfriars was built over the river in 1267 by Franciscans who arrived in England in 1224. *(Open in summer M-F 2-4pm. Free.)* The medieval **Poor Priests' Hospital,** also on Stour St., now houses the **Canterbury Heritage Museum** (tel. 452747), featuring a large collection of pilgrim badges from medieval souvenir shops as well as reconstructions of the city in various stages, from the Romans to Rupert. *(Open June-Oct. M-Sa 10:30am-5pm, Su 1:30-5pm; Nov.-May M-Sa 10:30am-5pm. £2.20, students and seniors £1.25, children £1.10.)*

At 1 St. Peter's St. stands the famous **Weaver's House,** where Huguenots lived during the 15th century. Walk into the garden to see an authentic witch-dunking stool swinging above the river. **Weaver's River Tours** (tel. 464660) runs cruises from here several times daily, except in time of drought. *(30min. £4, children £3.)*

Near the medieval city wall lie the **Dane John Mound and Gardens** and the massive, solemn remnants of the Norman **Canterbury Castle,** built for Conquering Bill himself. To the north on St. Dunstan's St., the vaults of **St. Dunstan's Church** contain a relic said to be the head of Sir Thomas More. Little remains of **St. Augustine's Abbey** (tel. 767345), built in 598, but older Roman ruins and the site of St. Augustine's first tomb (605) can be viewed outside the city wall near the cathedral. *(Open Apr.-Nov. daily 10am-6pm; Dec.-Mar. 10am-4pm. £2.50, students £1.90, children £1.30.)* Just around the corner from St. Augustine's on North Holmes St. stands the **Church of St. Martin,** the oldest parish church in England. Pagan King Ethelbert was married here to the French Christian Princess Bertha in 562. Joseph Conrad's heart sleeps in darkness inside the church.

Bath

Immortalized by Fielding, Smollett, Austen, and Dickens, Bath once stood second only to London as the social capital of England. Queen Anne's visit to the natural hot springs here in 1701 established Bath as one of the great meeting places for 18th-century British artists, politicians, and intellectuals.

ORIENTATION AND PRACTICAL INFORMATION

The **Pulteney** and **North Parade Bridges** span the **River Avon,** which bends around the city from the east. **The Roman Baths,** the **Abbey,** and the **Pump Room** are all in the city center. The **Royal Crescent** and the **Circus** lie to the northwest. The train and bus stations are near the south end of **Manvers Street,** at the bend in the river. From either terminal, walk up Manvers St. to the Terrace Walk roundabout and turn left onto York St. to reach the tourist office in the Abbey Churchyard.

Getting There: Bath is served by direct Intercity **rail** service (tel. (0345) 484950) from **Paddington** (1½hr., 1 per hr., £27) and **Waterloo** (2¼hr., 2 per day, £19.90). **National Express** (tel. (0990) 808080) operates **buses** from **Victoria coach station** (3hr., 9 per day, return £10.75-18.50).

Train Station: Railway Pl., at the south end of Manvers St. Booking office open M-F 5:30am-8:30pm, Sa 6am-8:30pm, Su 7:45am-8:30pm. Travel Centre open M-F 8am-7pm, Sa 9am-6pm, Su 9:30am-6pm.

Bus Station: Manvers St. (tel. 464446). Ticket office open M-Sa 8:30am-5:30pm. Information Centre open M-Sa 9am-5:30pm.

Taxis: Call **Abbey Radio** (tel. 465843) or **Orange Grove Taxis** (tel. 447777).

Bike Rental: Avon Valley Bike Hire (tel. 461880), behind the train station. £9 per ½ day, £14 per day; £250 deposit. Open Apr.-Oct. daily 9am-5:30pm; Nov.-Mar. M-Sa 9am-5:30pm, Su 10am-5pm.

Boat Rental: Bath Boating Station (tel. 466407), at the end of Forester Rd., about ½ mi. north of town. Punts and canoes £4 per person per hr., £1.50 each additional hr. Open daily summer 9am-9pm; winter 9am-5:30pm.

Tourist Office: Abbey Chambers (tel. 477101; fax 477787). Office gets crowded in summer. Map and mini-guide 25p. Pick up *This Month in Bath* (free). Open June-Sept. M-Tu and F-Sa 9:30am-6pm, W-Th 9:45am-6pm, Su 10am-4pm; Oct.-May M-Sa 9am-5pm, Su 10am-4pm.

Tours: Free guided **walking tours** given by the Mayor's Honorary Guides depart from the Abbey Churchyard daily at 10:30am and 2pm. Tours are very popular and range from good to excellent, depending on your guide. Open-topped, narrated 1hr. **bus tours** by **Guide Friday** (tel. 444102) depart from the bus station every 15min. daily 9:30am-5pm, and can be joined at various points on the route.

American Express: 5 Bridge St. (tel. 444757), just before Pulteney Bridge. Open M-Tu and Th-F 9am-5:30pm, W 9:30am-5:30pm, Sa 9am-5pm. Also in the tourist office (tel. 424416).

Emergency: Dial 999; no coins required.

Police: Manvers St. (tel. 444343), just up from the train and bus stations.

Hospital: Royal United Hospital (tel. 428331), Coombe Park, in Weston. Take bus #14, 16, or 17 from the rail or bus station.

Post Office: New Bond St. (tel. 445358), across from the Podium Shopping centre. Bureau de change. Open M-Sa 9am-5:30pm. **Postal Code:** BA1 1A5.

Internet Access: Midnight Express Café at the **Bath International Backpackers Hostel** (see below). 2 computers. £3 per 30min., £5 per hr. Open daily 5-7pm and 9-11pm, though hours may vary. Call 446787 for info.

Telephone Code: 01225.

ACCOMMODATIONS

B&Bs cluster on Pulteney Rd. and Pulteney Gdns. From the stations, walk up Manvers St., which becomes Pierrepont St., right onto N. Parade Rd. and past the cricket ground to Pulteney Rd. For a more relaxed setting, continue past Pulteney Gdns. A walk west toward **Royal Victoria Park** on Crescent Gdns. will reveal another front of B&Bs.

YHA Youth Hostel, Bathwick Hill (tel. 465674; fax 482947). From N. Parade Rd., turn left onto Pulteney Rd., then right onto Bathwick Hill. A footpath takes the hardy up the ever-ascending hill to the hostel (a steep 20min. walk). Save your energy for the city: Badgerline "University" bus #18 (6 per hr. until midnight; £1 return) runs to the hostel from the bus station or the Orange Grove roundabout. Secluded and graciously clean Italianate mansion overlooking the city. Don't underestimate the hill; you'll regret it. £9.75, under 18 £6.55. Breakfast £3, dinner £4.40. 117 beds. Showers, TV, laundry (£2.10 per load), lockers. No lockout, no curfew. In summer reserve a week in advance.

Lynn Shearn, Prior House, 3 Marlborough Ln. (tel. 313587). Convenient location on the west side of town beside the arbor of Royal Victoria Park. Easy 12min. walk, or take bus #14 from the station (6 per hr., get off at Hinton Grange). Look for the

Bath

ACCOMMODATIONS

- **G** International Backpackers Hostel
- **B** Lynn Shearn
- **D** Mrs. Guy
- **H** Mrs. Rowe
- **F** White Guest House
- **E** YHA Youth Hostel
- **C** YMCA International House
- **A** Camping

North Rd.
Sham Castle Ln.
Cleveland Walk
TO E (200m)
Sydney Rd.
Sydney Buildings
Beckford Rd.
Sydney Gardens
Holburne Museum
Sydney Pl.
Raby Pl.
Pulteney Rd.
Pulteney Gdns.
Bathwick St.
Great Pulteney St.
County Cricket Grounds
North Parade Rd.
Ferry Ln.
Broadway
Henrietta Rd.
Henrietta Park
Garden for the Blind
Laura Pl.
Pulteney Bridge
Orange Grove
Abbey
Pierrepont St.
S. Parade
Manvers St.
Book Museum
Train Station
Rossiter Rd.
St. John's Rd.
River Avon
Victoria Art Gallery
Guildhall
High St.
Cheap St.
Pump Room & Roman Baths
Stall St.
Southgate St.
Claverton St.
TO H (1/4 MILE)
The Building of Bath Museum
Walcot St.
Guinea Ln.
Assembly Rooms & Museum of Costume
Broad St.
Lansdown Rd.
Julian Rd.
Bennett St.
George St.
Milsom St.
Royal Photgraphic Society Octagon
Upper Borough Walls
Borough Walls
Westgate St.
St. James Parade
Corn St.
Museum of East Asian Art
THE CIRCUS
Gay St.
QUEEN SQUARE
Theatre Royal
James St. West
Green Park Rd.
River Avon
Crescent Ln.
Brock St.
Charlotte St.
Herschel House and Museum
Charles St.
Green Park
Lower Bristol Rd.
Wells Rd.
Royal Crescent
Royal Ave.
Upper Bristol Rd.
Midland Bridge Rd.
Marlboro Buildings
Marlboro Ln.
Royal Victoria Park
TO A4
TO A36 AND A (2 MILES)
N
0 200 yards
0 200 meters
Lower Oldfield Park

Let's Go sign in the window; among Bath's best values. Warm proprietors welcome you as friends. Doubles with full English breakfast £30, with bath £35. No smoking.

International Backpackers Hostel, 13 Pierrepont St. (tel. 446787; fax 446305). Extremely convenient location; up the street from the stations and 3 blocks from the baths. A self-proclaimed "totally fun-packed mad place to stay." Each room and bed is identified by a music genre and artist ("I'm sleeping in Rap"). Bordello-esque bar and lounge in the basement. £8-10, depending on season. Breakfast £1.

Mrs. Guy, 14 Raby Pl. (tel. 465120; fax 465283). From N. Parade Rd., turn left onto Pulteney Rd., then right up Bathwick Hill; Raby Pl. is the first row of buildings on the left. Luxuriate in this elegant Georgian home. TV/VCR lounge. Fresh seasonal fruits, yogurt, and homemade jams in Wedgwood dishes complement a generous English breakfast. Doubles £42-45, all with bath. No smoking.

FOOD AND PUBS

For fruits and veggies, visit the **Guildhall Market,** between High St. and Grand Parade (open M-Sa 8am-5:30pm). **Harvest Natural Foods,** 27 Walcot St. (tel. 465519), stocks a tremendous selection of organic produce (open M-Sa 9:30am-5:30pm).

Demuths Restaurant, 2 North Parade Passage (tel. 446059), off Abbey Green. Creative vegetarian and vegan dishes even the most devoted carnivore would enjoy. Fresh, colorful vegetables match the brightly colored paintings and fresh flowers; the lemon yellow walls may inspire you to try the luscious lemon sponge (£2.50). Entrees around £8. Open daily 10-11:30am, noon-4pm, and 6:30-10pm.

Tilleys Bistro, 3 N. Parage Passage (tel. 484200). Salivate over Tilleys's impressive Frenchie creations. Meat and veggie menus. Mushroom crepes under £5. Open M-Sa noon-2:30pm and 6:30-11pm, Su 6:30-10:30pm.

The Canary, 3 Queen St. (tel. 424846). Airy tea house serving tasty twists on light meals. Try the Somerset rabbit from an 18th-century recipe or the honey-spiced chicken; dishes £5-6. Open M-F 10am-5pm, Sa 9am-5:30pm, Su 11am-5:30pm.

If you're looking for a drink, **The Boater,** 9 Argyle St. (tel. 464211), overlooks the river with outdoor seating and a view of the lit-up Pulteney Bridge (open M-Sa 11am-11pm, Su noon-10:30pm). **The Garrick's Head,** St. John's Pl. (tel. 448819), is a scoping ground for the stage door of the Theatre Royal. For a late night, **The Huntsman,** North Parade (tel. 331367), at the Terrace Walk roundabout, is open Monday to Saturday until 2am.

SIGHTS AND ENTERTAINMENT

The **Roman Baths** (tel. 477759), once the spot for naughty sightings, are now a must-see for all. Long before the age of Hanoverian refinement, Bath flourished for nearly 400 years as the Roman spa city of Aquae Sulis. *(Open daily Apr.-July and Sept. 9am-6pm; Aug. 9am-6pm and 7-9pm; Oct.-Mar. 9am-5pm. Partial wheelchair access. £6.30, seniors £5.60, children £3.80, families £16.50; or buy a joint ticket to the Museum of Costume, £8.40, seniors £7.50, children £5, families £22. Avoid crowds by arriving early, or 1½hr. before closing.)* Guided tours run hourly from the main pool. Audio tours are also available.

Next door to the Baths, the 15th-century **Bath Abbey** (tel. 477752) towers over its neighbors, beckoning to visitors across the skyline. An anomaly among the city's first-century Roman and 18th-century Georgian sights, the abbey saw the crowning of King Edgar, "first king of all England," in 973. *(Open daily 9am-4:30pm; £1.50 donation requested.)* The whimsical west facade sports angels climbing ladders up to heaven—and two angels climbing down. The Abbey's **Heritage Vaults** (tel. 422462), below detail the millennia-spanning history of the stone giant. *(Open M-Sa 10am-4pm. £2, students, seniors, and children £1; wheelchair accessible.)*

The **Museum of Costume** (tel. 477752),Bennett St., houses a dazzling fashion parade of 400 years of catwalks, including a "generously cut" number worn by Queen Victoria. *(Open daily 10am-5pm. £3.80, seniors £3.50, children £2.70; or by joint ticket with Roman Baths; wheelchair access.)* The clothes are closeted in the basement of the

Assembly Rooms (tel. 477789), which staged fashionable social events in the late 18th century. *(Open daily 10am-5pm. Free.)* Although World War II ravaged the rooms, renovations duplicate the originals in fine detail. The **Building of Bath Museum** (tel. 333895), a few blocks over, recounts in precise detail how this Georgian masterpiece progressed from the drawing board to the drawing room. *(Open mid-Feb. to Nov. Tu-Su 10:30am-5pm. £3, students and seniors £2, children £1.50.)*

In the city's residential northwest corner, Nash's contemporaries John Wood, father and son, made the Georgian rowhouse a design to be reckoned with. Among notable inhabitants of the rowhouses, Jane Austen lived at 13 Queen Sq. ("Oh, what a dismal sight Bath is!"). From Queen Sq., walk up Gay St. to **The Circus,** which once housed Thomas Gainsborough, William Pitt, and David Livingstone. Proceed from there up Brock St. to **One Royal Crescent** (tel. 428126), a near-perfect replica of a 1770 townhouse, authentic to the last teacup and butter knife. *(Open Mar.-Oct. Tu-Su 10:30am-5pm; Nov. to mid-Dec. Tu-Su 10:30am-4pm. £3.80, students, seniors, and children £3.)* **Royal Victoria Park,** next to Royal Crescent, contains one of the finest collections of trees in the country, and its **botanical gardens** nurture 5000 species of plants from all over the globe. *(Park open M-Sa 9am-dusk, Su 10am-dusk. Free.)* For bird aficionados, there's also an aviary.

DAYTRIPS

The **Victoria Art Gallery,** Bridge St. (tel. 477772), holds a diverse collection of works including Old Masters and contemporary British art, such as Thomas Barker's "The Bride of Death"—Victorian melodrama at its sappiest. *(Open Tu-F 10am-5:30pm, Sa 10am-5pm, Su 2-5pm. Free. Wheelchair accessible.)* The museum sits next to the Pulteney Bridge—a work of art in its own right.

The **Museum of East Asian Art,** 12 Bennett St. (tel. 464640), displays objects from 5000 BC as well as amazing collections of jade and rhino horn carvings. *(Open Apr.-Oct. M-Sa 10am-6pm, Su noon-5pm. £3.50, students £2.50, seniors £3, children 6-12 £1, children under 6 free, families £8.)* Homesick Yankees and those who want to visit the United States vicariously (but haven't yet found a McDonald's) should stop by the **American Museum** (tel. 460503), perched above the city at Claverton Manor. *(Museum open late Mar. to early Nov. Tu-Su 2-5pm. Gardens open Tu-F 1-6pm, Sa-Su noon-6pm. House, grounds, and galleries £5, students and seniors £4.50, children £2.50; grounds, Folk Art, and New Galleries only £2.50, children £1.25.)* Climb Bathwick Hill to reach the manor, or let bus #18 (£1.20) save you the steep 2 mi. trudge.

Throughout the city lie stretches of green cultivated to comfort weary limbs (consult a map or inquire at the tourist office for the *Borders, Beds, and Shrubberies* brochure). **Henrietta Park,** laid out in 1897 to celebrate the Diamond Jubilee, was redesigned as a garden for the blind—only the most redolently pleasing flowers and shrubs were chosen for its tranquil grounds. Relax in the **Public Gardens** as the waters of the River Avon sweep by. *(Open daily 10am-8pm; £1, children 50p.)*

Classical and jazz concerts enliven **The Pump Room** during morning coffee (daily 9:30am-noon) and afternoon tea (2:30-5pm). In summer, buskers (street musicians) perform in the Abbey Churchyard, and a brass band often graces the Parade Gardens. Beau Nash's old haunt, the magnificent **Theatre Royal** (tel. 448844), Sawclose, at the south end of Barton St., produces opera, ballet, and pre- and post-London theater. *(Tickets £8-22; £1 student tickets M-Th. Box office open M-Sa 10am-8pm, Su noon-8pm.)*

The **Bizarre Bath Walking Tour** (tel. 335124; no advance booking required) begins at the Huntsman Inn at North Parade Passage nightly at 8pm. Punsters lead locals and tourists alike around, pulling pranks for about 1¼ hours. Tours vary from mildly amusing to hysterically funny and include absolutely no historical or architectural content. *(£3.50, students £3.)*

A night on the town could begin and end at cafe-bar **P.J. Peppers** (tel. 465777), on George St. The Bold and the Beautiful prance about, revealing more flesh in 15 minutes than the baths saw in all their years. *(Open daily 8am-11pm.)* A couple notches down on the pretty-boy meter, **The Pig and Fiddle** pub, on the corner of Saracen and Broad St., packs in a rowdy young crowd for pints around their large picnic table patio area. Bath nights wake up at **The Bell,** 103 Walcot St. (tel. 460426), an artsy pub that challenges its clientele to talk over the live jazz, blues, funk, and reggae. *(Open M-*

Sa 11am-11pm, Su 11am-3pm and 6:30-11pm.) At 14 George St., **Moles** (tel. 404445) burrows underground and pounds out techno and house music. Dress sharp and act smart. The club is "members only," but you might get in... if you can find it. *(Cover £5. Open M-Sa 9pm-2am.)* A final nightlife staple is **The Hush** (tel. 446288), on the Paragon at Lansdowne Rd. Head to this late-night pub before 10pm. *(Cover after 10pm £1-3 depending on the night. Open M-Sa 9:30pm-2am.)*

The renowned **Bath International Festival of the Arts,** over two weeks of concerts and exhibits, induces merriment all over town from late May to early June. Book well in advance for the **Bath International Music Festival** (box office tel. 463362; http://Bathfestivals.com) and its world-class maestri. *(Open M-Sa 9:30am-5:30pm.)* The **Contemporary Art Fair** (tel. 463362) opens the festival by bringing together the work of over 700 British artists. Musical offerings range from major symphony orchestras and choruses to chamber music, solo recitals, and jazz. For a complete festival brochure and reservations, write to the Bath Festivals Office, 2 Church St., Abbey Green, Bath BA1 1NL. The concurrent **Fringe Festival** (tel. 480097) celebrates music, dance, and liberal politics.

The Cotswolds

Stretching across the west of England, these whimsical hills enfold small towns barely touched by modern life—save periodic strings of antique shops and summer tourists. Hewn straight from the famed Cotswold Stone (termed "oolite" after the microscopic sea creatures that comprise it), Saxon villages and Roman settlements link a series of trails accessible to walkers and cyclists. Townspeople and tourists traverse the Cotswold terrain in harmony, skirting pastureland and treading near larger cities. Even the towns seem like scenes from a rustic past, and brilliant greens, golds, and purples color the entire area with natural beauty. Cheltenham makes a good base for exploring the Cotswolds by cycle or foot, but limited public transit means that daytrippers without cars will need to devote a few days to the area.

GETTING THERE AND GETTING AROUND

Cheltenham is served by frequent **trains** (2½ hr., 1 per hr., 7-day advance booking for M-Th return £18, F-Sa £34) from **Paddington** and **National Express** coaches (3hr., 1 per hr., £10) leave **Victoria.** The Cotswolds lie mostly in Gloucestershire, bounded by Banbury in the northeast, Bradford-on-Avon in the southwest, Cheltenham in the north, and Malmesbury in the south. The range hardly towers: a few areas in the north and west rise above 1000 ft., but the average Cotswold hill reaches only 600 ft. A 52 mi. long unbroken ridge, **The Edge,** dominates the western reaches of the Cotswolds.

Several **bus** companies operating under the auspices of the county government cover the Gloucestershire Cotswolds (most of the range) though many buses run only one or two days a week. Two unusually regular services are **Pulham's Coaches** (tel. (01451) 820369) from Cheltenham to Moreton via Bourton-on-the-Water and Stow-on-the-Wold (50min., M-Sa 7 per day, £1.40) and **Castleton's Coaches** (tel. (01242) 602949) from Cheltenham to Broadway via Winchcombe (about 1hr., M-Sa 4-5 per day, £1.45). The *Connection* timetable is free, indispensable, and available from all area bus stations and tourist offices. In Cheltenham pick up the tourist office's invaluable *Getting There from Cheltenham* pamphlet and have it bronzed.

Various firms offer **coach tours** of the Cotswolds, departing from Cheltenham, Cirencester, Gloucester, Stroud, and Tewkesbury. Inquire at the tourist information centers for more information. Cheltenham's tourist office (tel. (01242) 522878) offers less frantic tours of the North and South Cotswolds at a heftier £8.50 (students, seniors, and children £7.50). **Guide Friday** runs coach tours from Stratford-upon-Avon. If you prefer to run your own tour, **Country Lanes Cycle Center** (tel. (01608) 650065) hires bikes at the Moreton-on-the-Marsh train station. (£12 per day, plus 2

pieces of ID and refundable deposit. Gear and maps included.) Phone ahead—wheels are popular in these rolling hills (open daily 9:30am-5pm).

TOURIST OFFICES

Tourist offices in the area, which all book accommodations for a 10% deposit, include the following (listed north to south):

Chipping Campden: Noel Arms Courtyard, High St. Glos. GL55 6AT (tel. (01386) 841206). Open daily 10am-6pm.

Broadway: 1 Cotswold Ct., Worc. WR12 7AA (tel. (01386) 852937). Open Mar.-Oct. M-Sa 10am-1pm and 2-5pm. Booking service available year-round.

Stow-on-the-Wold: Hollis House, The Square, Stow-on-the-Wold GL54 1AF (tel. (01451) 831082). Open Easter-Oct. M-Sa 9:30am-5:30pm, Su 10:30am-4pm.

Cirencester: Corn Hall, Market Pl., Glos. GL7 2NW (tel. (01285) 654180). Open M 9:45am-5:30pm, Tu-Sa 9:30am-5:30pm; Nov.-Mar. daily 9:30am-5pm.

Cheltenham: 77 The Promenade, Glos. GL50 1PP (tel. (01242) 522878). Open July-Aug. M-Sa 9:30am-6pm, Su 9:30am-1:30pm; Sept.-June M-Sa 9:30am-5:15pm.

Gloucester: 28 Southgate St., Glos. GL1 1PD (tel. (01452) 421188). Open M-Sa 10am-5pm.

DAYTRIPS

ACCOMMODATIONS

The **Cheltenham YMCA,** Vittoria Walk, Cheltenham GL50 1PP (tel. (01242) 524024), offers clean, standard rooms, cafeteria, and continental breakfast. The office is open 24 hours and a porter lets guests in after 11pm (some singles available for £14). The *Cotswold Way Handbook* (£1.50) lists B&Bs along the Way; they are usually spaced in villages 3 mi. apart and offer friendly lodgings to trekkers. Alternatively, pick up *The Cotswolds Accommodation Guide* (50p). Call ahead in the morning to reserve same-day lodging. Savvy backpackers stay outside the larger towns to enjoy the silence. **YHA** has a number of **hostels** in the area:

Charlbury: The Laurels, The Slade, Charlbury, Oxford 0X7 3SJ (tel. (01608) 810202). On the River Evenlode, 1 mi. north of Charlbury, 5 mi. northwest of Blenheim Palace, 13 mi. northwest of Oxford; off the Oxford-Worcester rail line. From town center, follow road sign-posted *Enstone.* At B4022 crossroads, go straight across; hostel is 50 yd. on left. £7.70, under 18 £5.15. Breakfast £2.85, packed lunch £2.45, evening meal £4.25. Open July-Aug. M-Sa; Sept.-Oct. and Feb.-Mar. W-Su; Jan. F-Su; Apr.-June daily; closed Nov.-Dec.

Slimbridge: Shepherd's Patch, Slimbridge, Glos. GL2 7BP (tel. (01453) 890275; fax 890625), across from the Tudor Arms Pub, next to the swing bridge. Off the A38 and the M5, 4 mi. from the Cotswold Way and ½ mi. from the Wild Fowl Trust Reserve and Wetlands Centre. Easiest approach is by bus from Gloucester. Comes complete with its own ponds and wildfowl. 56 beds, showers, small store. £9.40, under 18 £6.30. Breakfast £3, packed lunch £2.55, evening meal £5. Open Mar.-Aug. daily; Sept.-Nov. M-Sa; Jan.-Feb. M-F; closed in Dec.

Stow-on-the-Wold: The Square, Cheltenham, Glos. GL54 1AF (tel. (01451) 830497). In the center of the village, between the White Hart Hotel and the Old Stocks. On the A424 highway; Pulham's bus passes about 1 per hr. from Cheltenham (17 mi.), Bourton-on-the-Water, and Moreton-in-Marsh (4 mi.). Bright rooms with wooden bunks; facilities are older but clean. Lovely, helpful warden. 56 beds; annex with 18 beds. Breakfast £2.85, packed lunch £2.45 or £3.25, and evening meal £4.25. Self-catering kitchen. Lockout 10am-5pm. £8.80, under 18 £6; students £7.80. 12mi. from Charlbury hostel. Open Apr.-Aug. daily; Sept.-Oct. M-Sa; Nov.-Dec. weekends; closed Jan.-Mar. Closed through Dec. 1998 for renovation. Call ahead for reopening date and definite hours.

HIKING THROUGH COTSWOLD VILLAGES

Experience England as the English have for centuries—by treading well-worn footpaths from village to village. Speed-walking will enable you to see several settlements

in a day, which proves especially convenient for daytrippers based in Cheltenham. Tourist office shelves strain with the weight of various books orchestrating your walk. B&Bs and pubs rest conveniently within reach of both the **Cotswold Way** and the **Oxfordshire Way.** Local roads are perfect for biking, and the rolling hills welcome casual and hardy cyclers alike; the closely spaced, tiny villages make ideal watering holes. Bear in mind that the Northern Cotswolds have a decidedly different feel than those in the South; many think the former are the more quaint and picturesque, while the latter suffer from less congestion. Check listings for local spring-time festivities like cheese rolling or woolsack races, where participants dash up and down hills laden with 60 pounds.

The more extensive of the two, the **Cotswold Way,** spans just over 100 mi. from Bath to Chipping Campden. The way affords glorious vistas of hills and dales, and fortunately tends to be uncrowded. The entire walk can be done in about a week at a pace of about 15 mi. per day. Due to pockmarks and gravel, certain sections of the path are not suitable for biking and horseback riding. What's more, many sections cross pastureland; try not to disturb Cotswold sheep and cattle, two breeds we're told it's fatal to mess with. Consult the **Cotswold Voluntary Warden Service** (tel. (01452) 425674) for details. Tourist information centers sell trail guides specially designed for the cyclist. Also available at the centers, the *Cotswold Way Map* (£5) provides a basic guide to the area, and *Cotswold Way* (£4) has maps and explicit directions. Tourist offices give out *Guided Walks and Events in the Cotswolds,* which tells about free guided walking groups led by informed locals. For additional reference, consult Ordnance Survey Maps 1:50,000: sheets 151 (Stratford), 150 (Worcester and the Malverns), 163 (Cheltenham), 162 (Gloucester), and 172 (Bath and Bristol), each £4.50. In addition, the Cotswolds Voluntary Warden Service provides guided walks through the Cotswolds, some with historical or ecological bents. The walks last from 1½ to 7½ hours and are free.

Years back, quiet **Chipping Campden** became the capital of the rampant Cotswold wool trade. Later, the village became a market center ("chipping" means "market"). The town is currently famous for its **Cotswold Olympic Games at Dovers Hill,** highlighted by the obscure sport of shin-kicking. *(Tickets available day of game.)* This sadistic activity was prohibited from 1852 to 1952, but has since been enthusiastically revived in late May and early June to the glee of local bone-setters.

Only 3 mi. west of Chipping Campden, restored Tudor, Jacobean, and Georgian buildings with thatch or Cotswold tile roofs scheme to make **Broadway** a museum. Since it became a stopover on the London-Worcester route in the 16th century, Broadway has bustled with visitors. **Broadway Tower** (tel. (01386) 852390) enchanted the likes of the decorator/designer/poet William Morris and his pre-Raphaelite comrade Dante Gabriel Rossetti. *(Open early Apr. to late Oct. daily 10am-6pm. £3, children £2.20, families £9.)* Built in the late 1700s in a superfluous attempt to intensify the beauty of the landscape, the tower affords a view of 12 counties.

A sleepy village that recently opened its eyes to protest a proposed supermarket, **Stow-on-the-Wold** features fine views of the surrounding countryside. Stow, "where the cold winds blow," will confirm your suspicion that Cotswold settlers looked no farther than their backyards for building materials. Stow also boasts one antique shop for every 33 residents. A few yards away from the stocks stands a **YHA Youth Hostel** (see **Accommodations and Food,** p. 299). Replenish glucose at **Cotswold Fruit Store,** the Square, or down a pint at **The King's Arms** across the way.

The Oxfordshire Way (65 mi.) runs between the popular hyphen-havens of Bourton-on-the-Water and Henley-on-Thames. A comprehensive *Walker's Guide* can be found in tourist offices. Plod over cow paddies to wend your way from Bourton-on-the-Water to Lower and Upper Slaughter along the **Warden's Way** (takes a half day). Parts of the footpaths are hospitable to cyclists, if slightly rut-ridden. Most adventurous souls can continue on to Winchcombe for a total of about 14 mi.

Like the proverbial lamb, travel a few miles southwest to the **Slaughters (Upper and Lower),** a pair of tranquil villages. Fortunately, your visit will be heralded by a host of lively sheep, not an unhinged butcher. Footpaths connect Upper and Lower

Slaughter and also lead to **Bourton-on-the-Water.** Rather inexplicably touted as the "Venice of the Cotswolds" (no gondolas, just a picturesque stream and a series of footbridges), Bourton hosts its fair share of tourists, including many polo-shirted English men and women in straw hats with real flowers. Many of the larger trails (The Cotswold Way, Oxfordshire Way) converge at Bourton. Between the olfactory heaven and hell of rose-laden gates and fields strewn with sheep dung lies **The Cotswold Perfumery** (tel. (01451) 820698) on Victoria St. The Perfumery houses a theater equipped with "Smelly Vision," that releases actual scents into the theater as they're mentioned onscreen. *(Open daily 9:30am-5pm, sometimes later in summer. £1.75, students, seniors, and children £1.50. Wheelchair accessible.)*

West of Stow-on-the-Wold and 6 mi. north of Cheltenham on the A46 lies **Sudeley Castle** (tel. (01242) 602308), neighboring the town of **Winchcombe.** Once the manor estate of King Ethelred the Unready, the castle was a prized possession in the Middle Ages, with lush woodland, a royal deer park, and Charles I's gloriously carved four-poster bed. The Queen's Garden is streamlined by a pair of yew-hedge corridors leading to rose and herb beds, while the newly planted Knot Garden was inspired by a pattern on a gown worn by Queen Elizabeth in 1592. **St. Mary's Chapel** contains the tomb of Henry VIII's Queen Katherine Parr. *(Open Apr.-Oct. daily 10:30am-5pm. £5.50, seniors £3.20, children £3; grounds only £4, seniors £3.20, children £1.80, families £15.)* The castle also schedules falconrie shows. Present occupants Lord and Lady Ashcombe welcome you and your admission fee into their home.

Prehistoric remains are stowed in the Cotswolds; archaeologists have unearthed some 70 ancient habitation sites. **Belas Knap,** a 4000-year-old burial mound, stands about 1½ mi. southwest of Sudeley Castle, accessible from the Cotswold Way. The **Rollright Stones,** off the A34 between Chipping Norton and Long Compton (a 4½ mi. walk from Chipping Norton), comprise a 100 ft. wide ring of 11 stones. Consult Ordnance Survey Tourist Map 8 (£4.25) for locations of other sites.

The Cotswolds contain some of the best examples of Roman settlements in Britain—most notably **Cirencester** and **Chedworth.** Sometimes regarded as the capital of the region, Cirencester is the site of Corinium, a Roman town founded in AD 49 and second in importance only to Londinium, which has continued to be the more successful sister. Cirencester today largely caters to its older population. The town is small and the pension crowd is large, so a queue forms at the post office 10 minutes prior to opening. Stay in Cheltenham or Gloucester and take a daytrip to see the Roman remains. Although only scraps of the amphitheater still exist, the **Corinium Museum** (tel. (01285) 655611), Park St., has culled a formidable collection of Roman paraphernalia, including a hare mosaic comprised of thousands of *tessarae,* tiny handworked bits of ceramic. *(Open Apr.-Oct. M-Sa 10am-5pm, Su 2-5pm; Nov.-Mar. Tu-Sa 10am-5pm, Su 2-5pm. £2.50, students £1, seniors £2, children 80p, families £5.)* The second longest yew hedge in England bounds Lord Bathwist's mansion in the center of town; the garden behind the home, scattered with Roman ruins, provides a good place for an afternoon stroll. On Fridays, the entire town turns into a bedlamic antique marketplace; a smaller craft fair appears every Saturday inside Corn Hall at the Marketplace (near the tourist office). Stop by the **Golden Cross** on Black Jack St. or the **Crown** at West Market Pl. near the Abbey for a pint. B&Bs cluster a few minutes from downtown along Victoria Rd. Prices are steep, but it is possible to bargain successfully.

Tucked away in the Chedworth hills southwest of Cheltenham is the well-preserved **Chedworth Roman Villa** (tel. (01242) 890256), equidistant from Cirencester and Northleach off the A429. *(Open Mar.-Nov. Tu-Su and bank holidays 10am-5pm. £3.20, children £1.60, families £8. Wheelchair accessible, but some parts are difficult.)* The famed Chedworth mosaics were discovered in 1864 when a gamekeeper noticed fragments of tile revealed by rabbits. The site now displays a water shrine and bathhouses just above the River Coln.

Fowl deeds will occur at **Slimbridge** (tel. (01453) 890065), 12½ mi. southwest of Gloucester off the A38, the largest of the Wildfowl Trust's seven centers in Britain. *(Open in summer daily 9:30am-5pm, grounds close 6pm; in winter daily 9:30am-4pm. £5, children £3, families £13.)* Sir Peter Scott cached the world's largest collection of wildfowl here, totaling 180+ different species. All six varieties of flamingos nest at Slimbridge,

and white-fronted geese visit from their Siberian homeland. In the tropical house, hummingbirds skim through jungle foliage. The visitor center has exhibits and food—don't ask for duck. The Slimbridge YHA Youth Hostel benefits from Sir Peter's aviary efforts, as well, hosting its own flocks of wild birds (see **Accommodations,** p. 299).

Just south of Slimbridge on the A38 rises the massive **Berkeley Castle** (BARK-lay), ancestral home of the Berkeley family (founders of a university in California). This stone fortress (tel. (01453) 810322) truly deserves the castle moniker, with its impressive towers, dungeon, and timber-vaulted Great Hall, where the barons of the West Country met before forcing King John to put quill to parchment and sign the Magna Carta. *(Open July-Aug. M-Sa 11am-5pm, Su 2-5pm; June and Sept. Tu-Sa 11am-5pm, Su 2-5pm; Apr.-May Tu-Su 2-5pm; Oct. Su 2-5pm. £5, students and seniors £4, children £2.60, families £13.50.)*

Dover

The sea is calm tonight.
The tide is full, the moon lies fair
Upon the straits;—on the French coast the light
Gleams and is gone; the cliffs of England stand
Glimmering and vast, out in the tranquil bay.

—Matthew Arnold, "Dover Beach"

ORIENTATION AND PRACTICAL INFORMATION

To reach the tourist office from the railway station, turn left onto Folkestone Rd. Continue until York St.; turn right and follow it to the end, where you turn left onto Townwall St.; the tourist office is on the left. From the bus station, turn left from Pencester onto Cannon St. Proceed through the pedestrian friendly city to Townwall St. and turn left. York St., which becomes High St. and eventually London Rd., borders the center of town. Maison Dieu Rd. graces the town's other side.

Getting There: Trains (tel. (0345) 484950) roll to Dover's Priory Station, off Folkestone Rd., from **Victoria, Waterloo East, London Bridge,** and **Charing Cross** approximately every 45min. (2hr., £17). Buses run regularly from **Victoria** (2¾hr., 15 per day, £13) into Dover's **Pencester Rd.** station (tel. (01304) 240024), between York St. and Maison Dieu Rd. Purchase tickets on the bus or in the ticket office. Open M-F 8:30am-5:30pm, Sa 8:30am-noon.

Tourist Office: Townwall St. (tel. 205108; fax 225498), a block from the shore. They post a list of accommodations after hours and supply ferry and hovercraft tickets. Open daily July-Aug. 8am-7:30pm; Sept.-June 9am-6pm.

Police: Ladywell St. (tel. 240055), right off High St.

Hospital: Buckland Hospital (tel. 201624), on Coomb Valley Rd. northwest of town. Take bus #D9 or D5 from outside the post office.

Postal Code: CT16 1PB.

Telephone Code: 01304.

ACCOMMODATIONS

Several of the hundreds of B&Bs on Folkestone Rd. (by the train station) stay open all night; if the lights are on, ring the bell. During the day, try the Castle St. B&Bs near the center of town. "White Cliffs Association" plaques outside homes indicate quality, moderately priced rooms. Most B&Bs ask for a deposit.

YHA Charlton House, 306 London Rd. (tel. 201314; fax 202236), with overflow at **14 Goodwyne Rd.** (closer to town center). Hostel is a ½ mi. walk from the train station; turn left onto Folkestone Rd., left onto Effingham St., past the gas station onto Saxon St., and left at the bottom of the street onto High St., which becomes London Rd. Be prepared to rub elbows with families. 69 beds; rooms with 2-10 beds. Lounge and game room with pool table. £9.75, under 18 £6.55. Breakfast £2.95, 3-

course dinner £4.40. Kitchen, forceful showers, and lockers available. Lockout 10am-1pm. Curfew 11pm.

YMCA, 4 Leyburne Rd. (tel. 206138); turn right off Goodwyne Rd. Men and women accepted. Basic accommodations. 47 mattresses (perfect if you have a sleeping bag, but sheets and blankets provided) in a co-ed room on a dance floor; also separate rooms for women. £5. Reception M-F 8:30am-noon and 6-10pm, Sa-Su 6-10pm. Curfew 10pm. Reservations recommended but not required.

Victoria Guest House, 1 Laureston Pl. (tel./fax 205140). The well-traveled Hamblins extend a friendly welcome to their international guests. Think twice about complaining of sore muscles; your neighbor might have just swum the Channel. Gracious Victorian rooms in an excellent location. Doubles £28-40; family room £48-54. Special 5-day rates available.

FOOD

Chaplin's, 2 Church St. (tel. 204870). Pictures of Charlie complement the classic feel of this Dover diner. Specials like roast chicken, vegetables, and potatoes (£4.50). Open M-Sa 9am-9pm, Su 9:30am-8:30pm.

The Lighthouse Café and Tea Room (tel. 242028), end of Prince of Wales Pier. View of castle and the White Cliffs as you sip tea from ½ mi. off shore. Open Mar.-Aug. M-F 9am-6pm, Sa-Su 9am-7pm; Sept.-Feb. Sa-Su 9am-5pm.

Pizza Pronto, 7 Ladywell (tel. 214234). Mouth-watering smells of take-away pizza waft down the street. Cheese pizza £3.70. Open daily 5pm-midnight.

SIGHTS

The view from Castle Hill Rd., on the east side of town, reveals why **Dover Castle** is famed both for its magnificent setting and for its impregnability. *(Hourly buses from the town center run daily Apr.-Sept., 45p. Castle and complex open daily Apr.-Sept. 10am-6pm; Oct.-Mar. 10am-4pm. £6.60, students and seniors £5, children £3.30, families £15. Partial wheelchair accessible.)* Many have launched assaults on it by land, sea, and air: the French tried in 1216, the English during the Civil Wars in the 17th century, and the Germans in World Wars I and II. Look down the long well shaft to discover how sophisticated the castle's (unfortunately lead-piped) plumbing system was. The **castle keep** showcases an odd medley of trivia and relics from the 12th century to the present. Boulogne, 22 mi. across the Channel, can (barely) be seen on clear days from the castle's top; it was from that coast that the Germans launched V-1 and V-2 rocket bombs in World War II. These "doodle-bugs" destroyed the **Church of St. James,** the ruins of which crumble at the base of Castle Hill. The empty **Pharos,** built in 43 BC, sits alongside **St. Mary's,** a tiled Saxon church. The only Roman lighthouse still in existence and certainly the tallest remaining Roman edifice in Britain, the Pharos' gaping keyhole windows testify to its original purpose. **Hell Fire Corner** is a 3½ mi. labyrinth of secret **tunnels** only recently declassified. Originally built in the late 18th century to defend Britain from attack by Napoleon, the graffiti-covered tunnels were the base for the evacuation of Allied troops from Dunkirk in World War II.

Relatively recent excavation has unearthed a remarkably well-preserved **Roman painted house** (tel. 203279), New St., off Cannon St. near Market Sq. *(Open Apr.-Sept. Tu-Su 10am-5pm. £2, seniors and children 80p.)* It's the oldest Roman house in Britain, complete with an under-floor central heating system. **The White Cliffs Experience** (tel. 214566), in Market Sq., employs costumed Roman soldiers, videos, and a rebuilt ferry deck to illustrate Dover's nearly two millennia of history. *(£5.50, students and seniors £4.25, children £3.75.)* On the third floor note the painted figure of Michael Jackson next to Charles II and Richard the Lionheart—all famous channel crossers. Check the White Cliffs Experience brochure, free at the tourist office, for discount coupons. Tickets purchased at White Cliffs include a tour of the **Dover Museum** (tel. 201066), Market Sq., which similarly displays curious bits of Dover history. *(Open daily Apr.-Oct. 10am-6pm; Nov.-Mar. 10am-5:30pm. £1.65, students, seniors, and children 85p. Wheelchair accessible.)*

A few miles west of Dover (25min. by foot along Snargate St.) sprawls the whitest, steepest, and most famous of the cliffs. Known as **Shakespeare Cliff** (look for the

signs), it is traditionally identified with eyeless Gloucester's battle with the brink in *King Lear.* Closer to town on Snargate St. is the **Grand Shaft** (tel. 201200), a 140 ft. triple spiral staircase shot through the rock in Napoleonic times to link the army on the Western Heights and the city center. *(Ascend July-Aug. W-Su 2-5pm; on bank holidays 10am-5pm. £1.20, seniors and children 70p.)* The first stairwell was for "officers and their ladies," the second for "sergeants and their wives," the last for "soldiers and their women." Other startling views can be found at **Samphire Hoe,** a well-groomed park created in the summer of 1997 from material dug to create the Channel. There are dozens of walks within a short distance of the center of town; consult the tourist office for more information.

Stonehenge

Stonehenge is a potent reminder that England seemed ancient even to the Saxons and Normans. The present stones—22 ft. high—comprise the fifth temple constructed on the site. The first probably consisted of an arch and circular earthwork, and was in use for about 500 years. Its relics are the Aubrey Holes (white patches in the earth) and the Heel Stone. The next monument consisted of about 60 stones imported up the River Avon from Wales around 2100 BC, used to mark astronomical directions. This monument may once have been composed of two concentric circles and two horseshoes of megaliths, both enclosed by earthworks. The present shape, once a complete circle, dates from about 1500 BC.

Many peoples have worshipped the Stonehenge site, from late Neolithic and early Bronze Age chieftains to contemporary mystics. In 300 BC the Druids arrived from the Continent and claimed Stonehenge as their shrine. The 1998 Summer Solstice saw the return of Druids worshipping at the site, absent since a storied confrontation with police ten years earlier.

Admission to Stonehenge includes a 40-minute English Heritage audio tour. English Heritage (tel. (01980) 625368) also offers guided personal tours throughout the day; ask the helpful guides. *(Open daily June-Aug. 9am-7pm; mid-Mar. to May and Sept. to mid-Oct. 9:30am-6pm; mid-Oct. to mid-Mar. 9:30am-4pm. £3.90, students, seniors, and unemployed £2.90, children £2. Wheelchair accessible.)*

Getting to Stonehenge takes two steps. **Trains** (2hr., 1 per hr., £22-30) run between **Salisbury** and **Victoria. National Express buses** (tel. (0990) 808080) run from **Victoria** Station (2¾hr., 3 per day, £9.25, return £12.50). Then take **Wilts and Dorset** bus #X4 (tel. (01722) 336855) to **Stonehenge** (40min., M-Sa 10 per day, Su 4 per day, £4.60). For the same price as a trip to Salisbury, get an **Explorer ticket,** which allows you to travel all day on any bus and use it to stop by **Avebury** (tel. (01672) 539425), a cousin of Stonehenge that is less crowded by tourists and more crowded by residents of the tiny village situated within the largest stone ring in Britain. Take bus #5 or 6 to Swindon (viewing free; wheelchair accessible).

Appendix

Bank Holidays and City Festivals

During Bank holidays, schools, businesses, and restaurants are closed; however, many museums and attractions stay open to accommodate the those who have a day off; it may be a good time to skip the British Museum in favor of a daytrip. London offers a multitude of festivals and special events year-round, including multicultural displays, renowned athletic competitions, and royal ceremonies Please note that the dates listed here are **tentative;** contact tourist offices for more information. .

Date	Event	Date	Event
January 1	New Year's Day; London Parade	**June 21-July 4**	Wimbeldon Lawn Tennis Championships
9-24	Mime Festival	**22-July 15**	City of London Festival
February 1	Chinese New Year Festival	**26-27**	Middlesex Show
March 17	St. Patrick's Day	**late June-early Sept.**	Kenwood Lakeside Concerts
19-April 13	Ideal Home Exhibition	**July 1-5**	Henley Royal Regatta
21-23	International Book Fair	**9-18**	Greenwich and Docklands International Festival
April 3	Oxford and Cambridge Boat Race	**mid-July-mid-Sept.**	BBC Henry Wood Promenade Concerts
12	Harness Horse Parade	**August 1**	Summer Rites
24	Good Friday	**3-7**	Great British Beer Festival
25	London Marathon	**29-30**	Notting Hill Carnival
27	Easter Monday	**late August**	Royal Academy Summer Exhibition
late April	Vietnam Festival	**31**	Summer Bank Holiday
May 1	Rugby League Challenge Cup Final	**September 4**	Great River Race
3	Early May Bank Holiday	**9-19**	Chelsea Antiques Fair
9	May Fayre and Puppet Festival	**12**	Thames Festival
15	FA Cup Final	**18-19**	London Open House
18-21	Chelsea Flower Show	**October 3**	Costermongers' Pearly Harvest Festival
22-30	Festival of Mind, Body, and Spirit	**3**	Punch and Judy Festival
24-June 6	BOC Covent Gdn. Festival	**17**	Trafalgar Day Parade
31	Spring Bank Holiday	**28-31**	Kensington Fine Art & Antiques Fair
June 1-August 15	Royal Academy Summer Exhibition	**late Oct.-early Nov.**	State Opening of Parliament
2-3	Beating the Retreat	**November 1**	London to Brighton Veteran Car Run
2-23	Spitalfields Festival	**4**	Bonfire Night

5	Fleadh Festival; Derby Day	**7**	Remembrance Sunday Ceremony
13	Trooping the Colour	**14**	Lord Mayor's Show
15-19	Royal Ascot	**late Nov.**	London Film Festival
19-20	International Kite Festival	**Nov.-Dec.**	Christmas Lights
19-July 4	Meltdown Music Festival	**December**	Christmas Tree
20-27	Covent Garden Flower Festival	**25-26**	Christmas Day-Boxing Day

Climate

Average high and low temperatures in degrees centigrade (Celsius) and the average yearly rainfall in centimeters during four months of the year:

January		April		July		October	
Temp	**Rain**	**Temp**	**Rain**	**Temp**	**Rain**	**Temp**	**Rain**
6°C/2°C	5.4cm	13°C/6°C	3.7cm	22°C/14°C	5.9cm	14°C/8°C	5.7cm

To convert from °C to °F, multiply by 1.8 and add 32.
To convert from °F to °C, subtract 32 and multiply by 5/9.

°C	100	35	30	25	20	15	10	5	0	-5	-10
°F	212	95	86	75	68	59	50	41	32	23	14

Telephone Codes

Australia	Austria	Canada	Ireland	New Zealand	South Africa	United Kingdom	United States
61	43	1	353	64	13	44	1

Time Zones

Though Greenwich Mean Time (GMT) is the standard by which much of the rest of the world sets its clocks, the British have a system of their own, with Winter Time (=GMT) and British Summer Time (late March-late Oct.; 1hr. later than GMT). British time is usually 5 hours ahead of Eastern Standard time.

Measurements

1 meter (m) = 1.09 yards	1 yard = 0.92m
1 kilometer (km) = 0.621 mile	1 mile = 1.61km
1 gram (g) = 0.04 ounce	1 ounce = 25g
1 kilogram (kg) = 2.2 pounds	1 pound = 0.45 kg
1 "stone" (weight—of man or beast only) = 14 pounds	1 pound = 0.071 stone
1 liter = 1.057 U.S quarts	1 U.S quart = 0.94 liter
1 liter = 0.88 Imperial quarts	1 Imperial quart = 1.14 liter
1 Imperial gallon = 1.193 U.S. gallons	1 U.S. gallon = 0.84 Imperial gallon
1 British pint = 1.19 U.S. pint	1 U.S. pint = 0.84 British pint

Speaking British

aubergine	eggplant
bap	a soft bun, like a hamburger bun
bed-sit, or bedsitter	one-room apartment
bevvy; bevvied	a drink, an alcoholic beverage; drunk
biscuit	if sweet, a cookie; if not, a cracker
boozer	pub
brilliant	cool, excellent
busker	street musician
cheers, cheerio	thank you, good-bye
chemist	pharmacist
chips	french fries
chuffed	excited; or disappointed
concession, "concs"	discount on admission
courgette	zucchini
crisps	potato chips
dicey, dodgy	problematic, sketchy
dosh	money
dustbin, rubbish bin	trash can
ensuite	with bath
fag	cigarette
fanny	female sexual organs
fortnight	two weeks
grotty	grungy
hire	rental
hoover	vacuum cleaner
iced lolly	popsicle
jelly	gelatin
jumper	sweater
kit	clothes (get one's kit off means to strip)
knickers	underwear
leader (in newspaper)	editorial
to let	to rent
lift	elevator
loo	restroom
lorry	truck
pensioner	senior citizen
phone box, or call box	telephone booth
take the piss out of, on	make fun of
pissed	drunk
pull	to "score"
punter	a guy, an average joe, a bar patron
public school	private school
queue; queue up, Q	a line; line up
return ticket	roundtrip ticket
ring up	telephone, call
rubber	eraser
self-catering	(accommodations with) kitchen facilities
shag, shagging, "fancy a shag?"	sexual intercourse
stroppy	crabby, grumpy
sultanas	raisins
swish	swanky
tights	pantyhose

tosser	loser, jerk
trainers	sneakers
wanker	jerk, tool
way out	exit
W.C. (water closet)	restroom
zed	the letter "Z,"

Blue Plaque Houses

Matthew Arnold	poet and essayist	2 Chester Sq., SW1
Hector Berlioz	composer	58 Queen Anne St., W1
James Boswell	author	8 Russell St., WC2
Elizabeth B. Browning	poet	99 Gloucester Pl., W1
Beau Brummell	dandy	4 Chesterfield St., W1
Thomas Carlyle	essayist and historian	24 Cheyne Walk, SW3
Frederic Chopin	composer	4 St. James's Pl., SW1
Sir Winston Churchill	statesman and soldier	28 Hyde Park Gate, SW7
Joseph Conrad	novelist	17 Gillingham St., SW1
Charles Darwin	naturalist	UCL Science Building
Charles Dickens	novelist	48 Doughty St., WC1
Benjamin Disraeli	statesman	19 Curzon St., W1
T.S. Eliot	poet and critic	3 Kensington Ct., W8
Benjamin Franklin	statesman and inventor	36 Craven St., WC2
Thomas Gainsborough	portrait artist	82 Pall Mall, SW1
Edward Gibbon	historian	7 Bentinck St., W1
George Frederick Händel	composer	25 Brook St., W1
Henry James	writer	34 De Vere Gdns., W8
Samuel Johnson	author / lexicographer	17 Gough Sq., EC4
Rudyard Kipling	poet and writer	43 Villiers St., WC2
Gugliemo Marconi	inventor of the wireless	71 Hereford Rd., W2
Karl Marx	economist/philosopher	28 Dean St., W1
Somerset Maugham	novelist and playwright	6 Chesterfield St., W1
Samuel Morse	inventor and painter	141 Cleveland St., W1
Wolfgang A. Mozart	composer	180 Ebury St., SW1
Sir Isaac Newton	physicist/mathematician	87 Jermyn St., SW1
Florence Nightingale	Crimean war nurse	10 South St., W1
Samuel Pepys	diarist	14 Buckingham St., WC2
Monty Python	tv & cinema humorists	Neals Yard, WC2
Sir Joshua Reynolds	portrait painter	Leicester Sq., WC2
Dante Gabriel Rossetti	poet and painter	16 Cheyne Walk, SW3
George Bernard Shaw	playwright and critic	29 Fitzroy Sq., W1
Percy Bysshe Shelley	Romantic poet	15 Poland St., W1
Vincent Van Gogh	impressionist painter	87 Hackford Rd., SW9
James A. McNeil Whistler	painter and etcher	96 Cheyne Walk, SW10
Oscar Wilde	wit and dramatist	34 Tite St., SW3

Index

INDEX

Q

R

S

INDEX

Z

About Let's Go

THIRTY-NINE YEARS OF WISDOM

Back in 1960, a few students at Harvard University banded together to produce a 20-page pamphlet offering a collection of tips on budget travel in Europe. This modest, mimeographed packet, offered as an extra to passengers on student charter flights to Europe, met with instant popularity. The following year, students traveling to Europe researched the first, full-fledged edition of *Let's Go: Europe,* a pocket-sized book featuring honest, irreverent writing and a decidedly youthful outlook on the world. Throughout the 60s, our guides reflected the times; the 1969 guide to America led off by inviting travelers to "dig the scene" at San Francisco's Haight-Ashbury. During the 70s and 80s, we gradually added regional guides and expanded coverage into the Middle East and Central America. With the addition of our in-depth city guides, handy map guides, and extensive coverage of Asia and Australia, the 90s are also proving to be a time of explosive growth for Let's Go, and there's certainly no end in sight. The maiden edition of *Let's Go: South Africa,* our pioneer guide to sub-Saharan Africa, hits the shelves this year, along with the first editions of *Let's Go: Greece* and *Let's Go: Turkey.*

We've seen a lot in 39 years. *Let's Go: Europe* is now the world's bestselling international guide, translated into seven languages. And our new guides bring Let's Go's total number of titles, with their spirit of adventure and their reputation for honesty, accuracy, and editorial integrity, to 44. But some things never change: our guides are still researched, written, and produced entirely by students who know first-hand how to see the world on the cheap.

HOW WE DO IT

Our series is completely revised and thoroughly updated every year by a well-traveled set of over 200 students. Every winter, we recruit over 160 researchers and 70 editors to write the books anew. After several months of training, researcher-writers hit the road for seven weeks of exploration, from Anchorage to Adelaide, Estonia to El Salvador, Iceland to Indonesia. Hired for their rare combination of budget travel sense, writing ability, stamina, and courage, these adventurous travelers know that train strikes, stolen luggage, food poisoning, and marriage proposals are all part of a day's work. Back at our offices, editors work from spring to fall, massaging copy written on Himalayan bus rides into witty yet informative prose. A student staff of typesetters, cartographers, publicists, and managers keeps our lively team together. In September, the collected efforts of the summer are delivered to our printer, who turns them into books in record time, so that you have the most up-to-date information available for your vacation. Even as you read this, work on next year's editions is well underway.

WHY WE DO IT

We don't think of budget travel as the last recourse of the destitute; we believe that it's the only way to travel. Living cheaply and simply brings you closer to the people and places you've been saving up to visit. Our books will ease your anxieties and answer your questions about the basics—so you can get off the beaten track and explore. Once you learn the ropes, we encourage you to put *Let's Go* down now and then to strike out on your own. You know as well as we that the best discoveries are often those you make yourself. When you find something worth sharing, please drop us a line. We're Let's Go Publications, 67 Mount Auburn St., Cambridge, MA 02138, USA (email: feedback@letsgo.com). For more info, visit our website, http://www.letsgo.com.

HAPPY TRAVELS!

Researcher-Writers

Rachel Greenblatt
A San Francisco native, Rachel's vivid descriptions and thoroughly researched copy were a joy to read. Despite a nomadic London existence, she covered everything from Covent Garden to Chiswick with an enthusiasm and attention to detail that was astounding, and she accompanied it all with hilarious illustrations. Whether musing over the woes of B&B interior decorating or researching pub history at the British Library, Rachel's cultural and social sensitivity gave her prose a refreshing insider's view.

Ben Jackson
From Scotland to America and back again, somehow Ben found the time to bring us his witty and insightful prose and extensive coverage. Through torrential rains and tube strikes, he still managed to unearth new finds and trek across town in search of a hostel or two. From the untamed capitalism of the City to the, um, untamed capitalism of the Docklands, Ben maintained his confidence and unrivaled sense of humor. Whether describing the Millennium Dome or an ATM, his writing was flawless and evocative, bringing the best of London to the page.

Tobie Whitman
A veteran England researcher, Tobie brought confidence and poise to the misty streets of London. Despite a virus-laden computer, she navigated the streets of posh Islington and swirling Piccadilly with unwavering dedication that resulted in flawless research and brilliant prose. She danced the night away in clubs and celebrated the World Cup, but still managed to create lively, evocative descriptions of the city that were thorough and well-written, accompanied by hilarious commentary.

Nick Grandy — *Bath, Oxford, Stratford, York*
Christa Franklin — *Brighton, Cambridge, Canterbury, Stonehenge*
Olivia Choe — *Editor, Britain and Ireland*
Alexandra Leichtman — *Associate Editor, Britain and Ireland*

Acknowledgments

Thanks to Måns Larsson, for great advice with a Swedish accent. To the Britain and Ireland pod (Olivia, Alex L., Brina and Jenny), for incredible interior decorating skills, lettuce, and great conversation, and to Lisa N. for answering my endless questions. Thanks to Alex S., editing guru, and the Production team (Dan V. and Maryanthe) for keeping this book intact. To Dan L., the map man, for making getting lost a little more difficult. Kudos to city guide editors (Josh, Rachel, Whitney, and Brian) for moral support and shared deadline frenzy. Thanks to all of the managing editors for making this process so much easier—and for doing it with a smile. Thanks to Anne Chisholm, Anna Portnoy, and Caroline Sherman for pulling everything together. Finally, I'd like to thank all of my researcher-writers—through rain, tube strikes, and the breakup of the Spice Girls, you still managed to do an incredible job.

Thanks to Mom, Dad, and Yannick for your constant love and support—I couldn't have done this without you. To my grandmother Blanche, my aunt Luraine, and my uncle Jon for helping me along the way—I love you all. To Sam for your love, patience, and encouragement—I can't thank you enough. *Grazie* to Mary and everyone at Lancaster Gate. Thanks to John McFadden and everyone at McFadden, Pilkington, and Ward for a great summer. **—SJD**

Rachel Greenblatt thanks her Mom and Dad, Ranti Williams, and everyone at Access Project. Ben Jackson thanks Derek Gadd, Denise Buford, Jo Beill, Kate Stocken, Jonathan Wheeler, and James Wheeler. Tobie Whitman thanks her Mom, Patrick, and Hazlitt Mews.

Editor	Shanya J. Dingle
Managing Editor	Måns O. Larsson
Publishing Director	Caroline R. Sherman
Publishing Director	Anna C. Portnoy
Production Manager	Dan Visel
Associate Production Manager	Maryanthe Malliaris
Cartography Manager	Derek McKee
Design Manager	Bentsion Harder
Editorial Manager	M. Allison Arwady
Editorial Manager	Lisa M. Nosal
Financial Manager	Monica Eileen Eav
Personnel Manager	Nicolas R. Rapold
Publicity Manager	Alexander Z. Speier
New Media Manager	Måns O. Larsson
Map Editors	Matthew R. Daniels, Dan Luskin
Production Associate	Heath Ritchie
Office Coordinators	Tom Moore, Eliza Harrington, Jodie Kirshner
Director of Advertising Sales	Gene Plotkin
Associate Sales Executives	Colleen Gaard, Mateo Jaramillo, Alexandra Price
President	Catherine J. Turco
General Manager	Richard Olken
Assistant General Manager	Anne E. Chisholm

Thanks to Our Readers...

Mano Aaron, CA; **Jean-Marc Abela,** CAN; **George Adams,** NH; **Bob & Susan Adams,** GA; **Deborah Adeyanju,** NY; **Rita Alexander,** MI; **Shani Amory-Claxton,** NY; **Kate Anderson,** AUS; **Lindsey Anderson,** ENG; **Viki Anderson,** NY; **Ray Andrews,** JPN; **Robin J. Andrus,** NJ; **L. Asurmendi,** CA; **Anthony Atkinson,** ENG; **Deborah Bacek,** GA; **Jeffrey Bagdade,** MI; **Mark Baker,** UK; **Mary Baker,** TN; **Jeff Barkoff,** PA; **Regina Barsanti,** NY; **Ethan Beeler,** MA; **Damao Bell,** CA; **Rya Ben-Shir,** IL; **Susan Bennerstrom,** WA; **Marla Benton,** CAN; **Matthew Berenson,** OR; **Walter Bergstrom,** OR; **Caryl Bird,** ENG; **Charlotte Blanc,** NY; **Jeremy Boley,** EL SAL; **Oliver Bradley,** GER; **A.Braurstein,** CO; **Philip R. Brazil,** WA; **Henrik Brockdorff,** DMK; **Tony Bronco,** NJ; **Eileen Brouillard,** SC; **Mary Brown,** ENG; **Tom Brown,** CA; **Elizabeth Buckius,** CO; **Sue Buckley,** UK; **Christine Burer,** SWITZ; **Norman Butler,** MO; **Brett Carroll,** WA; **Susan Caswell,** ISR; **Carlos Cersosimo,** ITA; **Barbara Crary Chase,** WA; **Stella Cherry Carbost,** SCOT; **Oi Ling Cheung,** HK; **Simon Chinn,** ENG; **Charles Cho,** AUS; **Carolyn R. Christie,** AUS; **Emma Church,** ENG; **Kelley Coblentz,** IN; **Cathy Cohan,** PA; **Phyllis Cole,** TX; **Karina Collins,** SWITZ; **Michael Cox,** CA; **Mike Craig,** MD; **Rene Crusto,** LA; **Claudine D'Anjou,** CAN; **Lizz Daniels,** CAN; **Simon Davies,** SCOT; **Samantha Davis,** AUS; **Leah Davis,** TX; **Stephanie Dickman,** MN; **Philipp Dittrich,**GER; **Tim Donovan,** NH; **Reed Drew,** OR; **Wendy Duncan,** SCOT; **Melissa Dunlap,** VA; **P.A. Emery,** UK; **GCL Emery,** SAF; **Louise Evans,** AUS; **Christine Farr,** AUS; **David Fattel,** NJ; **Vivian Feen,** MD; **David Ferraro,** SPN; **Sue Ferrick,** CO; **Philip Fielden,** UK; **Nancy Fintel,** FL; **Jody Finver,** FL; **D. Ross Fisher,** CAN; **Abigail Flack,** IL; **Elizabeth Foster,** NY; **Bonnie Fritz,** CAN; **J. Fuson,** OR; **Michael K. Gasuad,** NV; **Raad German,** TX; **Mark Gilbert,** NY; **Betsy Gilliland,** CA; **Ana Goshko,** NY; **Patrick Goyenneche,** CAN; **David Greene,** NY; **Jennifer Griffin,** ENG; **Janet & Jeremy Griffith,** ENG; **Nanci Guartofierro,** NY; **Denise Guillemette,** MA; **Ilona Haayer,** HON; **Joseph Habboushe,** PA; **John Haddon,** CA; **Ladislav Hanka,** MI; **Michael Hanke,** CA; **Avital Harari,** TX; **Channing Hardy,** KY; **Patrick Harris,** CA; **Denise Hasher,** PA; **Jackie Hattori,** UK; **Guthrie Hebenstreit,** ROM; **Therase Hill,** AUS; **Denise Hines,** NJ; **Cheryl Horne,** ENG; **Julie Howell,** IL; **Naomi Hsu,** NJ; **Mark Hudgkinson,** ENG; **Brenda Humphrey,** NC; **Kelly Hunt,** NY; **Daman Irby,** AUT; **Bill Irwin,** NY; **Andrea B. Jackson,** PA; **John Jacobsen,** FL; **Pat Johanson,** MD; **Russell Jones,** FL; **J. Jones,** AUS; **Sharon Jones,** MI; **Craig Jones,** CA; **Wayne Jones,** ENG; **Jamie Kagan,** NJ; **Mirko Kaiser,** GER; **Scott Kauffman,** NY; **John Keanie,** NIRE; **Barbara Keary,** FL; **Jamie Kehoe,** AUS; **Alistair Kernick,** SAF; **Daihi Kielle,** SWITZ; **John Knutsen,** CA; **Rebecca Koepke,** NY; **Jeannine Kolb,** ME; **Elze Kollen,** NETH; **Lorne Korman,** CAN; **Robin Kortright,** CAN; **Isel Krinsky,** CAN; **George Landers,** ENG; **Jodie Lanthois,** AUS; **Roger Latzgo,** PA; **A. Lavery,** AZ; **Joan Lea,** ENG; **Lorraine Lee,** NY; **Phoebe Leed,** MA; **Tammy Leeper,** CA; **Paul Lejeune,** ENG; **Yee-Leng Leong,** CA; **Sam Levene,** CAN; **Robin Levin,** PA; **Christianna Lewis,** PA; **Ernesto Licata,** ITA; **Wolfgang Lischtansky,** AUT; **Michelle Little,** CAN; **Dee Littrell,** CA; **Maria Lobosco,** UK; **Netii Ross,** ITA; **Didier Look,** CAN; **Alice Lorenzotti,** MA; **David Love,** PA; **Briege Mac Donagh,** IRE; **Brooke Madigan,** NY; **Helen Maltby,** FL; **Shyama Marchesi,** ITA; **Domenico Maria,** ITA; **Natasha Markovic,** AUS; **Edward Marshall,** ECU; **Rachel Marshall,** TX; **Kate Maynard,** UK; **Agnes McCann,** IRE; **Susan McGowan,** NY; **Brandi McGunigal,** CAN; **Neville McLean,** NZ; **Marty McLendon,** MS; **Matthew Melko,** OH; **Barry Mendelson,** CA; **Eric Middendorf,** OH; **Nancy Mike,** AZ; **Coren Milbury,** NH; **Margaret Mill,** NY; **David H. Miller,** TX; **Ralph Miller,** NV; **Susan Miller,** CO; **Larry Moeller,** MI; **Richard Moore,** ENG; **Anne & Andrea Mosher,** MA; **J. L. Mourne,** TX; **Athanassios Moustakas,** GER; **Laurel Naversen,** ENG; **Suzanne Neil,** IA; **Deborah Nickles,** PA; **Pieter & Agnes Noels,** BEL; **Werner Norr,** GER; **Ruth J. Nye,** ENG; **Heidi O'Brien,** WA; **Sherry O'Cain,** SC; **Aibhan O'Connor,** IRE; **Kevin O'Connor,** CA; **Margaret O'Rielly,** IRE; **Daniel O'Rourke,** CA; **Krissy Oechslin,** OH; **Johan Oelofse,** SAF; **Quinn Okamoto,** CA; **Juan Ramon Olaizola,** SPN; **Laura Onorato,** NM; **Bill Orkin,** IL; **K. Owusu-Agyenang,** UK; **Anne Paananen,** SWD; **Jenine Padget,** AUS; **Frank Pado,** TX; **G. Pajkich,** Washington, DC; **J. Parker,** CA; **Marian Parnat,** AUS; **Sandra Swift Parrino,** NY; **Iris Patten,** NY; **M. Pavini,** CT; **David Pawielski,** MN; **Jenny Pawson,** ENG; **Colin Peak,** AUS; **Marius Penderis,** ENG; **Jo-an Peters,** AZ; **Barbara Phillips,** NY; **Romain Picard**, Washington, DC; **Pati Pike,** ENG; **Mark Pollock,** SWITZ; **Minnie Adele Potter,** FL; **Martin Potter,** ENG; **Claudia Praetel,** ENG; **Bill Press,** Washington, DC; **David Prince,** NC; **Andrea Pronko,** OH; **C. Robert Pryor,** OH; **Phu Quy,** VTNM; **Adrian Rainbow,** ENG; **John Raven,** AUS; **Lynn Reddringer,** VA; **John Rennie,** NZ; **Ruth B.Robinson,** FL; **John & Adelaida Romagnoli,** CA; **Eva Romano,** FRA; **Mark A. Roscoe,** NETH; **Yolanda & Jason Ross,** CAN; **Sharee Rowe,** ENG; **W. Suzanne Rowell,** NY; **Vic Roych,** AZ; **John Russell,** ENG; **Jennifer Ruth,** OK; **William Sabino,** NJ; **Hideki Saito,** JPN; **Frank Schaer,** HUN; **Jeff Schultz,** WI; **Floretta Seeland-Connally,** IL; **Colette Shoulders,** FRA; **Shireen Sills,** ITA; **Virginia Simon,** AUS; **Beth Simon,** NY; **Gary Simpson,** AUS; **Barbara & Allen Sisarsky,** GA; **Alon Siton,** ISR; **Kathy Skeie,** CA; **Robyn Skillecorn,** AUS; **Erik & Kathy Skon,** MN; **Stine Skorpen,** NOR; **Philip Smart,** CAN; **Colin Smit,** ENG; **Kenneth Smith,** DE; **Caleb Smith,** CA; **Geoffrey Smith,** TX; **John Snyder,** NC; **Kathrin Speidel,** GER; **Lani Steele,** PHIL; **Julie Stelbracht,** PA; **Margaret Stires,** TN; **Donald Stumpf,** NY; **Samuel Suffern,** TN; **Michael Swerdlow,** ENG; **Brian Talley,** TX; **Serene-Marie Terrell,** NY; **B. Larry Thilson,** CAN; **J. Pelham Thomas,** NC; **Wright Thompson,** ITA; **Christine Timm,** NY; **Melinda Tong,** HK; **M. Tritica,** AUS; **Melanie Tritz,** CAN; **Mark Trop,** FL; **Chris Troxel,** AZ; **Rozana Tsiknaki,** GRC; **Lois Turner,** NZ; **Nicole Virgil,** IL; **Blondie Vucich,** CO; **Wendy Wan,** SAF; **Carrie & Simon Wedgwood,** ENG; **Frederick Weibgen,** NJ; **Richard Weil,** MN; **Alan Weissberg,** OH; **Ryan Wells,** OH; **Jill Wester,** GER; **Clinton White,** AL; **Gael White,** CAN; **Melanie Whitfield,** SCOT; **Bryn Williams,** CAN; **Amanda Williams,** CAN; **Wendy Willis,** CAN; **Sasha Wilson,** NY; **Kendra Wilson,** CA; **Olivia Wiseman,** ENG; **Gerry Wood,** CAN; **Kelly Wooten,** ENG; **Robert Worsley,** ENG; **C.A.Wright,** ENG; **Caroline Wright,** ENG; **Mary H. Yuhasz,** CO; **Margaret Zimmerman,** WA.

Let's Go 1999 Reader Questionnaire★

Please fill this out and return it to **Let's Go, St. Martin's Press,** 175 Fifth Ave., New York, NY 10010-7848. All respondents will receive a free subscription to ***The Yellowjacket***, the Let's Go Newsletter. You can find a more extensive version of this survey on the web at http://www.letsgo.com.

Name: ______________________________

Address: ______________________________

City: ____________ **State:** ______ **Zip/Postal Code:** ________

Email: ____________ **Which book(s) did you use?** ____________

How old are you? under 19 19-24 25-34 35-44 45-54 55 or over

Are you (circle one) in high school in college in graduate school employed retired between jobs

Have you used Let's Go before? yes no **Would you use it again?** yes no

How did you first hear about Let's Go? friend store clerk television bookstore display advertisement/promotion review other

Why did you choose Let's Go (circle up to two)? reputation budget focus price writing style annual updating other: ____________

Which other guides have you used, if any? Fodor's Footprint Handbooks Frommer's $-a-day Lonely Planet Moon Guides Rick Steve's Rough Guides UpClose other: ____________

Which guide do you prefer?

Please rank each of the following parts of Let's Go 1 to 5 (1=needs improvement, 5=perfect). packaging/cover practical information accommodations food cultural introduction sights practical introduction ("Essentials") directions entertainment gay/lesbian information maps other: ____________

How would you like to see the books improved? (continue on separate page, if necessary) ______________________________

____

How long was your trip? one week two weeks three weeks one month two months or more

Which countries did you visit? ____________

What was your average daily budget, not including flights? ____________

Have you traveled extensively before? yes no

Do you buy a separate map when you visit a foreign city? yes no

Have you used a Let's Go Map Guide? yes no

If you have, would you recommend them to others? yes no

Have you visited Let's Go's website? yes no

What would you like to see included on Let's Go's website? ____________

What percentage of your trip planning did you do on the Web? ____________

Would you use a Let's Go: recreational (e.g. skiing) guide gay/lesbian guide adventure/trekking guide phrasebook general travel information guide

Which of the following destinations do you hope to visit in the next three to five years (circle one)? Canada Argentina Perú Kenya Middle East Caribbean Scandinavia other: ____________

Where did you buy your guidebook? Internet independent bookstore chain bookstore college bookstore travel store other: ____________